Constructing Civil Libertie

Discontinuities in the Develo
American Constitutional Law

The modern jurisprudence of civil liberties and civil rights is best understood not as the outgrowth of an applied philosophical project involving the application of principles to facts, but as a developmental product of diverse, institutionalized currents of reformist political thought.
This book demonstrates that rights of individuals in the criminal justice system, workplace, and school were the endpoint of a succession of
progressive-spirited ideological and political campaigns of statebuilding and reform. In advancing this vision of constitutional development,
this book integrates the developmental paths of civil liberties law into
an account of the rise of the modern state and the reformist political
and intellectual movements that shaped and sustained it. In doing so,
Constructing Civil Liberties provides a vivid, multilayered, revisionist account of the genealogy of contemporary constitutional law and morals.

Ken I. Kersch is assistant professor in the Department of Politics
at Princeton University. He is recipient of the American Political Science Association's Edward S. Corwin Award (2000). His articles have
appeared in *Political Science Quarterly*, *Studies in American Political Development*, *The Public Interest*, and *The Washington Post*. He is the author of *Freedom of Speech: Rights and Liberties Under the Law* (2003)
and *The Supreme Court and American Political Development* (2005, with
Ronald Kahn).

For Barbara and Robert Kersch, and
In memory of Sylvia Schillinger

Constructing Civil Liberties

Discontinuities in the Development of American Constitutional Law

KEN I. KERSCH

Princeton University

CAMBRIDGE
UNIVERSITY PRESS

PUBLISHED BY THE PRESS SYNDICATE OF THE UNIVERSITY OF CAMBRIDGE
The Pitt Building, Trumpington Street, Cambridge, United Kingdom

CAMBRIDGE UNIVERSITY PRESS
The Edinburgh Building, Cambridge CB2 2RU, UK
40 West 20th Street, New York, NY 10011-4211, USA
477 Williamstown Road, Port Melbourne, VIC 3207, Australia
Ruiz de Alarcón 13, 28014 Madrid, Spain
Dock House, The Waterfront, Cape Town 8001, South Africa

http://www.cambridge.org

First published 2004

Printed in the United States of America

Typeface Sabon 10/12 pt.   *System* LATEX 2$_\varepsilon$ [TB]

A catalog record for this book is available from the British Library.

Library of Congress Cataloging in Publication Data

Kersch, Kenneth Ira, 1964–
Constructing civil liberties : discontinuities in the development of American constitutional
law / Ken I. Kersch.
    p. cm.
Includes bibliographical references and index.
ISBN 0-521-81178-3 (hardback) – ISBN 0-521-01055-1 (pbk.)
   1. Civil rights – United States – History.   2. Judicial review – United States.
3. Law and politics.   I. Title.
KF4749.K47   2004
342.7308′5–dc22   2003060534

ISBN 0 521 81178 3 hardback
ISBN 0 521 01055 1 paperback

Contents

Acknowledgments

Wisława Szymborska has described as "Fortune's darlings" those blessed enough to endlessly discover new challenges in their work, and thus to experience it as an ongoing adventure. I am clearly one of Fortune's darlings. The start of my good fortune was to have landed for graduate school in the government department at Cornell University, where the faculty encouraged me to ask and pursue big and interesting questions about politics. From the beginning, Ted Lowi, Richard Bensel, Isaac Kramnick, and Jeremy Rabkin guided my studies at Cornell and my work on this project. As I see it, this book is part of an ongoing conversation between me and each of these wonderful teachers, and among them. I have also been extremely fortunate after moving on from Cornell in finding colleagues and friends whose voices were added to this conversation and whose curiosity and sense of intellectual adventure have contributed immeasurably both to my thinking and to my continued delight in my work. Ron Kahn and Keith Whittington have become particularly valued friends and close intellectual companions. They have read multiple versions of this manuscript and have discussed it (and much else besides) with me at length. Clem Fatovic, Howard Gillman, Mark Graber, Scot Powe, Rogers Smith, and an array of anonymous readers spent a considerable amount of time with earlier versions of the manuscript and provided extensive, extremely helpful critiques. In addition, many generous and thoughtful people have read parts of the manuscript and offered highly useful criticisms and suggestions: Herman Belz, Matt Berke, Stephen Bragaw, Tom D'Andrea, Dan Dreisbach, Paul Frymer, Robert George, Lambert Gingras, Dennis Hutchinson, Larry Mead, Stephen Monsma, Alex Moon, Wayne Moore, Andy Moravscik, John Mueller, Carol Nackenoff, Julie Novkov, Grier Stephenson, Jim Stoner, and Art Swenson. I have also benefited over the years from related conversations with Jonas Pontusson, Elizabeth Sanders, Martin Shefter, and Sid Tarrow. Peter Fish and Murray Dry read the dissertation and provided encouragement and a sustaining vote of confidence at precisely the moment that it was needed. Paul Frymer,

Marie Gottschalk, Mike Klarman, Kevin Kosar, George Lovell, Karen Orren, and Stephen Skowronek kindly shared informative work in progress. Generous financial assistance was provided by the Andrew W. Mellon Foundation, the Russell Sage Foundation, Cornell University, the Princeton University Politics Department, Wiley Vaughan, and The James Madison Program in American Ideals and Institutions at Princeton (where I was the inaugural Ann and Herbert W. Vaughan Fellow during the 2001–2 academic year). The Madison Program provided me with a leave that not only gave me time to write, but also brought me into regular contact with a host of wonderfully informative, inquisitive, and friendly people who shaped this work in more ways than I could possibly describe. The Princeton Politics Department and its chair, Jeff Herbst, were unstinting in their support. It is hard to imagine a more stimulating environment in which to work. Lew Bateman at Cambridge University Press and Norrie Feinblatt provided expert editorial assistance. Clem Fatovic; James Goldman; Ted Holsten; Martin Krusin; Dan Peris; Bhamati Viswanathan; my students at Cornell, Lehigh, and Princeton; and the brothers at Lehigh's Phi Kappa Theta fraternity were bottomless sources of enthusiasm and encouragement.

The support and love of my parents, Barbara and Robert Kersch, have been steadiest and deepest of all. I dedicate this book to them, and to the memory of my grandmother, Sylvia Schillinger.

1

Introduction

This is a book about the paths of constitutional development culminating in the U.S. Supreme Court's landmark civil liberties and civil rights jurisprudence of the 1960s and 1970s. The roads to *Mapp v. Ohio* (1961) (search and seizure/privacy), *University of California Board of Regents v. Bakke* (1978) (affirmative action), *Engle v. Vitale* (1962) (separation of church and state), and other emblematic decisions marking the high tide of twentieth-century constitutional liberalism, I argue here, should be understood not as the issue of a single, linear and unidimensional path marked by the post–New Deal Court's newfound willingness to protect "personal" (as opposed to "economic") rights and liberties, and tracing out the implications for particular fact scenarios of abstract principles such as "privacy," "liberty," or "equality." These doctrinal landmarks are, rather, the diverse endpoints of a layered succession of progressive spirited ideological and political campaigns of statebuilding and reform. In the heat of these campaigns – whose center was typically outside the Court – it was apparent to the participants that key rights and liberties conflicted, and the meaning of both was contested. As such, it was understood by those animated by a strong substantive vision that some key rights and liberties would have to be jettisoned or circumscribed to advance others. Only after these campaigns succeeded, as part of the process of ideological institutionalization, were backwards-looking narratives created – off the Court and on – that worked to legitimate these achievements as rights-protecting triumphs and part of a linear, teleological march of progress.[1]

The narrative of constitutional development concerning rights and liberties that I characterize as backwards-looking pivots around the centerpoint of the New Deal. That narrative has shaped the agenda for constitutional scholars for most of the last century. One of its most significant characteristics

---

[1] *Mapp v. Ohio*, 367 U.S. 643 (1961); *Regents of the University of California v. Bakke*, 438 U.S. 265 (1978); *Engel v. Vitale*, 370 U.S. 421 (1962).

was that the developmental trajectory it imagines – a linear, teleological trajectory of barrier, breakthrough, and apotheosis – was highly court-centered. As such, it launched a raft of court-centered constitutional scholarship whose questions were framed by the pull of the narrative. At the core of this work were questions concerning judicial review, judicial activism, and judicial restraint. Since the reformers who made this constitutional revolution (chiefly Progressives and New Dealers) were at first outsiders to the role of shaping legal doctrine, they began their careers as critics of court power. Once they took hold of the reins of state and began to staff the courts themselves, however, the scholarship shifted, and they began to ask new and multi-layered questions that reflected this developmental sequence. Rather than simply decrying judicial review and judicial activism, their new task was to remain at least rhetorically consistent with the views on which their newfound power had been won, while moving, in turn, to justify both. This involved the formulation of new constitutional theories that set out in nuanced ways why judicial review and judicial activism were justified in some circumstances (for ends that they approved) and not others (for ends that they opposed). This new constitutional thinking began by stipulating a level of statism that was foreign (or fundamentally antagonistic) to the old constitutionalism. And it posited a new imperative involving the protection of civil liberties and civil rights. Structured as it was, the new constitutional scholarship was in its very sinews heavily implicated in the political project of justifying, institutionalizing, and (as conditions worked to decay its foundations) defending the New Deal constitutional regime.

In pivoting around barrier, breakthrough, and apotheosis, the foundational narrative of constitutional development I describe above – what I will call the "traditional narrative" – is a paradigmatic example of "progressive" history. And, indeed, this should hardly be surprising, as it is directly related to the work of the great progressive historians themselves, such as Charles Beard and Vernon Parrington, who served as the advance guard for the reformist program later institutionalized in the New Deal.[2] It is also a paradigmatic example of Whig history. Such histories, as historian Herbert Butterfield has described them, endeavor to cut "a clean path through ... complexity" through "an over-dramatization of the historical story" that pits the forces of progress against the forces of reaction. The historical task of the former is to remove the "obstructions" that are either thrown up by or defended by the latter. The Whig historian, Butterfield

---

[2] Charles A. Beard, *An Economic Interpretation of the Constitution of the United States* (New York: Macmillan, 1913); Vernon Parrington, "Introduction," in J. Allen Smith, *The Growth and Decadence of Constitutional Government* (New York: Henry Holt and Co., 1930). See William J. Novak, "The Legal Origins of the Modern American State," in *Looking Back at Law's Century: Time, Memory, and Change*, eds. Austin Sarat, Robert Kagan, and Bryant Garth (Ithaca, NY: Cornell University Press, 2002), 249–60.

writes, "very quickly busies himself with dividing the world into the friends and enemies of progress."[3]

Far from rendering narratives concerning historical trajectories implausible, the Whig approach is enormously seductive. Indeed, Butterfield concludes "[t]he truth is that there is a tendency for all history to veer over into Whig history" to the point where "it has been easy to believe that Clio herself is on the side of the Whigs." What is so seductive about Whig histories is that they are paeans to the illumination and glory of the present. Whig histories of the New Deal and the gradual achievement of court-protected civil rights and civil liberties have been so successful because, despite the anachronistic (and romantic) understanding of many of their purveyors as perpetual outsiders, in fundamental and gratifying ways they reflect and reinforce the discourse of power in contemporary thinking concerning twentieth-century American constitutional development.[4]

To say that constitutional thinking for most of the last century was written under the intense gravitational pull of the New Deal revolution is not to say that these histories are false in any broad sense or failed to yield important evidence and insights concerning the trajectory of American constitutionalism. After all, there was in fact a New Deal standoff. And it is undeniable that the agenda of the Supreme Court prior to the New Deal was different in important ways from the Court's agenda after it. Nor is it to gainsay that during the heyday of Whiggishness many detailed historical studies were written that effectively steered clear of the snares and perils of Whiggism. But in his anatomy of Whig histories, Butterfield himself noted that "[I]t is true that this tendency is corrected to some extent by the more concentrated labors of historical specialists." Nonetheless, he properly concluded, the tendency to Whig history is "so deep-rooted that even when piece-meal research has corrected the story in detail, we are slow in re-valuing the whole and reorganizing the broad outlines of the theme in light of these discoveries." There remains a persistent "tendency to patch the new research into the old story even when the research in detail has altered the bearings of the old subject."[5]

My contention in this book is that "research in detail" – my own (as presented here) and that of an ever-growing body of others (including Mark Graber, David Rabban, and G. Edward White's on the freedom of speech; Philip Hamburger's and John T. McGreevy's on the separation of church and state; David Bernstein's on the relationship between the state, the labor

---

[3] Novak, "Legal Origins of the Modern American State," 258 (referring to "the classic progressive trope: law as obstruction"). Herbert Butterfield, *The Whig Interpretation of History* (New York: W. W. Norton, 1965), 5, 29, 34.

[4] Butterfield, *Whig Interpretation*, 6, 8.

[5] Butterfield, *Whig Interpretation*, 5, 6. See also Paul Pierson, "Increasing Returns, Path Dependence, and the Study of Politics," *American Political Science Review* 94 (June 2000): 251–67, 260 ("understandings of the political world should themselves be susceptible to path dependence").

movement, and civil rights; Diane Ravitch's on progress in education; Kenneth Murchison's on prohibition; and Michael Klarman, Hugh Davis Graham, and John David Skrentny's on civil rights) has now accumulated to such an extent that it *fundamentally* undermines the plausibility of the third stage of the Whiggish New Deal constitutional narrative, and, in the process, of the entire narrative itself.[6] That third stage, involving the "end" – or the apotheosis – imagines what many today, under the pull of a still prevalent Whiggishness, would continue to call "civil rights and civil liberties," as the essence of the thing itself. Put otherwise, it sees the apotheosis as a "matter of principle."[7]

This book, in the spirit of the works cited above – which, in the nature of things, is a revisionist spirit – aspires, in a context long set by the pull of New Deal constitutional Whiggism, to unsettle our wonted assumptions. It does so by jettisoning the faith that the idiosyncratic and fundamentally contested policy end points that traditional legal scholars and political scientists dub "civil rights and civil liberties" represent in any broad sense an apotheosis of progress over reaction or the triumph of principle as if this were part of an

---

[6] David M. Rabban, *Free Speech in Its Forgotten Years* (Cambridge: Cambridge University Press, 1997); Mark A. Graber, *Transforming Free Speech: The Ambiguous Legacy of Civil Libertarianism* (Berkeley: University of California Press, 1991); G. Edward White, "Free Speech and the Bifurcated Review Project: The 'Preferred Position' Cases," in *Constitutionalism and American Culture: Writing the New Constitutional History*, eds. Sandra VanBurkeo, Kermit L. Hall, and Robert J. Kaczorowski (Lawrence: University Press of Kansas, 2002), 99–122; G. Edward White, "The First Amendment Comes of Age," *Michigan Law Review* 95 (1996): 299–392; Philip Hamburger, *The Separation of Church and State* (Cambridge, MA: Harvard University Press, 2002); John T. McGreevy, *Catholicism and American Freedom: A History* (New York: W. W. Norton, 2003); David E. Bernstein, *Only One Place of Redress: African Americans, Labor Regulations, and the Courts, from Reconstruction to the New Deal* (Durham, NC: Duke University Press, 2001); Diane Ravitch, *Left Back: A Century of Failed School Reforms* (New York: Simon and Schuster, 2000); Kenneth M. Murchison, *Federal Criminal Law Doctrines: The Forgotten Influence of National Prohibition* (Durham, NC: Duke University Press, 1994); Michael Klarman, "Rethinking the Civil Rights and Civil Liberties Revolutions," *Virginia Law Review* (February 1996): 1–67; Hugh Davis Graham, *Collision Course: The Strange Convergence of Affirmative Action and Immigration Policy in America* (New York: Oxford University Press, 2002); John David Skrentny, *The Ironies of Affirmative Action: Politics, Culture, and Justice in America* (Chicago: University of Chicago Press, 1996); John D. Skrentny, *The Minority Rights Revolution* (Cambridge, MA: The Belknap Press of the Harvard University Press, 2002). See also Eileen L. McDonagh, "The 'Welfare Rights State' and the 'Civil Rights State': Policy Paradox and Statebuilding in the Progressive Era," *Studies in American Political Development* 7 (Fall 1993): 225–74; Ken I. Kersch, "The Reconstruction of Constitutional Privacy Rights and the New American State," *Studies in American Political Development* 16 (Spring 2002): 61–87; Karen Orren and Stephen Skowronek, "What is Political Development?" paper presented at annual meeting of the American Political Science Association, San Francisco, California, August 29 – September 2, 2001.

[7] See Ronald Dworkin, *A Matter of Principle* (Cambridge, MA: Harvard University Press, 1985). See also Bruce Ackerman, *We the People: Foundations* (Cambridge, MA: The Belknap Press of the Harvard University Press, 1991).

ineluctable trajectory of history. In the absence of and in place of this faith, this book offers a series of empirical interpretive case studies involving three illustrative sites of constitutional order concerning constitutional rights and liberties – criminal process rights concerning privacy, workplace and labor rights, and civil liberties and civil rights in education – each culminating roughly (depending on the nature of the trajectory under study) with the Warren Court (1953–69) apotheosis, which the most influential scholars in the field have taken to be the high water mark of a judicial solicitude for civil rights and civil liberties. By taking a developmental approach that purposely rids itself of the gravitational pull of the Whiggish New Deal narrative (which many developmental histories do not) I offer, as a substitute for the field's wonted moralism and Whiggism, a sustained contemplation of the genealogy of contemporary constitutional morals.[8]

The Disintegration of the Historical Conditions that Produce Whiggish Constitutional Histories

While the traditional Whiggish narrative of contemporary rights and liberties – and the questions it perpetually throws up in legal scholarship – still defines the field, it is not nearly as predominant as it once was. Indeed, it is this decomposition in plausibility that has made possible both this study and other revisionist accounts of contemporary civil rights and civil liberties. Signs of the disintegration of the Whig narrative are apparent even in the work of leading constitutional Whigs such as Bruce Ackerman and Akhil Amar, who, for example, have both been influenced by the cyclical and decidedly non-progressive critical elections realignment theory of political scientists such as Walter Dean Burnham.[9] Although both Ackerman and Amar fashion teleological constitutional narratives that reach their apotheosis in contemporary constitutional liberalism, their pointed rejection of what Ackerman calls "the bicentennial myth" – which holds that the meaning of

---

[8] See Wendy Brown, *Politics Out of History* (Princeton: Princeton University Press, 2001), 91–120. See also Richard A. Posner, *Problematics of Moral and Legal Theory* (Cambridge, MA: The Belknap Press of the Harvard University Press, 1999). For the developmental accounts that laid the groundwork for this study by analyzing periodized trajectories of constitutional development, but (as I see it) in their structure remain vestigially wedded to the Whiggish (and moralizing) New Deal narratives, see Ackerman, *We the People*; Howard Gillman, "Preferred Freedoms: The Progressive Expansion of State Power and the Rise of Modern Civil Liberties Jurisprudence," *Political Research Quarterly* 47 (September 1994): 623–53; Howard Gillman, "Political Development and the Rise of the 'Preferred Freedoms' Rubric in Constitutional Law," paper presented at the University of Maryland Constitutionalism Discussion Group, College Park (April 2002).

[9] Bruce Ackerman, *We the People: Foundations*; Akhil Reed Amar, *The Bill of Rights: Creation and Reconstruction* (New Haven: Yale University Press, 1998); Walter Dean Burnham, *Critical Elections and the Mainsprings of American Politics* (New York: W. W. Norton, 1970).

the constitution is ineluctably tied to its meaning at one fixed time, located in a remote eighteenth-century past – plainly invites consideration of regimes and change into grand narratives of American constitutional history. Work in other areas, although not necessarily reflecting an express anti-Whiggism, clearly evinces a new attraction to questions that either challenge the traditional narrative and the conclusions scholars have drawn from its assumptions or, alternatively, originate wholly outside it. For instance, much of the new constitutional scholarship emphasizes the relative *unimportance* of judicial review as a political (and, hence, intellectual) problem, choosing to focus instead, even in explicitly constitutional studies, on either politics or the Constitution outside the courts. And even the work that does accord significant constitutional importance to courts increasingly treats those institutions as influenced by external political or ideological forces or heavily implicated in a regime-sustaining ideological endeavor. While puzzles of New Deal vintage, of course, continue to preoccupy many law professors and political theorists, this persistence is chiefly a matter of the institutional structure and politics of contemporary intellectual life (large ships turn slowly). In its most dynamic elements, the turn in the field is decidedly post–judicial review.[10]

These new preoccupations are not so much aberrations as a return, following a sustained and highly atypical period of elite consensus over

[10] See Barry Friedman, "The Birth of an Academic Obsession: The History of the Counter-majoritarian Difficulty: Part Five," *Yale Law Journal* 112 (November 2002): 153–259. See, e.g., Robert Dahl, "Decision-Making in a Democracy: The Supreme Court as a National Policy-Maker," *Journal of Public Law* 6 (1957): 279–95 (Supreme Court as part of broader governing coalition); Mark A. Graber, "The Non-Majoritarian Difficulty: Legislative Deference to the Judiciary," *Studies in American Political Development* 7 (1993): 35–73 (key landmark instances of judicial review represent the delegation by legislatures to courts of disruptive political issues); George Lovell, *Legislative Deferrals: Statutory Ambiguity, Judicial Power, and American Democracy* (New York: Cambridge University Press, 2003)(judicial review as part of the legislative agenda); Barry Friedman, "Dialogue and Judicial Review," *Michigan Law Review* 91 (1993): 577; Michael J. Klarman, "Rethinking the Civil Rights and Civil Liberties Revolutions," *Virginia Law Review* 82 (1996): 1–67 (arguing against the importance of countermajoritian judicial review in the development of twentieth-century civil rights and civil liberties); Gerald Rosenberg, *The Hollow Hope: Can Courts Bring About Social Change?* (Chicago: University of Chicago Press, 1991)(judicial review plays significantly lesser role than commonly thought in generating social change); John B. Gates, *The Supreme Court and Partisan Realignment: A Macro- and Micro-Level Perspective* (Boulder, CO: Westview Press, 1991); Keith E. Whittington, "Constitutional Theories and the Faces of Power," in *Alexander Bickel and Contemporary Constitutional Theory*, ed. Kenneth Ward (Albany: State University of New York Press, forthcoming); Keith E. Whittington, "To Support This Constitution: Judicial Supremacy in the Twentieth Century," in *Marbury v. Madison: Documents and Commentary*, eds. Mark A. Graber and Michael Perhac (Washington, DC: Congressional Quarterly Press, 2003); Keith Whittington, *Constitutional Construction* (Cambridge, MA: Harvard University Press, 1999)(significant features of our governing constitutionalism constructed outside the courts); *Judicial Independence in the Age of Democracy: Critical Perspectives*, eds. Peter H. Russell and David M. O'Brien (Charlottesville: University of Virginia Press, 2001), 7–8 (willingness of courts to void legislation no indication of judicial independence).

fundamental (and fundamentally political) constitutional commitments, to the contemplation of a normal state of affairs in American constitutional politics. Indeed, looked at retrospectively, the work of Rawls, Dworkin, and Ackerman seems to have been written at the high-water mark of contemporary constitutional liberalism, just before its tide began to recede. The realignment toward conservative national politics that began with Ronald Reagan's election to the presidency in 1980 ushered in a sustained challenge to key commitments of the New Deal regime (and its later outgrowths, such as the Great Society), including its basic assumptions concerning principles of structure and rights.[11] This political turn changed the composition of the federal judiciary (including the Supreme Court), and both altered and reflected shifting public attitudes toward centralization, statism, and long since reified contemporary definitions of civil liberties and civil rights.[12] Despite the institutional encrustation of statist liberalism within university faculties that tracked the imperatives and commitments of the prevailing regime, new paths of intellectual inquiry, both off campus and on, gradually opened up.

See also Stephen Skowronek, *Building a New American State* (courts as instruments of state and regimes, often serving distinctive institutional and ideological functions); Martin Sklar, *The Corporate Reconstruction of American Capitalism, 1890–1916* (New York: Cambridge University Press, 1988), 86–175; Ken I. Kersch, "The Reconstruction of Constitutional Privacy Rights" (courts as permeated by progressive thought concerning statebuilding and working to negotiate transitions from an old to a New American State). On the way in which elites have used judges to instituitonalize policy gains that they perceive as under siege, see Ran Hirschl, "The Struggle for Hegemony: Understanding Judicial Empowerment through Constitutionalization in Culturally Divided Polities," *Stanford Journal of International Law* 36 (2000): 73–118; Ran Hirschl, "The Political Origins of Judicial Empowerment through Constitutionalization: Lessons from Four Constitutional Revolutions," *Law and Social Inquiry* 25 (Winter 2000): 91–149; Ran Hirschl, *Toward Juristocracy: A Comparative Inquiry into the Origins and Consequences of the New Constitutionalism* (Cambridge, MA: Harvard University Press, 2004); Howard Gillman, "How Political Parties Can Use the Courts to Advance Their Agendas: Federal Courts in the United States, 1875–1891," *American Political Science Review* 96 (2002): 511–24. See also Philip Bobbitt, *Constitutional Fate: Theory of the Constitution* (New York: Oxford University Press, 1982) (focusing on judicial review, but radically removing it from foundationalist questions of constitutional philosophy and treating its study as a study of legalist justificatory and legitimating rhetorics or "argumentative modes"). Landmark works from the time when the problem of judicial review was at the center of the analysis include Alexander M. Bickel, *The Least Dangerous Branch: The Supreme Court at the Bar of Politics* (Indianapolis: Bobbs-Merrill, 1962); Ronald Dworkin, *Taking Rights Seriously* (Cambridge, MA: Harvard University Press, 1977); John Hart Ely, *Democracy and Distrust: A Theory of Judicial Review* (Cambridge, MA: Harvard University Press, 1980).

[11] See Ronald Kahn, *The Supreme Court and Constitutional Theory: 1953–1993* (Lawrence: University Press of Kansas, 1994). See Deborah A. Morris, "The Transmogrification of *United States v. Carolene Products*," paper presented at the annual meeting of the Western Political Science Association, Las Vegas, NV (March 2001) (noting that "Footnote Four lived in relative obscurity until the 1970s").

[12] See Thomas Keck, *The Most Activist Supreme Court in History: The Road to Modern Judicial Conservatism* (Chicago: University of Chicago Press, 2004).

The current Supreme Court commonly splits 5–4 on the most contentious issues of structure and rights. In an atmosphere in which both sides hurl charges of judicial activism on some issues and call just as vehemently for restraint on others, where charges of hypocrisy are endemic, and whereon some issues (most prominently, free speech) it is becoming increasingly difficult to label particular arguments and holdings as self-evidently "liberal" or "conservative," the intellectual and political influence of consensus theories positing a triumph of principle has sharply diminished.

Put otherwise, the study of American constitutionalism has once again assumed its place, not as a branch of consensus moral philosophy, but within the larger, messier, and decidedly less pristine study of American politics. To the extent that political practice implicates important creedal principles – and I believe it does – it also entails both contestation over the meaning of those principles and the perpetual imperative of making tragic choices between those principles – such as liberty and equality or privacy and publicity – when, as is commonly the case, one conflicts with another. The meanings are defined and choices made in concrete political circumstances and institutional contexts, with the decision in each case shot through with pull of specific, historically situated goals, aversions, hopes, and fears. As a distinctively political study (as opposed to a philosophical one), politics is constituted by contestation and by choice between incommensurables. As such, it is not linear.[13]

American constitutionalism is, however, developmental. To the extent that it represents the enshrinement of a choice or principle in either constitutional doctrine or another political institution, the subsequent meaning of that institutional achievement is not determined by the *intent* animating the initial achievement. Rather, that achievement lives in an "interinstitutional" environment characterized by patterns of intercurrence, where "different institutional rules and norms will abut and grate as a normal state of affairs." This is as true for civil rights and civil liberties as it is for any other aspect of law within political life. To the extent that it is a narrative positing a linear progression toward an equilibrium (such as "the protection of civil rights and civil liberties"), that narrative is not developmental in the sense in which we understand the processes of political development today. In this book, I provide a series of case studies canvassing the multifarious ways in which constitutional development concerning civil rights and civil liberties reflects the patterns of development and change identified in recent, groundbreaking work by scholars of political development.[14]

---

[13] See Samuel Huntington, *American Politics: The Promise of Disharmony* (Cambridge, MA: The Belknap Press of the Harvard University Press, 1981), 12–30; Isaiah Berlin, *Four Essays on Liberty* (New York: Oxford University Press, 1969), 164; Judith N. Shklar, "A Liberalism of Fear," in Judith N. Shklar, *Political Thought and Political Thinkers* (Chicago: University of Chicago Press, 1998).

[14] Karen Orren and Stephen Skowronek, "Institutions and Intercurrence: Theory Building in the Fullness of Time," in *Nomos 38: Political Order*, eds. Ian Shapiro and Russell Hardin (New

Traditional, linear, Whiggish narratives of constitutional development concerning civil rights and civil liberties make critical errors that successful developmental narratives attentive to processes such as intercurrence, path dependency, and unintended consequences would not. A Whiggish narrative may posit a normatively desirable constitutional policy choice as reflecting a sweeping and cross-institutional foundational commitment to a core political principle. So, for example, as I show in the substantive chapters that follow, a Whiggish narrative may imagine the forces of progress to be broadly committed to a "right to privacy" and to the value of privacy itself. But in doing so, it would need to focus almost exclusively on the end point – contemporary understandings of that right – and the issues of sexual and reproductive autonomy surrounding it. In the process, it would need to excise

York: New York University Press, 1996), 111–46); Ira Katznelson, "Structure and Configuration in Comparative Politics," in *Comparative Politics: Rationality, Culture, and Structure*, eds. Mark Irving Lichbach and Alan S. Zuckerman (Cambridge: Cambridge University Press, 1997), 81–111; Paul Pierson, "Not Just What, but *When*: Timing and Sequence in Political Processes," *Studies in American Political Development* 14 (Spring 2000): 72–92; Paul Pierson, "Increasing Returns, Path Dependence, and the Study of Politics," *American Political Science Review* 94 (June 2000): 251–67; Paul Pierson and Theda Skocpol, "Historical Institutionalism in Contemporary Political Science," in *Political Science: The State of the Discipline*, eds. Ira Katznelson and Helen V. Milner (New York: W. W. Norton, 2002), 692–721, 708 ("Functional interpretations of politics are . . . suspect because of the sizable temporal gap between actors' actions and the long-term consequences of those actions. Political actors, facing the pressures of the immediate or skeptical about their capacity to engineer long-term effects, may pay limited attention to the long run." It is the case, however, that "the long-term effects of institutional choices . . . are frequently the most profound and interesting ones." They are only understood by seeing them "as the *by-products* of social processes rather than embodying the goals of social actors."); Arthur Denzau and Douglass C. North, "Shared Mental Models: Ideologies and Institutions," *Kyclos* 47 (1): 3–31. For complementary approaches taken by legal scholars, see J. M. Balkin, "Ideological Drift and the Struggle Over Meaning," *Connecticut Law Review* 25 (1992–1993): 869–91; Richard H. Fallon Jr., *Implementing the Constitution* (Cambridge, MA: Harvard University Press, 2001), 7 ("by rejecting the mesmerizing notion that the Court's only proper role is identifying the Constitution's one, true meaning, we can get a richer picture of what the Court does and a more enlightening framework for considering what the Court ought to do. . . . [A]bandoning the view of doctrine as ideally being a perfect reflection of constitutional meaning helps us better appreciate the array of choices open to the Court in crafting [constitutional] rules and tests. We can begin to see different kinds of tests that the Court familiarly uses as available, but seldom necessary, mechanisms for protecting constitutional values." Moreover, Fallon argues, it is a mistake to assume "every case should furnish an occasion for judicial inquiry into the truth about what the Constitution means. The Supreme Court patently does not function in this way. In most cases, the Court proceeds on the tacit understanding that it will apply, without reexamining, frameworks that were crafted in earlier decisions" [43–4]. "In extraordinary cases, the Court concludes that it cannot resolve the question before it without either crafting new doctrine or reconsidering the wisdom or applicability of an existing doctrinal framework" [43]. Even in extraordinary cases, "the Court must go beyond the abstract moral principles rightly celebrated by the forum-of-principle model; the Justices must draw on psychology, sociology, and economics to craft doctrines that will work in practice, without excessive costs, and that will prove democratically acceptable" [77]).

from constitutional history the elaborate campaign *against privacy* and *for publicity* by the progenitors of the contemporary right to privacy who built the New American State, which serves as the foundation for the new constitutionalism to which it is currently committed. A Whiggish narrative will commonly define the contemporary legal landscape, to the extent that it is defined by what we today understand to be "civil libertarian" commitments, as uniquely the product of the pursuit of either founding or noble constitutional principles. But, as I demonstrate below in exploring the emergence of the contemporary civil libertarian doctrine concerning the separation of church and state, an archeological exploration of the genesis of that doctrine may demonstrate that its roots are actually in a unique convergence of half-understood and half-remembered (and, at times, highly ignoble) passions and prejudices, hopes and fears among progressive elites. In a similar dynamic, I demonstrate the way in which many contemporary "civil libertarian" criminal process protections have their roots not in reformist campaigns but in the resistance to the progressive-spirited campaign for prohibition. A Whiggish narrative will tend to view its great reformist breakthroughs as moments that largely clear the field, in the process sweeping away obstacles to a new and more enlightened order. While these breakthroughs often have precisely those effects along the policy dimension targeted by reformers, however, they are just as likely to set up new institutions that constitute new obstacles to the next reformist campaign – as I show in my discussion of the way in which progressive and New Deal labor constitutionalism represented a direct assault on American blacks and, as such, a new barrier to the cause of civil rights. To the extent they are undergirded by claims on behalf of democracy (and, in American constitutionalism, they typically are), Whiggish narratives skew the causal analysis of constitutional change toward society-centered, and away from state-centered, explanations, even though, in certain cases, the latter explanations are clearly predominant. For example, as I show in my discussion of the genealogy of contemporary concern for racial group rights, claims of that sort were alien to American blacks prior to the constitutional innovation according such rights to organized labor. Black Americans adopted self-understandings and a politics of group rights only after they became trapped in a constitutional order structured in significant part by the reformist campaigns of organized labor that constitutionally privileged such claims. Whiggish narratives of constitutional development typically position themselves as liberatory, evolutionary, and "living," in contradistinction to more constricting "conservative" constitutional understandings anchored in interpretive originalism or conceptual formalism.[15] But, as the history of affirmative action and my discussion of the process

---

[15] See Howard Gillman, "The Collapse of Constitutional Originalism and the Rise of the Notion of a 'Living Constituiton' in the Course of American Statebuilding," *Studies in American Political Development* 11 (Fall 1997): 191–247.

of institutionalizing group rights in the Supreme Court's labor picketing decisions shows, these narratives are just as likely to hew to regime-defining formalisms in the face of altered demographics and a shifting institutional environment, as are ostensibly conservative constitutional visions.

To be sure, Whiggish narratives of constitutional development do not evince all of these failings. Despite my criticism of Whiggish narratives for their formalism, for example, it would be inaccurate to characterize Whiggish narratives as thoroughly formalistic and their affinities for a "living constitutionalism" a myth. It is not my objective to substitute one linear model for another. My point is, first, that Whiggish narratives import a particular set of unifying myths into the study of constitutional development concerning civil rights and civil liberties. It is, second, that, as presented in the fullness of time, development is as rife with abrasions, abutments, agonisms, drift, and tensions as any other area of political life. As with any ideological system of meaning aimed at justifying a concrete and perpetually altering political order, it is the job of constitutional Whiggism to reconcile essentially irreconcilable commitments in an emotionally satisfying and, hence, politically plausible way.[16] As students of political development, with the aim of understanding the nature of change, it is our job to pull them apart.

Toward an Affirmative Theory of Constitutional Development in the New American State

Although I have spent some time here setting out the failings of traditional narratives of constitutional development concerning civil rights and civil liberties, and although I frame this book's substantive chapters in opposition to those narratives, my main purpose in the pages that follow is not negative but positive. In those chapters, I do not so much reject the Whig narrative of constitutional development as invite it in as an endogenous part of an affirmative, historically anchored theory of *constitutional* development that takes seriously the ideological process involving the construction of constitutional legitimacy.[17]

---

[16] See Judith N. Shklar, *Legalism: Law, Morals, and Political Trials* (Cambridge, MA: Harvard University Press, 1986), 1–28; Martin Shapiro, *Courts: A Comparative and Political Analysis* (Chicago: University of Chicago Press, 1981), 8, 11, 17–20.

[17] I consider *constitutional* development to be a distinctive part of the broader project of *political* development, with the former preoccupied with the task, under altering conditions and imperatives, with the perpetual construction and reconstruction of legitimate authority. As such, the study of constitutional development may be an empirical study, but it is also inevitably a study of ideas. Some, while sharing an interest in these dynamics concerning legitimacy, do not draw a sharp distinction between constitutional and political development. Orren and Skowronek, for example, argue that political development generally is about the construction of authority. Much of the ideological work in this area is

My central thesis here is that constitutional development in what I call the "New Constitutional Nation," a nation constructed beginning in the late nineteenth and early twentieth centuries and continuing to the present, has proceeded simultaneously on two tracks. One involved the building of the physical institutions and coercive apparatus of the modern "New American State."[18] And the second involved the ongoing ideological work of constructing that perpetually altering and expanding state – including, in its inception, the trimming and even jettisoning of commitments to long-standing creedal constitutional liberties and rights – as a legitimate source of national governing authority. Until quite recently, scholars of American

accomplished through constitutional discourse, which they implicitly fold into the category of political development. Wayne Moore, on the other hand, conceives of the construction of authority as, in its broadest sense, a *constitutional* problem, as I do here. See Stephen Skowronek, "Order and Change," *Polity* 28 (Fall 1995): 91–101; Karen Orren and Stephen Skowronek, *The Search for American Political Development?* (New York: Cambridge University Press, 2004); Wayne D. Moore, "Toward a Theory of Partial Constitutional Authority," paper presented at the annual meeting of the American Political Science Association, San Francisco, California (August 2001); Wayne D. Moore, "(Re)construction of Constitutional Authority and Meaning: The Fourteenth Amendment and the Slaughter-House Cases," in *The U.S. Supreme Court and American Political Development*, eds. Ronald Kahn and Ken I. Kersch. See also Pamela Brandwein, *Reconstructing Reconstruction: The Supreme Court and the Production of Historical Truth* (Durham, NC: Duke University Press, 1999); Pamela Brandwein, "The Civil Rights Cases and the Lost Doctrine of State Neglect," in Kahn and Kersch, *Supreme Court and American Political Development*; Kahn, *Supreme Court and Constitutional Theory*; Keith E. Whittington, "The Political Foundations of Judicial Supremacy," in *Constitutional Politics: Essays on Constitution Making, Maintenance, and Change*, eds. Sotirios Barber and Robert P. George (Princeton: Princeton University Press, 2001) (on the construction of the authority of the Supreme Court as an instituiton). Sociologist James Nolan sets out a useful, interactive, dialectical model of the construction of state authority by culture-state interaction that is compatible with my own. For Nolan, "legitimacy . . . refers to the cultural ideas and value systems that undergird the practical functions of the state . . . [or] the sources of legitimacy that give moral and philo-sophical justification (or 'normative dignity') to the laws, policies, and programs of a given state system." Nolan singles out court decisions in particular as exercises of state power in which "justifications for the existence of a given law" are commonly set out. He adds that "[a]n important and too often overlooked component of theories of state legitimation is a focus on the significant influence of the changing cultural codes of moral understanding that justify the laws, functions, and policies of the state. Recognizing that the state and culture exist in a dialectical relationship with each other . . . [leads us] to consider the cultural codes that [undergird] and [give] meaning to the state." Nolan, *Therapeutic State*, 26, 45; Bobbitt, *Constitutional Fate*, 243–4. I note that Bobbitt, while not denying that law is influenced by political, social, economic, and intellectual trends, makes a fairly sharp distinction between legitimating legal/constitutional arguments from these other spheres, which may influence constitutional law. I agree that the distinction is a useful one. But, as is evident in Bobbitt's work itself, it is far from hermetic. And my chief interest, unlike Bobbitt's, is precisely at the line between the two, which marks the fulcrum of constitutional legitimacy. See, generally, Shklar, *Legalism*; Shapiro, *Courts*.

[18] Or what Lowi calls "constitutive" public policy. Theodore J. Lowi, "Four Systems of Policy, Politics, and Choice," *Public Administration Review* 33 (July/August 1972): 298–310. Skowronek, *Building a New American State* (Cambridge: Cambridge University Press, 1982).

political development have devoted most of their time to the first part of this project. Scholars of *constitutional* development, however, as scholars of *constitutionalism*, are properly charged with devoting sustained attention to its second track. As empirical scholars concerned with the construction of legitimacy across time, it behooves them to avoid taking their cues from legalist intellectuals and legalist political theorists in formulating their models and categories and, as I do here, to treat them as endogenous and invested participants in this ongoing and ideologically charged process of constitutional construction.[19]

A Note on Periodization

I offer the previously outlined two-track model of constitutional development as a model uniquely appropriate to understanding American constitutionalism in the twentieth century. The case studies in constitutional development concerning civil rights and civil liberties presented here draw a distinction between an initial constitutional order – the constitutional adjunct of what Skowronek has characterized as the "state of courts and parties" (the "traditional constitutional order") – and a succeeding New Constitutional Nation, which took flight along with the rise of the New American State. This two-stage periodization is far from chronologically pristine: The transition from one stage to the other does not pivot on a "constitutional moment" or single transformative event. And, the legitimation-focused, regime-sustaining accounts of others notwithstanding, it does not align neatly with any critical election that serves to ratify its authority as a whole.[20] Internally, neither order is characterized by strict, unchanging

---

[19] See Whittington, *Constitutional Construction*. I share with Whittington a belief that the Constitution "must be constructed from the political melding of the document with external interests and principles." Whittington's interest is in constructions of the Constitution by the executive and legislative branches of government and in "altered constitutional practices [that] barely affected judicial doctrine." While I agree strongly that the constructions Whittington identifies are highly significant, I argue here for the additional importance of constructions arising in social, political, and intellectual life, as well as within formal governing institutions, and I am very much interested in the way that these ultimately affect judicial doctrine.

[20] See Wayne D. Moore, "Reflections of Constitutional Politics in the Early Judicialization of Reconstruction," paper presented at the annual meeting of the American Political Science Association, Boston, Massachusetts (29 August 2002). Wayne D. Moore, "(Re)construction of Constitutional Authority and Meaning," in Kahn and Kersch, *Supreme Court and American Political Development*. Here, I join the trend in studies of American constitutional development to decenter the narrative away from the New Deal. See Skowronek, *Building a New American State*; Whittington, *Constitutional Construction*; Barry Cushman, *Rethinking the New Deal Court: The Structure of a Constitutional Revolution* (New York: Oxford University Press, 1998); G. Edward White, *The Constitution and the New Deal* (Cambridge, MA: Harvard University Press, 2000); Graber, *Transforming Free Speech*; Lovell, *Legislative Deferrals*. See, generally, David R. Mayhew, *Electoral Realignments: A Critique of an American Genre* (New Haven: Yale University Press, 2002).

unities or settlements that necessarily cut across policy areas and institutions, though the first is decidedly more unified and less protean than its successor. Indeed, my chief interest is in the disharmonies and discontinuities and the protean character of civil rights and civil liberties in the New Constitutional Nation, as played against a persistent emotional, and hence political, imperative to reconstruct them as harmonious, continuous, and stable. Because, although roughly distinguishing the old order from the new, I do not posit any single, cross-cutting moment of transition, and because relatively rapid, disharmonious, and discontinuous transitions are a characteristic feature of the new order itself, I have decided to present my three case studies of substantive developmental trajectories in three rather long chapters unencumbered by the chapter breaks that would inevitably import a sharper periodization within these trajectories than that to which I would substantively wish to commit. To render these chapters more readable, however, I have broken them up into segments with numerous sections and subsections.

Following an introduction, as a baseline and a point of contrast, each chapter opens with a discussion of the substantive matter at hand under the traditional constitutional order. These beginnings emphasize, if not rigidity, immutability, and the strictest fidelity, then at least *relative* stability, or *relative* continuity within the processes of change. I take constitutional politics in this traditional order to have been distinctive, not only in its dynamics, but also in its substance. That politics, as Rogan Kersh has shown, was distinctively structured around an articulated set of tensions and competing, and commonly agonistic, principles and institutional commitments. The polarities of these traditional arrangements – Hamiltonianism versus Jeffersonianism, Jacksonianism versus Whiggism, and others – were lived chiefly in the realm of party politics and only rarely in the constitutional decisions of courts. These constitutive agonisms and antagonisms "had negative consequences aplenty, but [they] also permitted separate elements to be more or less peaceably combined, and addressed in American political debate: Hamiltonian nationalism and Jeffersonian localism; Jacksonian southerners' states rights views and Whigs' internal improvements carried out by the central government; individual rights and communal obligation; local civil society efforts and government assistance; and so forth," each of these tensions and themes was treated "in the context of sustained union," which lend a unity to a constitutional order constituted by its commitment to agonism. Under this order, "Americans could balance – if often precariously – political views otherwise perpetually in tension."[21]

Linear, unidimensional narratives of constitutional progress were alien to this order. Such directional unities, in the American context, at least, were not constitutional in the traditional sense; rather, they were religious. These

---

[21] Rogan Kersh, *Dreams of a More Perfect Union* (Ithaca, NY: Cornell University Press, 2001), 275. See, generally, Skowronek, *Building a New American State*.

unities, which would transform constitutional narratives into moral dramas, were first imported into the marrow of American constitutionalism by a religious reform movement: abolitionism. As abolitionism gained political saliency, it first called into question, and ended by shattering, the bona fides of a structurally balanced, Newtonian constitutionalism that preceded it, a constitutionalism that was understood as a way of managing conflict between different groups and within the government itself.[22] Abolitionism began as an irritant to the national government. But, with the Civil War and the Union's victory, it ultimately ended up laying the groundwork for the transformation of that government into a modern central state. In the process, its constitutional vision was imported into the sinews of the emerging state itself.[23]

Both the moral pull of the abolitionist vision (to the extent it was based on a broad understanding of human equality) and the claims of the Civil War central state, of course, were undermined on a variety of fronts by political and economic developments in the war's aftermath. Over time, especially with the end of Reconstruction, they faded significantly. But, for reasons that have been chronicled (and debated) by political development scholars, the process of statebuilding and nationbuilding, itself in important respects the product of successor reformist movements and campaigns (such as populism, Progressivism, and the labor movement, as well as feminism, and the temperance and social gospel movements), began anew in the late nineteenth and early twentieth centuries. Like abolitionism, these movements were, if not always religious, at least religious in their fervor and singleness of purpose. These movements, like abolitionism, had a singular sense of moral purpose and a belief that any and all means, including national power, could legitimately be used to achieve their goals. The movements imported this moralized constitutional vision into the void created by the disintegration of the traditional constitutional order.

As these developments played themselves out – haltingly and audaciously, partially and uniformly, loudly and *sub silentio* – constitutional arguments appealing to agonistic principles and institutional tensions and balances, were newly at a discount. In contrast, constitutional arguments endeavoring to reconcile conflicts in service of national goals and national movements toward progress, to rework apparently disparate and antagonistic parts and principles into a coherent monistic vision, were now at a premium. In the New Constitutional Nation, *reconciliation* became the order of the day. This

---

[22] See Alexander Hamilton, James Madison, and John Jay, *The Federalist Papers* (New York: Mentor Books, 1999), nos. 10, 48, 51, 54.

[23] Richard Franklin Bensel, *Yankee Leviathan: The Origins of Central State Authority in America, 1859–1877* (Cambridge: Cambridge University Press, 1990); Richard Franklin Bensel, *The Political Economy of American Industrialization, 1877–1900* (Cambridge: Cambridge University Press, 2000).

defining task and legitimating imperative of statebuilders ultimately led to the invention of modern field constitutional theory. In laboring over this project, public political theorists, such as Herbert Croly – the founder of modern constitutional theory – and, later, law school jurisprudes, played an indispensable role in aligning the mainstream of American constitutional thought with the ideological requirements and governing facts of the New American State. They invented, and continue to invent, the New Constitutional Nation. Croly's foundational contribution was to fashion an emotionally and politically plausible ideological defense of a level of statism in American politics that previously would have been understood, emotionally and politically, as wholly incompatible with a creedal and foundational antistatist Jeffersonian conception to freedom. By taking Croly's new statism as fundamental, later constitutional theorists laid the ideological foundations in monistic, reconciling terms for the political goals of one reformist enthusiasm after another, in a succession that has persisted to the end of the twentieth century. Because causes and imperatives shifted rapidly under this protean new order, *ingeniousness* – or an ever-proliferating (and often frantically rushing) cascade of efforts to legitimate by reconciling incommensurables – became the hallmark of modern constitutional theory. The task became one of a perpetual search, under constantly altering conditions, for the theory that would "work." Some, like Bruce Ackerman, had the grand, synthetic ambitions of the James Madison of contemporary constitutional theory himself, Herbert Croly. But even those with less comprehensive visions took Croly implicitly as their guide.

To a significant extent, the story of modern American constitutionalism is one of the choices reformers aligned with the cause of "progress" made – between statism and antistatism, rights and liberties, one right and another, and one liberty and another – all the while working frenetically and ingeniously to reconcile those choices in an emotionally and politically plausible way as having involved no choice at all, but rather as simply another step in the onward march of progress. Needless to say, a constitutionalism of this sort is especially susceptible to Whiggish understandings of its own history. It is hardly surprising that Whig histories, culminating always in the present on the verge of being born, became the definitive "constitutive stories" of the New Constitutional Nation.[24]

---

[24] Rogers M. Smith has argued that "civic myths" or "constitutive stories" are essential for mobilizing public support for political regimes and, indeed, to the project of imagining and building nations. Rogers M. Smith, *Civic Ideals: Conflicting Visions of Citizenship in U.S. History* (New Haven: Yale University Press, 1997), 6 (arguing that, to mobilize public support, political leaders have to craft civic myths); Rogers M. Smith, "Citizenship and the Politics of People-Building," *Citizenship Studies* 5 (2001): 73–95. See also Benedict Anderson, *Imagined Communities: Reflections on the Origin and Spread of Nationalism* (London: Verso, 1983); Paul Gerwitz, "Narrative and Rhetoric in the Law," in *Law's Stories: Narrative and Rhetoric in the Law*, eds. Peter Brooks and Paul Gerwitz (New Haven: Yale University Press, 1996). Readers

Cases: Three Sites of the Construction of Civil Liberties in the New Constitutional Nation

The core of this book is comprised of concrete historical-interpretive studies – the first involving criminal process rights and privacy, the second involving workplace and labor rights, and the third involving civil liberties and civil rights in education – that illustrate the workings of its theoretical model. Readers will find that some of this material covers territory that has been well trodden in constitutional histories. But because extensive historical erasures are essential to preserving the force and directionality of the predominant regime-sustaining Whiggish narratives, much of it will be new.[25]

The case selections may seem idiosyncratic. They were arrived at, in the first instance, inductively, after an immersion in certain areas of contemporary civil rights and civil liberties doctrine. Where this immersion led me to believe there might be telling genealogies that belied developmental narratives that seemed to be second nature, I investigated further. I was soon convinced, however, that these cases made conceptual sense as well. All, of course, involve civil rights and civil liberties, my chief focus in this book. The first section, on criminal process rights, covers not just what we would call "street crime," but, traced backwards, the building of the coercive regulatory apparatus of the modern administrative state. The second considers the construction of the modern constitutionalism of labor, which, as

---

will note that I use the term "progressive" throughout this book and that I do not apply it to any single, theoretically consistent outlook. I take "progressivism" (which I do not confine to the properly named early-twentieth-century political movement) to amount to an attitude and an inclination, not a logically coherent philosophy. At any given moment, this attitude jumbles together all manner of fashions, enthusiasms, prejudices, principles, convictions, and blind spots that are often flatly contradictory, both internally and with different "progressive" outlooks in different historical periods. To be progressive, in my account, is to be allied in what is taken to be a reformist cause with other people who also understand themselves working aggressively for progress and reform. In this sense, progressivism as I use the term here involves a certain vanguardism, or reformist self-conception. But, at base, I take as the measure of progressivism not adherence to any particular views, nor even some test asking whether the views advanced under the banner of progress represent challenges to the status quo (the "civil rights" leadership that currently takes itself to be "progressive," for example, is stand-pattist par excellence). When I wish to refer specifically to the early-twentieth-century "Progressive" political movement, I will do so by capitalizing the term.

[25] To date, the lion's share of work aimed at eliminating erasures in constitutional history has been directed toward giving voice to blacks, women, gays and lesbians, and other such groups. Far from challenging the traditional narrative and altering the Whiggish paradigm, by conceptualizing the trajectory of constitutional development as amounting, in its essence, to the story of the inclusion (or the failure of inclusion) of previously excluded "oppressed" groups, this work simply extends the program set out in the *Carolene Products* footnote and, in the process, reinforces it. *United States v. Carolene Products Co.*, 304 U.S. 144 (1938), n. 4. Systematic erasures of other types (even involving these very same groups), however, exist and are significant.

political development scholars have long recognized, was one of the formative influences on both American politics and the construction and nature
of the New American State. And the third involves education, a policy area
that to varying extents in different periods was charged with the construction
of modern citizens who would inhabit and sustain that state. As such, these
parts involve the building of the state itself and the construction of its workers and its people. When taken together, these case studies – which, strictly
speaking, I offer only illustratively – turn out to offer a fairly (if not fully)
comprehensive picture of trajectories of constitutional development concerning twentieth-century civil rights and civil liberties.

Each of these chapters involves a sustained consideration of a "site" of
constitutional development. My decision to study "sites" of development
arises out of an effort, in service of historical and theoretical illumination,
to steer a course between a clause-bound approach that traces the genealogy
of a single "right" or liberty – such as the freedom of speech, religious liberty, or the search and seizure provision of the Fourth Amendment – and an
approach spotlighting the broad, undifferentiated categories of "civil rights,"
"civil liberties," or "civil rights and civil liberties." Only by moving beyond
a clause-bound approach can we appreciate the ways in which developments
concerning one right or liberty influence and abrade against developments
concerning another – a key pattern in the trajectories of political development
characterized by intercurrence, path dependencies, and multiple orders. And
only by rejecting the broad, undifferentiated categories (which have been
swallowed whole, not only by normatively inclined constitutional Whigs, but
also by ostensibly value-neutral behavioralists) can we chart the processes
by which the innards of the categories shift, and certain rights and liberties –
or certain instantiations of those rights and liberties in altering contexts –
came to be preferred to others. When they are approached developmentally,
we can see that "civil rights," "civil liberties," and "civil rights and civil
liberties" as categories *never* move as broad unities in a single direction. Only
a middle-level, site-focused analysis can chart these developmental dynamics.

The following synopses begin with a description of the familiar Whiggish
narrative of development concerning each site. Taking account of patterns
of intercurrence, disharmony, and complexity, each then presents a counter-
narrative that I contend more accurately captures the nature of the trajectory
of constitutional development concerning that site.

Site One – Reconstituting Privacy and Criminal Process Rights

Traditional narratives of constitutional development concerning criminal
process rights, including Fourth and Fifth Amendment privacy rights, are
Whiggish narratives that posit an early lack of concern leading to a cresting solicitude for such rights in the Supreme Court's Warren and Burger
years. Within those narratives, progressive lawyer and civil libertarian Justice
Louis D. Brandeis is taken to have been an unwavering proponent of privacy

rights, and, as such, a trailblazer of the path that led to their linear, developmental apotheosis in the Supreme Court's abortion rights decision in *Roe v. Wade* (1973). This narrative became an institutional fixture of contemporary American constitutionalism, not because it provided a particularly rich or nuanced insight into the trajectory of development concerning constitutional privacy (and other criminal process rights), but rather because of the signal ideological service it provided in sustaining the prevailing (albeit now staunchly contested) post-1937 New Deal constitutional regime.

Free from the narrative requirements of Whiggishness, the trajectory of constitutional development concerning criminal process rights is best described as the issue of a series of sequential developmental struggles involving four distinct reformist political projects, only one of which does not involve what today would be considered classically "criminal" matters. The non–street crime project was the late-nineteenth- and early-twentieth-century fight by progressives to construct a powerful, fact-fortified New American State. Of the three street crime projects (which I take up successively), the first was the effort to secure the civil rights of the freedmen through the extension of central state jurisdiction and power. The second was the fight for alcohol prohibition in the teens and 1920s. And the third was the mid-twentieth-century fight to secure the civil rights of American blacks.[26]

The non–street crime part of this trajectory involved a sustained political and legal campaign by progressive intellectuals *against* constitutional privacy rights, a campaign that comprised a core part of their efforts to construct a powerful, seeing New American State that rendered legible and, hence, manipulable, formerly dark areas of the American political economy involving businessmen and business records. In this campaign, progressives argued frankly and audaciously that constitutional privacy rights (under the Fourth Amendment's search and seizure provisions, the Fifth Amendment's self-incrimination provisions, and the Constitution's structural provisions)

---

[26] In this case, that is, a layered succession of social movements played an important role in setting the path of development. I use the broader term "reformist movement" rather than "social movement" thoughout, however, because often intellectual movements not rising to the overtly political level of social movements are the key developmental force. On political development as a sequential, layered process, see Karen Orren and Stephen Skowronek, "Beyond the Iconography of Order: Notes for a 'New Institutionalism,'" in *The Dynamics of American Politics: Approaches and Interpretations*, eds. Lawrence C. Dodd and Calvin Jillson (Boulder, CO: Westview Press, 1994), 320; Kathleen Thelen, "How Institutions Evolve: Insights from Comparative Historical Analysis," in *Comparative Historical Analysis in the Social Sciences*, eds. James Mahoney and Dietrich Rueschemeyer (Cambridge: Cambridge University Press, 2003), 222, 226–8. Jeffrey K. Tulis, *The Rhetorical Presidency* (Princeton: Princeton University Press, 1987); Eric Schickler, *Disjointed Pluralism: Institutional Innovation and the Development of the U.S. Congress* (Princeton: Princeton University Press, 2001). On social movements and political development, see, e.g., Elizabeth Sanders, *Roots of Reform: Farmers, Workers, and the American State, 1877–1917* (Chicago: University of Chicago Press, 1999).

stood as a barrier to the statebuilding effort at the heart of the late-nineteenth-
and early-twentieth-century political agenda. Although the claims on behalf
of privacy against the progressive call for "publicity" at this time were mainly
asserted by businesses and businessmen, the ultimate defeat of those privacy
claims, once institutionalized, had pervasive, often unintended, effects upon
the value of privacy (if not the "right to privacy") under the new order. The
progressive triumph over the privacy claims made by economic actors in the
late-nineteenth and early-twentieth centuries gave the government broad,
seeing powers that left few limits on both the power of government to "see"
in the public interest (whether businesses were the target or not) and the
highly invasive discovery process in lawsuits through which (as the Clinton
impeachment usefully demonstrated) all sorts of noneconomic personal matters were potentially exposed to public view.

Progressives continued their frank assault on both privacy rights and criminal process rights, broadly considered, in their struggles on behalf of prohibition. Operating in the context of an expanded street crime jurisdiction that
was created to supervise the South's treatment of blacks and, in the wake
of the Civil War, sustain the Constitution's authority in the face of Southern resistance, however, the conservative Supreme Court in many respects
frustrated progressive assaults on privacy related and other criminal process rights. In resisting the progressive program concerning prohibition, the
Court played a major role in inventing the modern constitutional doctrine
of criminal procedure.

In subsequent years, the Fourth and Fifth Amendments, which had been
bled dry of the broad meanings they had held during the statebuilding process, and partially revived by a residually antistatist Supreme Court during
prohibition, were reinvented as part of the mid-twentieth-century Court's
antiracist policy program. As such, they were held to require an elaborate
new system of procedural protections for those accused of street crimes.

In some of these sequential reformist projects concerning criminal process
rights, the partisans of progress were the outspoken opponents of the cause
of rights protection. In fighting on behalf of the building of the powerful
and highly centralized New American State, for instance, the proponents of
progress rallied frankly and forcefully *against* the cause of rights protection,
whether pursuant to the Bill of Rights or otherwise. In the same struggle, they
also rallied *against* according broad constitutional protection for privacy
rights. Similarly, in championing the cause of the prohibition, proponents
of progress fought diligently against causes that today would be associated
with civil rights. For progressive prohibitionists, for instance, Catholics and
immigrants, as social groups, were taken to be enemies of a better future (as
progressive social scientific research in the realm of eugenics – in its statist,
reform Darwinist form, as opposed to its antistatist, Sumnerian form – was
demonstrating in this and other realms). Only the first and fourth of these
projects – those involving the post–Civil War and mid-twentieth-century

fight for civil rights for American blacks – can be readily characterized, in a contemporary sense, as, on balance, prorights and, in the second case, proprivacy. Even these projects for racial reform, however, were not free from ambiguities so far as the cause of rights was concerned, as much of the mid-twentieth-century project (the after-formulated legitimating rationalizations of liberal constitutional theorists notwithstanding) was often frankly and self-consciously antidemocratic. Contemporary Whiggish narratives positing a cresting progressive-spirited solicitude for privacy and criminal process rights as a "matter of principle" obscure these important developmental dynamics.

Site Two – Reconstituting Individual Rights: From Labor Rights to Civil Rights

Traditional narratives of the path of constitutional development spotlight both the achievement of the collective rights of labor in the 1930s and, at the same time, the launching of an upward progression toward the expansion of both collective civil rights and individual civil liberties. Such narratives systematically obscure the deep conceptual and political tensions between notions of collective or group rights and individual liberties. Although these tensions have been broadly acknowledged in other contexts (such as, for example, by political and legal theorists who devote their careers to attempting to reconcile them), they have not been usefully incorporated into nuanced narratives of constitutional development that forthrightly confront their persistence. When confronted with these tensions, historians writing within the Whig tradition, following the first principles set by philosophers, have systematically erased them. As I demonstrate in this chapter, over the course of the twentieth century, progressive-spirited reformers often loudly and frankly spurned claims on behalf of individual liberty in the interest of the advance of social collectivities. The theoretic proposition that those conflicts did not actually exist was the product not of those who initially changed the trajectory of constitutional development itself, but of the second stage of a two-track process in which serviceable ideologies were developed to legitimize and institutionalize those achievements. The reformers, put otherwise, proudly and defiantly made choices. In the interest of sustaining them, however, the ideologists, in turn, erased them.

I demonstrate these dynamics in this chapter within the constitutionalism of labor and civil rights by tracing a developmental path between the Supreme Court's neglected Norris-LaGuardia civil liberties decisions, *Senn v. Tile Layers Union* (1937) and *Lauf v. Shinner* (1938), and the mostly unacknowledged civil rights progeny of these labor law decisions, *New Negro Alliance v. Sanitary Grocery* (1938) and *Hughes v. Superior Court* (1950). By presenting this trajectory, as mediated by a series of institutional and intellectual intercurrences, I illuminate the profound (and, at times, plain) conflict between individual-oriented civil liberties and (contemporary) group-oriented civil rights that stood at the heart of twentieth-century constitutional practice.

To explore this path of development, I begin by recovering from narrative obscurity late-nineteenth- and early-twentieth-century civil rights individualism. As the statebuilding era began in the aftermath of Reconstruction, the chief test of one's progressive *bona fides* was not a solicitude for the plight of American blacks (indeed, progressivism was highly implicated in a commitment to an elaborate scientific racism). Rather, the test was one's fidelity to the advancement of organized labor and the cause of "industrial democracy." As it happened, however, in a turn that should long since have unsettled constitutional Whigs, American blacks at this time became some of the nation's most adamant opponents of labor unions and industrial democracy: They were highly individualistic, procapitalist, and antiunion, and, in significant numbers, strenuously backed the whole array of ostensibly "conservative" legal doctrines such as labor injunctions and the unconstitutionality of bans on yellow-dog contracts. Moreover, they subsequently opposed New Deal collective bargaining arrangements and the constitutional understandings that served to legitimate them, because those arrangements and understandings conferred unprecedented and fearsome state-sanctioned monopolistic powers to exclusionary, racist labor unions. Under these conditions, the cause of civil rights and labor rights were not harmonious but antagonistic.

As early as 1938, however, significant African Americans, who had previously hewed to (and fought for) highly individualist conceptions of civil rights, made a strategic calculation that their interests would now best be advanced not through individual but through class- or group-based arguments that given the Supreme Court's decisions in the Norris-LaGuardia cases and related developments outside the Court they calculated would inevitably be the wave of the constitutional future. Throughout the 1950s, however, the Court repeatedly parried claims that blacks were a cognizable constitutional class or group akin to labor. At the height of the Warren era "Rights Revolution," though, the Court, in the face of both relentless legal and intellectual argument and of highly publicized "movement" tactics borrowed directly from the repertoire of late-nineteenth- and early-twentieth-century labor, finally awarded blacks this new group status. As part of a Whiggish ideology of progress under which individual liberties did not conflict with group rights, however, the path-dependent link between the Warren-era group-oriented civil rights decisions concerning busing, voting rights, and (later) affirmative action and the earlier anti-individual rights decisions was severed. This was done through a reimagining, both on the Court and in the academy, of the Norris-LaGuardia decisions, not as corporatist, anti-individual rights decisions (as progressives frankly admitted them to be while defending them in the 1930s), but rather as "free speech" decisions that *advanced* rather than *limited* individual rights. In this creative project of ideological reconstruction, the group rights of both labor and blacks were conjoined with a solicitude for individual liberties as part of a purportedly seamless constitutional program in which group rights and individual rights were successfully harmonized. By recovering both the actual developmental link between the contemporary group-oriented understanding of civil rights and the progressive civil liberties sacrifices made in the Court's Norris-LaGuardia decisions, this chapter spotlights a crucial episode in the construction of constitutional memory in the interest of a regime-sustaining narrative of progress.

Site Three – Education Rights: Reconstituting the School

Traditional narratives of constitutional development concerning rights involving education and schools – typically First Amendment rights of free speech, free exercise, and nonestablishment – are Whiggish narratives, which, despite a nod to a handful of cases in the 1920s, are typically truncated. They begin only with the Supreme Court's parochial school aid case of *Everson v. Board of Education* (1947) and imagine the "civil libertarian" developments of the mid-twentieth century as a "matter of principle," or as a belated realization after a period of extended neglect, of the founding meaning of the First Amendment.

In this chapter, however, I situate these late, idiosyncratic constitutional developments in the broader stream of statebuilding and political development involving the schools and education. In a trajectory that until recently had been almost completely erased from narratives of constitutional development, there have been efforts from the country's very beginnings to build a national, centrally administered system of education with the aim of constructing truly "national" citizens. These efforts were frequently (though not exclusively) taken up in a reformist, progressive spirit. And they often targeted particular religious groups (such as Roman Catholics) and institutions of civil society (such as the family) that reformers argued were blocking the forward movement of this ambitious statebuilding and nationbuilding imperative.

For a variety of institutional and political reasons (some embryonic exceptions aside), these statebuilding and nationbuilding efforts concerning education were thwarted for much of American history. In the statebuilding era, however, these effects came closer to succeeding than ever before. At that time, progressive-spirited statists launched an ambitious reformist campaign involving compulsory education, English-only instruction laws, and the building of a national, centrally administered system of education. This campaign, espoused by John Dewey, Walter Lippmann, and others, was deeply rooted in visions of critical and rationalist scientific progress. At the time progressives were undertaking these initiatives, they argued frankly that statebuilding and nationbuilding goals concerning education were menaced by traditional institutions of civil society, such as church and family, and by a supportive substructure of constitutional doctrine (and allied political ideologies) concerning religious liberty, free exercise, and free association. In the Supreme Court cases of the 1920s striking down English-only instruction and compulsory public schooling laws, the "conservative" Old Court arrayed itself largely (though not completely) in opposition to this reformist campaign. These decisions contributed to the reasons that despite the more favorable conditions of the statebuilding era, the creation of a national system of education failed, as it had in earlier times.

At the same time, though, in the wake of the defeat of the statist programs for a national school system and in an environment newly hospitable to state power, progressives regrouped and worked through the federal courts (which they now controlled) to impose a secularizing, scientific centrally directed program upon a largely decentralized (or underdeveloped) education system. This reformist project proceeded on a number of fronts. In part because of intercurrent developments in ostensibly unrelated areas of the law, reformists were able to create legal doctrine that imagined the spur-of-the-moment, discretionary acts of local school officials as matters of "state" action and "state" policy. The progressive construction of the conduct of local school officials as "state" policy was supplemented by the further construction of these officials – particularly Roman Catholics or evangelical Protestants – as alien "others," and hence enemies of the emergent secular scientific state. Ironically, despite their frequent friendliness toward the Soviet Union (these enthusiasms waxed and waned with anfractuous turns in world events), progressives, in their school-focused nationbuilding campaign, made considerable headway in popularizing these constructions through open appeals to Cold War imperatives and fears. These fears and imperatives and longstanding progressive secularist scientific commitments at first spurred, and, in time, suffused the Court's mid-twentieth-century doctrine calling for the strict separation of church and state. With the advent of the liberalizing Second Vatican Council and a reimagination of religion as anchored less in theological doctrine and religious symbols and more in a commitment to toleration, justice, and fairness (the product, to a significant extent, of a new ecumenical and intercurring commitment to civil rights), the Cold War constitutional conflict over the Catholic menace subsided. Its doctrinal settlement, a civil libertarian commitment to strict separationism, however, was institutionalized as a late-twentieth-century pillar of "civil rights and civil liberties."

In this chapter, I demonstrate the singularity of the Supreme Court's mid-twentieth-century strict separationist jurisprudence, not only by setting out the above genealogy, but also by contrasting the structure of the pluralism that informed it with the very different form of pluralism the Court, at roughly the same time, deployed in grappling with the next great reformist campaign: the campaign for racial justice. Prior to this campaign, racial segregation in education had been accepted (and, indeed, advocated by Southern reformists) as a legitimate police measure that given prevailing attitudes was conducive to preserving the peace. As racial justice became the primary reformist imperative, however, the Court began to accept vigorous contention – and even violence – as the price of progress. To justify this turn, it imported into its race decisions involving schools arguments that it had previously developed in its progressive-spirited decisions concerning free speech that justified contention in terms of its contribution to scientific progress. It was these same arguments – which conceptualized blacks as the embodiment of truthful but unpopular ideas whose presence in integrated classrooms was essential to effective learning – that were used to justify affirmative action, both on the Court and off. This new imagining among civil rights reformers of the meaning of black people, I argue, stood in stark contrast to the reformist imagining of religious people, particularly those who continued to (atavistically) emphasize the importance of ritual, symbols, and doctrine. Whiggish narratives concerning civil rights and civil liberties in the Supreme Court's schools cases either shed no light on – or work actively to erase – these complicated developmental processes.

Toward a Genealogy of Contemporary Constitutional Morals

In the pages that follow, I present three case studies tracing, in three different areas, the genealogy of contemporary constitutional morals. These studies take as their end point the civil rights and civil liberties jurisprudence of the mid- to late-twentieth-century U.S. Supreme Court. Rather than treating this jurisprudence either as the triumph of principle following on the heels of the removal of the obstacles of formalism and laissez-faire or – because it is suffused with rights talk – as a categorical limitation on the state, I consider the rights creation undertaken in the wake of the New Deal standoff to be heavily implicated in the process of building the New American State and in the process of consolidating and legitimizing its authority and its power.

In conclusion, a word on the role of the Supreme Court in this process is perhaps in order. While exceptions exist, of course, there is a tendency in constitutional studies to assign a single institutional role or position to the Supreme Court within twentieth-century constitutional development: It is an instrument of law or of politics, an obstacle or a hope, active or restrained, formalistic or pragmatic, and, in its effects, central or insignificant. The developmental study that follows, however, suggests that efforts to pigeonhole the Court's jurisprudence into one of these categories simply will not avail. Given that political and constitutional orders are characterized in significant part by patterns of intercurrence and incongruities, the Court in the New Constitutional Nation, unsurprisingly, has never evinced a single, crosscutting orientation across policy areas for any significant length of time. Scholars get false positive readings in this regard mainly because they choose to follow what the Court is doing in policy areas they deem most salient at any given moment (like "the labor problem") and because they take as givens the ideological categories supplied by the Court and the discursive communities associated with it (such as law professors). Viewed critically and comprehensively, however, these unities and dichotomies fall apart. The Court, it turns out, is doctrinal and political, an obstacle and a hope, active and restrained, formalistic and pragmatic. Its jurisprudence is in some areas transformed by critical elections, and in others left relatively unchanged. It embraces new ideological visions, at times as wholes, but at others only in part. It takes these visions as it finds them in some cases, and actively transforms them in others. It resists change, negotiates change, and initiates change. The Court, in short, is a flashpoint or a crucible. It sits at the center of the conjunctions, multiple orders, and intercurrences that characterize the American political order, and, aware of its perpetually tenuous claim to authority, a claim based precariously on its status as a law follower rather than a law creator, labors to reconcile them plausibly in light of concrete, often crosscutting goals (and often in the absence of them). Only a developmental approach to American constitutionalism can hope to capture these complicated dynamics.

The end point of my case studies – the pronouncement by the Court of familiar, mid- to late-twentieth-century doctrines concerning civil rights and civil liberties – is the result not simply of intent (political or ethical), but also, inevitably, of the trajectories of development taken by political institutions and protean intellectual currents, of chance, unintended consequences, developmental paths, and pockets of resistance. It is, moreover, the result of choices made between rights and rights, liberties and liberties, and rights and liberties – choices that are often frankly acknowledged during the heat of reformist campaigns, but erased in a reconciling and institutionalizing project that follows. These choices are made in distinctive political, historical, social, and ideological contexts. The New Constitutional Nation's monistic philosophers and Whig historians are endogenous to this process. And they are committed by their first principles to obscuring its dynamics. It is the job of empirical developmental scholars to illuminate them.

2

Reconstituting Privacy and Criminal Process Rights

Introduction

Traditional narratives of constitutional development concerning the criminal process protections of the Bill of Rights, including the Fourth Amendment's search and seizure provision and the Fifth Amendment's self-incrimination clause (both of which I spotlight illustratively) are paradigmatically Whiggish. In those narratives, the promise of the Constitution's criminal process protections are by and large dormant – neglected, even – in a state of courts and parties preoccupied with the protection of economic rights. But then, at the urging of progressive and civil libertarian legal and political activists who cared about those rights, these protections were finally nursed to fulfillment, achieving their apotheosis during the Supreme Court's liberal Warren years (1953–69). Since then, the belatedly realized criminal process guarantees of the Bill of Rights are held to have either been institutionalized as a quasi-permanent part of the contemporary constitutional order, holding their place amidst either public indifference or even hostility; or, alternatively, they are held to be in genuine peril from the persistent predations of a political right that seeks to "turn back the clock" on those hard-won constitutional rights.

This familiar account of constitutional development concerning the criminal process provisions of the Bill of Rights is straightforward, elegant, and inspiring. In the style of a successful Aristotelian narrative, it has a beginning, a middle, and an end. It puts a moral project at its center. And it reminds us that threats to these achievements remain, while providing a continuing role for the veterans of the struggle, who are kept on the stage as vigilant sentries and reminders of darker days. This particular trajectory of progress has an added advantage as a narrative within modern American politics – indeed, the ultimate trump: It is joined in significant part to the signal moral achievement of twentieth-century American constitutionalism, the campaign for civil rights. From the Scottsboro cases in the 1930s, through the Warren era, the Supreme Court's power to hear appeals in criminal process cases was, in many instances, the last, best hope of black defendants facing down the brutality of the Jim Crow South. As such, the criminal process revolution was a key pillar of the civil rights revolution.

The appeal of this linear, teleological developmental narrative is apparent. But, like all Whiggish narratives, it distorts by beginning with the end. In so doing, it imagines the long stretch of constitutional development concerning the criminal process provisions of the Bill of Rights as the kernels of later developments, in the process obscuring key developmental trajectories involving constitutional criminal process rights.

One of the most misleading features of this narrative is the unambiguous pride it places in progressive-spirited political and constitutional thinkers as the founts of an expansive conception of human liberty. In fact, this unidimensional, linear narrative obscures the numerous ways in which the partisans of reform and progress held a much more ambiguous relation to the cause of freedom and the protection of civil liberties. In this area, constitutional development – far from amounting to a more or less linear, Manichaean struggle between the forces of reaction and the forces of progress, culminating in contemporary civil libertarianism – is more aptly described as a case of discontinuous development, in which progressives and civil libertarians were just as likely to be opponents of individualistic freedom as its champions.

Free from the narrative requirements of Whiggishness, the path of constitutional development concerning criminal process rights is best described as the issue of a series of sequential developmental struggles involving four distinct reformist political projects, one not involving what we today would take to involve classically "criminal" matters, and three that do. The non–street crime project was the late-nineteenth- and early-twentieth-century fight by progressives to construct a powerful, fact-fortified New American State. Of the three street crime projects (which I take up successively), the first was the effort to secure the civil rights of the freedmen through the extension of central state jurisdiction and power. The second was the fight for alcohol prohibition in the teens and 1920s. And the third was the mid-twentieth-century fight to secure the civil rights of American blacks. In some of these reformist projects, the partisans of progress were the outspoken opponents of the cause of rights protection. In fighting on behalf of the building of a powerful and highly centralized New American State, for instance, the proponents of progress rallied frankly and forcefully *against* the cause of rights protection, whether pursuant to the Bill of Rights or otherwise. In the same struggle, they also rallied *against* according broad constitutional protection for rights to privacy. Similarly, in championing the cause of the prohibition, proponents of progress fought diligently against causes that today would be associated with civil rights. For progressive prohibitionists, for instance, Catholics and immigrants, as social groups, were taken to be enemies of a better future (as progressive social scientific research in the realm of eugenics – in its statist, reform Darwinist form, as opposed to its antistatist, Sumnerian form – was demonstrating in this and other realms). Only the first and fourth of these projects – those involving the post–Civil War and mid-twentieth-century fight for civil rights for American blacks – can be readily characterized, in a contemporary sense, as prorights and, in the second case, pro-privacy. Even these projects for racial reform, however, were not free from ambiguities as far as the cause of rights was concerned, as (after-formulated legitimating rationalizations notwithstanding) they were often frankly and self-consciously antidemocratic.

Part of the political and ideological role of contemporary constitutional theory has been to craft the sorts of Whiggish narratives concerning the achievement of criminal process rights that institutionalize these successive achievements by eliminating historical ambiguities that would call into question a linear, developmental conception of civil libertarian progress. In the New Constitutional Nation, that task has involved the intricate intellectual labor of taking an agglomeration of deeply conflicted attitudes toward rights, liberties, and democracy, and reworking them into a linear, triumphalist constitutive story that erased these conflicts in favor of unidimensional progressive narrative. That familiar narrative has posited a century-long progressive struggle for civil liberties, civil rights, and democracy, culminating in the triumph of principle – as embodied in contemporary civil libertarian and Rawlsian legal liberalism. In the discussion that follows, I provide an account of the trajectory of rights and liberties concerning illustrative criminal process provisions of the Bill of Rights that jettisons that after-constructed, legitimating constitutional narrative.

The Project of Legibility, the Fourth and Fifth Amendments, and the New American State: Introduction

In the late nineteenth and early twentieth centuries, the United States underwent a profound transformation from a rural and agricultural to an urban and industrial society. A shift from a proprietary-competitive political economy to a corporate-administrative one undergirded this transformation. These political-economic transformations, in turn, were met and managed by an unprecedented course of American statebuilding, which marked a radically statist constitutional departure, culminating ultimately in the building of a New American State.[1]

---

[1] Stephen Skowronek, *Building a New American State: The Expansion of National Administrative Capacities, 1877–1920* (New York: Cambridge University Press, 1982); Martin Sklar, *The Corporate Reconstruction of American Capitalism* (New York: Cambridge University Press, 1986), 3. Specifically, Sklar defines "proprietary-competitive" as "capitalist property and market relations in which the dominant type of enterprise was headed by an owner-manager (or owner-managers), or a direct agent thereof, and in which such enterprise was a price-taker, rather than a price-maker, price being determined by conditions of supply and demand

Traditional understandings of the Bill of Rights extant at this time, along with the fundamental principles of liberty that undergirded them, were quite broad, and broadly antistatist (they were, in many ways, broader than their twentieth-century variants). As such, they posed ideological and institutional obstacles to this statebuilding project, a commitment to which came to define one as forward-looking and progressive. In fact, broad commitments to basic privacy rights – defended both as a general creed and as anchored in the Fourth Amendment's protection against unreasonable searches and seizures and the Fifth Amendment's self-incrimination privilege – came at this time to pose a particularly troublesome obstacle for these progressives. These privacy guarantees stood as institutional barriers to the fact-gathering powers that the New American State would need if it were to straddle and administer the nation's new political economy effectively. These constitutional provisions stood as potentially crippling limitations on the line of sight of the New American State, which needed to render many formerly dark corners of civil society visible in order to control and manipulate them.[2] James Scott has argued that the very essence of effective modern administrative states is their ability to see and read the civil society they seek to order. As such, one of their major tasks is to remake society into legible form – to undertake what Scott calls a "project of legibility."[3] This project is essential to the construction of corporate-administrative states because unseen or uncategorizable people or activities can only be manipulated if they are first observed and then assimilated onto an administrative grid – that is, in

beyond the control of the enterprise short of anticompetitive inter-firm collusion." By the new "corporate-administrative" order, he means a political economy characterized by the "capitalization of . . . property in the form of negotiable securities relatively widely dispersed in ownership, a corresponding separation of ownership title and management function, and management of the enterprise by bureaucratic-administrative methods involving a division, or a specialization of managerial function, and an integration, or at least a centralization, of financial control." It is meant to designate "a process occurring not merely in a few notable firms, or in a sector of the economy . . . but pervasively, and hence involving the change in the broader economy from price-competitive to administered, or 'oligopolistic,' markets." Sklar, *Corporate Reconstruction*, 4 n.1. See also Robert H. Wiebe, *The Search for Order, 1877–1920* (New York: Hill and Wang, 1967); Samuel P. Hays, *The Response to Industrialism: 1885–1914* (Chicago: University of Chicago Press, 1957); Alfred D. Chandler Jr., *The Visible Hand: The Managerial Revolution in American Business* (Cambridge, MA: The Belknap Press of the Harvard University Press, 1977).

[2] The Fourth Amendment provides that "[t]he right of the people to be secure in their persons, houses, papers, and effects, against unreasonable searches and seizures, shall not be violated, and no Warrants shall issue, but upon probable cause, supported by Oath or affirmation, and particularly describing the place to be searched, and the persons or things to be seized." U.S. Constitution, Amendment IV. In pertinent part, the Fifth Amendment provides that "[n]o person shall . . . be compelled in any criminal case to be a witness against himself. . . . " U.S. Constitution, Amendment V.

[3] James C. Scott, *Seeing Like a State: How Certain Schemes to Improve the Human Condition Have Failed* (New Haven: Yale University Press, 1998).

Scott's terms, if they are "made legible."[4] "Legibility," Scott writes, "is a condition of manipulation."[5] The "ongoing project of legibility," which is a prerequisite to statebuilding and statecraft, "is largely a product of internal colonization."[6] In this project, illegibility is a source of political autonomy. For that reason, legibility is often strenuously resisted.[7] Claims on behalf of rights and liberties were, in essence, claims to autonomy. It thus became a defining progressive imperative to take on and defeat those claims.

In the signal era of American statebuilding, powerful forces in American society advanced privacy arguments and aggressively wielded the Fourth and Fifth Amendments in staunch resistance to the New American State's project of legibility. At that time, in an effort to render legible increasingly large and politically and economically important entities, the federal government, at the behest of statist political progressives, undertook a succession of sustained efforts to compel the production of papers and records and to procure from private economic actors testimony regarding business practices. Those actors, who faced questions regarding joint ownership, rate structures, and pooling agreements, often refused to produce their books and papers and to testify under oath before government officials by claiming that such compelled testimony violated core constitutional protections for privacy as guraranteed them by the Fourth and Fifth Amendments. In 1886, in the case of *Boyd v. United States*, which involved government efforts to acquire business records in a customs duty dispute, these constitutional claims were given the authoritative imprimatur of the U.S. Supreme Court, dealing a potentially crippling blow to the entire progressive statebuilding project. The successful building of the New American State required that the *Boyd* ruling, and the broad constitutional protections for privacy rights it seemed to reinforce, be overcome. This was essential, as the possibility that a progressive constitutional triumph

---

[4] Scott, *Seeing Like a State*, 24. My main interest in Scott's work here is in his definition and description of state projects of legibility. Since my purpose here is primarily descriptive, I do not discuss Scott's normative critique of the interventionist hubris that has sometimes accompanied that process. The normative critique, however, constitutes a major theme of Scott's book.

[5] Scott, *Seeing Like a State*, 183. ("Any substantial state intervention in society – to vaccinate a population, produce goods, mobilize labor, tax people, and their property, conduct literacy campaigns, conscript soldiers, enforce sanitation standards, catch criminals, start universal schooling – requires the invention of units that are visible. The units in question might be citizens, villages, trees, fields, houses, or people grouped according to age, depending on the type of intervention. Whatever the units being manipulated, they must be organized in a manner that permits them to be identified, observed, recorded, counted, aggregated, and monitored. The degree of knowledge required would have to be roughly commensurate with the depth of the intervention. In other words, one might say that the greater the manipulation envisaged, the greater the legibility required to effect it.")

[6] Scott, *Seeing Like a State*, 80, 82.

[7] Scott, *Seeing Like a State*, 54, 68.

over privacy claims would fail to materialize, one scholar rightly declared, "posed a greater threat to activist government . . . than did substantive due process."[8]

In the heat of the political fight to build a New American State, forward-looking, public-spirited reformists were outspoken critics of rights rubrics generally and of the Bill of Rights in particular. They were similarly frank in their attacks on privacy rights; indeed, they repeatedly spoke out against the value of privacy, appealing instead to the promise of "publicity." Once they had succeeded in their task, however, in a pattern that this book demonstrates is common in American constitutional development, these reformers and their successors undertook an elaborate project of ideological reconstruction aimed at fashioning a compelling constitutive story that positioned their achievements as rights-protecting triumphs. To do so, they first read plausible interpretations of the Fourth and Fifth Amendments out of the lexicon of constitutional meaning. They then drew a serviceable ideological distinction between "economic" and "personal" privacy. The former, now consigned to a separate conceptual category, was declared socially counterproductive, a counterfeit privacy. This erasure left the Fourth and Fifth Amendments free to carry new sequential meanings that unlike the old meanings were consistent with the imperatives of the New American State. In time, the Fourth and Fifth Amendments, which had been bled dry of their late-nineteenth- and early-twentieth-century meanings, were reinvented as part of an elaborate system of procedural protections for those accused of street crimes, first by conservative justices Pierce Butler and James Clark McReynolds in resistance to progressive initiatives on Prohibition, and later as part of an antiracist policy program of the liberal Warren Court.[9] The value of "privacy" itself was reimagined as being protected by the due process clauses of the Fifth and Fourteenth Amendments, which now guaranteed a "right to privacy," a right which came to be associated primarily with claims to sexual and reproductive autonomy.[10]

---

[8] William J. Stuntz, "The Substantive Origins of Criminal Procedure," *Yale Law Journal* 105 (November 1995): 393–447, esp. 428. The defining substantive due process case of the era was *Lochner v. New York*, 198 U.S. 45 (1905) in which the U.S. Supreme Court invalidated a New York State law limiting the working hours of bakers on the grounds that the statute violated the liberty of contract as vouchsafed by the due process clause of the Fourteenth Amendment.

[9] See Lucas A. Powe Jr., *The Warren Court and American Politics* (Cambridge, MA: The Belknap Press of the Harvard University Press, 2000), 193–9; 379–444; Stuntz, "Substantive Origins"; William J. Stuntz, "Privacy's Problem and the Law of Criminal Procedure," *Michigan Law Review* 93 (March 1995): 1016–78. On Butler and McReynolds as the leaders of a push to revive a broad reading of the Fourth Amendment in Prohibition cases, see Kenneth M. Murchison, *Federal Criminal Law Doctrines: The Forgotten Influence of National Prohibition* (Durham, NC: Duke University Press, 1994), 74–101.

[10] *Griswold v. Connecticut*, 381 U.S. 479 (1965); *Eisenstadt v. Baird*, 405 U.S. 438 (1972); *Roe v. Wade*, 410 U.S. 113 (1973); *Bowers v. Hardwick*, 478 U.S. 186 (1986).

This trajectory of constitutional development, which in truth was highly ambivalent toward "privacy rights," broadly considered, came complete with a legitimating, progressive-spirited genealogy that constructed the trajectory as a linear progression toward the achievement of contemporary civil libertarian privacy rights. That genealogy, boldly enough, traced the concern with constitutional privacy back to one of the statebuilding era's staunchest proponents of "publicity," Louis D. Brandeis. The beginnings of the solicitude for privacy were thus traced back to the era of the construction of the New American State itself. And, since legitimating that state was the underlying imperative, the privacy commitments of the opponents of that state, such as Butler and McReynolds, were erased from that narrative. Finally, the chief progressive proponents of that state were imagined to be the progenitors of a modern concern for privacy, a concern that was folded into a narrative of cresting progressive solicitude for civil liberties.

Prologue: Fourth and Fifth Amendment Rights before the Statebuilding Era

Contemporary understandings of Fourth and Fifth Amendment constitutional rights emphasize primarily the criminal process aspects of rights. In the eighteenth and nineteenth centuries, however, under the state of courts and parties, criminal process rights, as applied to common crimes such as robbery, burglary, assault and battery, rape, and murder, were (for the most part) not Fourth and Fifth Amendment matters. Criminal procedure in such cases was a matter of state law, typically formulated by state judges sitting in state courts. For this reason, in their discussions of these amendments, the seminal constitutional treatises of the nineteenth century make few references to what we today would consider paradigmatic Fourth and Fifth Amendment matters involving searches and testimony in street crime cases.[11] In the eighteenth and nineteenth centuries, the arguments that prefigure and, in turn, expressly invoke the provisions of the Fourth and Fifth Amendments arise not in street crime cases, but rather in cases involving the assertion of the regulatory and administrative authority (in the case of the American colonies) of either the metropole or the American central state. They were, thus, broadly speaking, anticentralist and antistatist. As such, they were consistent with and, indeed, pillars of the prevailing structural features of the traditional constitutional order.

---

[11] James Kent, *Commentaries on American Law* (New York: W. Kent, 1851); Joseph Story, *Commentaries on the Constitution of the United States: With a Preliminary Review of the Constitutional History of the Colonies and States Before the Adoption of the Constitution* (Boston: Little, Brown and Co., 1858) 3rd edition, Secs. 1901–2; Thomas M. Cooley, *A Treatise on the Constitutional Limitations Which Rest Upon the Legislative Powers of the States of the American Union* (Boston: Little, Brown and Co., 1903), 424–36 (extended discussion of criminal procedure, but with emphasis on regulatory cases). There is notably more attention devoted to street crime issues in Christopher Tiedeman, *A Treatise on the Limitations of Police Power in the United States* (St. Louis: F. H. Thomas Law Book Co., 1886), Secs. 31–50.

Both of the amendments had English origins. In the case of the Fourth Amendment, those origins were relatively recent. The Fourth Amendment's proscription against unreasonable searches and seizures arose proximately in reaction to two politically galvanizing eighteenth-century English and colonial searches in seditious libel and tax collection cases, that of John Wilkes in England and that involving the Writs of Assistance in colonial Massachusetts. Both the controversies and the cases they generated involved substantive claims on behalf of the privacy of one's home and personal papers in the face of government regulatory schemes and revenue collection efforts.[12] The Wilkes case considered the propriety of general search warrants the Crown had issued authorizing its agents to ransack houses at will to discover who was churning out incendiary pamphlets sharply criticizing King George III. Through a succession of high-handed searches, Wilkes, a member of Parliament, was unmasked as their author. Rather than sinking quietly in the face of the disgorged evidence, Wilkes fought back against the manner in which his penning of the infamous North Briton #45 had been discovered by successfully suing the invading Crown officials for damages. In the process, Wilkes became a folk hero in the American colonies, polities that themselves were becoming impatient with the high-handed tactics of the British Crown.[13] The Writs of Assistance case, which echoed the Wilkes affair, involved the propriety of statutes giving colonial customs officials broad powers to enter any home or business and to search for and to seize forthwith any uncustomed imported goods. By issuing so-called "writs of assistance" colonial customs officers could force either colonial officials or private citizens to "assist" them in the stipulated search. These writs were deployed particularly aggressively in the port of Boston, and in a famous courtroom argument in resistance to a writs of assistance search, James Otis contended

---

[12] Stuntz, "Substantive Origins." *Entick v. Carrington*, 95 Eng. Rep. (K. B. 1765); *Wilkes v. Wood*, 98 Eng. Rep. 489 (C. P. 1763); Writs of Assistance, 1761–72, in *The Founder's Constitution*, Vol. 5, eds. Philip B. Kurland and Ralph Lerner (Indianapolis: Liberty Fund, 1987), 222–30, 230–1, 233–5. See Leonard W. Levy, "Origins of the Fourth Amendment," *Political Science Quarterly* 114 (1999): 79–101. The notions that "every man's house is looked upon by the law to be his castle of defense and asylum, wherein he should suffer no violence" and that "a *general* warrant to apprehend all persons suspected, without naming or particularly describing any person in special, is illegal and void for its uncertainty" had roots in English common law. See William Blackstone, *Commentaries on the Laws of England* (Chicago: University of Chicago Press, 1979), Book 3, 288; Book 4, 286–90.

[13] Wilkes's hero status remains well in evidence to this day in the number of American towns that were subsequently named for either Wilkes or Lord Camden, the judge who wrote the opinion finding for Wilkes in his damages action. Akhil Reed Amar, *The Constitution and Criminal Procedure: First Principles* (New Haven: Yale University Press, 1997), 184–5, n. 53; Pauline Maier, "John Wilkes and American Disillusionment with Britain," *William and Mary Quarterly* 20 (1963): 373–95. See also Levy, "Origins of the Fourth Amendment," 86–90; Bernard Bailyn, *The Ideological Origins of the American Revolution* (Cambridge, MA: The Belknap Press of the Harvard University Press, 1967), 110–12.

that suspicionless searches violated venerable guarantees of English liberty. Otis lost the battle but won the war: His failed courtroom oration found a wide popular following and ascended to rare political prominence. Moreover, it inspired patriot leader John Adams to compose and add a guarantee against unreasonable searches and seizures to the Massachusetts Constitution. It was this provision that served as the model for the U.S. Constitution's Fourth Amendment.

From the time of the Constitution's ratification until the late nineteenth century, the Fourth Amendment had two principal constitutional effects: to make certain that the issuance of general warrants at both the state and national levels would forever be considered beyond the pale of legitimate governmental practice; and, to institutionalize at both levels of government that search warrants be issued only upon a finding of probable cause, supported by a particularized sworn statement.[14] Since that time, these guarantees have been flouted in any obvious way.

There existed a *drôle de guerre* concerning the Fourth Amendment between the time of its ratification and the onset of the late-nineteenth-century project of legibility undertaken as a principal endeavor of the process of central-state construction. This was all but inevitable since, prior to the late nineteenth century, the provisions of the Bill of Rights were held to be restrictions on federal and not state conduct.[15] And, with relatively limited federal activity, criminal investigations were few and far between, and statist federal regulatory invasions and data collection efforts were distinct rarities. It is worth noting, however, that appeals to state constitutional proscriptions against unreasonable searches and seizures were similarly rare. Even at that level, these rights were not understood as ones that would be invoked by

---

[14] The Fourth Amendment's warrant requirement is separate from its prohibition on unreasonable searches and seizures. For a full explanation of the meaning and implications of this, see Amar, *Constitution and Criminal Procedure*, 1–45. So far as the Fourth Amendment's warrant requirement was concerned, the understanding was that search warrants were to be issued in criminal cases only. In *Constitutional Limitations*, for instance, Thomas Cooley stated that "[t]hey are only to be granted in cases where they are expressly authorized by law, and not until after a showing made before a magistrate, under oath, that a crime has been committed, and that the party complaining has reasonable cause to suspect that the offender or the property which was the subject or the instrument of the crime is concealed in some specified house or place." Thomas M. Cooley, *A Treatise on the Constitutional Limitations Which Rest upon the Legislative Power of the States of the American Union* (Boston: Little, Brown and Co., 1868), 304. "Search-warrants were never recognized by the common law as processes which might be availed of by individuals in the course of civil proceedings, or for that matter the maintenance of any mere private right; but their use was confined to cases of public prosecutions instituted and pursued for the suppression of crime, and the detection and the punishment of criminals." *Robinson v. Richardson*, 13 Gray 456 (J. Merrick), quoted in Cooley, *Constitutional Limitations*, 307, n. 1. He added: "The warrant is not allowed to obtain evidence of an intended crime; but only after lawful evidence of an offence actually committed." Cooley, *Constitutional Limitations*, 305.

[15] See *Barron v. Baltimore*, 32 U.S. 243 (1833).

common street criminals, but, in their more frequent instantiations, as rights against the heavy-handed assertion of governmental regulatory and administrative authority. Of course, in comparison with contemporary practice, state regulatory regimes were not especially invasive. And while there did develop a notable body of state court cases involving trespass suits against sheriffs for acting pursuant to defective search warrants, since no police forces existed at the time, and searches incident to (typically civilian) arrest were permitted, provisions of state constitutions proscribing unreasonable searches and seizures were rarely invoked by either civil or criminal defendants. Thus, during their first century of existence, the meanings of national and state constitutional search and seizure provisions, remained underdeveloped.[16]

Historically speaking, the origins of the Fifth Amendment's self-incrimination provisions run deeper in English constitutional history than those of the Fourth. As with the Fourth Amendment's search and seizure protections, the roots of the Fifth Amendment's self-incrimination protection are found not in concern for the rights of street criminals, but rather in political resistance to matters of substantive regulation. Arguments on behalf of a self-incrimination privilege were first advanced in English law when, in an effort to enforce religious uniformity, government officials insisted upon examining Catholic and Protestant dissenters under oath about both their own religious views and those of their friends and neighbors.[17]

---

[16] Stuntz, "Substantive Origins," 419–21. See *Walker v. Cruikshank*, 2 Hill 296 (January 1842 [NY]); *Rohan v. Sawin*, 59 Mass. 281 (5 Cush 281) (March 1850); *Walker v. Hampton*, 8 Ala. 412 (1845); *Commonwealth v. Dana*, 43 Mass. 329 (2 Met. 329) (March 1841); *Stone v. Dana*, 46 Mass. 98 (5 Met. 98) (October 1842); *Beaty v. Perkins*, 6 Wend. 382 (N.Y. 1831); *Robertson v. Richardson*, 79 Mass. 454 (13 Gray 454); September 1859); *Thurston v. Adams*, 41 Me. 419 (1856); *Parker v. Certain Lottery Tickets*, 59 Mass. 369 (5 Cust. 369) (March 1850); *Fisher v. McGirr*, 67 Mass. 1 (1 Gray 1) (March 1854); *Malcom v. Spoor*, 53 Mass. (12 Met.) 279 (1847). The influential nineteenth-century treatise writer Thomas Cooley (later, the first head of the Interstate Commerce Commission) described the constitutional proscription against unreasonable searches and seizures as hewing to "that maxim of the common law which secures to the citizen immunity in his home against the prying eyes of the government, and the protection, in person, property, and papers even against the process of the law, except in a few specified cases." Prior to the late nineteenth and early twentieth centuries, it was not at all clear whether the legibility imperatives of the New American State would fit into the category of the core of the protections or of its admitted exceptions. Cooley, *Constitutional Limitations*, 299. Joseph Story declared the Fourth Amendment to represent "little more than the affirmance of a great constitutional doctrine of the common law." Story, *Commentaries on the Constitution of the United States*, Sec. 1902. On this, however, he was mistaken.

[17] Stuntz, "Substantive Origins," 411–17. See also Leonard W. Levy, *Origins of the Fifth Amendment* (New York: Macmillan, 1969); John Langbein, "The Historical Origins of the Privilege Against Self-Incrimination at Common Law," *Michigan Law Review* 92 (1994): 1047–85; Ralph Rossum, "Self-Incrimination: The Original Intent," in Eugene W. Hickok Jr., *The Bill of Rights: Original Meaning and Understanding* (Charlottesville: University Press of Virginia, 1991), 273–87.

The privilege, in short, was asserted in resistance to an affirmative central statebuilding project involving the construction of uniform and cohesive national allegiances and identity. It was asserted in resistance to the nation-building project in England.

In the United States, a country founded by the members of the dissenting religious sects that the Crown took to be obstacles to this nationbuilding project, it was foreordained that if a Bill of Rights existed, it would contain a self-incrimination privilege of the sort fought for by their much-persecuted progenitors in England. The constitutionally guaranteed self-incrimination privilege had from the outset one very strong effect that operated at both the national and state levels and that was applicable in street crime cases: Criminal defendants in America were never forced onto the witness stand to testify against themselves. Between the time of its ratification and the onset of the project of legibility, there was a *drôle de guerre* concerning the meaning of the self-incrimination provision of the Fifth Amendment that paralleled that of the Fourth. Like the Fourth, the Fifth was widely understood to be a protection against federal and not against state conduct. Moreover, given the absence of police forces, the importance of pretrial questioning (to which the provision was inapplicable), the dearth of lawyers (which made a defendant's voluntary silence akin to an admission of guilt), and the unlikelihood of being examined under oath for regulatory purposes given the undeveloped nature of the state, the self-incrimination privilege was asserted in court only relatively rarely.[18]

That said, though, owing in part to its deeper roots in the English common law tradition, there was somewhat more flesh on the bones of the self-incrimination privilege in advance of the statebuilding era than there was on the relatively new constitutional protection against unreasonable searches and seizures. Between the time of the Fifth Amendment's ratification and the *Boyd* decision, those American courts that had considered the privilege's scope had repeatedly emphasized that the *constitutional* self-incrimination privilege was invocable only by criminal defendants facing questions in their own criminal trials. During this same time period, however, there did exist a simultaneous *nonconstitutional* common-law privilege against self-incrimination, known as the "witness privilege," that allowed witnesses in civil proceedings to refuse to answer questions on the grounds that their answers might incriminate them. As part of the resistance to the late-nineteenth-century project of legibility, these two self-incrimination privileges would be fused, constitutionalized, and joined with the search and seizure provisions

---

[18] Stuntz, "Substantive Origins," 411–17. Prior to the 1860s, neither the states nor the federal government allowed criminal defendants (or, for that matter, any person who had an interest in a case's outcome) to testify in courts on the grounds that such testimony was inherently unreliable. Rossum, "Self-Incrimination," 276; Katherine B. Hazlett, "The Nineteenth Century Origins of the Fifth Amendment Privilege Against Self-Incrimination," *American Journal of Legal History* 42 (1998): 235–60, n. 18.

in *Boyd* to provide a zone of privacy against the substantive fact-gathering efforts of the New American State.[19]

Stirrings of Change from the Center

A crucial difference between a common-law privilege such as the "witness privilege" and a constitutional privilege is that Congress (or, for that matter, any legislature) is institutionally bound by the latter, but has full power to abrogate the former. This difference became crucial to the dynamics of constitutional development concerning the Fifth Amendment, because from about the mid-nineteenth century onward, Congress began, at increasingly regular intervals in a series of historically isolated instances, to feel the imperative of seeing like a state. To enlarge the scope of its vision in these discrete instances, it began to pass a succession of immunity statutes aimed at compelling testimony before them through grants of immunity from prosecution.[20] The first of these immunity statutes, those of 1857 and 1862, were passed in response to a number of congressional corruption scandals.[21] But following the end of the Civil War, Congress began to put its immunity powers to use not simply in isolated and discrete corruption scandals, but increasingly in routine service of gathering a regular reading on the facts that seemed essential to a sustained statebuilding project. Unlike the scandal-driven immunity statutes, the post–Civil War congressional immunity statutes of 1868 and 1874 were

---

[19] Hazlett, "Nineteenth Century Origins," 235–60. This represents a paradigmatic example of the mediation and promotion of "two antagonistic tendencies – the centralization of power and the individualization of subjects," through the constitutionalization of law." William Novak, *The People's Welfare: Law and Regulation in Nineteenth Century America* (Chapel Hill: University of North Carolina Press, 1996), 240 [emphasis in original]. See also Novak, "Legal Origins of the Modern American State." It is worth specifying that Hazlett does not make clear that testimony that subjected one to a "penalty" or a "forfeiture" was considered "incriminating" testimony, and hence, if such testimony was at issue the witness could claim the privilege. If, however, the testimony was such that it would subject the witness to a debt action or a civil suit, the privilege was not available. The origins of this distinction postdate the ratification of the Fifth Amendment. They are found in the impeachment of Lord Melville in 1805 and a subsequent English court opinion and statute that influenced the development of the privilege under American law. See *Bull v. Loveland*, 27 Mass. 9 (10 Pick. 9) (September 1830); *Benjamin and Moore v. Hathaway*, 3 Conn. 528 (June 1821); *Taney v. Kemp*, 4 H & J 348 (June 1818 [Md]); *Planters' Bank v. George*, 6 Mart. (O.S.) 670 (June 1819 [La.]); *Copp v. Upham*, 3 N.H. 159 (February 1825); *Stoddert's Lessee v. Manning*, 2 H & G 147 (June 1828 [Md]).

[20] Hazlett, "Nineteenth Century Origins," 242–51. See also Akhil Reed Amar and Renee B. Lettow, "Fifth Amendment First Principles: The Self-Incrimination Clause," *Michigan Law Review* 93 (1995): 857–928, esp. 913–14; Amar, *Constitution and Criminal Procedure*, 46–88. Hazlett does not note that in their original state constitutions Delaware and Maryland did expressly extend the self-incrimination privilege to witnesses as well as defendants and beyond criminal trials to civil proceedings. See Levy, *Origins of the Fifth Amendment*, 407, 409, 411; Rossum, "Self-Incrimination," 275, 280.

[21] 11 Stat. 155 (1857); 12 Stat. 333 (1862).

both passed to aid in efforts at revenue collection, the *sine qua non* of that project.[22] The 1868 statute, while protecting the tax evader under congressional investigation from criminal prosecution, gave national revenue agents the power to compel the production of private books and records that would permit the government to determine the amount of taxes in arrears and, in turn, to then collect those taxes in a civil enforcement proceeding.[23] The 1874 statute also provided for the production of books and papers in civil revenue enforcement proceedings.[24] Unlike the earlier statute, however, the newer one, in a significant constitutional departure, did not preclude the use of the documents produced in subsequent criminal prosecutions.

Both the 1868 and 1874 statutes were challenged in court by parties resisting the reach of the relatively new national revenue laws and their novel fact-gathering enforcement provisions. It was in these challenges to the 1868 and 1874 immunity statutes that constitutional Fourth and Fifth Amendment claims – which seemed to apply by at least the Fifth Amendment's plain language only to "criminal case[s]" – were first raised by parties in civil proceedings. At this time, and consistent with the traditional understanding of the common-law privilege (which Congress had full power to abrogate) and the constitutional privilege (which applied only in criminal matters), the novel assertions of constitutional privilege were summarily dismissed.[25]

The easiest cases as far as federal courts were concerned arose under the earlier statute. By allowing the use of documents that had been produced in civil revenue collection proceedings as evidence in subsequent criminal prosecutions, however, the 1874 statute had upped the legal ante. In subsequent immunity cases, Fifth Amendment self-incrimination claims were quirks no more: They moved to center stage in the legal argument; in the 1870s, they were still a losing claim, to be sure, but a legal claim that in the face of a central state that had become more and more aggressive in its fact-gathering efforts had begun to be taken seriously nonetheless.[26]

---

[22] See Charles Tilly, "Reflections on the History of European State-Making," in *The Formation of National States in Western Europe*, ed. Charles Tilly (Princeton: Princeton University Press, 1975), 3–83. See also Scott, *Seeing Like a State*, 25–45.

[23] 15 Stat. 37 (1868).

[24] 18 Stat. 186 (1874).

[25] See, e.g., *In re Strouse*, 23 F. Cas. 261 (D. Nev. 1871) (rejecting joint Fourth and Fifth Amendment claims); *United States v. Williams*, 28 F. Cas. 670 (S.D. Ohio, 1872) (cases cited in Hazlett, "Nineteenth Century Origins").

[26] See, e.g., *United States v. Hughes*, 26 F. Cas. 417 (Cir. Ct. S.D.N.Y. 1875) (here, in an important tariff case involving imported merchandise, the court admitted the books and papers by dint of statutory interpretation by construing the 1874 act in light of the 1868 act, without mention of the Constitution); *United States v. Three Tons of Coal*, 28 F. Cas. 149 (E.D. Wis. 1875) (rejecting Fourth and Fifth Amendment claims in tax case involving a distillery); *United States v. Mason*, 26 F. Cas 1189 (N.D. Ill. 1875) (rejecting Fourth and Fifth Amendment claims in tax case involving a distillery).

The Project of Legibility: Preliminary Statebuilding Initiatives – and Constitutional Resistance

The broadening and deepening of the gaze of the central state began as a series of intermittent acts, a jumbled admixture of state-sustaining revenue collection cases and inquiries into vexed government institutions. In addition to the above-cited revenue cases, Congress simultaneously set up committees to investigate particular high-profile public scandals on a cornucopia of subjects. Joint House-Senate investigatory committees were first set up during the Civil War. In 1871, such a committee was created to investigate the status of the states of the defeated Confederacy. In 1874 and 1878, similar committees were set up to consider, respectively, the governance of the District of Columbia and the Indian Bureau.

Following the Civil War, however, the investigation of discrete scandals gradually began to dovetail with what were coming to be perceived as deep and sustained, nondiscrete, political-economic concerns. The lines between scandal, criminality, and regulatory imperatives began to blur in pregnant ways. In 1873, for instance, Congress set up prominent panels to investigate Crédit Mobilier and the financing of the Union Pacific Railway and, in 1874, to investigate the corrupt procuring of government subsidies for the Pacific Mail Steamship Company.[27]

At this time, it was far from clear that Congress had a right to collect the information it sought in sorting out these scandals. Certainly, the governmental powers to subpoena and compel testimony existed, but these had traditionally been powers reserved to judges, who had exercised them rarely and sparingly, and with a strong institutionally anchored pro-privacy bias. And judges typically exercised what they understood as part of their judicial role to be extraordinary powers in criminal cases. Whether these scandals were criminal or not was uncertain. If they were not, governmental fact-gathering powers were limited; if they were, then judicially guarded constitutional protections for searches and witnesses applied. The confusion, in a politically heated context, was a perfect recipe for the clash of wills concerning constitutional meaning.

In many cases, the legal fireworks proved to be intense. In the face of these nationally conducted investigations, key corporate witnesses defiantly refused to testify about what they claimed to be their private business affairs. A number of corporate witnesses were prominently imprisoned for their refusal.[28] Far from backing down in the face of this resistance throughout the 1880s and 1890s, both houses of Congress expanded the number and purview of their investigating committees, which moved beyond the unraveling of scandals to the consideration of an increasing array of social and

---

[27] Telford Taylor, *Grand Inquest: The Story of Congressional Investigations* (New York: Simon and Schuster, 1955), 45.

[28] See *Stewart v. Blaine* (S. Ct. Dist. Co. 1874); *Kilbourn v. Thompson*, 103 U.S. 168 (1880).

economic problems.[29] Some of the problems, particularly those involving the conduct and organization of railroads and economic trusts, became so serious and persistent that the need for gathering facts, for investigating, for seeing, was deemed by Congress to be permanent. Investigatory powers once asserted by Congress only in response to discrete scandals were now delegated to newly permanent governing institutions. Institutions such as the Interstate Commerce Commission were created which could devote their full efforts to the collection of facts from private economic entities that constituted a powerful sector of civil society.

Initially, the most strenuous resistance to the gaze of the New American State was mounted by small proprietor corporations like E. A. Boyd and Sons, businesses that personified the now disintegrating proprietary-competitive capitalist order. As concerns owned and managed by the same small group of people, these businesses felt the searing new gaze of the state keenly and personally. So, too, interestingly enough, did corporations like banks, railroads, and industrial conglomerates that precipitated and became pillars of the emerging corporate-administrative political economy. In the early stages of the nation's late-nineteenth-century political-economic transformation, many of these new conglomerates were Januses, with faces looking to both the old and the new order. In their reach and structure, they were modern. But at the same time, and significantly, many were still closely associated with a single individual, a J. P. Morgan, a Leland Stanford, an E. H. Harriman, or a John D. Rockefeller. The state's project of legibility thus was experienced even by the new corporations as an invasion of personal privacy of the books, papers, and diaries of these individuals. [30] Only as these corporations and their leaders came to recognize the benefits of a state-administered corporate order did their Fourth and Fifth Amendment privacy concerns fade. The Supreme Court's late-nineteenth- and early-twentieth-century Fourth and Fifth Amendment jurisprudence tracked this trajectory of resistance, mediation, and accommodation.

To justify an unprecedented ability to pry facts out of private economic entities, it was essential, first, to analogize these entities and the people who ran them to criminals. Identified as such, the personal dimension of their privacy claims became considerably less plausible. Investigating criminals would justify the strongest government evidence-gathering powers.

---

[29] Taylor, *Grand Inquest*, 51.

[30] See Sklar, *Corporate Reconstruction*, 27–8. See also Charles Francis Adams's characterization of Cornelius Vanderbilt as a man who had "combined the natural power of the individual with the factitious power of the corporation." Adams added, "The famous 'L'état, c'est moi' of Louis XIV represents Vanderbilt's position in regard to his railroads. Unconsciously he had introduced Caesarism into corporate life." Adams, of course, saw this less as a holdover from the old proprietary-competitive order than as a distinctive characteristic of the new corporate capitialism. Charles Francis Adams Jr., "A Chapter of Erie," in Charles Francis Adams Jr., and Henry Adams, *Chapters of Erie* (Ithaca, NY: Cornell University Press, 1968), 12.

The Social Construction of the "Criminaloid"

If sweeping fact-gathering governmental investigatory powers were typically justifiable only in criminal matters, then it was natural that those reformers who felt it imperative that these powers be broadly wielded came to see the potential targets of those powers as a new type of criminal. The moralization of economic behavior and the imagination of problematic economic behavior as a new type of criminality became a part of the ideological reconstruction essential to advance the progressive reformist program. This reconstruction was an ideological *sine qua non* of the project of legibility.

Signs of the moralization of economic behavior and (later) of regulatory transgressions are famously apparent in the work of the Progressive Era muckrakers. Perhaps most prominent in making the argument that economically undesirable behavior was a moral crime, and that business-class perpetrators were criminals was Edward A. Ross's book *Sin and Society* (1907), which appeared with a preface from Theodore Roosevelt.[31] In *Sin and Society*, Ross, a pioneering University of Wisconsin sociologist with close ties to Richard Ely and Lester Ward, made the progressive argument that "The sinful heart is ever the same, but sin changes its quality as society develops." "Modern sin," Ross declared, "takes its character from the mutualism of our time." "As society grows complex, it can be harmed in more ways." "A dense population lives in peace by aid of a protecting social order. Those who rack and rend this social order do worse than hurt particular individuals; they wound society itself."[32]

What Ross described as "this webbed social life" presented "sinister opportunities" and occasioned sinister acts that Ross believed caused moral rot and social damage fully comparable to that which resulted from traditional crime. The progressive professor complained:

> The man who picks pockets with a railway rebate, murders with an adulterant instead of a bludgeon, burglarizes with a "rake-off" instead of a jimmy, cheats with a company prospectus instead of a deck of cards, or scuttles his town instead of a ship, does not feel on his brow the brand of a malefactor.[33]

But, Ross continued, it is a progressive imperative that we recognize that

> [t]he stealings and slayings that lurk in the complexities of our social relations are not deeds of the dive, the dark alley, the lonely road, and the midnight hour. They require no nocturnal prowling with muffled step and bated breath, no weapon or offer of violence. Unlike the old-time villain, the latter-day malefactor does not wear a slouch hat and a comforter, breathe forth curses and an odor of gin, go about

---

[31] Edward A. Ross, *Sin and Society: An Analysis of Latter-Day Iniquity* (New York: Harper and Row, 1907).

[32] Ross, *Sin and Society*, 3, 6, 36.

[33] Ross, *Sin and Society*, 7.

his nefarious work with clenched teeth and an evil soul. . . . One misses the dramatic setting, the time-honored insignia of turpitude. Fagin, and Bill Sykes and Simon Legree are vanishing types.[34]

People simply "do not see that boodling is treason, that blackmail is piracy, that embezzlement is theft, that speculation is gambling, that tax-dodging is larceny, that railroad discrimination is treachery, that the factory labor of children is slavery, that deleterious adulteration is murder."[35] This is partly because these new sins are committed "without personal malice" and because those who commit them have all appearances of being pillars of the community.[36] After all, "[t]he government clerk who secretly markets advance crop information would hardly steal overcoats. . . . The life insurance presidents who let one another have the use of policy-holders funds at a third of the market rate may still be trusted not to purloin spoons."[37] Ross insisted:

Today, the villain most in need of curbing is the respectable, exemplary, trusted personage who, strategically placed at the focus of a spider-web of fiduciary relations, is able from his office chair to pick a thousand pockets, poison a thousand sick, pollute a thousand minds, or imperil a thousand lives. It is the great-scale, high voltage sinner that needs the shackle.[38]

Ross had a name for this new type of transgressor: "the criminaloid," which he defined as "a class . . . prosper[ing] by flagitious practices which have not yet come under the effective ban of public opinion," and is hence "quasi-criminal" notwithstanding his "counterfeit[ing] the good citizen."[39]

The hope lay, in Ross's progressive view, in the transformation of public opinion through visibility and light. "Public opinion," Ross declared, "is

---

[34] Ross, *Sin and Society*, 9–10.

[35] Ross, *Sin and Society*, 15.

[36] Ross, *Sin and Society*, 16.

[37] Ross, *Sin and Society*, 27.

[38] Ross, *Sin and Society*, 29–30.

[39] Ross, *Sin and Society*, 46–8, 61–2. Significantly, in extending Fourth and Fifth Amendment constitutional protections to a business in a civil proceeding in *Boyd v. United States*, Justice Bradley also alluded to the "quasi-criminal" nature of the case. *Boyd v. United States*, 116 U.S. 616 (1886), at 622. See also Charles Francis Adams Jr., "A Chapter of Erie," in Charles Francis Adams Jr. and Henry Adams, *Chapters of Erie* (Ithaca, NY: Cornell University Press, 1968) (essay originally published in 1868; book originally published in 1886) ("Pirates are commonly supposed to have been battered and hung out of existence when the Barbary Powers and the Buccaneers of the Spanish Main had been finally dealt with. Yet freebooters are not extinct; they have only transferred their operations to the land, and conducted them in more or less accordance with the forms of law. . . . ") Adams, "Chapter of Erie," 1 ("The unscrupulous [corporate] director is far less entitled to mercy than the ordinary gambler, combining as he does the character of the traitor with the acts of the thief"). Adams, "Chapter of Erie," 8 ("If the five years that succeeded the war have been marked by no exceptional criminal activity, they have witnessed some of the most remarkable examples of organized lawlessness, under the forms of law, which mankind had yet had an opportunity to study"). Charles Francis Adams Jr., "An Erie Raid," in Adams and Adams, *Chapters of Erie*, 138.

impotent so long as it allows itself to be kept guessing which shell the pea is under, whether the accountability is with the foreman, or the local manager, or the general manager, or the president, or the directors. How easily the general wrath is lost in this maze!"[40] He observed, however, hopefully, that "[e]ach of us emits a faint, compulsive beam, and since the agencies for focusing these into a fierce, withering ray of indignation become every day more perfect, public opinion as regulator of conduct steadily gains on priest and judge, and sheriff."[41] There is resistance, of course, to these rays of light. "[C]riminaloid philosophy" declares it "'un-American' to pry into 'private arrangements' between shipper and carrier, 'un-American' to fry the truth out of reluctant magnates."[42] This resistance, however, must be vanquished in the name of progress by an enlightened public that understands the true nature of the new political-economic order.

The construction of economic behavior as criminal, the imagination of the "criminaloid," was novel and striking to late-nineteenth-century commentators, as, of course, was the policy change it inspired. An extensive 1937 survey of substantive criminal law between 1887 and 1936 published by Harvard Law Professor Livingston Hall consigned street crime issues to a few insignificant late pages and ended up mainly as a survey of the era's massive criminalization of business practices.[43] "One result of this [progressive reform]," Hall observed, "has been to make everyone a criminal." "If the fines and short jail terms for which one was legally liable were actually enforced," he complained, "few would have any net income, or leisure out of jail in which to spend it."[44] Conspiracies in restraint of trade, transgressions of banking, securities, food and drug and tax laws, prohibition, and even the then-novel automobile regulation codes during the preceding half-century had become the focus of serious thinking at the time about criminal law. To Hall, the new order imported the moral presumptions of traditional criminal law into realms in which they had no place. "[N]o moral constraint dictates obedience to our modern bureaucracies," Hall pleaded. "Such an indiscriminate use of the criminal law weakens its hold as the arbiter of respectable conduct."[45] But Hall the critic was out

---

[40] Ross, *Sin and Society*, 125.

[41] Ross, *Sin and Society*, 24. We might go as far as to set Ross's vision of the statebuilding process here as amounting to an amalgamation of hundreds of thousands of light-projecting individuals as an interesting variant on the famous frontispiece to Hobbes's *Leviathan*. Thomas Hobbes, *Leviathan* (London: Penguin Books, 1968). In the frontispiece, however, the individuals comprising the state face inward rather than outward.

[42] Ross, *Sin and Society*, 65–6.

[43] Livingston Hall, "The Substantive Law of Crimes – 1887–1936," *Harvard Law Review* 50 (1937): 616–53. See also Herbert L. Packer, *The Limits of the Criminal Sanction* (Stanford: Stanford University Press, 1968), 13–14, 273–7, 354–63.

[44] Hall, "Substantive Law of Crimes," 622–3.

[45] Hall, "Substantive Law of Crimes," 623. See also Walter Lippmann, *Drift and Mastery: An Attempt to Diagnose the Current Unrest* (Madison: University of Wisconsin Press, 1985), 78.

of step with institutionalized developments. Ross and his allies had won the day.

Privacy and the Constitutional Resistance to the Progressive Imperative: The Initial Decisions of the 1880s

The progressive imperative that the state be empowered to see (as Ross had put it) "which shell the pea is under" and that "withering ray[s] of indignation" be trained on undesirable economic behavior acquired a rallying cry in the late nineteenth and early twentieth centuries: That rallying cry was the call for "publicity." The progressive push for publicity effectuated a subtle transformation in the meaning of the term. As far as matters of governance were concerned at the outset of the statebuilding era, the word "publicity" referred not to progressive efforts to expose the books and records of private business actors to public scrutiny, but rather to the imperative of establishing an open relationship between government bodies and the press.[46] But as private economic entities gradually came to be understood (and constructed) as having broad-ranging public effects, the word (and the progressive movement on behalf of) "publicity" assumed a new meaning. Now, the push for "publicity" referred to the effort to expose the inner workings of private businesses.[47]

[46] So, for example, in his chapter titled "Publicity" in his treatise *On Civil Liberty and Self Government*, Francis Lieber declared that publicity involved "the perfect freedom with which reporters may publish the transactions of public bodies." "Publicity, in connection with civil liberty," he announced, "meant publicity in the transaction of the business of the public, in all branches...." Such publicity was essential to making centralized, bureaucratic government free government. Lieber put it this way: "Bureaucracy is founded upon writing, liberty on the breathing word. Extensive writing, pervading the minutist branches of the administration, is the most active assistant of modern centralization.... [O]rality... [is] an important element of our civil liberty. I do not believe that a high degree of liberty can be imagined without widely pervading orality.... Whereas, [i]n former times secrecy was considered indispensable in public matters," now publicity must be understood as "at all events an alarm-bell, which calls public attention to the spot of danger." So governmental matters – quintessentially public matters – had to be seen and rendered visible. Francis Lieber, *On Civil Liberty and Self-Government* (Philadelphia: J. B. Lippincott & Co., 1877) (reprinted by Da Capo Press), 127–30. Alexander Hamilton had been a firm believer in this principle and practiced it throughout his career. See Forrest McDonald, *Alexander Hamilton: A Biography* (New York: W. W. Norton, 1982), 136–40, 188.

[47] The pioneering thinking on the imperative of a publicity-oriented seeing state was undertaken by government officials concerned with railroads. Foremost amongst them was Charles Francis Adams, who was from 1869 to 1879 the head of the nation's most significant early railway authority, the Massachusetts Board of Railroad Commissioners (MBRC), an agency that "was set up as a sort of lens by means of which the otherwise scattered rays of public opinion could be concentrated to a focus and brought to bear upon a given point." Adams, quoted in Thomas K. McCraw, *Prophets of Regulation: Charles Francis Adams, Louis D. Brandeis, James M. Landis, Alfred A. Kahn* (Cambridge, MA: The Belknap Press of the Harvard University Press, 1984), 23. See also Charles Francis Adams Jr., *Railroads: Their Origins and Problems* (New York: G. P. Putnam's Son's, 1880), 140–1 (asserting that the MBRC

In a series of prominent federal cases in the 1880s and 1890s, judges accustomed to the traditional privacy of the old proprietary-competitive order – an order under which "economic" and "personal" privacy were conflated – reacted with alarm to assertions of an imperative of publicity. In *Kilbourn v. Thompson* (1880), a scandal case involving the Jay Cooke real estate pool collapse, the U.S. Supreme Court held that a joint congressional investigating committee's attempt to force the pool's manager, Hallett Kilbourn, to fully discuss its operations amounted to a judicial act impermissibly undertaken by a legislative body. Congress has no such power, since no crime had been alleged. And, moreover, in the event that a crime had been alleged, it would be for a court and judge, not a legislature, to compel disclosure. "[W]hat authority," the Court asked, "has the House to enter upon this investigation into the private affairs of individuals who hold no office under the Government."[48]

The U.S. Supreme Court's *Boyd* case followed by a few years its staunchly privacy-protective *Kilbourn* ruling. Like those of *Kilbourn*, the facts of the *Boyd* case will not strike contemporary civil libertarians as those of a civil liberties landmark, involving, as it does, what we today might call "economic" as opposed to "personal" privacy. The *Boyd* decision was a tax case. In 1882, the supervising architect in charge of constructing new federal buildings in Philadelphia began accepting bids for glass to be used in the new structures.

"opened to light all the dark places," and making the claim that "[t]he indisputable fact was recognized that those [railway] corporations are so large and so removed from the owners of their securities, and the community is so deeply concerned in their doings and condition, that the law-making power both has a right and is duty bound to insist on that publicity as respects their affairs without which abuses cannot be guarded against"). It was Adams who created the nation's first "Sunshine Commission," which sought to regulate business primarily by exposing their "private" affairs to public view, a process Thomas McCraw has referred to as "regulation by publication." McCraw, *Prophets of Regulation*, 23. Adams's innovations in Massachusetts predate slightly the push for the criminalization of economic behavior. On the immense influence of railroads in setting institutional patterns of government administration, see Chandler, *Visible Hand*; Skowronek, *Building a New American State*. Under Adams's leadership, the MBRC, which had met staunch resistance to more coercive forms of regulation, devised an approach involving the production of information in reports and on forms arranged in a manner that the commissioners deemed to be most serviceable.

[48] *Kilbourn v. Thompson*, 103 U.S. 168, 195 (1880). In a private letter, Justice Miller, the author of the *Kilbourn* opinion, added: "I think the public has been much abused, the time of legislative bodies uselessly consumed and rights of the citizen ruthlessly invaded under the now familiar pretext of legislative investigation and that it is time that it was understood that courts and grand juries are the only inquisitions into crime in this country. I do not recognize the doctrine that Congress is the grand inquest of the nation, or has any such function to perform.... As regards needed information on subjects purely legislative no doubt committees can be raised to inquire and report, money can be used to pay for such information and laws may be made to compel reluctant witnesses to give it under proper guaranty of their personal rights. This is sufficient, without subjecting a witness to an unlimited power of a legislative committee or a single branch of a legislative body" (cited in Taylor, *Grand Inquest*, 50).

The architect asked those providing glass from abroad to submit bids consistent with the assumption that the glass would be admitted to the country duty-free. E. A. Boyd and Sons won the contract. Because the architect was rushed, however, he asked Boyd to supply him as soon as was practicable with glass on hand, glass on which duty had already been paid. In return, the architect guaranteed Boyd the future right to import an equivalent amount of glass duty-free.

Circumstances, however, soon conspired to lead Boyd into trouble. First, to fit his on-hand stock to order, Boyd had to cut, and in the process destroy, a larger quantity of glass than the square footage required for the federal building. Then, to make matters worse, a large amount of the glass that Boyd subsequently imported had shattered in transit. Soon, thirty-five cases of glass being imported by Boyd were seized by the customs inspector in the Port of New York on the grounds that Boyd had allegedly secured a duty-free permit from the U.S. Secretary of Treasury by making false statements that glass was to replace an equivalent amount used earlier in the construction of the Philadelphia federal building. In addition to the seizure, the U.S. attorney obtained a court order compelling Boyd to produce invoices for twenty-nine cases of glass previously imported by his company. Boyd was told that if he failed to produce these invoices, the allegations against him would be taken by the government as confessed. Boyd refused to supply the invoices, and a judgment was entered against him, leading to the permanent forfeiture of the thirty-five cases of glass. Boyd appealed, reasserting the sorts of arguments that had been made but had consistently been lost in lower federal courts in the 1870s, namely that the compulsory production of his business records violated his Fourth Amendment right against unreasonable searches and seizures and Fifth Amendment right against being forced to incriminate himself. By the late 1880s, however, when the statebuilding project and its accompanying project of legibility were well under way and when economic actors had begun to be imagined as criminals, the Supreme Court, in an opinion by Justice Joseph P. Bradley, held for Boyd against the claims of the U.S. government.

Justice Bradley's interpretation of the Fourth and Fifth Amendments, which had been adumbrated by losing arguments made in federal district courts in the 1870s, represented a departure from settled precedent and, by contemporary standards, was sweeping. The Fifth Amendment's constitutional self-incrimination privilege was traditionally invocable only by criminal defendants called to testify at their own trials. Bradley, apparently taking the reformers at their word that misbehaving economic actors in the new era were akin to criminals, extended the constitutional privilege to them in what he deemed to be "quasi-criminal" investigations.[49] He was able to

---

[49] *Boyd*, 116 U.S., at 622. Edward A. Ross later declared in *Sin and Society* (1907) that "[t]he real weakness in the moral position of Americans is not their attitude toward the plain criminal,

do this in part by constitutionalizing the common law "witness privilege," which itself had extended the self-incrimination privilege to nondefendants in civil proceedings. Moreover, *Boyd* extended the scope of the right to encompass papers seized in advance of the "quasi-criminal" trial. To do this, Bradley famously fused Fourth Amendment search and seizure limitations with common law and Fifth Amendment self-incrimination privileges. The understanding in *Boyd* of what constitutes a search and seizure was remarkably liberal. "It is true," he stated, in characterizing the facts of the *Boyd* case, "that certain aggravating incidents of actual search and seizure, such as forcible entry into a man's house and searching amongst his papers, are wanting [here]." But that is neither here nor there, since the government's assertion of its subpoena power in this case "accomplishes the substantial object . . . in forcing from a party evidence against himself."[50]

In *Boyd*, the Court upheld the joint rights-based Fourth and Fifth Amendment claims for the first time, in a provocative act of rights-based constitutional resistance to a perceived and actual growth of the invasive "seeing" powers of a rapidly expanding New American State. It did so on the grounds that the civil enforcement proceeding involved in the case was, for all intents and purposes, quasi-criminal and hence that constitutional guarantees typically extended to criminals were appropriate to those whose privacy was invaded by the newly seeing state. In form, the result was a classic civil liberties decision that elevated a common law right, the "witness privilege," and expanded it, by reading it into the self-incrimination privilege of the Fifth Amendment, with a boost from a simultaneous allusion to the Fourth Amendment's protection against unreasonable searches and seizures. The Supreme Court had engaged in a signal "juris-generative" act, for the first time making grand pronouncements on behalf of constitutional guarantees of personal privacy. This decision ushered in a heightened contemplation of constitutional privacy issues by the High Court – and, significantly, in that era's wider political culture.[51]

A ruling reinforcing the concerns of the landmark *Boyd* decision (and *Kilbourn v. Thompson*) was issued by Justice Stephen J. Field in a Circuit

---

but their attitude toward the quasi-criminal." Ross, *Sin and Society*, 46. Bradley's innovation was to accord quasi-criminals the constitutional protections of quasi-criminals.

[50] *Boyd*, 116 U.S., at 622. The opinion was long on history and placed the instant case alongside the famous Wilkes case. Of that case, Bradley declared that "the principles laid down in this opinion affect the very essence of constitutional liberty and security. . . . It is not the breaking of his doors, and the rummaging of his drawers, that constitutes the essence of the offence; but it is the invasion of the indefeasible right of personal security, personal liberty, and private property. . . ." *Boyd*, 116 U.S., at 630. The connection between the Fourth Amendment's search and seizure requirement and the Wilkes case and the American Writs of Assistance controversy were a staple of the expositions of the clause in the major nineteenth-century legal treatises. See, e.g., Cooley, *Constitutional Limitations*, 299–304.

[51] Robert M. Cover, "*Nomos* and Narrative: The Supreme Court 1982 Term Forward," *Harvard Law Review* 97 (1983): 4–68; Novak, "Legal Origins of the Modern American State," 251.

Court opinion one year later. *In re Pacific Railway Commission* involved the efforts of a commission specially authorized by Congress to investigate the Pacific Railway to compel Leland Stanford to disclose his private papers to the body.[52] In his opinion for the court, Field rebuffed the commission, citing separation of powers objections to making the federal court, which was called upon by the commission to assert its compulsory process powers, instruments of legislative or quasi-legislative bodies. To Field, this amounted to a misuse of the judiciary, plain and simple. And the issue appeared to him more than one of functional niceties: The separation of powers issues had plain civil liberties implications. A judicial hearing, Field asserted, was bound to be more solicitous of privacy claims than a decision made by either legislative or administrative fiat. "It is the forcible intrusion into, and compulsory exposure of, one's private affairs and papers, without judicial process, or in the course of judicial proceedings, which is contrary to the principles of a free government, and is abhorrent to the instincts of Englishmen and Americans," he wrote.[53] "[O]f all the rights of the citizen," he continued, "few are of greater importance or more essential to his peace and happiness than the right of personal security, and that involves, not merely the protection of his person from assault, but exemption of his private affairs, books and papers from the inspection and scrutiny of others. Without the enjoyment of this right, all other rights would lose half their value."[54]

The Launching of a Permanent Investigatory State – and Civil Libertarian Resistance

The *Kilbourn* case and Field's *Pacific Railway* opinion threw down the gauntlet on behalf of the prevailing institutional order. And *Boyd* grounded that prevailing order in new criminal process protections. But it soon became apparent that these staunch guarantees of privacy and civil liberties set out by Miller, Field, and Bradley represented a civil liberties jurisprudence that was radically at odds with the fact-gathering imperatives of the New American State.

The creation of the nation's first independent regulatory commissions – the Interstate Commerce Commission in 1887 and the Federal Trade Commission in 1914 – the passage of the Sherman Act in 1890, the 1894 federal income tax (struck down by the Supreme Court the following year but

---

[52] *In re Pacific Railway Commission*, 32 F. 241 (Circuit Court, N.D. California, 1887).

[53] *In re Pacific Railway Commission*, 32 F. at 251. Charles McCurdy has persuasively argued that Justice Field was not simply a laissez-faire justice acting in service of business interests but rather a major (and broadly concerned) constitutional theorist working to formulate and institutionalize socially useful and public-spirited legal guidelines concerning the separation of the public and private spheres. Charles W. McCurdy, "Justice Field and the Jurisprudence of Government-Business Relations: Some Parameters of 'Laissez-Faire' Constitutionalism, 1863–1897," *Journal of American History* 61 (1975): 970–1005.

[54] *In re Pacific Railway Commission*, 32 F. at 250.

ultimately prevailing following the 1913 passage of the Sixteenth Amendment),[55] the burgeoning budgets for the Internal Revenue and Customs Services, and, later, the passage of the Eighteenth Amendment and the Volstead Act, all brought important sectors of society into increasingly regular contact with the eyes and arms of the New American State. It was in dialogic response to this state expansion that the Supreme Court fashioned its first sustained jurisprudence of search and seizure and privacy.

In a series of cases involving challenges to the federal government's pioneering administrative body, the ICC, however, the entire Supreme Court set itself the task of reassessing the tenability of that regime given the emergent new political economy. While the Court was attentive to the concerns of Miller, Field, and Bradley, in the end it did not so much defend their staunch commitment to privacy as asserted in the *Boyd* decision as prudently negotiate its dismemberment. Wide-ranging investigatory powers were accorded to the ICC, while, at the same time, newly conceived outer limits were set.[56]

The Supreme Court held fast to its legibility-limiting, privacy-protecting commitments in its 1892 decision in *Counselman v. Hitchcock*.[57] In that case, Charles Counselman, a Chicago grain shipper who headed a small company with the assistance of seven employees, was brought before an Illinois grand jury to face direct questioning regarding whether the rates he paid for shipping grain on various railroads violated ICC-set tariffs and whether he received rebates, drawbacks, or commissions from the railroads. He repeatedly refused to answer, asserting (as had Boyd) a Fourth Amendment protection against unreasonable searches and seizures and a Fifth Amendment privilege against self-incrimination. Counselman was taken to jail for contempt and, in a federal habeas action, two federal courts upheld his ongoing imprisonment. In an opinion by Justice Samuel Blatchford, however, the U.S. Supreme Court unanimously reversed these decisions, holding

---

[55] *Pollack v. Farmers' Loan and Trust Co. v. United States*, 157 U.S. 429 (1895); 158 U.S. 601 (1895).

[56] This behavior involving a Court effort to work out a *modus vivendi* in the following Fourth Amendment legibility cases parallels the approach the Court used in assessing the novel assertion of ICC authority over railroad rates, an approach that was chronicled by Skowronek. Skowronek, *Building a New American State*, ch. 8. Regarding the ICC's new rate-making authority, Skowronek concluded that "[i]t is more than likely that the Court understood the volatile political nature of the question at hand and the growing precariousness of its own political position. In declaring its determination to refrain from unwarranted exercises of judicial power, the Court seemed to be searching for a new and more secure position before the growing democratic attack on the judiciary got out of hand and caused some real damage to its prerogatives and its prestige." Skowronek, *Building a New American State*, 260. This era witnessed escalating verbal attacks on the judiciary and proposals for the recall of both judicial decisions and judges themselves. See William G. Ross, *A Muted Fury: Populists, Progressives, and Labor Unions Confront the Courts, 1890–1937* (Princeton: Princeton University Press, 1994).

[57] *Counselman v. Hitchcock*, 142 U.S. 547 (1892).

that the Interstate Commerce Act would transgress the Fifth Amendment if read to compel a person to give testimony in a criminal case that subjected him to potential criminal prosecution.[58] The Court declared that for the information-eliciting provisions of the act to be valid, absolute immunity against future prosecution for the offense had to be granted.

The combined holdings of the Supreme Court in *Boyd* and *Counselman* landed a potentially crippling blow to the fact-gathering powers of the New American State. Two years later in *ICC v. Brimson* (a decision in which Justice Field did not participate), the High Court was more accommodating.[59] *Brimson* involved an informal complaint filed with the agency against the rates and charges of a number of railroads. The gravamen of the complaint was that the Illinois Steel Company was in collusion with certain railroads and thus gained preferential transportation rates. Suspicions were aroused that the steel company and the railroads were owned by the same people and, in an effort to confirm these suspicions, the ICC issued a series of subpoenas in an attempt to compel the company to produce its stock books. In a 5–3 decision, the *Brimson* Court held that a court could, at the ICC's request, compel production of the desired records. In doing so, the Court emphasized the practical necessity of its holding: "Any adjudication that Congress could not establish an administrative body with authority to investigate the subject of interstate commerce and with the power to call witnesses before it, and to require the production of books, documents, and papers relating to that subject, would go far toward defeating the object for which the people of the United States placed commerce among the states under national control," Justice John Marshall Harlan wrote for the Court.[60] At the same time, however, citing Justice Bradley's and Justice Field's respective opinions in

---

[58] Interestingly, the government unsuccessfully based its argument before the High Court on the contention that this was a regulatory rather than a criminal case. They stated specifically that "[a]n investigation before a grand jury is in no sense 'a criminal case.' The inquiry is for the purpose of finding whether a crime has been committed, and whether any one shall be accused of an offense. The inquiry [is] secret; there is no accuser, no parties, plaintiff or defendant. The whole proceeding is *ex parte*, the testimony being confined to one side, and the evidence adduced is not governed by the rules or the manner or method by which testimony is adduced or admitted on the trial of cases in court. Such an investigation is not a criminal case within the meaning of the Constitution." *Counselman*, 142 U.S. at 554–5.

[59] *Interstate Commerce Commission v. Brimson*, 154 U.S. 447 (1894). R. Erik Lillquist contends that the *Counselman* ruling represented a turning point in which the Court realized that it could not and should not interpose itself as a barrier to the project of legibility, given the massive changes at large in the wider political economy. R. Erik Lillquist, "Constitutional Rights at the Junction: The Emergence of the Privilege Against Self-Incrimination and the Interstate Commerce Act," *Virginia Law Review* 81 (October 1995): 1989–2042. In the pages that follow, however, I highlight what seems to me to be an ongoing process of negotiation concerning state development that took place over the course of the subsequent thirty or so years.

[60] *Brimson*, 154 U.S. at 474.

Boyd and *Pacific Railway*, Harlan emphasized in strongly worded dicta that "Neither branch of the legislative department, still less any merely administrative body established by Congress, possesses, or can be invested with, a general power of making inquiry into the private affairs of the citizen."[61] The counterposing of the early ICC cases of *Counselman* and *Brimson* in the Supreme Court signaled that the process of negotiating a *modus vivendi* between publicity and privacy in the era of the construction of the New American State had begun.

The Campaign for Legibility and Publicity

While the Supreme Court was an active participant in the privacy-publicity battles, important developments took place in other branches of the government as well as in the broader public discourse. A crucial sally in state development pertaining to the ongoing project of legibility was Theodore Roosevelt's 1903 establishment of the Bureau of Corporations in the Department of Commerce and Labor. While this bureau lacked direct regulatory power, it did possess broad authority to collect and publish data on American corporations. It possessed, that is, the power of publicity.[62] The Bureau of Corporations, the first executive branch agency established to monitor industry, sought, as had Charles Francis Adams's Massachusetts Board of Railroad Commissioners before it, to use publicity as its primary regulatory tool. Its goal was to open up corporations permanently to the eye of the New American State, to render them legible so that they could be administered. The Bureau of Corporations vowed to make stock ownership "as public as land titles," thus enabling public officials in Washington to see who within a corporation was making decisions and setting corporate policy.[63] Similarly, it sought to lay bare interlocking directorates and stock transactions so that the country's new regulatory laws could be targeted at real rather than fictitious interests. In service of these ends, it was proposed that national incorporation laws be established for companies operating in interstate commerce, with the privilege of incorporation being contingent upon corporate cooperation with the project of legibility, on the provision to the national

---

[61] *Brimson*, 154 U.S. at 478.

[62] Sklar has demonstrated the great coercive effect this power might have had in practice had the Hepburn bill strengthening the Bureau's publicity powers passed. Sklar, *Corporate Reconstruction*, 228–85. Theodore Roosevelt's commitment to publicity, in both his rhetoric and his substantive public policy proposals, closely tracks that of his advisor Herbert Croly, as well as that of Walter Lippmann (whose views are discussed subsequently). For an account of Roosevelt's rhetoric and commitment to publicity, see Arthur M. Johnson, "Theodore Roosevelt and the Bureau of Corporations," *Mississippi Valley Historical Review* 45 (March 1959): 571–90. The discussion of the Bureau that follows is drawn from Sklar, *Corporate Reconstruction*, 184–203.

[63] Sklar, *Corporate Reconstruction*, 190.

government, that is, of facts concerning corporate organization, accounting, and decision making. In addition, and more radically, it was proposed that a national licensing scheme be established for all corporations operating in interstate commerce, with the disclosure of requested facts a prerequisite to approval of the license.

These various government legibility initiatives, beginning with discrete congressional investigations and developing into the creation of permanent "seeing" institutions such as the ICC and the Bureau of Corporations, were supported by a broad cadre of progressive public intellectuals who assaulted the claims of privacy and vaunted the claims of publicity. In these progressive intellectual campaigns on behalf of the New American State's project of legibility, the visual metaphor used by James Scott in his book on state modernization crops up repeatedly.[64] A key progressive talking point, for instance, involved the power of the visible fact. Walter Lippmann, for example, argued in his influential early work that the collection of facts from individuals, businesses, and unions represented the first essential step in the creation of a scientific government characterized by mastery rather than drift. Lippmann defined mastery as the ability "to distinguish fact from fancy," a phrase he used repeatedly throughout his book.[65] "You cannot throw yourself blindly against unknown facts," he warned, "and trust to luck that the result will be satisfactory."[66] "Scientific discipline [is] where men...know fact from fancy...."[67] "The scientific spirit," he added, "is the discipline of democracy, the escape from drift, the outlook of a free man. Its direction is to distinguish fact from fancy; its enthusiasm is for the possible; its premise

---

[64] The widespread use of the visual metaphor in the formative years of the New American State serves as a notable parallel to the same era's deployment of the corporate metaphor, and seems to have served a similar naturalizing function vis-à-vis radically new and unfamiliar forms of governance. See Daniel P. Carpenter, "The Corporate Metaphor and Executive Department Centralization in the United States, 1888–1928," *Studies in American Political Development* 12 (Spring 1998): 162–203, esp. 166.

[65] Lippmann, *Drift and Mastery*, 156. Lippmann's book was of great significance because in many ways it captured perfectly the major themes of the "progressive" outlook of his times. It is worth noting, however, that over time Lippmann's views about the possibilities of democracy and democratic governance changed to the point where, after witnessing the rise of Nazi totalitarianism in Europe, Lippmann became a staunch opponent of New Deal collectivism and a proponent of natural law and laissez-faire economics. Walter Lippmann, *The Good Society* (Boston: Little, Brown, 1937). See Edward A. Purcell Jr., *The Crisis of Democratic Theory: Scientific Naturalism and the Problem of Value* (Lexington: University Press of Kentucky, 1973), 112–14, 152–4. See also David A. Hollinger, *In the American Province: Studies in the History and Historiography of Ideas* (Baltimore: Johns Hopkins University Press, 1985), 44–55; Ronald Steel, *Walter Lippmann and the American Century* (New York: Vintage Books, 1980), 315–17, 321–6. On the influence of the rise of European totalitarianism on legal (and political) thought more generally, see Richard A. Primus, *The American Language of Rights* (Cambridge: Cambridge University Press, 1999), 177–91.

[66] Lippmann, *Drift and Mastery*, 158.

[67] Lippmann, *Drift and Mastery*, 150.

is the shaping of fact to a chastened and honest dream."[68] In the name of progress, Lippmann called upon American society "to live ready, to lighten experience by a knowledge of its alternatives, to let no fact be opaque, but to make what happens transparent with the choices it offers."[69]

In a 1915 paean to publicity, Lippmann declared:

> The great healing effect of publicity is that by revealing men's motives it civilizes them. If people have to declare publicly what they want and why they want it, they cannot be altogether ruthless.... A special interest frankly avowed is no terror to democracy. It is neutralized by publicity.... The great virtue of democracy – in fact, its supreme virtue – is that it supplies a method for dragging the realities into the light, of summoning our rulers to declare themselves and to submit to judgment.[70]

This implied that for the sake of progress and democracy, a number of the traditional liberties assumed as part of the old proprietary-competitive order would have to be discarded:

> It is more than likely . . . that freedom in corporate accounting will have to be abolished, that all large enterprises will have to submit to publicly instituted systems of bookkeeping, and that their whole financial structure will become as visible as that of a railroad or a municipal corporation. For it is only by making publicly available to everyone the whole position of these enterprises that the relations of capital and labor, of corporation and investor, of industry and consumer can be lifted to a plane where transactions are really free because all the relevant facts are known. To preserve the reality of free contract it will almost surely be necessary to abolish the sham freedom of corporate secrecy.[71]

And the implications of these imperatives of the new corporate-administrative order would seep well beyond the targeted corporations themselves. Lippmann later took an additional step and insisted that in the interests of adequate regulation unions, too, would have to be opened up to public inspection, just as would any other powerful interests with a stake in the New American State.[72]

---

[68] Lippmann, *Drift and Mastery*, 151.

[69] Lippmann, *Drift and Mastery*, 174. I note that the connections between the seeing and hard fact-gathering imperative in the statebuilding project and the era's literary realism and naturalism (in the work of Dreiser and Norris, among others) seems strong. It appears that both policymakers and artists believed that strong, even dominant, social forces were at work, forces with which they had had very little contact and of which they lacked understanding. Factual knowledge was the prerequisite to understanding, and understanding, in turn, the prerequisite to mastery and control. See also Purcell, *Crisis of Democratic Theory*, 15–29.

[70] Walter Lippmann, *The Stakes of Diplomacy* (New York: H. Holt and Co., 1915), ch. 15, in *The Essential Lippmann: A Political Philosophy for Liberal Democracy*, eds. Clinton Rossiter and James Lare (New York: Vintage Books, 1965), 226–7.

[71] Walter Lippmann, *The Method of Freedom* (New York: Macmillan, 1934), Part 2, in *The Essential Lippmann*, 332.

[72] Walter Lippmann, "Regulating the Labor Unions," *Today and Tomorrow*, 29 May 1958, in *The Essential Lippmann*, 352–3. At the time of the proposal of the Sherman Act amendment

Lippmann's friend, the journalist and political theorist Herbert Croly, also made it plain in his book *Progressive Democracy* (1914) that the gathering of facts as part of the ongoing project of legibility might impinge upon rights once taken for granted under the rapidly passing proprietary-competitive political economy. This, for Croly, however, was simply the price of progress. Administrators, he said, have "more inspiring work to do" than to worry about an individual and his rights. "If the prevailing legalism and a repressive moral code are associated with the rule of live-and-let-live," he opined, "the progressive democratic faith finds its consummation rather in the rule of live-and-help-live." "Wherever the lives of other people are frustrated," Croly emphasized, fixed on the imperatives of a progressive statism and hence more or less indifferent to potential civil liberties concerns, "we are responsible for the frustration, just insofar as we have failed to do what we could for their liberation; and we can always do something on behalf of liberty."[73]

Key to the administrative success of the New American State, in Croly's view, was the "acquisition of social knowledge."[74] And the acquisition of that knowledge involved giving administrators the power to see further and deeper into what formerly had been considered purely private affairs. This for Croly was a matter beyond dispute. "The one demand made by critics of the traditional system upon its directors and beneficiaries, which the latter should recognize as being unequivocally helpful," he insisted, "is the demand for publicity." "Any part of the creed or the mechanism of the system which shuns the light," he concluded, "is necessarily a suspect."[75]

What at base was needed, in Croly's estimation, was a radically new conception of justice. He described progressive justice in arresting imagery by reimagining the symbol of justice itself:

Instead of having her eyes blindfolded, she would wear perched upon her nose a most searching and forbidding pair of spectacles, one which combined the vision of a microscope, a telescope, and a photographic camera. Instead of holding scales in her hand, she might perhaps be figured as possessing a much more homely and serviceable set of tools. She would have a hoe with which to cultivate the social garden, a watering pot with which to refresh it, a barometer with which to measure the pressure of the social air, and the indispensable typewriter and filing cabinet with which to record the behavior of society.[76]

---

involving the publicity powers of the Bureau of Corporations, it was proposed that labor unions would not be compelled to provide as much information to the bureau as was required from corporations. Sklar, *Corporate Reconstruction*, 232, 242–3.

[73] Herbert Croly, *Progressive Democracy* (New Brunswick, NJ: Transaction Publishers, 1998), 368–70, 426–7. Croly's constitutional philosophy is discussed well and succinctly in Brand, *Corporatism and the Rule of Law*, 54–61.

[74] Croly, *Progressive Democracy*, 369–70.

[75] Croly, *Progressive Democracy*, 26.

[76] Croly, *Progressive Democracy*, 369.

Louis D. Brandeis: The Push for Publicity and the "Right to Privacy"
Louis Brandeis is commonly categorized as a different sort of progressive
from Croly and Lippmann. Croly and Lippmann were New Nationalism
progressives who had made their peace with the large corporate conglomerates that characterized the nation's new political economy. They favored
the creation of strong central bureaucratic authorities to ensure that the new
agglomerations of private power operated ultimately in the public interest.
Brandeis, on the other hand, was a New Freedom progressive who ostensibly believed that democratic liberty would best be preserved by breaking
up concentrations of economic power and keeping the size of the central
administration relatively small. When it came to the imperatives of visibility,
however, these two commonly distinguished branches of progressivism were
cut from the same cloth.

Although typically remembered as an early and deep defender of "the
right to privacy," Brandeis, like Lippmann and Croly, was also a believer
in the salutary power of facts. And the creation of a full factual record
on any social problem typically involves prying out information that other
people are zealously committed to keeping private. In this regard, Brandeis's
commitment to privacy is well worth reconsidering. Brandeis plainly fits in
well with those public intellectuals who fought for limitations on privacy in
the name of publicity.

Conventional wisdom notwithstanding, in many senses Brandeis was
never a great defender of the "right to privacy" or of the "right to be let
alone." It is worth recalling at the outset that Brandeis invented neither
phrase: both were coined by staunch and prominent nineteenth-century advocates of limited government operating in the spirit of Justices Field and
Bradley. The former phrase was coined by *Nation* editor E. L. Godkin, a
classical liberal, in an 1890 article in *Scribner's Magazine*. The latter was
coined by Thomas Cooley in his 1888 treatise on torts.[77] Brandeis had been

---

[77] E. L. Godkin, "The Rights of the Citizen – To His Own Reputation," *Scribner's Magazine*
8 (July 1890): 58–67; Thomas M. Cooley, *A Treatise on the Law of Torts: Or the Wrongs
Which Arise Independent of Contract* (Chicago: Callaghan and Co., 1888), 2nd ed., 29. The
lineage is noted (and references to Godkin and Cooley made) in James H. Barron, "Warren
and Brandeis, The Right to Privacy, 4 Harvard Law Review 193 (1890): Demystifying a
Landmark Citation," *Suffolk Law Review* 13 (Summer 1979): 875, which, in conjunction
with the other sources listed in the ensuing notes, I draw upon for my subsequent discussion. Although Cooley has been frequently classified as a laissez-faire liberal, particularly in
the canonical, post–New Deal studies of laissez-faire constitutionalism (see, e.g., Benjamin
Twiss, *Lawyers and the Constitution: How Laissez Faire Came to the Supreme Court* [Princeton:
Princeton University Press, 1942]; Sidney Fine, *Laissez Faire and the General Welfare State: A
Study in Conflict in American Thought, 1865–1901* [Ann Arbor: University of Michigan Press,
1956]; Edward Corwin, *Liberty Against Government: The Rise, Flowering, and Decline of a
Famous Judicial Concept* [Baton Rouge: Louisiana State University Press, 1948]), Alan Jones
and, more recently, Howard Gillman, have argued convincingly that Cooley had no particular solicitude for property and economic rights as more important than other rights such

roped into writing the now famous *Harvard Law Review* article titled "The Right to Privacy," an article now commonly understood to be the progenitor of constitutional privacy rights, by Samuel Warren, his old friend and law partner, who, like many of his class in the new and unfamiliar age of the late-nineteenth-century mass circulation sensationalist press, was outraged about seeing his name in the Boston newspapers.[78] By contemporary standards, Warren had hardly been dragged through the muck of yellow journalism. Instead, Warren had simply been mentioned, and that, infrequently, as having been a guest at a few Boston society functions.

Warren and Brandeis certainly were straining toward a sort of privacy in penning their famous article, but the civil libertarian implications of that sort of privacy were dubious at best: These implications certainly would be characterized today as profoundly conservative, amounting to a form of press censorship. In their *Harvard Law Review* article, Warren and Brandeis arrayed themselves (to deploy Rochelle Gurstein's terms) with the "party of reticence" against the "party of exposure." The article essentially advanced the argument that if the press strayed from reporting news that was considered legitimate by the governing mugwumpish elites, there was an array of legal means available to rein them in.[79] But it must be said that even this reticence was more Warren's preoccupation than Brandeis's.

The first step in papering over the tension in Brandeis's thought between privacy (with which Brandeis's name is commonly associated in constitutional thought) and publicity, which was a statebuilding era progressive imperative that Brandeis worked tirelessly to advance, is apparent in his and Warren's 1890 article itself. Warren and Brandeis's initial argument for a

as free press and freedom of religion, and that Cooley's intellectual allegiances were actually derived from Jacksonian egalitarianism, and hence profoundly suspicious of economic and corporate power. As the first head of the ICC, Cooley believed strongly in appropriate regulatory schemes. Alan Jones, "Thomas M. Cooley and 'Laissez Faire Constitutionalism': A Reconsideration," *Journal of American History* 53 (March 1967): 751–71; Howard Gillman, *The Constitution Beseiged: The Rise and Demise of Lochner Era Police Powers Jurisprudence* (Durham, NC: Duke University Press, 1993), 55–9. That said, however, Cooley remained a firm believer in limited, constitutional governance.

[78] For illuminating discussions of the rise of the gossip-laden late-nineteenth-century sensationalist press, the way in which this rise was experienced by the middle class and elites such as Warren and Brandeis, and the efforts of some to secure privacy protections in the face of the onslaught, see Robert Mensel, "Kodakers Lying in Wait: Amateur Photography and the Right of Privacy in New York, 1885–1915," *American Quarterly* 43 (March 1991): 24–45, esp. 25, 32 (citing "a sense of social and psychological dislocation amongst bourgeois Americans" occasioned by urbanization, industrialization, secularization, and the pace of scientific discovery, reinforced, in light of the rise of the sensationalist press, by "a profound sense of exposure"); Rochelle Gurstein, *The Repeal of Reticence: A History of America's Cultural and Legal Struggles Over Free Speech, Obscenity, Sexual Liberation, and Modern Art* (New York: Hill and Wang, 1996), 146–78; Norman Rosenberg, *Protecting the Best Men: An Interpretive History of the Law of Libel* (Chapel Hill: University of North Carolina Press, 1986), 184–206.

[79] Barron, "Warren and Brandeis," 912.

right to privacy was, we should recall, an argument for a private and not a public right: The authors were advocating, and advocating only, an action in tort for its invasion. There was nothing constitutional about it. The primary defendants in such suits were imagined to be sensationalist newspapers, gossip columnists, and tabloid-style photographers. The article cites only private law cases. As such, and quite significantly, it neither mentions nor imagines that a right to privacy would be used as a shield against the invasion of the right by the government. Only after the Brandeis advocacy of intrusive government interventionism became deeply imbedded in the American political consciousness as part of the nation's governing philosophy under the New American State was it safe for the Warren Court to selectively invoke Brandeis's right to privacy in the service of targeted political constituencies without threatening all of the many intrusions upon privacy that Brandeis and his political heirs actively supported.[80]

Looked at in retrospect, however, Warren and Brandeis were paving the way for a regime-sustaining, post–New Deal ideology concerning the place of privacy (and civil liberty more generally) under the immensely powerful New American State. That ideology decoupled concerns about privacy from what progressives saw as the imperative project of legibility. It is significant that outside of his *Harvard Law Review* article, only when it came to Prohibition did Justice Brandeis prominently weigh in on the virtues of "privacy," in the *Olmstead* and the *Carroll* cases. And here, his record is mixed and no more civil libertarian than that of "conservative" Justices Bradley and James Clark McReynolds.[81]

Brandeis did not delude himself about his lack of commitment to privacy any more than did progressives Lippmann or Croly, neither of whom had cut a public figure as a protector of privacy rights. In a letter written to his friend Alice Goldmark in 1891, for instance, Brandeis noted:

Lots of things which are worth doing have occurred to me as I sit calmly here. And among others to write an article on "The Duty of Publicity" – a sort of companion

---

[80] *Griswold v. Connecticut*, 381 U.S. 479 (1965); *Eisenstadt v. Baird*, 405 U.S. 438 (1972) (Burger Court); *Roe v. Wade*, 410 U.S. 113 (1973) (Burger Court).

[81] In *Olmstead v. United States*, Justice Brandeis dissented from the Court's holding that an illegal wiretap used to enforce Prohibition laws did not violate the strictures of the Fourth Amendment. *Olmstead v. United States*, 277 U.S. 438 (1927). In *Carroll v. United States*, however, he voted with the majority to uphold an automobile search of motorists suspected of violating Prohibition laws. *Carroll v. United States*, 267 U.S. 132 (1925). See Philippa Strum, *Louis D. Brandeis: Justice for the People* (Cambridge, MA: Harvard University Press, 1984), 330. For Eileen McDonagh, "Prohibition legislation typif[ied] the anti-civil rights state institutionalized in the Progressive Era." Eileen L. McDonagh, "The 'Welfare Rights State' and the 'Civil Rights State': Policy Paradox and State Building in the Progressive Era," *Studies in American Political Development* 7 (Fall 1993): 225–74, esp. 245. Justices McReynolds and Sutherland dissented in the *Carroll* case. The most steadfast defenders of privacy rights in Prohibition cases were Justices Butler and McReynolds. Murchison, *Federal Criminal Law Doctrines*, 74–101.

piece to the last one that would really interest me more. You know I have talked to you about the wickedness of people shielding wrongdoers and passing them off (or at least allowing them to pass themselves off) as honest men. Some instances of that have presented themselves within a few days which have fired my imagination. If the broad light of day could be let in upon men's actions, it would purify them as the sun disinfects. You see my idea; I leave you to straighten out and complete that sentence.[82]

Brandeis made the same point in a published article many years later advocating the public disclosure of corporate financial arrangements. "Publicity," he stated there, "is justly commended as a remedy for social and industrial diseases. Sunlight is said to be the best of disinfectants; electric light is the most efficient policeman."[83]

In his advocacy for the creation of the Federal Trade Commission (1914), an agency that would ultimately absorb and expand upon the duties of Theodore Roosevelt's Bureau of Corporations (which itself had been modeled on Charles Francis Adams's "Sunshine Commission"), Brandeis emphasized the need for sweeping bureaucratic investigatory powers to put teeth into the powers of exposure. "In the complicated questions involved in dealing with 'Big Business,'" he wrote in *Harper's Weekly*, "the first requisite is knowledge – comprehensive, accurate, and up to date – of the details of business operations." "The current collection and prompt publication of . . . information concerning the various branches of business," he continued, "would prove of great value in preserving competition. The methods of destructive competition will not bear the light of day. The mere substitution of knowledge for ignorance – of publicity for secrecy – will go far toward preventing monopoly."[84]

To contemporaries, the conflict between the progressive investigatory vision and the commitment to privacy was clear. Section Nine of the Federal Trade Commission Act gave the Commission sweeping powers to probe, providing that the Commission and its agents shall have "access to, for the purpose of examination, and the right to copy any documentary evidence of any corporation being investigated or proceeded against." And Section Four of the act defined "documentary evidence" as "all documents, papers and correspondence in existence at and after the passage of this act." When read in combination with the FTC's vague mandate to move against all unfair methods of competition, it was not far from the mark for one railroad lawyer,

---

[82] Letter, Louis D. Brandeis to Alice Goldmark (February 26, 1891), in Louis D. Brandeis, *Letters of Louis D. Brandeis*, eds. Melvin Urofsky and David Levy, vol. 1 (Albany: State University of New York Press, 1971), 100, reprinted in Barron, "Warren and Brandeis," 912 (italics in original).

[83] Louis D. Brandeis, *Other People's Money and How the Bankers Use It* (New York: F. A. Stokes, 1914), 62, quoted in Barron, "Warren and Brandeis," at 912.

[84] Louis D. Brandeis, "The Solution of the Trust Problem," *Harper's Weekly* (November 8, 1913): 18.

Edward Jouett, to publicly assert that the act gave the agency "a roving commission to wander at will through all [of a business's] records and files." The FTC's mandate, Jouett complained, "exposes to outsiders a company's private business methods, trade secrets, and intimate correspondence. This may entail not only annoyance and humiliation but great financial loss."[85] This power was "not only unjust, unnecessary and un-American, but distinctly violative of the Fourth Amendment to the Constitution of the United States, which forbids unreasonable searches and seizure."[86]

This was squarely an issue of personal privacy, for the statute "lays bare to strangers and competitors not merely the impersonal record of the actual transactions of the company, but also the plans, hopes, fears, policies and opinions of its officials, and their correspondents, together with a great mass of private information as to men and things which a company necessarily receives and gives." "Letters necessarily involve the personal privacy of individuals," Jouett continued, "and this right of privacy is a substantial one which the laws of this free country should, and . . . do protect."[87]

Jouett's comments were part of a broad public policy debate in which concerns about "the microscopic espionage of the federal government" as part of the booming growth of the then hotly contested central regulatory state were much bruited.[88] And in this debate, it makes as much sense to align the ambivalent Louis Brandeis with those progressives advocating a restrictive view of privacy as with those enjoining government to keep its distance. In this regard, Brandeis was the wave of the future. During the 1920s, men who were to become prominent New Dealers, such as James Landis, Milton Handler, and David Lilienthal, all wrote articles defending the new fact-gathering powers claimed by the federal government. In 1926, the year after he completed his Supreme Court clerkship with Justice Brandeis, Landis, a pioneering scholar of the new administrative state later chosen by Franklin Delano Roosevelt to head the Securities and Exchange Commission, published a lengthy historical justification of an expansive view of

---

[85] Edward S. Jouett, "The Inquisitorial Feature of the Federal Trade Commission Act Violates the Federal Constitution," *Virginia Law Review* 2 (1915): 584, 586–7.

[86] Jouett, "Inquisitorial Feature," 585.

[87] Jouett, "Inquisitorial Feature," 588.

[88] Michael F. Gallagher, "The Federal Trade Commission," *Illinois Law Review* 10 (1915): 31–42; See also J. L. Mechem, "Fishing Expeditions by Commissions," *Michigan Law Review* 22 (June 1924): 765–76; Carman F. Randolph, "Inquisitorial Power Conferred by the Trade Commission Bill," *Yale Law Journal* 23 (1914): 672–81; Charles Willis Needham, "Federal Trade Commission," *Columbia Law Review* 16 (1916): 175–89; Wickersham, "Government by Commission" (address before Pennsylvania Bar Association, 1914). The commissions are defended in E.M.P., "Administrative Law, the Federal Trade Commission, Constitutionality of Its Investigatory Powers," *California Law Review* 8 (May 1920): 241–5; Gregory Hankin, "Validity of Federal Trade Commission Act," *Illinois Law Review* 19 (1924): 17–43; Milton Handler, "The Constitutionality of Investigations by the Federal Trade Commission: II," *Columbia Law Review* 28 (1928): 905–37.

congressional investigatory activities in response to charges that such activities made a hash of traditional separation of powers constraints.[89] Milton Handler of Columbia Law School addressed an array of constitutional objections to the sweeping investigatory powers of the FTC, among them objections that FTC probing violated privacy guarantees of the Bill of Rights. Handler believed that this defense was necessary in light of the Supreme Court's ruling in "the famous *Boyd* case," but he argued that only when an administrative agency demanded all of a business's papers, failing to put any bounds on its requests, or when it was unreasonable, did a privacy problem arise.[90] In Handler's view, privacy was not an issue when the government was gathering facts in a matter of public concern. He understood administrative agencies as impartial forces in pursuit of knowledge for the public good. An independent agency like the FTC had "no axe to grind, no incentive to misrepresent or suppress" in its "scientific investigation . . . for the benefit of the entire public rather than for a single group."[91] The Constitution, he concluded, is not "a bar to honest and scientific research. And where the needs of government demand it, it should not be in the power of individuals to block such research."[92]

David Lilienthal, a disciple of Brandeis's protégé Felix Frankfurter and later the head of the New Deal's most serious stab at social and economic planning, the Tennessee Valley Authority, saw a fussy traditionalism about the separation of powers of the sort articulated by Justice Field in his *Pacific Railway* decision as an unwelcome and antiprogressive brake on the engine of history. As a lawyer, Lilienthal recognized that traditionally testimony could only be compelled under extraordinary circumstances by a judicial tribunal. That, however, had to change with changing times – "[a] duty thus limited," he wrote, "met the needs and conformed to the traditions of a simple, predominantly rural and individualistic society."[93] In a regulatory era, "[t]o guide that regulation, to make it effective and intelligent, the regulators needed access to all the pertinent facts."[94] The practice of limiting compulsory disclosure to private disputes now had to "give way to the imperative

---

[89] James M. Landis, "Constitutional Limitations on the Congressional Power of Investigation," *Harvard Law Review* 40 (December 1926): 153–221. Thomas McCraw has called Landis's 1938 text, *The Administrative Process*, "the most thoughtful analysis of regulation by an experienced commissioner to appear since Charles Francis Adams' Railroads: Their Origins and Problems (1878)." McCraw, *Prophets of Regulation*, 153. For a broader profile of Landis, including his commitment to publicity, see McCraw, *Prophets of Regulation*, 153–209.

[90] Handler, "The Constitutionality of Investigations by the Federal Trade Commission: II," 911.

[91] Handler, "Constitutionality of Investigations," 934–6.

[92] Handler, "Constitutionality of Investigations," 935.

[93] David E. Lilienthal, "Power of Government Agencies to Compel Testimony," *Harvard Law Review* 39 (1926): 694–724, 695.

[94] Lilienthal, "Power of Government Agencies," 696.

needs of government regulation."[95] In reaching these conclusions, Lilienthal understood himself to be staking out new territory as a social engineer. "We know little of the technique of publicity as a method of social control," he mused. "[I]ts potentialities seem limitless. It may well be that the welfare of the nation, perhaps the very integrity of our economic life, will some day depend upon the power of a public tribunal to secure full, complete, and continuous access to the facts."[96]

Negotiating a Sustainable Legal Order for the New American State

By the early twentieth century, the partisans of publicity had begun to gain the upper hand in public debate as in institutional developments. It was at this time that the U.S. Supreme Court began repeatedly to distance itself from the most sweeping readings of its *Boyd* and *Counselman* precedents and to negotiate a rapprochement with the perceived imperatives of the New American State. The Court extended its permissive interpretation of the ICC's investigatory powers in three early-twentieth-century decisions, *ICC v. Baird*, *ICC v. Goodrich Transit Co.*, and *Smith v. ICC*.[97] In *Baird*, a freight-pooling case, the Court parried Fourth, Fifth, and Tenth Amendment claims raised by coal companies resisting the ICC's insistence that they produce their purchase and transportation contracts and give testimony about them, by ruling that under the Interstate Commerce Act, the contracts and testimony fell within the ambit of legitimate Commission inquiry. The *Goodrich* decision made it clear that under its organic statute the Commission could compel regulated businesses to keep their financial records in a certain form – a form, that is, designed to render them legible to the New American State.[98] And the *Smith* decision considered compulsory testimony concerning political contributions by businesses to be a legitimate area of ICC inquiry, when the agency was directed by a Senate resolution to conduct a wide-ranging investigation into anticompetitive and politically corrupt conduct by railroads.

---

[95] Lilienthal, "Power of Government Agencies," 698. Along the same lines, Herbert Croly had argued that "[t]he conscientious and competent administrator of an official social program would need and be entitled to the same kind of independence and authority in respect to public opinion as that which has traditionally been granted to a common law judge." Croly, *Progressive Democracy*, 361.

[96] Lilienthal, "Power of Investigations," 721.

[97] *Interstate Commerce Commission v. Baird*, 194 U.S. 25 (1904); *Interstate Commerce Commission v. Goodrich Transit Co.*, 224 U.S. 194 (1912); *Smith v. Interstate Commerce Commission*, 245 U.S. 33 (1917).

[98] In this regard, it is worth noting that the project of legibility in many cases involves not only securing a state's access to preexisting facts but the very construction (and then use) of what constitutes a fact. It is also worth noting here that the Court avoided as much as possible a constitutional interpretation and made recourse to statutory interpretation in negotiating an interpretive turn in constitutional doctrine. It made similar choices in later interpreting the Volstead Act and the Wagner Act's duty of fair representation.

These rulings seemed to embolden the ICC, and in two major cases, *Harriman v. ICC* and *U.S. v. Louisville and Nashville Railroad Co.*, an apparently worried Court rallied to hem in some of the Commission's less circumscribed investigations.[99] The *Harriman* case involved ICC orders to the head of the Union Pacific, E. H. Harriman, and his banker to answer questions concerning Harriman's stock ownership and purchasing arrangements involving other roads. Justice Oliver Wendell Holmes Jr., who wrote the opinion in *Harriman*, considered the case to be a major civil liberties milestone. Holmes was plainly infuriated by the claims made by the ICC, which he told Harold Laski "made my blood...boil and...made my heart sick to think that they excited no general revolt."[100]

Holmes, who did not draw the after-constructed distinction between economic and personal privacy, was outraged by the Commission's high-handed wielding of its investigatory powers. As he characterized it:

The contention of the Commission is that it may make any investigation that it deems proper, not merely to discover any facts tending to defeat the purposes of the [Interstate Commerce Act] but to aid it in recommending any additional legislation relating to the regulation of commerce that it may conceive to be within the power of Congress to enact; and that in such an investigation it has power, with the aid of the courts, to require any witness to answer any question that may have a bearing upon any part of what it has in mind.[101]

The ICC had the audacity to suggest, Holmes continued, that "whatever might influence the mind of the Commission in its recommendations is a subject upon which it may summon witnesses before it and require them to disclose any fact, no matter how private, no matter what their tendency to disgrace the person whose attendance has been compelled."[102] Holmes concluded that fidelity to basic principles of Anglo-American common law dictated that testimony be compelled only when a sacrifice of privacy was necessary, that is, where a specific transgression of the law was being alleged. The decision once again was made on statutory grounds, but Holmes suggested that had the Court not construed the statute in this way, the Commission's conduct would likely have run afoul of constitutional requirements.

---

[99] *Harriman v. Interstate Commerce Commission*, 211 U.S. 407 (1908); *United States v. Louisville and Nashville Railroad Co.*, 236 U.S. 318 (1915).

[100] Letter, Oliver Wendell Holmes Jr. to Harold Laski, 15 September 1916, in *Holmes-Laski Letters*, ed. Mark De Wolfe Howe, vol. 1, abridged by Alger Hiss (New York: Athenaeum, 1963), 19.

[101] *Harriman*, 211 U.S. at 417. In a letter to Herbert Croly, Holmes explicitly linked the principles enunciated in his *Harriman* opinion to his strenuous opposition to the U.S. Postmaster General's denial of mailing privileges to periodicals allegedly evincing a "seditious tendency." Letter, Oliver Wendell Holmes Jr. to Herbert Croly, 12 May 1919, in *Holmes-Laski Letters*, ed. Howe, 152.

[102] *Harriman*, 211 U.S. at 417.

The *Louisville and Nashville* decision of 1915 also limited what the Court saw as ICC investigatory overreaching. There, the Commission was seeking to have its agents inspect and examine a wide range of a railroad's internal accounts, records, and memoranda. The railroad balked, asserting a Fourth Amendment defense that all sorts of requested materials – memoranda between department heads and with legal counsel, proposed construction plans, intelligence on rivals, and labor relations – were private papers to which the ICC had no legitimate claim. The Court, in an opinion by Justice William Rufus Day, upheld on statutory grounds the Commission's right to review certain relevant papers. At the same time, however, it concluded that the Commission did not have the right to see either the railroad's business correspondence or the correspondence between the railroad and its counsel. By construing the statute in this way, the Court noted, it need not reach the more vexing constitutional issues raised by the more sweeping right to search claims made by the agency.

At the same time it was wrestling with its ICC cases, the Court was also fashioning a search and seizure jurisprudence in antitrust cases. Perhaps the most widely known search and seizure case of the statebuilding era after *Boyd* was *Hale v. Henkel*, a case which involved a Sherman Act prosecution of both the American Tobacco Company and the MacAndrews and Forbes Company, the major supplier of licorice (a key ingredient in tobacco products) to the ATC.[103] Hale, the Secretary and Treasurer of MacAndrews and Forbes, was subpoenaed to appear before a grand jury investigating the case. Hale, however, resisted the subpoena. Even after being guaranteed immunity from prosecution, he refused either to testify before the grand jury or to produce corporate documents called for by the subpoena on the grounds that he had a right to both assert the corporation's protection against unreasonable searches and seizures under the Fourth Amendment and against self-incrimination under the Fifth.

In its *Hale* opinion, the Court for the first time held that corporations are protected under the Constitution from unreasonable searches and seizures. It went on to conclude that in the case before it, the scope of the subpoena was too broad to be reasonable. At the same time, though, it decided that Hale could not refuse as a blanket matter to produce any books and documents properly requested by the grand jury as part of its investigation.[104]

---

[103] *Hale v. Henkel*, 201 U.S. 43 (1906).

[104] *Hale*, 201 U.S. at 76. Here we see an instance of what Stephen Holmes has argued is a systematically underappreciated dynamic in constitutional politics: the way in which rights creation is commonly deployed as a means of empowering (rather than limiting) state power. Stephen Holmes, *Passions and Constraint: On the Theory of Liberal Democracy* (Chicago: University of Chicago Press, 1995), 101–2. Here, at the same time that the Court extended unprecedented Bill of Rights protections to corporations, it empowered the federal government to gather broad information from them. See also William J. Novak, "The Legal Origins of the Modern Administrative State," in Austin Sarat, Robert Kagan, and

In reaching this conclusion, the Court explicitly cited the imperatives of a functional regulatory regime, saying that a contrary ruling "would result in the failure of a large number of cases where the illegal combination was determinable only upon the examination of such papers."[105]

In another prominent decision involving the Tobacco Trust, Justice Holmes wrote a strong opinion for the Court clipping the investigatory presumptions of the FTC, just as he had done to the ICC in the *Harriman* case. In *FTC v. American Tobacco Co.*, the FTC had claimed an unlimited right of access to the ATC's papers, citing the possibility that the company had violated key provisions of the Federal Trade Commission Act. "The mere facts of carrying on a commerce not confined within state lines and of being organized as a corporation," Holmes, again failing to draw an economic/personal privacy distinction, wrote, "do not make men's affairs public.... Anyone who respects the spirit as well as the letter of the Fourth Amendment would be loath to believe the Congress intended to authorize one of its subordinate agencies to sweep all our traditions into the fire ... and to direct fishing expeditions into private papers on the possibility that they

Bryant Garth, *Looking Back on Law's Century: Time, Memory, and Change* (Ithaca, NY: Cornell University Press, 2002), which mounts a sustained criticism of the thesis that until the New Deal "breakthrough," law served as a brake on the development of the New American State. Law, in Novak's view, played a central role, a "juris-generative" role in helping to constitute that state.

[105] *Hale*, 201 U.S. at 74. For the common law doctrine, see *Chitty on Criminal Law* (1816) and Archbold, *Criminal Pleading, Evidence and Practice*, 29th ed. 1934), cited in "Illegally Seized Evidence," *Southern California Law Review* 15 (1941): 65. Interestingly enough, at the same time that corporate ownership was being depersonalized and dispersed, American legal doctrine was redefining corporations as "persons" for purposes of constitutional law. *Santa Clara County v. Southern Pacific R.R.*, 118 U.S. 394 (1886). Morton Horwitz has argued that the "natural entity" or "corporate personality" theory of the corporation was not inherent in the *Santa Clara* decision, as is usually supposed, but instead became retrospectively attributed to it in hindsight. He roots the corporate personality theory in the 1905 *Hale v. Henkel* decision, which is a key Supreme Court legibility decision and is discussed at some length above. Morton Horwitz, "*Santa Clara* Revisited: The Development of Corporate Theory," *West Virginia Law Review* 88 (1985): 173–224. The importance Horwitz attributes to *Hale v. Henkel* further underscores the significance of the Court's legibility decisions. See also Morton Horwitz, *The Transformation of American Law, 1870–1960* (New York: Oxford University Press, 1992), 65–107. Broadly speaking, the idea that corporate entities are to be treated, for certain purposes, like "natural persons" dates back to English common law. Blackstone, *Commentaries*, Book 1, ch. 18, 467. For discussions of similar Fourth and Fifth Amendment issues arising out of antitrust investigations, see "Fourth and Fifth Amendments and Visitorial Power of Congress over State Corporations," *Columbia Law Review* 30 (January 1930): 103–8; Henry W. Taft, "The Tobacco Trust Decisions," *Columbia Law Review* 6 (1906): 375–87; "Powers of Federal Trade Commission to Demand Documentary Evidence," *Harvard Law Review* 36 (January 1923): 340–1; *Federal Trade Commission v. American Tobacco Co.*, 264 U.S. 298 (1924); *Wilson v. United States*, 221 U.S. 361 (1911). For a lower court application of the *Hale* holding to a Fifth Amendment privilege assertion against a Bureau of Corporations demand for information, see *United States v. Armour and Co.*, 142 F. 808 (N.D. Illinois, 1906).

may disclose evidence of crime."[106] "The interruption of business, the possible revelation of trade secrets, and the expense that compliance with the Commission's wholesale demand would cause are the least considerations. It is contrary to the first principles of justice to allow a search through all the respondents' records, relevant or irrelevant, in the hope that something will turn up."[107]

Federal "Street Crime" Criminal Process Rights and the Reintegration of the Southern Periphery into the National Core

Under the state of courts and parties, criminal process rights applied to street criminals – as opposed to socially constructed, business-class "quasi-criminals" – were for the most part not considered matters of concern or interest to the central state. They were quintessential matters of state law, and often of state, judge-derived common law.[108] There were, however, two

---

[106] *Federal Trade Commission v. American Tobacco Co.*, 264 U.S. 298 (1924), 305–6.

[107] *American Tobacco*, 264 U.S. at 306. In a letter to Harold Laski, Holmes pithily described the case as involving a "right claimed by the Trade Commission to go through all the books, correspondence, and papers of a corporation engaged in interstate commerce to see if they couldn't find out something to its disadvantage." Letter, Oliver Wendell Holmes Jr., to Harold Laski, 16 March 1924, in *Holmes-Laski Letters*, ed. Howe, 418. For another vigorous Holmes opinion concerning the Fourth Amendment, this involving the recklessly improper seizure of corporate books and documents, see *Silverthorne Lumber Co. v. United States*, 251 U.S. 385 (1920).

[108] In his categorization of cases coming before the Court in 1875, 1925, and every five years thereafter, David O'Brien observes that between the 1870s and the mid-1940s, the Court decided only about two or three cases each year involving the constitutional rights of the accused. Richard Pacelle notes that only during the peak years of the Warren Court does O'Brien discern a spike in the number of criminal procedure cases. David M. O'Brien, *Storm Center: The Supreme Court in American Politics*, 3rd ed. (New York: W. W. Norton, 1993), 261. See also Richard L. Pacelle Jr., *The Transformation of the Supreme Court's Agenda from the New Deal to the Reagan Administration* (Boulder, CO: Westview Press, 1991), 143–9; Charles Epp, *The Rights Revolution: Lawyers, Activists, and Supreme Courts in Comparative Perspective* (Chicago: University of Chicago Press, 1998), 27; Howard Gillman, "Political Development and the Rise of the 'Preferred Freedoms' Rubric in Constitutional Law," paper presented at the University of Maryland Discussion Group on Constitutionalism, College Park, MD (April 2002). See *Barron v. Baltimore*, 32 U.S. 243 (1833). A court docket that regularly applied the limitations of the Bill of Rights as restrictions on the states did not surface until the middle of the twentieth century. In 1884, the Court seemed to underscore the distance it intended to keep from the law of criminal process in its decision in *Hurtado v. California*, 110 U.S. 516 (1884). With the hangman's noose focusing his mind squarely on the ascendant doctrine of substantive due process, Joseph Hurtado appealed his conviction for murder in California on the grounds that his prosecution, which followed an information filed by the district attorney rather than an indictment by a grand jury, violated his Fifth Amendment rights. These rights, Hurtado argued, had been incorporated as a proscription against the states by the due process clause of the Fourteenth Amendment. In an opinion in which only Justice Harlan dissented, the Court rejected Hurtado's claim. Just a few years later, in 1892, the Court, on procedural grounds, refused to pass on the possible violation of the

exceptions to this rule. The first, less significant for our purposes, was a catch-all category of issues arising out of common street crime – theft, assault, homicide – occurring in federal jurisdictions like the military, the territories, and the District of Columbia.[109] The second, however, was of major developmental significance: It involved the central state's project of governing, administering, and (to a degree much attenuated, but still worth following after the end of Reconstruction) supervising the defeated South. While the project of legibility eventually succeeded more or less completely, and its achievements, both practical and ideological, were incorporated into the sinews of the modern administrative state, the project involving the reintegration of the South into the nation succeeded only partially; and as far as black Americans were concerned, it failed completely. The initial failure of the nationbuilding ambitions of the latter project left it as a goal to be achieved over the course of the twentieth century. This pattern set the context conducive to the construction of the Whiggish legal liberal narratives of constitutional development concerning criminal process that predominated in the late twentieth century. That narrative, of course, was premised on the erasure from the constitutive story of constitutional development in this area of the earlier battles between privacy and publicity.

Beginning with the Civil War, the Republican Congress passed a series of statutes that radically extended the power of the federal judiciary to try criminal cases in order to advance Northern control over renegade Southern institutions and, in particular, to protect both occupying Northern officials, their families, and allied freed slaves from Southern oppression. The

---

Eighth Amendment rights of a man sentenced to fifty-four years of hard labor for violating state liquor laws. *O'Neil v. Vermont*, 144 U.S. 323 (1892). In dicta, the Court reiterated that the Eighth Amendment was not a constitutional limit on the conduct of the states. *O'Neil*, 332. The Court similarly sidestepped efforts by litigants to nationalize the rights of criminal defendants in *Maxwell v. Dow* (1900) and *Twining v. New Jersey* (1908). *Maxwell v. Dow*, 176 U.S. 581 (rejecting an appeal on Fifth and Fourteenth Amendment grounds of a man convicted of robbery after an information rather than a grand jury indictment, and a trial before a jury of eight rather than twelve); *Twining v. New Jersey*, 211 U.S. 78, 114 (holding that the "exemption from compulsory self-incrimination in the courts of the States is not secured by any part of the Federal Constitution," in a case involving a criminal conviction for the intentional deception of a bank examiner).

[109] These decisions provide a useful point of reference for assessing the views of federal judges on substantive criminal process issues, as compared with the views of their state court counterparts in the same era. In the late nineteenth and early twentieth centuries, the Supreme Court did articulate federal standards for trial by jury, double jeopardy, and cruel and unusual punishment (to name a few areas), but its decisions on these matters were not innovative. See *Thompson v. Utah*, 170 U.S. 343 (1895) (trial by jury); *United States v. Zucker*, 161 U.S. 481 (1896) (trial by jury); *Callan v. Wilson*, 127 U.S. 549 (1888) (trial by jury); *Crossley v. California*, 168 U.S. 640 (1898) (double jeopardy); *Gilbert v. Minnesota*, 254 U.S. 325 (1920) (double jeopardy); *Wilkerson v. Utah*, 99 U.S. 134 (1879) (cruel and unusual punishment); *Badders v. United States*, 240 U.S. 391 (1916) (cruel and unusual punishment).

Reconstruction-era expansion of the jurisdiction of the federal courts was, in its time, the most extensive expansion of the jurisdiction of those courts since 1789.[110]

The most significant of the new jurisdictional laws were those granting sweeping habeas corpus powers to the federal courts and those giving litigants the power to remove cases from state to federal courts. The Habeas Corpus Act of 1863 authorized the removal of civil and criminal cases involving official acts performed under the direction of a national official. And the 1867 Habeas Act granted those held in state detention the right to a federal habeas hearing. In addition, other substantive legislation, like the Civil Rights Act of 1866, the Internal Revenue Act of 1866, and the Voting Rights Enforcement Act of 1871, provided for removal of cases involving particular policy areas. The Jurisdiction and Removal Act of 1875, a landmark statute still in effect, established federal question jurisdiction in the federal courts, permitting removal in all suits arising under the Constitution, laws, and treaties of the United States. Taken together, these new statutes both gave Southern blacks recourse to federal courts to challenge their criminal prosecution by Southern law enforcement officials and simultaneously empowered federal judges to preside over the trials of whites charged with criminal violations of Reconstruction legislation.[111]

These Reconstruction-era extensions of central state judicial powers were part of the larger Northern effort to conquer, control, and reconstruct the American South in the 1860s and 1870s, which included the ratification of the Civil War Amendments, the passage of a series of civil rights acts, and occupation by a conquering army, along with cadres of administrative officials. During this period, Southern blacks were incorporated (though briefly) within the American nation. They voted and were elected to office (including the U.S. Congress), participated freely as jurors and witnesses in court proceedings, attended public schools, and sat side by side with whites in streetcars and places of public amusement and accommodations. This

---

[110] For a developmental model of courts as instruments of the consolidation of central state power that is applicable here, see Martin Shapiro, *Courts: A Comparative and Political Analysis* (Chicago: University of Chicago Press, 1981), 17–28.

[111] Stanley Kutler, *Judicial Power and Reconstruction Politics* (Chicago: University of Chicago Press, 1968), ch. 8; William M. Wiecek, "The Reconstruction of Federal Judicial Power, 1863–1876," in *American Law and the Constitutional Order*, eds. Lawrence M. Friedman and Harry N. Scheiber (Cambridge, MA: Harvard University Press, 1988), 237. On war in general, and the Civil War in particular, as an occasion for the expansion of central state power, see *Shaped by War and Trade: International Influences on American Political Development*, eds. Charles Tilly, Ira Katznelson, and Martin Shefter (Princeton: Princeton University Press, 2002); Bartholomew H. Sparrow, *From the Outside In: World War II and the American State* (Princeton: Princeton University Press, 1996); Richard Bensel, *Yankee Leviathan* (Cambridge: Cambridge University Press, 1990).

relative equality persisted, though in forms that slowly began to attenuate, even after the end of Reconstruction in 1877.[112]

By the late 1880s, however, the status of Southern blacks took a decided turn for the worse, and the new and deviant "Jim Crow" political order, with its denial of voting and civil justice rights; segregated and unequal public amusements, accommodations, and schools; and debt peonage systems, was instituted in the southern United States. The combination of a persisting racism, the economic downturn of the times, and the decline in political power of the wealthy, paternalistic white elite in favor of populist farmers and the white working class (who, to a significant extent, measured their social status by the degree to which they stood above the neighboring blacks) all contributed to the emergence of the Jim Crow South. Unfortunately for Southern blacks, at about the same time, Northern solicitude for the fate of Southern blacks was also rapidly fading. There, massive immigration from southern and eastern Europe, as well as influxes of blacks into northern cities (where previously they had been uncommon) led white, Anglo-Saxon Northerners to harbor new sympathies for the racial policies of the South they had previously condemned. Indeed, the simultaneous rise of racism in the North – fed by the developing sense of the "white man's burden," the sense of an immigrant invasion diluting the white racial stock, and the trying presence of impoverished blacks – and the consolidation of the Jim Crow South in many ways knit together a new (white) nation that had for so long been torn asunder. Nationbuilding pageants signaling the sectional reconciliation of the white North and the white South, such as joint Union–Confederate veteran reunions, were held for the first time. Critical views of Reconstruction, so evident in the new Dunning School historiography and in films like D. W. Griffith's *Birth of a Nation* (1915), took hold of the intellectual and popular imaginations. Thus, national identity in the late nineteenth and early twentieth centuries – the transition from "Union" to "Nation" – was forged and consolidated in significant part by the withdrawal of that power from the American South. A racialized narrative of national identity (which excluded blacks, and, to a lesser extent, others) substituted for the exercise of direct, coercive power of the central state in drawing the conquered South back into the national fold.[113]

---

[112] Michael J. Klarman, *From Jim Crow to Civil Rights: The Supreme Court and the Struggle for Racial Equality* (New York: Oxford University Press, 2004), 10.

[113] Klarman, *From Jim Crow to Civil Rights*, 10–15; David Blight, *Race and Reunion: The Civil War in American Memory* (Cambridge, MA: The Belknap Press of the Harvard University Press, 2001), 354–61; Rogers M. Smith, *Civic Ideals*, 371–85; Rogan Kersh, *Dreams of a More Perfect Union* (Ithaca, NY: Cornell University Press, 2001), 242–76; Gary Gerstle, *American Crucible: Race and Nation in the Twentieth Century* (Princeton: Princeton University Press, 2001); Eric Foner, *Reconstruction: America's Unfinished Revolution, 1863–1877* (New York: Perennial Library, 1988), 581.

In this context, rather than serving as a highly coercive instrument of state power, the constitutional criminal process decisions that emerged from the South in the late nineteenth and early twentieth centuries served primarily to set outer constitutional limits on Southern oppression, in the process negotiating the terms of retreat in the exercise of coercive authority in service of a sustainable reconciliation of the white nation. These criminal process decisions did little, if anything, to mitigate the actual oppression of Southern blacks. What they did do, however, in evincing a commitment to what Michael Klarman has called "minimalist-constitutionalism," is perform the signal ideological function of reaffirming the legitimacy of the Constitution itself, and of the Court as an authoritative interpreter of it, in the aftermath of *Dred Scott* and the Civil War. In doing so, the Court in these cases, even if "ineffective" when judged by traditional tests of judicial power, played an important role in the post–Civil War nationbuilding process.[114]

The new federal laws governing habeas and removal jurisdiction were particularly important in preparing the way for the reconsolidation of national constitutional authority. It was these jurisdictional statutes, for instance, that made possible a series of 1880 Supreme Court rulings that held explicit race-based exclusions of blacks from juries to be unconstitutional. In *Strauder v. West Virginia* (1880), the Court sided with a black defendant who challenged his criminal conviction by an all-white jury selected under a state statute expressly limiting jury service to "all white male persons," agreeing that the conviction ran afoul of the Fourteenth Amendment's equal protection guarantee. The Court issued a similar ruling the same year in *Neal v. Delaware* (1880), where the jury was selected from voter rolls and the state's suffrage was legally restricted to white males. And in *Ex Parte Virginia* (1880), the High Court upheld the criminal indictment of a state judge who systematically excluded blacks from the state's jury rolls.[115]

In these decisions, which predated the consolidation of the Jim Crow regime in the later 1880s, the Court announced the outer constitutional limits beyond which the South could not go in explicitly limiting black civil and political rights. Federal courts also supervised the central state's use of constitutional criminal process jurisdiction to police Southern regulation of voting rights.[116] At about the same time, though, the Court clearly signaled

---

[114] Klarman, *From Jim Crow to Civil Rights*, 78, 99, 117–35.

[115] *Strauder v. West Virginia*, 100 U.S. 303 (1880); *Neal v. Delaware*, 103 U.S. 370 (1880); *Ex Parte Virginia*, 100 U.S. 339 (1880). See Klarman, *From Jim Crow to Civil Rights*, 39–43.

[116] Many of these cases involved criminal prosecutions of Southern whites for interfering with blacks' right to vote. In *Ex Parte Yarbrough*, the Court read Congress's power to regulate the election of its members under Article I, Section 4, and the right of blacks to vote under the Fifteenth Amendment broadly to uphold the federal criminal conviction of Klansmen charged with beating a black man to prevent him from voting. *Ex Parte Yarbrough*, 100 U.S. 651 (1884). In other important cases, however, including those involving the 1870 Force Act and the 1871 Ku Klux Klan Act, the Court retreated, limiting the scope of federal

the lines beyond which it would not go. In *Virginia v. Rives* (1880), *Williams v. Mississippi* (1898), and *Martin v. Texas* (1906), the Court announced that it would not consider the simple absence of blacks from juries an equal protection violation. Nor would it concern itself with the effect on jury composition of poll taxes and literacy tests. Only direct, state-sanctioned racial exclusion, the Court held, was constitutionally forbidden.[117]

In a number of procedural decisions, the Court also signaled that, despite its ostensible power to do more, it did not wish to aggressively supervise the conduct of state criminal trials. In 1886, the Court introduced the Exhaustion Doctrine that committed it to hearing habeas petitions only after all possible avenues of state court relief had been pursued.[118] In 1891, it held that lower federal courts should revisit federal constitutional questions raised in habeas petitions only when the state court that decided them lacked jurisdiction over either the person or the cause.[119]

The perils of the Court's hands-off supervision of irregularities in state criminal trials were occasionally spotlighted in notorious cases that seized widespread public attention. Perhaps the first was the Leo Frank case (1915), a case that did not involve blacks. There, Frank, the Jewish owner of an Atlanta pencil factory, was convicted and sentenced to death in an atmosphere of mob violence and intimidation for murdering one of his employees, a thirteen-year-old girl. In that case, the Supreme Court held that mob

government's powers to criminally prosecute those impeding the access of blacks to the ballot in the Southern states. *United States v. Cruikshank*, 92 U.S. 542 (1876) (invalidating Force Act prosecution of several hundred armed whites who surrounded and burned a Louisiana courthouse in which blacks were holding a public meeting concerning a disputed election, leading to about one hundred deaths, on the grounds that there was not evidence of racial discrimination involving the right to vote and that the Fourteenth Amendment applied only to state action); *United States v. Reese*, 92 U.S. 214 (1876) (invalidating Force Act indictment of a Kentucky electoral official for failure to register a black man to vote in a municipal election on a narrow construction of the Fifteenth Amendment); *James v. Bowman*, 190 U.S. 127 (1903) (invalidating federal authority under the Fifteenth Amendment to criminally prosecute a private citizen who used bribery to interfere with voting by blacks in a congressional election). See also *Civil Rights Cases*, 109 U.S. 3 (1883). In line with its staunch commitments to minimal constitutional standards (that is, aimed at upholding the legitimacy of the Civil War Amendments), though, the Court did uphold federal prosecutions under the Peonage Abolition Act of 1867. A wave of these prosecutions came before the Court in the early years of the twentieth century and, as it had with the *de jure* corruption of jury trials, the Court drew the line at what came perilously close to the literal reintroduction of slavery. *Bailey v. Alabama*, 219 U.S. 219 (1911); *United States v. Reynolds*, 235 U.S. 533 (1914). See also *Clyatt v. United States*, 197 U.S. 207 (1905).

[117] *Virginia v. Rives*, 100 U.S. 313 (1880); *Williams v. Mississippi*, 170 U.S. 213 (1898); *Martin v. Texas*, 200 U.S. 316 (1906). Klarman notes that "[b]etween 1904 and 1935, the Court did not reverse the conviction of even one black defendant on the ground of race discrimination in jury selection, even though blacks were universally excluded from Southern juries." Klarman, *From Jim Crow to Civil Rights*, 43.

[118] *Ex Parte Royall*, 117 U.S. 241 (1886).

[119] *In re Wood*, 140 U.S. 278 (1891).

intimidation of the jury did not deny Frank the due process of law, and that any improprieties in his trial had been vitiated by the appeals process in the state courts of Georgia. Shortly after Georgia's governor commuted his sentence to life in prison, Frank was lynched by a mob.[120]

In sum, the Supreme Court's late-nineteenth- and early-twentieth-century criminal law jurisprudence concerned with race and Reconstruction is significant as an integral part of the negotiation of a new *modus vivendi*, a negotiation in which judicial assertiveness and quiescence – as with the Court's legibility decisions of roughly the same period – were both important parts of the process. In the wake of the Civil War, Congress had radically expanded both the scope and reach of federal criminal law as well as the power of the federal courts to try cases under that law and to apply national constitutional standards to state criminal law prosecutions. The Court's willingness to use this newfound authority, however, hewed roughly to the prevailing political will, but was distinctively important as a legitimating process nonetheless. By the mid-1870s, the political will behind the radical Republican cause was waning, as was the nation's attentiveness to the problem of Southern blacks. Steeped as it was in an Anglo-American tradition of liberty under law, a free labor ideology, and a basic commitment to the constitutional legitimacy of the Civil War Amendments (and to the Constitution more generally), the Court, uniquely charged with sustaining the authority of the Constitution, stood firm against the most explicitly defiant assaults on basic constitutional guarantees, particularly those on trial by jury and debt peonage. Beyond this, however, the courts would not – indeed, could not – go. Rather than focus on the Court's failure in this era to lead by launching the Warren era rights revolution a half century early – a failure highlighted in Whiggish narratives of civil rights progress (and true enough, though it hardly could have been otherwise) – what should be emphasized in empirical accounts of constitutional development is the important role the Supreme Court played in helping to negotiate a reconciliation of the white North and the white South and to lend legitimacy to that reconcilation through a skillful commitment to constitutional minimalism concerning criminal process and race.[121]

The Next Reformist Campaign: Prohibition

The period running from Reconstruction through the New Deal witnessed three major campaigns involving fundamental rights and liberties that touched upon matters of criminal law and criminal process and were

---

[120] *Frank v. Mangum*, 237 U.S. 309 (1915). On the Frank Case, see Steve Oney, *And the Dead Shall Rise: The Murder of Mary Phagan and the Lynching of Lee Frank* (New York: Pantheon Books, 2003). Only in later years did the Court take tentative steps to supervise more aggressively state behavior on this front. *Moore v. Dempsey*, 261 U.S. 86 (1923); *Powell v. Alabama*, 287 U.S. 45 (1932).

[121] For an extended argument against the familiar claim that the Court could have taken a different path, see Klarman, *From Jim Crow to Civil Rights*.

mediated by the constitutional involvement of the U.S. Supreme Court: the rights-restricting, state-fortifying project of legibility; the Reconstruction-era civil rights initiatives; and – our next topic – the statebuilding and nation-building initiatives concerning Prohibition. As we have seen, the reformist campaign for legibility was a campaign that was avowedly both antirights and antiprivacy. Its express aim was to force the delimitation of prevailing understandings of key provisions of the Bill of Rights in the interest of building a powerful, seeing central state that could effectively straddle and administer the emergent corporate capitalist political-economic order. This progressive-spirited, antirights initiative was largely successful. The reformist antialcohol initiatives discussed below were also self-consciously progressive, and – as described by their own partisans – were just as expressly antirights and antiprivacy. Here, however, the reformist project met with more public and political resistance and must be considered in some respects a developmental failure, with conservative, prorights opposition to its broader ambitions ultimately prevailing over its progressive, anti–civil liberties agenda.

As we have seen, in the late nineteenth and early twentieth centuries, the meaning of the Fourth and Fifth Amendments' search and seizure and self-incrimination clauses were explored most prominently by the Supreme Court in cases involving central state efforts to secure the production of business records in the service of effective national economic regulation. As the regulatory scope of the national government expanded, as federal police powers expanded, and, in a related development, as the revenue needs of the New American State became increasingly voracious, the Fourth and Fifth Amendments came to be invoked in federal courts in new contexts, in cases involving gambling, alcohol, and drugs that today would be more readily recognized as "criminal." Despite the fact that the Court had long since come to terms with the project of legibility, its rulings in these cases continued to draw upon the highly rights-protective spirit of Justice Bradley's opinion in *Boyd*.

The modern exclusionary rule, for instance, which is often associated in the popular imagination with the criminal process rights revolution of the Warren era, was actually created by the Court in *Weeks v. United States* (1914), a case involving the use of the mail to transport lottery tickets. In *Weeks*, the police, who had no search warrant, found a key to the defendant's house, entered it while he was at work, and rifled through his room and drawers for evidence of a crime, which they promptly found by discovering the lottery tickets. The Court, in this *Lochner*-era decision, however, boldly refused to admit the evidence obtained by this illegal search.[122]

---

[122] *Weeks v. United States*, 232 U.S. 383 (1914). In 1903, in a closely divided vote, the Court had upheld the authority of the national government to regulate the sale of lottery tickets and, implicitly, to exercise extensive national powers of police. *Champion v. Ames*, 188 U.S. 321 (1903).

Far from being champions of these rulings, progressively minded people in the statebuilding era were ambivalent – if not hostile – to them. It was progressives, after all, who were among the leading proponents of passing these morals laws at the national level and were committed to seeing them effectively enforced. In no area was the antirights zeal of the party of progress more apparent than in the campaign for Prohibition. Indeed, contemporary Fourth Amendment doctrine in particular was essentially invented – first in outraged resistance, then in negotiated accommodation, and, finally, in renewed resistance to this prominent progressive imperative – in a flood of Prohibition-era appellate and Supreme Court decisions (1920–33). At the outset, according to the legal historian who has studied the issue most extensively, "the [Supreme] Court abandoned the rule of liberal construction of the protections afforded by the Fourth Amendment ... [and] ... interpreted the amendment to permit a variety of intrusive enforcement actions by Prohibition authorities."[123] Gradually, though, as the public's hostility to Prohibition intensified, the Court – led not by Justices Holmes and Brandeis, but rather by Justices Butler and McReynolds – extended the broader Fourth Amendment protections associated with resistance to the project of legibility to Prohibition criminal process cases. This important strand of constitutional criminal process rights, in short, was crafted in resistance to progressive reformist imperatives and not in their service.

The New Court Initiative on Street Crime: Protecting Privacy in the Face of the Antialcohol Crusade

In accounts of American political development, Prohibition should properly be considered a part of the statebuilding era's broader project of central state construction. During Prohibition, the central state seized an unprecedented degree of direct regulatory power – so much, in fact, that even its proponents considered a constitutional amendment essential to authorizing it. Prohibition, moreover, like the assertion of regulatory power over other aspects of economic life at the time, was understood as a progressive measure and a full part of the progressive political program. Like other progressive initiatives, it was supported by cutting-edge studies of the new social sciences, which sought to reduce social harms in the interest of rational and disciplined public policy. The obstacles to progress in this area, as in other areas such as machine politics and education, were immigrants, Catholics, and other traditional ethnic communities, all of whom, in contrast to the forward-looking reformers who were in tune with the imperatives of modernity, remained stubbornly attached to their old, costly, corrupt, unhealthy, and inefficient ways.

---

[123] Between 1920 and 1933, the Court issued twenty Fourth Amendment opinions. Murchison, *Federal Criminal Law Doctrines*, 48, 68, 71, 75, 83–4. See also *Harris v. United States*, 331 U.S. 145 (1946) (J. Frankfurter, dissenting).

Prohibition was a part of both the statebuilding and the "disciplinary" nationbuilding project involving the reconstruction of the citizen of the New Constitutional Nation on the model of sober, white, native-born, Protestants. Here, as was common with many of the modernizing initiatives advanced at this time, American progressives looked to European practice as a developmental model. The Europeans – who these progressives lamented were out ahead of them in the task of constructing a forward-looking modern state, after all – had in recent years taken noted steps toward the tighter regulation of (and, in some cases, bans on) alcohol.[124] National Prohibition was also a constituent part of the heavily statist, antirights, disciplinary project associated with the war. Prohibition drew from the impetus of the war the renewed imperative to produce sober farm, factory, and battle-ready Protestant citizens. Indeed, the campaign against alcohol addressed itself expressly to the practical imperatives of a wartime state. Although temperance advocacy had a long history in the United States, at this time the argument that drink rendered soldiers unfit to fight and prevail against Germany gave Prohibition proponents a major boost.

The road to the ratification of the Eighteenth Amendment, which took effect on January 16, 1920, began well before the war and the Roaring Twenties. The wave of antialcohol agitation that culminated in the Eighteenth Amendment began in earnest in 1907.[125] After successfully fending off objections that it represented an unconstitutional federal effort to regulate intrastate commerce, in 1913, overriding the veto of President Taft, Congress passed the Webb-Kenyon Bill banning any interstate traffic in liquor that would run afoul of the laws of the state into which it was being imported.[126] The outbreak of war in Europe added a transnational competition over productive efficiency to the domestic debate over Prohibition. Britain, France, and Russia had all launched campaigns against traffic in alcohol as part of their efforts to shore up their military strength. Well aware of

---

[124] Gary Gerstle properly places Prohibition alongside the debilities placed upon Japanese immigrants in the western states and the passage of the Espionage and Sedition Acts in 1917 and 1918. Gerstle, *American Crucible*, 91, 114, 135; Pegram, *Battling Demon Rum*, 89–90, 136–7. During its resurgence in the 1920s, the Ku Klux Klan became one of the chief supporters of the rigorous enforcement of Prohibition laws. Pegram, *Battling Demon Rum*, 170–3. See also McDonagh, "Welfare Rights State and 'Civil Rights State' "; Mark Mazower, *Dark Continent: Europe's Twentieth Century* (New York: Vintage Books, 1998), 76–103.

[125] Pegram, *Battling Demon Rum*, 85.

[126] Timberlake, *Prohibition and the Progressive Movement*, 162; Pegram, *Battling Demon Rum*, 134–5. The law's constitutionality was ultimately upheld by the Supreme Court in *Clark Distilling Co. v. Western Maryland Railway Co.*, 242 U.S. 311 (1917). The power of Prohibition politics is evident in this ruling, which runs against the grain of the Court's strong, late-nineteenth- and early-twentieth-century jurisprudence under the commerce clause limiting state and national regulation in the interest of constructing a national market. See Bensel, *Political Economy of American Industrialization*, 321–33.

these efforts, American Prohibitionists began to argue that the unwillingness of Americans to ban liquor traffic put the nation at a perilous disadvantage in readying the state for war (a dynamic that gained momentum with the beginning of the American war preparedness program in 1915). It was in this context that the Anti-Saloon League (founded by Howard H. Russell, a graduate of liberal, reformist Oberlin College), the leader of the Prohibitionist forces, began to achieve victory after victory at the state level. Twenty-six states – containing over half of the American people – were dry by 1917.[127] War, of course, was hardly the only motivation behind this trend. But it did play a major role in efforts to move Prohibition from the state to the national level. The discourse linking the cause of Prohibition to war preparedness was prominent. In his widely read book *Why Prohibition!* (1918), social gospel minister Charles Stelzle opens with the declaration that

America needs patriots – not only those who will go to the battle line in France, but also men and women, too, who will strengthen the hands of the boys who have gone to the Front. Our greatest peril is that of waste – and the greatest waster in our country is the liquor traffic. To strengthen America by precept and practice is a distinct obligation resting upon every citizen of this Republic.[128]

In the book's body, Stelzle continued, "There never was a time when America so needed her sober senses as to-day – it is a time when selfishness must be subordinated to the great task of winning the war." Referencing the European antialcohol initiatives of Lloyd George and Marshal Joffre, Stelzle added: "[T]here's one fact that stands out clear and sharp as we take a world-wide view of the war – namely, that we've got to reckon not only with 'Kaiser Bill Hohenzollern' but with 'Kaiser John Barleycorn.'" The manufacture of liquor wasted vital foodstuffs (chiefly grains) in the midst of a national wartime food conservation campaign. It wasted vital labor "at a time when every man is needed in some useful occupation to help win the war." And it significantly shortened the lives of bartenders, brewery workers, and waiters – "too great a price for the nation to pay."[129]

---

[127] Timberlake, *Prohibition and the Progressive Movement*, 165–6; Pegram, *Battling Demon Rum*, 113, 136, 144–7.

[128] Charles Stelzle, *Why Prohibition!* (New York: George H. Doran, 1918), vii.

[129] Stelzle, *Why Prohibition!*, 22–42; Timberlake, *Prohibition and the Progressive Movement*, 164, 178; James A. Morone, *Hellfire Nation: The Politics of Sin in American History* (New Haven: Yale University Press, 2003), 312–14, 321–2. The war also dealt a major blow to the influence of the National German-American Alliance, which had been a forceful voice for the nation's brewers and beer drinkers and a powerful prohibition opponent. Pegram, *Battling Demon Rum*, 144–5. On the significance of international influences, and war in particular, on the dynamics of state construction and American political development, see Ira Katznelson, "Rewriting the Epic of America," in *Shaped by War and Trade*, eds. Katznelson and Shefter, 3–23. See also Tilly, *Coercion, Capital, and European States, AD 990–1990* (Oxford: Basil Blackwell, 1990); Skowronek, *Building a New American State*; Bensel, *Yankee Leviathan*; Theda Skocpol, *Protecting Soldiers and Mothers: The Political Origins of*

National Prohibition actually predated the effective date of the Eighteenth Amendment and the passage of the Volstead Act. The 1918 War Prohibition Act, an emergency wartime measure, banned the manufacture of beer and wine after May 1, 1919 (adding to a preexisting ban on whiskey), and, after June 30, 1919, the sale of all intoxicating drinks. These bans remained in force even after the armistice ending the war (November 11, 1918) and carried the nation right up through the effective date of the Eighteenth Amendment.[130]

The claim that Prohibition was a wartime imperative dovetailed with other strands of the early-twentieth-century progressive political vision. The movement was fueled by a pronounced moral fervor and was sometimes expressly religious in inspiration (as, for example, with the Women's Christian Temperance Union and with social gospel ministers like Stelzle and Robert Raushenbush). But it was also fueled by a strong set of secular imperatives, including a faith in science, reason, and worldly progress. Drink addled the mind, laid waste to people's health, and caused all manner of social problems. Prominent progressive social Darwinists like E. A. Ross – also a key proponent of the project of legibility – argued for Prohibition on elaborate (and, to the contemporary ear, strange) natural selection grounds. To advance the social organism, its head – the state – needed to take an enlightened stand against the consumption of alcohol. Although not adopting Ross's reasons, many of the popular magazines for intelligent, well-educated, forward-looking middle-class people – *Harper's*, *The Atlantic Monthly*, *Collier's*, *McClure's*, *The Outlook* – gave proposals for alcohol bans full and, typically, sympathetic treatment throughout the early twentieth century.[131]

In one sense, the early-twentieth-century campaign to ban the manufacture and consumption of alcoholic beverages was a campaign waged on behalf of human liberty – on behalf, that is, of the liberation of individual reason from the fetters of drink.[132] But for many progressives, in this

Social Policy in the United States (Cambridge, MA: The Belknap Press of the Harvard University Press, 1992); Gerstle, *American Crucible*.

[130] Timberlake, *Prohibition and the Progressive Movement*, 178, 180. Timberlake concludes: "In speeding the amendment through Congress and the state legislatures, the war undoubtedly played an important part. Although ratification was practically assured by the elections of 1916, the magnitude and speed of the victory owed much to the idealism and spirit of sacrifice called forth by the war. More important than the size and speed of the victory, however, was the kind of amendment the war made possible, for what the people got was not temperance but almost total abstinence." Timberlake, *Prohibition and the Progressive Movement*, 178.

[131] Timberlake, *Prohibition and the Progressive Movement*, 2, 24, 53, 60, 156; Pegram, *Battling Demon Rum*, 114–15. For similar progressive visions seizing European governing elites at the same time, see Mazower, *Dark Continent*, 76–103.

[132] In this sense, the campaign for temperance can be seen as of a piece ideologically with the free labor case against actual chattel slavery. Lincoln himself once famously articulated

as in so many other areas, appeals to individual liberty made in resistance to the moment's progressive imperative were rapidly and frankly (and often haughtily) dismissed as reactionary obstacles to the achievement of a golden and newly glimpsed social future. In 1914, for instance, *The Gospel of the Kingdom*, the monthly magazine of the American Institute of Social Service (edited by Josiah Strong and W. D. P. Bliss), attributed the nation's swelling Prohibitionist sentiment to a cresting commitment to democracy and its newly recognized handmaiden: state power. The editors declared:

Personal liberty is at last an uncrowned, dethroned king with no one to do him reverence. The social consciousness is so far developed, and is becoming so autocratic, that institutions and government must give heed to its mandate and shape their life accordingly. We are no longer frightened by that ancient bogy – 'paternalism in government.' We affirm boldly, it is the business of government to be just that – paternal.... *Nothing human can be foreign to a true government.*[133]

Indeed, when the Eighteenth Amendment finally took effect, some even went so far as to advise the Supreme Court to interpret that amendment as having implicitly repealed the Fourth Amendment in liquor cases.[134] As the central state radically expanded its powers with the coming of Prohibition, those resisting the highly invasive procedures used to enforce it turned to the Fourth Amendment, as had the businessmen resisting the project of legibility

this understanding, declaring in his address to the Washingtonian Temperance Society in Springfield, Illinois (22 February 1842) that in the "temperance revolution...we shall find a stronger bondage broken, a viler slavery manumitted, a greater tyrant deposed....And what a noble ally this [is] to the cause of political freedom....And when the victory shall be complete – when there shall be neither a slave nor a drunkard on the earth – how proud the title of that land which may truly claim to be the birthplace and the cradle of both those revolutions that shall have ended in the victory. How nobly distinguished that people who shall have planted and nurtured to maturity both the political and moral freedom of their species," in Abraham Lincoln, *Selected Speeches and Writings* (New York: Library of America, 1992), 34–43. The Washingtonians, of course, took their name from the hero of American independence. Pegram, *Battling Demon Rum*, 27, 36, 55. See, generally, Eric Foner, *Free Soil, Free Labor, Free Men: The Ideology of the Republican Party before the Civil War* (New York: Oxford University Press, 1970).

[133] *The Gospel of the Kingdom* 6 (July 1914): 97–8, cited in Timberlake, *Prohibition and the Progressive Movement*, 27. See also Stelzle, *Why Prohibition!*, 84 ("In law and in civilization the first consideration is not the individual, but society. Therefore, whatever injures society is not permitted. The greater our civilization, the more restricted become our liberties. You may enjoy civil liberty only as you are willing to sacrifice personal liberty."). It is worth noting that in a move that adumbrates the trajectory of contemporary progressive crusades, after playing a major role in securing the ratification of the Eighteenth Amendment, the Anti-Saloon League immediately went on to create the World League Against Alcoholism, with the aim of securing a worldwide ban on the consumption of alcoholic beverages. Timberlake, *Prohibition and the Progressive Movement*, 180; Pegram, *Battling Demon Rum*, 136–7; Murchison, *Federal Criminal Law Doctrines*, 188 (on narrow readings of Bill of Rights by Prohibition proponents).

[134] Johnson, "Some Constitutional Aspects of Prohibition Enforcement," *Central Law Journal* 97 (1924): 113, 122–3, cited in Murchison, *Federal Criminal Law Doctrines*, 71.

before them. In the process, they spurred the Supreme Court to move toward the modern instantiations of those rights.[135]

In the early years of Prohibition, the Court, having recently made its peace with the project of legibility, acted quite progressively – that is, it narrowly construed the protections afforded by the Bill of Rights, ushering them out of the way of statist progressive policy, statebuilding, and nationbuilding goals.[136] In *Carroll v. U.S.* (1925), for example, a relatively early Prohibition decision, police officers searched the car of two men on the mere hunch that they were transporting liquor in violation of the Volstead Act. The officers had no search warrant and no justification for stopping the car. Rejecting the Fourth Amendment claims of the defendants, the Court's majority, including Justice Brandeis, distinguished the search of automobiles from that of private dwellings. In his dissent, Justice McReynolds, joined by Justice Sutherland, acknowledged the distinction but dismissed the contention that it made any difference: "What of it?" he asked. McReynolds insisted that suspicion alone did not justify a warrantless search.[137]

Decisions like *Carroll* – which I use only as an illustration in a familiar case of a rights-restricting trend in early Prohibition cases – prompted much discussion and, in some cases, outrage. One commentator from the (then highly conservative) legal academy, for example, wrote in the *Virginia Law Review*:

I cannot but think it unfortunate that any judicial tribunal should be so indifferent to [the Fourth and Fifth Amendments] as to emasculate them in order to secure convictions. Courts are established to administer justice, according to the spirit as well as the letter of constitutional and statutory requirements, enacted for their guidance and the protection of all citizens, including lawbreakers, and it seems to me that courts should be extremely careful in giving effect to provisions that are equally if not more binding on them, than any other class of persons.... In the exercise of their great powers courts have no higher duty to perform than those involving the protection of the citizen in the civil rights guaranteed to him by the Constitution, and if at any time the protection of these rights should delay or even defeat the ends of justice in the particular case, it is better for the public good, that this should happen than that an old and great constitutional mandate should be nullified.[138]

---

[135] Well into the 1940s, in fact, long after Prohibition's demise, surveys of constitutional doctrine concerning search and seizure plainly looked at liquor interdiction cases as paradigmatic. See Murchison, *Federal Criminal Law Doctrine*, 48. See also, e.g., E. C. Arnold, "Search and Seizure Problems," *Tennessee Law Review* 16 (April 1940): 291–303. Antialcohol crusades had intermittently thrown up legal questions concerning unreasonable searches and seizures in state courts as early as the 1850s. Pegram, *Battling Demon Rum*, 41.

[136] *Olmstead v. United States*, 277 U.S. 438 (1928).

[137] *Carroll v. United States*, 267 U.S. 132 (1925).

[138] See, e.g., "Search and Seizure in the Old Days," *American Bar Association Journal* 8 (November 1922): 712; J. D. Carroll, "The Search and Seizure Provisions of the Federal and State Constitutions," *Virginia Law Review* 10 (December 1923): 124–40; F. T. R., "Is a Man's House No Longer His Castle?" *Notre Dame Lawyer* 5 (December 1929): 144–7; Forrest

As time went on and public opinion shifted against Prohibition, the Court, led by its most conservative justices, became more protective of civil liberties in criminal Fourth Amendment cases. Justice Brandeis's dissent in *Olmstead v. United States* (1928), which involved the admission of wiretap evidence in a Prohibition case, became emblematic among later civil libertarians. Though the leading legal historian of these cases praises Brandeis's *Olmstead* dissent, he clearly gives Justices Butler and McReynolds, then the Court's leading antistatists, pride of place as the chief architects of the Court's criminal process rights protection revival in Prohibition's later years. It seems that Brandeis's chief contribution here was his decision to anchor the Constitution's Fourth Amendment rights in a broader theory of intellectual freedom (a matter of particular concern to the legal and intellectual elites who constructed him as a civil liberation hero). Brandeis anchored his eloquent defense of "the right to be let alone" in this appeal to intellectual freedom. Obviously, this appeal was not relevant in the *Carroll* case, where Brandeis sided with those narrowly construing the search and seizure provisions of the Fourth Amendment.[139]

Once it became law, three aspects of Prohibition proved to be crucial in fixing its trajectory within American constitutional development. The first was its peculiar social incidence as a matter of criminal law. As John Barker Waite pointed out in the *Pennsylvania Law Review* in a post mortem on Prohibition in the 1930s, "with the enactment of the Prohibition law tens of thousands of erstwhile more or less law-abiding citizens became at least technical lawbreakers and exceedingly fearful of search, whether reasonable or otherwise."[140] The potential criminals included the friends and neighbors

Revere Black, *Ill-Starred Prohibition Cases: A Study in Judicial Pathology* (Boston: R.G. Badger, 1931). Carroll, "Search and Seizure Provisions," *Virginia Law Review* 10 (December 1923): 124–46, 143–4. See also Murchison, *Federal Criminal Law Doctrine*, 52, 68–70.

[139] In *Olmstead*, Brandeis said of the Fourth and Fifth Amendments that "they sought to protect Americans in their beliefs, their thoughts, their emotions, and their sensations." Autos, unlike wiretaps, were harder to link with "man's spiritual nature . . . his feelings . . . and his intellect." *Olmstead*, 277 U.S. at 478. My analysis here is consistent with G. Edward White's view that free speech issues represent the true core of contemporary civil liberties. G. Edward White, "Free Speech and the Bifurcated Review Project: The 'Preferred Position' Cases," in *Constitutionalism and American Culture: Writing the New Constitutional History*, eds. Sandra F. VanBurkleo, Kermit L. Hall, and Robert J. Kaczorowski (Lawrence: University Press of Kansas, 2002), 99–122.

[140] John Barker Waite, "Reasonable Search and Research," *University of Pennsylvania Law Review* 86 (April 1938): 623–37, esp. 626. The Wickersham Commission reported that "many of the best citizens in every community, on whom we rely habitually for the upholding of law and order, are at most lukewarm as to the National Prohibition Act. Many who are normally law-abiding are led to an attitude hostile to the statute by a feeling that repression and interference with private conduct are carried too far." National Commission on Law Observance and Enforcement ("Wickersham Commission"), *Report on the Enforcement of the Prohibition Laws of the United States* (1931), 54. This creation of a new class of criminals in the service of national policy goals tracked the course of the criminalization of business

of lawyers and judges, which had a number of legal consequences. Chief among them was that it made the federal exclusionary rule (created earlier in *Boyd* and *Weeks*) more popular with state judges than it ever would have become had it been invoked in traditional street crime cases such as burglary, rape, and murder. In response to Prohibition, judges in state after state began to aggressively import this federal criminal process rule into their own jurisprudence.[141]

The second aspect was that debate over the proper scope of searches and seizures and the spread of the exclusionary rule dovetailed fortuitously with broader philosophical debates among legal elites over the relationship between positive and natural law. Before long, the Fourth Amendment and the judge-made rules of evidence associated with it were swept into the larger debates involving the relationship between the Fourteenth Amendment and the Bill of Rights and between positive law and natural law. By the time the Supreme Court first seriously considered incorporating the Fourth Amendment and the exclusionary rule as restrictions on the states via the due process clause of the Fourteenth Amendment in *Wolf v. Colorado* (1949), influential Supreme Court justices were asserting that the states had adopted the exclusionary rule in droves because they had considered it a fundamental part of Fourth Amendment liberties.[142] The course taken by state judges in the 1920s in response to a law that many were coming to appreciate as draconian (a course that might even be characterized as a mild form of nullification), was later constructed by the Supreme Court as evidence of an emerging moral consensus in favor of a universal rule of justice applicable in all criminal cases, no matter how mainstream the law and no matter how dangerous the criminal.

The third crucial aspect of Prohibition was that it created a nationwide crime wave that soon was considered a major national problem. Indeed, it was Prohibition – not civil rights – that played the primary role in transforming crime and criminal process issues from state level to national political issues.[143] It did so through a rather byzantine path, however, that has little

behavior. While federal laws did not prohibit individual possession and consumption of alcohol, the "baby Volsteads" of many states did. Pegram, *Battling Demon Rum*, 152, 159.

[141] Murchison, *Federal Criminal Law Doctrines*, 97; Waite, "Reasonable Search and Research," 626.

[142] *Wolf v. Colorado*, 338 U.S. 25 (1949). By a 6–3 vote, *Wolf* accepted the incorporation of the Fourth Amendment but not of the exclusionary rule, which Frankfurter's opinion for the Court (joined by Hugo Black) considered only a rule of evidence. *Wolf* was eventually overruled in *Mapp v. Ohio*, 367 U.S. 643 (1961).

[143] Kenneth Murchison rightly contends (and demonstrates at length) that "The thirteen years of constitutional prohibition should be regarded as the formative era of modern criminal law and procedure at the federal level." Murchison, *Federal Criminal Law Doctrine*, 170. See also Epp, *Rights Revolution*, 27 ("[T]he Court's agenda on criminal procedure began to grow in the early thirties…long before justices with liberal attitudes toward criminal procedure gained control of the Court").

to do with progressive people taking the fight for the rights of criminals to the national level. Rather, constitutional criminal process went national because progressive-spirited people, through legislation and Constitutional amendment, *created* a new class of criminals, in the process contributing markedly to the level of violent crime within American society. This turned street crime, formerly a classic state issue, into a national problem. In criminalizing the manufacture, sale, and transport of nearly all the alcohol in the United States, and in criminalizing not only those acts, but also an array of secondary acts associated with them, Prohibition virtually created the modern world of organized crime and criminal gang warfare. Approximately 70 percent of the criminal cases in the federal courts during Prohibition were Volstead Act cases. This inevitably led the federal courts into the byways of criminal procedure. The volume of these cases, in fact, was so large that it quickly led to what amounted to administrative decisions by courts to cut back on traditional rights to trial by jury and to rely broadly on a system of plea bargaining in criminal cases. Many cities even went as far as initiating "bargain days," on which the court would trade a promise of no jail time for a quick guilty plea to spare the court system the time and expense of a constitutionally well-appointed trial. And in a related development, the modern boom in prison construction had begun.[144]

Herbert Hoover's 1929 inaugural address was the first by an American president to identify crime as a national issue. In that address, Hoover proposed the formation of a national commission with a broad-ranging mandate to study this new national problem. In 1931, the National Commission on Law Observance and Enforcement – popularly known as the Wickersham Commission – issued a series of fourteen separate reports on crime and law enforcement issues.[145] The Wickersham Commission's *Report on the Enforcement of the Prohibition Laws of the United States* (1931) opened by noting the unprecedented levels of federal power that the Eighteenth Amendment created – attributing that development to the roots of Prohibition in the perceived imperatives of war.[146] The Commission scored

---

[144] See Henry Alan Johnston, *What Rights Are Left* (New York: Macmillan Co., 1930), 26; Murchison, *Federal Criminal Law Doctrines*, 154, 159–60, 166, 171–5; Pegram, *Battling Demon Rum*; Morone, *Hellfire Nation*, 232, 325–9, 343. See also Marie Gottschalk, "Unlocking the Doors of the Past: The Nationalization and Politicization of Law and Order in American Political Development," paper presented at the annual meeting of the American Political Science Association, Boston, MA (29 August 2002).

[145] See James D. Calder, *The Origins of the Development of Federal Crime Control Policy: Herbert Hoover's Initiatives* (Westport, CT: Praeger, 1993), 1–6, 77–102.

[146] "The Eighteenth Amendment was submitted and ratified during a great war. The National Prohibition Act was passed immediately thereafter. During a period of war the people readily yield questions of personal right to the strengthening of government and the increase of its powers. These periods are always characterized by a certain amount of emotionalism. This was especially true of the World War." See also Johnston, *What Rights Are Left*, 26 ("The National Prohibition Act . . . [is] . . . a revolutionary departure from the contemplated

the assumption of the zealous federal authorities "that [the Prohibition Act] was of paramount importance and that constitutional guarantees and legal limitations on agencies of law enforcement and on administration must yield to the exigencies or convenience of enforcing it." It then openly discussed the widespread violation of rights that Prohibition had occasioned, declaring, on a hopeful note that "[t]hese enlargements of governmental power, at the expense of individual right, are always followed by reactions against the abuses of that power which inevitably occur." Chief among these reactions were those made under the Fourth and Fifth Amendments on behalf of the right to privacy. "[A]dvocates of the law," the Commission wrote, "have constantly urged and are still urging disregard or abrogation of the guarantees of liberty and of sanctity of the home." "Unfortunate public expressions by advocates of the law, approving killings and promiscuous shootings and lawless raids and seizures and deprecating the constitutional guarantees involved" made matters all the worse. "Many . . . accepted and observed the law when once it was passed," the Commission observed. But "[w]hen it became apparent that the results expected were not being realized, when the effects of the operations of the law and of the methods of enforcement which they deemed invasions of private rights became manifest, their opposition became aroused." "High-handed methods, unreasonable searches and seizures, lawless interference with personal and property rights" were now suddenly, in the criminal process context, a matter of major national concern.[147]

A contemporaneous study of the legal dimensions of Prohibition, Henry Alan Johnston's *What Rights Are Left* (1930) listed the Fourth and Fifth Amendments first in its chapter laying out the "enforcement problem" attendant to Prohibition, declaring, "These rights are inalienable. They are not derived from the Constitution, but are natural rights which antedate the Constitution; they are rights which the Colonists insisted on as Englishmen, rights which they brought to America from the mother country, and rights which they would not permit England or any government on earth to deprive them of."[148]

scheme and purpose of the Federal Government . . . necessitating the setting up of a national police force of unusual powers"). As such, Prohibition should properly be placed alongside the Espionage Act as one of the wartime regulatory initiatives crucial to the trajectory of constitutional development concerning civil rights and civil liberties. It is worth considering whether there are contemporary political/ideological reasons why this, to date, has not been done.

[147] *Report on the Enforcement of the Prohibition Laws of the United States*, 45–46, 51, 57. Pegram, *Battling Demon Rum*, 175. See Calder, *Origins and Development of Federal Crime Control Policy*, 108–15.

[148] Johnston, *What Rights Are Left*, 28–9, 79. The search warrant provision of the Volstead Act, incidentally, was copied from the search warrant provision of the now anathematized Espionage Act (1917). Johnston, *What Rights Are Left*, 70.

A conservative backlash against violations of fundamental privacy and criminal process rights and against the unprecedented assertion of national power in this area brought on by progressive legislation played a major role in ginning up opposition to Prohibition, and the ultimate repeal of the Eighteenth Amendment by the Twenty-first in the 1930s.[149]

Incorporation and the Black-Frankfurter Debate

The question of whether the Bill of Rights or portions of it should be understood as restrictions on the conduct of the states – typically discussed either in the context of the original intent of the framers of the Fourteenth Amendment or, later, in quasi-abstract metaphysical speculation about the meaning of "ordered liberty" (in Justice Benjamin Cardozo's 1937 *Palko* decision and the Black-Frankfurter debate) – attracted the sustained attention of the Supreme Court for the first time in Prohibition-era criminal process cases. Indeed, President Hoover underlined the nation's commitment to the "maintenance of ordered liberty" in his inaugural address focusing on federal crime control policies.[150] Moreover, the very issue involved in the Court's famous *Palko* decision, the Fifth Amendment's double jeopardy provision, had been raised prominently and repeatedly during the previous decade in a run of cases involving successive state and federal prosecutions, first under state prohibition laws and then pursuant to the Volstead Act. In 1922, the Supreme Court, announcing a dual sovereignty exception to the double jeopardy protection, unanimously declared such prosecutions to be fully consistent with the Constitution, an exception that remains part of the constitutional law of criminal process to the present day.[151]

At first, the Court's ruling in this case met with the nearly universal approbation of the law reviews. Over time, however, this sanguine professional view of the dual sovereignty exception began to change (a transition that was also apparent in the newspapers). Writing toward the end of the 1920s, one contemporaneous commentator declared that in its decision "the Court seemed to lose sight of the fact that double punishment for the same offense is, and always has been, utterly opposed to every conception of justice, whether under the Mosaic, the Roman, the Common law, or any other system. It is a fundamental concept of Liberty." It is this very affront to

---

[149] Pegram, *Battling Demon Rum*, 179; Morone, *Hellfire Nation*, 282, 310–11, 331. See, generally, David Kyvig Jr., *Repealing National Prohibition* (Chicago: University of Chicago Press, 1979).

[150] Inaugural Address of Herbert Hoover (4 March 1929), in *Inaugural Addresses of the Presidents of the United States from George Washington 1789 to Richard Milhous Nixon 1969* (Washington, DC: United States Government Printing Office, 1969), 227. Justice Cardozo (whose use of the phrase "ordered liberty" in *Palko* is more widely known than Hoover's) was appointed to the Supreme Court by Hoover in 1932. *Palko v. Connecticut*, 302 U.S. 319 (1937).

[151] *United States v. Lanza*, 260 U.S. 377 (1922). See also *Hebert v. Louisiana*, 272 U.S. 312 (1926).

liberty – the possibility of double jeopardy – to which New York Governor Al Smith referred in 1923 when he signed the repeal of the Prohibition laws of New York state.[152]

The *Palko* case became seminal not because the issues it raised first came to the Court's attention in that case: The issues had become familiar to the Court during Prohibition. *Palko* became seminal because in that decision the debate over those issues was conceptually recast by the intersection of the Prohibition-era double jeopardy issues with emergent jurisprudential debates amongst progressives – who that same year were about to wrest control of the federal courts from the conservatives – about the proper exercise of judicial power. Beginning in the late 1930s, Franklin Delano Roosevelt's appointees to the Court initiated an unusual period of judicial philosophizing over seemingly abstract questions involving the possibilities of objectivity and the implications of human subjectivity for the judicial role. The origins of this philosophic turn had nothing in particular to do with Prohibition. The turn arose, rather, out of the progressive reformist fight against "government by judiciary" in struggles over "the labor problem," the defining progressive reformist fight of the statebuilding era. It was essentially a debate concerning the nature of judicial power under a new regime in which progressives had vanquished – and replaced – their old judicial nemeses. Now that *they* were the judges, the question became how could their own power be both cabined

---

[152] Johnston, *What Rights Are Left*, 40, 41. This theme emphasizing the injustice and unfairness of the result gained ascendency in the law reviews. Murchison, *Federal Criminal Law Doctrines*, 116–17, citing Anthony A. Goerner, "Constitutional Law: Double Jeopardy: Double Liability," *Cornell Law Quarterly* 12 (1927): 212–16; Max P. Cohen, "Recent Cases, Criminal Law – Former Jeopardy Power of the State and the Federal Government to Prosecute," *Boston University Law Review* 7 (1927): 57–9; Recent Cases, Intoxicating Liquors – Eighteenth Amendment – Concurrent Power of Congress and the Several States," *Minnesota Law Review* 11 (1927): 173–4; J. A. C. Grant, "The *Lanza* Rule of Successive Prosecutions," *Columbia Law Review* 32 (1932): 1309–31; J. A. C. Grant, "The Scope and Nature of Concurrent Power," *Columbia Law Review* 34 (1934): 994–1040. See also Wickersham Commission, *Report on the Enforcement of the Prohibition Laws of the United States* (1931), 52–3. ("Nor was it merely that a radical change was made when the federal government was given jurisdiction over matters internal to the states. It was necessary also to adjust our federal polity to a conception of two sovereignties, each engaged independently in enforcing the same provision, so that, as it was supposed, wherever and whenever the one fell down the other might step in. Endeavor to bring about a nationally enforced universal total abstinence, instead of limiting the power devolved on the federal government to those features of the enforcement of the amendment which were naturally or traditionally of federal cognizance, invited difficulty at the outset. But difficulties inhered also in the conception of the amendment that nation and state were to act concurrently, each covering the whole of the same ground actually or potentially; each using its own governmental machinery at the same time with the other in enforcing provisions with respect to which each had a full jurisdiction"). The Court's earlier jurisprudence on double jeopardy focused almost exclusively on seriatim prosecutions initiated by the federal government. Murchison, *Federal Criminal Law Doctrines*, 104–25.

and husbanded to proper effect? How, in other words, could it be exercised legitimately?

These matters were played out most famously on the Court in the debate between two Roosevelt appointees: Felix Frankfurter argued that judges could be trusted to discern the meaning of vague concepts such as due process and the fundamentals of Anglo-Saxon liberty by hewing to objective standards of judgment; and Justice Hugo Black insisted that only by relying on the constitutional text (he meant the Bill of Rights) could the subjectivity-run-rampant that he saw at work in the economic rights decisions of the old, pre–New Deal Court be reined in and real constitutional standards be applied.[153]

As far as criminal process issues were concerned, Justice Black positioned himself as heir to a series of lone dissents in criminal cases by the first Justice John Marshall Harlan, which were after-constructed by legal scholars (following Black) as early, principled commitments to a rights-protective theory of incorporation.[154] The establishment of a genealogical provenance in a series of lone Harlan dissents proved of special value in the mid-twentieth century, as Harlan had at the same time also issued a series of lone dissents in civil rights cases – and by the mid-twentieth century the race problem had replaced the labor problem as the defining reformist political commitment.[155] Although, as part of his debates with Black over incorporation, Frankfurter implicitly agreed with Black's genealogy by dismissing Harlan as "an eccentric exception," in his views in his criminal process dissents, Harlan's actual dissents in those cases support Frankfurter's views as much as Black's. Since Harlan had not been primarily concerned with the "problem" of ostensibly uncabined judicial power concerning the labor problem – as were legal progressives and later New Dealers like Frankfurter and Black – while certainly for a broad conception of natural rights, Harlan did not distinguish between approaches to those rights anchored in the Bill of Rights and those deriving generally from the fundamentals of "Anglo-Saxon institutions," "due process," "privileges and immunities," or "the peculiar privileges of Englishmen."[156] In this, the Bill of Rights were not determinative but rather served an evidentiary function. To move back and forth between these anchors for judicially enforced constitutional rights did not especially trouble

---

[153] See, generally, Mark Silverstein, *Constitutional Faiths: Felix Frankfurter, Hugo Black, and the Process of Judicial Decisionmaking* (Ithaca, NY: Cornell University Press, 1984).

[154] *Hurtado v. California,* 110 U.S. 516 (1884); *Chicago, Burlington and Quincy Railroad v. Chicago,* 116 U.S. 226 (1897); *O'Neil v. Vermont* (1892); *Maxwell v. Dow,* 176 U.S. 581 (1900); *Patterson v. Colorado,* 205 U.S. 454 (1907); *Twining v. New Jersey,* 211 U.S. 78 (1908). See, e.g., Tinsley Yarbrough, *Judicial Enigma: The First Justice Harlan* (New York: Oxford University Press, 1995), 226–7.

[155] *Civil Rights Cases,* 109 U.S. 3 (1883); *Plessy v. Ferguson,* 163 U.S. 537 (1896); *Berea College v. Kentucky,* 211 U.S. 45 (1908).

[156] *Hurtado,* 110 U.S. at 539, 543.

Harlan, as a progressive legal ideology profoundly suspicious of judicial power more or less postdated his career. It was not, however, good enough for Frankfurter or Black. The problem of judicial power raised by the so-called *Lochner* court set the agenda of constitutional thinking in their formative years.

On a new, post-*Lochner* Court that with each new FDR appointment saw itself as increasingly progressive, the civil liberties problem became one of how to guarantee constitutional standards of justice in criminal trials while at the same time (and in the old progressive spirit) strictly tethering federal judicial power. The problem was front and center of the Court's *Palko* decision, which involved a Fourteenth Amendment challenge to a man's conviction for first degree murder in Connecticut.[157] The man was initially convicted of second degree murder, but under a Connecticut law that allowed the state to appeal decisions in criminal cases, this verdict was overturned, a new trial granted, and Palko this time was convicted of first degree murder. Palko alleged that by placing him twice in jeopardy for the same offense, his new conviction violated the Fifth Amendment, which acted as a restriction upon the states via the due process clause of the Fourteenth.

In his opinion for the Court in *Palko*, Justice Cardozo conceded that if the federal government had done to Palko what the state of Connecticut had, it would have run afoul of the Fifth Amendment's double jeopardy protections. As for the argument that the standards of the Bill of Rights are the same as those to be applied to the states, however, he concluded (echoing the conclusions that had been debated widely and arrived at by the courts during Prohibition) that "there is no such general rule."[158] The Fourteenth Amendment due process test was different. It forbade "practice[s] repugnant to the conscience of mankind" and required only procedures that "have been found to be implicit in the concept of ordered liberty," without which, "a fair and enlightened system of justice would be impossible," and "neither liberty nor justice would exist if they were sacrificed."[159] As for Palko's predicament, Cardozo asked, "Is that kind of double jeopardy to which the statute has subjected him a hardship so acute and shocking that our polity will not endure it? Does it violate those 'fundamental principles of liberty and justice' that lie at the base of all our civil and political institutions?" Absolutely not, he concluded. "This is not cruelty at all, nor even vexation in any immoderate degree."[160] It would remain to be seen how long, in a new context, with new intellectual agendas and newly emerging reform

[157] *Palko v. Connecticut*, 302 U.S. 319 (1937).

[158] *Palko*, 302 U.S. at 323.

[159] *Palko*, 302 U.S. at 325, 326.

[160] *Palko*, 302 U.S. at 328. See Murchison, *Federal Criminal Law Doctrine*, 104–25. In the Warren years, the sentiment was quite otherwise, and the *Palko* decision concerning double jeopardy was overruled in *Benton v. Maryland*, 395 U.S. 784 (1969).

imperatives, this understanding of the scope of constitutionally guaranteed national rights would stand.

From Prohibition to Race: The Nationalization and Standardization of Police Procedures

The American system of government is exceptional in leaving much of the task of law enforcement to a loose patchwork of town, city, county, and state police forces. In Europe, police forces are part of the central state bureaucracy and, as such, are highly responsive to policy changes ordered by the state. Here, the system is less centralized and messier. As with the public schools (which in Europe are also run by national bureaucracies), when it comes to criminal process policy, central state efforts to nationalize and standardize policy have historically been initiated not by national administrative bureaucracies but rather by federal judges wielding constitutional doctrines and constitutional principles.[161]

In *Building a New American State* (1982), Stephen Skowronek posited a general (albeit "patchwork") movement in American political development from a nineteenth-century "state of courts and parties" to a twentieth-century New American State – a marked departure from the earlier regime. Skowronek's recent work (written with Karen Orren) has placed additional emphasis upon patterns of intercurrence, in which incongruities or even contrary orderings of state power coexist within a single temporal period. American statebuilding with regard to criminal process in the twentieth century (like education, but unlike with railroads and the military) represents a twentieth-century anachronism. Despite the fact that a New American State had by that time been built, a significant amount of statebuilding involving criminal process was not through bureaucracy, but rather by judicial ruling, a system of national criminal process regulation that persists to the present day.[162]

A sustained and ultimately successful project to nationalize and standardize criminal procedure as applied to street crimes began in the interlude

---

[161] There is, of course, variation in Europe. Nonetheless, the contrast with the United States is strong. Generally speaking, the continental police forces are the most highly centralized. But even in Great Britain, a relatively highly decentralized system, the structure of the system is set by national legislation and local practices monitored by the Home Secretary. David H. Bayley, "The Police and Political Development in Europe," in *The Formation of National States in Western Europe*, ed. Charles Tilly (Princeton: Princeton University Press, 1975), 328–79.

[162] Karen Orren and Stephen Skowronek, "Institutions and Intercurrence: Theory Building in the Fullness of Time," in *Nomos: XXIII: Political Order*, eds. Ian Shapiro and Russell Hardin (New York: NYU Press, 1996), 111–46. In both cases, the most important courts in this regard are the federal courts – in contradistinction to the common law courts that were the chief instruments of (localized) policymaking for most of the nineteenth century. As such, it is not inconsistent to discuss court practice in education and criminal law as a matter of central state construction. See, generally, Shapiro, *Courts*.

between the First and Second World Wars, and involved two progressive-spirited reformist initiatives. The first, as we have seen, was Prohibition. The second involved civil rights. In particular, it involved an effort of the central state to grapple with the outlier status of the South in its treatment of blacks in their criminal justice systems (and, subsequently, in other areas as well). The problem of the outlier status of the South as far as criminal process was concerned assumed political salience in a series of prominent cases that garnered national media attention.[163] The imperative of national standardization, the persisting progressive suspicion of judicial power, and the increasingly apparent outsider status of the South met in the court's consideration of a series of racially inflected criminal process cases that arose in the interwar years. The Court began to negotiate a national constitutional *modus vivendi* on fair trials in a series of cases that arose out of highly publicized racial incidents in the South: the Leo Frank affair, the Elaine riots, and Scottsboro.[164]

The *Frank* case involving the Jewish pencil factory owner in Georgia discussed previously served as a prelude to the interwar cases involving blacks.[165] In reviewing the Georgia court decision sentencing Frank to death, the U.S. Supreme Court, in a 7–2 opinion, was deferential to the sectional claims of the South. Justice Mahlon Pitney wrote:

[I]t is perfectly well settled that a criminal prosecution in the courts of a state, based upon a law not in itself repugnant to the Federal Constitution, and conducted according to the settled course of judicial proceedings as established by the law of the state, so long as it includes notice, and a hearing, or an opportunity to be heard, before a court of competent jurisdiction, according to established modes of procedure, is "due process" in the constitutional sense.[166]

By the early 1920s, however, the Court was already showing signs of insisting upon more stringent minimal national standards of criminal process. *Moore v. Dempsey* (1923) was a case in point. *Moore* rose out of the Elaine,

---

[163] Michael Klarman, a legal historian, has argued in various places that "the Justices seem least reluctant to expand constitutional rights when doing so involves simply holding a few outlier states to the norm already espoused by a vast majority of them." See Klarman, "Racial Origins," 18. Klarman, "Is the Supreme Court Sometimes Irrelevant? Race the Southern Criminal Justice System in the World War II Era," University of Virginia School of Law Working Paper 01-9 (December 2001); Klarman, *From Jim Crow to Civil Rights*, 78–79, 85, 136–7, 236, 453–4. This view, which is in dialogue with Gerald Rosenberg's work, provides a useful developmental perspective on court power. See Rosenberg, *The Hollow Hope*.

[164] Many of these cases, including the Elaine and Scottsboro cases, were placed on the Supreme Court's agenda through the work of the relatively new National Association for the Advancement of Colored People (NAACP), founded in 1910. See Epp, *Rights Revolution*, 21. See, generally, Michael Klarman, "The Racial Origins of Modern Criminal Procedure," Working Paper 00-5, University of Virginia School of Law (May 2000); Klarman, *From Jim Crow to Civil Rights*, 117–35.

[165] *Frank v. Mangum*, 237 U.S. 309 (1915).

[166] *Frank v. Mangum*, 237 U.S. at 326.

Arkansas race riots in which blacks meeting in a church to strategize how to protect themselves from extortion by white landowners were attacked by a white mob.[167] In the ensuing melee, five whites and two hundred blacks were killed. Despite the fact that the whites had instigated the violence and the blacks had been murdered disproportionately, in the prosecutions following the incident, five blacks were sentenced to death in a trial lorded over by a mob that had threatened to lynch the defendants; the crowd had been held at bay only by the trial court's solemn promise in advance of the trial to convict the black defendants and sentence them to death. In writing for the Court in *Moore*, Justice Holmes declared the trial to be a plain violation of the Fourteenth Amendment's due process clause.[168]

In *Powell v. Alabama* (1932), one of the Scottsboro cases, the Court took an additional step toward setting national criminal process standards when it held that the hasty trial and rape conviction of nine black youths who were denied the assistance of counsel violated the Fourteenth Amendment's due process clause.[169] That amendment, declared Justice Sutherland, guaranteed every defendant a fair trial. Sutherland's opinion in *Powell* was anchored in the Fourteenth Amendment and not in the Sixth. But he discussed the Sixth Amendment in his opinion, and the Court held that at least where poor, ignorant, and friendless blacks were charged in capital cases like this one, states were required to provide the defendants with counsel.[170]

---

[167] *Moore v. Dempsey*, 261 U.S. 86 (1923).

[168] See also *Mooney v. Holohan*, 294 U.S. 103 (1935) (sharply criticizing the first-degree murder conviction of a California man on Fourteenth Amendment due process grounds after the man was convicted on the sole basis of perjured testimony knowingly used by the prosecutors, who had also suppressed exculpatory evidence; the case, however, was dismissed because the defendant had not yet exhausted all of his potential state court remedies). Klarman plausibly attributes the different result reached in *Moore* than in *Frank* to the NAACP's aggressive antilynching campaign in the intervening years (which garnered the support of prominent national political figures from both parties, including A. Mitchell Palmer, Elihu Root, and Charles Evans Hughes), the focus trained on the problem of interracial violence in the wake of the deadly race riots that took place in the intervening years, and the emergent antilynching commitments of the Republican Party. Klarman, "Racial Origins;" Klarman, *From Jim Crow to Civil Rights*, 121–3.

[169] Counsel actually had been appointed but were only given a half hour to research and prepare their defense. *Powell v. Alabama*, 287 U.S. 45 (1942). See also *Norris v. Alabama*, 294 U.S. 587 (1935). See Dan T. Carter, *Scottsboro: A Tragedy of the American South*, rev. ed., 1979; James E. Goodman, *Stories of Scottsboro* (New York: Pantheon Books, 1994). Michael Klarman provides evidence for the interesting argument that for many in the South, the quick (and unfair) trial of the sort held in the South in *Moore* and the Scottsboro cases was considered a step forward from the lynchings that had previously been widespread (by the 1920s, lynchings had declined dramatically since the 1890s). The substitution of blatantly unfair trials for lynchings, however, still fell woefully short of national, minimal constitutional standards. Klarman, "Racial Origins"; Klarman, *From Jim Crow to Civil Rights*, 119.

[170] The Sixth Amendment was ultimately incorporated during the Warren years in *Gideon v. Wainwright*, 372 U.S. 335 (1963). See also *Brown v. Mississippi*, 297 U.S. 278 (1936) (voiding

The Supreme Court's *Powell* decision prominently highlighted a disjunction in the Court's jurisprudence between its requirements in federal and state criminal cases. In federal prosecutions, the Court had held that the Sixth Amendment required the appointment of counsel in all serious criminal matters. But its *Powell* opinion declared that the appointment of counsel was only required in a presumably more limited class of cases in which the failure to appoint such counsel would be unfair. The standards of fairness for state criminal trials thus seemed to be lower than those for their federal counterparts, and the so-called "fair trial rule" interpretation of the due process clause of the Fourteenth Amendment seemed set off against a higher standard of justice anchored in an alternate approach more closely tethered to the Bill of Rights. The interaction between the Sixth and the Fourteenth Amendments in one of the most famous cases of the time helped to set the terms of the debate over the requirements of fundamental justice in the constitutional law of criminal procedure.

The Ascendancy of an Antiracist Reform Imperative

In the aftermath of the New Deal, in which a settlement had been reached concerning both the labor problem and the constitutional legitimacy of the radical augmentation of central state administrative power, a new reform imperative – the race problem – was rapidly emerging. This problem, of course, had long existed in American society. But after the end of Reconstruction, it had more or less been removed from the agenda of the central state, which, in subsequent years, had negotiated a rapprochement with the South and, in the interest of national reconciliation and institutional settlement, made peace with its racial policies. Moreover, in the era of Jim Crow, the connection between being a partisan of progress – whether as a populist, a progressive, or another sort of political reformer – and a proponent of racial equality or antiracism had long since been severed. Certainly, some on the left at this time were principled antiracists (such as many members of the Knights of Labor). But at the same time, many capitalist Republicans hostile to the power of labor unions, strongly in favor of economic rights, and (later) vocally hostile to Roosevelt's New Deal were more reliably pro-equality and antiracist than many of those on the political left. Antiracism at this time, simply put, was not part of the definition of what it meant to be a reformer.

Beginning in the early twentieth century, however, in response to epochal demographic, cultural, and political forces, that began to change. Foremost among these forces, perhaps, were seismic alterations in the electoral landscape created by blacks migrating from the South, where they could not vote, to northern cities, where they could. Northern politicians moved to

a murder conviction based solely on a confession procured by torture as a violation of Fourteenth Amendment due process rights).

take strategic advantage of those shifts. In addition, a 1944 Supreme Court decision declaring white primaries unconstitutional significantly increased the political power of Southern blacks in urban areas, where they were less isolated and, hence, less subject to violent retribution for exercising their political rights. Superimposed on these demographic changes and their attendant politics was the freighted ideological and political fallout of the Second World War, a war in which the United States and its Allies were locked in mortal battle with an expansionist power that had placed state-sanctioned racism at the core of its self-definition. The fight against racist totalitarianism now publicly vexed the accommodations and evasions concerning race that had characterized the American constitutional and political order. Specifically, the passage of the Nuremberg Laws (1935) and the subsequent German internal war against Jews, Gypsies, and other nonracial minorities like Jehovah's Witnesses, suddenly threw America's treatment of its own minority groups, and blacks in particular, into high relief. This was partly a matter of cognitive dissonance on the part of white Americans. But, as Daniel Kryder has emphasized, it also went beyond this. A black population increasingly vocal about its own oppression threatened the ground-level political disruptions that could derail the nation's war mobilization efforts. It was in this context that the African-American press became increasingly outspoken on the issue, taking up the fight for a "War on Two Fronts" of "Double-V" against racism abroad and at home.[171]

The audacity of Hitler's racist articulations at once made familiar American "traditions" suddenly seem foreign to proper conceptions of national identity. It soon became apparent that Southerners probing the way of life of their region at this time, like W. J. Cash and William Faulkner, were becoming self-conscious and defensive about Dixie folkways.[172] Southern traditions were becoming newly identified not with homespun American values but rather with European fascism, an identification reinforced by the publication during the 1940s of two monographs on race in America that were

---

[171] Daniel Kryder, *Divided Arsenal: Race and the American State during World II* (New York: Cambridge University Press, 2000); William C. Berman, *The Politics of Civil Rights in the Truman Administration* (Columbus: Ohio State University Press, 1970), 42; David W. Southern, *Gunnar Myrdal and Black-White Relations: The Use and Abuse of an American Dilemma, 1944–1969* (Baton Rouge: Louisiana State University Press, 1987), 51–2. Philip A. Klinkner and Rogers N. Smith, *The Unsteady March: The Rise and Decline of Racial Equality in America* (Chicago: University of Chicago Press, 1999), 136–201. See also Brenda Gayle Plumer, *Rising Wind: Black Americans and U.S. Foreign Affairs, 1935–1960* (Chapel Hill: University of North Carolina Press, 1996), 83–124; John D. Skrentny, *The Minority Rights Revolution* (Cambridge, MA: The Belknap Press of the Harvard University Press, 2002), 21–5.

[172] See W. J. Cash, *The Mind of the South* (New York: Alfred A. Knopf, 1941); James Baldwin, "Faulkner and Desegregation," in *Nobody Knows My Name* (New York: Dell Publishing Co., 1961), 98–104. On the defensive reaction of Southern liberals in the face of a burgeoning civil rights movement, see Southern, *Gunnar Myrdal and Black-White Relations*, 77–8.

widely read and reported on, with major cultural effect: Gunnar Myrdal's *American Dilemma* (1944) and the report of the President's Committee on Civil Rights, *To Secure These Rights* (1947).[173]

Both studies characterized the race problem as first and foremost a problem of morality. Myrdal opened his book with a declaration of that characterization, and went on to call attention to the nation's long "suppressed moral conflict," to portray a country "continuously struggling for its soul," and to conclude that "that status accorded to the Negro in America represents nothing more and nothing less than a century-long lag of public morals."[174] The Truman Committee report similarly claimed that morality was the foremost reason for national action on civil rights, condemning "a kind of moral dry rot which eats away at the emotional and rational bases of democratic beliefs."[175]

Both studies drew a portrait of sharp and unflattering contrast between ideals and practice in American life, especially in the country's treatment of its black citizens. Myrdal famously referred to the nation's ideals as the "American Creed," a professed commitment to liberty, equality, justice, and fair opportunity for all. At the same time, Myrdal – a foreign observer imported to give a presumably unbiased analysis – saw a nation suffering from a clash between "the consciousness of sins and the devotion to high ideals." "The Negro is a 'problem' to the average American," he contended, "partly because of a palpable conflict between the status actually awarded to him and [the nation's] ideals."[176] While Myrdal recognized the ambiguity inherent in the broad terms like "liberty" and "equality" that defined the American Creed, he maintained that their meaning for the "Negro problem" was clear: "The Creed is expressive and definite in practically all respects of importance for the Negro problem. . . . In principle the Negro problem was settled

---

[173] Gunnar Myrdal, *An American Dilemma: The Negro Problem in Modern Democracy* (New York: Harper and Bros., 1944); *To Secure These Rights: The Report of the President's Committee on Civil Rights* (Washington, DC: U.S. Government Printing Office, 1947). It is notable that the idea for an extensive social scientific study of blacks in America was first broached at the Carnegie Corporation by one of the corporation's trustees, Newton D. Baker, in 1935. At that time, Baker had just completed his service as a prominent member of the Wickersham Commission on Crime in America. Southern, *Gunnar Myrdal and Black-White Relations*, 1–2. After being importuned to do so in a September 1946 meeting with Walter White, the NAACP's executive director, and other black leaders, Truman created the Committee by Executive Order 9808, 11 Fed. Reg. 14153 (5 December 1946), thus bypassing congressional opposition to a federal spotlighting of the race problem. Truman made key parts of the Committee's recommendations part of his 1948 special message to Congress, but the legislature refused to act on the proposals. Civil Rights Program Message from the President of the United States, 80th Congress, 2nd Session (House Doc. 516) (2 February 1948).

[174] Myrdal, *American Dilemma*, xlv, xlvi, 4, 24.

[175] *To Secure These Rights*, 139.

[176] Myrdal, *American Dilemma*, 22, 23.

long ago."[177] The Truman Committee report also spoke of the chasm between ideals and practice, and the failure to meet goals.[178] In the view of both books, in the way it handled race, America was simply failing to be America.

For Myrdal and the President's Committee, as for many others, the unsettling echoes of fascism in U.S. race policies were all too apparent. *An American Dilemma* explicitly defined the American Creed as the antithesis of Nazism and totalitarian fascism.[179] The Truman Committee denounced "the totalitarian arrogance which makes one man say that he will respect another man as his equal only if he has 'my race, my religion, my political views, my social position.'"[180] The report went on to claim that the international implications of America's race policies were one of the three main reasons for reforming them (the other reasons being moral and economic).[181] In the wake of its triumph over the Axis powers, the United States was poised to assume a leadership role worldwide. The nation's race policies, however, embarrassed it before the world, undercut the respect accorded to its diplomats overseas, and made its professed ideals seem hollow. All of this rendered the country vulnerable to criticism from the communist world at a time in which it was locked in competition with that world for international preeminence. At the height of the era of American internationalism, race relations could no longer be written off as a purely parochial concern. [182]

Race, the Police, and Constitutional Criminal Procedure

A significant part of what America saw itself as standing for in the world was the rule of law and an adherence to basic standards of due process. As early as 1931, during the Hoover administration, a national commission had undertaken a study of "third-degree" police tactics and declared them to be uncivilized. But given the lack of any particular constituency for the hardcore criminal defendants likely to be subject to those tactics, especially after the repeal of Prohibition, and the financial constraints imposed by the

---

[177] Myrdal, *American Dilemma*, 24.

[178] *To Secure These Rights*, 9. While of major significance during these years, the political appeal to the contrast between American ideals and actual practice was not new in these reports, but has recurred, to more or less political affect, throughout American history. See Samuel Huntington, *American Politics: The Promise of Disharmony* (Cambridge, MA: The Belknap Press of the Harvard University Press, 1983).

[179] Myrdal, *American Dilemma*, 6.

[180] *To Secure These Rights*, 4.

[181] *To Secure These Rights*, 139.

[182] *To Secure These Rights*, 100, 110–11, 146–8. See also Mary L. Dudziak, *Cold War Civil Rights: Race and the Image of American Democracy* (Princeton: Princeton University Press, 2000); Azza Salma Layton, *International Politics and Civil Rights Policies in the United States, 1941–1960* (Cambridge: Cambridge University Press, 2000).

Great Depression, no serious reforms were forthcoming.[183] An awakening to the nature of Soviet tyranny, however, helped to rectify the prevailing public indifference to such rights. The brutality of Stalin's Moscow show trials (1936–8), chronicled for American readers in Arthur Koestler's nightmarish 1941 fictional account, *Darkness at Noon*, once again confronted many Americans – including members of the Supreme Court – with self-knowledge through antithesis.[184] Arrest without cause, beatings at the hands of authority, lack of access to a lawyer, *pro forma* trials with preordained results were exposed as a key pillar of communist totalitarian regimes. An admission that in some ways a variant of this un-American approach to justice was happening at home was bound to be more disturbing to many in an atmosphere of staunch anticommunism than in times past.

The theme of the innocent wrongly sentenced, which had fallen on deaf ears in the immediate aftermath of the Wickersham Commission Report, acquired a new resonance at this time. It became a staple of some of the era's most prominent films, which appeared in a sort of cultural trajectory, starting out with veiled references to Southern problems and culminating in an aggressive outspokenness about them. The quiet commentary began in the years following Scottsboro (but well before the 1950 ascendancy of Joseph McCarthy) with the Henry Fonda vehicle *The Ox-Bow Incident* (1942), a monitory tale based on a 1940 book by Walter Van Tilburg Clark of the mistaken lynching of an innocent man accused of cattle rustling in the most symbolically American of settings, the Old West.[185] Sydney Lumet's *Twelve*

[183] Wickersham Commission, *Lawlessness in Law Enforcement*; Calder, *Origins of Federal Crime Control Policy*, 96; Michael Klarman, "The Racial Origins of Modern Criminal Procedure, 24; Klarman, *From Jim Crow to Civil Rights*, 129–30, 155; Powe, *Warren Court*, 387.

[184] Arthur Koestler, *Darkness at Noon*, trans. Daphne Hardy (New York: Bantam Books, 1941).

[185] Clark acknowledged that his story had been fueled emotionally by the rise of Hitler and the Nazis in Germany, but insisted "that it was a kind of American Nazism that I was talking about. I had the parallel in mind, all right, but what I was most afraid of was not the German Nazis, or even the Bund, but that ever-present element in any society which can always be led to act the same way, to use authoritarian methods to oppose authoritarian methods. What I wanted to say was, 'It can happen here. It has happened here, in minor but sufficiently indicative ways, a great many times.'" Clark, quoted in conversation with Walter Prescott Webb, Afterword, Walter Van Tilburg Clark, *The Ox-Bow Incident* (New York: New American Library, 1960), 223–4. In a 1954 essay in the *Partisan Review* (the year, of course, of the Supreme Court's decision in *Brown v. Board of Education*), Robert Warshow wrote: "In *The Virginian* [1929], which is an archetypal western movie . . . there is a lynching in which the hero (Gary Cooper), as leader of a posse, must supervise the hanging of his best friend for stealing cattle. With the growth of American 'social consciousness,' it is no longer possible to present a lynching in the movies unless the point is the illegality and injustice of the lynching itself; *The Ox-Bow Incident*, made in 1943, explicitly puts forward the newer point of view and can be regarded as a kind of 'anti-western.' But in 1929, when *The Virginian* was made, the present inhibition about lynching was not yet in force; the justice, and therefore the necessity, of the hanging is never questioned – except by the schoolteacher from the East,

Angry Men (1957), which also starred Henry Fonda (who later, and not coincidentally, starred in *Gideon's Trumpet*, a dramatization of the Warren Court's 1963 criminal procedure landmark *Gideon v. Wainwright*) followed the deliberation of a contemporary jury in New York City as a group of white men, influenced in part by racial prejudice against Puerto Ricans, came perilously close to convicting the wrong man for murder.[186] Finally, in 1963, Hollywood confronted racist Southern justice directly in the film version of Harper Lee's *To Kill a Mockingbird*, with Gregory Peck starring as Atticus Finch, a small-town Southern lawyer who takes on, and ultimately loses, the case of a black man wrongly accused of rape. These widely seen films were a sign of the public's increasing willingness to confront head-on the barbarities of a racist system of crime and punishment.

Here the pro–criminal process rights currents of anticommunism and antiracism joined with each other. Civil rights activists added a new dimension to this relation by strategically playing upon the dynamics of the nation's twilight struggle against the homicidal, totalitarian, and expansionist Soviet Union. As these activists aggressively insisted, American racism put the nation at a distinct disadvantage in winning the hearts and minds of the inhabitants of third world countries – for which America went toe-to-toe with the Soviet Union during the long course of the Cold War. The presence of racial injustice at home, moreover, became one of the chief recruiting points of the Communist Party (commonly known as CPUSA), the domestic political party run secretly by Moscow, and a nest of domestic espionage. (The Rosenberg's opposition to racial discrimination is one of the reasons that despite their work on behalf of totalitarian mass murderers, they were – and, to many, remain – heroes of the American Left.) In addition, the treatment of American blacks, particularly in criminal trials in the South, could not help but bring to mind images of Soviet justice. Thus, a dynamic that had its origins in domestic demographic and political developments that

---

whose refusal to understand serves . . . to set forth more sharply the deeper seriousness of the West. . . ." Robert Warshow, "Movie Chronicle: The Westerner," *Partisan Review* (March–April 1954), reprinted in Warshow, *The Immediate Experience: Movies, Comics, Theatre and Other Aspects of Popular Culture* (Cambridge, MA: Harvard University Press, 2001), 105–24, esp. 112. See also Klinkner and Smith, *The Unsteady March*, 185.

[186] *Gideon v. Wainwright*, 372 U.S. 335 (1963) (holding that the Sixth and Fourteenth Amendments guaranteed indigent defendants the right to court-appointed counsel when charged with serious criminal offenses in state courts). The film was based on a best-selling recounting of the case by Anthony Lewis. Anthony Lewis, *Gideon's Trumpet* (New York: Random House, 1964). On Fonda as a "representative [figure] who help[ed] citizens to construct, through mass-mediated imagery their nation's constitutional culture," see Norman Rosenberg, "Constitutional History and the 'Cultural Turn': Cross-Examining the Legal Realist Narratives of Henry Fonda," in *Constitutionalism and American Culture: Writing the New Constitutional History*, eds. Sandra F. Van Burkleo, Kermit Hall, and Robert Kaczorowski (Lawrence: University Press of Kansas, 2002), 381–409.

opened new opportunities for domestic political activism and had been reinforced by the ideological imperatives of World War II was further energized
by the ongoing politics of the Cold War.[187]

In this context, issues of guaranteeing fair criminal process protections
nationwide assumed a new and major political prominence in a way it had
not since the demise of Prohibition. Four full chapters of Myrdal's *American
Dilemma* were devoted to the problem of blacks and criminal justice. After casual and economic contacts, the author listed criminal contacts as the
third most important field of black-white relationships. These contacts led
whites, in many ways unfairly, to view blacks as a largely criminal class.
For their part, however, blacks saw and resented a strong pattern of "prejudiced treatment from the police and the courts."[188] Myrdal's social scientific
tome, which ended up before a mass audience, stripped away the myths and
revealed the self-fulfilling nature of the characteristic white view of crime.
It also documented and lent authoritative (white) voice to the truthfulness
of previously ignored black plaints. Ultimately, Myrdal proposed a specific
criminal justice corollary to his American Creed, the now unremarkable assertion that "Negroes are entitled to justice equally with all other people;"

[187] See *Smith v. Allwright*, 321 U.S. 649 (1944); Michael J. Klarman, "The White Primary
Rulings: A Case Study in the Consequences of Supreme Court Decisionmaking," *Florida
State University Law Review* 29 (October 2001) 55–107; Klarman, *From Jim Crow to Civil
Rights*, 182–4, 219, 291, 299–300, 375–96; Doug McAdam, *Political Process and the De-
velopment of Black Insurgency*, 1930–1970 (Chicago: University of Chicago Press, 1982);
Dennis Chong, *Collective Action and the Civil Rights Movement* (Chicago: University of
Chicago Press, 1991); Richard Primus, "A Brooding Omnipresence: Totalitarianism in Post-
War Constitutional Thought," *Yale Law Journal* 106 (November 1996): 423–57; Richard
Primus, *The American Language of Rights* (Cambridge, MA: Cambridge University Press,
1999); Kryder, *Divided Arsenal*; Skrentny, *Minority Rights Revolution*, 27–37. The role of
Cold War politics in spurring on Truman-era civil rights politics has long been known.
See, e.g., Berman, *The Politics of Civil Rights in the Truman Administration*, 63–7; Donald
R. McCoy and Richard T. Reutten, *Quest and Response: Minority Rights in the Truman Ad-
ministration* (Lawrence: University Press of Kansas, 1973); Southern, *Gunnar Myrdal and
Black-White Relations*, 102; Robert Cushman, "Our Civil Rights Become a World Issue,"
New York Times Magazine, 11 January 1948. Perhaps because of the increasing interest of
politically progressive contemporary academics in using transnational bureaucracies and
social movements to change domestic public policy, there has recently been a revival in
scholarly interest in this dynamic. See, e.g., Dudziak, *Cold War Civil Rights*; Layton, *Inter-
national Politics and Civil Rights Policies*; Thomas Borstelmann, *The Cold War and the Color
Line: American Race Relations in the Global Arena* (Cambridge, MA: Harvard University
Press, 2001); Carol Anderson, *Eyes off the Prize: The United Nations and the African American Struggle for Human Rights, 1944–1955* (New York: Cambridge University Press, 2003);
Plumer, *Rising Wind*, 167–216; Klinkner and Smith, *Unsteady March*, 202–41. See also James
A. Miller, Susan D. Pennybacker, and Eve Rosenhaft, "Mother Ada Wright and the Inter-
national Campaign to Free the Scottsboro Boys, 1931–1934," *American Historical Review*
106 (April 2001): 387–403.

[188] Myrdal, *American Dilemma*, 979, 655.

that is, that justice should be administered impartially without regard to race, creed, or color.[189]

An American Dilemma identified local police forces as a leading cause of racial problems. Brutality, arbitrary arrest, coerced confessions, and private punishment, Myrdal told the nation, were common practices that took place right here on American soil, typically when black suspects (and frequently innocent ones) were involved. The situation may have been invisible to most Americans, Myrdal explained, because the degree of police misconduct varied by region. Myrdal found a "sharp division" between the behavior of police officers in the North and those in the South.[190] In the North, blacks got a rough approximation of legal justice. The South, however, was another country. There, Myrdal found "a strange atmosphere of consistent illegality around the activity of the officers of the peace and the whole judicial system in the South."[191] Repeating the patterns of slavery times, the white Southern policeman, "a crucial and strategic factor in race relations," acted as an agent of white planters and employers to enforce black obedience. As part of a system of social subordination, the Southern policeman not only arrested but also summarily sentenced and punished blacks, commonly without the trouble of a trial.[192]

This lawless lawman was a brutal menace, a poorly trained and ill-educated white man of low social status, taught from an early age to despise Negroes. The chief way this man rose in the world was by carrying a gun and wielding the power that came with it. He was, in short, a "weak man with ... strong weapons,"[193] who, like Polyphemus, lorded over any exit from the dank cave of Southern racial subordination: "As far as the cultural and social adjustment of the Negroes is concerned," Myrdal concluded, "the Southern police system is undoing much of what Northern philanthropy and

---

[189] Myrdal, *American Dilemma*, 525. The mistreatment of blacks at the hands of Southern police had not gone unnoted by experts in earlier times. But when it was noted it was only in passing. Only later did it vault to the center of national consciousness. See, e.g., Edwin H. Sutherland, *Criminology* (Philadelphia: J. B. Lippincott Co., 1924), 190 (citing fee system for payment of police officers leading to arrest of the innocent and helpless: "[P]articular instances of this are reported from some of the southern states where the negroes are the victims, but the practice prevails, also, in other sections"). Michael Klarman has argued that some judges, even in the South, were disturbed by this treatment, although the threshold of acceptibility remained decidedly different in North and South. Southern courts sometimes policed the more egregious instances of mistreatment, but became resistant to doing so when Southern practices were challenged from outside the region in the post–World War I era. In any case, there was little significant attention to, or improvement of, these matters at that time. Klarman, "Racial Origins of Modern Criminal Procedure," 3; Klarman, *From Jim Crow to Civil Rights*, 117–35.

[190] Myrdal, *American Dilemma*, 528–9.

[191] Myrdal, *American Dilemma*, 536.

[192] Myrdal, *American Dilemma*, 544.

[193] Myrdal, *American Dilemma*, 538–41, esp. 540.

Southern state governments are trying to accomplish through education and by other means."[194]

President Truman's Committee on Civil Rights, which was modeled on the Prohibition-era Wickersham Commission and directly and heavily influenced by *An American Dilemma*, saw the situation in a similar light and devoted a section of its final report to police brutality, citing violent physical assaults by policemen on suspects, the widespread use of third-degree tactics to extort confessions, abuse of search and seizure powers, prolonged detention, unwarranted and arbitrary arrests, and even complicity with lynch mobs. The Truman Committee report, moreover, found that these departures from lawfulness were markedly higher in cases involving blacks, especially in the South. While it devoted most of its attention to the racial aspects of renegade police forces, the Truman Committee, however, went beyond *An American Dilemma* in generalizing its claims: "In one place the brunt of illegal police activity may fall on suspected vagrants, in another on union organizers, in another on unpopular racial and religious minorities, such as Negroes, Mexicans, or Jehovah's Witnesses. Unpopular, weak, or defenseless groups," the Committee concluded, "are most apt to suffer."[195]

While both of the reports identified Southern police forces as the most vexing problem, they also recognized that blacks were hardly guaranteed equal justice simply by having survived the ordeal of the squad car and making it to the courthouse steps. From his interviews with Southern blacks, Myrdal discovered that many of them viewed the courthouse less as a public institution than as the personal property of local white folks.[196] Their reasons for this were both concrete and legion: Punishment was meted out unequally on the basis of the relative races of perpetrator and victim; black criminal guilt was frequently presumed, leading to convictions on flimsy evidence after irregular trials; black defendants faced juries from which those of their race had been meticulously weeded out; and the bail and bond system was wielded as a racial weapon. Moreover, blacks, like other poor defendants, were typically forced to run this frightening racist gauntlet alone, without the assistance of competent counsel.[197] The conclusion was ineluctable: "This whole judicial system of courts, sentences, and prisons in the South is over-ripe for fundamental reforms. It represents a tremendous cultural lag in progressive twentieth-century America. Reform in this field – especially in

---

[194] Myrdal, *American Dilemma*, 540.
[195] *To Secure These Rights*, 25–7, 115–28, 155–7. On the Myrdal's influence on the Truman Committee report, see Southern, *Gunnar Myrdal and Black-White Relations*, 114–88. Truman formed the committee as competition for black votes was heating up, and in the wake of the Democratic Party's massive losses in the 1946 congressional elections. On the political dynamics leading to the formation of the commission, see Berman, *Politics of Civil Rights in the Truman Administration*, 54–5, 57.
[196] Myrdal, *American Dilemma*, 537.
[197] Myrdal, *American Dilemma*, 548–54. See also *To Secure These Rights*, 27–9.

the courts – would be strategic in the efforts to improve the Negro people and their living conditions and, consequently, to improve race relations."[198] "[I]n principle," Myrdal announced, "the average white Southerner is no longer prepared to defend racial inequality of justice.... [I]t is in the interest of society" – and not just blacks – "to care for the Negro – and even for the criminal Negro."[199]

The Criminal Procedure Reform Imperative and the Problem of Democracy

Regime-sustaining Whiggish constitutional narratives typically characterize the Warren Court's assault on injustice in the criminal justice system as simultaneous triumphs for principles of liberty, equality, justice, and democracy.[200] As we have seen, however, when actually in the thick of a reformist fight, reformers have been more forthright about the tensions and tragic choices that typically characterize the most ambitious reformist projects. This was also the case with regard to national, court-led criminal process reform. Indeed, in *An American Dilemma*, Gunnar Myrdal himself identified an excess of democracy as a *barrier* to reform in this area – as an obstacle that needed to be overcome.

Myrdal explained this position at length in his opening chapter on the administration of criminal justice in the South. As he understood it, the problem was specifically one of police forces, prosecutorial teams, and a judiciary that was too close to the people. All were more politicized in the South than elsewhere, meaning that all were more likely to be staffed by officials who were popularly elected on the basis of frequent electoral campaigns. The problem with the police was that they were not sufficiently professionalized, not removed enough from popular control to do what Myrdal, and most of us, would consider to be right.[201] For this reason, Myrdal in *An American Dilemma* felt it necessary to oppose a new notion of democracy to the old one and to do so without denying the claims to authority of the older definition. "The *extreme democracy* in the American system of justice," he wrote, "turns out... to be the greatest menace to *legal democracy*," especially when it is "based on the restricted political participation [of blacks] and an ingrained tradition of caste suppression."[202]

Creating a "legal democracy," as Myrdal set out to do, however, was actually to mitigate the claims of democracy by placing greater emphasis on issues of constructing the rule of law, a task properly accounted as a dimension of liberalism. Liberalism and democracy, of course, are different

---

[198] Myrdal, *American Dilemma*, 555.
[199] Myrdal, *American Dilemma*, 556.
[200] See, e.g., Morton J. Horwitz, *The Warren Court and the Pursuit of Justice: A Critical Issue* (New York: Hill and Wang, 1998).
[201] Myrdal, *American Dilemma*, ch. 24. See also *To Secure These Rights*, 19, 155–7.
[202] Myrdal, *American Dilemma*, 524 (emphasis added).

matters, with the former dealing with the reach of sovereign power and the other with its source. The two need not go together and, in Myrdal's view, the treatment of blacks in the South by the police is a good example of a case where clearly they did not: The liberal principal of the rule of law, impartially administered, is threatened by an administration of justice that he has deemed excessively democratic.

In one limited sense, Myrdal in *An American Dilemma* is advocating more democracy in the South. Plainly, he believed that part of the solution to the race problem involved ensuring unhindered black access to the ballot and the jury boxes, thus adding an element of equality to the democratic process. But Myrdal's language suggests that he hardly considered this sufficient. What Myrdal has christened "legal democracy" and we imprecisely might call a commitment to "democratic values" is actually a commitment to liberal values – administered by enlightened professionalized elites.

This became clearer in Myrdal's discussion of the relationship between constitutionalism and legal formalism and racial justice. The relationship sketched by Myrdal was highly paradoxical because, for him, the creation of legal democracy – rule-of-law liberalism – involved the jettisoning of any overly scrupulous commitment one might have to a constitutionalism that was formally rigorous. As far as the reform of criminal justice in the South was concerned, the constitutional rule of law, strictly speaking, needed to be set aside. At least in this context, constitutionalism and legalism were more the problem than the solution.

"The worship of the Constitution," Myrdal told his readers near the outset of his book, "is a most flagrant violation of the American Creed which, as far as the technical arrangements for executing the power of the people are concerned, is strongly opposed to stiff formulas."[203] Echoing the then familiar arguments of Charles Beard and J. Allen Smith, Myrdal went on to condemn both the Constitutional Convention as "nearly a plot against the common people" and the nation more generally for its habitual adherence to the letter rather than the spirit of the law.[204]

One might take this as a simple reiteration of the Progressive historian's view married to the changing constitution formulation first advanced by Chief Justice Marshall in *McCulloch v. Maryland* (1819) and given new life by the New Deal Court – were it not for Myrdal's oddly backward ending to his articulation of a vision of the Constitution as unwarranted obstacle. "[T]he 150-year-old Constitution," he contends, "is in many respects impractical and ill-suited for modern conditions and . . . furthermore, the drafters of the document made it technically difficult to change *even if there were no popular*

---

[203] Myrdal, *American Dilemma*, 12–13.
[204] Myrdal, *American Dilemma*, 13, 18. See J. Allen Smith, *The Spirit of American Government: A Study of the Constitution, Its Origin, Influence, and Relation to Democracy* (New York: Macmillan, 1912).

feelings against change."[205] The last part of the sentence suggests not that the Constitution is being used to block popular change as in the Progressive view, but instead that proper change advocated in the name of progress and "democracy," though clearly not accompanied by a popular groundswell or demand, is being thwarted even though no one is mobilizing *against it*. In other words, a traditional progressive would have substituted the words "even if there were popular feelings for it" for Myrdal's quite different ending. This small shift in terminology is an early indication of the transformation from the claims of New Deal to Warren Court constitutionalism in response to a new set of social problems.

Prompted by the problem of the treatment of Southern blacks, Myrdal reformulated the term "democracy" so that it harmonized with rule-of-law liberalism – the perceived imperative – within the relevant policy areas. In doing so, he wrote out of the story both the rule-of-law problems raised by his assault on constitutionalism and the loss of the people's traditional (majority rule) democratic powers, which his new direction entailed.

Myrdal's ideological reconstruction of civil libertarian progress adumbrated the path that would be taken by both legal liberal jurisprudential thought and the U.S. Supreme Court a decade later. An immersion in the race problem had led Myrdal to the conviction that national leadership elites had to take policy steps toward a solution in the spirit of the American Creed and that those steps would define our Constitution, that is, who we are as a nation. Our meaning, in other words, would be defined by the Creed and not by the text. "The Supreme Court," he explains, "pays its reverence to [the American Creed] when it declares what is constitutional and what is not."[206] More importantly, the Court should take these steps in the absence of popular outcry against these steps. In short, the Court should be an aggressive policy leader, much in the way that a relatively insulated central state bureaucratic agency would act as an instrument of state policy: It should proceed forward in the absence of opposition rather than in line with the prevailing democratic views of the populace. This is hardly popular democracy as we have known it. Legal democracy was on the verge of assuming its place as an instrument of statebuilding and as the new coin of the constitutional realm.[207]

---

[205] Myrdal, *American Dilemma*, 12 (emphasis added).

[206] Myrdal, *American Dilemma*, 4.

[207] Myrdal's criticism of the conduct of Southern police forces was brought to the attention of the legal community in a review of the book in the *Harvard Law Review* by Charles Wyzanski Jr. As early as the late 1940s, the critique of police practices made in *An American Dilemma* began to influence police conduct, at least in the northern and western United States. Police departments in Boston, Cincinnati, Chicago, and (statewide) in California were all tutored on Myrdal's findings concerning police practices vis-à-vis African Americans and trained to steer their behavior in more approved directions. Most police departments, however, did not receive this training, and Southern police forces remained a particular problem. Charles E. Wyzanski Jr., "Book Review: An American Dilemma," *Harvard Law Review* 58 (1944): 285–91; Southern, *Gunnar Myrdal and Black-White Relations*, 110, 128.

While Myrdal's report contributed to the construction of the ideological underpinning of modern legal liberalism and the allied activist civil liberties jurisprudence of the Warren Court, the Truman Committee provided the Court, as well as the legislative and executive branches, with a more serviceable blueprint for action. *An American Dilemma* paved the way for changes in the spirit of the law and the Truman Committee for developments in its letter.

It was not likely, after all, that the Court, the key legitimating institution of the American central state, would follow Myrdal in dismissing the written Constitution as "impractical and ill-suited to modern conditions," or as "a plot against the common people," or that it would unmask American veneration of the document as "a most flagrant violation of the American Creed." The President's Committee on Civil Rights argued that a vigorous national legislative program to advance civil rights would, despite aberrant and antiquated High Court rulings suggesting otherwise, now be upheld as a constitutionally legitimate exercise of national power. Following the obligatory citation to John Marshall's notion of a living Constitution, the Truman Committee backed up its claims with specific textual citations. Among them were the Civil War Amendments, including the due process, equal protection, and privileges and immunities clauses of the Fourteenth Amendment, the power to regulate interstate commerce, and the taxing and spending powers, all of which would soon become part of the legal foundation of the Warren Court Rights Revolution. The report, in short, clothed Myrdal's Creedal constitutionalism with the language of the constitutional text. The stage was set for, among other things, a populist-spirited, elite-driven, and professionally administered revolution in the constitutional rules of criminal procedure.

Alternative Paths: International Human Rights Standards or the Constitution?

At mid-century, the antiracist reform imperative grew so strong and its proponents grew so frustrated by the remaining institutional barriers to reform that lawyers, judges, political activists, and legal academics began to cast about for novel means of accomplishing their reforms in ways that had some pretense to constitutional legitimacy. One potential path to constitutional revolution on behalf of blacks that was seriously considered but ultimately not taken was the tenth on the Truman Committee's list: the "Power derived from the treaty clause in Article II, Section 2 of the Constitution, to protect civil rights which acquire a treaty status."[208] Article II gives the president the right to bind the nation by treaty, provided he has the consent of

---

[208] *To Secure These Rights*, 110. This road-not-taken is of special interest today, as lawyers, judges, and others interested in contemporary criminal process and civil rights reform (as well as reform in other areas) are moving toward following a similar path. For a fuller discussion, see this book's concluding chapter.

two-thirds of the Senate for any such agreement. When read in conjunction with the Supremacy Clause of Article VI, making treaties (along with the Constitution and the laws of the United States) the supreme law of the land, Article II presented a powerful route to legal legitimacy for a civil rights and criminal process revolution.

The Truman Committee's suggestion that the treaty power might serve the cause of civil rights had special purchase in the immediate postwar era.[209] During the mid- to late 1940s, the United States had participated in a wave of international lawmaking that many Americans knew could have sweeping domestic consequences. As a response to racist totalitarianism, much of this lawmaking set foundational standards for the new, apolitical, and world-wide category of "human rights." Signatories to the treaties, and support-ers of the declarations and covenants pledged themselves to be measured – certainly morally, and perhaps legally – by these new standards.[210] Four of these international agreements in particular – the United Nations Charter (1945), the Universal Declaration of Human Rights (1948), the Covenant on the Prevention and Punishment of the Crime of Genocide (1948), and the Proposed Covenant on Human Rights (1948) – could prove relevant domes-tically, both to matters of policy and to questions of constitutional law.

The agreement with the surest legal reach was the U.N. Charter, which, unlike the other three, the United States Senate had officially ratified as a treaty.[211] The charter's preamble opened with a reaffirmation of a "faith in fundamental human rights, in the dignity and worth of the human per-son, [and] in the equal rights of men and women." The articles with the most potential to transform civil rights law in the United States, however,

---

[209] As the Truman Committee noted, moreover, such a path to change could be anchored in more than just the constitutional text. The Supreme Court in its 1920 decision in *Missouri v. Holland* had put its imprimatur on a potent reading of the treaty power. *Missouri v. Holland*, 252 U.S. 416 (1920). The *Holland* case arose when the state of Missouri sought an injunction against a U.S. game warden in the state who was charged with enforcing federal antihunting regulations made pursuant to the Migratory Bird Treaty Act of 1918. That Act had been passed by Congress to implement a treaty between the United States and Great Britain for the protection of migratory birds crossing the United States on their way to and from Canada. Citing earlier lower-court decisions on a similar law passed without the authority of a treaty, Missouri challenged the Migratory Bird Treaty Act on the grounds that states had sovereign authority over the birds within their borders and that, consequently, the Act was a violation of the Tenth Amendment, which reserves all undelegated powers under the Constitution to the states or to the people. In his opinion for the Court's 7–2 majority, Justice Holmes read Article II, Section 2; Article VI; and the necessary and proper clause of Article I, Section 8 together to reject the state's claims and hold that the power to make treaties was a delegated national power and that treaties were without qualification the law of the land and, as such, superseded any contrary state laws.

[210] A leading student of international law, Louis Henkin, has characterized these standards as rhetorical rather than philosophical and as having been imposed on a prostrate world, without a political hashing out, by diplomatic and political elites. Louis Henkin, *The Age of Rights* (New York: Columbia University Press, 1990).

[211] Charter of the United Nations, 59 Stat. 1031, T.S. 993, 3 Bevens 1153 (26 June 1945).

were Articles fifty-five and fifty-six – both of which were cited in full by the President's Committee on Civil Rights.[212]

Article fifty-five of the U.N. Charter provided:

With a view to the creation of conditions of stability and well being which are necessary for peaceful and friendly relations among nations based on respect for the principle of equal rights and self-determination of peoples, the United Nations shall promote:

 a. higher standards of living, full employment and conditions of economic and social progress and development;
 b. solutions of international economic, social, health, and related problems; and international cultural and educational cooperation; and
 c. universal respect for, and observance of, human rights and fundamental freedoms for all without distinction as to race, sex, language, or religion.

Article fifty-six added:

All Members pledge themselves to take joint and separate action in cooperation with the Organization for the achievement of the purposes set forth in Article 55.

Unlike the U.N. Charter, the Universal Declaration of Human Rights was not a treaty but a formal proclamation made by the members of the U.N. General Assembly, including the U.S.[213] It comprised thirty articles and reads very much like a compendious Bill of Rights, with Article Two proclaiming: "Everyone is entitled to all the rights and freedoms set forth in this declaration, without discrimination of any kind, such as race, colour, sex, language, religion, political or other opinion, national or social origin, property, birth, or other status." The declaration's stated guarantees are many, including rights to privacy, honor and reputation, marriage, property, thought, conscience, religion, opinion, expression, emigration, asylum, nationality, assembly, association, equal suffrage, equal pay for equal work, just and favorable remuneration, rest and leisure, an acceptable standard of living, education, and the right to freely participate in cultural life, enjoy the arts, and share in scientific advancement. Articles Five through Eleven announce universal rights for criminal defendants, including the right to equal protection of the law; to a presumption of innocence; and to not be subjected to torture or to cruel, inhuman, or degrading treatment or punishment or arbitrary arrest or detention. Moreover, signatories to the declaration specifically pledged themselves in Article Eight to having a national judicial tribunal act effectively to vindicate the violation of any fundamental rights guaranteed to people by the Constitution or by law.

The Covenant on the Prevention and Punishment of the Crime of Genocide was adopted by the General Assembly a day before the Universal

---

[212] *To Secure These Rights*, 111.
[213] United Nations General Assembly Resolution 217 (10 December 1948).

Declaration of Human Rights, although U.S. ratification of the genocide agreement was slow in coming.[214] The genocide agreement pledged its signatory countries to prohibit not only national, ethnic, racial, or religious killings or the infliction of serious bodily harm, but also bringing about serious "mental harm" to a member of a persecuted group. During the same fecund year of 1948, with the assistance of Eleanor Roosevelt, the U.N. began work on a binding Covenant on Human Rights that would make many of the protections outlined in the Universal Declaration of Human Rights enforceable under the terms of international law.[215]

The potential effect of foundationalist internationalist antiracism on American law became apparent in American courts almost immediately. In the decade between the end of World War II and the mid-1950s, judges in constitutional civil rights cases were simultaneously bombarded with *amicus* brief citations to Myrdal's *American Dilemma* and to the U.N. Charter and other prominent international agreements.[216] It was not long before law professors inclined toward civil rights began to pick up on the suggestion of the Truman Commission – and the demands of civil rights movement advocates – and to argue with considerable stridency that the U.N. Charter was now a legally binding part of the American Constitution.[217]

Despite the fact that the U.N. Charter was cited in a "substantial number of cases" in the postwar period, the Supreme Court itself invoked the charter specifically in only one: *Oyama v. California* (1948). In that case, however, it did so prominently. *Oyama* involved a constitutional challenge to California's Alien Land Law, which prohibited aliens ineligible for American citizenship from owning, occupying, leasing, or transferring agricultural

---

[214] 78 U.N.T.S. 277 (9 December 1948); 28 I.L.M 789 (1989). The United States ratified the Genocide Convention only in 1988, and then only with stated reservations.

[215] See, generally, Mary Ann Glendon, *A World Made New: Eleanor Roosevelt and the Universal Declaration of Human Rights* (New York: Random House, 2001).

[216] On Myrdal in the Supreme Court, see Southern, *Gunnar Myrdal and Black-White Relations*, 127–50. On appeals to international agreements in American courts during precisely the same period, see Bert B. Lockwood Jr., "The United Nations Charter and United States Civil Rights Litigation: 1946–1955," *Iowa Law Review* 69 (1983–4): 901–56. Layton, *International Politics and Civil Rights Policies*, 111–18. Myrdal himself prophesied that international developments would help advance the domestic interests of black Americans. Myrdal, *American Dilemma*, 426, 998, 1,004–9, 1,013–23.

[217] See Paul Sayre, "*Shelley v. Kraemer* and United Nations Law," *Iowa Law Review* 34 (1948): 1–11, esp. 3; Lockwood, "United Nations Charter," 916–17. The U.N. Human Rights Commission was formed in 1946. In 1947, the NAACP, under the direction of W. E. B. DuBois, Milton Konvitz, Earl Dickerson, and others filed An Appeal to the World with that Commission detailing the mistreatment of American blacks. On this and other movement appeals to the United Nations at the time, see Reutten and McCoy, *Quest and Response*, 67–8; Berman, *Politics of Civil Rights in the Truman Administration*, 65–6; Dudziak, *Cold War Civil Rights*, 11–12, 43–5, 63; Plummer, *Rising Wind*, 178–85; Klarman, *From Jim Crow to Civil Rights*, 183–84, 213.

land.[218] In that case, a son, a U.S. citizen, who had received a parcel of such land from his father, who was an unnaturalizable Japanese citizen, alleged that the escheat of the land to the state after the land transfer was invalidated was a violation of the privileges he was entitled to as a citizen, as well as his right to the equal protection of the laws. The father also challenged the escheat on equal protection, due process, and takings grounds.[219]

The Supreme Court in *Oyama* held that California's Alien Land Law deprived the son of the privileges to which he was entitled as a citizen as well as violated his equal protection rights. Of particular interest, however, was part of Justice Black's concurrence, joined by Justice William O. Douglas. There, Black expressed his agreement with the grounds for the Court's majority opinion. But at the same time, he expressed his view that the opinion had not gone far enough:

There are additional reasons now why [the Alien Land Law] stands as an obstacle to the free accomplishment of our policy in the international field. One of these reasons is that we have recently pledged ourselves to cooperate with the United Nations to "promote . . . universal respect for, and observance of, human rights and fundamental freedoms for all without distinction as to race, sex, language, or religion." How can this nation be faithful to this international pledge if state laws which bar land ownership and occupancy by aliens on account of race are permitted to be enforced?[220]

Black then cited Articles 55(c) and 56 of the U.N. Charter as well as the ratifying statute passed by Congress.

Justice Frank Murphy, in his concurrence in the *Oyama* case (joined by Justice Wiley Rutledge), advanced similar views. Murphy was troubled by the international implications of California's law, and he declared that the statute "has been more than a local regulation of internal affairs. It has overflowed into the realm of foreign policy; it has had direct and unfortunate consequences on this country's relations with Japan."[221]

Murphy continued:

Moreover, this nation has recently pledged itself, through the United Nations Charter, to promote respect for, and observance of, human rights and fundamental freedoms for all without distinction as to race, sex, language and religion. The Alien Land Law stands as a barrier to the fulfillment of that national pledge. Its inconsistency with

---

[218] *Oyama v. California*, 332 U.S. 633 (1948). Lockwood, "United Nations Charter and Civil Rights," 917. The purported relevance of the charter had been called to the Court's attention in the briefs submitted by the petitioner and by the ACLU.

[219] The "takings clause" of the Fifth Amendment provides "nor shall private property be taken for public use without just compensation." U.S. Constitution, Fifth Amendment. This provision has been applied as a restriction on the states via the due process clause of the Fourteenth Amendment.

[220] *Oyama*, 332 U.S. at 649–50.

[221] *Oyama*, 332 U.S. at 672–3.

the Charter, which has been duly ratified and adopted by the United States, is but one more reason why the statute must be condemned.[222]

The law, Murphy wrote, "does violence to the high ideals of the Constitution of the United States and the Charter of the United Nations."[223] That four of the nine justices on the Court cited the U.N. Charter was no small event. It was not long before litigants in some cases involving racial discrimination in the South began making strategic use of what four members of the Court had signaled as a newly opening path of constitutional development concerning civil rights and civil liberties, proffering legal arguments in court appealing in part on the dictates of the U.N. Charter.[224]

Perhaps the high watermark in judicial recognition of the legal authority of international human rights standards occurred in a middle-level appeals court decision in California in the *Sei Fujii* case, which became a constitutional *cause célèbre* in the early 1950s, and which one commentator has described as "the legal shot heard around the nation.[225] *Sei Fujii* involved a challenge to the part of California's Alien Land Law still standing in the wake of the *Oyama* decision – the part involving the rights of the non-naturalizable alien to own land. Perhaps feeling constrained because the U.S. Supreme Court

---

[222] *Oyama*, 332 U.S. at 673.

[223] *Oyama*, 332 U.S. at 673.

[224] See *Shelley v. Kraemer*, 334 U.S. 1 (1948); *Hurd v. Hodge*, 334 U.S. 24, 28, n. 4 (1948) (restrictive covenants); *Hurd v. Hodge*, 162 F.2d 233 (D.C. Cir. 1947); *Boyer v. Garrett*, 183 F.2d 582 (4th Cir. 1950) (segregation of public parks and playgrounds in Baltimore); *Sweatt v. Painter*, 339 U.S. 629 (1950); *Rochin v. California*, 342 U.S. 165 (1952). For a comprehensive accounting of appeals to the U.N. Charter in Supreme Court civil rights cases of the time, see Lockwood, "United Nations Charter and Civil Rights." In a different context, Chief Justice Vinson, writing for himself and Justices Stanley Reed and Sherman Minton, cited America's obligation under the U.N. Charter to preserve international peace and security, as part of his dissent from the Court's invalidation of President Truman's seizure of the nation's steel mills during the Korean War. *Youngstown Sheet and Tube Co. v. Sawyer*, 343 U.S. 579, 668–9 (1952).

[225] *Sei Fujii v. California*, 217 P.2d 481 (District Court of Appeal, Second District, Division 2, California, 1950). Lockwood, "United Nations Charter and Civil Rights," 925. Lockwood adds that "[p]erhaps no other decision of a state appellate court received as much attention in the legal periodicals" and provides an extensive overview of that commentary. The following *Sei Fujii* case notes are referenced: *New York University Law Review* 25 (1950): 924–32; *Virginia Law Review* 36 (1950): 804–6; *North Dakota Law Review* 27 (1951): 56; *Texas Law Review* 29 (1950): 263–5; *Minnesota Law Review* 35 (1951): 333–8; *Washington University Law Quarterly* (1951): 117–24; *West Virginia Law Review* 53 (1951): 79–82; *Georgia Bar Journal* 13 (1950): 110; *Mercer Law Review* 2 (1950): 276; *Miami Law Quarterly* 5 (1951): 333; *Notre Dame Law Review* 26 (1950): 137–42; *Tulane Law Review* 25 (1950): 117–19; See also Oscar Schacter, "The Charter and the Constitution: The Human Rights Provisions of American Law," *Vanderbilt Law Review* 4 (1951): 643–59; Comment, "The Application of the United Nations Charter to Domestic Law," *Fordham Law Review* 20 (1951): 91–7; Wright, "National Courts and Human Rights – the *Fujii* Case," *American Journal of International Law* 45 (1951): 62–82.

had specifically upheld such legislation in cases such as *Terrace v. Thompson* (1923), in the *Sei Fujii* case, the California court cited the U.N. Charter not as one of many grounds for its decision striking down the law, but as legally decisive.[226] The U.N. Charter, the court declared, was self-executing. As the supreme law of the land, "every state in the Union [was obligated to] accept and act upon the Charter according to its plain language and its unmistakable purpose and intent."[227] The court then proceeded to do just that, parsing the language of the U.N. Charter (and the Universal Declaration of Human Rights as well) at length as if the words were from American statutes.

The judicial flirtation with treaties and international human rights agreements in the immediate postwar years occasioned a swift and serious political response, which ultimately led to a sustained attempt to root out the problem at its source by amending the Constitution to overturn *Missouri v. Holland* (1920). A Pulitzer Prize in journalism (1951) was awarded to a series of articles calling for such an amendment. The *American Bar Association Journal* published an aggressive series of articles taking a similar line. And the following year, the American Bar Association House of Delegates signed on to the campaign for a constitutional amendment to restrict the application of treaties within domestic law. Although it went through many forms, the core of the amendment proposed in 1951 by Senator John Bricker, Republican of Ohio, ensured that a "treaty shall become effective as internal law in the United States only through legislation which would be valid in the absence of the treaty."[228]

Politicians, groups, and individuals backed the Bricker Amendment for a variety of reasons, including apprehensions of runaway executive power in the wake of Yalta and Potsdam, as well as fear of bootstrapped policymaking via treaties in areas such as labor law and the provision of medical care. But foremost in the mind of Southern supporters of the amendment was the threat that the United Nations and other international agreements posed to the autonomy of the Southern states in their regulation of race relations.[229]

---

[226] *Terrace v. Thompson*, 263 U.S. 197 (1923).

[227] *Sei Fujii*, 217 P.2d at 486. See also *Namba v. McCourt*, 185 Or. 579, 204 P.2d 569 (1949).

[228] Arthur E. Sutherland Jr., "Restricting the Treaty Power," *Harvard Law Review* 65 (1951–2): 1305. Sutherland cites the following articles from the *A.B.A. Journal*: Duetsch, "The Treaty Making Clause: A Decision for the People of America," *A.B.A. Journal* 37 (1951): 659; Fleming, "Danger to America: The Draft Convention on Human Rights," *A.B.A. Journal* 37 (1951): 739, 816; Ober, "The Treaty-Making and Amending Powers: Do They Protect Our Fundamental Rights?" *A.B.A. Journal* 36 (1950): 715; Holman, "Treaty Law-Making: A Blank Check for Writing a New Constitution," *A.B.A. Journal* 36 (1950): 707. Sutherland, "Restricting the Treaty Power," 1305, n. 2. The political history of the Bricker Amendment is treated comprehensively in Duane Tananbaum, *The Bricker Amendment: A Test of Eisenhower's Political Leadership* (Ithaca, NY: Cornell University Press, 1988).

[229] Tananbaum, *Bricker Amendment*, 33, 39, 54, 71, 199. See also Bruce Ackerman and David Golove, "Is NAFTA Constitutional?" *Harvard Law Review* 108 (February 1995): 799–930, esp. 898.

The struggle over the Bricker Amendment was hard fought and politically prominent during the 1950s. In the end, the amendment was defeated largely through the aggressive anti–Bricker Amendment campaign launched by President Eisenhower, who was concerned less about human rights than about any proposed limitations on the president's power over foreign affairs.[230] Eisenhower acted with savvy to defuse support for the amendment, in part by actively consulting Congress over policy in Indochina and Formosa (Taiwan). In addition, through Secretary of State John Foster Dulles, Eisenhower informed Congress in 1953 that he would not ask the Senate to ratify the U.N. Genocide Convention and, moreover, that he would withdraw the United States from all efforts to draft a legally binding international covenant on human rights.[231]

The virulent political reaction against the use of the treaty power to advance human rights at home also seems to have affected the judiciary. Following a flurry of critical commentary, both scholarly and political, about the apparent willingness of tribunals to treat treaties like the U.N. Charter as self-executing, courts dropped the sort of bold reasoning deployed by Justices Black and Murphy and the intermediate appellate court in California and found other grounds for their decisions. In 1952, the California Supreme Court upheld the lower appellate court's invalidation of the state's Alien Land Law, but did so exclusively on Fourteenth Amendment equal protection grounds. In its opinion, the court expressly repudiated the lower court's reliance upon Articles 55 and 56 of the U.N. Charter.[232] Soon thereafter, other courts also summarily rejected legal arguments anchored in the U.N. Charter.[233] Before long, citations to the charter by litigants appeared only in oddball political lawsuits aimed less at the prospect of legal victory than at mobilizing political movements. Although essentially a dead letter from a legal standpoint, the charter continued to be invoked from time to time by political activists in cases challenging nuclear testing, for example, or the war in Vietnam.[234]

---

[230] Tananbaum, *Bricker Amendment*, 67, 71–9, 138–56.

[231] Tananbaum, *Bricker Amendment*, 199.

[232] *Sei Fujii v. California*, 242 P.2d 617 (1952). A "self executing" treaty is held to be legally binding upon domestic political actors from the moment it is ratified; no further congressional legislation implementing the treaty is necessary. Mark W. Janis, *An Introduction to International Law* 2nd ed. (Boston: Little, Brown and Co., 1993), 85–9.

[233] *Rice v. Sioux City Memorial Park*, 349 U.S. 70 (1955) (race discrimination by cemetery); *Sipes v. McGhee*, 316 Mich. 614, 25 N.W.2d 638 (Supreme Court of Michigan, 1947); *Vlissidis v. Anadell*, 262 F.2d 398, 400 (7th Cir. 1959) (allegations of racially discriminatory immigration laws).

[234] See *Pauling v. McElroy*, 164 F.Supp. 390 (D.D.C. 1958), aff'd, 278 F.2d 252 (D.C. Cir. 1960) (nuclear testing); *Autenrieth v. Cullen*, 418 F.2d 586 (9th Cir. 1969) (Vietnam); *United States v. Owens*, 415 F.2d 1308 (6th Cir. 1969) (Vietnam); *United States v. Spock*, 416 F.2d 165 (1st cir. 1969). Militant black activists, such as Malcolm X, continued to evoke the charter as authority in their political speeches. Malcolm X joined this to a repudiation of

In his opinion for the Court in *Reid v. Covert* (1957), Justice Black himself hemmed in the menace of his *Oyama* concurrence and of *Missouri v. Holland* more generally, by holding in a criminal case involving an overseas military trial of an American serviceman's wife for murder, that "no agreement with a foreign nation can confer power on the Congress, or any other branch of government, which is free from the restraints of the Constitution."[235]

Justice Black could now safely take this step without yielding one inch on the domestic civil rights front. In the fight against racial discrimination in the South, specific recourse to the U.N. Charter and other international human rights agreements became increasingly unnecessary because, as the California Supreme Court had recognized and others had now come to appreciate, the same result could be achieved through domestic law with a more expansive reading of the Fourteenth Amendment.[236] Writing in the *American Journal of International Law*, for example, Charles Fairman argued that the *Sei Fujii* court's reliance upon the legal authority of the U.N. Charter was an embarrassment to the cause of human rights because it rushed too quickly to a needlessly exposed position, unleashing an unfortunate political backlash.[237] Fairman contended that the U.N. Charter was best viewed as "a fresh impulse to the historic process whereby the guarantees of 'liberty' and 'equal protection' receive an ever-broadening construction." "It would seem, indeed," he added, "a reproach to our constitutional system to confess that the values that it establishes fall below any requirement of the Charter."[238]

And reproach it seemed to be. For the Supreme Court stuck to the equal protection revolution that had begun in 1954 with *Brown v. Board of Education*, a decision reinforced by the use of federal military force in Little Rock in 1957 and by federal legislation such as the Civil Rights Act of 1964 and the Voting Rights Act of 1965. The Court's newly expanded understanding of the commerce power and of state action soon substituted for an aggressive reading of the treaty power. In the end, the same results were achieved by what now seemed like less vulnerable and more authoritatively legitimate constitutional means.

---

his identity as an American, which was a sure prescription for the political marginalization of his arguments. Malcolm X, "The Ballot or the Bullet," speech delivered to the Cory Methodist Church, Cleveland, OH, 3 April 1964.

[235] *Reid v. Covert*, 354 U.S. 1 (1957). See Tananbaum, *Bricker Amendment*, 211–14.

[236] See Lawrence Preuss, "Some Aspects of the Human Rights Provisions of the Charter and Their Execution in the United States," *American Journal of International Law* 46 (1952): 289–96 (advocating use of the Fourteenth Amendment rather than the U.N. Charter to advance civil rights in the United States).

[237] Charles Fairman, "Editorial Comment: Finis to Fujii," *American Journal of International Law* 46 (1952): 682–90, esp. 682–3.

[238] Fairman, "Finis to Fujii," 689.

The Waning of Fourth and Fifth Amendment Rights
in Service of the New Administrative State

In the late 1930s and the 1940s, at the very time the Court was beginning to undertake a sustained effort to reform the constitutional law of criminal process in the interest of (national) civil rights, it was working to consolidate and institutionalize the constriction of Fourth and Fifth Amendment privacy rights as part of its (regulatory) statebuilding agenda. As we have seen, a major part of the effort to construct a smoothly functioning New American State involved the vanquishing of legal resistance of privacy rights. In the late nineteenth century, when progressive partisans of the project of legibility sought to advance their cause through a morally charged rhetoric of criminality, partisans of privacy, such as Justice Bradley, responded by according civil defendants and resisters to the seeing state constitutional rights that had traditionally been vouchsafed only to federal criminal defendants. They also (understandably enough, given their roots in the old proprietary-competitive political-economic order) refused to draw a new distinction between the economic privacy of businesses and businessmen and a more delimited sphere of "personal" privacy.

Justice Bradley's bold civil libertarian step, however, with its broad new protections for privacy rights, proved too protective, given the needs of the newly emergent central state: It posed a potentially serious obstacle to the entire statebuilding project, an obstacle at least as menacing as the Court's more often discussed "liberty of contract" jurisprudence. The Court itself soon recognized this, and in a series of ICC and antitrust cases, gradually negotiated away its earlier proclaimed Bill of Rights privacy protections. This narrowing of the scope of privacy rights was a *progressive* and not a conservative project. And this whittling down of Fourth and Fifth Amendment protections, it is worth noting, was thought necessary despite the fact that many of the new regulatory violations were now, thanks to the legislative successes of the progressive program, no longer quasi-criminal but *actually* criminal and, as such, potentially subjected violators to both large fines and lengthy spells in state or federal prisons.[239]

It is only in this context that we can appreciate why in the 1930s and 1940s some of the Supreme Court justices now most strongly identified as civil libertarians, such as Louis Brandeis (who left the Court in 1939) and William O. Douglas, turned out to be among the justices most opposed to expansive readings of criminal process rights in (criminal) regulatory cases. In such cases, dispatch, efficiency, and a smoothly functioning regulatory system were the chief imperatives, and broad readings of the criminal process

---

[239] See Livingston Hall, "Substantive Law of Crimes;" Packer, *Limits of the Criminal Sanction*, 13–14, 273–7, 354–63.

provisions of the Bill of Rights to advance "privacy rights" would only prove to be obstacles to progressive goals.[240]

The Supreme Court's 1937 decision in *District of Columbia v. Clawans*, the Court's "switch-in-time" term, is illustrative. *Clawans* involved the trial of a man in police court without a jury for the sale of merchandise without the required license. The punishment for this regulatory violation was significant: a fine of $300 or ninety days in jail. In a 7–2 opinion joined by Justice Brandeis, the Court (despite the plain-language strictures of the Sixth and Seventh Amendments, the former of which the Court had ostensibly evinced a burgeoning affinity for in the Scottsboro cases of only a few years before) found no constitutional violation. The reason? The case involved regulation in the public interest. In contrast, justices who today are considered "anticivil libertarian," James McReynolds and Pierce Butler, dissented in *Clawans*, calling the Court's decision a "grave danger to liberty." In their view, even if the regulatory case were classified as civil rather than criminal, since the case concerned well over $20, the right to a jury trial could not be denied. The *Clawans* decision was an early indication that the new constitutional order had implications that would sweep beyond the large corporations it was initially designed to straddle and administer. [241]

Three important 1946 decisions anchored the new order. In *Davis v. United States* and *Zap v. United States*, two Fourth Amendment opinions penned by William O. Douglas, the Court shunted aside the constitutional claims made by defendants who ran afoul of regulatory regimes.[242] *Davis* in fact held that if the place to be searched is a publicly regulated business or if the things to be

---

[240] Interestingly enough, Justice Douglas's opinion for the Court in *Skinner v. Oklahoma*, 316 U.S. 535 (1942), striking down a law providing for the sterilization of habitual criminals, is often cited (as is Brandeis's 1890 law review article) as seminal in the development of the "right to privacy." This is the case even though the *Skinner* opinion makes no mention of "privacy" and is decided squarely on equal protection grounds. On the new positivist state, see Karen Orren, *Belated Feudalism: Labor, the Law, and Liberal Development in the United States* (Cambridge: Cambridge University Press, 1991); Stephen Skowronek, *Building a New American State*. See also Lustig, *Corporate Liberalism*, 25 ("[M]odern developments [change] the form of law, what fundamentally is. Rather than a settled framework of activity, rooted in precedent, known to citizens, and focused on the judicial individual, "law" becomes equated with changing policies and social purposes as defined by powerful groups. It also becomes oriented toward future goals. Administrative law, rather than contract law, becomes the paradigmatic form of law in the modern state."). See also Lustig, *Corporate Liberalism*, ch. 7. The institutionalization of this dispatch and efficiency in criminal regulatory cases constituted an important part of what Orren and Skowronek have called "the settlement of the 1940s." Karen Orren and Stephen Skowronek, "Regime and Regime Building in American Government: A Review of Literature on the 1940s," *Political Science Quarterly* 113 (1999): 689–702.

[241] *District of Columbia v. Clawans*, 300 U.S. 617 (1937). See *Powell v. Alabama*, 287 U.S. 45 (1942) (Justices Butler and McReynolds dissenting).

[242] *Davis v. United States*, 382 U.S. 582 (1946); *Zap v. United States*, 382 U.S. 624 (1946).

seized are either property or records held pursuant to that regulatory regime, the Court's constitutional scrutiny of ostensibly unreasonable searches and seizures would be significantly reduced.

Davis was a wartime Office of Price Administration case involving the owner of a New York City filling station who apparently sold gas to undercover federal agents without the required coupons and at an illegally inflated price. After the sale took place, the agents tried to determine if the total amount of receipts on hand at the station matched the measurements there for the amount of gas sold. At some point, the owner of the station alleged that he had the full complement of receipts in a locked storage room on the premises, a room to which he refused admission to the agents. The testimony is disputed about whether the agents then threatened to break down the door to the storage room or whether the station owner was coerced by them in other ways, but at some point he relented and let the agents into the room. Counterfeit coupons were found. And the filling station owner alleged an unconstitutional search and seizure that violated the Fourth Amendment.

Justice Douglas's opinion for the Court rejected the station owner's claim, asserting the facts justified a lower level of Fourth Amendment scrutiny for two reasons. The first, Douglas argued, was that the search and seizure involved not private but public papers and documents.[243] And the second was that the filling station was not a private residence but a place of business, which, moreover, was searched during the course of regular business hours.[244] In other words, the case involved the core of the regulatory process.

Justice Frankfurter's dissent in the case (which was joined by Justices Murphy and Rutledge) was of a different tenor. Plainly irate, Frankfurter declared the *Davis* case to be "directly related to one of the great chapters in the historic process whereby civil liberty was achieved and constitutionally protected against future inroads" and insisted that, in his opinion for the Court, Justice Douglas had made a "travesty" of the Fourth Amendment.[245] Answering Douglas's argument, Frankfurter admitted that there were relevant distinctions between private and public papers. Private papers, he contended, could not be seized even through legal process because such a seizure would violate the Fifth Amendment provision regarding self-incrimination. Public papers, on the other hand, could be seized, but only through a properly safeguarded search.

As for Douglas's distinction between the relative protections accorded to places of business and private residences, Frankfurter asserted:

If this is an indirect way of saying that the Fourth Amendment only secures homes against unreasonable searches and seizures but not offices – private offices of

---

[243] By statute, the gasoline coupons remained the property of the Office of Price Administration and were subject to inspection by it at all times. *Davis*, 328 U.S. at 588.

[244] *Davis*, 382 U.S. at 592.

[245] *Davis*, 382 U.S. at 594–5.

physicians and lawyers, of trade unions and other organizations, of business and scientific enterprises – then indeed it would constitute a sudden and drastic break with the whole history of the Fourth Amendment and its applications by this Court.[246]

"It is easy," Frankfurter argued (in a pungent reversal of the invocation used by later Warren-era civil libertarians to defend according full constitutional protections to street criminals and political radicals) "to make light of insistence on scrupulous regard for the safeguards of civil liberties when invoked on behalf of the unworthy. It is too easy. History bears testimony that by such disregard are the rights of liberty extinguished, heedlessly at first, then stealthily, and brazenly in the end."[247] If it begins with the businessmen just because they are unpopular, Frankfurter in effect asks, where will it all end?

Justice Frankfurter asserted that the *Davis* decision "opens an alarming vista of inroads upon the right of privacy." As he pointed out, most businesses in the country were in possession of Office of Price Administration documents. And if one considered all documents that federal and state governments require be kept – an ever-expanding category – the prospect for government intrusion would be all but unlimited.[248]

For reasons similar to those he set out in *Davis*, Frankfurter also dissented from Justice Douglas's opinion for the Court in *Zap v. United States*, which was decided the same day. In that case, which involved procurement fraud by a Navy contractor, the defendant had given the government the right to inspect his accounts and records as part of the deal to secure the government contract. One such inspection turned up a fraudulent check. Both the majority and the dissenters in *Zap* agreed that here the search was lawful. The check, however, was seized from the contractor under a defective warrant. In allowing the check to be admitted as evidence against the defendant at trial, Justice Douglas made much of the fact that it was discovered and taken at a business during business hours without coercion. And besides, he added, a valid warrant could have been issued. In Justice Frankfurter's estimation (again joined by Justices Murphy and Rutledge), "the fact that this evidence might have been secured by a lawful warrant seems a strange basis for approving a seizure without a warrant." "The Fourth Amendment," he concluded, "stands in the way."[249]

The narrowing of Fourth Amendment privacy protections in the service of a smoothly functioning fact-fortified New American State continued in yet another case from 1946, *Oklahoma Press v. Walling*.[250] The *Oklahoma Press* case involved the constitutional propriety of the *pro forma* judicial enforcement of a subpoena issued to the paper by the Department of Labor under the

---

[246] *Davis*, 382 U.S. at 596.
[247] *Davis*, 382 U.S. at 597.
[248] *Davis*, 382 U.S. at 602.
[249] *Zap*, 382 U.S. at 633.
[250] *Oklahoma Press v. Walling*, 327 U.S. 186 (1946).

Fair Labor Standards Act (FLSA) (a statute that had copied its enforcement provisions verbatim from Wilson and Brandeis's Federal Trade Commission Act). Under the FLSA, the administrator was authorized to "enter and inspect such places and such records (and make such transcriptions thereof), question such employees, and investigate such facts, conditions, practices, or matters as he may deem necessary or appropriate to determine whether any person has violated any provision of this Act."[251] The Labor Department had sought information from the newspaper company in an effort to discover whether it was violating the Act. No allegations of illegality against the Oklahoma Press Company were pending. The paper resisted a federal court's *pro forma* enforcement of the subpoena, countering with a traditional Fourth Amendment argument of the sort Justice Field had made in his 1887 *Pacific Railway* opinion. It asserted that a court had to fully adjudicate the issue before such a subpoena could be enforced. This time, however, with only Justice Murphy dissenting, the Court declared that Oklahoma Press's argument "raise[d] the ghost of controversy long since settled adversely to their claim."[252] "What petitioners seek," the Court intoned dismissively, "is not to prevent an unlawful search and seizure. It is rather a total immunity to the Act's provisions, applicable to all others similarly situated, requiring them to submit their pertinent records for the Administrator's inspection."[253] "It is not necessary," the Court added, "that a specific charge or complaint of violation of law be pending. . . . It is enough that the investigation be for a lawfully authorized purpose, within the power of Congress to command." "This has been ruled most often . . . in relation to grand jury investigations," the Court noted, citing *Hale v. Henkel* and *Wilson v. United States*, "but also frequently in respect to general or statistical investigations authorized by Congress."[254] The Court then characterized in circular fashion the Fourth Amendment doctrinal "compromise [that] has been worked out" to support the New American State: The modern understanding of the Fourth Amendment "secure[s] the public interest and at the same time [guards] the private ones affected against the only abuses from which protection rightfully may be claimed." These are "the interests of men to be free from officious intermeddling." Any other construction of the Fourth Amendment, the Court concluded, "would stop much if not all of investigation in the public interest at the threshold of inquiry. . . . " Besides, the Court noted, its fact-gathering

---

[251] FSLA, Sec. 11(a).
[252] For this proposition, the Court cited Milton Handler on the constitutionality of Federal Trade Commission investigations and the entire array of ICC and antitrust cases discussed earlier at length: *Hale v. Henkel*, *Wilson v. United States*, *ICC v. Brimson*, *ICC v. Baird*, *ICC v. Goodrich Transport*, *Smith v. ICC*, *Harriman v. ICC*, and others. *Oklahoma Press*, 327 U.S. at 204, n. 31, 32.
[253] *Oklahoma Press*, 327 U.S. at 196.
[254] *Oklahoma Press*, 327 U.S. at 208–9, citing the late-nineteenth- and early-twentieth-century ICC cases and Handler.

rules went no further than the discovery rules of the Federal Rules of Civil Procedure (FRCP).[255]

The lone dissenter, Justice Murphy, declared that "[i]t is not without difficulty that I dissent from a procedure the constitutionality of which has been established for many years." "But," he stated, "I am unable to approve the use of non-judicial subpoenas issued by administrative agents." Murphy followed the now lonely task of tilting to the civil liberties commitments made by the Court in the waning days of the old proprietary-competitive order:

Perhaps we are too far removed from the experiences of the past to appreciate fully the consequences that may result from an irresponsible though well-meaning use of the subpoena power. To allow a non-judicial officer, unarmed with judicial process, to demand the books and papers of an individual is to open invitation to abuse of that power.[256]

"Only by confining the subpoena power exclusively to the judiciary can there be any insurance against this corrosion of liberty. . . . Liberty is too priceless," he ended, "to be forfeited through the zeal of an administrative agent."[257]

The Institutionalization of the Fourth and Fifth Amendment Retreat: The Federal Rules of Civil Procedure

When these developments are considered as part of the narrative concerning the trajectory of twentieth-century protections under the Bill of Rights – as they should be – that narrative becomes considerably less Whiggish. One prominent legal scholar has recently declared, given these constitutional developments concerning the building of the New American State, "[B]y about 1950, Fourth and Fifth Amendment law was almost an empty shell."[258] As it happened, by the 1940s, the appeal to the traditional constitutional protections of the pre-Progressive order was more quixotic than even Justice Murphy, as a lone dissenter in *Oklahoma Press*, may have suspected. Murphy apparently failed to recognize that the role of judges under the new regime had been redefined in ways that moved them away from the mindset of traditional common law judges solicitous of individualist due process protections and toward the mindset of the administrators that Murphy had so fervently – and anachronistically – hoped they would control. Crucial, and noted as justificatory in the *Oklahoma Press* opinion, were the New Deal amendments to the discovery rules of the Federal Rules of Civil Procedure, which were soon copied by the states and thus pervaded American law.[259]

---

[255] *Oklahoma Press*, 327 U.S. at 186, 216 n. 55.
[256] *Oklahoma Press*, 327 U.S. at 218–9.
[257] *Oklahoma Press*, 327 U.S. at 219.
[258] Stuntz, "Substantive Origins of Criminal Procedure," 434.
[259] The significance of FRCP amendments for contemporary privacy is emphasized by Walter K. Olson in *The Litigation Explosion: What Happened When America Unleashed the Lawsuit*

Prior to the 1938 amendments to the federal rules, the scope of discovery – the process of fact gathering backed by the coercive power of the state – was severely limited and, where it was allowed, judges were charged with keeping the discovery process on a tight leash. Only facts legally relevant to the cases, with relevance strictly construed, could be elicited. Moreover, lawyers could only request information relevant to their own case, and not to their opponent's case, a limitation known as the "own-case-only rule."[260] To secure a fuller discovery, parties had to apply for a special "bill of discovery" that amounted to a relatively rare exception to the general rule.[261]

At the time of the triumph of the project of legibility, however, the discovery rules were altered to mimic the new constitutional power given to the public-spirited fact-gathering powers of the administrators of the New American State. Under the new FRCP 26(b), the own-case-only rule was jettisoned, as were the strictures confining inquiry to facts relevant to the issues in the case. Now lawyers in private lawsuits had a right to inquire into any facts that might lead them to other facts that might be of use in a trial.[262] Any

---

(New York: Dutton, 1991), which I draw from (and supplement) in the following discussion. I note that Justice Murphy himself (an FDR appointee, after all) was apparently unaware of the relation, with benefit of historical perspective, from which I am about to draw. In *Hickman v. Taylor*, Murphy boldly asserted: "The deposition discovery rules are to be accorded a broad and liberal treatment. No longer can the time-honored cry of 'fishing expeditions' serve to preclude a party from inquiry into the facts underlying his opponent's case. Mutual knowledge of all the relevant facts gathered by both parties is essential to proper litigation. To that end, either party may compel the other to disgorge whatever facts he has in his possession." *Hickman v. Taylor*, 329 U.S. 495, 501 (1947). See also *Lloyd v. Cessna Aircraft*, 74 F.R.D. 518 (E.D. Tenn., 1977) (accepting "fishing expedition" under contemporary discovery rules); *United States v. AT&T*, 461 F.Supp. 1314 (D.D.C. 1978) (noting that in complex antitrust litigation, discovery will inevitably, and acceptably, amount to a fishing expedition). These cases are cited in Moore's *Federal Practice* (New York: Matthew Bender, 1996), Vol. 4, Sec. 26.07[1] n. 12.

[260] Moore's *Federal Practice*, Sec. 26.03.

[261] See *Bruch Machine Tool Co. v. Aluminum Co. of America*, 63 F.2d 778 (2nd Cir., 1933) (bill of discovery granted in Clayton Act antitrust case).

[262] "The scope of discovery in the federal courts is broad and requires nearly total mutual disclosure of each party's evidence prior to trial. The discovery rules are to be accorded broad and liberal treatment.... The information sought need not be admissible at the trial if the information appears reasonably calculated to lead to the discovery of admissible evidence. The purpose of discovery is to allow a broad search for facts.... FRCP 26(b) envisions generally unrestricted access to sources of information." 10 Fed. Proc. L. Ed. Sec. 26:64. Section 26:68 states "It is, in fact, a matter of no significance that broad discovery will disclose large quantities of material which would be completely inadmissible in evidence." See *Report of the Advisory Committee on Rules for Civil Procedure Appointed by the Supreme Court of the United States Containing Proposed Rules of Civil Procedure for the District Courts of the United States* (April 1937); *Final Report of the Advisory Committee on Rules for Civil Procedure Appointed by the Supreme Court of the United States* (November 1937); *Notes to the Rules of Civil Procedure for the District Courts of the United States* (March 1938). It is worth noting that in 1946 – the same year as what I have called the Supreme Court's "Decisions of '46," FRCP 26(b) was amended to remove inadmissibility at trial as grounds for objection

inquiry relevant to the (ill-defined and broadly construed) subject matter of the litigation was fair game, with relevancy very broadly construed.[263] As a contemporary federal procedure manual described it, under FRCP 26 "[t]he requirement of relevancy must be construed liberally with common sense rather than measured by precise issues framed by the pleadings or limited by other concepts of narrow legalisms. . . . [D]iscovery should ordinarily be allowed unless it is clear that the information sought can have no possible bearing upon the subject matter of the action. . . . A request for discovery should be considered relevant if there is any possibility that the information sought may be relevant to the subject matter of the action."[264] The fact-gathering needs of the New American State had not simply moved the judge and his wonted doctrines out of the way of modern administrators: They had also transformed the very nature of judicial power itself. The result was not only a new, powerfully seeing state, but also, as the new privacy ethos spread from the administrative sphere to the broader legal system, to the contemporary private lawsuit that permits lawyers to gaze deeply into the private lives of individuals, and allows all manner of "fishing expeditions" by now unconstrained lawyers in a strategic effort to gain advantage. In the heady days of the new regime, a 1945 note in the *Columbia Law Review* stated frankly that "the [new discovery] rules . . . permit 'fishing' for evidence *as they should*" [emphasis added].[265] Under this regime, Walter Olson quotes one California attorney as saying, "Attorneys must inquire into everything and prepare for everything, because no court will tell them where to stop or permit them to stop an adversary."[266] This new role as pretrial investigator, one commentator has suggested, is behind the transformation of people who used to be known as "trial lawyers" into "litigators."[267] In ways that formerly would have been barred by key provisions of the Bill of Rights, now every attorney has assumed the power of a progressive administrator. The result has been an explosion in the time and expense of lawsuits and an unprecedented assault on what even we today would call "privacy." These uncabined New Deal discovery rules have affected both low and high, reaching even the president of the United States.[268] Thus, the fate of privacy under

---

during a deposition where "the testimony sought appears reasonably calculated to lead to the discovery of admissible evidence." Moore's *Federal Practice*, Sec. 26.01[2]. See also Sec. 26.01[6] and Sec. 26.01[7] (Committee Note of 1946 to amended subdivision (b) stating purpose of the amendment to "allow a broad search for facts").

[263] FRCP 26(b)(1) allows discovery of any nonprivileged matter "which is relevant to the subject matter of the pending matter."

[264] 10 Fed. Proc. L. Ed. Sec. 26:67.

[265] Note, *Columbia Law Review* 45 (1945): 482. See also *Hickman v. Taylor*, op cit. at n. 117.

[266] Olson, *Litigation Explosion*, 114.

[267] Maurice Rosenberg, "Federal Rules of Civil Procedure in Action: Assessing Their Impact," *University of Pennsylvania Law Review* 137 (1989): 2197, 2203.

[268] See Jeffrey Rosen, *Unwanted Gaze*. Rosen focuses on recent changes in the discovery rules in sexual harassment cases. Walter Olson demonstrates, however, that invasions of privacy

the fact-gathering ethic of the progressive legal order begat in significant part the fate of privacy in the contemporary one.[269]

While they clearly have implications for privacy as a value, these developments, under which both the government asserting a claim of public interest and private lawyers acting on behalf of their clients have sweeping and unprecedented state-supported fact-gathering powers, no longer raise serious questions under the Fourth and Fifth Amendments or under what the Supreme Court has declared (under the Fifth and Fourteenth Amendment due process clauses) to be "the right to privacy." Given this developmental trajectory, the Fourth and Fifth Amendments and the "right to privacy" were free to carry wholly new meanings and policy agendas. In the years after the New Deal – and culminating in the Warren years – the Fourth and Fifth Amendments were drafted into service as part of the Supreme Court's antiracist criminal process revolution, where their meaning is perpetually refined in a seemingly endless succession of street crime cases.[270] "The Right to Privacy" has been developed mainly in cases involving sexual autonomy, beginning with birth control, moving to abortion and gay rights. The distinction between personal and economic privacy is strongly institutionalized in legal doctrine. Although the Fourth and Fifth Amendments and "the right to privacy" are taken very seriously, the fate of privacy as a value within the contemporary constitutional order remains decidedly ambiguous.

---

have become routine features of discovery in a wide variety of cases, not just those involving sexual harassment. Olson, *Litigation Explosion*, ch. 6. These developments, I insist here, are direct institutional legacies of progressive reforms undertaken as part of the effort in the late nineteenth and early twentieth centuries to create a New American State.

[269] William Stuntz declares that today "subpoenas are subject to only the weakest of legal constraints." Stuntz, "Substantive Origins of Criminal Procedure," n. 161. They are "practically unregulated; as long as the request is relevant to some legitimate investigation and compliance is not too burdensome [a limit, as Olson suggests, very rarely found], the target of the subpoena must hand over the goods (or papers). . . . [T]his bottom line is nonsense in privacy terms. Subpoenas can and do require disclosure of material that is much more private than the sorts of things police officers find in car searches, yet the subpoenas are much less heavily regulated than the searches. On the other hand, given the reliance of administrative agencies on the subpoena power, any other decision would pose real problems for much of the government outside the realm of ordinary criminal procedure." Stuntz, "Substantive Origins of Criminal Procedure," 444–5. For a detailed historical account of the profound changes wrought by the 1938 discovery rules, see Stephen N. Subrin, "Fishing Expeditions Allowed: The Historical Background of the 1938 Federal Discovery Rules," *Boston College Law Review* 39 (May 1998): 691–745. Subrin's account of the discussion and scholarly, professional, and political debate surrounding the adoption of the new discovery rules suggests a strong (and derivative) relationship between the content of the new discovery rules and the content of the perceived imperatives of the earlier progressive statebuilding project.

[270] Powe, *Warren Court and American Politics*, 193–9, 379–444; Stuntz, "Origins of Criminal Procedure;" Stuntz, "Privacy's Problem."

Race and the Warren-Era Criminal Process Revolution: The March of Domestic Atrocities

To integrate the progressive-spirited reformist struggle *against* broad readings of the Fourth and Fifth Amendments and *against* the value of privacy should not lead us to adopt a model of constitutional development that is simply the mirror image of the traditional Whiggish progressive narratives – to present, that is, a narrative of pure decline. The fate of liberty in the modern constitutional order, I wish to argue, was complicated, contradictory, vexed, and mixed in ways that characterize the nature of the regime itself.

As we saw earlier, beginning in the late 1920s and early 1930s, the Court became decidedly more protective of the rights of criminal defendants in street crime cases, including those implicating the search and seizure provisions of the Fourth Amendment. In doing so, the Court acted in a state-limiting way. But its new solicitude for civil liberties in this area was *not* a progressive project. Rather, it was a conservative one, an act of resistance to the presumptions of one of the defining progressive policy initiatives of the early twentieth century: Prohibition. But when the Court subsequently moved to extend these criminal process protections in cases involving the Southern system of racial subordination in the 1930s and 1940s (and beyond), it was acting in concert with a reformist imperative that was friendly to state power – the power of the (Northern) central state over the outlier section of the South (or, put otherwise, it was a state-friendly civil rights initiative arrayed in the doctrinal clothing of state-limiting civil liberties).

Prohibition inaugurated a new era in the modern Court's concern with the application of the Bill of Rights to street criminals. This new substantive preoccupation gained momentum as it became part of the Court's cresting solicitude for civil rights. Between 1938 and 1952, the Court decided 168 criminal procedure cases, which, in the early years of the period, amounted to 6.2 percent of its docket and about twice as much – 12 percent – toward the early 1950s. Between 1953 and 1972, at the peak of the civil rights era, the number of criminal cases on the Court's docket rose to 514, taking up twice that – close to a quarter of the Court's time – in the early 1970s.[271]

The perceived need to reform Southern law enforcement as part of a national constitutional program of racial justice had been pressed upon the Court not only by the highly publicized reports of Gunnar Myrdal and the Truman Committee, but also by the deliberate efforts of social movement actors who, one-by-one, brought a succession of criminal cases involving blacks to the Court. As we have seen, the Court got a glimpse of these matters in the 1930s in cases like *Powell v. Alabama* (1932) and *Brown v. Mississippi* (1936). In those cases, the Court dealt with Southern justice firmly but narrowly. Police cases percolating up from the South after *Powell* and *Brown*, though,

---

[271] Pacelle, *Transformation of the Supreme Court's Agenda*, 147, Table 6.2.

made it clear to the Court that not only were there ongoing problems with the Southern criminal justice system, but also that these problems, far from being aberrations, were an institutional pillar in an elaborate social system devoted to racial subordination and oppression. Confronted with a stream of cases designed to showcase the systemic brutality and inequality of Southern law enforcement – in the context of increasingly disruptive social movement activity, hot war, and, in time, the international competition of the Cold War era – the Court was now subject to intense incentives, arising out of the way it saw the world, to accord increasing constitutional protections to criminal defendants in street crime cases.[272]

Doctrinal change in a wide variety of areas of constitutional criminal procedure was driven by a series of cases in which racial oppression was clearly the underlying issue. In 1945, the Court was pushed by the case of *Screws v. United States* to expand its conception of state action to permit federal criminal prosecution of Southern lawmen.[273] There, a county sheriff in Georgia, Screws, who had been having a disagreement with a thirty-year-old black man named Hall, rounded up a deputy and a local policeman and the three headed off to a local bar to fortify themselves for a night of violence. Late into the night, when the officers had had their fill, the three men headed out to Hall's home, where they arrested him for allegedly stealing a tire. Immediately after removing Hall from the squad car at police headquarters, Screws and his companions began beating Hall with a two-pound, eight-inch-long blackjack and with their fists. The beating continued for fifteen to thirty minutes until Hall was unconscious. He died shortly thereafter. The Supreme Court held in the case that the officers could be prosecuted for acting "under color of state law" under a Reconstruction-era civil rights law, even though their actions had been illegal under the laws of the state of Georgia.[274]

A black petitioner who had, at least as of the date his case reached the Supreme Court, survived his beatings, however, lost in court in *Sweeney v. Woodhall* (1952).[275] In *Sweeney*, a black man who had served six years in an Alabama prison for burglary had escaped from prison and fled to Ohio. Once recaptured, the man attempted to halt his extradition to Alabama on

---

[272] On the extensive involvement of civil rights groups in criminal process litigation, see Charles Epp, *Rights Revolution*; Jack Greenberg, *Crusaders in the Courts: How a Dedicated Band of Lawyers Fought for the Civil Rights Revolution* (New York: Basic Books, 1994); Mark Tushnet, *The NAACP's Legal Strategy Against Segregated Education, 1925–1950* (Chapel Hill: University of North Carolina Press, 1987).

[273] *Screws v. United States*, 325 U.S. 91 (1945).

[274] In his 1954 Gaspar G. Bacon lectures on the Constitution at Boston University Law School, Albert Beisel used the *Screws* case (as well as *Watts v. Indiana*) at the outset of his speech as a concrete illustration of "the concept of 'police lawlessness.'" Albert R. Beisel Jr., *Control Over the Illegal Enforcement of the Criminal Law: Role of the Supreme Court* (Boston: Boston University Press, 1955).

[275] *Sweeney v. Woodhall*, 344 U.S. 86 (1952).

the grounds that it would constitute cruel and unusual punishment. Back in Alabama, the convicted burglar had been repeatedly beaten to unconsciousness in prison and permanently scarred by lashes from a nine-pound strap studded with sharp metal prongs. In addition, he was forced into sexual slavery to the other prisoners at night, following days in which he was driven to work all day in the broiling sun, stripped to the waist, without rest. In *Sweeney*, settled legal doctrine concerning federalism made the prisoner's extradition all but inevitable – he was a fugitive and had not made any effort to vindicate his constitutional claims in Alabama's courts. But Justice Douglas, at least, heaved the legal niceties aside and decried in dissent any decision holding that "this Negro must suffer torture and mutilation or risk death to get relief in Alabama."[276]

Many of the constitutional criminal procedure cases of this era with deep racial undertones involved coerced confessions. In a case argued by Thurgood Marshall, *Chambers v. Florida* (1940), the Supreme Court overturned the conviction of four young black men for the murder of an elderly white man on the grounds that the central evidence in the case, the men's confessions, had been coerced, in the process violating the suspects' Fourteenth Amendment due process rights. After the murder, the local police, without warrants, had rounded up forty black men and interrogated them nonstop for a week, all the while refusing the men access to friends, relatives, and counsel. In addition, there was some conflicting testimony suggesting that threats and physical harassment were employed.[277]

The Court's initiatives to nationalize criminal procedure reached full force during the heyday of the civil rights era, when the Court further institutionalized its prior work on coerced confessions. In 1966, the Court overturned on due process grounds the conviction and death sentence meted out to a black man with a long criminal record for the rape and murder of an elderly white woman after the man – who was, the Court noted, impoverished and debilitated by low mental abilities – confessed to the crime following a two-week interrogation during which he was barely fed and allowed to speak to no one but the police. The defendant, Davis, also alleged that he had been beaten, cursed at, and threatened by the police. In its brief to the Court, the State of North Carolina defended its treatment of the defendant in part by stating, "Surely, Davis was not such a sensitive person, after all his years in prison, that 'cussing' and being called 'nigger' constituted any degree of fear or coercion."[278]

An Alabama effort to force a black man to confess to the rape and murder of a white woman was overturned the following year on similar due process

---

[276] *Sweeney*, 344 U.S. at 92.

[277] *Chambers v. Florida*, 309 U.S. 227 (1940). See also *Brown v. Mississippi*, 297 U.S. 278 (1936); Klarman, *From Jim Crow to Civil Rights*, 227–31, 269–70, 282–6.

[278] *Davis v. North Carolina*, 384 U.S. 737, 741 n. 2 (1966).

grounds. The suspect, Beecher, was a fugitive from the police when they shot him in the leg. After he fell, the local police chief pressed a loaded gun to his face while another officer put a rifle against the side of his head. Beecher was then asked if he had raped and killed the white woman. He denied it. He was then angrily called a liar and told that if he denied it again they would kill him. Beecher then confessed to the crime, a confession he later signed in a formal version while in the hospital in a drug-induced stupor.[279]

Miranda v. Arizona (1966), the emblematic case of the Warren Court's criminal process revolution, was decided during the same term as the *Davis* case and just before *Beecher*, and like those cases it set new standards for ensuring the voluntariness of criminal confessions.[280] On its face, although it involved the conviction of a member of a racial minority – Ernesto Miranda was described by the Court as "an indigent Mexican defendant" – *Miranda* does not seem to have much to do with blacks. A closer look, however, suggests that the Court was clearly thinking about transforming the way in which the police treated blacks, especially in the South, in reaching its decision.

Near the beginning of his opinion for the Court, Chief Justice Warren drew attention to "a series of cases decided by this Court [since the 1930s, in which] the police resorted to physical brutality – beating, hanging, whipping – and to sustained and protracted questioning incommunicado in order to extort confessions."[281] In the footnote spotlighting the problem he characterized as all but intractable, Warren cited ten cases to underline his point. Of these, the first seven dealt with the mistreatment of blacks accused of a crime in the South, and the opinions in many of these cases make it clear that the Court believed that the suspect was mistreated because he was black.[282] Later in

---

[279] *Beecher v. Alabama*, 389 U.S. 35 (1967) (case argued by Jack Greenberg, head of the NAACP Legal Defense and Education Fund). See also other coerced-confession cases in which the defendant's race was raised either implicitly or explicitly as an explanation for the ill treatment of the suspect: *Upshaw v. United States*, 335 U.S. 410 (1948) (race noted at 433 n. 25); *Fikes v. Alabama*, 352 U.S. 191, 196 (1957) ("Here the prisoner was an uneducated Negro, certainly of low mentality, if not mentally ill," who was apprehended by a group of whites. Case argued by Jack Greenberg); *Culombe v. Connecticut*, 367 U.S. 568, 641 (1961) ("The system of police interrogation under secret detention falls heaviest on the weak and illiterate – the least articulate segments of our society.... The indigent who languishes in jail for want of bail ... or the member of a minority group without status or power who suffers most when we leave the constitutional right to counsel to the discretion of the police.") (Justice Douglas, concurring).

[280] *Miranda v. Arizona*, 384 U.S. 436 (1966).

[281] *Miranda*, 384 U.S. at 446.

[282] *Miranda*, 384 U.S., n. 6, citing *Brown v. Mississippi* (1936); *Chambers v. Florida* (1940); *Canty v. Alabama*, 309 U.S. 629 (1940) (In the state supreme court's decision in the case of a black man convicted of murder, a police officer is quoted as testifying: "I haven't mistreated him, that negro, not one single time, and very little I have had to do with him. I have not abused that negro in any way. He has absolutely been treated better than a lot of white folks I know of. He has had everything he wanted, coca colas to drink, all he wanted to

the opinion, Warren warned, "Interrogation procedures may even give rise to a false confession. The most recent conspicuous example occurred in New York, in 1964, when a Negro of limited intelligence confessed to two brutal murders and a rape which he had not committed."[283] In his dissent from the Court's opinion, Justice Harlan contended that in it, "the Court portrays the evils of normal police questioning in terms which I think are exaggerated."[284] If we only look at the subgroup of cases through which Warren and the other justices in the majority seemed to imagine the problem, however, it is quite likely that the diagnosis fit the disease.

In other cases, it was not the police but what appeared to be a racist double standard applied by judges that seemed to drive doctrinal development. Besides stating the facts, the Supreme Court did not mention race at all in *Duncan v. Louisiana* (1968). Apparently, the Magna Carta, Blackstone, and Anglo-American tradition dictated the Court's holding that the Sixth Amendment right to a jury trial in all criminal cases was incorporated against the states via the Fourteenth Amendment. But *Duncan* involved an absurdly small racial incident that had yielded the defendant, Duncan, a wildly disproportionate sentence. Duncan, a black teenager of nineteen years, had come across two of his younger cousins talking by the side of the road with four white boys about the same age. Worried because he had heard about racial tensions at the nearly all-white high school to which his cousins had transferred, Duncan said, "Let's go," to his cousins. As the three left, the testimony was conflicted over whether Duncan had slapped one of the white boys on the elbow or had merely brushed up against him. For this, Duncan was tried without a jury (available in the state only in capital cases or cases where hard labor was a potential penalty) for battery and sentenced to two months in prison and a $150 fine. [285]

The following year, the Court set new federal standards for ensuring that guilty pleas were entered voluntarily, holding that the standards were dictated by the emanations from a series of constitutional clauses, including those involving self-incrimination, trial by jury, and one's right to confront

---

eat, and if he wanted them, both, he got them." 191 So. 260 (1939); *White v. Texas*, 310 U.S. 530 (1940) (black man accused of rape and sentenced to death following confession after police beating; during investigation, sixteen blacks in the area were taken into custody without warrants or charges being filed); *Vernon v. Alabama*, 313 U.S. 547 (1941) (black man convicted of murder); *Ward v. Texas*, 316 U.S. 547 (1942) (The opening sentence of the Court's opinion reads: "Petitioner William Ward, a negro, was indicted at the September 1939 term of the District Court of Titus County, Texas, for the murder of Levi Brown, a white man"); *Ashcraft v. Tennessee*, 322 U.S. 143 (1944) (case involving two defendants, one black, one white). The last three cases cited do not involve blacks: *Malinski v. New York*, 324 U.S. 401 (1945); *Leyra v. Denno*, 347 U.S. 556 (1954); *Williams v. United States*, 341 U.S. 97 (1951).

[283] *Miranda*, 384 U.S. at 455 n. 24, citing news accounts.

[284] *Miranda*, 384 U.S. at 517.

[285] *Duncan v. Louisiana*, 391 U.S. 145 (1968).

witnesses testifying against him. It did so in *Boykin v. Alabama* (1969), a case in which a twenty-seven-year-old black man with no prior criminal record was sentenced to death on each of five counts of common law robbery involving holdups of a series of grocery stores and other small shops. Only one of the holdups had involved a shooting – when the defendant's gun accidentally went off while pointed away from the victim – but the bullet ricocheted off an object, hitting the store owner in the leg. The NAACP filed an amicus brief in the *Boykin* case.[286]

The succession of cases kept coming to the Court throughout the 1960s. But at the same time the political context that serves to create meaning was undergoing important changes, changes that seem not to have been apparent to the Court's justices, who, for the past decade had become enthusiastic participants in a morally compelling project of national constitutional criminal process reform in street crime cases. From the vantage point of the justices, who saw themselves as key participants in an ongoing reformist project, the *Miranda* decision may have simply been the next logical developmental step in the cause of doctrinal reform aimed at guaranteeing civil rights through an expansion (in certain contexts) of constitutional criminal process rights. By the time *Miranda* was handed down in 1966, however, the political context had been altered by a series of landmark legal changes. With the *Brown* decision (1954), the Civil Rights Act (1964), and the Voting Rights Act (1965), the civil rights movement had achieved most of the goals on which it had hopes of winning a national consensus – goals aimed at full legal and political equality. As Scot Powe has rightly observed, *Gideon v. Wainwright* (1963) "was the last important purely Southern criminal procedure case." "For the rest of [the 1960s]," Powe writes, "the Court decided cases that applied equally to existing Northern practices as they did to Southern practices."[287]

The developmental dynamic involving the assertion of federal judicial power to integrate an outlier region into a national regulatory regime had run its course. Now the Court was no longer engaged in a project of sectional integration. It had moved on to the project of setting national policy, pure and simple. In this new context, criminal procedure cases were no longer broadly understood to be disguised race cases implicating national standards of basic justice. They were now overtly race cases, and their meaning had changed. In the emergent post–civil rights era, the Court's criminal process decisions involving blacks no longer called to mind the helpless Southern black wrongly accused (except among the old guard of the earlier civil rights struggle, who continued to fight the fight). Rather, for the broader public and many non-racist politicians, they began to call to mind the hardened, predatory urban black criminal in an increasingly violent and chaotic society. The decision of the leadership of the Black Power movement (in line with a prominent sliver

[286] *Boykin v. Alabama*, 395 U.S. 238 (1969).
[287] Powe, *Warren Court and American Politics*, 386.

of the educated white liberal/left political and literary elite) to romanticize violence, rioting, and criminality utterly changed the meaning of taking a "progressive" stance on the continued expansion of criminal suspects' constitutional rights.

Race, Privacy, and the New Court-Led Regulation of Search and Seizure in Street Crime Cases

Illegal search must be viewed in the context of the total criminal law process – arrest, search and seizure, interrogation, arraignment. Poor police performance in one of these areas is likely to mean poor performance in all. Illegal searches are therefore only part of the general problem of police lawlessness, which includes illegal arrest, brutality toward suspects, subtler forms of coercion, and illegal detention without arraignment. These illegal acts tend to be interrelated.[288]

Fourth Amendment cases constituted a major part of the mid-twentieth-century criminal process revolution. The flush of activity in the area during Prohibition subsided until it once again became hot in the heyday of the civil rights movement. Between 1938 and 1952, the Court handed down only seventeen search and seizure decisions, only one of which was decided between 1938 and 1942. However, between 1953 and 1972, the number of search and seizure opinions more than quadrupled to seventy-eight.[289] The rate of growth of search and seizure cases as a segment of the Supreme Court's docket surpassed even the growth rate of the Court's racial equality cases, which jumped from twenty-two in the 1938–52 period to seventy-three in 1953–72.[290] Roughly speaking, though, the amount of Court energy devoted to the Fourth Amendment and that devoted to racial equality moved together in the same direction, in similar quantities, and at a similar rate of growth. The developments, in short, were parallel.

Simply to cite Supreme Court statistics on the Fourth Amendment (and, no doubt, on cases involving racial equality), however, is to miss the monumental change in the legal landscape that took place after 1954. A recent hard-bound volume of the United States Code Annotated devoted to listing Fourth Amendment decisions by both federal and state courts (with brief case descriptions of a few sentences) runs over 1,000 pages and is divided into over 4,000 subcategories of law. The overwhelming majority of the search and seizure cases are federal court decisions handed down after 1954.[291]

I will not attempt to untangle the massive doctrinal skein that these cases, when considered together, have created: Weighty tomes are now written on the subject, and even they have trouble teasing out coherent patterns. I will

---

[288] Jacob W. Landynski, *Search and Seizure and the Supreme Court: A Study in Constitutional Interpretation* (Baltimore: Johns Hopkins University Press, 1966), 177.

[289] Pacelle, *Transformation of the Supreme Court's Agenda*, 145, Table 6.1.

[290] Pacelle, *Transformation of the Supreme Court's Agenda*, 159, Table 6.4.

[291] USCA Constitutional Amendment Four (1987).

simply note that the cases regulate the behavior of law officers by examining that behavior through the prism of a number of prominent categories: cases involving the scope of the warrant requirement, searches incident to lawful (and unlawful) arrests, stop-and-frisk procedures, eavesdropping, wiretapping, and automobile searches.

A key element of the constitutional jurisprudence of the Fourth Amendment in this era was the exclusionary rule, as articulated in the Court's 1961 decision in *Mapp v. Ohio*. As we saw earlier, the Court did not invent this rule in the early 1960s. For that reason, it serves as a useful illustrative vehicle for tracing the trajectory of meaning of an institutionalized Fourth Amendment right over time. Most of the Court's doctrinal creativity concerning the admissibility of improperly seized evidence had taken place in the *Boyd* decision (1886), penned by Justice Bradley, a decision reinforced by the Court in *Weeks* (1914). *Boyd*, in fact, was in some ways a more sweeping decision than *Mapp* or *Weeks* ever was; after all, it considered the rule applicable to a wide array of searches, extending well beyond the context of criminal prosecutions. In the end, although *Mapp*'s holding was narrower, its applicability was wider. For *Mapp v. Ohio* newly applied the Fourth Amendment as a restriction on the conduct of states, which in practice meant that its standards were to govern the behavior of every policeman walking the beat in the United States, from the sleepiest small towns to the most bustling cities.

In *Mapp*, the Court effectively overruled its decision in *Wolf v. Colorado* (1949), which had held, in the heyday of the Black-Frankfurter debate and the era of transition from a jurisprudence of minimal standards to something new and as yet uncertain, that while baseline Fourth Amendment search-and-seizure protections were incorporated under the Fourteenth Amendment as limits upon the states, the exclusionary rule was not. In *Mapp*, which took place near the end of the period in which criminal procedure cases were broadly understood as disciplining an outlier region, the Court was faced with the conviction of a black woman, Dollree Mapp, for the possession of lewd and lascivious books, pictures, and photos in the wake of a brazen and high-handed search of her home by the Cleveland Police. Looking for suspects wanted in connection with a recent bombing, the police knocked on the door of Mrs. Mapp's home and insisted that they be admitted. After telephoning her lawyer (whom she had retained on an unrelated civil matter), she informed them that she would not let them in without a warrant. The police then retreated, but returned three hours later. When Mapp, who was at the other end of the house, did not respond to their knock immediately, they broke through her front door, manhandled her, and brandished a paper they said was a warrant. It was not. They then began rifling through her papers, dressers, closets, and suitcases. When her attorney arrived, the police held him outside the house and away from Mrs. Mapp. Eventually, they found material in a suitcase that led to her conviction, though

Mapp insisted that the suitcase was not hers and had been left by a recently departed border. In *Mapp*, the Court overturned Mrs. Mapp's conviction on the grounds that the search had been illegal, and, as such, the evidence obtained from it should not have been admitted as evidence against her.

Mapp was yet another racially inflected criminal process case, and the Court was almost certainly thinking of race when it widened the applicability of Justice Bradley's rule. In *Draper v. United States* (1958), Justice Douglas, who was later in the *Mapp* majority, had explicitly suggested that blacks were likely to be the victims of any laxness of Fourth Amendment scrutiny of law enforcement by the High Court.[292] In *Monroe v. Pape* (1961), which the Court decided only one month prior to hearing arguments in *Mapp*, Justice Douglas's worries were made strikingly real.[293]

In *Monroe*, the Court was confronted with police racism and brutality in sickening splendor. In the middle of the night, thirteen Chicago policemen broke into the home of Mr. Monroe, a black man, roused him, his wife, and six children from bed and made them stand together naked in the living room, while the police ransacked every room, recklessly destroying the family's possessions in the process. One of the officers, Detective Pape, struck Monroe several times with his flashlight, all the while calling him "nigger" and "black boy" as he stood naked before his family. Monroe was then hauled off to police headquarters on open charges and questioned for ten hours about a two-day-old murder. During this time, he was not allowed to speak to an attorney or his family, nor was he brought before an available magistrate (as was required by state law). Eventually, he was released without charges. Neither a search warrant nor an arrest warrant had ever been issued in the case.

Strictly speaking, *Monroe* set no precedent for *Mapp*. *Monroe* was not a Fourth Amendment case – and the exclusionary rule was irrelevant because Mr. Monroe was never charged with any crime. *Monroe* involved the legitimacy of a claim under 42 U.S.C. 1983 (the 1871 Ku Klux Klan Act, which provides a legal remedy for the violation of a person's civil liberties under the color – that is, aegis – of state law). But the relationship between *Monroe* and *Mapp* is obscured by a narrow focus on legal doctrine. The Court held that while a federal remedy under Section 1983 was available to Monroe, the doctrine of sovereign immunity precluded any action against the City of Chicago.

Like *Sweeny v. Woodhall* (1952) – the case brought by the black man who had escaped to Ohio and was fighting extradition back to a brutal Alabama prison – *Monroe* involved an apparent war between the "attitudinal" policy preferences of the justices and their simultaneous commitment to remaining

---

[292] *Draper v. United States*, 358 U.S. 307, 321 (1958) (Justice Douglas, dissenting) (upholding warrantless search in train station of black man matching description of drug courier).

[293] *Monroe v. Pape*, 365 U.S. 167 (1961).

faithful to the dictates of the law.[294] In his opinion in *Monroe* (concurring in part and dissenting in part), Felix Frankfurter compared the behavior of the police in Chicago to the "modern totalitarianism" he saw in the world around him.[295] And it is difficult to see how his brethren could have disagreed. At the same time, though, the Court ran right up against the ancient doctrine of sovereign immunity, which seemed to leave them very little choice in what they could do. In this case, legal obligations trumped policy preferences, and the Court was constrained to offer only a compromise remedy to Mr. Monroe: Under federal law, he was free to sue the officers who had abused him as individuals. This option was not likely to get him any significant financial judgment. Nor would it chasten the Chicago Police Department, which, given the large number of officers who had participated in the mistreatment of Monroe both on the street and at headquarters, seemed to be fully complicit in the behavior of the individual cops.

Through the application of the exclusionary rule to the police (that is, its incorporation through the Fourteenth Amendment), however, the Court could move to rein in the police. Given the *Boyd*, *Weeks*, and *Wolf* cases, the doctrine in these areas of the law was more pliable – and had fewer potential side-effects in wholly unrelated policy areas. Other related areas of criminal procedure were also being nationalized at the same time, and, moreover, the social forces driving this trend – the reaction against the lawless treatment of American blacks – seemed to dictate that *Monroe* not be the remedial end of the line for lawless searches undertaken by racist police officers. The *Mapp* case was argued a month later, and its decision to incorporate the exclusionary rule followed hot on the heels of the argument. The holding was almost automatic.

Although the exclusionary rule was subsequently applied in many – and, no doubt, a majority of – cases in which black defendants were not paired off as litigants against white police forces, the empathetic engine of the rule seemed to lie in black-white confrontations. In the 1960s, an important part of the NAACP Legal Defense and Education Fund's work under the leadership of Jack Greenberg involved action as counsel or *amicus curiae* in criminal procedure cases generally, and exclusionary rule cases in particular.[296]

It would be wrong to say that in its decisions in this area over the course of the 1960s, the Court simply backed black defendants, no questions asked, in helping them to face down their police oppressors. Facts still mattered. But

---

[294] The attitudinal or behaviorialist model of judicial decision making is advanced most prominently in the work of Jeffrey A. Segal and Harold J. Spaeth, *The Supreme Court and the Attitudinal Model Revisited* (New York: Cambridge University Press, 2002).

[295] *Monroe*, 365 U.S. at 209.

[296] See *Bumper v. North Carolina*, 391 U.S. 543 (1968) (Greenberg *amicus curiae*); *Terry v. Ohio*, 392 U.S. 1 (1968) (Greenberg *amicus curiae*); *Davis v. Mississippi*, 394 U.S. 721 (1969) (Greenberg counsel). See also *Warden v. Hayden*, 387 U.S. 294 (1967).

the goal of the Court now seemed to be to instill some balance and fairness into the system. It would be accurate to say, however, that the specter of racial tension between the police and blacks in one way or another haunted most exclusionary rule cases (and most criminal cases). From time to time, when they upheld the actions of the police, as the Court did in *Terry v. Ohio* (1968) – a case assessing the decision by an experienced police officer to stop-and-frisk a black man acting suspiciously on the street – the Court found it necessary to apologetically reassert its awareness of antagonisms between racial minorities and the police.[297] As Earl Warren announced in his opinion for the Court in *Terry*:

Proper adjudication of cases in which the exclusionary rule is invoked demands a constant awareness [of these tensions]. The wholesale harassment by certain elements of the police community, of which minority groups, particularly Negroes, frequently complain, will not be stopped by the exclusion of any evidence from any criminal trial. Yet a rigid and unthinking application of the exclusionary rule, in futile protest against practices which it can never be used effectively to control, may exact a high toll in human injury and frustration of efforts to prevent crime.[298]

Warren then went on to insist that nothing in the Court's opinion should be construed as condoning any inappropriate conduct by the police.[299] In short, in its search and seizure cases of this era, the Court was self-conscious about its role as a regulatory referee between the frequently renegade police

---

[297] Interestingly enough, though race is a subtext in the case, the Court's opinion nowhere mentions the race of the defendant.

[298] *Terry*, 392 U.S. at 14–15. Further mention of police/minority tensions is made in the opinion at 12, 14, 14 n. 11. In Justice Brennan's memorandum in this case, Terry's race is mentioned explicitly.

[299] See also *Bartkus v. Illinois*, 359 U.S. 121, 163 (1958) (double jeopardy case) ("Inevitably the victims of such double prosecutions will most often be the poor and weak in our society, individuals without friends in high places who can influence prosecutors not to try them again. The power to try a second time will be used, as have all similar procedures, to make scapegoats of helpless, political, religious, or racial minorities and those who differ, who do not conform and who resist tyranny." Justice Black, dissenting); *Culombe v. Connecticut*, 307 U.S. 568, 641 (1961) (coerced-confession case) ("The system of police interrogation under secret detention falls heaviest on the weak and illiterate – the least articulate segments of our society.... The indigent who languishes in jail for want of bail ... or the member of a minority group without status or power is the one who suffers most when we leave the constitutional right to counsel to the discretion of the police." Justice Douglas, concurring) ("Police officers are charged with the fair and impartial administration of the law. Yet, in many locations, there are sharp and shocking contrasts in the kind of 'law' administered to different groups of citizens.... [P]eople lacking special status or 'pull' may be pushed around, roughed up, arrested on vague and even false charges, and treated generally as second-class citizens. This is especially true of dwellers in slum areas with high crime rates – and even more especially of poverty-ridden Negroes and other minority groups – where police raids on tenement homes are sometimes made on slight suspicion without the benefit of search warrants.") Justice Douglas, concurring, quoting Deutsch, *The Trouble with Cops* (1955) at 63; *Culombe*, 367 U.S. at 641 n. 3.

and the right of black Americans to live free and equally under a tenable system of law.

Conclusion

Traditional narratives of constitutional development concerning the criminal process protections of the Bill of Rights are linear and structured around a progressive-spirited political project that transcended a constitutional jurisprudence focused on economic (as opposed to personal) rights and then moved belatedly toward the fulfillment of the true promise of the Bill's criminal process protections. The modern (post–New Deal) Supreme Court is accorded a central role in this process. The path of the development of constitutional criminal process rights presented here, by contrast, is decidedly nonlinear. It does not move teleologically toward the fulfillment of some monistic principle, such as privacy. And it is not authorized or legitimized as the outgrowth of either a critical election or a constitutional moment. In this trajectory, the Supreme Court plays multiple roles, from aggressive, creative rights protection, to setting minimal national standards, to working for transformative policy reform, to negotiating ongoing broad transformations of the political-economic order. In this, the Court is neither a follower of pure legal doctrine nor a mere echo chamber for partisan politics. The Court's thinking throughout was permeated by political and intellectual currents abroad in the country at large and cognizant of changes in formal institutions taking place around it. In some cases, it assimilated these changes. In other cases, it reacted against them. And in some cases, it worked to negotiate and legitimate ongoing transformations.

One thing, however, is clear throughout: The Court is a national political institution that draws its legitimacy in significant part from its role as a forum for rights protection. In performing this task, it stands at the center of what Karen Orren and Stephen Skowronek have called "patterns of intercurrence," or multiple (often contradictory) orderings of authority or incongruities, in the face of specific (often reformist) pressures for institutional change. As far as criminal process rights were concerned, the Court at first worked to defend and expand traditional Fourth and Fifth Amendment criminal process protections concerning privacy in the face of efforts to create a powerful, centralized, and seeing New American State. When that reformist statebuilding effort became all but inevitable, the Court – long before the New Deal constitutional revolution of 1937 – began negotiating away these rights. The Court, again in response to a progressive-spirited reformist campaign, also negotiated away fundamental rights that at first would have frustrated Prohibition. It then turned and, in the face of multiple outrages, grew more protective of those rights, launching the contemporary Court's modern criminal process jurisprudence. That development might have been stillborn with Prohibition had its trajectory not been fueled by another reformist campaign, that for civil rights. At the close of the Civil War, Congress had given the federal courts expanded criminal process jurisdiction to use to supervise the newly conquered South. Following the close of Reconstruction, the Court used these powers mainly to set minimal constitutional standards, sustain sectional reconciliation, and rekindle broad, cross-sectional constitutional authority. As political and cultural conditions altered beginning in the early twentieth century, and as civil rights replaced the labor problem as the chief reformist imperative, the Court began aggressively to use its constitutional criminal process powers to set national criminal process standards, first imposing them on the South and then on the North. The Court became swept up in this project and continued it even after the civil rights movement had achieved its major goals. This, in turn, led to a political reaction against the Court that slowed movement along this developmental path.

Over the course of the last century, the Court both limited and extended constitutional criminal process rights and weighed rights claims in some areas against conflicting rights claims in others. Whiggish narratives positing an initial lack of concern and then a cresting solicitude for personal rights and privacy fail to capture these distinctive developmental dynamics.

3

Reconstituting Individual Rights

From Labor Rights to Civil Rights

Introduction

Traditional narratives of the trajectory of constitutional development concerning civil rights and liberties are quintessentially Whiggish narratives, which posit, first, the vanquishing of reactionary constitutionalism of outmoded economic liberties that characterized the premodern state of courts and parties, and, second (and coincident with the consolidation of the modern state), a linear post-breakthrough progression upward toward an increasing solicitude for personal individual liberties. This linear, progressive narrative, which is structured around barrier, breakthrough, and apotheosis, serves as an ideological adjunct of the process of legitimizing and institutionalizing the policy architecture of the New American State. In its unidimensional developmental structure, however, this narrative has worked systematically to erase the choices that were made in the ongoing process of constructing that state between contentious, agonistic creedal commitments and multiple institutional orders. Instead, as part of the process of inventing the New Constitutional Nation, it has worked systematically to construct those choices and settlements as a monistic triumph of principle.

In this chapter, I spotlight some of the key erasures that have helped to consolidate the Whiggish developmental narrative by focusing on two major – indeed, central – areas of twentieth-century constitutional reform that are typically treated separately: labor rights and civil rights. To say they are treated separately, however, is perhaps not quite right. In traditional narratives of constitutional development, the paths of development of labor rights and civil rights are treated sequentially, and, indeed, these sequential reforms constitute the spine of these unidimensional Whiggish narratives. First came the recognition of the rights of labor, then of blacks, and then of others, in a movement – delays and setbacks notwithstanding – toward the triumph of civil rights and individual freedom.

At the center of the decidedly less Whiggish account I present here, which emphasizes tragic choices and intercurrence, however, is a frank and aggressive campaign by early-twentieth-century progressives and liberals to curtail and delegitimize individual rights claims in favor of group rights. While defenders of modern, group-oriented conceptions of rights commonly present those conceptions as the issue of a burgeoning commitment to the principles of freedom, democracy, and equality, a consideration of their genealogy paints a picture that is considerably more complex and rife with conflicts, settlements, and sacrifices of important individual rights and foundational creedal commitments. To demonstrate this, I trace the origins of the modern civil rights jurisprudence of group rights back to its founding moments, when it was deployed not on behalf of African Americans, but rather on behalf of organized labor. The simultaneous consideration of the political contestation involving individual and group rights claims between labor and blacks illustrates both how sacrifices between incommensurable commitments to basic rights and liberties are made in constitutional development and also how such sacrifices and settlements are institutionalized in significant part by erasing them from constitutional memory in the service of the ideological, regime-sustaining narratives of progress.

Specifically, in the pages that follow, I argue that the U.S. Supreme Court's late-twentieth-century group-oriented civil rights jurisprudence as reflected in busing and affirmative action cases such as *Swann v. Charlotte-Mecklenberg* (1971) and *United Steelworkers of America v. Weber* (1979), respectively, does not represent a philosophical project of the sort imagined by constitutional theorists aligned with the new regime.[1] It is, rather, more accurately depicted as the legitimating cap to a strategically informed and highly politicized project of ideological reconstruction taken up by black Americans (and many of their supporters) to avail themselves of the potentially useful limitations on individual liberty that were an essential part of the early-twentieth-century statebuilding process. These black Americans undertook the project in this form not because they believed it advanced the cause of justice in an abstract philosophical sense, but because it served to advance their interests as a corporatist group within the novel institutional environment of the New American State.

This path of constitutional development concerning contemporary conceptions of civil rights becomes apparent if, after setting out the settlements that characterize the preexisting institutional order, we trace the relation between the U.S. Supreme Court's neglected New Deal Norris-LaGuardia civil liberties decisions involving labor injunctions – *Senn v. Tile Layers Union* (1937) and *Lauf v. Shinner* (1938) – and their mostly unacknowledged civil

---

[1] *Swann v. Charlotte-Mecklenberg*, 402 U.S. 1 (1971) (This case is discussed more fully in the subsequent chapter on civil liberties in education); *United Steelworkers of America v. Weber*, 443 U.S. 193 (1979).

rights progeny – *New Negro Alliance v. Sanitary Grocery* (1938) and *Hughes v. Superior Court* (1950). In the *Senn* and *Lauf* cases, the Court upheld the constitutionality of the Norris-LaGuardia Act and, in the process, played an important role in the institutionalization of a novel group conception of the rights of labor. At the same time, at the urging of progressive and liberal reformers, the Court frankly, forthrightly, and even brutally privileged that conception of those rights over the competing claims of individual workers to pursue a livelihood without hindrance or harassment. Recognizing this radical shift in constitutional doctrine and the institutional environment of which it was a part, black Americans abandoned their longstanding traditional commitment to an individualist conception of civil rights and began to advance their cause in a way that was attuned to the newly institutionalized imperatives of the New American State. In the subsequent *New Negro Alliance* and *Hughes* cases, the Court signaled that it was willing to consider welcoming blacks as a group into this new statist order by treating civil rights pickets as a category of labor dispute. In so doing, the Court began the process of according blacks the same group protections that had benefited organized labor (and had trumped individual rights claims), helping to set the path of constitutional development concerning civil rights for the rest of the twentieth century.[2] It is worth noting, however, that the Court's certification of blacks as a class within the new regime was not immediate. Throughout the 1950s, the Court continued to parry claims that blacks were a constitutional class akin to labor. At the height of the Warren-era "Rights Revolution," however, the Court was finally ready to negotiate the award of Norris-LaGuardia – like class status for constitutional purposes to blacks.

As part of the process of constructing a regime-sustaining Whiggish ideology of progress under which individual liberties did not conflict with group rights, the developmental link between the Warren-era group-oriented civil rights decisions concerning busing, voting rights, and (later) affirmative action and the earlier anti–individual rights decisions was severed. This was accomplished through a reimagining both on the Court and in the academy of the Norris-LaGuardia decisions not as corporatist, anti–individual rights decisions (as progressives had frankly admitted them to be while defending them in the 1930s), but rather – in a pattern repeated throughout this book – as "free speech" decisions, which advanced rather than limited individual rights.[3] Thus, the group rights of both labor and blacks were conjoined with a solicitude for individual liberties as part of a purportedly seamless

---

[2] *Senn v. Tile Layers Union*, 301 U.S. 468 (1937); *Lauf v. Shinner*, 303 U.S. 323 (1938); *New Negro Alliance v. Sanitary Grocery*, 303 U.S. 552 (1938); *Hughes v. Superior Court*, 339 U.S. 460 (1950).

[3] On the central ideological role of free speech in contemporary American constitutionalism, see G. Edward White, "Free Speech and the Bifurcated Review Project: The 'Preferred Position' Cases," in *Constitutionalism and American Culture*, eds. VanBurkleo, Hall, and Kaczorowski, 99–122.

constitutional program in which group rights and individual rights harmoniously coexisted. By exploring both the actual developmental link between the contemporary group-oriented understanding of civil rights and the progressive civil liberties sacrifices made in the Court's Norris-LaGuardia decisions, this chapter spotlights an important episode in the construction of constitutional memory in the interest of a regime-sustaining ideology of civil rights and civil liberties progress.

Labor Individualism and Liberty: The Traditional Ideological Benchmark

The foundations of modern American constitutionalism were forged, to a significant extent, in the fires of reformist opposition to deeply rooted understandings of the nature of work and the moral meaning of the individual worker, which stood as an institutional pillar of the state of courts and parties. These understandings, which imagined the worker as a free-standing, autonomous individual operating within a captialist economic order, had themselves at one time been the fruit of a radically reformist emancipatory political project – the liberation of the autonomous individual from the shackles of feudalism.[4] While plainly individualist in many respects, the imagining of the worker that prevailed in the United States through the end of the nineteenth century was simultaneously informed by a strong conception of the common good, a perception tied to the producer ethic rooted in the Puritan concept of the calling.[5] This moralized vision of callings and work

---

[4] The target, in the earlier case, was a feudal order premised upon status rather than contract. Capitalist individualism represented a liberation of the worker from the constraints imposed upon him by feudalism. See Sir Henry Sumner Maine, *Ancient Law: Its Connection with the Early History of Society and Its Relation to Modern Ideas* (n.p.: Dorset Press, 1986)[1861], 141; Isaac Kramnick, *Republicanism and Bourgeois Radicalism: Political Ideology in Late Eighteenth-Century England and America* (Ithaca, NY: Cornell University Press, 1990), 4–18. Louis Hartz, *The Liberal Tradition in America: An Interpretation of American Political Thought Since the Revolution* (New York: Harcourt, Brace and World, Inc., 1955). On the way in which the meaning of rights is constructed in a dialectical response to adversity, see Primus, *The American Language of Rights.*

[5] See John Patrick Diggins, *The Lost Soul of American Politics: Virtue, Self-Interest, and the Foundations of Liberalism* (New York: Basic Books, 1984). The religious undergirding of this imagination is apparent in the writings of the English Puritans, whose influence upon American thought was direct. The writings of sixteenth-century Cambridge theologian William Perkins reflected this suffusing spirit well: "A vocation or calling," Perkins explained, "is a certain kind of life, ordained and imposed on man by God, for the common good.... The author of every calling, is God himself...." "The finall cause or end of every calling," the theologian continued, is "for the common good: that is, for the benefite and good estate of mankinde. In mans body there be sundry parts and members, and every one hath his severall use and office, which it performeth not for it selfe, but for the good of the whole bodie; as the office of the eye, is to see, of the eare to heare, and the foote to goe. Now all societies of men, are bodies...and in these bodies there be severall members which are men walking in severall callings and offices, the execution whereof, must tend to the happy and good estate of the

was reflected both in the religious presuppositions and the Lockeanism of the early Americans, who, inverting the commitments of classical republicanism, spoke repeatedly of the sanctity of work and of devotion to calling.[6]

The sweeping geographic expanse and the striking economic abundance of the United States ensured that the cultural and religious disposition of its inhabitants to value work and its derivative, property, would not die young. The simple fact that there was an abundance of productive land made it relatively easy for men of humble origins to assume the status of craftsmen, landowners, and freeholding farmers. Whether Americans actually worked harder than people in other countries is an open question. But it was clearly the case that Americans came to an unusual degree to define themselves by their work. They famously took a peculiar pride in their status as independent producers.[7]

The producer ethic was one of the central axes of American political thought for much of the nineteenth century. Jefferson and the Jeffersonians placed the independent and self-sufficient property-owning agrarian producer at the center of their political thought, and imagined him to be the veritable bulwark of a free government.[8] Locke's labor theory of value and emphasis on property rights was a fundamental component of the

rest. . . . The common good of men stands in this, not onely that they live, but that they live well, in righteousness and holines, and consequently in true happinesse. And for the attainment hereunto, God hath ordained and disposed all callings, and in his providence designed the persons to beare them." William Perkins, "A Treatise of the Vocations or Callings of men, with sorts and kinds of them, and the right use thereof," in *Puritan Political Ideas, 1558–1794*, ed. Edmund Morgan (Indianapolis: Bobbs-Merrill, 1965), 36, 39.

[6] C. B. Macpherson, *The Political Theory of Possessive Individualism: Hobbes to Locke* (London: Oxford University Press, 1962). Locke himself derived the right to property from the duty to labor. John Locke, *Second Treatise of Government*, ed. C. B. Macpherson (Indianapolis: Hackett Publishing Co., 1980)[1690], 18–30; Kramnick, *Republicanism and Bourgeois Radicalism*, 1. Michael Sandel, as part of an intellectual project attempting to trace out an American republican tradition, refers to this moralized vision of labor as "republican." In its valorization of work and production, however, it is actually rather distant from classical republicanism, which emphasized the advantages of leisure over work. See Michael Sandel, *Democracy's Discontent: America in Search of a Public Philosophy* (Cambridge, MA: The Belknap Press of the Harvard University Press, 1996), 193. William Forbath similarly mistakes the Protestant underpinnings of liberalism for republicanism. See Forbath, "The Ambiguities of Free Labor: Law and Labor in the Gilded Age," *Wisconsin Law Review* (1985): 767.

[7] See Robert Wuthnow, *Poor Richard's Principle: Recovering the American Dream Through the Moral Dimension of Work, Business, and Money* (Princeton: Princeton University Press, 1999) (on the real and, he argues, widely emulated, work habits of Benjamin Franklin).

[8] See Joyce Appleby, *Liberalism and Republicanism in the Historical Imagination* (Cambridge, MA: Harvard University Press, 1992); Douglass G. Adair, *The Intellectual Origins of Jeffersonian Democracy: Republicanism, the Class Struggle, and the Virtuous Farmer*, ed. Mark E. Yellin (Lanham, MD: Lexington Books, 2000); Thomas Jefferson, *Notes on the State of Virginia*, in *The Portable Thomas Jefferson*, ed. Merrill D. Peterson (New York: Penguin, 1975), 217; Jean Yarbrough, *American Virtues: Thomas Jefferson on the Character of a Free People* (Lawrence: University Press of Kansas, 1998), 55–101.

political thought of Federalists like John Marshall.[9] Andrew Jackson and the Jacksonians mounted a militant egalitarian defense of the small producer against the idle, nonproducing classes who, as the Jacksonians saw it, sought to appropriate state power to advance corrupt and self-interested ends.[10] In a sign of the grip that the producer ethic had on the imagination of Americans, Benjamin Franklin's paeans to industry remained national bestsellers through much of the nineteenth century, long after they had first been penned.[11]

The centrality of the producer ethic and the independent worker to the country's social and political self-conception was only reinforced by the emergent struggle over chattel slavery, a central episode in American political development. The fires of that struggle recast the individualist producer ethic into a distinctive free labor ideology, which, in a new context, once again put the small property-owning producer at the heart of American notions of political liberty.[12] As Jefferson and Jackson had, each in his own way, nourished and sustained these preoccupations in his own time, Lincoln and the Republican Party advanced them in a distinctive form in the mid-nineteenth century. In turn, two Republican appointees to the Supreme Court, Stephen J. Field, a Democrat appointed by Lincoln, and Joseph Bradley, a Republican appointed by Grant, played prominent parts in importing this most recent instantiation of the liberal producer ethic into that Court's constitutional decisions.

---

[9] See *Johnson v. M'Intosh*, 21 U.S. 543 (1823); Charles F. Hobson, *The Great Chief Justice: John Marshall and the Rule of Law* (Lawrence: University Press of Kansas, 1996), 170–80; James T. Ely Jr., *The Guardian of Every Other Right: A Constitutional History of Property Rights* (New York: Oxford University Press, 1992), 42–58.

[10] This understanding of Jacksonianism (at least in its most influential guise) was advanced most prominently in Arthur M. Schlesinger Jr., *The Age of Jackson* (Boston: Little, Brown and Co., 1946). See also Robert V. Remini, *Andrew Jackson and the Bank War: A Study in the Growth of Presidential Power* (New York: W. W. Norton, 1967). Schlesinger made an explicit link between the Jacksonians and their Jeffersonian predecessors. Others (in my view, rightly) have placed more emphasis on the consensus entrepreneurial-capitalist (as opposed to oppositionist-egalitarian) aspects of Jacksonianism. See Richard Hofstadter, *The American Political Tradition and the Men Who Made It* (New York: Alfred A. Knopf, 1959). Bray Hammond, *Banks and Politics from the Revolution to the Civil War* (Princeton: Princeton University Press, 1948). See also Marvin Meyers, *The Jacksonian Persuasion: Politics and Belief* (Stanford: Stanford University Press, 1957).

[11] J. A. Leo Lemay and P. M. Zall, eds., *Benjamin Franklin's Autobiography: An Authoritative Text, Backgrounds, Criticism* (New York: W. W. Norton, 1986), xiii. See Nain-Sheng Huang, *Benjamin Franklin in American Thought and Culture, 1790–1990* (Philadelphia: American Philosophical Society, 1994), 42–107. For a further discussion of the producer ethic, see Hattam, *Labor Visions*, ch. 3; Diggins, *Lost Soul of American Politics*; Sandel, *Democracy's Discontent*.

[12] Eric Foner, *Free Soil, Free Labor, Free Men: The Ideology of the Republican Party before the Civil War* (New York: Oxford University Press, 1970). See Abraham Lincoln, "Address before the Wisconsin State Agricultural Society, Milwaukee, Wisconsin" (September 30, 1859), in Abraham Lincoln, *Selected Speeches and Writings* (New York: Vintage Books, 1992), 233–7.

In the wake of the Union victory in the Civil War and in the heyday of what Richard Bensel has called the Civil War Party State, a constitutionalism of callings became a fixture of the Court's constitutional jurisprudence. This was apparent in the Court's first decision interpreting the Fourteenth Amendment, the *Slaughterhouse Cases* (1873), only a few years after Lee's surrender at Appomattox. Fittingly enough, the argument in *Slaughterhouse* evincing a foundational commitment to the dignity of labor and the sanctity of property was advanced by an old Jacksonian Democrat (and former Supreme Court justice), John Archibald Campbell, the attorney for the plaintiffs. And it was also fitting that that argument was both adopted and defended by the Free Labor Lincoln and Grant appointees, Justices Bradley and Field.[13]

Slaughterhouse involved a constitutional challenge to a New Orleans butchering monopoly law that threw hundreds of the city's independent butchers out of business. As Campbell told the Court, the constitutional problem with the law was plain:

The only question then is this: "When a state passes a law depriving a thousand people, who have acquired valuable property, and who, through its instrumentality, are engaged in an honest and necessary business, which they understand, of their right to use such their own property, and to labor in such their honest and necessary business, and gives a monopoly, embracing the whole subject, including the right to labor in such business, to seventeen other persons – whether the state has abridged any of the privileges or immunities of these thousand persons?"[14]

Quoting Thiers (and the Puritans), Campbell reminded the Court of the religious imperative of labor: "[T]he obligation to labor," Campbell emphasized, "[is] a duty, a thing ordained of God, and which if submitted to faithfully, secured a blessing to the human family." Tracing out the implications of this obligation with Lockean logic, he then explained that a right to property arose from fidelity to this duty. The implications of this lineage for the New Orleans butchering monopoly, Campbell contended, were plain: "[T]he right to labor, the right to one's self physically and intellectually, and to the product of one's own faculties, is past doubt property, and property of a sacred kind." Thus, any deprivation of this right by legislative decree was a deprivation of liberty and property without due process of law. The question went to the core of traditional constitutional rights.[15]

---

[13] In the context of his times, Campbell, a native Georgian, was a moderate on slavery. He had voted with the Court in its infamous *Dred Scott* (1857) decision – decided on property rights grounds. At the same time, "He believed free labor would gradually and peacefully displace the less efficient 'peculiar institution.'" Tony Freyer, "John Archibald Campbell," in *The Oxford Companion to the Supreme Court of the United States*, eds. Kermit L. Hall, et al. (New York: Oxford University Press, 1992), 116–17.

[14] *Slaughterhouse Cases*, 83 U.S. 36 (1873) at 55.

[15] *Slaughterhouse*, 83 U.S. at 50–6.

The Free Labor Republican dissents in the *Slaughterhouse* case meshed seamlessly with the argument advanced by the plaintiff's Jacksonian Democratic counsel. Writing soon after emancipation and animadverting against the monopoly, Justice Field vehemently defended what he called "the right of free labor, one of the most sacred and imperscriptable rights of man." He defined this right in part as the "right to pursue one of the ordinary trades or callings of life," a right that he declared, "appertain[s] solely to the individual." Moreover, the "right to pursue the ordinary avocations of life" was for Field not simply a matter of liberty, but also the essence of equality, entitling each American "to enjoy equally [with the others] the fruits of his labor." "[A]ll grants of exclusive privileges in contravention of this equality," he added in a Jacksonian echo, "are against common right and void."[16]

In a separate dissent in the case, Justice Bradley launched similar arguments at the Court's majority. "[T]he right of any citizen to follow whatever lawful employment he chooses to adopt (submitting himself to all lawful regulations) is one of his most valuable rights, and one which the legislature of the state cannot invade. . . ." he declared. Bradley added:

[T]he individual citizen, as a necessity, must be left free to adopt such calling, profession, or trade as may seem to him most conducive [to the preservation of his rights to life, liberty, and the pursuit of happiness]. Without this right he cannot be a freeman. This right to choose one's calling is an essential part of that liberty which it is the object of government to protect, and a calling, when chosen, is a man's property and right. Liberty and property are not protected where these rights are arbitrarily assailed.[17]

Slaughterhouse proved just the beginning of a constitutional jurisprudence anchored in considerations of callings, property, and labor. As the nation's political economy began to undergo radical transformations in the late nineteenth and early twentieth centuries and the regulatory claims of an emergent central state multiplied, the Court was repeatedly called upon both to remove state-level barriers to the construction of a national market (under its commerce clause jurisprudence) and to draw lines and distinguish legitimate state police power regulations from illegitimate special interest or "class legislation" (pursuant to the Fourteenth Amendment).[18] Given the prevailing ideological order, class legislation was considered a constitutional abomination because it was understood as the issue of self-interested individuals or groups using the power of government for their own private advantage and profit while circumscribing the God-given property and labor rights of

---

[16] *Slaughterhouse*, 83 U.S. at 88–110.

[17] *Slaughterhouse*, 83 U.S. at 116.

[18] Richard Franklin Bensel, *The Political Economy of American Industrialization, 1877–1900* (Cambridge: Cambridge University Press, 2000), 321–49.

others.[19] In striking down class legislation infringing upon God-given private rights, the Court did not imagine itself as either a tool of rapacious capitalists, a bastion of inequality, or an opponent of democratic self-government. Rather, it understood itself to be a champion of liberty and equality and a faithful steward of American constitutional democracy.[20]

At the dawn of the statebuilding era, the Court undertook the task of separating legitimate laws from illegitimate class legislation with a sense of high purpose, invalidating only those laws that it was convinced were passed pursuant to private rather than public purposes.[21] In the same year that it decided *Slaughterhouse* – which had upheld the New Orleans butchering law, albeit narrowly – the Court upheld by a broad margin the constitutionality of an outright ban on liquor sales in Iowa. In his concurrence in this case, Justice Bradley distinguished a ban on alcohol motivated by genuine public health and safety concerns from "the right to pursue such lawful avocation as a man chooses to adopt, unrestricted by tyrannical and corrupt monopolies."[22] Justice Field agreed, writing, "It was because the act of Louisiana transcended the limits of police regulation, and asserted a power in the state to farm out the ordinary avocations of life, that dissent was made

---

[19] Howard Gillman charts at length the history of the efforts of judges to draw these distinctions, in the process reintroducing twentieth-century scholars to the once widely-known textbook law of the last century. On the emergent state itself, see Robert H. Wiebe, *The Search for Order, 1877–1920* (New York: Hill and Wang, 1967); Skowronek, *Building a New American State.*

[20] Two prominent dissents from the orthodox narrative of the laissez-faire capitalist judge in self-interested service to his class are Charles McCurdy, "Justice Field and the Jurisprudence of Government-Business Relations: Some Parameters of Laissez-Faire Constitutionalism, 1863–1897," *Journal of American History* 61 (1975): 970–1005; and Gillman, *The Constitution Besieged.* Nor was the Court simply enforcing relations established through a feudal inheritance. See, e.g., Karen Orren, *Belated Feudalism: Labor, the Law, and Liberal Development in the United States* (New York: Cambridge University Press, 1991); Eric Foner, *The Story of American Freedom* (New York: W. W. Norton, 1998), 124–30.

[21] The "laissez-faire" Court actually upheld the constitutionality of an overwhelming amount of public interest legislation. Sizing up in the 1920s the run of Fourteenth Amendment police power decisions, Harvard Law School Professor Charles Warren concluded that: "[i]t may fairly be said that the support which the Court has thus given to the police power of the states has been one of the most remarkable features of its career. Certainly a litigant who hopes to overturn the deliberate judgment of a state legislature as expressed in this form of legislation has a very scanty hope of assistance from the Court." Charles Warren, *The Supreme Court in United States History,* Vol. II (Boston: Little, Brown, 1926), 742. Warren's view has been confirmed by Melvin Urofsky. Urofsky, "Myth and Reality: The Supreme Court and Protective Legislation in the Progressive Era," *Yearbook of the Supreme Court Historical Society* (1983): 53–72. See also Urofsky, "State Courts and Protective Legislation during the Progressive Era: A Re-evaluation," *Journal of American History* 72 (1985): 63–91. On the pervasiveness of nineteenth-century regulatory statutes that either survived or escaped court scrutiny, see William J. Novak, *The People's Welfare: Law and Regulation in Nineteenth Century America* (Chapel Hill: University of North Carolina Press, 1996).

[22] *Bartemeyer v. Iowa,* 85 U.S. 129, 136 (1873) (Justice Bradley, concurring).

to the judgment of the Court." Here, Field saw no "parcel[ing] out to fa-vored citizens the ordinary trades and callings of life."[23] Relying on similar reasoning, the Court subsequently upheld (among other things) laws regulat-ing grain elevators, the insurance industry, banking, fishing, and education, and outright bans on the operation of billiard halls and the manufacture of oleomargarine.[24]

During the initial years of the statebuilding era, the justices frequently disagreed about whether a particular law was passed to advance public or private interests (in retrospect, the oleomargarine opinion seems clearly to have been a mistake). And when their best judgment told them that the private interest motivation had been paramount, the justices immediately fixed their attention on those whose livelihood and honest calling had been sacrificed by the self-serving commandeering of the coercive powers of gov-ernment. In his dissent in the grain elevator case, for instance, Justice Field was angered by what he took to be a private interest power grab and de-fended the fundamental liberty of all Americans "to pursue such callings and avocations as may be most suitable to develop his capacities, and give to them their highest enjoyment."[25] Field took the same position in his lone dis-sent in the oleomargarine case, though Justice Harlan insisted in his majority opinion for the Court that the regulation in question did nothing to inhibit "the privilege of pursuing an ordinary calling or trade, and of acquiring and selling property," which "is an essential part of [a person's] rights of liberty and property, as guaranteed by the Fourteenth Amendment."[26]

From Calling to Class: The Ideological Construction of the Union Worker

The ideological reconstruction concerning work and labor that accompa-nied the building of the New American State is most evident in the contrast between two types of late-nineteenth- and early-twentieth-century labor cases. The first, where change was assimilated and the ideological bench-mark was repeatedly reinforced, involved cases in which the assertion of new

---

[23] *Bartemeyer*, 85 U.S. at 139 (Justice Field, concurring). See also *Mugler v. Kansas*, 123 U.S. 623 (1887) (upholding Kansas law prohibiting the manufacture and sale of intoxicating liquors).

[24] *Munn v. Illinois*, 94 U.S. 113 (1877) (Justice Field dissenting) (upholding rate regulation scheme for Chicago grain elevators); *Noble State Bank v. Haskell*, 219 U.S. 104 (1911) (up-holding Oklahoma law assessing banks for purpose of setting up a deposit guarantee fund); *Lawton v. Steele*, 152 U.S. 133 (1894) (upholding New York State law limiting fishing to prevent the exhaustion of the fish supply); *German Alliance Ins. Co. v. Lewis*, 233 U.S. 389 (1914) (following *Munn* in upholding rate regulation in insurance industry); *Berea College v. Kentucky*, 211 U.S. 45 (1908) (upholding state law forbidding private colleges chartered by the state from educating black and white students together); *Murphy v. California*, 225 U.S. 623 (1912) (upholding municipal ordinance banning billiard halls); *Powell v. Pennsylvania*, 127 U.S. 678 (1888) (upholding oleomargarine ban).

[25] *Munn*, 94 U.S. at 142.

[26] *Powell*, 127 U.S. at 692.

regulatory police powers ran into long-legitimate claims of individual rights. The second, however, proved to be a crucible of ideological transformation. These cases involved the efforts of labor activists and reformers to seek novel legitimacy for the collective power of labor unions. Such powers had long been tightly constrained. Under the common law that prevailed in the state of courts and parties, trade unions had been legal. But they had not been legal in a form that political progressives involved in the process of building a New American State found serviceable. The old common law labor union simply could not fulfill its function in a modern order comprised (as progressive lawyer Louis D. Brandeis put it) of plants and businesses rather than tools and trades.[27]

The status of trade unions had long been governed by English common law, which had been imported to North America both before and subsequent to the Revolution. At common law, an institutional pillar of governance under the state of courts and parties, it had long been considered a criminal conspiracy for workmen to combine against their masters for any purpose – including for the purpose of demanding a wage increase or a change in work conditions. Even when legislation was passed in England in 1825 legalizing labor combinations, the reforming statute made it clear that intimidation by labor unions would not be tolerated.[28]

The theory underlying this approach derived from *sic utere tuo* legal liberalism.[29] Individuals had a right to come together in groups in any way they pleased. And so the law held there was nothing illegal per se about trade unions. However, once these groups directed the power of their combination toward their employers, they acted in a way that invaded the right of another to conduct a lawful trade or business free from disturbance. (Under the prevailing producer ethic, both the employer and the employee were considered producers.) Those invading this right of others through combination were subject to civil damages. Under English law, individuals were at full liberty to take their grievances to their employers. If they were denied legitimate redress, they were free to quit and seek employment elsewhere.

In the United States (as in England), common law damages were available for the enticement of servants away from their employers and for

---

[27] *New State Ice v. Liebmann*, 285 U.S. 262, 282 (1932) (Justice Brandeis, dissenting).

[28] Thomas S. Cogley, *The Law of Strikes, Lockout and Labor Organizations* (Washington, D.C.: W. H. Lowdermilk & Co., 1894), Sec. 28. See, generally, Hattam, *Labor Visions and Labor Power*, 30–75; Daniel R. Ernst, *Lawyers Against Labor: From Individual Rights to Corporate Liberalism* (Urbana: University of Illinois Press, 1995), 72–6. On the reception of English common law concerning labor into the American political order, see Orren, *Belated Feudalism*.

[29] It was not a theory premised on feudal ideas. Karen Orren has argued that the preprogressive legal order amounted to a "feudal" holdover within what many have otherwise taken to be a liberal polity. Orren, *Belated Feudalism*. See also Louis Hartz, *The Liberal Tradition in America* (New York: Harcourt, Brace & World, Inc., 1955).

conspiracies promoting such enticements. The law looked upon such behavior as a tortious interference with a lawful business. Under traditional American law (and for similar underlying reasons), a business owner could also sue for damages caused by boycotts. Courts conceptualized those boycotts as illegitimate deployments of the powers of combination aimed at injuring and invading the right of the business owner to earn his keep and ply his trade. Equitable remedies such as injunctions, moreover, were available against related, tortious "nuisances" like parading with banners or picketing in front of businesses. These actions were understood in the same light as acts of enticement and boycotts – as intentional attempts, that is, to inflict injury upon a lawful business.[30]

The common law could always be amended by statute. But given the preexisting understandings of property and labor that had become institutionalized within America's constitutional jurisprudence, statutory efforts to legitimize boycotts and strikes, which had long been considered illegally coercive assaults on fundamental producer rights, were taken by courts as ploys to advance not the rights of individual workers, but rather of labor as a political-economic class. And, indeed, labor unions openly anchored their claims with appeals to group, as opposed to individual, power. In their strikes and boycotts, labor unions proudly subsumed the individual within the bosom of the group. Breaking ranks was considered scabbing and betrayal, and the consequences of doing so ranged from personal hostility to physical violence. Unions were clearly private entities that achieved their goals through the exercise of coercion – not simply against employers, but also, and importantly, against fellow employees as well.

It was in this context that the Court defended the constitutional rights of employers and employees to agree, as part of an individually negotiated labor contract, that the employees would not join a labor union. Such agreements, referred to by their critics as "yellow-dog contracts" (a term of opprobrium), originated in the New England textile industry in the 1870s and later became common nationwide. Animated by the same individual (and equal) rights-based outlook that led him to pen his famous dissent in the segregation decision of *Plessy v. Ferguson*, Justice Marshall Harlan wrote the majority opinion in *Adair v. United States* (1908), a decision invalidating a federal law prohibiting interstate carriers from asking their workers to sign yellow-dog contracts and from firing employees for union activities.[31] Adverting to a long line of dignity-of-labor precedent, Justice Harlan insisted

---

[30] Under traditional American law, the recourse to the equitable powers of courts was deemed necessary to head off civil damage suits in cases where either irreparable harm to a lawful business was likely to occur or the ultimate calculation of actual damages to that business would be impossible to measure. Cogley, *Law of Strikes, Lockouts, and Labor Organizations*, Secs. 30, 32, 33. See Ernst, *Lawyers Against Labor*, 69–89.

[31] *Adair v. United States*, 208 U.S. 161 (1908).

on "the right of the person to sell his labor upon such terms as he deems proper." This right, he contended, was "the same as the right of the purchaser of labor to prescribe the conditions upon which he will accept such labor from the person offering to sell it." The Act was pure class legislation, Harlan concluded, with no reasonable relationship to public health, safety, and morals. The Court applied the same analysis in the *Coppage* (1914) decision to strike down a Kansas state law outlawing similar contracts. Such decisions from the High Court, of course, proved to be serious obstacles to the development of a powerful American labor movement.[32]

Thus, as the United States entered the statebuilding era, a commitment to the dignity of labor and the sanctity of calling stood at the heart of the law of strikes, boycotts, pickets, and unions. Within this architecture of understanding, constructed upon a producer ethic foundation, employers and employees alike were conceptualized as "workers" or "laborers." The law of this era was directed at ensuring that each individual laborer, whether employer or employee, was given the freest possible field in which to govern his working life. By the lights of this moralized and individualized vision, the exercise of coercive power by labor unions was adjudged pernicious. And the notion of employees constituting a distinct and differentiated laboring class was alien.[33] The primary means of preserving this order – and the fundamental rights that had been guaranteed within it – against what was taken by many as a deeply disturbing onslaught was the law of conspiracy.[34]

Taking on this powerful and deeply institutionalized vision of work and labor – and the entire constellation of individual common law and constitutional rights that embodied it – would prove a major undertaking for the labor movement and allied progressive political reformers. That undertaking has typically been taken by Whiggish narratives of constitutional development as a negative task – one of clearing the way of legal, political, and ideological barriers, of old, outmoded thinking. But, although there was certainly much negative work involved, these accounts underemphasize the affirmative, substantive content of the reformist vision concerning labor, a significant failing given that that vision would come to form a crucial part of the ideological architecture of the New American State.

The task for labor reformers of the late nineteenth and early twentieth century was to forge a new, affirmative ideology that was powerful enough

---

[32] *Coppage v. Kansas*, 236 U.S. 1 (1915). See also *Hitchman Coal & Coke Co. v. Mitchell*, 245 U.S. 229 (1917) (rejecting constitutional challenge to injunctions against union activities said to induce the breach of yellow-dog contracts). See Gillman, *Constitution Besieged*; William E. Forbath, *Law and the Shaping of the American Labor Movement* (Cambridge, MA: Harvard University Press, 1991).

[33] Daniel R. Ernst, "Free Labor, the Consumer Interest, and the Law of Industrial Disputes, 1885–1900," *American Journal of Legal History* 36 (January 1992): 19.

[34] Hattam, *Labor Visions, passim.*

to rival – and ultimately displace – the dignity-of-labor, anticlass legislation ideology and jurisprudence. At the center of this vision was an unabashed – and, in the American context, novel – statism. A critical mass of forward-looking reformist thinkers came to believe that a strong central state was essential to managing the nation's political economy in a way that checked the excesses of private power, including the power of employers over workers, in the new era of urbanization and industrial combination. For these partisans of the statebuilding project, judges who interposed their views of whether economic legislation was directed toward public or private purposes stood as potential (and unpredictable) obstacles to the construction of new lines of political and regulatory authority. Indeed, many of these reformers took judges to be members of (and, hence, agents of) the very capitalist classes the New American State was charged with taming. But even if one held a more charitable view of the personal motivations of the judges themselves, it seemed to many that the doctrinal rubrics they were committed to applying in constitutional cases were nettlesome relics of an increasingly outmoded and ill-adapted state of courts and parties. The notion that there was a fundamental "right" to pursue an honest trade or calling, in particular, was, for progressive legalists, a right that was clearly associated with a dying order. It was an obstacle to statebuilding and needed to be excised from the constitutional imagination and prevailing institutional order.

The campaign to do so was not simply a matter of the negative project of overruling legal precedent. The changes could be institutionalized only through an affirmative project of ideological reconstruction. The individualist, dignity-of-labor jurisprudence, after all, had been institutionalized not simply (or even primarily) through judicial power, but by the mutual reinforcement of the discourses and decisions of courts by an ambient ideology of work and labor. Any sustainable defeat of this dignity-of-labor constitutionalism had to be buttressed by a countervailing ideology that would fuse a new, state-friendly labor jurisprudence with broader and supportive currents in modern political practice and thought.

Progressive Legalism: The Deconstructive and Reconstructive Project
Two of the chief architects of both the negative project of deconstruction and the affirmative project of reconstruction were Oliver Wendell Holmes Jr. and Louis D. Brandeis. Writing in the *Harvard Law Review* in 1894, the hard-edged skeptic Oliver Wendell Holmes sounded the call for a new constitutionalism of work and labor. In Holmes's estimation, tradition and the moral commitment to work and calling, which had long constituted the ideological foundation of old-style judging on the subject, were now bankrupt. What was needed was a new workplace constitutionalism that issued not from traditions and age-old moral visions but rather from a forthright engagement with the world at hand. "[V]iews of policy," he contended in speaking of law, "are taught by experience of the interests of life." "These

interests," the Civil War veteran and social Darwinist explained using a martial metaphor, "are the field of battle."[35]

Boycotts, Holmes boldly contended, are not infringements of vested rights. Rather, they are battles for power. And the legal question of "whether and how far a privilege [such as the privilege of boycotting] shall be allowed is a question of policy." He continued:

Questions of policy are legislative questions, and judges are shy of reasoning from such grounds. Therefore, decisions for or against the privilege, which really can stand only upon such grounds, often are presented as hollow deductions from empty general propositions like *sic utere tuo et alienum non laedas*, which teaches nothing but a benevolent yearning, or else are put as if they themselves embodied a postulate of the law and admitted of no further deduction, as when it is said that, although there is temporal damage, there is no wrong; whereas, the very thing to be found out is whether there is a wrong or not, and if not, why not.[36]

As to whether the courts should enjoin union-led labor boycotts, Holmes, beholding a vast Darwinian struggle for existence, declared that "[b]ehind all this is the question whether the courts are not flying in the face of the organization of the world which is taking place so fast, and of its inevitable consequences."[37]

This assessment of the trajectory of history was strongly influenced by the waves of railroad and other strikes (and other upheavals and outbreaks of disorder) that Holmes had seen all around him in the late nineteenth century. When judges met these strikes by aggressively wielding antistrike injunctions, Holmes, a pioneering innovator within legal scholarship, chose to interpret these events as the embodiment of a Darwinian battle of class against class, of labor against capital. While a skeptic like Holmes felt comfortable looking upon this disorder and calling it war, others preferred to cast it in a far more positive light. Holmes's friend, the influential progressive reformer Louis D. Brandeis, found it more congenial to look upon the same disorders and construct them not as war, but rather as a form of forward-looking democratic struggle.

The most prominent clash in the war – or struggle – occurred one year after the publication of Holmes's landmark *Harvard Law Review* piece. At that time, the Supreme Court upheld the contempt citation of Eugene V. Debs, the socialist head of the American Railway Union. Acting in sympathy with striking Pullman Company workers, Debs had persisted in leading a nationwide railway worker boycott of trains containing Pullman cars in the teeth of a court injunction against such an action. For this, Debs had been charged with criminal conspiracy. In a unanimous opinion by Justice

[35] Oliver Wendell Holmes Jr. "Privilege, Malice and Intent," *Harvard Law Review* 8 (April 1893): 3, 7. Holmes's essay is discussed in Ernst, *Lawyers Against Labor*, 81–5.
[36] Holmes, "Privilege, Malice and Intent," 3.
[37] Holmes, "Privilege, Malice and Intent," 3.

David Brewer, the Court upheld the federal antiboycott injunctions, arguing that the Railway Union's actions were a restraint on trade, interfered with interstate commerce and the mails, and constituted both a public nuisance and an attack on the legitimate property rights of the railroads.[38]

As the dignity-of-labor constitututionalists had been informed by currents of thought in the wider polity and culture, so, too, were Holmes and Brandeis. In challenging the traditional constitutionalism of work and labor, both found it useful to draw upon the age's ambient Social Darwinism, albeit a Darwinism of a different variety from that imputed (in much exaggerated form) to their "laissez-faire" constitutional opponents.[39] What many consider the "reactionary" Darwinism focused on a struggle of individual against individual. The "progressive" Darwinism of Holmes and Brandeis, however, centered on a struggle of class against class.[40]

Holmes and Brandeis's inclination to import Darwinism into American constitutionalism proved to be inspired. Beginning in the late nineteenth century, the ascendance of science and scientific theories of history had already begun to undercut the intellectual authority of the moralized understanding of labor that had undergirded the traditional American imagination of work and labor. With its secularism and scientism, its privileging of power over right, and its commitment to notions of historical and social destiny (along with agnosticism concerning the ultimate destination of the ordained new order), Darwinism provided a grounding for a new constitutionalism that was amenable to the imperatives of a New American State. The nation's courts had long troubled the statebuilding project through their unpredictable wielding of doctrinal rubrics concerning class legislation. Now, in response, both Holmes and Brandeis boldly countered the charge of class legislation with the Darwinian argument that if the laboring classes were

---

[38] *In re Debs*, 158 U.S. 564 (1895). See also *Gompers v. Buck's Stove and Range Co.*, 221 U.S. 418 (1911). See Ernst, *Lawyers Against Labor*, 76–7. Neither Holmes nor Brandeis was yet serving on the Court.

[39] It is one of the commonplaces of constitutional narratives, of course, that it was the Court's "laissez-faire" justices such as Justice Field who were the social Darwinists. And it is undeniable that many defended the Supreme Court's decisions striking down workplace regulation laws in the pervasive social Darwinist rhetoric of the day. But the sort of rights-based constitutionalism hewed to by Field and the like-minded justices, as we have seen, long predates *The Origin of Species* (1859). The rise of the progressive jurisprudence of Holmes and Brandeis, on the other hand, is coincident with the heyday of Darwinist ideas themselves.

[40] That Brandeis (and, to a much lesser extent, Holmes) was convinced that their jurisprudence was fundamentally anti-Darwinist is simply a testament to the centrifugal pull of ideas as powerful as social Darwinism. See *Lochner v. New York*, 198 U.S. at 75 ("The Fourteenth Amendment does not enact Herbert Spencer's Social Statics"). (Justice Holmes, dissenting). See, generally, Richard Hofstadter, *Social Darwinism in American Political Thought*; Eric Goldman, *Rendezvous with Destiny: A History of Modern American Reform* (New York: Alfred A. Knopf, 1952), 92–3. See also Morton G. White, *The Origin of Dewey's Instrumentalism* (New York: Columbia University Press, 1943).

destined to triumph socially and legislatively, the Court and the Constitution could not, and should not, stand in their way. This argument was anchored in claims not of right but of power. It imagined society as a growing organism. For such a state, a "living constitutionalism" was of necessity the order of the day.[41]

Despite the similarity of many of their commitments, Holmes's and Brandeis's Darwinisms were not of a piece. Holmes's was dour and fatalistic. He looked upon the proliferation of regulations governing labor and the workplace and the effusion of legislation and institutions that constituted the statebuilding project as the effluvia of an ongoing war of class against class in which the strongest would inevitably prevail. Efforts by courts to interpose themselves in this war, as he saw it, were futile. Holmes's votes in support of the collective bargaining arrangements that came to define the

---

[41] See Herman Belz, *A Living Constitutionalism or Fundamental Law? American Constitutionalism in Historical Perspective* (Lanham, MD: Rowman and Littlefield, 1998); Gillman, "The Collapse of Constitutional Originalism and the Rise of the Notion of a 'Living Constitution' in the Course of American Statebuilding," *Studies in American Political Development* 11 (Fall 1997): 191–247, esp. 193. The imagination of the American constitutional system as a "living" organism, of course, is appropriate for those with a Darwinian view. As metaphor, it is usefully contrasted with the Newtonian imagination of the Constitution as "a machine that would go of itself." See Michael Kamman, *A Machine That Would Go of Itself: The Constitution in American Culture* (New York: Vintage Books, 1986). For a discussion of the naturalizing functions served by metaphors in the statebuilding era (albeit looking at a different metaphor), see Daniel P. Carpenter, "The Corporate Metaphor and Executive Department Centralization in the United States, 1888–1928," *Studies in American Political Development* 12 (Spring 1998): 162–203, esp. 166. Most attention on the relationship between social thought and American constitutionalism has focused on pragmatism rather than on social Darwinism. This, needless to say, lends a rhetorical appeal to the narrative of constitutional change that the invocation of "social Darwinism" (even of a reformed variety) would not. The emphasis on pragmatism in contemporary constitutionalism may also be due to its utility in a field concerned in the first instance with practice and guides to social conduct. Such considerations, however, should not be foremost to those tracing seminal conceptual shifts that inform American constitutional thought. For purposes of American constitutionalism, most of the relevant conceptual shifts were inherent in the "reform Darwinism" of thinkers such as Lester Ward, who preceded and, in many ways, formed the intellectual core of pragmatism (also influential in America was the English Reform Darwinist Thomas Henry Huxley). Such thinkers were the first to reimagine society as a living organism. As reformers, they considered the state to be its thinking head. Pragmatism was a reinforcement of (and, in some ways, less foundational to modern American constitutionalism than) reform Darwinism. See generally Goldman, *Rendezvous with Destiny*, 85–160 (including, at 134, a discussion of the "legal reform Darwinism" of Holmes and Brandeis); on Ward, see Hofstadter, *Social Darwinism in American Thought* (Boston: Beacon Press, 1955), 67–84, 137–8; The seminal work is Lester Ward, *Dynamic Sociology* (2 vols.) (New York: D. Appleton & Co., 1883, 1897). On Huxley, see Hofstader, *Social Darwinism*, 95 (employing horticulture as metaphor for the modern state), 138–9. Thomas Henry Huxley, *Evolution and Ethics and Other Essays* (1920). On the way in which pragmatism was "profoundly influenced by Darwinism," see Hofstadter, *Social Darwinism*, 123–42, esp. 124; Goldman, *Rendezvous with Destiny*, 158–9 (describing John Dewey as "the Herbert Spencer of reform Darwinism").

new constitutional order concerning labor under the New American State were a product not of a belief in either any inherent "rights" of labor or a sympathy with the laboring class. Rather, they followed his inclination to ratify what he took to be the outcome in the continuing struggle for social advantage that constituted all of human life.[42] "I quite agree," he wrote to Felix Frankfurter in 1914, "that a law should be called good if it reflects the will of the dominant forces of the community even if it will take us to hell." As for whether the courts should stand in the way, Holmes declared that "[i]f you can pay for your ticket and are sure you want to go, I have nothing to say."[43]

Brandeis's Darwinism, in contrast, was optimistic – a variant of the popular reform Darwinism of his time.[44] Brandeis was famously committed to the gathering of evidence as part of a hopeful project of experimentation aimed at discovering what in the science of government and regulation worked. Unlike Holmes, Brandeis had high hopes for regulation and economic planning, although he repeatedly expressed reservations about the wisdom of centralizing state administrative capacities.[45] Absent artificial barriers (such as those interposed by the courts wielding doctrines concerning economic rights that were suited to a passing order), Brandeis believed the people would ultimately triumph and society would progress to a more modern system of governance.

Under the traditional constitutionalism of work that characterized the state of courts and parties, police legislation concerning work was subject to an earnest (if at times hasty and shallow) judicial debate in which both sides agreed upon a fundamental right to pursue an honest calling, subject only to public-spirited health, safety, and morals regulation. At issue was the application of these settled principles to the novel facts of a particular case.

---

[42] Albert Alschuler, *Law Without Values: The Life and Legacy of Justice Holmes* (Chicago: University of Chicago Press, 2000), 67–8; David Lowenthal, *No Liberty for License: The Forgotten Logic of the First Amendment* (Dallas: Spence Publishing, 1997), 43–68.

[43] Letter, Oliver Wendell Holmes Jr. to Felix Frankfurter, March 24, 1914, in *Holmes and Frankfurter: Their Correspondence*, 19; Letter, Oliver Wendell Holmes Jr. to Canon Patrick Sheehan, November 23, 1912, in *The Holmes–Sheehan Correspondence: The Letters of Justice Oliver Wendell Holmes and Canon Patrick Sheehan*, 52, 52–3 (Port Washington, NY: Kennikat Press, 1976), both cited in Alshuler, *Law Without Values*, 59 n. 40, 41.

[44] Because of this, it was not "ironic," as Philippa Strum states, that "Brandeis, who scorned social Darwinism, was greatly influenced by Holmes, a social Darwinist." Philippa Strum, *Brandeis, Beyond Progressivism* (Lawrence: University Press of Kansas, 1993), 57. For an explication of the clear Darwinian strain in Brandeis's free-speech opinions, see Lowenthal, *No Liberty for License*, chs. 2, 4, 5. See also Goldman, *Rendezvous with Destiny*, 134. For the conceptual outlines of reform Darwinism, see Hofstadter, *Social Darwinism*, 67–84.

[45] See Woodrow Wilson, *The New Freedom: A Call for the Emancipation of the Generous Energies of a People* (New York: Doubleday, Page & Co., 1914); Martin Sklar, *The United States as a Developing Country: Studies in U.S. History in the Progressive Era and the 1920s* (Cambridge: Cambridge University Press, 1992), 102–42.

Holmes's and Brandeis's rejections of the very terms of this debate, however, altered the discourse of contention concerning the constitutional legitimacy of the emergent modern regulatory state.

The late nineteenth and early twentieth centuries provided grounds upon which the struggle between the old and new constitutional visions could be fought. The stakes of the struggle between the adherents to the traditional constitutionalism of callings and those (such as Holmes and Brandeis) opposed to that constitutionalism has been minimized by a regime-reinforcing focus on emotionally resonant cases involving sweatshops and protective legislation for women and children. Progressive legislation was certainly passed for these purposes. Such legislation, however, was also passed simultaneously on almost every other front imaginable. The statebuilding project involved public-spirited regulation. But it also involved significant efforts to appropriate public power for private purposes.[46] The defeat of the traditional ideology of work and labor and the displacement of courts as the institutional guardians of that constitutionalism opened the door to the assertion of unprecedented levels of state power in the service of *both* public and private purposes.

The Supreme Court's early-twentieth-century labor cases proved to be one of the major battlefields on which the armies of the old constitutional order squared off against the swelling legions of the new. Traditional understandings prevailed, for example, in *Adams v. Tanner* (1917), a case in which the Court considered the constitutionality of progressive legislation forbidding employment agencies from collecting fees from workers for whom they found jobs. When invalidating the law (in defense of job-seeking workers), Justice McReynolds, writing for the Court, grounded his analysis in the traditional ideology of work and labor. "We have held employment agencies are subject to police regulation and control," he wrote, "[b]ut we think it plain that there is nothing inherently immoral or dangerous to public welfare in acting as paid representative of another to find a position in which he can earn an honest living. On the contrary, such service is useful, commendable, and in great demand." McReynolds continued:

Because abuses may, and probably do, grow up in connection with this business, is adequate reason for hedging it about by proper regulations. But this is not enough to justify destruction of one's right to follow a distinctly useful calling in an upright way. Certainly there is no profession, possibly no business, which does not offer peculiar

---

[46] This has been demonstrated in various spheres by historically oriented public-choice scholars and other scholars. See, e.g., David E. Bernstein, *Only One Place of Redress: African Americans, Labor Regulations, and the Courts* (Durham, NC: Duke University Press, 2001); Hadley Arkes, *The Return of George Sutherland: Restoring a Jurisprudence of Natural Rights* (Princeton: Princeton University Press, 1994). For a careful exposition of the contrary view, see William G. Ross, *A Muted Fury: Populists, Progressives, and the Labor Unions Confront the Courts, 1890–1937* (Princeton: Princeton University Press, 1994). See also Gillman, *The Constitution Besieged.*

opportunities for reprehensible practices; and as to every one of them, no doubt, some can be found quite ready earnestly to maintain that its suppression would be in the public interest. Skillfully directed agitation might also bring about apparent condemnation of any one of them by the public. Happily for all, the fundamental guaranties of the Constitution cannot be freely submerged if and whenever some ostensible justification is advanced and the police power invoked.[47]

Holmes and Brandeis dissented (along with Justices John H. Clarke and Joseph McKenna), with Brandeis arguing on behalf of the public interest in preventing "general demoralization."

A few years later, in *Meyer v. Nebraska* (1923), the Court, in much the same spirit, invalidated a law sharply restricting instruction in public and private schools in modern languages other than English. The Court in *Meyer* condemned the Nebraska legislature specifically for "interfer[ing] with the calling of modern language teachers," "callings [that] always ha[ve] been regarded as useful and honorable, essential, indeed, to the public welfare." This interference, Justice McReynolds wrote for the Court, violated "the right of the individual to . . . engage in any of the common occupations of life."[48] Justice Holmes dissented.

Holmes and Brandeis similarly dissented in subsequent cases where the traditional dignity-of-labor constitutionalism continued to carry the day. They dissented in *Burns Baking* (1924), which struck down as unreasonable a state statute that fixed the permissible weights for loaves of bread. And they dissented in *Liggett v. Baldridge* (1928) in which the Court invalidated a law that required all corporations owning drugstores and pharmacies to have only stockholders who are licensed pharmacists.[49]

Despite their commitments to the triumph of legislative power, even these two justices did hew to some outer limits. In 1920, Kansas passed a state Industrial Relations Act that provided for compulsory arbitration in a specialized state court of all labor disputes in the food, clothing, and fuel industries. This special court, moreover, was given authority (in prescribed circumstances) to govern all matters affecting labor. It could, for instance, set wages and working conditions and judicially supervise strikes and lockouts. Writing for a unanimous Supreme Court striking down the Kansas law, Chief

---

47 *Adams v. Tanner*, 244 U.S. 590, 593–5 (1917).
48 *Meyer v. Nebraska*, 262 U.S. 390, 399–400 (1923).
49 *Burns Baking Co. v. Bryan*, 264 U.S. 504 (1924); *Liggett Co. v. Baldridge*, 278 U.S. 105 (1928) (citing *Meyer* and *Pierce* for the proposition that a state cannot "under the guise of protecting the public arbitrarily interfere with private business or prohibit lawful occupations or impose unreasonable and unnecessary restrictions upon them"). See also *Smith v. Texas*, 233 U.S. 630 (1914) (striking down on liberty of contract grounds Texas statute making it a misdemeanor for any person to act as a conductor of a freight train without having previously served for two years as a brakeman on such trains) (Justice Holmes, dissenting).

Justice William Howard Taft stated (leading with a Whitmanesque song of occupations):

It has never been supposed, since the adoption of the Constitution, that the business of the butcher, or the baker, the tailor, the wood chopper, the mining operator or the miner was clothed with such a public interest that the price of his product or his wages could be fixed by state regulation. It is true that in the days of the early common law an omnipotent Parliament did regulate prices and wages as it chose, and occasionally a colonial legislature sought to exercise the same power; but nowadays one does not devote one's property or business to the public use or clothe it with a public interest merely because one makes commodities for, and sells to, the public in the common callings which the above mentioned are instances.[50]

From there, Taft went on to formulate what he hoped would be a working definition of the types of businesses that are clothed with a public interest and thus subject to public regulation. This definition represented a creative effort on Taft's part to negotiate a serviceable settlement between the new and old orders. First, he said, came those businesses carried on under the authority of public grants or privileges, such as railroads, common carriers, or public utilities. Second came certain exceptional occupations such as innkeepers, cab drivers, and grist millers, whose public role had been long recognized by the law. And third were businesses that had not been public at their inception but, over time, had risen to assume a widely acknowledged public purpose.[51]

If Chief Justice Taft thought this formulation would serve as a guide for courts and legislatures in the statebuilding era (or even for those members of the Court who had specifically joined in his Kansas Industrial Relations Act opinion), he was mistaken. In the *New State Ice* (1932) case nine years later, in which the Court struck down an Oklahoma law that forbade the manufacture, sale, or distribution of ice without a certificate of public necessity, the Court was once again called upon to assert itself against the increasingly prevalent progressive view that "engagement in the business is a privilege to be exercised only in virtue of a public grant, and not a common right to be exercised independently by any competent person conformably to reasonable regulations equally applicable to all those who chose to engage therein."[52]

---

[50] *Wolff Packing Co. v. Court of Industrial Relations*, 262 U.S. 522, 537 (1923). See Domenico Gagliardo, *The Kansas Industrial Court: An Experiment in Compulsory Arbitration* (Lawrence: University of Kansas Press, 1941); James Gray Pope, "Labor's Constitution of Freedom," *Yale Law Journal* 106 (January 1997): 941–1031.

[51] *Wolff Packing*, 262 U.S. at 535.

[52] *New State Ice v. Liebmann*, 285 U.S. 262, 273 (1932). See Gillman, who rightly characterizes the constitutionalism of the New American State as one of "general powers" and "residual privileges." Howard Gillman, "Preferred Freedoms: The Progressive Expansion of State Power and the Rise of Modern Civil Liberties Jurisprudence," *Political Research Quarterly* 47 (September 1994): 623–53. See also Paul L. Murphy, *World War I and the Origin of Civil Liberties in the United States* (New York: W. W. Norton, 1979). This transformation marked a radical departure from James Madison's constitutional vision. Madison distinguished the

"Plainly," Justice Sutherland added in his opinion for the Court, "a regulation which has the effect of denying or unreasonably curtailing the common right to engage in a lawful private business . . . cannot be upheld consistent with the Fourteenth Amendment."[53]

Justice Brandeis, however, dissented. In doing so, he now expressly rejected the longstanding conceptualization of workers and businessmen as devotees of callings to which they possessed individual and constitutionally guaranteed rights. Brandeis shared Justice Sutherland's reading of the constitutional tradition. He agreed that under that tradition it was unheard of that certificates of public convenience and necessity be issued for what had long been understood as common occupations. But, unlike Sutherland, Brandeis concluded that society had changed in fundamental ways that had transformed that tradition into a relic. Certificates of public convenience and necessity, Brandeis announced, are "creature[s] of the machine age in which plants have displaced tools and businesses are substituted for trades." A new world of administered aggregations was now being born. And in such a world, "whether the local conditions are such as to justify converting a private business into a public one is a matter primarily for the determination of the state legislature."[54]

Parallel Developments: Aggregations, the Law of Antitrust, and the New Judicial Power

In the years immediately following the Civil War, the common law of conspiracy, a pillar of the state of courts and parties, had been one of the major legal devices governing conflicts between employers and employees. Between 1885 and 1895, as the path of statebuilding gained momentum, however, this regulatory system was radically altered. By 1895, aggrieved employers began to turn toward the labor injunction and away from the conspiracy laws in seeking a remedy for labor disputes. In a time of heightened industrial strife, conspiracy prosecutions proved increasingly unwieldy. They were criminal matters, requiring the presentation of evidence before a jury and a determination

American constitution from European constitutions by describing it as "a charter of power granted by liberty rather than a charter of liberty granted by power." Madison, quoted in Gordon Wood, *The Creation of the American Republic, 1776–1787* (New York: W. W. Norton, 1969), 601.

53 *New State Ice*, 285 U.S. at 278.

54 *New State Ice*, 285 U.S. at 281–4 (Justice Brandeis, dissenting). This, incidentally, amounts to a direct repudiation of Justice John Marshall's landmark decision in *Dartmouth College v. Woodward*, 17 U.S. 518 (1819). Brandeis was one of the great creators of what John M. Jordan has called "Machine Age Ideology," a man who "catapulted efficiency [of people such as Frederick Winslow Taylor] into the public imagination." Jordan, *Machine Age Ideology: Social Engineering and American Liberalism, 1911–1939* (Chapel Hill: University of North Carolina Press, 1994), 42; Samuel Haber, *Efficiency and Uplift: Scientific Management and the Progressive Era, 1890–1920* (Chicago, 1964). Brandeis, in fact, invented the term "scientific management." Jordan, *Machine Age Ideology*, 41–2.

of individual guilt or innocence. Injunctions, on the other hand, did not operate primarily against individuals, but could blanket whole industries or
areas. Injunctions could be issued quickly, on the order of a single judge.
And, ironically, by taking labor disputes out of the realm of all-or-nothing
criminal prosecutions, injunctions proved to have considerable advantages,
at least initially, in helping to shore up the legitimacy and authority of the
federal courts in contentious times.[55]

The path to this major alteration in the legal landscape governing the
relations of employers and employees was paved to a significant extent by
the successes of two important reformist campaigns. The first was a negative
reform and involved the long struggle undertaken by organized labor, joined
by progressive intellectual elites, against the application of conspiracy laws
to labor actions. The second was a positive reform and involved the successes of Populists and Progressives in winning the passage of powerful new
antimonopoly laws. The courts used the commitments against consolidated
power of the second reformist campaign to fill the intellectual and regulatory vacuum that (as they saw it) had been created by the successes of the
first. In the process, they reconstructed what had formerly been considered
"conspiracies" as "restraints of trade," with the latter, thanks to the new antimonopoly laws, carrying new and more powerful sets of judicial remedies.
While it is easy enough in retrospect to interpret this turn by the courts as a
product of pure, antilabor animus, it is actually better understood as a sign
of the persistent power of the ideological vision of the traditional constitutionalism of labor. The recourse the courts made to the new antimonopoly
laws in labor cases was made plausible by the fact that those laws privileged right over power in the economic sphere. As such, those new laws
reinforced the underlying ideological dynamics of the traditional constitutionalism of labor, which had been built upon similar commitments. That
the courts would turn to these laws in the face of ongoing labor disputes was
a natural and predictable development.

The Sherman Antitrust Act (1890), a progressive law targeting the consolidation of industrial power that characterized the late nineteenth century,
imposed sweeping prohibitions – backed by unprecedented (federal) criminal penalties and fines – upon "every contract, combination . . . or conspiracy
in restraint of trade or commerce."[56] No sooner had the law taken effect
than it was challenged in court on constitutional grounds by businesses with
the financial means to undertake a vigorous litigation campaign and with a
financial interest in limiting its scope.

Five years after the Sherman Act's passage, the American Sugar Refin-
ing Company successfully persuaded the Supreme Court to sharply limit the

---

[55] Hattam, *Labor Visions*, 161–2.
[56] See, generally, Hans Thorelli, *The Federal Antitrust Policy: Origination of an American Tradition* (Stockholm, 1954).

compass of the Act. In the *E. C. Knight* case (1895), the Court held that the Sherman Act did not apply to manufacturing monopolies (such as American Sugar's) but only to interstate commerce – that is, to interstate trade itself.[57] Despite this apparent setback, the government achieved some important victories under the Sherman Act in a series of landmark rulings in 1911. But in handing the government those victories, the Court at the same time held that it would be guided not by the literal words of the antitrust act but instead by a vague (and hence unreliable and unpredictable) "rule of reason."[58] In time, despite their many antagonisms, both businesses and progressives who sought to rein in industrial power were unhappy with the interpretative uncertainties that resulted from the Court's decision to adopt a rule of reason. Both pushed for a clarifying statutory supplement to the Sherman Act and got it when Congress passed the Clayton Antitrust Act in 1914. Although both groups had pressed for antitrust reform, progressives could claim the lion's share of the victory in shaping the terms of the new statute.

For them, one of the chief frustrations wrought by the Sherman Act's prohibition on contracts, combinations, and conspiracies in restraint of trade had been that the courts had transmogrified the act's statutory prohibitions – which had been targeted at particular aggregations of political-economic power: industrial combinations – into a license for the courts to wield their injunctive powers against what they understood as altogether different aggregations of political-economic power: labor unions. In the Danbury Hatter's case, the Court had held that labor unions amounted to combinations in restraint of trade under the terms of the act.[59] And subsequently, in a period

---

[57] *United States v. E. C. Knight Co.*, 156 U.S. 1 (1895). The sharp distinction drawn between manufacturing and commerce in this decision came to pervade the Court's jurisprudence under the commerce clause at this time. See, e.g., *Hammer v. Dagenhart*, 247 U.S. 251 (1918) (invalidating the federal Keating-Owen Child Labor Act barring goods made by children from interstate commerce). The distinction is traceable as far back as the Marshall Court. See *Gibbons v. Ogden*, 22 U.S. 1 (1824).

[58] *Standard Oil Co. v. United States*, 221 U.S. 1 (1911) (using a common law understanding of reasonableness to dissolve the Oil Trust); *American Tobacco Co. v. United States*, 221 U.S. 106 (1911).

[59] *Loewe v. Lawlor*, 208 U.S. 274 (1908) (holding unanimously that an AFL effort to unionize hatters in Danbury, Connecticut, using a secondary boycott was a violation of the Sherman Act, which forbade "every contract, combination . . . or conspiracy, in restraint of trade or commerce." Sherman Act, 26 Stat. 209, Sec. 1 (1890). As such, treble damages against the union were in order, by the terms of the act. The common law, as we have noted, in quite similar language forbade conspiracies in restraint of trade. These common law proscriptions had long been held to apply to labor unions. See Ernst, *Lawyers Against Labor*, 69–76. The Court majority, still drawing upon the common law tradition, contended that it was not holding the existence of the union itself a violation of the law and that secondary boycotts were not lawful and legitimate. Justice Brandeis in dissent accused the majority of disregarding the plain import of the act. The Danbury Hatters decision galled progressives, who contrasted it with the Court's 1895 *E. C. Knight* case holding that a national monopoly on sugar production did not violate the act.

of highly destabilizing labor unrest, federal courts repeatedly recurred to that act when confronted by assertions of power by organized labor in industrial disputes. Organized labor lobbied hard to put a stop to this by inserting corrective language into the new Clayton Act.[60]

Section Six of the Clayton Act seemed to be a clear victory for reformist progressives and their chief political constituency: organized labor. In explicit language, Section Six severed the equivalence that traditional American law, under the influence of a highly institutionalized producer ethic, had made between the employee as producer and the employer as producer. It first drew a sharp distinction between an industrial product and human labor. It then stipulated plainly what most progressives thought should have long since been obvious: that not all aggregations of power were the same, and that the aggregation of political-economic power in labor unions was radically distinguishable from the aggregation of such power in an industrial trust. Thus, the act stated:

That the labor of a human being is not a commodity or article of commerce. Nothing contained in the Anti-trust laws shall be construed to forbid the existence and operation of labor...organizations...or to forbid or restrain individual members of such organizations from lawfully carrying out the legitimate objects thereof; nor shall such organizations, or the members thereof, be held or construed to be illegal combinations or conspiracies in restraint of trade under the Anti-trust laws.[61]

Building upon the distinctions set out in Section Six of the act, Section Twenty then moved to curtail the power of federal courts to issue injunctions in labor disputes. It provided that

[n]o restraining order or injunction shall be granted by any court of the United States...in any case between an employer and employees, or between employers and employees, or between employees, or between persons employed and persons seeking employment, involving, or growing out of a dispute concerning terms or conditions of employment...unless necessary to prevent irreparable injury to property, or to a property right, of the party making the application.[62]

It added, moreover, that

[n]o such restraining order or injunction shall prohibit any person or persons...from ceasing to perform any work or labor, or from recommending, advising, or persuading others by peaceful means so to do; or from attending at any place where such person or persons may lawfully be, for the purpose of peacefully obtaining or communicating information, or from peacefully persuading any person to work or to abstain from working, or from ceasing to patronize or to employ any party to such dispute, or

---

[60] Hattam, *Labor Visions*, 163; Frankfurter and Greene, *Labor Injunction*, 165–98; Forbath, *Law and the Shaping of the American Labor Movement*, 156–8.
[61] Clayton Act, 38 Stat. 730, Sec. 6 (1914).
[62] Clayton Act, 38 Stat. 730, Sec. 20 (1914).

from recommending, advising, or persuading others by peaceful and lawful means so to do.[63]

The passage of the Clayton Act strongly reinforced the modern movement toward defining the power of labor organizations as a distinctive and legally cognizable form of group power.

Constructing the New Imperative of Labor Power: Labor Power as Industrial Democracy

Without democracy in industry . . . there is no such thing as democracy in America.[64]

There was much discussion among progressives in the late nineteenth and early twentieth centuries of the imperative of according power to organized labor as a collectivity. Much of this discussion was rooted (as in Holmes's thinking) in notions of an ongoing struggle for power, as against claims of right, or, alternatively (as in Brandeis's thinking), in a notion of an unfolding experimental state conceptualized as an ever-evolving organism. The varieties of social Darwinism, however, with their frank championing of the claims of power over claims of right, as a product of class war or the sweep of history, proved to be a poor means of legitimating a new constitutional order in the context of American politics. As constitutive stories, Darwinian narratives lacked the moral authority of the old dignity-of-labor constitutionalism the progressive constitutionalists were endeavoring to replace. For constitutional purposes, it was imperative that "the labor problem" be reimagined on more principled, more "American" grounds.

John Dewey, the era's seminal progressive philosopher, took the lead in the ideological project of defending the new constititutionalism of labor – in which labor was reconceptualized as a class rather than an individual matter – in terms that would win it sustained political support within the American political tradition. With refinements and alterations, Dewey's reconstruction of the constitutional imagining of labor was incorporated into the thinking of highly influential first-order political journalists such as Herbert Croly and Walter Lippmann. It was then, in turn, taken up by the lawyer-intellectuals such as Louis Brandeis and Felix Frankfurter, who, under the banner of modernity and progress, carried it at last into the world of lawyers and the U.S. Supreme Court.[65] As these ideas gained credence in both progressive intellectual and legal circles, and as they came to shape constitutional doctrine, they were strategically adopted by advocates and applied to other types of reform, most prominently, later in the century, by those advancing the cause of civil rights.

---

[63] Clayton Act, 38 Stat. 730, Sec. 20 (1914).

[64] Walter Lippmann, *Drift and Mastery*, 59.

[65] Steve Fraser specifically refers to both Brandeis and Frankfurter as "architects of industrial democracy." Fraser, "The Labor Question," in *The Rise and Fall of the New Deal Order, 1930–1980*, eds. Gary Gerstle and Steve Fraser (Princeton: Princeton University Press, 1989), 69.

Dewey's contribution to the ideology of modern American constitution-alism (along with that of like-minded thinkers) was to reimagine a fight for labor power that had previously been conceptualized as a Darwinian power struggle as instead a fight for "industrial democracy" or "industrial freedom."[66] The chief appeal of this reimagining, of course, was its noble creedal ring. And, indeed, at the outset, there was little to Dewey's vision beyond that; for just what "industrial democracy" and "industrial freedom" meant in concrete terms was as unclear to Dewey as it was to others. What was known was that "the labor question" – the abiding social and political problem of the statebuilding era – needed to be solved and that Americans were normatively committed to the idea of democracy. The rest would have to be worked out. As it became apparent over time, the solution forward-looking thinkers alighted upon would involve the reimagining of the work-place as a public rather than a private sphere.[67]

As early as 1894 (the year of the Pullman strike), Dewey had added "in-dustrial democracy" to civil and political democracy as the third pillar of his vision of a truly democratic society. As he saw it, the belief that the work-place was a private space was more than an economic problem. It was rather a problem implicating the meaning of humanity itself. To see the workplace as a private space was to stand in the way of the realization of the full eth-ical potential of human beings and, in turn, the ethical potential of society. "[A]ll industrial relations," Dewey wrote in *Ethics and Politics*, "are to be re-garded as subordinate to human relations, to the law of personality. . . . They are to become the material of an ethical realization; the form and substance of a community of good (though not necessarily of goods) wider than any now known."[68] Plainly influenced by Marx, Dewey argued in his classroom

---

[66] On the carry over of the rhetoric of "industrial democracy" into New Deal–era labor strug-gles, see David Plotke, *Building a Democratic Political Order*, 98–9; Ruth Horowitz, *Political Ideologies of Organized Labor: The New Deal Era* (New Brunswick, NJ: Transaction Books, 1978), 175–7.

[67] Fraser has demonstrated that progressives of this era of all varieties saw "that the 'labor question' was not merely the supreme economic question but the *constitutive* moral, polit-ical, and social dilemma of the new institutional order," and "the central dilemma of the social order" [emphasis added]. Fraser, "The Labor Question," in Fraser and Gerstle, *Rise and Fall of the New Deal Order*, 55, 56. At the moment in which "the labor question" pre-dominated in American political life, the phrase "industrial democracy," Fraser declared, evoked a "thousand and one subtle nuances of meaning" and involved all manner of "polit-ical scheming and social dreaming." He adds, "no one had any really firm ideas of just what the message of industrial democracy meant." Fraser, in Gerstle and Fraser, *Rise and Fall of the New Deal Order*, 58, 62. See also Edward Bellamy, *Looking Backward*, in which the labor question is dubbed the "Sphinx's riddle of the nineteenth century," and its having been solved is the very first topic taken up between Doctor Leete and Julian West after the latter's long sleep. Bellamy, *Looking Backward: 2000–1887* (New York: Penguin Books, 1986 [1888]), 61.

[68] John Dewey, *Ethics and Politics* (1894), quoted in Robert B. Westbrook, *John Dewey and American Democracy* (Ithaca, NY: Cornell University Press, 1991), 49. Across the ocean, the Fabian socialists in England were also calling for "industrial democracy." The phrase, and

lectures that the private control of wage labor served, in a zero-sum way, to benefit employers at the expense of their employees. Under this exploitative system, the employee was thwarted in his efforts to realize his full human potential. Unless the relations between employer and employee were somehow transformed, both individual and social realization would be permanently blocked. The class divisions of industrial capitalism thus had to be transcended by what Dewey called industrial democracy.[69]

Underlying Dewey's political theories was a bedrock commitment to a broadly democratic polity. Just as citizens should actively govern their civil and political life, so, too, in Dewey's view, should they govern their lives as workers. Dewey emphasized this participatory ideal in his scholarly blueprints for progressive education, and he put them into practice at the Lab School he founded and supervised at the University of Chicago.[70] There, the teachers (who were, of course, employees at the school) actively governed their own workplace. And in Dewey's vision of education, the students themselves were to be trained through active, participatory learning.[71] Part of that participatory project involved learning about the interconnections between the work of each and the collective social functioning and social good. The building of character fit for self-government in all (interconnected) realms, including the world of work, was the goal of a progressive Deweyan education.

Outside of the school setting, the practical implications of Deweyan notions of industrial democracy remained hazy. Those who were inspired by the philosopher, however, most prominently the men who formed the magazine *The New Republic*, in turn moved to anchor and develop Dewey's thought. In a seminal early work, Walter Lippmann, for example, made it plain that he identified industrial democracy and industrial citizenship with what labor

the push for it, were thus transnational. See Sidney and Beatrice Webb, *Industrial Democracy* (London: Longmans, Green, and Company, 1897); Nelson Lichtenstein, *State of the Union: A Century of American Labor* (Princeton: Princeton University Press, 2002), 10. Indeed, in many cases industrial democracy was referred to in the United States as "The British Way." Fraser, "The Labor Question," in Gerstle and Fraser, *Rise and Fall of the New Deal Order*, 57–9. See, generally, James T. Kloppenberg, *Uncertain Victory: Social Democracy in European and American Thought, 1870–1920* (New York: Oxford University Press, 1986). See also Arthur Mann, "British Social Thought and American Reformers of the Progressive Era," *Mississippi Valley Historical Review* 42 (March 1956): 672–92; Hofstadter, *Social Darwinism*, 81–2. The imagination of the path of progress as a transnational (and, more particularly, a European) cause at this time became a characteristic predisposition of twentieth-century political progressivism, one that is especially strong within elite progressive thought at the beginning of the twenty-first century.

[69] Westbrook, *John Dewey*, 50.
[70] See Diane Ravitch, *Left Back: A Century of Failed School Reforms* (New York: Simon & Schuster, 2000), 57–8, 171–4.
[71] John Dewey, *The School and Society* (Chicago: University of Chicago Press, 1900); John Dewey, *Democracy and Education: An Introduction to the Philosophy of Education* (New York: Macmillan Co., 1944).

unions were fighting for.[72] Traditional Jeffersonian, Jacksonian, and Free Labor strains of American political thought held that only the autonomous individual was fit for and capable of self-government. Picking up on Dewey's industrial republicanism, Lippmann denied this, claiming that only the man who participated collectively in industrial governance acquired the political education that prepared him to govern the United States. If labor unions, as currently constituted, did not seem up to that ambitious educative mission, it was because they had yet to be trusted with the kind of responsibility that would hone their democratic and republican instincts and skills:

> If labor is apathetic, hostile to efficiency, without much pride, it is because labor is not part of industrial management. People don't take a sympathetic interest in the affairs of state until they are voting members of the state. You can't expect civic virtue from a disenfranchised class, nor industrial virtues from the industrially disenfranchised.[73]

"Private industry," Lippmann warned, "has got to prepare itself for democratic control."[74] "Men are fighting for the beginning of industrial self-government," he announced. "They have got to win civilization, they have got to take up the task of fastening a worker's control upon business."[75]

What would that control look like? Lippmann expected that it would involve worker partnerships with management, the right of laborers to choose their own foremen, to elect company directors, and to share company profits. Joint employer-worker governance would eventually expand outward. In due course, it would become a crucial part of a nationwide system of economic governance in which the tasks of industrial planning would be coordinated with governing plans of both consumers and the state. The goal would be "to adjust ... conflicts and to reach some working plan."[76]

At the heart of this process, in Lippmann's view, would be unions and unionization. The effort to build unions, he declared in *Drift and Mastery*, represented "the extension of civilization into the wilderness ... the first feeble effort to conquer the industrial jungle for democratic life." Its failure, he insisted (not without some irony as an advocate of a politics of groups) would fix American life into a structure of permanent classes.[77]

This was plainly a constitutional vision, as was apparent in Lippmann's choices of metaphors. Employers, he observed:

> fight unions as monarchs fight constitutions, as aristocracies fight the vote. When an employer tells about his own virtues, he dilates upon his kindness, his fairness, and all the good things he has done for his men. That is just what benevolent autocrats do: they try to justify their autocracy by their benevolence. Indeed, the highest vision

---

[72] See Lippmann, *Drift and Mastery*, ch. 5.
[73] Lippmann, *Drift and Mastery*, 64.
[74] Lippmann, *Drift and Mastery*, 59.
[75] Lippmann, *Drift and Mastery*, 60.
[76] Lippmann, *Drift and Mastery*, 65.
[77] Lippmann, *Drift and Mastery*, 59–60.

of those who oppose unions is that the employer will develop the virtues of a good aristocrat.[78]

To put unions in control, in fact, was to raise anew all the problems of a constitutional founding:

In this movement to eat into economic absolutism, very perplexing questions, of course, arise. What is the proper structure for a union? Shall it be organized by crafts, or occupations, or industries? With amalgamation or by federation? How shall the unions be governed: by representative or by direct vote? In fact, there is hardly a problem of constitutional government which doesn't appear in acute form among the workers. And in passing, one might suggest that scholars who wish to see sovereignty in the making cannot do better than to go among the unions.[79]

Herbert Croly also followed Dewey in making his own case for industrial democracy. Like Lippmann, Croly argued that the practice of industrial democracy would amount to a "genuinely formative popular political experience," conducive to "individual and social fulfillment." "As the result of such action," he contended, "a progressive democracy will gradually learn to be progressively democratic.... The creation of an industrial organization... will serve to make individual workers enlightened, competent, and loyal citizens of an industrial commonwealth."[80]

In Croly's analysis, a decision by the nation to seize the promise of industrial democracy was a decision to seize the only opportunity that remained to preserve its freedom in the face of the profound political-economic shifts that had come to pass during his lifetime (1869–1930). During those years, Croly had watched the country transform from a nation of property-holding freeholders to one of salary-drawing wage earners. Worrying in the era of the strike, the boycott, and the labor injunction over what was perhaps the central problem taken up by American political thinkers since Lincoln, Croly

---

[78] Lippmann, *Drift and Mastery*, 57. See also William Leiserson, "Constitutional Government in American Industries," *American Economic Review* 12 (Supp. 1922): 56, 60–1; Lichtenstein, *State of the Union*, 7, 36; Katherine Van Wezel Stone, "The Post-War Paradigm in American Labor Law," *Yale Law Journal* 90 (1981): 1509–80, esp. 1514–16; Reuel E. Schiller, "From Group Rights to Individual Liberties: Post-War Labor Law, Liberalism, and the Waning of Union Strength," *Berkeley Journal of Employment and Labor Law* 20 (1999): 1–73, esp. 5–6.

[79] Lippmann, *Drift and Mastery*, 65.

[80] Herbert Croly, *Progressive Democracy* (New Brunswick, NJ: Transaction Publishers, 1998) (originally published 1914), 378, 379, 390. The book *Progressive Democracy* is comprised of the Godkin Lectures Croly delivered at Harvard in 1913–14. Both *Drift and Mastery* and *Progressive Democracy*, which appeared at about the same time, were effusively praised by Theodore Roosevelt, who declared that "No man who wishes seriously to study thought and action so as to work for national betterment in the future can afford not to read these books through and through and to ponder and digest them." Theodore Roosevelt, "Two Noteworthy Books on Democracy," *Outlook* 108 (November 18, 1914): 648–51. The imagination of industrial democracy as an explicitly *constitutional* order was one of its defining features in the American context. In this imagination, Lippmann's characterization is illustrative rather than distinctive. See Fraser, "The Labor Question," in Gerstle and Fraser, *Rise and Fall of the New Deal Order*, 59–60.

argued that "the wage system in its existing form creates a class of essential economic dependents." The worker in this new era, he explained, "faces a Hobson's choice among masters." "The wage system itself," he concluded, "will have to be transformed in the interest of an industrial self-governing democracy."[81]

One ray of hope for a wage-earning society that Croly rejected outright was that the workers would accept the existing system based on wage labor, property ownership, and individual rights. This was a prospect Croly was convinced was plainly unhealthy. "The wage-earner whose greatest stimulus to work is assumed to be the ultimate chance of becoming a property owner, may be a hard worker, but he will rarely be a good worker or a desirable citizen in an industrial democracy." Such a worker would be too fixed on his private goal rather than on his job. "[H]is motives will be interested and self-involved rather than disinterested and social."[82]

Like Lippmann's, Croly's vision was also constitutional:

> The wage-earner must have the same opportunity of being consulted about the nature and circumstances of his employment that the voter has about the organization and policy of the government. The work of getting this opportunity for the wage-earner is the most important task of modern democratic social organization.[83]

Only by granting the worker legal security in and control of his work life on par with the legal security and effective control enjoyed by the property owner would the worker cease "to separate himself from his fellows by becoming a property owner" and join in a socialized democracy.[84] Labor unions would play a crucial role in this process. Participation in a union would counteract the tendency of the individual in a capitalist society to separate himself from his fellows and to stake his claims to freedom as an autonomous individual. "[Making] the economic emancipation of the individual depend on the emancipation of the whole class" – unions, that is – would counteract the atomistic tendencies of modern capitalism.[85]

Notwithstanding his commitment to organized labor, Croly was nonetheless critical of the objectives of the contemporaneous labor movement. Focusing on the extraction of collective bargaining agreements and concrete, but limited, concessions from employers, unions were insufficiently radical. They were self-seeking in aiming at the acquisition of property – class property, perhaps, but property all the same. In *Progressive Democracy*, Croly condemned the old craft unionism as "a parasite" and decried the union appropriation of a reactionary property-holding ideology. Instead,

[81] Croly, *Progressive Democracy*, 383–4.
[82] Croly, *Progressive Democracy*, 385–6.
[83] Croly, *Progressive Democracy*, 384–5.
[84] Croly, *Progressive Democracy*, 384–5.
[85] Croly, *Progressive Democracy*, 386.

while distancing himself somewhat from syndicalist methods involving the revolutionary seizure of the means of production by unions, he praised the syndicalist ideal and called for the establishment of "industrial constitutionalism," a "constitutional government in industry" in which workers would ultimately control the structure of production and of their own lives. In doing so, they would inevitably be wiser than the unscientific capitalist entrepreneurs he saw all around him, whom he characterized as "sportsmen," "pioneers," and "Napoleons," out for their own "personal aggrandizement." Those running a true industrial constitutional system would know enough to hire "a well-equipped general staff" of "expert administrators" to lead them into a successful democratic industrial future.[86]

Louis Brandeis, the future Supreme Court justice, saw the same targets of reform spotlighted by Dewey, Lippmann, and Croly. For Brandeis, part of the "curse of bigness" in corporations was that it stifled creativity and individual initiative in workers, in the process subtracting from the sum total of human happiness. Besides making businesses smaller, one of Brandeis's chief antidotes to "industrial absolutism" involved the empowerment of workers by inviting them to be active participants in "industrial government."[87] Such government, he argued:

will make the employee to a very much larger extent a thinker; it will make him realize that his work is his best field for development, and he will look to that as the employer looks to that – as a place for his greatest satisfaction in life.[88]

Brandeis, like Croly, believed that labor unions would play an important part in this new industrial-republican order. "America must breed only free men," Brandeis insisted. "It must develop citizens. It cannot develop citizens unless the workingmen possess industrial liberty; and industrial liberty is impossible if the right to organize be denied."[89] Like Croly, however, Brandeis, who also spoke in constitutional terms, saw craft unionism as only an intermediate stage on the road to industrial democracy:

We have already had industrial absolutism. With the recognition of the unions, this is changing into a constitutional monarchy, with well-defined limitations placed about

---

[86] Croly, *Progressive Democracy*, 386–402. In his earlier book, Croly had spoken more favorably of collective bargaining arrangements. Croly, *Promise of American Life*, 389–93. There, however, he did say that "the spirit and methods of collective bargaining between the employers and the labor organizations [needed to be] very much improved." Croly, *Promise of American Life*, 392.

[87] Louis Brandeis, quoted by Treadwell Cleveland Jr. in *LaFollette's Weekly Magazine* (24 May 1913) cited in Louis Brandeis, *The Brandeis Guide to the Modern World*, ed. Alfred Lief (Boston: Little, Brown and Company, 1941), 93.

[88] Brandeis, *Boston Sunday Post*, 14 February 1915, cited in Brandeis, *Brandeis Guide*, 96. See Karl Marx, "Economic and Philosophic Manuscripts of 1844," in *The Marx-Engels Reader*, 2nd ed., ed. Robert C. Tucker (New York: W. W. Norton, 1978), 66–125.

[89] Brandeis, "Trusts, Efficiency, and the New Party," *Collier's Weekly* (14 September 1912), 15.

the employer's formerly autocratic power. Next comes profit sharing. This, however, is only to be a transitional, halfway stage. Following upon it will come the sharing of responsibility, as well as of profits. The eventual outcome promised to be full-grown industrial democracy.[90]

Brandeis's friend and disciple, Felix Frankfurter echoed these now-familiar themes. Frankfurter – who was also a future Supreme Court justice and a major influence on the development of labor law through, among other things, his treatise opposing labor injunctions[91] – scored modern industry for "its grinding pressure and spiritual starvation...its failure to use the creative qualities of men, its deadening monotony and its excessive fatigue." Frankfurter worried:

Nowhere, save in directive and professional work, is there the opportunity for individual expression which was characteristic of the medieval handicraft. The result is to ensure a stunted citizenship, since only in a really adequate leisure and a training in the facility of its use can the qualities of democratic life be made manifest. For it is very certain that without facilities for the cultivation of the amenities of civilized life the mass of the people will remain incapable of disciplined democracy.[92]

In some ways, Frankfurter's vision of industrial democracy was more restrained and pragmatic than that of Dewey, Croly, Lippmann, and even Brandeis. Frankfurter, for instance, put in a good word for the social value of "leisure," one of the labor movement's decidedly nonrevolutionary goals. And he notched the rhetoric of industrial democracy down a pitch by implying that in many ways corporatist collective bargaining and craft unionism represented not the fledgling beginnings of a move toward the *beau idéal* of industrial democracy proper, but rather the achievement of the thing itself. Frankfurter's decision to accept collective bargaining and craft unionism went a long way toward domesticating the concept and reworking it into a form that was broadly acceptable politically.

Central for Frankfurter was stemming the tide of industrial unrest. Labor disturbances are "bound to continue," Frankfurter contended, "just so long as the present state of mind and feeling of workers is generated by growing disparity between their participation in politics and their exclusion from industrial direction." Collective bargaining, in Frankfurter's estimation, showed promise as a starting point for a solution. "This principle," he argued, "must, of course, receive ungrudging acceptance. It is nothing but belated recognition of economic facts – that the era of romantic individualism

---

[90] Brandeis, quoted in Cleveland, *LaFollette's Weekly Magazine*, 24 May 1913, cited in Brandeis, *Brandeis Guide*, 93–4.

[91] Felix Frankfurter and Nathan Greene, *The Labor Injunction* (New York: The Macmillan Company, 1930).

[92] Felix Frankfurter, "The Eight Hour Day," *Boston Herald*, 9 October 1916, reprinted in Frankfurter, *Law and Politics: Occasional Papers of Felix Frankfurter, 1913–1938*, eds. Archibald MacLeish and E. F. Pritchard Jr. (New York: Harcourt Brace, 1939), 203–4.

is no more." "The collectivity," he declared, "must be represented and must be allowed to choose its representatives."[93]

The Clayton Act Comes to the Court: Toward a Class-Based Constitutionalism of Collectivities

At the behest of organized labor and allied political progressives, in drafting the Clayton Act, Congress drew an express distinction between the assertions of political-economic power of organized labor and assertions of such power by capital. Nonetheless, the fact remained that the court-curbing language of the Clayton Act would inevitably be subject to interpretation by the federal courts – the ostensible object of the reformist legislation. In a major Clayton Act decision, however, the High Court, drawing once again from the well of traditional dignity-of-labor constitutionalism, counterattacked, narrowly interpreting the Act's new restrictions on federal judicial power.[94]

This Clayton Act case, *Duplex Printing v. Deering* (1921), involved the propriety of an injunction sought by a manufacturer of newspaper printing presses in Battle Creek, Michigan, against a machinist's union that had instigated a secondary boycott of the company's products. Duplex Printing was one of only four companies nationwide that manufactured such presses. By the time the union had called for the boycott against Duplex, it had induced each of the other three companies to become closed shops, in the process recognizing the union, establishing an ongoing relationship with it, and agreeing to minimum-wage and maximum-hour standards. Two of these three companies, however, were threatening to pull out of their agreement with the union unless Duplex Printing was brought into it. As it stood, the holdout at Duplex Printing undercut the competitiveness of the three other press manufacturers vis-à-vis the un-unionized shop. Duplex countered that the effort to force it to set up a closed shop was a conspiracy in restraint of trade that was illegal under federal antitrust law.

The Supreme Court's decision in the *Duplex Printing* case rested upon what might seem to be a narrow issue of statutory construction under the Clayton Act: whether the union members against whom a court injunction

---

[93] Frankfurter, "Law and Order," *Yale Review* (Winter 1920), reprinted in Frankfurter, *Law and Politics*, 213–15. This concern was paramount for many New Dealers. See Klare, "The Quest for Industrial Democracy and the Struggle Against Racism: Perspectives from Labor Law and Civil Rights Law," *Oregon Law Review* 61 (1982): 157–200, esp. 170–2; Karl E. Klare, "Labor Law as Ideology: Toward a New Historiography of Collective Bargaining Law," *Industrial Relations Law Journal* 4 (1981): 450–82, esp. 452, 456.

[94] *Duplex Printing Co. v. Deering*, 254 U.S. 443 (1921). See also *American Steel Foundries v. Tri-City Central Trades Council*, 257 U.S. 184 (1921); *Bedford Cut Stone v. Journeymen Stone Cutters' Association of North America*, 274 U.S. 37 (1927). On the political impetus for the act, as well as the sources of its many ambiguities, see George Lovell, *Legislative Deferrals: Statutory Ambiguity, Judicial Power, and American Democracy* (New York: Cambridge University Press, 2003).

was sought were covered (that is, protected) by the act, which by its terms applies to disputes "in any case between an employer and employees, or between employers and employees, or between employees, or between persons seeking employment, involving, or growing out of, a dispute concerning terms or conditions of employment." The interpretative difficulty arose from the fact that the union members who were boycotting Duplex Printing had no direct connection to either that company generally or to its Battle Creek plant. The only articulable connection those union members had to Duplex was that they worked in the same industry. If one interpreted the Clayton Act language forbidding courts from issuing injunctions in labor disputes as applying to disputes between employers and employees (actual or potential) in a particular business, then the boycott was probably unlawful and the Court remained free to issue an injunction in this case. If, however, one took the terms "employers" and "employees" in the Act to stand not for antagonistic sides in a dispute taking place at a particular business in a particular geographic location, but rather as designations of two broad and distinctive economic classes, the result would be altogether different.

The opinions in the case clearly set out these distinct interpretive alternatives. Justice Mahlon Pitney's opinion for the Court upholding the injunction against the machinist boycott plainly reads the Clayton Act in the former way. Justice Brandeis's dissent in the case (joined by Justices Holmes and Clarke), adopting a class-based interpretation of the Act, plainly reads it in the latter.

In his opinion for the Court, Pitney first made it clear that the undisputed peaceableness of the boycott at issue was irrelevant: It is the conspiracy itself that was unlawful. Next, he deemed it obvious that Section Twenty of the Clayton Act, by its plain meaning, referred to "parties standing in proximate relation to a controversy such as is particularly described," that is, it referred to "parties to an actual dispute respecting the terms or conditions of their own employment, past, present, or prospective," a construction that came to be known as "the proximate relations doctrine."[95] In contrast, Pitney explained, "The majority of the circuit court of appeals [which had affirmed a dismissal of the injunction] appear to have entertained the view that the words 'employers and employees' as used in Section Twenty, should be treated as referring to 'the business class or clan to which the parties litigant respectively belong.'"[96] However, it "would do violence to the guarded language employed were the exemption extended beyond the parties affected in a proximate and substantial, not merely a sentimental or sympathetic sense by the cause of the dispute." "Congress had in mind particular industrial controversies," the Court's majority concluded, "not a general class war."[97]

---

[95] *Duplex Printing*, 254 U.S. at 471, 472.
[96] *Duplex Printing*, 254 U.S. at 471.
[97] *Duplex Printing*, 254 U.S. at 472.

In his dissent, however, Justice Brandeis read Section Twenty of the Clayton Act as applying not simply to two parties to a bounded dispute, but rather as part of a broader framework of governance involving an ongoing project of administering the relations of antagonistic social classes. After first laying out the organizational architecture of the printing press industry in the United States, Brandeis then went on to conclude that Duplex's status as the last open-shop in the industry "threatened the interest not only of such union members as were its factory employees, but even more of all members of the several affiliated unions employed by [their] competitors."[98] "[T]he contest between the company and the machinists' union," he added, thus "involves vitally the interest of every person whose co-operation is sought."[99] The Clayton Act, Brandeis explained, "was the fruit of unceasing agitation, which extended over more than twenty years, and was designed to equalize before the law the position of workingmen and employer as industrial combatants."[100] The state, in passing that act, had deliberately sought to domesticate this class struggle. It had done so by counterposing "centralization in the control of business [to a] corresponding centralization in the organization of workingmen." In so doing, the "processes of justice" were substituted for "the more primitive method of trial by combat."[101] In light of these developments in state–society relations, the Clayton Act could only be construed as speaking of employers and employees in their broadest collective sense.

The Supreme Court's decision in the *Duplex Printing* case, which interpreted legislation that strained toward the adoption of a new constitutional vision in the spirit of the old, shocked the American labor movement. More particularly, *Duplex Printing* underlined for that movement that the Clayton Act had not freed it from the aggressive equitable policing of its strikes and pickets by the federal courts. To get out from under that debility, it seemed, labor activists and progressives would need to do more than simply pass legislation. They would need to reconstruct the underlying interpretive ethos. Now, more than ever, this was plainly the task at hand.[102]

---

98 *Duplex Printing*, 254 U.S. at 480.

99 *Duplex Printing*, 254 U.S. at 481.

100 *Duplex Printing*, 254 U.S. at 484.

101 *Duplex Printing*, 254 U.S. at 482, 488. As will be discussed, Brandeis's view eventually prevailed, first in the structure of the Norris-LaGuardia anti-injunction act (1932) and subsequently in the architecture of the labor laws and Court decisions structuring and ratifying the New Deal.

102 See "Labor to Organize as Political Party: State and Local Bodies of Federation Will Co-Operate with Central Committee," *New York Times*, August 28, 1921, 6 (announcing AFL national "campaign of investigation and education, to protect the rights of the wage earners against the encroachments of corporate power in significant part in response to "[t]he action of the United States Supreme Court in taking the heart out of the labor sections of the Clayton Law . . . in the decision of the Duplex Printing Company case"); "Special Conference in Washington: Union Leaders Draft Bill to Protect Unions, Seek Rehearing of Case of

Lean Years for the Reconstructive Project

No sooner had the calls for a transformative, reconstructive industrial democracy and a new constitutionalism of labor reached a fever pitch than the fever broke. In 1920, even Felix Frankfurter, one of the most pragmatic proponents of industrial democracy, had confidently announced that "the era of romantic individualism is no more." At that very moment, however, the mood of the country began to shift. A growing indifference to the labor problem, even among "the working class" itself, was palpable. Efforts by progressive intellectual elites to fan the flames of reformism proved feckless.

The new mood was apparent in Middletown, the midwestern city put under the sociological microscope of Robert and Helen Merrell Lynd. In the 1890s, the Lynds reported that Middletown was "one of the best organized cities in the United States," with nearly 4,000 AFL members living there. New unions, the Lynds reported, were founded there, and union conventions were held there. Labor unions, moreover, played an active role in the city's civic life. Labor unions sponsored libraries, and educational and leisure activities in abundance. The unions were also agitating continually for new laws concerning wages, health and safety, and death and disability benefits.[103]

By the early 1920s, things were different. "Labor Day," the authors reported, "a great day in the nineties, is today barely noticed." The Lynds quoted the secretary of one national union as stating that "the organized labor movement in [Middletown] does not compare with that of 1890 as one to one hundred." Civic boosters now openly boasted that Middletown was an "open shop town."[104] "The social function of the union has disappeared in this day of movies and the automobile," the Lynds found, "save for sparsely attended dances at Labor Hall." "[P]ublic opinion," they added, "is no longer with organized labor." Many members of the Middletown "working class" no longer perceived themselves as such and had great hopes for the social mobility of their children through education. Their own lives were no longer touched, as they saw it, by the great industrial injustices of fifty years earlier. Middletown residents were focused increasingly instead on the pursuit of leisure and consumption.[105]

Duplex Printing Press Company, Plan Fight Against Open Shop Campaign," *New York Times*, 23 February 1921, 15, col. 8; "U.S. Supreme Court Decides It Does Not Permit Labor Unions to Employ Secondary Boycott Against Interstate Trade of Employers, in Injunction Suit of Duplex Printing Company Case Against International Association of Machinists," *New York Times*, 4 January 1921, 1, col. 1; "S. Gompers Assails Decision, Says U.S. Supreme Court Has Joined Forces with Anti-Union Shop Movement," *New York Times*, 5 January 1921, 10, col. 5; "Gautier Hints at United Action by Organized Labor," *New York Times*, 7 January 1921, 2, col. 6; "Union Leaders Seek Rehearing of Case, at American Federation of Labor Special Conference in Washington," *New York Times*, 23 February 1921, 15, col. 8.

[103] Robert S. and Helen Merrell Lynd, *Middletown: A Study in American Culture* 76–7.

[104] Lynd and Lynd, *Middletown*, 78.

[105] Lynd and Lynd, *Middletown*, 78–82.

The patterns the Lynds observed in Middletown proved emblematic of nationwide trends during the 1920s. In a time of postwar prosperity, salaries, free time, consumption, and productivity all were up, as were, as labor historian Irving Bernstein argued, materialism and individualism. Studies of the era showed, in fact, that during the 1920s members of unions entering into collective bargaining agreements gained little more than those employees who were not affiliated with unions. When it came to wages and hours, one was actually likely to be worse off in the 1920s with a collective bargaining arrangement than without one.[106]

Bernstein, a partisan of progressive and New Deal labor constitutionalism that helped form Whiggish developmental narratives, famously dubbed the prosperous 1920s – in which workers perceived themselves as better off than they had ever been – as "The Lean Years," a decade of "paternalism," which witnessed a succession of employer efforts "to check unionism," such as stock ownership, profit sharing and bonuses, old-age pensions, worker health insurance, employee cafeterias and athletic facilities, social halls, paid vacations, and unemployment relief. During the 1920s, Bernstein complained, "[t]he social functions of the unions were assumed by the factory."[107]

It was only in a teleological spirit that defined progress as necessarily culminating in either worker control of factories or a statist organization of the workplace (or some combination of both) that the extention of profit sharing, health insurance, and paid vacations to workers could be characterized as a misfortune, and the prosperous years that witnessed these developments labeled "lean years" vexed by "the perils of prosperity."[108] These events, nonetheless, forced Bernstein to think hard about how things had gotten so bad for the working class in the 1920s:

Employers had several motives for this paternalism, perhaps most important being the desire to prevent labor trouble by removing its causes. In addition, they perceived a relationship between the worker's morale and his productive efficiency. Finally, some felt a social responsibility for their employees since bargaining hardly existed.[109]

The sudden and unexpected achievement of these goals was a problem because the winning benefits for the workers was not the first-order goal of progressives – though, of course, they wanted workers to be better off rather than worse off. Their primary goal was to midwife and institutionalize a new, group-oriented constitutional order. And the prosperity of the 1920s frustrated movement toward that goal, thwarting progress along the proper trajectory of state development. Since prosperity "retarded unionism," it

---

[106] Irving Bernstein, *The New Deal Collective Bargaining Policy* (Berkeley: University of California Press, 1950), 2–6.

[107] Bernstein, *New Deal Collective Bargaining Policy*, 14. See also Irving Bernstein, *The Lean Years: A History of the American Worker, 1920–1933* (Boston: Houghton Mifflin, 1960).

[108] William E. Leuchtenburg, *The Perils of Prosperity, 1914–1932* (Chicago: University of Chicago Press, 1958).

[109] Bernstein, *New Deal*, 14.

was a form of poverty. Developmentally speaking, the 1920s were lean years indeed.[110]

Some rump resistance remained, of course, even in the 1920s (labor problems plagued the railroads, spurring important institutional innovations in labor management relations). As courts continued to issue labor injunctions during that decade and as their use was repeatedly upheld by the Supreme Court, organized labor and allied progressive intellectuals muted some of their more visionary theorizing and began to mount an aggressive and practical campaign against the federal court's injunctive powers. In their widely read 1930 book *The Labor Injunction*, Felix Frankfurter and Nathan Greene spotlighted this assertion of judicial power as an ongoing problem. Greene, a member of the American Civil Liberties Union's Committee on the Labor Injunction, and Frankfurter, then a Harvard law professor and a protégé of Louis Brandeis (the author of the *Duplex Printing* dissent), not only wrote the book, as it were, but (serving as advisors to Congress) also wrote the law – the 1932 federal anti-injunction statute, popularly known as the Norris-LaGuardia Act, which was passed in the early years of the Great Depression. Book and statute united to form a common front against the recalcitrant courts. As Columbia University's P. F. Brissenden noted at the time, "[O]ne may say...with truth, that the [Norris LaGuardia Act], to which the book is a footnote, is a footnote to the book."[111]

Besides declaring that workers have broad collective bargaining and organizing rights, the Norris-LaGuardia Act restricted the power of the federal courts to issue injunctions in labor disputes, as had the Clayton Act before it.[112] This time, however, the statute explicitly adopted the broad, class-based understanding of a labor dispute advanced by Justice Brandeis in his *Duplex Printing* dissent and rejected the narrower, traditional approach in the majority opinion of Justice Pitney. The new act stated that a labor dispute covered by the act exists "when the case involves persons who are engaged in the same industry, trade, craft, or occupation," or has a "direct or indirect interest therein, or is a member, officer, or agent of any union which deals with employers or has employees engaged in that industry, trade, craft, or occupation." Under that Act, a labor dispute is any controversy "concerning terms or conditions of employment regardless of whether or not the disputants stand in the proximate relation of employer and employee."[113]

---

[110] Bernstein, *New Deal*, 14.

[111] P. F. Brissenden, "The Labor Injunction," *Political Science Quarterly* 48 (September 1933): 413–50. In these efforts, Frankfurter and Greene were joined by progressives and future New Dealers Edwin Witte, Herman Oliphant, and Donald Richberg. O'Brien, *Workers' Paradox*, 153. See, generally, Melvin J. Segal, "The Norris-LaGuardia Act and the Courts" (Ph.D. dissertation, 1938, University of Illinois at Urbana-Champaign).

[112] 47 Stat. 70 (1932).

[113] I should note here that my insistence that the Act by the terms quoted treats labor as a class seems to run directly counter to Ruth O'Brien's claim that what is distinctive about

Crisis and the Revival of the Reconstructive Imperative

The transformed understanding of the nature of the relationship between capital and labor manifested in the Norris-LaGuardia Act owed much to the crisis atmosphere in which it was passed. The collapse of the American economy in 1929, which brought fears of the permanent collapse of capitalism itself, added weight to appeals for a new, group-oriented governing ethos and the imperative of "industrial democracy." In this regard, in contrast to the lean years of the 1920s, the 1930s would be a time of pronounced abundance. During the economic crisis, the progressive elites who had been so active in the century's first two decades were finally able to push through collective bargaining legislation that transferred an unprecedented amount of public power to the political-economic aggregates of labor unions. This political development, which ran counter to longstanding individualist, dignity-of-labor traditions of American constitutionalism, progressively inclined politicians plainly acknowledged, could not have been achieved in more prosperous times.[114] While Americans evinced little interest in labor unions in the years prior to the 1920s collapse (and would again gradually lose interest after the

the Norris-LaGuardia Act is that it "withdrew equitable relief for certain types of activities or conduct and not for special classes or agents," that it made "injunctive relief dependent on conduct rather than agency." O'Brien, *Workers' Paradox*, 149. O'Brien properly draws attention to the fact that the Act does not grant unions immunity from equitable relief, as they had sought (with particular vehemence in the face of unfavorable court constructions of the Clayton Act) and that instead, it settled upon an action-based scheme that lessoned labor union vulnerability. She declares that the law thus "avoid[ed] any association with class legislation," which in the prevailing constitutional environment would render it vulnerable to constitutional challenge. O'Brien, *Workers' Paradox*, 154. While this is all true, so far as it goes, it seems to me crucial – as we shall see plainly in the way in which the law of injunction developed post-1937 – that the statutory definition of a "labor dispute" under the Act left open the possibility that courts could (and, indeed, would) deploy the Act as a form of class legislation (a battle adumbrated in the Pitney-Brandeis dispute in the *Duplex Printing* decision). One can miss the features of the Act that are class (as opposed to action) based by not according due attention to the way in which the Act defines a cognizable "labor dispute." That definition proved crucial to the path of constitutional development and the way in which the nature of labor rights came to shape the later meaning of civil rights.

[114] Franklin Roosevelt, David Kennedy noted, was actually troubled by signs at the outset of his second term that economic recovery might be around the corner. This was because, in his view, he had not yet had the opportunity to institutionalize the changes in the nation's governing structures that a deep crisis had afforded him the opportunity to make. Indeed, the perils of a crisis ended prematurely was a theme Roosevelt mused upon repeatedly in speeches and private letters. Kennedy, *Freedom from Fear*, 323–4. In England, similarly, the Depression-era Labour Party, which was committed to using the crisis brought on by the war in Europe to lay the groundwork for a postwar socialist order, fought and defeated economic policies promoted by John Maynard Keyes, which made use of time-limited statism (such as compulsory savings, refundable to taxpayers on demand after the war had concluded). Labour insisted on high tax interventionism specifically because that approach would be most likely to outlast the immediate crisis. See Robert Skidelsky, *John Maynard Keyes, Vol. 3: Fighting for Freedom, 1937–1946* (New York: Viking, 2001),

Second World War), in this aberrant time, desperate, and open to experimentation and trying anything that might work, the American public acquiesced in New Deal labor and collective bargaining laws.

The depths of the economic crisis of the 1930s soon made it seem as if the indifference of the 1920s had never existed. Recalling the push for collective bargaining arrangements just a few years after the first such measures were instituted, Roosevelt aide Hugh Johnson declared, "In this stage of [industrial] specialization [one] can no more stop the rush of economic trend than the Dane, Canute, could sit on the seashore and stop the incoming tide." "Even some of our very courts of justice," he contended, "threw their judgments against the rights of men by invoking the common law doctrines of feudalism in an industrialized nation of the nineteenth century. But the onward sweep of human events was stirring the ranks of labor."[115] "The dikes of paternalism against the spread of unionism," Irving Bernstein declared later, "were swept away in the flood of the Great Depression."[116]

After heralding the death of paternalism, Bernstein immediately argued that it was the weakness of labor unions and their inability to govern themselves that made the New Deal collective bargaining initiative an imperative. The first step in this crisis period in constructing state power to nurse a broad-based unionism into being had been the passage of the Norris-LaGuardia Act in 1932, which severely limited the ability of the federal courts to issue injunctions in labor disputes.[117] But following this initiative, the next step was unclear. One obstacle was that Roosevelt had little of the progressive interest in unionism or collective bargaining that had so inspired Brandeis and Frankfurter and their intellectual predecessors. He had barely discussed unionism in his 1932 campaign. Nor did Frances Perkins, FDR's Labor Secretary, see the labor movement as any sort of solution to importunate social problems.[118] The first New Deal collective bargaining measures came together more in the spirit of acquiesence and experimentation than of deliberate and rational planning. The collective bargaining measures were passed

---

58–68. On the importance of economic crisis as a necessary, if not sufficient, cause of the passage of the Wagner Act, see Plotke, *Building a Democratic Political Order*, 101–8.

[115] Hugh S. Johnson, *The Blue Eagle from Egg to Earth* (Garden City, NY: Doubleday, Doran & Co., 1935), 323, 325. Though exhibiting a penchant for millennial rhetoric, Johnson was ultimately bitten by it, to the extent it served to justify anything that came down the pike in the name of the New Deal. Johnson (along with Donald Richberg), for instance, seriously resisted many of the specifics of the collective bargaining laws hashed out by Robert Wagner and others on Roosevelt's NIRA labor boards. See William Leuchtenburg, *Franklin Delano Roosevelt and the New Deal* (New York: Harper Torchbooks, 1963), 107–8. Like "the Dane, Canute," he also ended up with wet feet.

[116] Bernstein, *New Deal*, 14.

[117] Norris-LaGuardia Act, 47 Stat. 70, 73 (23 March 1932). Donald Richberg, a top labor lawyer and soon-to-be FDR's leading labor advisor, played a leading role in drafting the Norris-LaGuardia Act.

[118] Kennedy, *Freedom from Fear*, 297–8, 319–21.

as part of the hastily cobbled together National Industrial Recovery Act (NIRA), a hodgepodge of legislation that represented less a carefully considered and coherent approach to the sea of troubles brought on by the Depression than part of a defensive plan providing an alternative to Senator Hugo Black's proposed "thirty-hour bill" (which banned from interstate commerce goods produced in factories whose workforce worked more than thirty hours a week, a ban Roosevelt was convinced would prove economically disastrous), and, at the same time, showcasing the administration's seriousness about fighting the Great Depression.[119] The NIRA comprised a grab bag of initiatives. Under the NIRA, businesses were granted broad exemptions from the nation's antitrust laws to enable them to come together, under the supervision of the National Recovery Administration (NRA), to draft code agreements limiting "destructive" competition in their industries. Under this arrangement, vast numbers of government planners of the *New State Ice* variety were given broad new powers to license business.[120] The NIRA created the Public Works Administration (PWA), which was authorized to spend $3.3 billion on pump-priming public works projects. And in Section 7(a) of the act, labor unions were guaranteed collective bargaining rights and minimum-wage and maximum-hour protections under the new labor codes.[121] By organizing businesses and seeking to govern through them, the NIRA, in a time of crisis, imposed a radically new group-oriented corporatist order upon the nation's business sector. This new order dovetailed with the increasing government solicitude for labor cartels, which were to be institutionalized through collective bargaining arrangements. A new constitutional order anchored in the creation and government supervision of groups was taking shape.[122] United Mine Workers leader John Lewis compared the NIRA's Section 7(a) to the Emancipation Proclamation. And, in truth, his histrionic analogy was not far off. That section played a major role in relegating the old individualist dignity-of-labor constitutionalism concerning the workplace to the status of museum piece of the constitutional past.[123]

The crisis-time drafters of the NIRA, however, had moved with so little concern for constitutional proprieties that the law was quickly invalidated

---

[119] National Industrial Recovery Act, H.R. 5755, June 16, 1933, Public Laws of the United States (Seventy-Third Congress) (Washington, D.C.: Government Printing Office, 1934); Kennedy, *Freedom from Fear*, 150–3.

[120] The new NRA quickly ballooned, with a staff of forty-five hundred, drafting approximately thirteen thousand pages of codes and issuing eleven thousand rulings in its short two-year life. Kennedy, *Freedom from Fear*, 185–6.

[121] Leuchtenburg, *Franklin D. Roosevelt*, 57–8.

[122] It is worth noting that the business cartels ultimately collapsed in the face of business defectors. The Wagner Act, however, ensured that such defections among the ranks of labor would be minimized.

[123] Fraser, "The Labor Problem," in Gerstle and Fraser, *Rise and Fall of the New Deal Order*, 68.

by the U.S. Supreme Court – in a unanimous opinion to which even the Court's most liberal members subscribed.[124] Following the High Court's invalidation of the NIRA, a small group of committed policymakers, meeting behind closed doors in round-the-clock sessions, hashed out a new collective bargaining bill that accorded state-sponsored power to labor unions. In signing the legislation that emerged from these sessions, which advanced a new governing constitutionalism for the workplace, Franklin Roosevelt "had little idea what he was letting himself in for. . . ." The president, "perturbed at being cast in the role of midwife of industrial unionism" said his "administration was uncertain about what 7(a) meant or how it could be enforced."[125]

Someone who was happy to be cast in this role, however, was Senator Robert F. Wagner of New York, a leader of the core elite of the liberal politicians of the day and the only member of Congress who had had any serious influence on the NIRA's secret drafting.[126] Wagner skillfully constructed the new order upon the foundations of the rather weak labor boards the president had set up under that act to implement 7(a). Wagner accorded the central state the power to conduct secret union elections and, following the outcome of those elections, to confer power upon majority-selected unions to exercise exclusive bargaining rights for all. Wagner's labor boards also were given the power to enforce good faith bargaining between labor and management and to mandate that all collective bargaining disputes end in agreement.[127]

The authority accruing to Wagner in taking these initiatives was augmented by a sense of instability and widespread political violence. In 1933 and 1934, a series of especially violent strikes swept American industry, leaving a swath of injury and destruction in their path. Employers armed themselves in a way that harked back to the bloody labor disputes of the previous

---

[124] *Schecter Poultry v. United States*, 295 U.S. 495 (1935) (the statute was invalidated on the grounds that it controvened the Constitution by delegating legislative power to the executive, and by empowering Congress to regulate local, as opposed to interstate, commerce).

[125] Leuchtenburg, *Franklin D. Roosevelt*, 107. Others have similarly emphasized the unformed positions of labor unions concerning the nature of the arrangements they were seeking at the time the Wagner Act was being drafted, as well as the president's (and the Democratic Party's) initial lack of interest in the bill. See Plotke, *Building a Democratic Political Order*, 99, 105. Alan Brinkley has argued that unlike the early "brains trusters" and early-twentieth-century progressives, core New Dealers rejected the "associational vision" as set out by the NRA. Alan Brinkley, "The Idea of the State," in Fraser and Gerstle, *Rise and Fall of the New Deal Order*, 88. The ambivalent origins of this order are apparent in the shape of the narrative crafted by Peter Irons in his book *New Deal Lawyers*, a carefully researched and informative book that argues simultaneously that the New Deal legislation was hashed out behind closed doors by young, hurried, and inexperienced elite lawyers to serve vested interests and that the Supreme Court, in striking it down, stood athwart a great tide of democratic lawmaking plainly directed at advancing the wider public interest. Irons, *The New Deal Lawyers* (Princeton: Princeton University Press, 1982).

[126] Plotke, *Building a Democratic Political Order*, 108–17.

[127] Plotke, *Building a Democratic Political Order*, 107.

century. In the face of this rising unrest, the essentially mediative offices of the Section 7(a) National Labor Board offered little relief.[128]

In his efforts to construct state power in a way that would prove more effective in the management of labor disputes, Wagner built on the "common law" that had been cobbled together by the labor board during its short existence and the governing precedent established by the 1926 Railway Labor Act. That pathbreaking law had set up a comprehensive collective bargaining scheme for railroad workers, though it lacked either provisions for union elections or an effective enforcement mechanism (which were to be added by an amendment in 1934). Wagner's accomplishment was to borrow the railway precedent, strengthen and improve it, and then apply it across the board to employer/employee relations in every state and in the major sectors of the modern American political economy.

Wagner (following a wonted pattern of progressive argument) treated the bargaining arrangements of the Railway Labor Act as an experiment in a single sector that, because it proved successful, was now worthy of universal adoption. He chose not to emphasize the uniqueness of the railroad industry and, hence, the distinction between employee-management relations in railroads and such relations in the nation's other industries. Railroads, after all, were common carriers and, as such, had been legally charged with advancing the public interest since the Granger laws of the 1870s.[129] In 1887, an independent federal body, the Interstate Commerce Commission, was set up for the sole purpose of regulating railroads. And labor disputes on the rails were so potentially harmful to the national interest that the railroads were actually seized by the federal government during the First World War. When they were returned to private hands in 1920, a rather toothless Railway Labor Board was set up to try to stave off labor contention in the industry. A national strike shut down the railroads in 1922. By 1926, the federal government, still seeking a solution to the bedeviling problems of national commerce and national security (given the perceived lessons of the war), had passed the Railway Labor Act.[130]

In the interest of the construction of state power in a period of crisis, Wagner drew an analogy: Just as labor violence and unrest in railroads had proved a menace to national commerce and national security, now labor

---

[128] Irving Bernstein, *Turbulent Years: A History of the American Worker, 1933–1941* (Boston: Houghton Mifflin, 1970), 172–4. Plotke, *Building a Democratic Political Order*, 101–2. The most prominent and violent of the confrontations in these years, all of which involved fatalities, included the Electric Auto-Lite Company strike in Toledo, Ohio, the San Francisco longshoreman's strike, the Minneapolis Teamsters strike, and the nationwide textile workers strike. Kennedy, *Freedom from Fear*, 291–6. See also Klare, "The Quest for Industrial Democracy," 170–2; Klare, "Labor Law as Ideology," 452, 456.

[129] See Elizabeth Sanders, *Roots of Reform: Farmers, Workers, and the American State, 1877–1917* (Chicago: University of Chicago Press, 1999), 108, 179, 183.

[130] Bernstein, *New Deal*, 40–2, 60.

violence in every other sector was proving a menace to national commerce
and national security. A system of government-supervised collective bargaining, he contended, could stanch and manage this labor antagonism. However,
it failed to do so on equitable and effective terms in the railroad industry
because government supervision and the means of enforcement had been
lax. That deficiency would now be corrected, both on the railroads and
elsewhere, with the National Labor Relations Act (the NLRA, or "Wagner
Act"), which the senator shepherded successfully through Congress and presented to the president for signature.[131] A form of "industrial democracy"
had finally been instituted and union power permanently ensconced as a
defining feature of a reconstructed, group-oriented constitutionalism. When
in 1947, in the early days of the Cold War, a Freedom Train toured America
with originals of some of the nation's iconographic documents – the Declaration of Independence, the Mayflower Compact, the Gettysburg Address –
the Wagner Act was slated to go on tour with them. Only the intercession
of the American Heritage Foundation, a business-backed sponsor, prevented
its taking a symbolic place alongside the nation's other constitutive texts.[132]

The Wagner Act transformed the entire constitutional conception of the
workplace, shifting it once and for all from one characterized by employers
and employees freely contracting to one that envisaged a bargain between
the collectivities of "business" and "labor," which the state now conceptualized as a recognized constitutional class. The Wagner Act put the power
of the federal government behind labor as a class. It prohibited company
unions (where, ostensibly, workers were compelled to become outsiders to
their class by working too closely with the capitalist-managerial class). The
act obligated employers to accept rather than fight unionization. And it set
up the sort of workplace governance that many of the progressive proponents of "industrial democracy" had dreamed of, providing labor unions
with exclusive power within plants and workplaces to represent the interests
of all workers as a class, with the representing union to be determined by
government-supervised elections.[133]

---

[131] National Labor Relations Act of 1935, 29 U.S.C. 151–169 (1994). James MacGregor Burns,
Roosevelt: The Lion and the Fox (New York: Harcourt, Brace & World, Inc., 1956), 244.

[132] Eric Foner, *The Story of American Freedom* (New York: W. W. Norton, 1998), 249–50. Also
slated to go but eliminated was an original of FDR's order establishing the Fair Employment
Practices Commission.

[133] Leuchtenburg, *New Deal*, 150–2. Schiller, "From Group Rights to Individual Liberties,"
9–23; Stone, "Post-War Paradigm," 1521–5; Klare, "Quest for Industrial Democracy,"
165. Tomlins and others have characterized the act as amounting to a failure of a more
radical labor vision. It was, however, by and large an achievement of the progressive vision for labor. See Christopher L. Tomlins, *The State and the Unions: Labor Relations, Law,
and the Organized Labor Movement in America, 1880–1960* (Cambridge: Cambridge University Press, 1985); Lichtenstein, *State of the Union*, 148–62; Klare, "Quest for Industrial
Democracy," 166. For a critique of the "deradicalization theorists" for failing to situate
the post–New Deal system of labor governance within the context of broader, dominant,

Putting the Constitutional Imprimatur on the New Group-Oriented Order

To the surprise of everyone (including the Roosevelt administration), the Supreme Court ratified this new group-oriented constitutionalism, putting its imprimatur on the Wagner Act in its *Jones and Laughlin Steel* decision.[134] The "Four Horsemen," of course, objected, insisting upon the traditional constitutional guarantees under the Fifth and Fourteenth Amendments concerning the rights of employers and employees to bargain over their labor contracts free from the coercive hand of governmental power. For the majority, however, the government interest in stanching the labor unrest and violence in those unusual times justified the unprecedented insertion of government authority into the workplace on behalf of the public interest (which was identified with the perceived interests of both stability and labor). The Court's holding in the *Jones and Laughlin Steel* case was soon imagined within the new constitutional order to have been not simply a necessary, though unusual, emergency measure but rather a permanent progressive-spirited alteration of the meaning of the constitutional rights of labor.[135]

The Supreme Court's *Jones and Laughlin* decision was clearly one of the most dramatic of the New Deal. Less heralded, but of equal institutional consequence, were the Court's Norris-LaGuardia decisions of about the same time. In those decisions, the Court announced the end of the traditional dignity-of-labor constitutionalism that had been the focus of contention in a long series of precrisis cases and statutes involving labor injunctions. In these Norris-LaGuardia decisions of the 1930s, the Court at last adopted the constitutional ethos concerning labor-management relations expressed in Justice Brandeis's *Duplex Printing* dissent, and discarded once and for all Justice Pitney's traditional constitutional vision.

The Norris-LaGuardia Act, as we have seen, represented what many hoped would be the coup de grâce in a long institutional battle between "conservative" courts and labor activists and progressive legislators over labor-management relations in late-nineteenth- and early-twentieth-century America. The question posed after the act's passage was how would the federal courts interpret this new and relatively clear statutory language, which

---

interest group pluralist understandings of the nature of political life, see Schiller, "From Group Rights to Individual Liberties." See, generally, Kahn, *Supreme Court and Constitutional Theory.*

[134] *National Labor Relations Board v. Jones and Laughlin Steel Corp.*, 301 U.S. 1 (1937).

[135] The primary argument in defense of the constitutionality of the NIRA (the precursor to the NRA) in the Supreme Court had been that the government's unprecedented powers were justified by an economic emergency. *Schecter Poultry v. United States*, 295 U.S. 495 (1935). See also *Home Building and Loan Association v. Blaisdell*, 290 U.S. 398 (1934). One of the central points of contention within labor scholarship has been over the degree to which the state's interest in stability and the interests of labor were in conflict. See Tomlins, *State and the Unions*; Lovell, *Legislative Deferrals.*

was specifically crafted to clip their institutional power.[136] In the immediate aftermath of the act's passage, most courts gave it a broad construction in line with Congress's apparent intent. But the Seventh Circuit Court of Appeals in the upper Midwest continued to give a limited construction to the phrase "labor dispute" in anti-injunction statutes. In two closely divided decisions, however, the U.S. Supreme Court nipped the Seventh Circuit's resistance in the bud.[137]

The first of the Supreme Court's Norris-LaGuardia decisions, *Senn v. Tile Layers Union* (1937) was something of a trial run for the Court.[138] It involved not the Norris-LaGuardia Act itself, but rather Wisconsin's "little Norris-LaGuardia Act" (which was the fruit of labor activism by many of the same people who had pushed for passage of the federal act, including Felix Frankfurter and Nathan Greene). Importantly, however (and unlike many of the grand industrial disputes of the previous half-century), it was not at all clear in the *Senn* case that justice lay on the side of the union organizers. Because of the partial inversion of the emotional dynamics of the case, the decision provides an unusually clear glimpse into the institutional implications of the new act.[139]

Paul Senn was the proprietor of a small Milwaukee tile-laying company. Although Senn had a small showroom elsewhere in the city, he ran his business primarily out of his home. He did much of his company's tile-laying work with his own hands, though, depending on the number of jobs his company had lined up, it was not unusual for him to sign on one or two journeyman tile layers and one or two helpers. The net income of his company in 1935

---

[136] The contrast was with the language of the Clayton Act, whose (minimal) ambiguities had been seized by the Court. See, generally, Lovell, *Legislative Deferrals*.

[137] See *Lauf v. Shinner*, 82 F.2d 68 (7th Cir. 1936); *United Electric Coal Co. v. Rice*, 80 F.2d 1 (7th Cir. 1935), *cert. denied*, 297 U.S. 714 (1936); *Newton v. Laclede Steel Co.*, 80 F.2d 636 (7th Cir. 1935); *Scavenger Service Corp. v. Courtney*, 85 F.2d 825 (7th Cir. 1936). See also Erwin B. Ellmann, "Comment: When a 'Labor Dispute' Exists within Meaning of the Norris-LaGuardia Act," *Michigan Law Review* 36 (1938): 1146–76, esp. 1152, 1154.

[138] *Senn v. Tile Layers Union*, 301 U.S. 468 (1937).

[139] For a progressive argument from the statebuilding era supporting this view, see Croly, *Promise of American Life*, 387–8 ("In the majority of discussions of the labor question the non-union laborer is figured as the independent working man who is asserting his right to labor when and how he prefers against the tyranny of the labor union. . . . [He is conceptualized as] fighting the battle of individual independence against the army of class oppression. Neither is this estimate of the non-union laborer wholly without foundation. The organization and policy of the contemporary labor union being what they are, cases will occasionally and even frequently occur in which the non-union laborer will represent the protest of an individual against injurious restrictions imposed by the union upon his opportunities and his work. But such cases are rare compared to the much larger number of instances in which the non-union laborer is to be considered as essentially the industrial derelict. . . . [U]nder existing conditions, [independence] must be bought by association. Worthy individuals will sometimes be sacrificed by this process of association; but every process of industrial organization or change . . . necessarily involves individual cases of injustice").

was $1,500, $750 of which went to Senn himself. Senn's income from his business, the trial record makes clear, was insufficient to support him and his family – consisting of a wife and four children.

Tile laying in Milwaukee was a union industry, and the local tile layer's union had approached Senn about converting his business into a union shop. Senn was sympathetic to the union and thus expressed an openness toward the possibility of doing so. Once he began to discuss the conversion with union officials, however, problems arose. The first was that the prevailing union rules required that a tile setter who performed journeyman-type work, as Paul Senn did, have acquired his practical experience through a three-year tile-laying apprenticeship. Senn, however, had not done so. The second problem was that the union rules were premised upon – and forced – a sharp distinction between labor and management. Specifically, Article III of the rules of the Tile Layer's Union required that "no individual member of a partnership or corporation engaged in the Tile Contracting Business shall work with the tools or act as [a] Helper." Because Senn was both the owner and the principal laborer in his small firm, he impermissibly straddled the distinct categories set out in Article III.[140]

Senn did not see these problems as serious obstacles to organizing his tile-laying business as a union shop. In talks with the union, he expressed a willingness to join, as long as he was exempted from those rules that forbade him personally from practicing his trade. Along these lines, Senn informed the union's representatives that he was willing to hire only union employees. He likewise told them that he would follow all their rules regarding wages, hours, and working conditions. He even went as far as declaring a willingness to refrain from working himself when there was sufficient work in the shop to allow him to do so. At the moment, however, that was not possible because, as he told them, if he stopped working now, his business would go bankrupt.

The Milwaukee Tile Layer's Union was not sympathetic. It dismissed Senn's pleas for special treatment and spurned his offer. Shortly thereafter, the union undertook a sustained campaign to destroy his business. The union picketed his shop with signs declaring that Senn's tile-laying business was "unfair" to the Tile Layers Protective Union. Its members followed him from home to work and picketed his jobs.

Under the traditional constitutional order in which the individual's right to a livelihood was a constitutionally guaranteed individual liberty interest, Senn would have had a right to pursue his work without harassment. To enforce that right, he might have successfully sought a court order enjoining the union's efforts to drive him out of business. Wisconsin, however,

---

[140] The union's insistence on labor and management as hermetically antagonistic classes is consistent with the longstanding imagination of the "labor problem" by progressive intellectuals. It clearly fits with the vision of Justice Brandeis as expressed in his *Duplex Printing v. Deering* dissent.

was a pioneer of the new constitutional order concerning labor, which was premised on a solicitude for the rights of labor as an aggregate group or class (the same solicitude apparent in Justice Brandeis's *Duplex Printing* dissent). The state's new little Norris-LaGuardia act, part of the state-level assault on the *Duplex Printing* majority, limited the injunctive power of Wisconsin courts over the sort of picketing that was a common feature of labor disputes.

Given the temporal proximity of the traditional order (which created uncertainty regarding its continuing legitimacy), Senn and his lawyer instinctively made claims in court that would have been both cognizable and persuasive only a few years before. The Fourteenth Amendment's due process and equal protection clauses, they argued, forbade legislation that conferred public power upon a special interest or class, thereby permitting that class to advance its own collective interests at the expense of an individual freely exercising his or her lawful constitutional rights – here, the liberty to work and to earn a living. Thus, as applied, he asserted, the Wisconsin Labor Code was not a legitimate health, safety, or morals measure within the rightful police powers of the state.

Tracking the proximate relations logic set out by Justice Pitney in the *Duplex Printing* majority, Senn's lawyer argued that the Wisconsin Labor Code, which prevented the Court from enjoining picketers (who belonged to unions with no proximate relation with his business) attempting to deny Senn his right to work, had deprived him of his property rights without due process of law. As such, the code was directed not at advancing the constitutionally cognizable interests of individuals, but instead at advancing the interest of employees as a class over the interests of employers as a class. Senn was being compelled to give up his fundamental rights to further these class interests.[141] These class interests were advanced through the portion of the Wisconsin Labor Code that broadly defined labor disputes: Had the unions not represented other workers in the same line of business as that in which Senn himself employed others, an injunction would certainly have been issued.

In an opinion written by Justice Brandeis, however, the Court categorically rejected Senn's arguments. Not surprisingly, Brandeis's theoretical assumptions in *Senn* tracked those of his earlier *Duplex Printing* dissent. Foremost among these was the assumption of economic interdependence, a defining feature of the new constitutionalism,[142] and the consequent need for a

---

[141] Citing *Traux v. Corrigan*, 257 U.S. 312; *Butchers' Union v. Crescent City Live Stock Co.*, 111 U.S. 746; *Hitchman Coal & Coke Co. v. Mitchell*, 245 U.S. 229; *Coppage v. Kansas*, 236 U.S. 1; *Traux v. Raich*, 239 U.S. 33; *Adair v. U.S.*, 208 U.S. 161. See, generally, Gillman, *Constitution Besieged*.

[142] This assumption was at the core of the posttraditional constitutional order. See *NLRB v. Jones and Laughlin Steel*, 301 U.S. 1 (1937); Thomas L. Haskell, *The Emergence of Professional Social Science: The American Social Science Association and the Nineteenth Century Crisis of Authority* (Urbana: University of Illinois Press, 1977); Theodore J. Lowi, "The Welfare State: Ethical Foundations and Constitutional Remedies," *Political Science Quarterly* 101

broadly conceived, society-wide, systems-regarding constitutional vision. Brandeis began not with Senn's individual rights, but rather with the observation that the tile industry was in a "demoralized state" at the time the union made its demands upon him. The Wisconsin law permitted the union to combine and act for what the Court now readily held was a thoroughly legitimate purpose, namely to "[enhance] their opportunity to acquire work for themselves and those whom they represent," to "[protect] . . . themselves as workers and craftsmen in the industry." Because they were advancing their collective interests, there was nothing wrong with what they had done. Following the test laid out by Holmes in his influential 1893 law review article, Brandeis concluded that here "[t]here is no basis for a suggestion that the unions' request that Senn refrain from working with his own hands . . . was malicious; or there was a desire to injure Senn." Moreover, "[t]here was no effort to induce Senn to do an unlawful thing." "There was no violence, no force was applied, no molestation or interference, no coercion."[143] "Each member of the unions, as well as Senn, has the right to strive to earn his living," Brandeis explained. "Senn seeks to do so through the exercise of his individual skill and planning. The union members seek to do so through combination." So far as the Constitution is concerned, Brandeis summarily concluded, this was all a matter of state policy and "not our concern. The Fourteenth Amendment does not prohibit it." "[A] hoped-for job is not property guaranteed by the Constitution."[144]

In his opinion for the Court, Justice Brandeis passed quickly over the question of whether the situation in *Senn* amounted to a "labor dispute" under the Wisconsin Labor Code, which tracked the definition of the federal Norris-LaGuardia Act. "Those issues involved the construction and application of the [state] statute and the Constitution of the state," he explained. "As to them," he held, "the judgment of [the state's] highest Court is conclusive."[145]

(1986): 197–220; Morton White, *Social Thought in America: The Revolt Against Formalism* (Boston: Beacon Press, 1957); *Wickard v. Filburn*, 317 U.S. 111 (1942); *West Coast Hotel v. Parrish*, 300 U.S. 379 (1937). The critique of the notion that the nation's economy could be managed by a decentralized federalism that imagined "a widespread similarity of local conditions" and that the states could manage the complexities of the regulation of interstate commerce in the statebuilding era had long been advanced by progressives outside the Court before it finally made its way into Court doctrine. David W. Levy, *Herbert Croly of the New Republic: The Life and Thought of an American Progressive* (Princeton: Princeton University Press, 1985), 110–13.

[143] *Senn*, 301 U.S. at 480–1. See Oliver Wendell Holmes Jr., "Privilege, Malice and Intent," *Harvard Law Review* 8 (April 1893): 3, 7; Ernst, *Lawyers Against Labor*, 81–5; Lovell, *Legislative Deferrals*, ch. 2.

[144] *Senn*, 301 U.S. at 481–2. Needless to say, this assertion would in time be rejected as antiprogressive when the next reformist movement, that of civil rights, took hold. The position advanced by Brandeis in *Senn*, incidentally, was supported by the ACLU in an *amicus* brief filed in the case.

[145] *Senn*, 301 U.S. at 477.

In his discussion of Article III of the Tile Layers' Union contract, which, had he signed it, would have obligated Senn to give up his trade, Brandeis deployed the same group- or class-based approach to labor that he had outlined in his *Duplex Printing* dissent. He noted, first, that however unfair to Senn this section of the contract might seem, given the "necessities of employment within the industry and [the need] for the protection of themselves as workers and craftsmen in the industry," it was (as the state courts had concluded) "a reasonable rule."[146] "The unions acted, and had the right to act as they did, to protect the interests of their members against the harmful effect upon them of Senn's actions. . . . Because his action was harmful, the fact that none of Senn's employees was a union member, or sought the union's aid, is immaterial."[147]

While Brandeis applied a class and society-level systems analysis in the *Senn* case, Pierce Butler (joined by McReynolds, Van Devanter, and Sutherland) appraised the situation from the perspective of the aggrieved individual. Eschewing Brandeis's abstract and distancing systems analysis, Butler focused instead on the seemingly absurd predicament into which Paul Senn had been placed. What the case amounted to, Butler pointed out, was a union refusal to allow Senn either to unionize or to carry on his business solely because he personally worked with his hands. This, Butler declared, was an unlawful purpose. Under the law, he declared, strikes and picketing for unlawful purposes are plainly illegal. As such, the *Senn* decision "violat[ed] a principle of fundamental law: That no man may be compelled to hold his life or the means of living at the mere will of others."[148]

The *Senn* decision, which dealt with a state labor law, was a prelude for the Court's ultimate construction of the federal Norris-LaGuardia Act itself in another case from Wisconsin: *Lauf v. Shinner* (1938). *Lauf* involved the efforts of an unincorporated AFL – affiliated union to organize about thirty-five workers at a small chain of privately owned Milwaukee meat markets. By all accounts, these workers were content with their jobs and their relationships

---

[146] In this regard, it is interesting to juxtapose Brandeis's opinion in *Senn* to the majority and dissenting opinions in *Lochner v. New York*, 198 U.S. 45 (1905). In his famous dissent in that case, Justice John Marshall Harlan asked the Court to look past the formalities of the doctrine of liberty of contract to the actual unequal bargaining power between an employer and an employee. Brandeis's opinion in *Senn* is actually closer in spirit to Justice Peckham's majority opinion in *Lochner* in its formalist assumptions: Senn had a choice to make, and, as far as Brandeis was concerned, it was a choice made in total freedom – either give up his trade or go out of business. It seems that the chief difference between Peckham and Brandeis is not one of formalism versus antiformalism, but rather in their respective commitments to individualist or collectivizing goals. For a further elaboration of this point, see Kersch, "The New Deal Triumph as the End of History? The Judicial Negotiation of Labor Rights and Civil Rights," in *Supreme Court and American Political Development*, eds. Kahn and Kersch.

[147] *Senn*, 301 U.S. at 480.

[148] *Senn*, 301 U.S. at 491.

with their employers. They had organized in their own employee association and were pleased with that as well. At some point, however, the union officials, who had no connection to either the meat markets or its employees, called up the owner of the markets and demanded that all his employees join the union. The owner told the union representative that the employees had their own association and that he did not think they would be interested in an outside union. Nonetheless, he told the union that he would raise the issue with them, and he did so, telling his employees that the union had expressed an interest in organizing them and that they were free to join up if they wanted to. The employees responded that they were not interested, a message the owner in turn relayed back to the union. The union responded by informing the owner of its intention "to declare war on you."

The union then demanded that the owner present his employees with an ultimatum: Join the union and designate it as your exclusive agent and collective bargaining representative or be fired. When the owner refused (as, indeed, he was obligated to do under the labor laws, which prohibited him from using the threat of dismissal in any way to coerce his employees regarding their decisions about whether to join a labor union), the union declared that the owner was "unfair to labor." It picketed, marched, threatened, and intimidated the owner and the meat market employees.

The lower court in *Lauf* had held that, under these circumstances, no labor dispute had existed under the federal (or state) law, since Shinner was bound to allow its employees a free choice concerning whether to join a labor union. It was thus entirely appropriate for a court to issue an injunction against the union prohibiting it from coercing the meat market owner into dismissing his employees for failing to make the "proper" choice. The Supreme Court granted certiorari on the basis of an apparent conflict with its ruling in *Senn*.[149]

In an opinion by Justice Roberts (who had just recently broken the standoff between the Court and the president by joining his pro–New Deal colleagues in the 5–4 majorities in *West Coast Hotel* (1937) and *Jones and Laughlin Steel* (1937)), the Court found rather easily that the district court's interpretation of the Wisconsin labor law diverged from the state court's interpretation of its own statutes. This divergence, it held, was impermissible and in error. As for the federal act, the Court was obligated to follow its own lights. Adopting the ethos and ideology of the state court decision interpreting the little Norris-LaGuardia Act (if not strictly speaking, following it as a matter of law), the Court quickly and peremptorily held that the lower courts had not made the legal findings necessary to justify an injunction. And for good measure, it held that there was no employee associational right that warranted such an injunction.

---

[149] *Lauf v. Shinner*, 82 F.2d 68 (7th Cir. 1936); *Lauf v. Shinner*, 90 F.2d 250 (1937).

As he had done in *Senn*, Justice Butler penned an impassioned dissent in *Lauf*, reminding the Court in emphatic italics that there had been "a demand by the union that [Shinner] compel its employees, on pain of dismissal from their employment, to join the union and constitute it their bargaining representative and agent." Because the employer refused to use coercion to defeat individual choice in the interest of consolidating an emergent, group-oriented corporatist constitutional order, the union falsely declared that he was "unfair to labor" in banners, picketing, and placards.[150]

In issuing an injunction, Butler insisted, the lower courts had simply enforced the provisions of the Norris-LaGuardia Act that stated clearly that the unorganized worker should remain "free to decline to associate with his fellow workers" and that he should "have full freedom of association, self-organization, of representatives of his own choosing" and should "be free from the interference, restraint, or coercion of employers of labor, or their agents, in the designation of such representatives."[151] By yielding and coercing his employees into a union, Butler contended, Shinner would be "join[ing] a conspiracy."[152] To call the efforts of an outside union to compel an employer to coerce his employees to join a labor union against their will a "labor dispute" in which courts could not use their equitable powers of injunction was to defeat the very purpose of the act. "If a demand by a labor union that an employer compel its employees to submit to the will of the union, and the employer's refusal, constitute a labor controversy, the highwayman's demand for the money of his victim, and the latter's refusal to stand and deliver constitute a financial controversy."[153]

---

[150] *Lauf*, 303 U.S. at 332.

[151] *Lauf*, 303 U.S. at 333, citing 29 U.S.C. Section 102 (Section 2 of the Norris-LaGuardia Act, March 23, 1932, 47 Stat. 70).

[152] *Lauf*, 303 U.S. at 334. On the defeat of the conspiracy doctrine to which Butler was appealing, see Hattam, *Labor Visions*; Ernst, *Lawyers Against Labor*, 69–89.

[153] *Lauf*, 303 U.S. at 336. It should be noted that the rhetoric of "choice" concerning a worker's decision whether or not to join a labor union had hardly been at the core of progressive thought. Herbert Croly, for instance, frankly argued in 1908 that because, in a new, modern order, the power of "labor" as a collectivity was needed to counterbalance the power of capital as a collectivity, workers who refused to join a union had to be stripped of their right to work. Croly asserted that "[t]he labor unions deserved to be favored [by the state], because they are the most effective machinery which has yet been forged for the economic and social amelioration of the laboring class...."; "As a type the non-union laborer is a species of industrial derelict. He is the laborer who has gone astray and who either from apathy, unintelligence, incompetence, or some immediately pressing need prefers his own individual interest to the joint interests of himself and his fellow laborers. From the point of view of a constructive national policy he does not deserve any special protection. In fact, I am willing to go farther and assert that the non-union industrial laborer should, in the interest of a genuinely democratic organization of labor, be rejected; and he should be rejected as emphatically ... as the gardener rejects weeds in his garden for benefit of fruit- and flower-bearing plants." See Croly, *Promise of American Life*, 387. Along the same lines,

The Institutionalization of the New Order Concerning Labor

Although the Norris-LaGuardia Act itself predated the New Deal, the Supreme Court's landmark decisions interpreting that act coincided with the New Deal constitutional revolution of the late 1930s. The statist, anti-individualist, group-oriented ethos they reflected did not originate in these opinions. It had been a part of progressive reformist political thought since the late nineteenth century and had been a feature of the dissenting opinions on the Court in earlier labor law cases. But with the Norris-LaGuardia decisions, it was clear that the Court had made its peace with the departure from traditional constitutionalism in this area and accepted the new order.

This new ideological vision was being institutionalized in Supreme Court opinions such as *Senn* and *Lauf* and simultaneously being consolidated in the political realm. The creation of the new statist regime involving labor-management relations, overseen by the National Labor Relations Board (NLRB), quickly worked to manufacture its own supportive political constituency. After the passage of the NLRA, union membership quintupled, which immediately helped to institutionalize reforms that had only been enacted in an atmosphere of crisis.[154] By availing themselves of crisis conditions and a wave of violent outbreaks during that crisis, a cadre of policy elites had effectively transformed a small constituency into an army of voters. The process of elite-driven bureaucratic construction, followed by the post-hoc creation of a supportive political constituency, accompanied by a justificatory, legitimating ideological project (in which the Supreme Court played an important part), created the modern regime of labor regulation. This project of ideological reconstruction gave constitutional sanction to a new constitutionalism of groups and aggregates rather than a constitutionalism of individuals. In these senses, the National Labor Relations Act *created* or *constituted* the people necessary for its institutionalization. Part of that project of ideological reconstruction involved the invention of a Whiggish narrative by which "we the people" rose up to demand "industrial democracy." In fact, constitutional development in this area moved in precisely the opposite direction. Political democracy did not create industrial democracy. Rather, an elite-constructed vision of industrial democracy, once created, worked to construct modern understandings of the political democracy concerning labor. Ideological reconstruction and institutional development went hand-in-hand.

Croly condemned "[t]he politician who solemnly declares that he believes in the right of the laboring man to organize, and that labor unions are deserving of approval, but... also believes in the right of the individual laborer to eschew unionism whenever it suits his individual purpose or lack or purpose...." Croly, *Promise of American Life*, 388. See also Levy, *Herbert Croly*, 114.

[154] Bernstein, *New Deal*, 148; Kennedy, *Freedom from Fear*, 319–22.

Civil Rights and Labor Rights: Constitutional Progress Creates a New Barrier

During the heat of reformist campaigns concerning the labor problem, progressive partisans of industrial democracy openly framed their campaigns as both anti-individual rights and, in many cases, even as anticonstitutionalist. After all, they associated "individual rights" with the rights of property and capital. To the extent such reformers talked about rights at all, they were concerned with the rights and liberties not of individuals but of classes, and, in particular, of the laboring class.[155]

The system of collective bargaining created under the Wagner Act marked the defeat of important claims of individual rights in the American constitutional system, in particular those rights associated with traditional "dignity-of-labor" individualism, which had deep roots in the American political tradition. Because of what has long been understood to be the compelling justifications behind the defeat of those claims, the scope of the institutional consequences of the disappearance of those rights has been underappreciated. Among those consequences was a serious blow to civil rights.

In the statebuilding era, some of the staunchest partisans (and greatest beneficiaries) of the traditional, individualist, dignity-of-labor constitutionalism enunciated by, among others, the "old" Supreme Court, were American blacks. A 1930 study of African American workers conducted by the Urban League declared American blacks to be "the most individualistic of workers."[156] While perhaps jarring today, this pervasive black individualism, which predominated among African Americans from emancipation until about the time of the New Deal, was hardly surprising at the time. An individualist-oriented free labor ideology was intricately tied with the struggle that led to emancipation itself. In their staunchly individualist attitude toward work, African Americans, in this sense, as in others, were the "omni-Americans."[157]

Given these commitments, African Americans were among those Americans least interested in seeing the New American State develop along a

---

[155] For the anticonstitutionalism of progressives, see, e.g., Croly, *Progressive Democracy*, 29–62; White, *American Social Thought*, ch. 8; Richard Hofstadter, "Charles Beard and the Constitution," in *Charles Beard: An Appraisal*, ed. Howard K. Beale (Lexington: University of Kentucky Press, 1954); Felix Frankfurter, *Mr. Justice Holmes and the Constitution: A Review of His Twenty-Five Years on the Supreme Court* (Cambridge, MA: Dunster House Bookshop, 1927). Holmes and Brandeis were also thinking of the battle of class against class when they initiated their early defense of free speech rights. Only through the free competition of ideas in the marketplace – as expressed by communists and labor activists – they believed, would the best class win (Brandeis expected it would be labor; Holmes was indifferent).

[156] Department of Research and Investigations, National Urban League, *Negro Membership in Labor Unions* (New York: Negro Universities Press, 1969) (originally published, 1930), 165.

[157] Albert Murray, *The Omni-Americans: New Perspectives on Black Experience and American Culture* (New York: Outerbridge and Dienstfrey, 1970).

trajectory that augmented the political-economic power of organized labor. African Americans of the statebuilding era – unlike many lawyers and scholars of labor law who, for many years, were engaged as active partisans in the project of ideologically institutionalizing the new constitutional order concerning labor – neither romanticized nor favored the reformist political agenda of the white working class. Blacks were in regular contact with working-class whites, and found them, as a group, to be hostile and dangerous.

It has been insufficiently emphasized in Whiggish narratives of constitutional development (which prefer to focus on Jim Crow exclusionism in railroad cars, hotels, and places of public amusement) that "the first large-scale exclusion of Negroes by private organizations in the post-bellum period was the handiwork of organized labor."[158] Prior to the mid-1960s, union power meant black exclusion. Any political development that entailed state sanctioning of the union shop promised to completely exclude blacks from the American workplace. In this context, every victory for labor was a defeat for blacks. Civil rights and labor rights were antagonistic programs.

White workers resented the potential competition for their jobs from black workers. Moreover, they refused blacks admission to their "brotherhoods" on the grounds that this would force them to associate with blacks as social equals. They were less comfortable with the white working class than with white capitalists, with whom they had been allied since the founding of the Republican Party. When this longstanding loyalty to the Republican Party is combined with the racist and self-seeking behavior of the (largely Democratic) union movement, the black valorization of capitalism and capitalists was not in any sense Uncle Tomism. After noting that many poor whites were sympathetic to socialism, a typical black steelworker in 1912 defended capitalism to one researcher:

I am afraid of the poor white men; they don't see that we Negroes have to live as well as they, and they are not willing to give us a chance. So far as I am concerned, I let socialism and all that sort of thing alone; and I stand by the man that stands by me, that is the rich man every time.... No Negro ought to have anything to do with socialism.[159]

---

[158] Rayford W. Logan, *The Negro in American Life and Thought: The Nadir, 1877–1901* (New York: Dial Press, 1954), 142. See, generally, Herbert Hill, *Black Labor and the American Legal System: Race, Work, and the Law in the American Legal System* (Madison: University of Wisconsin Press, 1985); David E. Bernstein, *One Place of Redress: African Americans, Labor Regulations, and the Courts from Reconstruction to the New Deal* (Durham, NC: Duke University Press, 2001); John Hope Franklin and Alfred A. Moss Jr., *From Slavery to Freedom: A History of Negro Americans*, 6th ed. (New York: Knopf, 1988); Eric Arnesen, *Brotherhoods of Color: Black Railroad Workers and the Struggle for Equality* (Cambridge, MA: Harvard University Press, 2001); Lichtenstein, *State of the Union*, 40–2, 73.

[159] Quoted in Sterling T. Spero and Abram L. Harris, *The Black Worker: The Negro and the Labor Movement* (New York: Columbia University Press, 1931), 402. This was the case despite the relatively welcoming disposition of class-oriented socialists toward blacks. Lichtenstein,

Capitalism, in the mind and experience of many blacks, was color-blind: It looked only to the abstraction of profit. Collectivist unionism, on the other hand, promised ironclad exclusion. Columbia University researchers repeatedly ran up against such sentiments in talking to black workers during the 1920s and early 1930s. "The excuse, 'I have no objection to hiring colored labor but my employees would quit if I did,' has been heard so often by Negro job seekers," the (progressive) scholars noted somewhat incredulously, "that they have come to believe it and to assume that if only the opposition of white labor were removed the Negro could find ready employment."[160]

Perhaps the broadest and most influential articulation of procapitalist, dignity-of-labor individualism amongst American blacks was undertaken by Booker T. Washington in his widely read (and soon to be widely attacked) 1901 book *Up From Slavery*. Washington, the founder of the Tuskegee Institute (which held its ribbon cutting with studied symbolism on July 4, 1881), was an optimist about the future of the country as well as the future of African Americans within it. "[T]he ten million Negroes inhabiting this country," he declared, ". . . are in a stronger and more hopeful condition, materially, intellectually, morally, and religiously, than is true of an equal number of black people in any other portion of the globe."[161] The key to the advancement of blacks, in Washington's view, lay in individual industriousness and punctiliousness, a zeal for self-improvement, and a pride in work. Washington declared himself to have "no patience with any school for my race in the South which did not teach its students the dignity of labor."[162] He hoped that at Tuskegee "the students themselves would be taught to see not only utility in labor, but beauty and dignity, would be taught, in fact, how to lift labor up from mere drudgery and toil, and would learn to love work for its own sake."[163] "The individual," he declared, "who can do something that the world wants done will, in the end, make his way regardless of his race."[164] Washington reiterated these commitments in his Atlanta Exposition address, in which he declared:

Our greatest danger is that in the great leap from slavery to freedom we may overlook the fact that the masses of us are to live by the productions of our hands, and fail to keep in mind that we shall prosper in proportion as we learn to dignify and glorify common labor and put brains and skill into the common occupations of life. . . . No

State of the Union, 76–7. By the time the powerful, nondiscriminatory Congress of Industrial Organizations (CIO) was created in 1935, a change in black attitudes toward the labor movement (as chronicled below) was under way.

[160] Spero and Harris, *Black Worker*, 133–4. It seems that, to the extent that this was actually true, there would have been sharp sectional differences. It may have been more likely in the North and West, and much less so in the South. I do not explore these differences here.

[161] Booker T. Washington, *Up from Slavery* (New York: Gramercy Books, 1993), 13.

[162] Washington, *Up From Slavery*, 54.

[163] Washington, *Up From Slavery*, 109.

[164] Washington, *Up From Slavery*, 114.

race can prosper till it learns that there is as much dignity in tilling a field as in writing a poem.[165]

    This was certainly the position of Marcus Garvey, an admirer of Washington.[166] He wrote:

It seems strange and a paradox, but the only convenient friend the Negro worker or laborer has in America at the present time is the white capitalist. The capitalist being selfish – seeking only the largest profit out of labor – is willing and glad to use Negro labor whenever possible on a scale reasonably below the standard union wage ... but if the Negro unionizes himself to the level of the white worker, the choice and preference of employment is given to the white worker. ... If the Negro takes my advice he will organize by himself and always keep his scale of wage a little lower than the whites until he is able to become, through proper leadership, his own employer; by doing so he will keep the good will of the white employer and live a little longer under the present scheme of things.[167]

    Neither Marcus Garvey nor black workers, of course, were so naive as to think that the rich did not believe in white racial superiority. But the sense of superiority of wealthy whites was at least softened by a certain paternalism. White capitalist philanthropy, for instance, had recently helped to build black colleges – and blacks knew it. Blacks in the statebuilding era were less likely to contrast that paternalism with a nonpaternalist ideal than with something much more immediate and worse: white working-class brutality. Understandably enough, African Americans preferred the relatively benign paternalism of the rich to the ruthless brutality of the partisans of labor. Andre Siegfried, a French sociologist who interviewed American blacks while touring the United States in the years following World War I, put it this way: "Circumstances have developed in [African Americans] an extraordinary instinct for judging people and knowing what they can get out of them. ... With the rich they quickly adopt a flattering attitude, but they utterly despise the 'poor whites.'"[168]

---

[165] Washington, *Up from Slavery*, 161.

[166] Ronald Takaki, *A Different Mirror: A History of Multicultural America* (Boston: Little, Brown, 1993), 355–6.

[167] Spero and Harris, *The Black Worker*, 136. Once "the rights of labor" began to be recognized by the centralized state, Garvey's program for black advancement took a direct hit. The 1931 Davis-Bacon Act required that all workers receive the "prevailing" local wage, making it impossible for blacks to appeal to capitalist self-interest to get a foot in the labor market in the way that Marcus Garvey had advised them to do. Davis-Bacon Act, 46 Stat. 1494 (1931). See Bernstein, *One Place of Redress*, ch. 4.

[168] Andre Siegfried, *America Comes of Age: A French Analysis by Andre Siegfried*, trans. H. H. Hemming and Doris Hemming (New York: Harcourt Brace and Company, 1927), 101, quoted in Spero and Harris, *The Black Worker*, 428. As David Bernstein notes, many unions, particularly those in the railroad industry, were "fraternal" organizations, stylized as "brotherhoods." The implication of social equality, recalling the relations of blood kinship, only deepened the hostility that white workers had toward inviting black workers

Given that the chief partisans of a corporatist, group-oriented constitutionalism were allied with the cause of organized labor, it should hardly
be surprising that African Americans were vigorous backers of traditional,
individualist constitutional visions (visions that are today commonly categorized as "conservative"). Labor unions and strikes, of course, did not sit
well with traditionalist constitutionalists. During the summer following his
second year as a student at the Hampton Institute, Washington recalled, he
returned to his home in West Virginia to find the coal mines and salt furnaces
shut down by a labor strike. The strike, to Washington's great annoyance,
prevented him from finding the work he desperately needed to pay his way
through Hampton. As he saw it, strikes in that part of the country tended
to occur when the workers got two or three months ahead in their savings.
When their savings ran out, they slogged back to work. And in this way, they
failed to accumulate any capital. "Before the days of strikes in that section
of the country," Washington recalled, "I knew miners who had considerable money in the bank, but as soon as the professional labor agitators got
control, the savings of even the more thrifty ones began disappearing."[169]
In his Atlanta Exposition address, Washington famously called upon white
capitalists to "cast down your bucket among these people who have, without strikes and labor wars, tilled your fields, cleared your forests, builded
your railroads and cities, and brought forth treasures from the bowels of
the earth." "We shall stand by you," he added, "with a devotion that no
foreigner can approach."[170]

In many ways, the capitalists did cast down their buckets. The era of the
First World War was a particular boon to black workers. The war and legal
restrictions on immigration afterward brought to a halt the massive foreign
influx of earlier years, in the process improving the employment opportunities for American blacks. At the same time, blacks benefited from the emigration back to their nations of origin by many foreigners who had entered
the country earlier. The war itself, moreover, stoked the fires of American
industry, and conscription put industrial labor in even shorter supply. At the
end of Reconstruction, the opportunity for Southern blacks to move freely
to take advantage of the nation's postwar economic expansion had been seriously hindered by the passage of a wave of emigrant agent laws. These laws,
whose constitutionality was upheld in a series of court challenges, assessed
ever-escalating taxes and license fees on employment agents who came to recruit Southern (black) workers.[171] The labor shortage at the time of the First

---

into their unions. Bernstein, *One Place of Redress*, 46–7; See, generally, Arnesen, *Brother-
     hoods of Color.*
[169] Washington, *Up from Slavery*, 51.
[170] Washington, *Up from Slavery*, 162.
[171] Bernstein, *One Place of Redress*, ch. 1; *Shepperd v. County Commissioners*, 59 Ga. 535 (1877);
     Williams v. Fears, 35 S.E. 699 (Ga.); aff'd., 179 U.S. 270 (1900).

World War, however, broke down some of these old barriers to recruitment. This time, Northern capitalists were able to successfully recruit black industrial labor. Between 1915 and 1928, over 1.2 million blacks migrated from southern to northern states, taking up positions in factories and stockyards throughout the North.[172]

These black workers carried with them a willingness to act as strikebreakers and undercut the wages of white union workers. Strikebreaking, in fact, became a major means of advancement for blacks who had been shut out of industry by the exercise of private power by white working-class unions. In the railroad, steel, meat-packing, and coal-mining industries, strikebreaking proved a major route for African Americans to higher wages, shorter hours, and better working conditions.[173] As Communist Party leader William Z. Foster noted at the time, strikebreaking was zealously advocated by leading black intellectuals who emphasized repeatedly the menace any intervention of the state on behalf of organized labor posed to African Americans. These intellectuals, Foster observed, argued vigorously that strikebreaking was "a legitimate and effective means of Negro advancement." "They have seen their people, by use of it," he added, "readily work their way into trades and industries previously firmly sealed against them by white workers and white employers' prejudices."[174]

Indeed, a fair overview of African American political thought and activism in the statebuilding era undercuts Whiggish narratives of constitutional development, which place primary emphasis on a linear, developmental progression concerning labor rights and civil rights, culminating in the (admittedly, much delayed) incorporation of blacks into the new, group-oriented order. These familiar narratives begin by acknowledging the discriminatory practices of the labor movement (and effusively praising the less discriminatory wing of that movement, comprised of industrial unions such as the Congress of Industrial Organizations (CIO)). And they operate under the teleological assumption that it was the underlying destiny of blacks to join with labor in what would eventually, through struggle and law, become nondiscriminatory unions. Once they began focusing on black exclusion from labor unions (a relatively recent preoccupation, coinciding with the fraying of the New Deal consensus), such narratives naturally placed stories of the black struggles for admission to and equal treatment within labor unions at their center. They have, however, been systematically reluctant to discuss fully the aggressive black antiunionism of the statebuilding

[172] Bloch, *Circle of Discrimination*, 93–6. See Carole Marks, *Farewell – We're Done and Gone: The Great Black Migration* (Bloomington: Indiana University Press, 1989); Takaki, *A Different Mirror*, 340–69; James R. Grossman, *Land of Hope: Chicago, Black Southerners, and the Great Migration* (Chicago: University of Chicago Press, 1989).

[173] National Urban League, *Negro Membership*, 165–9.

[174] William Z. Foster, *The Great Steel Strike and Its Lessons* (New York: B. W. Huebsch, Inc., 1920), 207, 210, quoted in National Urban League, *Negro Membership*, 166.

era. Whiggish narratives of constitutional development have minimized the degree of sustained black support for a wide array of retrospectively "conservative," antiprogressive, and antistatist causes and judicial doctrines in the early twentieth century.[175]

Instead, twentieth-century scholars of African-American, labor, and constitutional history, reflecting prevailing constitutive stories concerning the path of development of the new regime have repeatedly grouped blacks and labor together as aligned categories of "the oppressed" and constructed them as (sequentially) liberated by the constellation of public policies that came to constitute twentieth-century liberalism. Driven by the imperatives of the regime, such scholars have either ignored or minimized the degree of black support for the "conservative" court doctrine regarding, for example, boycotts, labor injunctions, and yellow-dog contracts, the defeat of which have been taken as veritable litmus tests for progressive New Deal breakthrough-oriented models of constitutional development.[176] Many African Americans were prominent opponents of Eugene V. Debs's much-lionized 1894 Pullman strike.[177] And they opposed the campaigns to cabin judicial power, campaigns that played a central role in defining early-twentieth-century progressivism and in shaping the substantive commitments of New Deal constitutional liberalism. Over the course of many years, many African Americans actively fought the passage of federal anti-injunction bills. In his testimony before the Senate Judiciary Committee against such a bill, Harry E. Davis, a prominent black politician from Ohio, asserted, for example, that

if a colored worker is denied the protection which union membership gives him, even where he is willing to become a member, there is only one place where he can have his employment rights protected if they are assailed and that is in our courts. For all practical purposes the proposed bill would take away this right from a group of independent workers for whom I am speaking and it would mean their subjection to a state of economic serfdom.[178]

When the Norris-LaGuardia Act was passed and, in turn, successfully defended against constitutional challenges in the *Senn* and *Lauf* cases in the

---

[175] See, e.g., Derrick Bell, *Race, Racism, and American Law*, 2nd ed. (Boston: Little, Brown and Co., 1980), 37 n. 9. On Bell's presentist reading of black history, see Bernstein, *One Place of Redress*, 54. A fictional narrative similar to Bell's has also been imported into the ostensibly "revisionist" narratives of multiculturalists. See, e.g., Takaki, *A Different Mirror*, 368–9.

[176] See, e.g., Forbath, *Law and the Shaping of the American Labor Movement*; Orren, *Belated Feudalism*. For contrasting (shared) views, see the work of prominent African-American historian (and member of "the Howard Group," which included Ralph Bunche, Abram Harris, and E. Franklin Frazier) Rayford Logan and "conservative" public-choice scholar David Bernstein. Logan, *Negro in American Life*, 153; Bernstein, *One Place of Redress*, 54–5.

[177] Arnesen, *Brotherhoods of Color*, 29–30.

[178] Hearings Before Subcommittee of the Committee on the Judiciary, U.S. Senate, 70th Congress, 1st Session on S. 1482, 1928, 603–14, quoted in Spero and Harris, *The Black Worker*, 139.

late 1930s, many African Americans saw themselves as having sustained a stinging defeat. A pro-court, pro-injunction, antiunionism was considered, in proper context, a pro–civil rights constitutionalism. Only in retrospect would these contours of constitutional struggle be erased from narratives of American constitutional development.[179]

The Black Appropriation of the Class Approach: From the "Old Crowd" to the "New Negro"

With the political triumph of the progressive statebuilding project in the early twentieth century, African American leaders were forced to reconsider their longstanding individualist commitments. During the First World War, the progressive administration of Woodrow Wilson – the century's most racist[180] – had supported the stabilization of wartime production by encouraging an unprecedented number of collective bargaining arrangements in industry. Railroad unions were granted unprecedented collective bargaining power by the 1926 Railway Labor Act.[181] After "the [developmentally] lean years" of the prosperous 1920s, the Norris-LaGuardia Act and the New Deal labor legislation accorded important and apparently permanent new powers to labor unions. To persist in opposing a fait accompli of state construction and its accompanying ideology countenancing a system of governance by social collectivities or groups now, to many African Americans, seemed futile.

A pivotal figure in catalyzing the transformation of black constitutional thinking and black strategy was the head of the Pullman porters' union, A. Philip Randolph, soon to become famous nationwide as "Mr. Black Labor."[182] The Pullman Company, the crucible for Randolph's ideological project, it turns out, was not one of the worst employers for blacks but, indeed, one of the best (many said that "Lincoln freed the slaves, and the Pullman Company hired 'em").[183] The company, while far from being a paragon by contemporary standards, paid relatively generous wages to its

---

[179] For a narrative to be erased from narratives of "constitutional development" is *not* the same as being erased from history. The account presented here, of course, draws from the work of many excellent historians who have studied African-American and labor history. Our constitutional narratives, however, have been typically teleological in a broadly progressive, New Deal sustaining way. Such narratives, while touching upon race discrimination by labor unions as an obstacle to be overcome, focus their attention on black efforts to join unions on a nondiscriminatory basis, rather than on black antiunionism. This, I contend, distorts our understanding of the path of constitutional development.

[180] See Kendrick A. Clements, *The Presidency of Woodrow Wilson* (Lawrence: University Press of Kansas, 1992), 45–6.

[181] O'Brien, *Workers Paradox*, 120–47; Skowronek, *Building a New American State*.

[182] Beth Tompkins Bates, *Pullman Porters and the Rise of Protest Politics in Black America, 1925–1945* (Chapel Hill: University of North Carolina Press, 2001), 145.

[183] Bates, *Pullman Porters*, 20.

porters. It gave freely to black organizations, such as hospitals, YMCAs, and political groups like the Urban League. The relative goodwill the Pullman Company evinced toward its employees was a direct outgrowth of the philosophy of its founder and president, George Pullman, who believed "that capital and labor must cooperate for their mutual benefit, that the task of the employer was to improve employee morale by alleviating the squalor of city life, and introducing workers to the advantages of reading rooms, libraries, and concert halls."[184]

Randolph, leader of a movement that came to be known as the "New Negroes," took on those blacks whose inclination was to work on amicable terms with George Pullman and his company. In a sweeping ideological critique, Randolph set himself to stigmatizing blacks who were pro-individualist, procapitalist, and who looked favorably on paternalistic "patron-client" relationships between relatively benign white employers and black employees as the "Old Crowd" Negroes. As Randolph saw it, not only was the Old Crowd servile, but it had also had long been hostile to unionism. Randolph, in contrast, saw unionism as the wave of the future. As a socialist, Randolph, departing from the outlook of generations of African-American intellectuals before him, committed himself resolutely to labor union power and to effectuating a transformation in the African-American mind from an individual to a collective consciousness.[185] Randolph, moreover, situated the fight for racial freedom within a broader quest for social and economic justice (in the process marking himself as a progenitor of contemporary twentieth-century liberalism).[186] To achieve his political and ideological goals, he deliberately appropriated the "repertoire of contention" of organized labor, which was group-oriented, mass-based, and confrontational and reimagined that politics as the core of a new politics of civil rights.[187]

---

[184] Bates, *Pullman Porters*, 43.

[185] Bates, *Pullman Porters*, 98.

[186] Bates, *Pullman Porters*, 35. Joining the fight for racial justice to the cause of "social justice" was, of course, a defining feature of the politics of prototypical twentieth-century liberals. See., e.g., William H. Chafe, *Never Stop Running: Allard Lowenstein and the Struggle to Save American Liberalism* (New York: Basic Books, 1993); Lois Schlarf, *Eleanor Roosevelt: First Lady of American Liberalism* (Boston: Twayne Publishers, 1987). See also Plotke, *Building a Democratic Political Order*, ch. 9; Alan Brinkley, *Liberalism and Its Discontents* (Cambridge, MA: Harvard University Press, 1998), 99–100.

[187] Bates, *Pullman Porters*, 10–11; See Tilly, *The Contentious French* (Cambridge, MA: Harvard University Press, 1986), 2. In a refinement of Tilly, Sidney Tarrow has referred to "the capacity of a form of collective action to be utilized by a variety of social actors, against a variety of targets, either alone or in combination with other forms, as "modular collective action." "As word of successful – and learnable – collective action spread[s] to other social groups," Tarrow writes, "movements develop a rolling, spiraling dynamic." Sidney Tarrow, *Power in Movement: Social Movements, Collective Action, and Politics* (New York: Cambridge University Press, 1994), 31–47, esp. 46.

Through his leadership of the Brotherhood of Sleeping Car Porters, Randolph worked to join the collective interests of labor as a class with the collective interests of blacks as a class. Part of this process involved a sustained intellectual and political project aimed at repositioning as reactionary the once progressive (indeed, liberationist) free labor individualism held by the vast majority of American blacks. The aggregationist "New Negroes" saddled their opponents with the pejorative of "Old Crowd Negroes." They declared Uncle Tom "an individualist."[188] And in a radical act of ideological subversion, they recast the once emancipationist Republican free labor ideology, long a touchstone of progressive African-American thinking, as a form of slavery.[189] "The Brotherhood liberally laced its discourse with images and references to slavery."[190] Membership in a company union or individualist antiunionism was analogized in porters' union rhetoric to bondage itself. The porters declared that the Pullman Company had "girded... our loins with a new form of slavery," and they demanded their "emancipation." Under the leadership of Randolph and the porters, that is, the collective power of a labor union was reconstructed within black political thought as the very definition of "free labor" itself. Beth Tompkins Bates reports that large segments of the black community came to support the slavery analogy.[191]

At the same time, under Randolph's leadership, the porters' union, worked aggressively to associate the reconstructed concept of "free labor" with a reconstructed concept of "free men" in a New Constitutional Nation. At the 1928 Negro Labor Conference, the Brotherhood had declared the right to

---

[188] Bates, *Pullman Porters*, 97.

[189] Indeed, this act of ideological reinvention stands as a counterpart in twentieth-century constitutionalism to Madison's reinvention of the term "republican" in his defense of the American Constitution. James Madison, Alexander Hamilton, and John Jay, *The Federalist Papers*, eds. Clinton Rossiter and Charles R. Kesler (New York: Mentor, 1999), 49–50, Federalist No. 10.

[190] Bates, *Pullman Porters*, 92.

[191] Bates, *Pullman Porters*, 89–93. The nature of this as a departure is evident from Arnesen's characterization of the mid-1930s amendments to the Railway Labor Act outlawing company unions and corporate interference with worker associations as "a critical victory for the white [railway] brotherhoods." Arnesen, *Brotherhoods of Color*, 126. Indeed, Willard Townsend, the highest black official in the CIO and the head of the red caps unions, claimed that following the "triumph" of the New Deal labor legislation concerning railroads, "the Negro railroad worker finds himself in much the same position as Dred Scott, the runaway slave, who had entered a free state and was ordered back to slavery by the United States Supreme Court," quoted in Arnesen, *Brotherhoods of Color*, 128. The slavery analogy was one that had been adopted in the broader labor movement. Pope, "Labor's Constitution of Freedom;" James Gray Pope, "Labor and the Constitution: From Abolition to Deindustrialization," *Texas Law Review* 65 (1987): 1071. While Pope effectively explicates the deployment of a rhetoric of slavery in the labor movement of the statebuilding era, he underemphasizes the individualist roots of the (antislavery) Republican Party in the Civil War era and, hence, of the genesis of the Thirteenth Amendment itself. See Foner, *Free Soil, Free Labor, Free Men*.

organize to be an inherent right of American citizenship, in the same way that the equal protection of the laws was a citizenship right. The labor struggle and the civil rights struggle were declared (again, in a marked ideological departure) to be one and the same. Randolph announced at that conference that "the Negro's next gift to America will be economic democracy." The triumph of the labor movement was reconstituted in Randolph's innovative constitutional thought as the rightful legacy of the Civil War and, by implication, the constitutional legacy of the Civil War amendments.[192]

This New Negro collective consciousness was forged not only on paper and in speeches, but also in the smithy of concrete political struggle. Foremost among these struggles was Randolph's campaign, beginning in the 1920s, to unionize the Pullman porters. In these organizing efforts, Randolph met stiff resistance, not only from the Pullman Company, but also, and significantly, from the black porters, the black press, black intellectuals, and the black middle class.[193]

Randolph's organizing efforts at the Pullman Company were not the only crucible of this new constitutional vision uniting the interests of blacks as a class and labor as a class. The political fight over Republican President Herbert Hoover's 1930 nomination of Judge John J. Parker for a seat on the U.S. Supreme Court also proved to be a signal event in this project of ideological reconstruction. Opposition to the Parker nomination came from two fronts. Many progressives opposed Parker because they believed that as a judge on the Fourth Circuit court of appeals he had shown solicitude for yellow-dog contracts, one of the major labor issues of the day (it was for this reason that the AFL helped lead the fight against his confirmation).[194] Many

---

[192] Bates, *Pullman Porters*, 86, 92, 97. Strictly speaking, the Constitution's equal protection clause applied not only to citizens but to all "persons." Randolph, of course, was also now joining the civil rights movement to the fight not just for labor unions, but to the broad progressive push for "industrial democracy."

[193] These efforts, and the resistance to them, have been well chronicled in the recent work of such historians as Bates, Arnesen, and others.

[194] At issue was Judge Parker's decision in *United Mine Workers v. Red Jacket Coal and Coke Company*, 18 F.2d 839 (1927) upholding an injunction against union organizing by the UMW in the West Virginia coal fields following a violence-ridden organizing campaign waged against a company whose workers had signed yellow-dog contracts. Parker, whose views on labor (and other issues) were rather progressive, claimed that he was compelled to reach the decision he did in the *Red Jacket* case by the Supreme Court's precedential holding in *Hitchman Coal and Coke Co. v. Mitchell*, 245 U.S. 229 (1917) and *Coppage v. Kansas*, 236 U.S. 1 (1915). Organized labor, however, countered that in his Red Jacket opinion, Parker did not express any reservations about the *Hitchman Coal* precedent. See John Anthony Maltese, *The Selling of Supreme Court Nominees* (Baltimore: Johns Hopkins University Press, 1998), 58–66. This was important, as William Green, the president of the AFL, characterized *Hitchman Coal* as "labor's *Dred Scott* decision." "The effect of the *Dred Scott* decision was to perpetuate human slavery," Green wrote. "The effect of the *Hitchman Coal* decision is to establish and perpetuate industrial servitude. No inferior court could follow the *Dred Scott* decision merely because of precedent and no enlightened jurist, who

blacks, however, including the NAACP and the Brotherhood of Sleeping Car Porters, opposed Judge Parker's confirmation on the basis of a statement he had made ten years earlier during his 1920 North Carolina gubernatorial campaign that blacks were unfit for political participation.[195] Despite the fact that both labor groups and civil rights groups were opposed to seating Judge Parker on the Supreme Court, Beth Tompkins Bates reports that, "neither . . . wanted to connect its protest to that of the other."[196] Misgivings notwithstanding, however, the NAACP decided to assume a leadership role in the Parker fight, a decision that necessitated a moderation of its hostility to labor unions.

The NAACP itself, it is worth noting, was at this time a relatively new organization that lacked a foundation in traditional black individualism. Indeed, in a landmark work by one of its founders, *The Souls of Black Folk* (1903), W. E. B. DuBois had mounted a strenuous challenge to the hard work and individual rights program for black advancement that had been championed by Booker T. Washington.[197] The NAACP's willingness to step

appreciates the character of human relations in modern industry, would follow the decision in the *Hitchman* case, without expressing his disapproval of the rule laid down in the famous decision. Letter, William Green to President Herbert Hoover (April 16, 1930), quoted in Maltese, *Selling of Supreme Court Nominees*, 58. Following his defeat, Parker continued to serve on the court of appeals, where he compiled a thoroughly progressive record on labor issues. Maltese, *Selling of Supreme Court Nominees*, 69.

[195] Parker's racial comments were made during the heat of a Southern campaign. Just as Parker's personal views on labor were not well represented in his *Red Jacket* opinion, so his off hand campaign remarks did not reflect an especially virulent racism in the man himself. See Kenneth W. Goings, *The NAACP Comes of Age: The Defeat of Judge John J. Parker* (Bloomington: Indiana University Press, 1990). In defending himself against Democratic charges that he was actively seeking black votes and pushing black political power, Parker had said that "the Negro as a class does not desire to enter politics" and that "the participation of the Negro in politics is a source of evil and danger to both races and is not desired by the wise men in either race or by the Republican Party of North Carolina." At the same time, though, Parker added, "I say it deliberately, there is no more dangerous or contemptible enemy of the state than the man who for personal or political advantage will attempt to kindle the flame of racial prejudice or hatred." W. T. Bost, "Republicans Happy in Progress of Negroes to Democratic Party," *Greensboro Daily News* (April 19, 1920), quoted in Maltese, *Selling of Supreme Court Nominees*, 59–60. Following his defeat, as a judge on the court of appeals, Parker compiled a strong civil rights record that was praised by the NAACP. Maltese, *Selling of Supreme Court Nominees*, 69.

[196] Bates, *Pullman Porters*, 108. Maltese, *Selling of Supreme Court Nominees*, 61. Interestingly enough, in his study focusing on Supreme Court (and, hence, constitutional) history (as opposed to Bates's African-American history), Maltese calls attention to organized labor's hostility to blacks, while omitting any mention of the counterposing black hostility to organized labor. By constructing his narrative in this (unidirectional) way, Maltese (most likely unconsciously) had effectively integrated the story of the Parker fight into the teleology (and ideology) of the New Deal narrative of twentieth-century constitutional development. See Maltese, *Selling of Supreme Court Nominees*, 61.

[197] W. E. B. DuBois, *The Souls of Black Folk* (New York: Bantam Books, 1989)[originally published in 1903].

gingerly to the side of labor in the Parker fight was consistent with DuBois's principles (like Randolph, DuBois was also a socialist). The position taken by the Brotherhood of Sleeping Car Porters in the Parker fight, though, went much farther. In their house organ, *The Black Worker*, the porters declared that Parker's hostility toward the collective interest of labor and the collective interest of blacks were two sides of the same coin, "for the Negro," the paper boldly announced, "is essentially a worker."[198] The decision of both the NAACP and the porters union to side with organized labor over the Parker nomination and their collective victory in a close vote in the Senate charted the path of a future labor–civil rights alliance.[199]

The NAACP emerged from its success in the Parker fight with new authority, as did Randolph's Brotherhood of Sleeping Car Porters.[200] Their political triumph, in alliance with organized labor, proved to be a harbinger of the formation of a new constitutional vision. The old bootstraps dignity-of-labor individualism was now under double-barreled assault. As organized labor and state power were conjoined two years later with the passage, in sequence, of the Norris-LaGuardia anti-injunction act and the Wagner Act, Randolph had effectively positioned blacks to take advantage of the emergent new institutional order.

The next developmental step for American blacks would involve a political and legal struggle to open (white) labor unions to black membership. In this civil rights project, group-oriented, pro-union black leaders such as Randolph deliberately appropriated the (white) labor movement's repertoires of contention. Randolph's effective use of the threat of a massive black March on Washington in 1941 to advance the struggle against job discrimination in the wartime defense industries (which effectively forced Franklin Roosevelt against his will to issue an executive order creating the Fair Employment Practices Commission (FEPC)), pushed the black community to reimagine its understanding of the nature of the struggle for "civil rights."[201] "African-Americans," concluded Bates, "viewed [Roosevelt's] executive order as a legitimation of protest politics." Randolph's success "encouraged

---

[198] Bates, *Pullman Porters*, 109.

[199] It also represented one of the earliest examples of interest group involvement in Supreme Court nominations, a form of politics that became institutionalized by the 1960s. The Parker confirmation battle (and that involving Charles Evans Hughes just before it) was "the first truly 'modern' Senate confirmation proceedings for Supreme Court nominees," in a new environment shaped by the direct election of senators and open Senate hearings. On this particular labor-black alliance as a seminal moment in interest group politics, see Maltese, *Selling of Supreme Court Nominees*, 5, 52–69; Richard L. Watson Jr., "The Defeat of Judge Parker: A Study in Pressure Groups and Politics," *Mississippi Valley Historical Review* 50 (September 1963): 216.

[200] Goings, NAACP; Bates, *Pullman Porters*, 109.

[201] Executive Order 8802 (1941). Daniel Kryder sets out in useful detail the dimensions of the pressures on Roosevelt in the face of Randolph's threats to march on Washington. Kryder, *Divided Arsenal*, 53–66.

using mass demonstrations as a tool for changing power relations."[202] "By 1941, many agreed that the era of gratitude toward paternalistic white liberals for their good intentions in lifting black Americans out of second-class status was over."[203] The civil rights vision of the Old Crowd, which had been anchored in the postbellum individualist free labor ideology, was increasingly rejected by many blacks. The New Crowd, aggregationist ideology of a reimagined "free labor" was ascendant.

Once it was clear to the New Negroes that the labor movement, despite continuing racism and, in many cases, openly exclusionary policies, would come to define the new order of state-society relations, and, once pioneering New Negro socialists like Randolph had assimilated labor movement ideology into civil rights thinking, grassroots civil rights groups independent of the Pullman porters began to follow the modular tactics (and adopt the supporting ideology) pioneered in the black community.

The Constitutional Politics of the New Negroes

New Negro constitutional politics positioned itself within the institutional architecture of the New Deal regime in two ways, both of which jettisoned the formerly prevailing black hostility to labor unions generally and to organized labor's repertoires of contention. First, the New Negroes, having come to accept unions, initiated a sustained campaign to desegregate them. And second, they embraced the political tactics that had been successfully deployed by organized labor – and the constitutional theories and ethos devised to legitimate them – in the fight for civil rights.[204]

These initiatives represented a radical departure – a reversal, even – in thinking about civil rights among both blacks and whites who were allied with their cause. As late as the mid-1940s, for example, Gunnar Myrdal, one of the central figures in drawing public attention to civil rights, remained uneasy with this turn toward labor unions – despite his being a (Swedish) socialist. In his classic work, *An American Dilemma*, Myrdal fretted openly: "[T]here are grave risks . . . in the increased union power. A greatly strengthened union movement holding power over employment might, if dominated by monopolistic and prejudiced white workers, finally define the Negro's 'place' as outside industrial employment."[205] Myrdal continued to stress the longstanding antagonism between labor rights and civil rights, made more menacing in the wake of the New Deal by the reinforcement of the power of labor unions by the newly built powers of the American central state.

---

[202] Bates, *Pullman Porters*, 160, 175.

[203] Bates, *Pullman Porters*, 152.

[204] On repertoires of contention and political change, see Doug McAdam, Sidney Tarrow, and Charles Tilly, *Dynamics of Contention* (Cambridge: Cambridge University Press, 2001), 48–50.

[205] Gunner Myrdal, *American Dilemma*, 401. See also Myrdal, *American Dilemma*, 643, 787.

The problem was that the powers that had been newly conferred upon organized labor as a group and on the central state as patron of that group, had been fought for, justified, and legitimated by a longstanding ideological project that constructed labor union power as a pillar of democracy. Throughout the statebuilding era, the traditional individualist dignity-of-labor constitutional vision concerning labor had been under assault as constituting a barrier to the achievement of "industrial democracy." And intellectuals including John Dewey, Walter Lippmann, Herbert Croly, Louis Brandeis, and Felix Frankfurter all had devoted considerable intellectual energies to explaining why according power to labor unions to govern themselves, overseen benignly by the state, if necessary, was fundamental to the modern meaning of democracy. But the problem of civil rights as seen by the New Negroes involved, to a considerable degree, an effort to limit the power and autonomy of those now thoroughly legitimized labor unions. Thus, it was essential, after having devoted years to explaining why allowing labor unions to govern themselves was the quintessence of democracy, that a reformist campaign to sharply limit that autonomy also be a campaign for "democracy."

Central to this highly ideological project was the statism at the heart of the New Deal order concerning labor – a statism that was condemned at the time and subsequently by proponents of a labor union voluntarism that might have been. Statism, of course, though viewed with skepticism by some labor leaders (including very important ones, such as Samuel Gompers, at least as far as labor unions were concerned), had long been viewed warmly by progressives and, indeed, as the key developmental imperative. Statist understandings of industrial democracy had long been legitimized by appeals to republicanism in response to charges that they trampled upon individual (private) rights.[206] Although the policy contours of that republicanism varied among these thinkers, what proponents of "the new republic" that made industrial democracy one of its centerpieces shared was a commitment to reconstituting wide swathes of what was formerly considered the private sphere – such as labor-management relations – as elements of the public sphere, and hence subject, accordingly, to public regulation.[207] This

---

[206] By "republicanism" here, I mean to follow a conception of the term emphasizing a widespread participation in democratic self-governance. See Michael J. Sandel, *Democracy's Discontent: America in Search of a Public Philosophy* (Cambridge, MA: The Belknap Press of the Harvard University Press, 1996), 5–6, 208.

[207] See *Munn v. Illinois*, 94 U.S. 113 (1877). On the Court, as we have seen, the process of expanding the meaning of public interest had begun in earnest in the 1870s, with constitutional consideration of the Granger Laws. It continued throughout the Progressive Era and was ratified by the New Deal. It should be noted that Walter Lippmann's views over time strayed further and further from Deweyan ideals. I associate him here with the views he held that harmonized most fully with the thinking of his fellow progressives. See John W. Coffey, "The Five Faces of Walter Lippmann," *Reviews in American History*

republican rhetoric, of course, sat uneasily with simultaneous appeals for labor power through labor autonomy, which, in many ways, retained vestigial affinities for the old constitutional thinking. New initiatives concerning civil rights would need to negotiate these tensions and, in the process, construct a serviceable ideology for the new constitutional order concerning labor rights and civil rights.

The republican strain within progressive thought concerning labor, with its inclination to collapse the barriers between public and private spheres and (in the United States in this era) its statism, now made labor unions, at the very moment that a campaign for their autonomy had ostensibly succeeded, potentially porous to state regulation. The progressive constitutionalism of the statebuilding era had long since looked suspiciously on the claims of the private sphere as amounting to little more than an ideologically loaded rhetorical gesture aimed at undermining the legitimacy of much-needed public-spirited legislation. Their targets had, of course, typically been business corporations. But once this understanding had been transformed as applied to business corporations, there was no reason that the logic could not be applied equally to other social and economic institutions. Corporations, many had said, were ultimately creations of state power and served public purposes. They were thus broadly regulable in the service of public ends. Now, however, it was easy enough to see labor unions the same way. And, henceforth, they would be no more inviolate than business corporations in the new constitutional order.

Even though the Wagner Act instituted a regime governing labor-management relations that rejected the strong version of labor voluntarism in favor of a more statist regulatory model, an ethos respectful of claims of labor union autonomy remained an important part of the ideology of the new order. The problem was, however, that after these reforms had been achieved, a new reformist imperative – civil rights or antiracism – began to move to center of the self-understandings of people who saw themselves as being forward-looking and politically and constitutionally progressive. In the face of this new imperative, organized labor, whom progressives had long devoted their lives to empowering, became a barrier to reform.[208]

---

2 (December 1974): 546–52; Walter Lippmann, *The Good Society* (Boston: Little, Brown, 1937); Edward A. Purcell Jr., *The Crisis of Democratic Theory: Scientific Naturalism and the Problem of Value* (Lexington: University Press of Kentucky, 1973), 112–14, 152–4. See also David A. Hollinger, *In the American Province: Studies in the History and Historiography of Ideas* (Baltimore: Johns Hopkins University Press, 1985), 44–55; Ronald Steel, *Walter Lippmann and the American Century* (New York: Vintage Books, 1980), 315–17, 321–6.

[208] See Plotke, *Building a Democratic Political Order*, ch. 9, emphasizing the sequential nature of the movement from a labor-oriented reformist imperative among progressive liberals to one centered around civil rights. This movement away from the labor-oriented reformist imperative was partly the result of the success of labor in achieving recognition and collective bargaining arrangements during the New Deal, the subsequent institutionalization of those

The new regulatory regime concerning labor proved a serious potential obstacle to the cause of civil rights. In particular, the state's conferral of majority rule collective bargaining power on labor unions handed those unions a state-sanctioned and enforced monopoly power over the supply of labor in key areas, a power that true to their traditions, they quickly deployed to dismiss black workers and hand over the newly liberated positions to whites. That this would occur under the new regulatory order concerning labor was hardly unanticipated at the time the new labor laws were under consideration. During the Depression, union incentives to act this way had been especially strong because whites at that time were especially desperate for jobs.[209] The NAACP, the Urban League, and other black groups had lobbied hard to get an antidiscrimination provision added to the Wagner Act. The efforts of these civil rights groups were strenuously opposed at that time by the AFL, the erstwhile ally of blacks in the Parker confirmation fight, and they failed. African American civil rights leaders saw themselves as suffering a double defeat when, in what is viewed as a great progressive triumph, a provision was written into the act requiring the ultimate dismissal of all strikebreakers and the rehiring of all striking employees.[210] One of the New Deal's central achievements posed serious institutional barriers for the cause of civil rights.

At the same time, though, the perceptive Gunnar Myrdal was able to discern that other strains in progressive political thought that had informed

gains during the war and postwar economic recovery and boom, and the gradual transformation from a heavily unionized manufacturing-based economy to (beginning as early as the 1940s), to a postindustrial service economy. Daniel Bell, *The Coming of Post-Industrial Society* (New York: Basic Books, 1976). See also Karen Orren and Stephen Skowronek, "Regimes and Regime Building in American Government," *Political Science Quarterly* 113 (1998–9): 689–702. On the emergence of a civil rights program as a central state imperative, see Dudziak, *Cold War Civil Rights*. For an ideational perspective emphasizing the fight against totalitarian ideas, see Primus, *American Language of Rights*.

[209] Writing of the prolabor amendments to the railway labor laws in the mid-1930s, the leading historian of black railway workers concluded that those "progressive," prolabor revisions "placed new and powerful weapons in the hands of white workers who were determined to eliminate their black competitors...." He adds that "these legislative changes continued to exert a largely negative influence on the fortunes of African-American railroaders through the early 1960s." "African-American firemen, brakemen, and porter-brakemen," he continues, "found the rules governing union elections devastating.... Such representation "was worse than no representation at all," for it empowered whites to drive them out of the industry. He concludes, "The New Deal Revolution in labor legislation...not only offered black operating craft workers no benefits, but it provided whites with powerful weapons against them." Arnesen, *Brotherhoods of Color*, 126, 127, 128; Bernstein, *One Place of Redress*, 46–62 (railway labor laws), 85–110 (New Deal Labor Laws). Bernstein, in fact, attributes the origins of the divergence of the black and white unemployment rates in twentieth-century America to New Deal labor laws. Bernstein, *One Place of Redress*, 103–10.

[210] Wolters, "Closed Shop and White Shop," in Cantor, *Black Labor*, 137–52.

the ethos of the New Deal triumph concerning labor, strains emphasizing republicanism, and the collapse of longstanding public-private distinctions, and statism, might render the internal affairs of labor unions porous to regulation in the service of civil rights, despite apparently countervailing commitments to labor union autonomy. And indeed, no sooner had U.S. unions succeeded in winning broad rights to free association[211] than at least a few political leaders (most of whom had led the fight for labor union autonomy) began appealing to republican and statist strains of progressive political thought and calling for the policing of those rights to ensure that they harmonized with public purposes to which perhaps a majority of workers themselves had been vocally and notoriously hostile.

In the wake of the New Deal, for instance, socialist Norman Thomas began calling for the increased government control of unions to guarantee democracy *within* them. Specifically, Thomas stated:

I propose that every union, to be entitled to recognition as the agency of the workers in collective bargaining (and without that recognition most every union would be doomed), must conform to certain minimum standards of democracy. Its doors must be open to all qualified workers, regardless of race, creed, or color, and practices must provide for orderly elections at reasonable intervals. And finally, a disciplinary procedure must be set up which will protect members of the union from arbitrary punishment more serious than most judges or juries can impose. Possibly some other requirements might be laid down, for instance, with regard to votes on strikes, but those which I have mentioned seem to me essential.[212]

Similarly, Myrdal contended that "industrial democracy," so recently seen as a culminating reformist triumph, in many ways ran counter to the nation's creedal democratic commitments. "It is likely," he wrote, "that the war emergency will help [organized labor] to get union shop agreements in an increasing part of the labor market." "But such power," he declared, "can be tolerated in a democratic country only if the doors to the unions are kept open and if democratic procedures within the unions are amply protected."[213]

Indeed, it was Myrdal's view that labor union mistreatment of black workers posed such a fundamental challenge to America's understanding of itself that it would foment a thoroughgoing reconsideration of just what a commitment to democracy in the workplace actually meant. "In the course of time," he predicted correctly, "it will become evident that government support is followed by government influence." The impending federal government

---

[211] See *Hague v. CIO*, 307 U.S. 496 (1939) (Justice Stone, concurring). The case is of conceptual significance for many reasons, not the least of which is that it represents an important instance of the assertion of judicial injunctive power *in favor of* public picketing by labor unions.

[212] Norman Thomas, "How Democratic Are Labor Unions?" *Harper's Monthly* (May 1942), 655–62, quoted in Myrdal, *American Dilemma*, 408.

[213] Myrdal, *American Dilemma*, 407.

campaign to keep employment levels high following the end of the war, he believed, would spur new government initiatives to democratize labor unions internally. "[I]t is simply incredible," he maintained, "that the government will undertake tremendous financial efforts to create employment and leave to the trade unions the power of partly sabotaging this policy" by leaving African-American workers out of the equation.[214]

This process, of course, did not take place solely in the realm of ideas, but also in the realm of concrete political action. Perceptive black leaders understood well the parameters of the new institutional order concerning labor: Many had spent considerable time opposing it. A few, however, had favored it. And once that new order became a fait accompli, these few, such as A. Philip Randolph, were especially well positioned to begin to fashion a campaign for civil rights that could work for reforms within the institutions and governing ideology of that order. Randolph's success in getting Roosevelt to create the Fair Employment Practices Commission inserted the federal government into the center of disputes over racial discrimination in the workplace for the first time.[215] As the new commission was accorded only mediatory powers, however, its practical effects were few. It was one thing, after all, for Roosevelt to declare he would police the behavior of the government and private businesses. Both were fully consistent with New Deal politics. In the 1940s, however, those politics were still too closely joined to cause of labor union autonomy for Roosevelt to take more aggressive steps to police the conduct of labor unions.[216] This was an ongoing problem for blacks. After all, businesses commonly and accurately declared in hearings before the commission that black workers were excluded from their shop floors not through the policies of employers but rather by those of the very labor unions the federal government forced them to deal with. In any case,

---

[214] Myrdal, *American Dilemma*, 407–8. See Kryder, *Divided Arsenal*, 5–11 (emphasizing threat of disruption of war mobilization effort behind civil rights developments; he contrasts this thesis to Myrdal's "ideational model," which emphasized the war's effects on the creedal consciousness of Americans). While outlining Myrdal's views, Kryder himself emphasizes the threat the possibility of black civil disruption posed for the effort to mobilize the society for war played in spurring change in central state civil rights policies. I consider my account here, while different in its emphases from Kryder's, consistent with that account. See also Dudziak, *Cold War Civil Rights* (emphasizing that, following World War II, interstate Cold War competition between the United States and the Soviet Union as an engine of civil rights progress in the United States).

[215] Kryder, *Divided Arsenal*, 53–66.

[216] Indeed, this continuing opposition of "labor rights" and "civil rights," both in general and, increasingly, within Democratic Party politics, was part of the dynamic that limited civil rights progress in this period. See Kryder, *Divided Arsenal*, 103–4. State imperatives of this era created conflicting dynamics. On the one hand, the ceding of state power to (white) labor unions was itself intended as a stabilizing step, following the labor disorder of the mid-1930s. On the other, unhappiness by African Americans about their exclusion from labor unions was itself a potential source of wartime disorder.

facing opposition from Southerners and organized labor, Congress failed to appropriate funds for the commission for a second year, and this precedent-setting, but largely symbolic, initiative died a quick and quiet death.

Once "the labor problem" faded as a reformist imperative and "the race problem" took its place, it was the Supreme Court that began to renegotiate the various strands of progressive political thought concerning labor to create the ideological space for reform involving workplace civil rights. The question centered around the degree to which labor unions were autonomous – as far as their internal policies concerning race were concerned – in the new constitutional order. This issue was brought before the Court in two wartime cases arising soon after the demise of the FEPC: *Railway Mail Association v. Corsi* (1944) and *Steele v. Louisville and Nashville Railroad* (1944). In both, the NAACP and the ACLU argued on behalf of the black plaintiffs and against the rights to democratic self-government and associational freedom asserted by the labor union defendants.[217] At issue in *Corsi* was a New York State civil rights law that provided that no labor organization shall deny a person membership by reason of race, color, or creed, nor deny to any of its members by reason of race, color, or creed equal treatment in the designation of its members for employment, promotion, or dismissal by an employer. In Article III of its constitution, the Railway Mail Association, an AFL affiliate group of 22,000 postal clerks of the Railway Mail Service, in a provision typical of racial exclusions practiced by many American labor unions (either tacitly or explicitly), limited membership to those who were either white or American Indian. Strikingly enough, given that the case was heard a full seven years after the constitutional revolution of 1937, *the labor union defendant* in *Corsi*, in a precise echo of the ostensibly dead formalist arguments that employers had used in an attempt to deflect state regulation in the interests of organized labor, defended itself by asserting that the New York law trampled its Fourteenth Amendment due process liberty rights to choose its own members, to have those members freely contract with each other, and to manage its own property as it saw fit.

The Court began its opinion in *Corsi* by rebuffing the union's efforts to revive these pre–New Deal forms of argument in service of the ends of the substantive winners of the New Deal: organized labor. As the New Deal Court had ultimately rejected these constitutional claims when employers had made them in resistance to progressive labor laws (including those aimed at advancing the interest of organized labor), the Court now, in turn, rejected the same claims made by organized labor in resistance to African-American claims on behalf of civil rights. The Court parried the union's claims to autonomy, asserting that the union was an organization "functioning under

---

[217] *Railway Mail Association v. Corsi*, 326 U.S. 88 (1944); *Steele v. Louisville and Nashville Railroad Co.*, 323 U.S. 192 (1944).

the protection of the state" and as such was subject to state regulation in the service of state-declared policy interests. One such policy was that against racial discrimination. In opposing the Wagner Act's collective bargaining provisions, many blacks had complained of the adverse position in which they would be placed by state's conferral of monopoly power on labor unions. In *Corsi*, the Court in effect took judicial notice of this complaint. Because "the terms imposed by a dominant union apply to all employees, whether union members or not," it wrote, African Americans were deprived of all means of protection from unfair treatment by the racially discriminatory policies and practices of labor unions. Thus, the state could now act to regulate the internal affairs of labor unions.[218]

The *Steele* case raised a related question under the terms of the pioneering 1926 Railway Labor Act, which had served as a model for New Deal collective bargaining legislation. The Brotherhood of Locomotive Firemen had been granted the exclusive collective bargaining authority for train firemen under the terms of the Railway Labor Act – a law marking a major step forward for the cause of industrial democracy. Besides participating in shaping the terms of their own employment through collective bargaining, the Brotherhood itself operated democratically – that is, by majority rule.[219] The problem was that the majority of union members were white, and by the terms of the act, the black union members were thus subject to governance by a white majority.

Changes in the nature of railroad work led to the dispute that brought about the *Steele* case. Technological advances in the industry had made the job of a railway fireman cleaner (hence, more desirable). Given the high unemployment levels during the Great Depression, the fireman's job, formerly a "Negro position," had become more attractive to whites. It was in the context of these changes that the railway brotherhood, acting by majority vote, began systematically to drive black workers out of the firemen's slots and into less attractive positions. As part of this effort, the *Steele* plaintiff and his black peers were pushed out of their jobs as locomotive firemen and replaced by white men with less seniority and no more professional competence. The black firemen were then reassigned to lower-paying and less attractive jobs.

---

[218] *Corsi*, 326 U.S. at 94. See also *J. I. Case v. National Labor Relations Board*, 321 U.S. 332 (1944) (reaffirming majority rule principle of the Railway Labor Act).

[219] See *Virginian R. Co. v. System Federation*, 300 U.S. 515, 545 (1937) (holding that the majority of any craft has the right to determine who shall be the representative of the class for purposes of collective bargaining with the employer); Arnesen, *Brotherhoods of Color*, 126–7. It is worth noting that the ethos – rather than the law being interpreted – is crucial. Here, the case involves not the National Labor Relations Act, but rather the Railway Labor Act. And it involves statutes rather than the Constitution itself. But the ethos or construction is what is underlying all three situations and bleeds across them. Being overly legalistic in one's analysis can lead one to miss these dynamics.

In its decision invalidating these union initiatives, which had been defended with appeals both to autonomy and democracy, the *Steele* Court – urged on by *amicus* briefs filed by the Justice Department and the NAACP – made a jurisgenerative argument anchored in an analogy between a labor union and a legislature. Interestingly enough for a Court that had recently abandoned its requirement of legislative neutrality in cases involving contention between capital and labor,[220] the Court then went on to assert that it was a *statutory* requirement under the Railway Labor Act that all legislatures operate impartially. (Chief Justice Harlan Fiske Stone, the author of the *Steele* opinion, would not go as far as reading this as a *constitutional* requirement.)[221] This the Court held despite the fact that the Railway Labor Act lacked any nondiscrimination provision and despite the fact that in passing the act in the 1920s, there was no legislative intent to impose racial integration on the railway labor unions. The Court explained:

If, as the state court has held, the Act confers this power on the bargaining representative of a craft or class of employees without any commensurate statutory duty toward its members, constitutional questions arise. For the representative is clothed with power *not unlike that of a legislature* which is subject to constitutional limitations on its power to deny, restrict, destroy or discriminate against the rights of those for whom it legislates and which is also under an affirmative constitutional duty equally to protect those rights.[222]

This "union as legislature" had, in the Court's estimation, a fiduciary *duty* to act impartially with the best interests of all in mind – a duty that came to be known as the "duty of fair representation." Chief Justice Stone continued: "We think that the Railway Labor Act imposes upon the statutory representative of a craft at least as exacting a duty to protect equally the interests of the members of the craft as the Constitution imposes upon a legislature to

---

[220] See Gillman, *The Constitution Besieged*. This appeal to democracy and its rhetoric was serviceable in this context in significant part because, as most people conversant in the politics of the era knew, the labor movement itself had relied upon arguments concerning the "right of representation" as part of their fight to secure the passage of the Wagner Act in 1935 (as in many instances before). See Plotke, *Building a Democratic Political Order*, 97–8. I borrow the concept of juris-generative ideas from Robert M. Cover, "Nomos and Narrative: The Supreme 1982 Term Forward," *Harvard Law Review* 97 (1983): 4–68.

[221] Stone was unwilling at this point to declare that the union was acting unconstitutionally. Justice Frank Murphy, however, with a characteristic disdain for legalistic euphemisms and evasions, would have taken such a step, as he explained in his *Steele* concurrence.

[222] *Steele*, 323 U.S. at 198 (emphasis added). See also, e.g., Archibald Cox, "The Duty of Fair Representation," *Villanova Law Review* 2 (1957): 151–77, esp. 152. On the recourse made by labor lawyers (and the Court) to broader theories of governance – an understanding that I have shown repeats patterns pioneered by earlier twentieth-century progressive political thought more generally – see Karl Klare, "Labor Law as Ideology: Toward a New Historiography of Collective Bargaining Law," *Industrial Relations Law Journal* 4 (1981): 450, 458–80; Klare, "Quest for Industrial Democracy," 196–7; Stone, "Post-War Paradigm in American Labor Law," 1514–16; Lichtenstein, *State of the Union*, 7, 36.

give equal protection to the interests of those for whom it legislates."[223] In *Steele*, that is, Chief Justice Stone read the Railway Labor Act as proscribing class legislation favoring one race over another, thus signaling a major constitutional revival of the old pattern of constitutionalism in a new context and for an altered purpose.

The reasoning of Justice Murphy's concurrence in *Steele* was more straightforward about the sources of the class discrimination found in the case. As African Americans had long maintained, discrimination had to be laid at the feet of Congress, which, under the 1926 act, had buttressed the power of the Brotherhood with all the authority of the central state. "While such a union is essentially a private organization," Murphy emphasized, "its power to represent and bind all members of a class or craft is derived solely from Congress." Unlike Stone, who interpreted the act in line with what he saw as newly emerging policy imperatives, Murphy correctly noted that the act, which evinced a broad trust in industrial democracy, "contains no language which directs the manner in which the bargaining representative shall perform its duties." For the Court to assert that unions such as the Brotherhood were limited in the ways in which they could govern themselves and take positions in their dealings with management was to make a constitutional rather than a statutory decision. Murphy insisted that the Court should base its holding not on statutory grounds, but on the grounds that unless interpreted in this way, the statute (and presumably other collective bargaining arrangements that were based upon its model) was in contravention of the Constitution's Fifth Amendment.

The Court, however, was not yet ready to forthrightly apply the Fifth Amendment as a guarantee of equal protection of the laws in race discrimination cases (that would have to wait until 1954 in *Bolling v. Sharpe*). And it would never be ready to admit to the ultimate constitutional incommensurablility between industrial democracy and the rights of African Americans. The Court (and the country), of course, eventually arrived at Murphy's position (just as it did with his views on incorporation). But its ideological commitments drove the Court to reach that same position by a more tortured and roundabout doctrinal path.[224]

---

[223] *Steele*, 323 U.S. at 202. Bernstein characterizes Stone's intellectual moves in the *Steele* decision as "legal gymnastics," which were "perhaps" disingenuous. Bernstein, *One Place of Redress*, 63. Without denying some truth in this characterization, it is important to note the way in which, admittedly animated by a reformist policy goal, Stone is rethinking the nature of representative democracy within American constitutionalism. His patterns of thought, as revealed in the *Steele* decision, are notable (and will prove influential) in ways that extend beyond his decision to vote "for" civil rights, in line with his policy preferences. My conceptual point here is similar to Kahn's. Kahn, *Supreme Court and Constitutional Theory*.

[224] *Bolling v. Sharpe*, 347 U.S. 497 (1954). The *Steele* opinion, of course, applied only to unions that already had black members. It did not require unions to admit blacks as members. Nor did it alter other antiblack operating rules within labor unions. In any case, as Bernstein

Labor and the Construction of Blacks as a Class: The Picketing Cases
As we have seen, civil rights initiatives were taken that sought, in the interest of civil rights, to circumscribe the autonomy of labor unions, a cause that had recently sat so close to the heart of what it meant to be a political progressive. At about the same time, however, other civil rights initiatives were taken that were at peace with the new constitutional status accorded to labor unions and aimed at taking advantage of the central state's – and the law's – new acceptance of that power. New Deal labor decisions, such as the Court's Norris-LaGuardia decisions in *Senn* and *Lauf* in the late 1930s, along with other developments, had signaled to American blacks the altered nature of the political and constitutional opportunity structure under the new regime. Of particular importance was the retreat of the courts from narrow interpretations of the term "labor dispute" (in, for example, formulating the "proximate relations doctrine"), to which they had hewed, even after the passage of the Clayton Act, in upholding their authority to issue injunctions in cases involving such disturbances. The *Senn* and *Lauf* decisions in particular signaled that courts would now categorize a more expansive array of social disturbances as "labor disputes," in the process sharply restraining their injunctive powers. The collective, coercive powers of organized labor could be asserted – even in frontal assaults on plausible individual rights claims (as was the case in the rather disturbing *Senn* and *Lauf* decisions themselves) – and, as a matter of central state policy, would meet with no rights-protective judicial intervention from that state. The new civil rights leadership soon learned that it could work to advance the interests of blacks as a class if it could get the courts to categorize race discrimination disputes as a type of class-based "labor dispute."

During the 1930s, urban American blacks launched a series of "Don't Buy Where You Can't Work" campaigns against white business owners operating in black neighborhoods. These campaigns, which had a special intensity given the dearth of jobs in the depths of the Depression, deployed an array of direct action tactics that had been appropriated from the repertoires of contention of organized labor, including publicity, boycotts, and pickets. The demands of the Don't Buy Where You Can't Work campaigns of the 1930s were straightforward: Targeted businesses were asked to either hire all-black staffs or to fulfill a specified proportion or quota of black

notes, the *Steele* opinion was not energetically enforced. Bernstein, *One Place of Redress*, 64. For a fuller account of the negotiation (on the Court and off) of the integration of labor unions in the aftermath of these decisions in such cases as *Graham v. Brotherhood of Locomotive Firemen and Enginemen*, 338 U.S. 232 (1949); *Brotherhood of Railroad Trainmen v. Howard*, 343 U.S. 768 (1952); and *Oliphant v. Brotherhood of Locomotive Firemen and Engineers*, 262 F.2d 359 (1958), *cert. denied*, 359 U.S. 935 (1959); and in a series of NLRB administrative rulings in the early 1960s, see Kersch, "The New Deal Triumph as the End of History? The Judicial Negotiation of Labor Rights and Civil Rights," in *Supreme Court and American Political Development*, eds. Kahn and Kersch.

workers.[225] Failure to do so would be to bring a hail of protest down upon the defiant business.

Two of the earliest legal rulings arising out of these campaigns, *A. S. Beck v. Johnson* (1934) and *Green v. Samuelson* (1935), were issued by state courts.[226] In *A. S. Beck*, a white-owned Harlem shoe store was systematically picketed by a group of blacks having no connection with the store, its employees, or, for that matter, with any labor organization (and, thus, no "proximate relation" to the business). The picketers demanded that the store employ a fixed percentage of black workers and urged Harlem residents not to shop there if the store refused. Resisting these threats, A. S. Beck sought and won an injunction against the picketing. The New York Supreme Court (a trial court) based its decision on the *sic utere tuo* principle that Beck's business was being hurt by an organized protest campaign that lacked a lawful purpose, a ruling that seemed to fit more comfortably with the old order's constitutional ethos than the new one's. Picketing in New York State (as elsewhere) had recently been accorded statutory protection from judicial injunctions. But the pickets at issue in *A. S. Beck*, the court plausibly declared, were different: Since they were aimed at having the store dismiss white employees so that black workers could be hired to replace them, the pickets lacked a lawful purpose. The New York court also held, again quite plausibly, that the confrontation did not involve a labor dispute. It was, rather, a racial dispute. Thus, although blacks were deploying labor movement tactics in *A. S. Beck*, the fact remained that they were not a recognized class like organized labor, and their use of those tactics to advance their interests as a group did not fall under the anti-injunction laws as applied to labor disputes. Under these circumstances, individual rights considerations of the sort that were at the heart of the old order concerning labor regulations would remain decisive.[227]

---

[225] In the discussion of the political campaigns and cases that follow, I have profited from Paul D. Moreno, *From Direct Action to Affirmative Action: Fair Employment Law and Policy in America, 1933–1972* (Baton Rouge: Louisiana State University Press, 1997), ch. 2. See also Klinkner and Smith, *The Unsteady March*, 144–5; Lichtenstein, *State of the Union*, 73; Plummer, *Rising Wind*, 67–9.

[226] *A. S. Beck Shoe Corporation v. Johnson*, 274 N.Y. Supp. 946 (Sup. Ct. 1934); *Green v. Samuelson*, 178 A. 109 (Court of Appeals of Maryland 1935). These early harbinger cases predate the Supreme Court's Norris-LaGuardia decisions and Randolph's proposed march on Washington. However, they postdate his organizing fight for the porters, the John J. Parker confirmation battle, and the passage of the Norris-LaGuardia Act itself. As such, they come at the center of the project of ideological reconstruction I am presenting in this chapter.

[227] *Beck*, 274 N.Y. Supp. at 946. Keith Whittington has suggested to me that a dispute of the sort at the center of the *A. S. Beck* case – which involved employment and who would get it – has more in common with quintessential "labor disputes" in picketing cases than when, say, Earth First! pickets McDonald's over the use of Amazon River Basin coffee. This is certainly true. What I argue here is not that the conceptualization of the Don't Buy Where You Can't Work pickets is either fanciful or a stretch, but rather that it expanded the labor dispute category or (in legal jargon) it "extended" the earlier precedent.

In *Green v. Samuelson*, another state case decided the following year, the Jewish owners of a number of stores in black neighborhoods in Baltimore were targeted by civil rights boycotts and pickets, insisting they hire only black workers. At the time the boycotts and pickets began, some of these Jewish-owned stores had staffs that were a full 50 percent black, a percentage the protesters had deemed inadequate. In issuing a permanent injunction against black pickets and boycotts, the Maryland court, as in *A. S. Beck*, cited the *sic utere tuo* principle and maintained that it was inappropriate to invoke the rules applicable to labor disputes in a race case, which involved different issues. "In our opinion," the Maryland court concluded, "this is a racial or social question, and as such, the rules heretofore announced and applied to labor disputes have no application." In 1935, the effort "to promote the interests of the colored race generally" was still seen as constitutionally distinct from analogous efforts on behalf of organized labor.[228]

Soon after these decisions were announced, however, some of the nation's most elite law journals began the process of ideologically reconstructing their meaning. This began in articles that were supportive of the rulings. Even there, however, transformative ambitions were apparent. In backing the *A. S. Beck* decision, for example, a comment in the *Harvard Law Review* was quick to call attention to the fact that "the picketing in the instant case, definitely for the purpose of aiding members of the Negro race, seems similar to the organized labor cases in that it involves the possibilities of riots and injury to the business of the employer as well as a demand for the betterment of the position of the picketing class." The crucial difference for the commentator, however, was "the lack of any policy favoring racial privileges comparable to that favoring labor demands." This difference, he concluded, "seems an adequate reason for a different result."[229]

A commentator writing in the *University of Pennsylvania Law Review* took a different approach. The author first noted the court's holding that the case "involved no dispute over working conditions, and no attempt to unionize." This, the court had held, had essentially dictated that the protesters possessed no right to avail themselves of the "privilege" of picketing. To this line of reasoning, however, the commentator objected:

[T]he impossibility of fitting the situation into the category of a labor dispute should not necessitate such a result. There may well be considerations in favor of giving such privileges to the negro race quite as compelling as those which have brought about the liberalization of the judicial attitude toward labor.[230]

---

[228] *Green*, 178 A. at 114.
[229] Comment, *Harvard Law Review* 48 (1935): 691.
[230] Comment, *University of Pennsylvania Law Review* 83 (1935): 383–5, esp. 384.

The commentator continued the conceptual analogy between blacks and labor as cognizable groups or classes:

Some degree of violence seems to be an inevitable concomitant of any self-enforced improvement in the lot of previously subjected groups, as the turbulence of many labor disputes will bear witness. The alternative of abandoning all attempts at progress is scarcely preferable.... The essential purpose behind the liberal attitude toward labor would seem to be the advisability of raising living standards and ultimately reducing the sociological and economic burdens upon the community as a whole which accompany the subjugation of any large group therein. The economic progress of the negro race should, for this same reason, be a proper subject of community concern.[231]

The issues raised in these state court decisions soon reached the Supreme Court. And it was not long before the Court, in turn, adopted as the law of the land the analogy urged by the University of Pennsylvania law student, an analogy, of course, that sat well, if not with the law, per se, then at least with the new, group-oriented constitutional ethos.

The High Court took the key step in the term immediately following its "switch-in-time" decisions in the *West Coast Hotel* and *Jones and Laughlin Steel* and at about the same time as its Norris-LaGuardia decisions. The opinion in which it applied this new constitutional ethos was *New Negro Alliance v. Sanitary Grocery* (1938), a decision penned by Justice Owen Roberts (and an alumnus, professor, and, later, dean of the University of Pennsylvania Law School – and thus a man who was likely to have perused the school's law review comment involving the state court picketing decisions).[232] In *New Negro Alliance*, the Court held, contrary to the thrust of the state-level *A. S. Beck* and *Green* decisions, that antirace discrimination picketing *does* constitute a labor dispute under the terms of the Norris-LaGuardia Act. And the Court further held that this was the case even if the picketers had no employment relationship with the targeted business. In so ruling, the Court, for picketing purposes at least, elevated blacks as a class to the same status of labor as a class within the parameters of the new constitutional order.

New Negro Alliance involved the legality of the picketing of a Washington, D.C. grocery store by a black civic and racial improvement association. The store, Sanitary Grocery, operated in a black neighborhood and employed both white and black employees. None of the employees at the store were affiliated with the New Negro Alliance.[233] The Alliance insisted both that the store employ more blacks and that those blacks newly hired in response to

---

[231] Comment, *University of Pennsylvania Law Review*, 383, 384.

[232] *New Negro Alliance v. Sanitary Grocery Co.*, 303 U.S. 552 (1938).

[233] As we have seen, Justice Brandeis had long argued that a "proximate relation" between employers and employees should not be a requirement for bringing a dispute under the statutory auspices of progressive legislation regulating labor disputes. *Duplex Printing v. Deering* (Justice Brandeis, dissenting). Brandeis wrote these views into law in his opinions for the Court in its Norris-LaGuardia decisions.

their protests be appointed to sales and managerial positions. When Sanitary Grocery refused to accede to the Alliance's demands, its members threatened to boycott and ruin the business. As part of their protest campaign, they paraded in front of the store with signs reading, "Do your Part! Buy Where You Can Work! No Negroes Employed Here!"

In his opinion in *New Negro Alliance*, Justice Roberts brought African Americans – not as individuals but as a group or class – under the wing of the new state-administered order set out by the Norris-LaGuardia anti-injunction act. Roberts justified the Court's decision to do so with the argument that race discrimination in employment was "quite as important" as discrimination arising out of labor union affiliation or other grievances about the conditions of employment. (The *University of Pennsylvania Law Review* article had called it "quite as compelling.") "The [Norris-LaGuardia] Act," Roberts wrote, "does not concern itself with the background and motives of the dispute."

The desire for fair and equitable conditions of employment on the part of persons of any race, color, or persuasion, and the removal of discriminations against them by reason of their race or religious beliefs is quite as important to those concerned as fairness and equity in terms and conditions of employment can be to trade or craft unions or any form of labor organization or association. Race discrimination by an employer may reasonably be deemed more unfair and less excusable than discrimination against workers on the ground of union affiliation.[234]

Two years later in yet another workplace picketing decision, the Court reinforced the normative constitutional foundations of this innovative interpretation of the term "labor dispute" by declaring, additionally and for the first time, that peaceful labor picketing constituted a form of constitutionally protected free speech (formerly, picketing had been considered not "speech" but "conduct").[235] While the ascension of "speech plus conduct"

---

[234] *New Negro Alliance*, 303 U.S. at 561.
[235] *Thornhill v. Alabama*, 310 U.S. 88 (1940). See also *Hague v. CIO*, 307 U.S. 496 (1939). Free speech arguments had been urged by labor activists in public discourse and in courts – and rejected in courts – from the earliest years of the twentieth century. Rabban, *Free Speech in Its Forgotten Years*, 169–73. For example, in 1911, Samuel Gompers made free speech arguments central to his case against an injunction of an AFL labor boycott. *Gompers v. Buck's Stove and Range Co.*, 221 U.S. 418 (1911). For this, he was criticized by labor activists for abandoning class-based arguments and appealing to individual rights. Ernst, *Lawyers Against Labor*, 133–5. Once labor had achieved class-based recognition at the time of the New Deal, it was ideologically safer for it to make individual rights arguments – and for the courts to adopt them in cases such as *Thornhill* (in the process inventing what is called "speech plus" in contemporary constitutional doctrine). On the ideological usefulness of free speech in the new regime, see White, "Free Speech and the Bifurcated Review Project." Under the constitutionalism of earlier times, picketing had always been considered conduct, not speech. See Ken I. Kersch, "How Conduct Became Speech and Speech Became Conduct: A Political Development Case Study in Labor Law and the Freedom of Speech," paper presented at the University of Maryland Constitutionalism Discussion Group (March 2004). See also *Milk Wagon Drivers Union v. Meadowmoor Co.*, 212 U.S. 287 (1941); *AFL v. Swing*,

is typically understood in the legal academic literature as a philosophical development tracing out the implications of an underlying principle of free "expression,"[236] the engine of this development was actually a concrete political goal, namely to reinforce structurally and ideologically the preferred position of organized labor as a class within the New Deal constitutional order.[237] This dynamic is all the more apparent in the Court's decision to declare such conduct by organized labor noncoercive at the very moment that, in a series of separate decisions (discussed in detail below), the National Labor Relations Board (NLRB) and the lower federal courts were beginning to declare the (antiunion) "pure speech" of employers to be coercive, even when no link was found between that speech and any sort of implicit threat by employers to pro-union workers. In these cases, the Court developed what became known as the "laboratory conditions" doctrine, which held that certain substantive statements, if uttered in certain contexts, were inherently threatening and coercive (this doctrine was a clear progenitor of contemporary "hostile environment" harassment codes, which opponents have appropriately referred to as "speech codes"). Under the laboratory conditions doctrine, employer speech critical of unions was, as a legal matter, presumed to be coercive.[238]

These developments in the Court's jurisprudence – the decision to consider private labor unions permeable to state regulation in the public interest and subject to constitution-like standards of democratic fairness, to treat labor as a class for purposes of the new anti-injunction laws, to, in turn, treat blacks as a class for the same purposes, and to consider labor union behavior as a form of protected speech (while, at the same time, restricting the "pure speech" that was critical of unions by employers) and, in a culminating final step taken in *Hague v. CIO* (1939), for the Court for the first time to affirmatively wield its injunctive powers in service of labor union free speech rights – were all constituent parts of a newly constructed constitutional vision. As reconfigured in the Court's constitutional imagining at this time, the collective

---

312 U.S. 321 (1941); *Hotel Employees' Local v. Board*, 315 U.S. 437 (1942); *Carpenters' Union v. Ritter's Café*, 315 U.S. 722 (1942); *Allen-Bradley Local v. Board*, 315 U.S. 742 (1942); *Bakery and Pastry Drivers and Helpers Local v. Wohl*, 315 U.S. 769 (1942). See Orren and Skowronek, "Regimes and Regime Building in American Government."

[236] See, e.g., Pope, "Labor's Constitution of Freedom," *Yale Law Journal* 106 (January 1997): 941.

[237] In some senses, it was a ratification by legal elites of an argument made by activists in the organized labor movement. See James Gray Pope, "Labor's Constitution of Freedom," 941–1028. The effects of this reconstruction of conduct as speech would be broad-ranging, extending well beyond the interests of organized labor. This, of course, is a common dynamic in constitutional development. See, generally, Rogers M. Smith, "Political Jurisprudence, the 'New Institutionalism,' and the Future of Public Law," *American Political Science Review* 82 (1988): 84–108. Howard Gillman, *The Constitution Besieged*; Kahn, *The Supreme Court and Constitutional Theory*.

[238] See, e.g., *Indianapolis Glove Co.*, 5 NLRB 231 (1938); *NLRB v. Ford Motor Co.*, 114 F.2d 905 (6th Cir., 1940); *General Shoe Corp.*, 77 NLRB 124 (1948).

rights of labor, the civil (equal) rights of blacks, and the individual right to the freedom of speech – once highly antagonistic political commitments – (not to mention the aggressive assertion of judicial power) were no longer incommensurable.[239] In the new constitutional imagining, individual liberty and group equality now went hand-in-hand. The foundations of contemporary constitutional liberalism had been constructed. And a new "common sense" – contemporary constitutional liberalism – was created.[240]

Reconstituting and Institutionalizing Contemporary "Civil Rights and Civil Liberties"

Part of the process of institutionalizing this vision – of making it into a fixture of contemporary liberal constitutionalism's common sense – involved having it adopted and reinforced not only by political interest groups, but also by constitutional interest groups with strong normative claims to be acting on behalf of creedal commitments to justice, equality, and freedom. In the 1930s, the national civil liberties and civil rights leadership, which routinely made such claims, had only the most tenuous connection to the locally organized Don't Buy Where You Can't Work campaigns for quotas and proportional hiring of African Americans. By 1950, however, both the NAACP and the ACLU had embraced these initiatives (the ACLU, which frankly worked to advance the substantive interests of labor as a class in its early years, had successfully argued as far back as in the *Senn* case (1937) on behalf of broad picketing powers for labor unions). By actively supporting these initiatives, both groups played an important ideological role in laying the groundwork for constitutional legitimation of racial allocations and quotas, which were later created to quell social disturbances and win support from more transparently self-seeking political interests.[241]

[239] *Hague v. CIO*, 307 U.S. 496 (1939) (upholding the grant of an injunction against Jersey City, New Jersey Mayor Frank Hague's blanket refusal to grant permits to labor unions to distribute pro-union literature in city parks and streets). Felix Frankfurter, a proponent of the fight against government by injunction, voted with the Court in the *Hague* case.

[240] For a discussion of the way in which the Court, in cases that wove together its fair representation and its injunction jurisprudence (both chronicled here), in the processes moving toward banning race discrimination by labor unions (or, in terms of developmental theory, describing how, in the aftermath of *Steele*, the Court further negotiated the conflicting claims of two sequentially preferred groups), see Kersch, "The New Deal Triumph as the End of History? The Judicial Negotiation of Labor Rights and Civil Rights," in *The Supreme Court and American Political Development*, eds. Kahn and Kersch.

[241] On the ACLU's commitment to organized labor in its early years, see Donohue, *Politics of the American Civil Liberties Union*, 30–56. On race preferences and quotas as the product of interest group politics and efforts to allay social disturbances, see, generally, Hugh Davis Graham, *The Civil Rights Era: Origins and Development of National Policy, 1960–1972* (New York: Oxford University Press, 1990). Hugh Davis Graham, *Collision Course: The Strange Convergence of Affirmative Action and Immigration Policy in America* (New York: Oxford University Press, 2002), 65–92. See also John David Skretney, *The Ironies of Affirmative Action: Politics, Culture, and Justice in America* (Chicago: University of Chicago Press, 1996), 177–221.

An important moment in this ongoing project of ideological reconstruction and institutionalization involved the Supreme Court's decision in *Hughes v. Superior Court* (1950).[242] In that case, the NAACP and the ACLU, joined now by the CIO (with Arthur Goldberg drafting the union brief), all signed on simultaneously to the new constitutional liberalism in which a normatively desirable commitment to the cause of "civil rights" would entail support for the rights of labor and blacks as distinct (but analogous) constitutional classes, a commitment to "civil liberties" would entail an expansive definition of a generic right to free speech, and a commitment to "civil rights and civil liberties" would entail support for race-based hiring quotas.

The *Hughes* case involved the picketing of a California grocery store by the Progressive Citizens of America, who demanded that the percentage of black employees at the store match the percentage of the store's customers who were black (which was approximately 50 percent). In a unanimous opinion written by Felix Frankfurter, the Court held that the Progressive Citizens could not conspire to injure the store's business to coerce it through picketing to accede to an unlawful practice, namely, to undertake a race-based hiring program.[243] A driving force behind the Norris-LaGuardia Act, Frankfurter simply refused to trace out the implications of the class-based ethos of the new constitutionalism that he had helped midwife into being. That vision, Frankfurter concluded, simply could not be understood as conferring legitimacy upon racial quotas. Others, however, grasped the implications of the new constitutionalism more fully, it seems, than Frankfurter himself. Legislative initiatives and administrative practices that fit more easily with the new class-based constitutional ethos were not far off.

Still, as Frankfurter's resistance indicated, the Court was not ready in the 1950s to take such bold steps. The constitutional approval of race quotas would not be immediate but rather would have to be negotiated by the Court over time. In its landmark early civil rights decisions, such as *Sweatt v. Painter* (1950), which was decided the same term as *Hughes*, as the Court marched incrementally forward toward *Brown* (1954), it insisted upon anchoring its jurisprudence as firmly as possible in universal (as opposed to group-oriented) claims of justice. To take bold steps concerning race in the teeth of potentially sharp political resistance, the Court seemed especially mindful of the need to appeal to consensus creedal principles such as the equality of individuals before the law. An appeal to the interests of the advancement of blacks as a group would shatter whatever fragile consensus might exist over the

---

[242] *Hughes v. Superior Court*, 339 U.S. 460 (1950). See Moreno, *From Direct Action to Affirmative Action*, ch. 4. On the way in which preferential policies, whatever their initial goals, (and, indeed, if cross-national empirical studies are to be believed, inevitably) tend to be expanded to encompass more and more groups, see Thomas Sowell, *Preferential Policies: An International Perspective* (New York: William Morrow and Co., 1990), 120–2.

[243] See also *Giboney v. Empire Storage & Ice Co.*, 336 U.S. 490 (1949).

meaning of fundamental fair play. At the same time though, a counterethos that had been institutionalized outside the Court in the bureaucracy of the New American State, an ethos that had long since made its peace with a group-oriented interest group liberalism (or pluralism), had become a major part of the governing constitutional order. It was this ethos that eventually came to infuse the Court's jurisprudence, giving constitutional sanction to "hard," quota-based affirmative action.[244]

In this regard, what the NLRB was to the labor movement in the 1930s and 1940s, the Equal Employment Opportunity Commission later became to the civil rights movement in the 1960s and 1970s. Both were captured agencies that consolidated the interests of the class within the bosom of the central state and, importantly, legitimated those interests with normative appeals to be acting on behalf of "the rights of labor" and "civil rights." While President Franklin Roosevelt had presided over the institutional triumph of corporatist group rights over individual rights as a settlement of "the labor problem," FDR Jr., as the first head of the EEOC (1965), presided over the institutional triumph of corporatist group rights over individual rights as a settlement of a new order concerning civil rights.

As we have seen, the demands of some African Americans that they be treated as members of a power-seeking group entitled to collective benefits did not originate in the mid-1960s, but rather in the 1930s with the labor-inspired Don't Buy Where You Can't Work campaigns. Driven to desperation by the Great Depression and inspired by the recent success of organized labor in winning exemptions from common law rules limiting parading and picketing with the intent to injure lawful businesses, black participants in these campaigns pushed aggressively for group hiring quotas. By the 1950s, both the ACLU and the NAACP, while not yet themselves calling for quotas, were actively supporting the lawfulness of pickets that had insisted upon them.

In the meantime, the federal government, pushed at times by the threat of mass protests and nudged by the new politics of the Great Migration, took a series of steps to accord blacks the basic guarantees of equal rights as individual rights. In the wake of the demise of these, many states passed nondiscrimination laws and set up fair employment practices commissions of their own (a state fair employment law, which targeted the chief obstacle to black employment opportunity, organized labor, was at issue in the 1944 *Corsi* case). In 1953, President Dwight Eisenhower, availing himself of the power that accompanied the largesse of the postwar military industrial

---

[244] *Sweatt v. Painter*, 339 U.S. 629 (1950). See Theodore J. Lowi, *The End of Liberalism: The Second Republic of the United States* (New York: W. W. Norton, 1979); Grant McConnell, *Private Power and American Democracy* (New York: Alfred A. Knopf, 1966). For an argument that, in time, the Court fully assimilated into its jurisprudence the pluralism of the New Deal State, see Kahn, *Supreme Court and Constitutional Theory*.

complex, set up by executive order the President's Committee on Government Contracts (PCGC), which relied on "education, conciliation, mediation, and persuasion" to enforce nondiscrimination clauses in government procurement contracts.[245] Aside from its absence of enforcement power, the failure of the PCGC to police unions meant that it was destined to have little or no practical effect. In March of 1961, however, Eisenhower's successor, John F. Kennedy, signed an executive order that created the President's Committee on Equal Employment Opportunity (PCEEO), a body with the power to force government contractors to submit compliance reports outlining the racial practices of their unions. President Kennedy's executive order prohibited racial discrimination in government contracting and employment. Significantly, although it was firmly anchored in the tradition of individual equality constitutionalism, the order used the term "affirmative action" for the first time, asking contractors and unions to sign "plans for progress" regarding not quotas or timetables but instead a movement toward a policy of equal openness to black workers. The phrase "affirmative action," however, would soon be reconstituted to take on a new meaning consistent with the group-oriented ethos of the new constitutional order.[246]

Ironically, the vehicle for the ideological reconstruction of the meaning of "affirmative action" in line with the governing ethos of the New American State would be the Civil Rights Act of 1964 (CRA), which, in Title VII, was the first federal law that expressly prohibited racial discrimination by unions or employers. Both the language of the act and the debate on its adoption in the U.S. Congress clearly demonstrate that the CRA, hewing as close as possible to political consensus, was aimed at the protection of equal individual and not group rights. It was the CRA that created an EEOC with the power to receive complaints arising under the terms of the act, to attempt to settle them through "conference, conciliation, and persuasion," and, if necessary, to authorize an aggrieved party to bring a civil discrimination suit for CRA violations. The CRA also authorized the U.S. Attorney General to file civil discrimination suits on his own initiative and gave the commission the power to institute compliance proceedings in federal courts.[247]

---

[245] Eisenhower, on another occasion, of course, had warned against the political effects of that complex. Dwight D. Eisenhower, *Farewell Address* (January 17, 1961). The committee seniority system in Congress gave Southern congressmen a virtual veto power over civil rights legislation. Given this legislative obstacle, presidents often found it easier to pursue civil rights policy, to the extent they were interested in doing so, through the issuance of executive orders and other exercises of executive power.

[246] Ray Marshall, *The Negro and Organized Labor* (New York: John Wiley & Sons, Inc., 1965), 212–25. See also Herman Belz, *Equality Transformed: A Quarter Century of Affirmative Action* (New Brunswick, NJ: Transaction Publishers, 1991).

[247] U.S. Equal Employment Opportunity Commission, *Legislative History of Titles VII and VI of Civil Rights Act of 1964* (Washington, D.C.: U.S. Government Printing Office, n.d.); Moreno, *Direct Action to Affirmative Action*, 208–10, 213–19, 229–30; Graham, *Collision Course*,

No sooner had the EEOC been created, however, than the civil rights groups – whose turn away from individual and toward group rights had been adumbrated as far back as the 1950s in their *amicus* briefs in the *Hughes* case – captured the policymaking levers of the administrative agency in much the same way that organized labor had captured the NLRB.[248] The political campaign to capture the new agency was initiated by Jack Greenberg, head of the NAACP Legal Defense and Education Fund (LDF). In his memoirs, Greenberg discussed this campaign openly as a calculated strategic effort, and proudly deemed it to be "almost on par with the campaign that won *Brown.*"[249] Greenberg's strategy was to deluge the newly-created EEOC with so many complaints that administrative exigencies would force it to regard blacks as a group rather than as aggrieved individuals. The sheer volume of complaints, Greenberg adroitly calculated, would simply make it too time consuming and expensive for the agency to either conciliate or adjudicate individual claims. The day that Roosevelt Jr.'s EEOC opened for business, the LDF was standing at the door ready to file nearly 500 complaints. A few weeks later they were ready with an additional 400 more.[250] Soon, class action race discrimination lawsuits became the order of the day, and Title VII claims were assessed not on the basis of whether a complaining individual had been discriminated against because of his race, but whether blacks as a group were statistically underrepresented in a workplace.

The emphasis on statistics and patterns in racial discrimination suits, pushed by a team of LDF lawyers in league with a stable of foundation-funded social scientists, was given special impetus by Greenberg's calculated campaign. But it also would have made bureaucratic sense even without it, because the search for an "intent to discriminate" was inherently difficult and time consuming. When the campaign was considered alongside an ethical disposition to treat blacks as a group and considerations of bureaucratic efficiency, it made special sense. The group-oriented statistical approach also saved the agency time and effort by enabling employers to calculate for themselves whether or not the EEOC would find that they were discriminating on the basis of race. The group-oriented statistical pattern-regarding approach permitted them to seek a safe harbor through "voluntary" quota hiring. This

26–38; Skrentny, *Ironies of Affirmative Action*, 7–8; Kersch, "The New Deal Triumph as the End of History? The Judicial Negotiation of Labor Rights and Civil Rights," in *Supreme Court and American Political Development*, eds. Kahn and Kersch.

[248] See Graham, *Collision Course*, 74–6; Thomas Sowell, *Civil Rights: Rhetoric or Reality* (New York: Quill/William Morrow, 1984), 39. On the NLRB, see Tomlins, *State and the Unions*; James Q. Wilson, *Bureaucracy: What Government Agencies Do and Why They Do It* (New York: Basic Books, 1989), 67. On the capture of administrative agencies generally, see Wilson, *Bureaucracy*, 75–83; Lowi, *The End of Liberalism*.

[249] Jack Greenberg, *Crusaders in the Courts* (New York: Basic Books, 1994), 412.

[250] Greenberg, *Crusaders in the Courts*, 413.

helped insulate them from many discrimination suits, in the process doing the EEOC's work without occupying the EEOC's time.[251]

The emphasis on race quotas emerging in the central state bureaucracy fit well with the political and institutional environment of the mid-to-late 1960s. A series of race riots, beginning with the 1965 Watts section of Los Angeles, put increasing political pressure on governments to take public steps to advance the interests of blacks as a group.[252] So, too, did an intragovernmental bureaucratic rivalry that developed between the Office of Federal Contract Compliance (OFCC) (created by Lyndon Johnson in 1965) and the EEOC. That rivalry set in motion an interagency competition that spurred the OFCC to attempt to outdo the EEOC in its adoption of policymaking by pattern and statistics.[253] This new direction in central state policymaking concerning race was reinforced by the constitutional imprimatur placed on it by the Supreme Court in *Griggs v. Duke Power* (1971), which was argued by Jack Greenberg.[254] By the late 1970s, the Court was explicitly upholding the constitutionality of racial quotas in employment of the very type it had condemned in the *Hughes* case as part of its equal opportunity push culminating in *Brown*.[255] The constitutional ethos institutionalized in the bureaucratic structures of the New American State had finally been ratified by the civil rights jurisprudence of the nation's highest court.

By the 1970s, an individual right to labor, a pillar of the old constitutional order, had long since been written out of the lexicon of American constitutionalism in the interest of conferring state-sanctioned power on organized labor. In the 1930s, as part of the process of constructing the constitutional legitimacy of group rights, the Supreme Court had then reimagined the group rights conferred upon organized labor as closely joined to the individual right to free speech. In the wake of the success of this project of constitutional reconstruction, African Americans (who had long been the reliable opponents of the group claims of organized labor) strategically positioned themselves within this newly constructed constitutional architecture. At first, courts held

---

[251] A fuller discussion of the (partial) roots of affirmative action in the bureaucratic imperatives of the EEOC is provided in Skrentny, *Ironies of Affirmative Action*, 110–44.

[252] Skrentny, *Ironies of Affirmative Action*, 67–110; Graham, *Collision Course*, 30–4.

[253] Belz, *Equality Transformed*, 29–34.

[254] *Griggs v. Duke Power*, 401 U.S. 424 (1971) (inaugurating the Court's "disparate impact" approach in striking down tests for hiring and promotion not meeting EEOC guidelines requiring that however neutral in terms or intent, those terms in their effects not statistically hold back blacks more than whites; the test at issue involved a high school graduation requirement for power plant workers). See Moreno, *Direct Action to Affirmative Action*, 267–82.

[255] *United Steelworkers of America v. Weber*, 443 U.S. 193 (1979) (specifically approving for the first time preferential treatment accorded to blacks in the workplace as constitutional and not in violation of Title VII); *Fullilove v. Klutznick*, 448 U.S. 448 (1980) (upholding constitutionality of racial set-asides for minority businesses under the Public Works Employment Act of 1977).

coercive pickets undertaken by African Americans seeking to force businesses to engage in (unlawful) race-based hiring to be illegal assaults on individual rights (as organized labor's pickets had been held beforehand). By the early 1970s, however, both the Court (in *Griggs*) and the administrative state (at the EEOC and elsewhere) had conferred constitutional legitimacy on the group rights of American blacks, thus welcoming them as a full-fledged class for purposes of maneuvering within the institutional order of the New American State. The final step in this extended project of ideological and constitutional reconstruction was taken the year after *Griggs*, in the Supreme Court's *Mosley* decision – another picketing case. There, the Court, in an important ideological move echoing the pattern it had followed earlier involving organized labor, explicitly associated the Fourteenth Amendment's equal protection clause with the individual right to freedom of speech. In so doing, the Court announced that aggregate group rights and individual rights in the realm of race were one and the same under the new constitutional order.[256]

Police Department of Chicago v. Mosley involved the constitutionality of a Chicago ordinance banning picketing in front of schools, but exempting peaceful picketing by labor unions from that prohibition. A solitary African American picketer who had been parading in front of the school carrying a sign accusing the school of race discrimination sought an injunction against the enforcement of the ordinance against his actions. In an opinion by justice Thurgood Marshall (who, as an NAACP lawyer, had argued unsuccessfully on behalf of the Progressive Citizens Alliance picketers in the *Hughes* case), the Court voided the ordinance on equal protection grounds, reasoning that the law treated picketers with one message differently from picketers with another.[257]

Mosley would seem to be a rather straightforward content discrimination case under the First Amendment. And, initially, legal academics were disposed to treat it as such.[258] Nevertheless, Justice Marshall rather willfully

---

[256] The similar ideological move concerning labor took place in *Hague v. CIO* and *Thornhill v. Alabama*, as discussed above. On the unique legitimacy the new order conveyed by a decision made on free speech grounds, see White, "Free Speech and the Bifurcated Review Project."

[257] *Police Department of Chicago v. Mosley*, 408 U.S. 92 (1972).

[258] See Kenneth Karst, "Equality as a Central Principle of the First Amendment," *University of Chicago Law Review* 43 (1975): 20–68, esp. 27 ("Despite the Court's choice of an equal protection ground for decision, its opinion speaks chiefly to first amendment values and primarily cites first amendment cases as authority"); Roy A. Black, "Equal But Inadequate Protection: A New Look at *Mosley* and *Grayned*," *Harvard Civil Rights and Civil Liberties Law Review* 8 (1973): 469–85. Karst declares *Mosley* to be a "landmark first amendment decision" in which equality has finally stepped out of the shadows and asserted itself as a "central principle of the first amendment." "[T]he idea of equal treatment," he opines, "has a special emotional appeal, not only to the justices, but to the Court's varied constituencies, including the public." Karst, "Equality as a Central Principle of the First Amendment," 28, 67.

decided to frame the central issue in the case as one of equal protection. This decision is a strange one as a matter of constitutional law. If one considers it from the developmental perspective outlined throughout this discussion, a perspective emphasizing the Supreme Court's participation in an affirmative project of ideological construction, however, that choice makes considerably more sense. The original default rule under the traditional constitutionalism of the state of courts and parties was to forbid picketing altogether (picketing, recall, was considered not speech but rather fully regulable conduct). Around the time of the New Deal, after a considerable period of progressive activism and theorizing, labor was accorded special statutory privileges as a constitutionally preferred collectivity or group. One of those privileges exempted labor, and labor alone, from the traditional common law prohibition on picketing. Seeking to take advantage of that special exemption conferred upon labor as a group, African Americans began picketing employers, frequently demanding proportional racial hiring or quotas. To defend their actions in court, they (including Thurgood Marshall himself, prior to his ascendency to the Court) argued that regardless of the lack of connection between civil rights picketers and the targeted businesses, their pickets were statutorily privileged because they fell within the ambit of a "labor dispute."[259] Marshall's opinion for the Court in *Mosley*, written as an equal protection rather than a First Amendment opinion, reflects the arrival of African Americans as an aggregate class for purposes of constitutional analysis. Blacks, Marshall announced implicitly in *Mosley*, were now like labor. As such, they were no longer obligated to piggyback their picketing claims on the special privileges accorded to labor as a group. A ruling issued on purely First Amendment grounds would not convey this conviction. A ruling anchored in the equal protection clause, however, would.

In this regard, the Court's opinion in *Mosley* evinces a close ideological kinship with *Griggs*, as well as with subsequent landmark affirmative action decisions in the *Bakke* (1978) and *United Steelworkers v. Weber* (1979) cases of about the same time.[260] In these 1970s affirmative action decisions, the Court undertook a sustained repudiation of the ethos underlying its Don't Buy Where You Can't Work decisions of the civil rights era, which rejected group-based understandings of race and was actively engaged in the process of legitimating such understandings as a form of constitutionally sanctioned state policy. Put otherwise, at the very moment equality was being announced as a central principle of the First Amendment, it was being read out as a central principle of the Fourteenth.

[259] See *Duplex Printing v. Deering*, 254 U.S. 443 (1921); *New Negro Alliance v. Sanitary Grocery*, 303 U.S. 552 (1938).
[260] *Regents of the University of California v. Bakke*; 438 U.S. 265 (1978); *United Steelworkers of American v. Weber*, 443 U.S. 193 (1979).

These ideological developments, interestingly enough, were apparent at the time – and decidedly unpalatable – to many of the civil libertarians of an earlier era who were unwilling to reconstruct their understandings of individual rights to fit a new ideology of race. The founder of the ACLU, Roger Baldwin, for example, was still around in the 1970s and was scandalized by his group's decision to advocate the conferral of special group-oriented constitutional privileges upon blacks, a decision that struck this pioneering civil libertarian as a very strange development indeed. As far as affirmative action was concerned, Baldwin told an interviewer during this time: "I think the ACLU is wrong. I'm on the other side. . . . I think it was a great mistake. I think the ACLU is false to its own principles when it supports a quota. We've always opposed quotas. Never supported quotas . . . [W]e have played favorites with people who are disadvantaged. I understand it. I'm very sympathetic with it, but it destroys another principle. And they've chosen the wrong one."[261] In holding this view, Baldwin, of course, allied himself within the ideological architecture of the new regime with the ostensible enemies of "civil rights."

The new vision of civil rights was a direct assault on the individual rights of many people who happened not to be African American to be hired, promoted, admitted, and otherwise judged and evaluated on the basis of factors other than their race. To oppose this vision, however, soon became widely stigmatized in the late twentieth century as racist. For a black person to oppose it (as Justice Clarence Thomas has) was to be vehemently attacked by progressive and civil rights elites as, at best, ignorant of one's history and, at worst, anti–civil rights and a traitor to one's race. Soon, however, this new vision of the meaning of civil rights began to affect not just civil rights but "civil liberties" as well.[262]

[261] Roger Baldwin, quoted by Donohue, *Politics of the ACLU*, 79–80. In a similar vein, one of the leading historians (and partisans) of early-twentieth-century reform, Eric Goldman, left his position as a celebrated professor of history at Princeton profoundly embittered by the institutionalization of racial preferences at the university. Goldman was convinced that such preferences did violence to the core egalitarian principles to which he had devoted much of his life. Daniel J. Kelves, "Eric Frederick Goldman," in *Luminaries: Princeton Faculty Remembered*, ed. Patricia H. Marks (Princeton: Association of Princeton Graduate Alumni, 1996), 106. The chief organizer of the 1963 March on Washington for Jobs and Freedom, the legendary civil rights activist Bayard Rustin, was also an outspoken critic of affirmative action.

[262] See Carol Swain, "Double Standard, Double Bind: African American Leadership after the Thomas Debacle," in *Race-ing Justice, En-Gendering Power: Essays on Anita Hill, Clarence Thomas, and the Construction of Social Reality*, ed. Toni Morrison (New York: Pantheon Books, 1992), 215–31. For a late-twentieth-century racialist progressive identification of race preference policies with "civil rights" itself, see Derrick Bell, "A Radical Double Agent," in *Court of Appeal: The Black Community Speaks Out on the Racial and Sexual Politics of Clarence Thomas vs. Anita Hill*, eds. Robert Chrisman and Robert L. Allen (New York: Ballantine Books, 1992), 36–7; Ronald N. Wolters, "Clarence Thomas and the Meaning of Blackness," in *Court of Appeal*, 215–18; "Questions and Answers on the

New Restraints on Civil Liberties in the Interest of (Reconstituted) "Civil Rights"

During their statebuilding-era reform campaigns aimed at solving the labor problem, many progressive partisans of industrial democracy openly characterized their efforts as both anti–individual rights and even anticonstitutionalist. These reformers, after all, associated "individual rights" primarily with the rights of property and capital. When they did speak in favor of rights, it was mostly not the rights of the individual but rather the rights accruing to social classes, particularly the laboring class.

The collective bargaining provisions of the Wagner Act represented the culmination of this reformist campaign and, as such, the defeat of the key individual rights claims arising out the traditional dignity-of-labor constitutionalism that had long stood as a barrier to such an achievement. Although certainly not all members of the labor movement would have advocated the same reforms that were institutionalized as part of the New Deal, the passage of the Wagner Act was nonetheless a great progressive triumph that marked the end of the labor problem as the central progressive political project within American politics. Because the Wagner Act was perceived as such a political and institutional imperative, the defeat of the individual rights claims on

NAACP's Position on Judge Clarence Thomas," in *Court of Appeal*, 275–7; Toni Morrison, "Introduction," in Morrison, *Race-ing Justice* (arguing that Thomas had "internal[ized] the master's tongue" (xxv) and that the judge inhabited an "expediently deracialized self" (xxviii); A. Leon Higginbotham Jr., "An Open Letter to Judge Clarence Thomas from a Federal Judicial Colleague," in Morrison, *Race-ing Justice*, 1–39 (Thomas's positions, including that on affirmative action, reflect "a stunted knowledge of history and an unformed judicial philosophy"); Manning Marable, "Clarence Thomas and the Crisis of Black Political Culture," in Morrison, *Race-ing Justice*, 61–85 (Clarence Thomas's climb to power is directly related to his "abandonment of the principles of the black freedom struggle," including the fight for affirmative action (62); "ethnically, Clarence Thomas has ceased to be African American" (82); Hearings Before the Committee on the Judiciary, United States Senate, 102nd Congress, 1st Session, on the Nomination of Clarence Thomas to Be Associate Justice of the Supreme Court of the United States (S-Hrg. 102-1084, Part 2 – J – 102-40 (September 17, 1991); Statement of the Congressional Black Caucus on the Nomination of Judge Clarence Thomas as Associate Justice of the United States Supreme Court (September 19, 1991), 2568–84; Testimony of Eleanor Cutri Smeal, president, The Fund for the Feminist Majority on the Nomination of Clarence Thomas for Associate Justice of the Supreme Court (September 20, 1991), 2945–53; Testimony of Panel Consisting of Benjamin L. Hooks, executive director, National Association for the Advancement of Colored People, Rev. Dr. Ames C. Brown, The National Baptist Convention, U.S.A., Inc., Rev. Archie Le Mone, The Progressive National Baptist Convention (September 20, 1991), 3010–156; Statement by The Center for Constitutional Rights Against the Nomination of Judge Clarence Thomas to the U.S. Supreme Court (September 20, 1991), 3444–57. It was not long before other racial and ethnic groups were accorded preferential treatment under affirmative action plans, a move that helped institutionalize these public policies. See Skrentny, *Minority Rights Revolution*, 85–164; Peter H. Schuck, *Diversity in America: Keeping Government at a Safe Distance* (Cambridge, MA: The Belknap Press of the Harvard University Press, 2003), 139.

which it was based has rarely been treated as an important loss. The conceptualization of the Wagner Act as a triumph, however, had tended to obscure studies of the full range of consequences of the curtailment of those rights. For example, it is only recently that scholars have begun to discuss at length the ways in which the triumph of labor rights represented a setback for civil rights.

This same triumph was also made possible at the expense of significant curtailments of important civil liberties. Although the new order, as we have seen, was reconstructed in the Supreme Court as a triumph for First Amendment free speech rights in a number of New Deal–era picketing cases, at the same time the broad protection for free speech rights was soon understood in other contexts to pose a threat to the new, state-sanctioned rights of labor as a class. One important problem was that the speech of individual workers, if aggressively protected, could undermine the power of labor unions as collectivities or groups. And so the Supreme Court and other courts, while protecting the free speech rights of labor as a group in cases such as *Thornhill v. Alabama* and *Hague v. CIO*, routinely spurned the free speech claims of individual union members when asserted against the group. They often did so with frank declarations that under the new order the rights of the group trumped the rights of the individual. The Supreme Court declared in 1948, for example, in a statement suggestive of its new commitments, that "the expression of bloc sentiment is and always has been an integral part of our democratic and legislative processes."[263] And, notwithstanding its ringing declaration in the Jehovah's Witness flag salute case that no one should be coerced into making statements that ran counter to that individual's beliefs, the Court consistently refused repeated opportunities, in the face of a run of First Amendment claims, to hold that unions could not use their compulsory dues to subsidize political speech with which dissenting union members disagreed. In a 1950 decision upholding a requirement of the Taft-Hartley Act (1947) that union officials sign affidavits swearing that they were not members of the Communist Party, Chief Justice Fred Vinson stated explicitly that the benefits of the new order were premised on the sacrifice of key rights. "Because of the necessity to have strong unions to bargain on equal terms with strong employers, individual employees are required to sacrifice rights which in some cases are valuable to them," Vinson wrote. But "the loss of individual rights for the greater benefit of the group [ultimately] results in a tremendous increase in the power of the group – the union."[264]

---

[263] *United States v. CIO*, 335 U.S. 106, 144 (1948) (Justice Wiley Rutledge).

[264] See *Railway Employees' Department v. Hanson*, 351 U.S. 225 (1956) (holding the union's contract to be state action, but refusing to rule on the First Amendment claim); *West Virginia State Board of Education v. Barnette*, 319 U.S. 624 (1943). See also *DeMille v. American Federation of Radio Artists*, 31 Cal.2d. 139 (1947); *American Communications Association v. Douds*, 339 U.S. 382, 401 (1950) (communist affidavit decision). The above discussion is drawn

Another important problem arose under the new order when employers insisted on trying to persuade their employees verbally to choose not to join labor unions. If such speech was broadly protected, however, it might have had the effect of persuading a large number of workers not to join labor unions. But if this came to pass, the promise the new order presented to thoroughly restructure the governing order the world of work in the United States would also be threatened. Thus, in the interest of sustaining the new regime, the freedom of speech in this previously protected sphere would have to be limited. "Until the enactment of the Wagner Act in 1935 the issue of what an employer might lawfully say to his employees in the course of a labor dispute was no issue at all; neither statute nor common law rule...stayed his tongue,"[265] one commentator concluded. That act, however, as the foundation of the new order, declared that "it shall be an unfair labor practice for an employer to interfere with, restrain, or coerce employees in the exercise of their [collective bargaining] rights" set out elsewhere in the act.[266] Such a provision, of course, was not a direct restraint on free speech. But it was not long before the NLRB, as part of its project of consolidating the power of the new regulatory order, began interpreting this provision as rendering antiunion statements made by employers as "unfair labor practices." In the 1930s and early 1940s, for example, statements by employers accusing unions of "causing trouble," of being "outside agitators," "shyster outfits," or "a bunch of Bolsheviks" all subjected employers to NLRB sanctions.[267] These administrative decisions stand in particularly stark contrast to the Supreme Court's decision in *Senn v. Tile Layers Union* (1937), in which the Court held that the aggressive picketing of a small business owner being hectored out of his trade by claims that he was "unfair to labor" was not "coercive" in any way.

from Schiller, "From Group Rights to Individual Liberties," 31–8, which treats the subject more comprehensively than I do here. See also Klare, "Labor Law as Ideology," 454.

[265] Thomas G. S. Christensen, "Free Speech, Propaganda and the National Labor Relations Act," *New York University Law Review* 38 (1963): 255.

[266] National Labor Relations Act, Sec. 8(a) (1).

[267] See *Indianapolis Glove Co.*, 5 NLRB 231, 239 (1938) (employer accusation that unions were causing trouble); *American Manufacturing Concern*, 7 NLRB 753 (1938) (employer statement referring to union organizers as "outside agitators"); *Huch Leather Co.*, 11 NLRB 394, 401 (1938) (employer statement that unions amounted to "a bunch of Bolsheviks"); *Leitz Carpet Corp.*, 27 NLRB 235, 237–8 (1940) (employer statement referring to unions as "shyster outfits"). These cases are cited in Ian M. Adams and Richard L. Wyatt Jr., "Free Speech and Administrative Agency Deference: Section 8(c) and the National Labor Relations Board – An Expostulation on Preserving the First Amendment," *Journal of Contemporary Law* 22 (1996): 19–50, esp. 22 n. 19. Along the same lines in 1937, the ACLU (in a memo written by Nathan Greene, the progressive coauthor with Felix Frankfurter of *The Labor Injunction* and an ACLU board member in the 1930s) backed the NLRB in this endeavor, ostensible devotion to the freedom of speech and the press notwithstanding, and supported the NLRB's efforts to track down the author of an unsigned antiunion editorial in a Pennsylvania newspaper. Samuel Walker, *In Defense of American Liberties*, 101.

The free speech consequences of the Wagner Act, though now largely forgotten, proved contentious in the immediate aftermath of its passage. Perhaps the most famous dispute involving this issue took place at the Ford Motor Company, where in 1938, the company ran afoul of the NLRB for, among other things, distributing antiunion literature to its employees during a United Automobile Workers of America (UAW) organizing campaign.[268] Among these were pamphlets titled "Ford Gives Viewpoint on Labor" and cards with sayings on them (dubbed "Fordisms" by the company) such as "A monopoly of JOBS in this country is just as bad as a monopoly of BREAD."[269]

Given the First Amendment's free speech guarantee, the federal government's claim that it could ban the dissemination of such pamphlets would seem to be highly dubious. Nonetheless, the Ford case split even the ACLU down the middle, provoking a bitter battle within the group over whether it should side with Ford or the NLRB. When employers approached the ACLU seeking their support and asked the civil liberties group whether or not the Constitution's right to free speech applied to them, too, Roger Baldwin reported that the group's governing board told them: "No, you have no rights of free speech against unions now because the right to form a union is now a fundamental one under the National Labor Relations Act." When the employers then asked if they at least had the right to talk, the ACLU responded by saying, no, they no longer had a right to talk. Ultimately, the ACLU did back Ford in the case. But they did so on the limited basis that they were prepared to defend only "noncoercive" employer speech.[270]

In its subsequent decisions, the NLRB evinced a sustained and decided preference for the tight regulation of employer speech concerning labor unions.[271] The Board initially took the position that employers could say nothing at all about unions (the "strict neutrality" approach). But, nudged by the Supreme Court, it soon adopted a distinction between coercive and noncoercive speech, the same distinction that the ACLU had arrived at in its dealings with Ford.[272] The Board, however, soon began to interpret the

---

[268] See William A. Donohue, *The Politics of the American Civil Liberties Union* (New Brunswick, NJ: Transaction Books, 1985), 47–50, from which I draw and quote. See also Samuel Walker, *In Defense of American Liberties* (New York: Oxford University Press, 1990), 101–4.

[269] Donohue, *Politics of the American Civil Liberties Union*, 47.

[270] Donohue, *Politics of the American Civil Liberties Union*, 48; Walker, *In Defense of American Liberties*, 103; *NLRB v. Ford Motor Company*, 114 F.2d 905 (6th Cir. 1940).

[271] See, generally, Adams and Wyatt, "Free Speech and Administrative Agency Deference." See also Julius Getman, "Symposium: Directions in Labor Law – Concern for the Dignity of the Worker: Labor Law and Free Speech: The Curious Policy of Limited Expression," *Maryland Law Review* 43 (Fall 1984): 4–22.

[272] *National Labor Relations Board v. Virginia Electric and Power Co.*, 314 U.S. 469 (1941) (holding that employer utterances alone, without threat of retaliation, do not amount to prohibited speech).

category of "coercion" broadly. In response, Congress, as part of the Taft-Hartley Act, amended the Wagner Act to make clear that

[t]he expressing of any views, argument, or opinion, or the dissemination thereof, whether in written, printed, graphic, or visual form, shall not constitute or be evidence of an unfair labor practice under any of the provisions of this Act if such expression contains no threat of reprisal or force or promise of benefit.[273]

Following (and in partial resistance to) Taft-Hartley, the NLRB adopted a "laboratory conditions" standard that left it with broad leeway to regulate employer speech during a union election campaign. The Board justified its assertion of this regulatory authority by asserting a federal interest in maintaining a "pure" dialogue, untainted by (employer) overstatement (an approach, of course, that strayed far from Holmes's "marketplace of ideas" model of First Amendment liberties).[274] Rather than falling by the wayside in the era of Alexander Meikeljohn, Thomas Emerson, and William Brennan, as free speech protections ostensibly got broader and broader, federal regulatory efforts requiring pure dialogue, free of overstatement, were accepted without challenge from civil libertarians right through the Warren-era rights revolution. Indeed, in 1969, at the height of constitutional free speech latitudinarianism, the Supreme Court in its *Gissel* opinion put its express imprimatur on the NLRB's "laboratory conditions" doctrine.[275]

The new constitutional recognition accorded to classes did not just affect the civil liberties of employers. The decision to give preference to the rights of labor as a group over the rights of capital, as we have seen, inspired other groups to seek recognition as privileged classes. African Americans were innovators in this regard. But others followed. In due course, the women's movement, in working toward its political objectives within the architecture

---

[273] 29 U.S.C. Sec. 158(c) (1988).

[274] *General Shoe Corp.*, 77 NLRB 124 (1948). See *Abrams v. United States*, 250 U.S. 616 (Justice Holmes, dissenting) (1919). See also *New York Times Co. v. Sullivan* 376 U.S. 254, 270 (alluding to "a profound national commitment to the principle that debate on public issues should be uninhibited, robust, and wide-open").

[275] *National Labor Relations Board v. Gissel Packing Co.*, 395 U.S. 575 (1969). In *Gissel*, the president of a company warned during a union organizing drive that the Teamsters Union was a "strike happy" outfit and that another strike at the company could drive them out of business, at the cost of the employees' jobs. The Court held that the employer had no right to mention the possibility of a plant closing, stating that to be allowed, "such a prediction must be carefully phrased on the basis of objective fact to convey an employer's belief as to demonstrably probable consequences beyond his control." Quoting the appellate decision below, the Court stated that "conveyance of the employer's belief, even though sincere, that unionization will or may result in the closing of the plant is not a statement of fact unless... the eventuality of closing is capable of proof." *NLRB v. Gissel Packing*, 395 U.S. at 618–19. *Brandenburg v. Ohio*, 395 U.S. 444 (1969), a cross-burning decision, is commonly taken as the high point of free speech latitudinarianism.

of the new order, self-consciously followed the path of blacks, as blacks had followed labor. Like blacks, women's group-oriented claims also started with the (individual rights-oriented) 1964 Civil Rights Act, which called for equal treatment of women in employment without regard to sex.[276] Women's groups, like blacks before them (although the women met more initial bureaucratic resistance) effectively staked a clientist claim to the Equal Employment Opportunity Commission, harnessing the power of the central state to advance a particular vision of feminist group ends. In addition, feminist groups further reconstructed ideological understandings of the relationship between individual and group rights through lawsuits and ideologically pregnant law review advocacy scholarship.[277] Catherine MacKinnon's *Sexual Harassment of Working Women* (1979) was published the same year as the Supreme Court's *United Steelworkers v. Weber* decision. And the EEOC issued its first *Guidelines on Sexual Harassment* in the same year as *Fullilove v. Klutznick* (1980). The group rights claims made by women at this time evinced the same ambivalence toward important individual rights as advocates of new conceptions of civil rights demonstrated in their defenses of racial quotas (feminist groups, as a key constituency of late-twentieth-century constitutional liberalism, came to support and benefit from affirmative action). As with labor, the group rights claims of women also ended up in important instances opposing broad understandings of the freedom of speech.[278]

In accord with the new constitutional ethos, federal courts have looked favorably upon feminist group rights claims, even when those claims have been countered by highly plausible appeals to the freedom of speech. Interpreting Title VII of the Civil Rights Act, courts have held that employers have an affirmative obligation to "prevent... bigots from expressing their opinions in a way that abuses or offends their co-workers."[279] Along these lines, not only ill-intentioned remarks but also "well-intentioned compliments" subject employers to potential liability.[280] Acting pursuant to governmental

---

[276] The sex discrimination provision of the Act was inserted by conservative Virginia Representative Howard W. Smith as a killer amendment that in his view would render the legislation so preposterous that no one but the most pie-eyed radicals would vote for it. Smith's strategy, of course, backfired. See Graham, *Civil Rights Era*, 134–9.

[277] On the trajectory of sex discrimination advocacy within and enforcement by the EEOC, see Graham, *Civil Rights Era*, 205–32.

[278] Catherine A. MacKinnon, *Sexual Harassment of Working Women* (New Haven: Yale University Press, 1979).

[279] *Davis v. Monsanto Chemical Co.*, 858 F.2d 315, 350 (6th Cir. 1988).

[280] *Ellison v. Brady*, 924 F.2d 872, 880 (9th Cir. 1991). Both of these references are drawn from Kingsley R. Browne, "Workplace Censorship: A Response to Professor Sangree," *Rutgers Law Review* 47 (Winter 1995): 579. Title VII provides specifically that "[i]t shall be an unlawful employment practice for an employer... to discriminate against any individual with respect to his compensation, terms, conditions, or privileges of employment, because of such individual's race, color, religion, or national origin." Title VII of the Civil Rights

policies set by the courts and the EEOC at the behest of women's groups, employers today commonly ban sexist speech (typically defined broadly as any remarks that might make some women feel uncomfortable), the use of sexual metaphors, and dirty jokes.[281] Despite a prominent concern for the "chilling effect" of overbroad or vague regulation concerning speech in other contexts, the Supreme Court has never invalidated "hostile environment" regulations under the First Amendment.

Restrictions on sex-related workplace speech were derived most immediately from preceding restrictions that had been placed on speech that was deemed racially harassing. In the early 1970s, a federal court held for the first time that race-related remarks could lead to an improper and illegally hostile workplace environment.[282] This earlier limitation on speech, in turn, is traceable to the restrictions the NLRB placed on workplace speech critical of labor unions in the immediate post–New Deal era, restrictions that the Board justified by the laboratory conditions doctrine in a position ratified by the Supreme Court. And, in fact, contemporary feminist legal scholars have made this lineage explicit by citing *Gissel* and other NLRB decisions from the 1940s as precedents justifying the curtailment of sex-related workplace speech. One such scholar, for instance, in arguing for such limits, asserted:

Even employers have limited rights of expression on the job. For example, an employer cannot engage in speech that could unfairly interfere with a union election [citing *Gissel*]. This restriction on employer expression is justified by the state's interest in ensuring the adequate protection of workers' rights. A similar logic may be applied to sexual harassment law.[283]

Act of 1964, 78 Stat. 255, 42 U.S.C. 2000e-2(a) (1994). EEOC Guidelines make sexual harassment a violation of Title VII. 29 C.F.R. 1604 11(a) (1993).

[281] See, generally, Jonathan Rauch, "Offices and Gentlemen," *The New Republic*, June 23, 1997, 22–8; Walter K. Olson, *The Excuse Factory: How Employment Law Is Paralyzing the American Workplace* (New York: Martin Kessler Books, 1997); Eugene Volokh, "How Harassment Law Restricts Free Speech," *Rutgers Law Review* 47 (Winter 1995): 563–77; Kingley R. Browne, "Title VII as Censorship: Hostile Environment Harassment and the First Amendment," *Ohio State Law Journal* 52 (1991): 481–550.

[282] *Rogers v. Equal Employment Opportunity Commission*, 454 F. 2d 234 (5th Cir. 1971). See also *Firefighters Institute for Racial Equality v. St. Louis*, 549 F.2d 506 (8th Cir. 1977). The court in *Rogers* did assert at the time, though, that it did "not wish to be interpreted as holding that an employer's mere utterance of an ethnic or racial epithet which engenders offensive feelings in the employee" triggers Title VII protection. *Rogers*, 454 F.2d at 283.

[283] Deborah Epstein, "Free Speech at Work: Verbal Harassment and Gender-Based Discriminatory (Mis)Treatment," *Georgetown Law Journal* 85 (February 1997): 649–66, esp. 657. See also Amy Horton, "Of Supervision, Centerfolds, and Censorship: Sexual Harassment and the Contours of Title VII," *University of Miami Law Review* 46 (1991): 423–31 (citing *Gissel* in support of the proposition that limits on sex-related speech in the workplace do not violate the First Amendment).

It is clear that the new constitutional ethos constructed at the behest of organized labor in the first half of the twentieth century had broad-ranging and unanticipated legal and ideological implications.

Conclusion

Traditional narratives of constitutional development are structured around, first, a New Deal–era breakthrough clearing the way for (among other things, but importantly) the rights of labor and, in turn, a gradual progression toward court-protected guarantees concerning civil liberties and civil rights. The trajectory of constitutional development presented here concerning labor rights, civil liberties, and civil rights is linear in significant parts and nonlinear in others. The New Deal breakthrough concerning labor, I emphasize here, was not simply a negative affair. It was sustained by an affirmative substantive political vision that emphasized a constitutionalism of classes and groups fashioned in progressive thought and Supreme Court decisions long before the New Deal, a vision that was in many respects frankly opposed to individual rights. That vision was ultimately institutionalized in the collective bargaining provisions of the National Labor Relations Act. While well suited to ending "the labor problem," the animating axis of reform politics in the statebuilding era, this "breakthrough" created new developmental problems. First, by putting state power behind labor unions, it actually created a new developmental obstacle to the achievement of the next reformist imperative: civil rights. And, second, to institutionalize the new regime, its antirights underpinnings needed to be reconstructed as pro–individual rights. These problems were both political and ideological. In many ways, the traditional characterization of the "Old" Supreme Court as a barrier to the guarantees of the "rights of labor" is accurate. (After all, that narrative is itself derived largely from constitutional struggles concerning "the labor problem.") Once that barrier falls, however, the role played by the courts is complicated and hardly fits into the simple characterization of regaining its power, but now in the service of "civil liberties" and "civil rights." The Court, during this period, follows neither the dictates of partisan politics nor those of legal doctrine – at least not in any simple way. Rather, it is immersed in a highly ideological process, taking place both within the Court and outside of it (such as in the thinking of A. Philip Randolph or in the bureaucratic structures of the NLRB), of working to institutionalize and legitimize the new order, while at the same time, in response to new reformist pressures, to negotiate changes within it. These involved, among other things, negotiating the extension of the class status of labor to blacks, in the process limiting labor union autonomy and the civil rights of nonblacks, and restricting free speech rights in some areas (such as workplace speech) and expanding them in others. In this, the Court stood at the rather messy center of what Orren and Skowronek have called intercurrence – or multiple, often contrary orderings or incongruities – in the face of specific, often reformist, pressures for institutional change. The Court exercised both restraint and activism, and was pro–civil rights and anti–civil rights, prolabor and anti-labor, pro–civil liberties and anti–civil liberties. Whiggish unidimensional narratives of constitutional development fail to capture these important dynamics.

4

Education Rights

Reconstituting the School

Introduction: The Absence of Education from Narratives of American Statebuilding

Our formative understandings of the nature and trajectory of American political development are rooted in longstanding conventions concerning American exceptionalism. Beginning in the nation's infancy, foreign political observers and thinkers as eminent as Alexis de Tocqueville and Georg Friedrich Hegel fixed on the United States as an oddly "stateless" entity, as measured against the baseline of the purported continental European norm. More recently, however, Stephen Skowronek has influentially argued that this characterization of the United States as stateless was not quite right, even at the time that Tocqueville and Hegel were writing. The United States, Skowronek contended, has long been possessed of a "state." Only its form was distinctive. The American state prior to the crucial statebuilding era of the late nineteenth and early twentieth centuries was best characterized as a "state of courts and parties," a unique institutional order, that set the United States apart from the European model.[1]

Continental European states remained the point of comparison as the process of "building a new American state" began in earnest in late-nineteenth-century America. That baseline, though, proved to be a moving target, as European states around the same time, under the influence of leaders such as Germany's Prince Otto von Bismarck and Great Britain's Benjamin Disraeli, responded to many of the same political-economic transformations and social pressures that were affecting the United States and began to assume new dimensions as modern social welfare states. As these transformations took place in Europe, a new yardstick of development was invented, one that was crafted less along the lines of the old European states that served as models for

---

[1] Skowronek, *Building a New American State*, 5–10. See, generally, Seymour Martin Lipset, *American Exceptionalism: A Double-Edged Sword* (New York: W. W. Norton, 1996).

Tocqueville and Hegel, and more according to the specifications of Bismarck, Disraeli, and newly influential Fabian Socialists such as Sidney and Beatrice Webb. As this bold new project of institutional building took hold in Europe, many progressive-spirited, forward-looking Americans found their groping, would-be, or "patchwork" efforts to match the Europeans in the trajectory of state construction to be wanting. America's effort at modernizing through the construction of a powerful and efficient modern, centralized welfare state was ultimately thwarted, many believed, by longstanding ideologies and institutional (including constitutional) arrangements, which precluded the necessary statism in the service of dubious, atavistic attachments to individual and constitutional rights.

For a core group of scholars of American political development, who begin from Marxian and socialist historical or social scientific presuppositions (even if they are not Marxists or socialists themselves), the key to the "problem" of the aberrant and underdeveloped American state has long been attributed to the unique relationship between capital and labor across American political history. Thus, for these scholars, questions involving the sources of the problematic nature of the American state have long been understood to be a variant of the root question, "Why no socialism?" As such, the failure of Americans to develop a modern social welfare state is commonly traced back to the failure of socialist political movements in American politics. And the question of why these movements failed becomes synonymous with the question of why the United States lacks a fully developed modern state. Given that, in Europe and for much of American history, socialist movements were closely identified with the labor movement, the labor problem and the statebuilding problem were, in the eyes of many, one and the same. A modern, advanced state was defined, to a significant extent, by whether or not it accorded "proper" status to the working class, a class that itself was understood (again along the European model) to be embodied and defined by organized labor. American exceptionalism concerning labor thus came to constitute the core of American exceptionalism itself. It is for this reason that the formative studies of American political development have accorded pride of place to the labor question.[2]

Given the centrality of "the labor question" in the statebuilding era, this focus on labor makes considerable sense. At the same time, though, too relentless a focus on the reformist developmental imperative concerning labor has – at least within studies of American political development – obscured other important facets of America's distinctive path of state construction that are only tenuously linked to the problem of labor. One such facet involves state development concerning issues of cultural politics such as education

---

[2] Karen Orren, for one, has explicitly declared that political development concerning labor is central to American political development. See Orren, "The Primacy of Labor in American Constitutional Development," *American Political Science Review* 89 (June 1995): 377–88.

and religion. The United States is developmentally exceptional in many ways. One of the most important is its failure to construct a nationwide system of education and in its (perhaps partially related) "failure of secularization."[3] For students of American constitutional development, given that these issues have cropped up repeatedly in the jurisprudence of the twentieth-century Supreme Court, this attention should be considered indispensable.

Education and the American State before the Statebuilding Era[4]

Despite the contemporary perception that the very idea of creating and implementing education policy at the level of the nation-state is wholly alien to the American political tradition, the truth is that at least some national political actors, beginning in the country's very earliest years, publicly contemplated proposals for some form of active central state involvement in American education. In the 1780s, for instance, a run of prominent founders, including Benjamin Rush, Charles Pinkney, John Adams, Thomas Jefferson, Alexander Hamilton, and Edmund Randolph, all advocated the establishment of a national university. And while serving as president, George Washington himself pushed zealously for the establishment of such an institution. For reasons of expense, however (which should be considered in light of the central state's limited revenue-raising capacity at that time), Congress never followed through on these proposals.[5]

Others, however, even in the nation's earliest years, had even grander designs. In the 1790s, Samuel Knox, a minister and prominent public figure, lobbied Maryland's legislature to pass a resolution that would have put the state on record as supporting not a single national university (as Washington and others had called for), but a national system of education. In an essay that

---

[3] David Hollinger has called "the failure of secularization" in America "[t]he parallel to the Sombartian interrogative . . . " and said, appropriately, that "[t]he relative slowness and limited extent of a de-Christianization in modern American history even down to the present is an event of the same order as the failure of the American Left to develop social democratic movements comparable to those of Great Britain, France, and Germany." Hollinger, *Science, Jews, and Secular Culture: Studies in Mid-Twentieth Century American Intellectual History* (Princeton: Princeton University Press, 1996), 21. I want to emphasize that in using the term "failure," I do not wish to convey any sort of normative judgment. It is quite possible that America's failure to develop along European lines in this and other areas was either particularly suited to American circumstances or, alternatively, an improvement on European conditions.

[4] Kevin Kosar has rightly noted that "educational historians have produced little research on congress, presidents, and federal education policy and politics prior to 1960." I am indebted to Kosar's chapter "Congress, Presidents, and the Politics of Education, 1785–1945" in the brief overview that follows. Kevin Kosar, *National Education Standards and Federal Politics* (Ph.D. dissertation, New York University, 2002), *passim*. I thank Lawrence M. Mead for bringing Kosar's work to my attention.

[5] Lorraine Smith Pangle and Thomas L. Pangle, *The Learning of Liberty: The Educational Ideas of the American Founders* (Lawrence: University Press of Kansas, 1993), 147–52.

won a prize from the American Philosophical Society in 1797 for the best essay submitted on the subject of establishing a national education system (that
a contest on this topic was held by such a prominent body is itself significant),
Knox argued that such a system would perform an essential nationbuilding
role. "[I]n a country circumscribed and situated as the United States, a considerable local diversity in improvement, whether with respect to morals or
literature, must be the consequence." "Nothing," Knox wrote, "might be
supposed to have a better effect towards harmonizing the whole in these
important views than an *uniform system of national education.*" However,
similar to the proposals for a national university, proposals such as Knox's
calling for the creation of a national education system also failed to rally
committed political support. And for most of early American history, federal
involvement in education was confined to occasional sales of federal lands
to fund small gifts to special-needs schools, such as schools for the deaf. [6]

The fleeting nature of early interest in the creation of a national education system is understandable in light of the nation's prevailing institutional
order. That order, and the emergent state of courts and parties, placed tight
constitutional constraints upon the powers of the national government. The
Constitutional text itself – whose structural provisions were taken more seriously than they are today and played a significant part in constituting the
terms of political debate – did not grant the federal government any express
authority to establish a national education system. Moreover, the framework
of government set up by that text limited the government's revenue-raising
capacities, in the process placing sharp practical limitations on the successful
creation of any such system. Demographics conspired against the establishment of a national education system as well. Prior to the late nineteenth
and early twentieth centuries, the bulk of the population in this frontier
nation was rural and dispersed. In line with these patterns of population
dispersal, towns, states, churches, charities, and parents – often under the
sway of strongly Protestant beliefs – had from the beginning made do without any central state assistance in educating their children. The instruction
provided by these institutions and entities of civil society and local government, broadly speaking, proved satisfactory, either in their final results or in
laying the foundation for further efforts individuals were expected to take
to educate themselves. In this context, the radical innovation of constructing a national school system never became a high priority. When sectional
antagonisms over states' rights (accompanied by the rise of Jacksonian constitutional strict constructionism) were added to constitutional constraints,

---

[6] Samuel Knox, "An Essay on the Best System of Liberal Education," in Frederick Rudolph,
Essays on Education in the Early Republic (Cambridge, MA: The Belknap Press of the Harvard
University Press, 1965), 311, 357–67 (italics in original). See also Rev. Benjamin O. Pears,
*American Education: or Strictures on the Nature, Necessity, and Practicability of a System of
National Education Suited to the United States* (New York: John S. Taylor, 1838).

inadequate revenues, demographic dispersal, and functional substituting institutions, the prospect of a national school system seemed even less likely. These antagonisms, of course, became even more intense as the controversy over slavery moved to center stage in national politics.[7]

The first successful, large-scale central state initiative concerning education was a direct result of the centralizing and nationalizing effects of the Civil War.[8] Justin S. Morrill introduced a bill in 1857 to establish state colleges providing students with practical training in agricultural and industrial trades by giving federal grants to states drawn from monies raised from the sale of federal lands. This bill, which was proposed the same year as the Supreme Court's provocative *Dred Scott* decision, was vehemently opposed prior to the Civil War by Southerners and Westerners in Congress, who denounced it as an assault on states' rights and a constitutional abomination. After only narrowly squeaking through Congress and being vetoed by James Buchanan in 1859, however, the bill sailed through the Civil War Congress in 1861, with little discussion or opposition. Abraham Lincoln signed the Morrill Act into law in 1862.[9]

Similarly, it was during what Richard Bensel has called the Civil War Party State that the Republican Congress in 1867 created (as a sub-bureau of the Interior Department) the country's first bureaucratic agency "to promote the cause of education throughout the country," the United States Bureau of Education. The Bureau's very existence was a statebuilding landmark of sorts. But it was accorded few powers and charged with only limited functions. The Bureau's organic act set out its highly circumscribed purpose, which was to collect "such statistics and facts as shall show the condition and progress of education in the several states and territories, and [to diffuse] such information respecting the organization and management of schools and school systems, and methods of teaching, [to] aid the people of the United States in the establishment and maintenance of efficient school systems." The Bureau was statutorily obligated to report to Congress on its investigations and activities.[10] Over time, the Bureau took on new responsibilities, albeit

---

[7] Bensel, *Yankee Leviathan*, 73 n. 115 ("[T]he South at this point opposed every measure that promised to strengthen the federal government except those favoring slavery"). Kosar notes that in this context, "even the effort to create the Smithsonian Institution [which happened eventually in 1846]...required eight years of negotiation among congressmen and executives." Kosar, *National Education Standards*.

[8] See Bensel, *Yankee Leviathan*, 1–4. See, generally, *Shaped by War and Trade: International Influences on American Political Development*, eds. Ira Katznelson and Martin Shefter (Princeton: Princeton University Press, 2002).

[9] Bensel, *Yankee Leviathan*, 69–73; Sanders, *Roots of Reform*, 315–16.

[10] 14 Stat. 434 (2 March 1867), reprinted in Darrell Hevenor Smith, *The Bureau of Education: Its History, Activities and Organizations* (Baltimore: Johns Hopkins University Press, 1923), 2–3, a useful Institute for Government Research monograph, which presents federal legislation concerning education from the Civil War through the 1920s, as well as budgets and narrative descriptions of bureau endeavors. Donald R. Warren's *To Enforce Education: A History of the*

only within a highly limited range. Typical was the issuance of reports on topics of interest to educators and on the education of children living in United States possessions and territories.

Additional initiatives concerning education were proposed by national political actors at about the same time. Most of these either failed completely (as did Massachusetts Representative George F. Hoar's call for a national system of education) or, as a result of opposition, were tightly circumscribed. The 1866 appropriation for the Freedmen's Bureau (created in 1865) earmarked 7 percent of its funds for educational purposes. Efforts by the national government to fund the education of freed blacks in the South, predictably enough, provoked intense Southern opposition. President Ulysses S. Grant fought this opposition and repeatedly called on Congress to ameliorate the problem of illiteracy among the recently freed slaves. To clear the way of constitutional obstacles, Grant asked Congress to draft a Constitutional amendment compelling the states to create adequate systems of public schooling. Subsequently, both during and after Reconstruction, bills were introduced in Congress (in 1872 and 1879) aimed at funding the education of freed blacks via federal land sales. No such bill was ever passed.[11]

The boldest and most politically salient initiatives concerning education at this time trained attention on the role public education, a traditional function of the American states, could play in the nationbuilding task of constructing truly "American" citizens. The chief "problem" in need of reform in this regard was "sectarianism," or the allocation of public monies to religious schools. There were two strands of political criticism of public support for religious education, one a secularist strain that was broad in its criticism of public support for both Protestant and Catholic schools, and another that focused exclusively on the intellectual slavery imposed by Roman Catholic education on students who would otherwise learn to think for themselves. While one of these strains was secularist and the other heavily Protestant in its underlying motivations, both were vehemently anti-Catholic and were closely intertwined with the ambient nativism that played so prominent a role in American politics for much of the late nineteenth and early twentieth centuries.

Founding Years of United States Office of Education (Detroit: Wayne State University Press, 1974) is a useful history, but it concentrates primarily on the 1860s and 1870s. The creation of the bureau was vigorously opposed by constitutional strict constructionists, states' rights advocates, and Southern congressmen (who were sometimes the same people), with many raising concerns involving fears of cultural domination of the South by the North (including that involving racial issues). See Kosar, *National Education Standards*. The objections were defeated under the Civil War Party State, though their influence is evident in the bureau's limited authority.

[11] On the post–Civil War initiatives, see Kosar, *National Education Standards*; Gordon Canfield Lee, *The Struggle for Federal Aid, First Phase: A History of the Attempts to Obtain Federal Aid for the Common Schools, 1870–1890* (New York: Teachers College Press, 1949), 51–3, 72–3, 81–6.

President Grant, who had been an anti-Catholic Know-Nothing before the war, and who, as the head of the victorious Grand Army of the Republic, had become a hero to and symbol of a triumphant and unified nation, was the first American president to devote sustained attention to issues involving public education. His attentions were focused on two issues. First, Grant called for the widespread establishment of public schools across the United States. And second (as he put it in a speech in Des Moines, Iowa, in 1875), he insisted that, as a matter of federal constitutional law, "not one dollar appropriated to [state public schools] shall be supplied to the support of any sectarian school."[12] Taking up Lincoln's project of midwifing a new birth of American freedom, Grant proposed a Constitutional amendment that required states both to provide public schools and to forbid the appropriation of public dollars to sectarian schools.[13]

Grant's ambitious and constitution-altering nationbuilding proposal was soon taken up by Maine Republican Congressman James G. Blaine, who in 1875 introduced what came to be known as the Blaine Amendment in Congress, which would have instituted a national ban on (state) public school funds going to any "religious sect." Blaine's proposal was far from obscure: The congressman was launching a serious bid for the presidency at the time he proposed it. And although he lost that bid to Rutherford B. Hayes, the Republican Party platform went on record in support of the Blaine Amendment, which, although passed by a landslide in the House, narrowly failed to garner the required two-thirds vote in the United States Senate.

This nativist and largely anti-Catholic movement for church and state separation in the schools, of which the Grant and Blaine Amendments were prominent parts, did not die with the narrow defeat of the latter amendment. "Little Blaine Amendments" were passed in many states, and anti-Catholic initiatives aimed at public schools – typically proposed (as by the Ku Klux Klan) on the grounds that Catholic education failed to provide the training in free and critical thought that was essential to a meaningful conception of American citizenship – continued throughout the nineteenth and twentieth centuries.[14]

---

[12] Quoted in Philip Hamburger, *Separation of Church and State* (Cambridge, MA: Harvard University Press, 2002), 322.

[13] It was assumed at the time that the Constitution did not require either of these things. Hamburger demonstrates at length how the notion of a separation of church and state was constructed by a series of secularist, nativist, and anti-Catholic political movements long after the founding and the adoption of the Bill of Rights. Hamburger, *Separation of Church and State*. Grant's proposed amendment also called for the taxation of church property and for making education compulsory by the disenfranchisement of all those who could not read or write. Hamburger, *Separation of Church and State*, 323.

[14] The contemporary Supreme Court's "civil liberties" doctrine concerning the separation of church and state is a direct, if not necessarily self-aware, outgrowth of these movements. See Hamburger, *Separation of Church and State*. Its patterns of analysis and stable of cultural and political fears are also reflected in contemporary civil libertarian and Rawlsian liberal

In the early 1880s, while anti-Catholic sentiments continued, the broader, secularist separationists (including those associated with the National Liberal Party) had fallen into schism and disarray, as various separationist sects splintered over the issue of obscenity.[15] Different problems concerning federal education policy came to eclipse the issue of separationism at that time. These led to renewed calls for federal funding for education.

In the 1880s, partly in response to disturbing census data concerning illiteracy rates and partly in an effort to disperse an accumulating treasury surplus, which proved to be a liability to partisans of the tariff, New Hampshire Senator Henry Blair introduced a series of bills (which were supported by President Rutherford B. Hayes) that would have made federal aid available to public schools.[16] The statebuilding and nationbuilding party of the Civil War era, the Republicans (creators of the U.S. Bureau of Education and the Freedmen's aid bills and leaders in the fight for a separationist public schools amendment) backed the Blair bills.[17] Some Democrats, particularly those from the states of the Confederacy, perhaps feeling less threatened by Northern (central state) power in the wake of the end of Reconstruction in the late 1870s and a movement toward sectional reconciliation – or more needy in the aftermath of the ravages of the war (they were likely to get most of the money) – supported the distribution of federal largesse. Democrats from the border states and the North, however, were perhaps less needy – and more skeptical. They opposed it, with a barrage of arguments invoking both the Constitution and the anticipated expense. The potential racial implications of the bill also proved important. And, indeed, the defeat of the Blair bill marked an important constitutional episode, as it was the era's "most politically promising alternative to federal noninterference" in the lives of freed blacks in the aftermath of Reconstruction.[18]

constitutional and political thought. See, e.g., Stephen Macedo, *Diversity and Distrust: Civic Education in a Multicultural Democracy* (Cambridge, MA: Harvard University Press, 2000).

[15] Hamburger, *Separation of Church and State*, 328–34.

[16] Sanders, *Roots of Reform*, 486 n. 5. In his Inaugural Address, Hayes declared that "at the basis of all prosperity, for [the South] as well as for every other part of the country, lies the improvement of the intellectual and moral condition of the people. Universal suffrage should rest upon universal education. To this end, liberal and permanent provision should be made for the support of free schools by the state governments, and, if need be, supplemented by legitimate aide from national authority." Rutherford B. Hayes, Inaugural Address (5 March 1877), in *Inaugural Addresses of the Presidents of the United States from George Washington 1789 to Richard Milhous Nixon 1969* (Washington, D.C.: United States Government Printing Office, 1969), 137. See also Henry L. Swint, "Rutherford B. Hayes, Educator," *The Mississippi Valley Historical Review* 39 (June 1952): 45–60.

[17] The Republican Party platforms of 1884 and 1888 gave explicit support to federal aid to education. *National Party Platforms, 1840–1972*, eds. Donald Bruce Johnson and Kirk H. Porter (Urbana: University of Illinois Press, 1972), 73, 81.

[18] Daniel W. Crofts, "The Black Response to the Blair Education Bill," *The Journal of Southern History* 37 (February 1971): 41–65, esp. 41, 43. Crofts notes that the Blair bill would have required a strict adherence to equal expenditures in education of both state and federal money

Subsequently, a series of agricultural extension acts aimed at farm constituencies passed between 1887 and 1914 and marked a succession of breakthroughs in the history of central state involvement in education. Farmers, who bore the weight of high taxes on property and sales and yet had little wealth, became staunch advocates of federal aid to education in the late nineteenth and early twentieth centuries. In 1887, at the behest of the Grange, the Farmers Alliance, and other farm groups, Congress passed the Hatch Act, which funded the instruction of farmers in agricultural techniques and was "the first federal education legislation to support a specific curricular subject."[19] This agricultural extension program on the model of the Morrill Act was first funded by federal land sales. Soon, however, the program was given an annual appropriation. In 1890, farm constituencies strongly supported the second Morrill Act, which led to the creation of additional land grant colleges, all of which gave prominence to vocationally oriented agricultural curricula.[20]

The Common Law Order, Child Labor, and Compulsory School Attendance: Early Stirrings of State Construction

To say that America lagged behind Europe in the development of central state capacity concerning education is not to say that Americans lagged behind Europeans in the provision of education. Indeed, owing to both its democratic-egalitarian ethos and its Protestantism (which made much of the ability of each individual to read and make sense of the Bible without

for education under federal supervision. It is interesting to consider how constitutional development culminating in *Brown v. Board of Education* (1954) might have been different had the Blair bill become law. The "aid to education" movement ended in 1890 – at the very moment of the rise of Jim Crow (and, as Philip Hamburger has noted, the beginning of the rise of the notion of an "American" set of nationally guaranteed rights under the Supreme Court's "incorporation" doctrine). The broader constitutional objections were answered with allusions to the precedent of the Morrill Act land grants and the U.S. Bureau of Education appropriation for education in the territories and for Indians, as well as federal disaster aid following the Great Chicago Fire. Others responded that if such aid were considered constitutional, so, too, in due course, would be prohibition, pure food and drug laws, socialized medicine, and minimum-wage and maximum-hours laws. See Allen J. Going, "The South and the Blair Education Bill," *The Mississippi Valley Historical Review* 44 (September 1957): 267–90, 280–4; Sanders, *Roots of Reform*, 316. Hamburger, *Separation of Church and State*, 439–41. Kosar notes that Senator Blair, stung by the repeated defeats of his education aid bills, attributed those losses to the machinations of Jesuits. In years to come, of course, Catholic groups would be among the most skeptical of plans for national systems of education (indeed, they were at times the stated target of such schemes). Kosar, however, suggests that there was no evidence of a Catholic campaign against the federal aid bills of the 1880s. On the federal initiatives of the 1880s, in addition to Kosar, see William A. Mitchell, *Federal Aid for Primary and Secondary Education* (Ph.D. dissertation, Princeton University, 1948), 48–121; Sanders, *Roots of Reform*, 316.

[19] Kosar, *National Education Standards*, 42; Sanders, *Roots of Reform*, 316.
[20] Sanders, *Roots of Reform*, 317.

priestly assistance), mass education actually had significantly deeper roots in America than it had in Europe. What was distinctive about education in America was that it was controlled at the state and local level and, until the twentieth century, was undertaken primarily by nonstate actors.[21]

Compulsory education laws as United States public policy – the requirement that children be educated on pain of legal penalty – is almost exclusively a twentieth-century phenomenon.[22] In the state of courts and parties, the primary legal obligation facing American parents concerning education was set by common law and not by statute. This less-than-menacing common law duty required that parents educate their children in a manner "suitable to their station in life."[23] As one later reform-minded scholar described the dictates of this duty, "so long as the parent did not put the child to death too suddenly, very little interest was manifest about its welfare."[24]

Over the course of the late nineteenth and early twentieth centuries, powerful segments of civil society had often united in opposition to the occasional quixotic attempt to enact state-level compulsory education laws. Both parents and employers, after all, were habituated and committed to putting children to work, and, indeed, at that time the young were pervasively integrated into the country's economic life, assuming productive places beside adults in the home, on the farm, and in the factory. Children pitched in as well in a full array of miscellaneous jobs that were popularly associated with people their age. Young people, in fact, came to define the jobs of shop helpers, newspaper and message delivery boys, and bootblacks. Prior to the institutionalization of compulsory schooling, children formed a vital and broadly accepted part of the nation's workforce.

The compulsory education statutes that did pass seemed to later reformers with a more ambitious and systematic agenda to be "half-hearted measures, emasculated by those who regarded any interference with parental control over children as undemocratic, or jockeyed out of the possibility of effective enforcement by designing men who were profiting by the unrestricted labor of children."[25] Looking back from the early twentieth to the

---

[21] See Alexis de Tocqueville, *Democracy in America* (Harvey C. Mansfield, ed.; Delba Winthrop, trans.), (Chicago: University of Chicago Press, 2000), 652.

[22] The country's first compulsory school attendance law had been passed fifty years earlier, in 1852, in Massachusetts, at the behest of labor activists and social reformers. The Massachusetts statute, however, was an outlier. Moreover, it called for only twelve weeks of part-time school attendance and provided no means of enforcement.

[23] See *Board of Education v. Purse*, 101 Ga. 422, 28 S.E. 896 (Supreme Court of Georgia, 1897). This duty was characterized by Justice McReynolds as a "natural" duty in his opinion in *Meyer v. Nebraska* (1923), one of the most prominent of the U.S. Supreme Court's early pronouncements on education. *Meyer v. Nebraska*, 262 U.S. 390, at 400.

[24] C. C. Liebler, "Court Decisions Affecting the Enforcement of Compulsory Education," *American School Board Journal* 77 (October 1928): 49–50.

[25] Forest Chester Ensign, *Compulsory School Attendance and Child Labor* (Iowa City: Athens Press, 1921), 3.

mid-nineteenth century, these statist reformers found the widely made arguments that compulsory education laws "were undemocratic and out of harmony with American principles of government" to be "strange," the product of the "retarding influences" and of the "selfishness of employers and poverty of parents, unwilling to sacrifice their real or fancied interests to the social good."[26]

The most strident case for the transformative potential of compulsory education laws was initially made by secular, late-century political radicals. Under the influence of Hegel, Marx, and Darwin, Socialist Laurence Gronlund, for example, envisaged a major role for a state-directed education system in serving as midwife to a new and more just social order. Gronlund considered the prevailing discourse in opposition to such laws concerning the liberty of parents (which was asserted in opposition to compulsory attendance laws and, later, in the *Pierce v. Society of Sisters* (1925) case by Justice McReynolds) to be little more than reactionary cant. As he put it in *The Cooperative Commonwealth and Its Outlines* (1884):

To hear some fathers talk of what is commonly called "compulsory" education, one should suppose that a man's children were literally a part of himself. When they are not allowed to be masters over their offspring, to choose what is wrong for their children – and we know that as to education the greater the need the greater is the dislike – they call that an infringement of their "liberty"; they do not value *liberty*, but irresponsible *power*. Children do not belong to their parents; they belong to society.... [T]he education of children is of far more importance to the state than to the parents, since the effects of it will be felt by society, and principally *after* these parents are dead and gone. It is because through it society accomplishes the end of its being, that all education is a public *trust*.[27]

In an intellectual construction that would prove crucial to the path of statebuilding over the course of the twentieth century concerning education (including via Court-formulated mid-twentieth-century constitutional doctrine), Gronlund, a pioneering reform Darwinist and one of the era's most prominent intellectuals, imagined science and religion as fundamentally antagonistic ways of understanding the world.[28] In the project of actualizing

---

[26] Ensign, *Compulsory School Attendance*, 234–5.

[27] Laurence Gronlund, *The Cooperative Commonwealth and Its Outlines* (Boston, 1884), in *American Writings on Popular Education: The Nineteenth Century*, ed. Rush Welter (Indianapolis: Bobbs-Merrill Co., 1971), 346–7. [Emphasis in original]. Gronlund was also the nation's "first expositor of Marx." Hofstadter, *Social Darwinism*, 114–15; Kloppenberg, *Uncertain Victory*, 206.

[28] Prior to the late nineteenth century and the rising influence of Darwinism (on *all* thought, both laissez-faire *and* progressive), both religion and science were understood as forms of reasoned inquiry, with each form of inquiry imagined as broadly compatible with the other. Beginning in the late nineteenth century, however, social actors in the United States (including, influentially, many progressive reformers) increasingly came to imagine the domain of science as uniquely the realm of reason, and religion as the realm of divine revelation or faith.

and incarnating society in a fully developed state, Gronlund placed both secular private and religious schools, including colleges, whether Protestant or
Catholic, alongside other institutions he declared "incompetent to teach,"
such as family and church. Condemning Quaker-affiliated Swarthmore College as a case in point, Gronlund insisted that "the New Order cannot get
along with such one-sided, awry, cramped men and women as necessarily
must issue from such a one-sided school."[29] "The Coming Commonwealth,"
he added, "must radically do away with all and any form of quackery and
amateurship, in educational matters especially. Education is essentially a
scientific labor."[30] How to accomplish this task? Gronlund proposed that
education in the United States be run as a national system, supervised by a
National Board of Administration. This approach, he predicted, would, as it
had in Germany, usher in a new era of intellectual freedom in which religion
would play no role and science would reign supreme.[31]

    While they were in many ways more cautious, early-twentieth-century
progressive reformers shared with Gronlund both the sense that education
was moving along a developmental trajectory and that progress in education,
to the extent that it continued, depended upon the active involvement of
the American central state. Education reformer Forest Ensign divided this
trajectory into three stages: the fumbling beginnings of the middle nineteenth
century; the late-nineteenth-century dawning of new faith in state power;
and the successful start of serious forward movement in the early twentieth,
marked by the national campaigns for the universal schooling of children
and against child labor.[32]

    Political-economic transformations involving industrialization and ur-
banization, which transformed the nature of certain forms of work and
were occasioned by the rise of a powerful labor movement, led an array
of reformers to reimagine the traditional integration of the young into the
mainstream of the country's economic life as a new social problem known as
"child labor." During the years of their peak influence, from the mid to late
1880s, the Knights of Labor, motivated mainly by the prospect of eliminating
the competition that the young provided for well-paying jobs, launched the
first important campaign for broadly conceived restrictions on child labor.
As the power of the Knights waned in the last decade of the nineteenth century, however, the reformist campaign on behalf of child labor laws wilted. A
textile boom in the South during the same decade, though, helped revive the

---

Gronlund's thoughts concerning education clearly reflected these trends. Vestigial remnants
of this nineteenth-century Darwinian today constitute a prominent part of contemporary
Rawlsian liberalism. See John Rawls, *Political Liberalism* (New York: Columbia University
Press, 1993); Macedo, *Diversity and Distrust*.
[29] Gronlund, *Cooperative Commonweath*, 347.
[30] Gronlund, *Cooperative Commonwealth*, 347.
[31] Gronlund, *Cooperative Commonwealth*, 348.
[32] Ensign, *Compulsory School Attendance*, 3, 246.

focus on child labor and revitalize the imagination of child labor as a serious social problem. After all, as many as a quarter of the workers tending the Southern spinning machines in what was suddenly becoming a huge industry were children. In 1904, picking up where the Knights left off, a National Child Labor Committee was set up with the ultimate goal of abolishing child labor in the United States. The National Child Labor Committee drew its support from women's clubs, labor organizations, and the mainstream of both major parties. It conducted investigations and publicized conditions, published reports and a regular bulletin, and both proposed and lobbied for model child labor legislation, which set minimum ages, maximum hours, and health and safety regulations for youth.

The child labor campaign, which had localist roots, had decided to go national not long before, with the introduction in 1906 of the first congressional proposal to regulate child labor. The Supreme Court's decision in *Hoke v. United States* (1913) gave the advocates of national child labor laws further hope for the constitutionality of such laws when it upheld in a Mann Act case the right of Congress to use its commerce power to advance policies directed at public morals.[33] In 1914, the Palmer-Owen bill was passed by Congress, buoyed by the support of all three major parties (the third being the Progressives). Somewhat unexpectedly, however, the Supreme Court, influenced in part by arguments about a coming statist assault upon family life, bit back. The new federal child labor law was struck down in a stunning 5–4 decision.[34] Congress and the advocates of child labor laws then regrouped. Encouraged by a different line of Supreme Court precedent, Congress's next move was to pass a law with similar aims, but this time it grounded its authority in its taxing rather than its commerce powers. Once again, though, the Supreme Court thwarted its efforts.[35] The next step was to propose a National Child Labor Amendment to the Constitution, which passed the Congress pursuant to Article V and was sent out to the states for ratification.[36]

As a way to advance the enforcement of child labor laws, the committee also lobbied aggressively on behalf of the symbiotic passage of compulsory schooling laws. As state after state moved to restrict child labor in the late nineteenth and early twentieth centuries, each moved simultaneously to pass

---

[33] *Hoke v. United States*, 227 U.S. 308 (1913).

[34] *Hammer v. Dagenhart*, 247 U.S. 251 (1918). See Sanders, *Roots of Reform*, 364–5. In 1912, following a vigorous campaign led by reformer Florence Kelley and supported by an alliance of academics, women's groups, and social workers, the first bureaucratic agency devoted to the well-being of children, the Children's Bureau, was created. Its purpose was to collect statistics and other information on the state of the nation's children. Sanders, *Roots of Reform*, 342, 343, 349.

[35] *Bailey v. Drexel Furniture*, 259 U.S. 20 (1922).

[36] David E. Kyvig, *Explicit and Authentic Acts: Amending the Constitution, 1776–1995* (Lawrence: University Press of Kansas, 1996), 255–61.

statutes mandating school attendance.[37] Ensign described this legislative era as one in which "[t]he state began to discover its own power and to be more keenly aware of its responsibility."[38] In 1890, not long after the Knights of Labor had reached its peak of influence, Connecticut passed the nation's first enforced full-time attendance law, which proved to be a harbinger of things to come. Within ten years, more than thirty states and the District of Columbia had followed suit. The South lagged somewhat behind. But even there, a raft of compulsory school attendance laws were passed between 1900 and 1918, with Mississippi bringing up the rear following the First World War.[39]

As this new order took shape, widely read legal treatises and state court judges seconded it without objection. Ernst Freund's influential treatise on the police power, in language that Justice McReynolds later appropriated for his opinion in *Pierce v. Society of Sisters* case, declared in 1904 that "one of the most important of parental rights is that of directing the education of the child." But Freund added, as did McReynolds in the *Pierce* case, that although heretofore the right had been left free and unregulated, it was hardly beyond the scope of the state's police power. Many states, Freund noted, had recently enacted compulsory education laws and, he reported approvingly, their constitutionality had uniformly been sustained.[40]

The first constitutional green light given by judges to compulsory attendance laws had come in the closing years of the nineteenth century.[41] In the

---

[37] Elizabeth Sands Johnson, "Child Labor Legislation," in John R. Commons, *History of Labor Legislation in the United States, 1896–1932* (New York: Macmillan, 1935) (Vol. III, ed. Elizabeth Brandeis), 403–11; Kim Voss, *The Making of American Exceptionalism: The Knights of Labor and Class Formation in the Nineteenth Century* (Ithaca, NY: Cornell University Press, 1993), 113, 115.

[38] Ensign, *Compulsory School Attendance*, 234–5.

[39] Lawrence Kotkin and William F. Aikman, *Legal Foundations of Compulsory School Attendance* (Port Washington, NY: Kennikat Press, 1980), 24–6; Johnson, "Child Labor Legislation," 410–13; Lawrence A. Cremin, *American Education: The National Experience: 1783–1876* (New York: Harper and Row, 1980), 155.

[40] Ernst Freund, *The Police Power: Public Policy and Constitutional Rights* (Chicago: Callaghan and Co., 1904), Sec. 264. Here again, as was the case with privacy rights, we see the way in which the process of rights creation is intimately related to the process of the construction of state power. See Holmes, *Passions and Constraint*: 101–2; Novak, "The Legal Origins of the Modern Administrative State," in *Looking Back on Law's Century*, eds. Garth, Kagan, and Sarat. See also Skowronek, *Building a New American State*, ch. 8, on the way in which rights declarations by courts are often first steps in broader developmental projects – in which courts are only one participant – aimed at arriving at a governing constitutional *modus vivendi*.

[41] *Quigby v. State*, 5 Ohio Cir. Ct. 638 (1891); *Ex Parte Liddell*, 93 Cal. 633, 29 P. 251 (Supreme Court of California, 1892). See also *State v. Bailey*, 157 Ind. 329, 61 N.E. 730 (1901); *State v. Jackson*, 71 N.H. 552 (1902); *Commonwealth v. Edsall*, 13 Pa. D.D. 509 (1903); *State v. McCaffrey*, 69 Vt. 85, 37 A. 234 (1896) (sustaining constitutionality of truancy laws – which were unknown at common law – as a valid exercise of the police power).

years that followed, state courts from time to time filled in gaps in this new regulatory regime, giving, for instance, a constitutional go-ahead to state initiatives to compel attendance beyond grade school and even onward into high school.[42] New York courts held that parents could not sidestep the state's compulsory education requirements by simply refusing to vaccinate their children.[43] And, at least when they had not notified local public school authorities and gotten their approval, state courts announced that home schooling, even by demonstrably capable parents, simply would not suffice.[44]

The court cases involving the country's new compulsory education statutes are instructive; but arising as they did prior to the ascendance of judicial governance in the mid-twentieth century, there simply were not very many of them. Between 1871 and 1925, the courts took up only forty-six challenges to compulsory attendance laws.[45] Common law courts by and large supported the construction of a new regime characterized by state-compelled compulsory education and school attendance laws. Although they were important participants in the constitutional project, however, courts were not its primary engine.

Education in the Statebuilding Era: The Social Construction of Autonomous Intellectual Inquiry and the American State

We are now on our way, but what is our destination?[46]

For many reformers, the passage of compulsory attendance laws in the American states in the late nineteenth and early twentieth centuries signaled not the end of their work but rather the beginning. Even as the campaign for compulsory attendance laws was just beginning, many saw it as an early stage in a developmental trajectory that would ultimately transform the relationship between the child and the state along radically progressive lines. Compulsory education was clearly imagined as the first step in a much broader statebuilding and nationbuilding project. As such, it is properly considered alongside efforts to create a seeing state capable of straddling and managing corporate power and successfully administering industrial and labor relations.

---

[42] *State v. O'Dell*, 187 Ind. 84, 118 N.E. 529 (1918); *Miller v. State*, 77 Ind. App. 611 (1922), respectively.

[43] *People v. Eckerold*, 211 N.Y. 386 (1911); 105 N.E. 670, 160 N.Y. App. Civ. 930; *Shappee v. Curtis*, 142 N.Y. App. Div. 155 (1911). *Contra: State v. Turney*, 12 O.C.C. N.C. 33, 210 C.C. 222 (Ohio); *O'Bannon v. Cole*, 220 Mo. 697, 119 S.W. 424, 22 L.R.A. [N.S] 986 (1909).

[44] *State v. Cournort*, 124 P. 910 (1912). *Contra: State v. Peterman*, 32 Ind. App. 665; 70 N.E. 550 (1904).

[45] John Frederick Bender, *The Functions of Courts in Enforcing School Attendance Laws* (New York: Teachers College, Columbia University, 1927), 10.

[46] William D. Parkinson, "The Limits of Compulsory School Attendance," *Journal of Education* 110 (November 4, 1929): 381.

The heady sense by progressives that they were witnessing the take-off of a developmental trajectory that would revolutionize the role of the state in education has all but disappeared from accounts of statebuilding – and even of progressive politics – in this era. This selective memory has been possible, however, only because, looking backward, we know how things have turned out so far as the creation of centralized, bureaucratic, and hierarchically organized national system of education was concerned.[47] This omission might at first glance be dismissed by citing the commonplace of American federalism that education is a function of state and local governments. But all sorts of similar commonplaces of federalism and of long-respected constitutional limitations were challenged and cast aside in this same era: The regulation of employment agreements and manufacturing, poor relief, and even moral conduct (such as gambling and prostitution) were all once characteristic examples of areas that were consigned by settled constitutional doctrine to states and local communities. Why should education necessarily have been perceived as impervious to these wider constitutional and political trends?[48] The assumption of a failed trajectory of development in the effort to set up a national education system in this era is also obscured by a failure to give courts – the invisible instruments of statebuilding spotlighted by Skowronek – their due as potentially powerful arms of government policy. Through their doctrines concerning church-state separation, in particular, courts actually acted aggressively as instruments of central state policy concerning education, and in the mid- to late twentieth century, came to involve themselves heavily in an extended nationbuilding project of major developmental importance.

---

[47] See, e.g., Skowronek, *Building a New American State*; Weibe, *The Search for Order*, which do not mention education as a part of the era's statebuilding agenda. Some historians not associated with the statebuilding literature, however, have from time to time done better. See Diane Ravitch, *Left Back: A Century of Filed School Reforms* (New York: Basic Books, 2000); Lynn Dumenil, "The Insatiable Maw of Bureaucracy: Antistatism and Education Reform in the 1920s," *Journal of American History* 77 (September 1990): 499–524.

[48] See William H. Kilpatrick et al., *The Educational Frontier* (New York: D. Appleton-Century, Co., Inc., 1933), 108–9 ("It is...with no apology that we propose the putting of the educational function not only prominently, but uppermost, in the work that belongs to every special interest in society. Something of this sense may have been implicit in the development of the universal public school in America, but it has remained implicit.... Will such a place be given to education in our country? Is it conceivable that in such scope it could become a public charge? For the short view the answer is no. But the longer view is not entirely discouraging. If we had told the fathers on the *Mayflower* that we should ever in the new country be carrying on at public charge the education of the army of youth which now considers it the thing to do to attend high school and college and university, he would have been suspected of witchcraft. If the function of the Interstate Commerce Commission had been hinted to the first Continental Congress, the hint would have fallen on deaf ears. And instances could be multiplied to show how matters of a supposedly private concern are not only becoming sensitive to public interest but are being held to public interest at public charge. How far ahead, then, shall we have to look to see society making education its chief concern?").

As the dual federalist order came under siege in the late nineteenth and early twentieth centuries, education seemed to contemporaries to be of a piece with other policy areas. At the state level, governments began vigorously asserting their powers over schooling, in the process diminishing the governing authority of families, churches, and other institutions of civil society. At the federal level, the new state initiatives were praised, but at the same time doubts arose as to whether a state-by-state approach was up to the task of educating a modern nation, a nation that was characterized by a growing – almost European – sense of state and was charged with new and important responsibilities at home and in the wider world.[49] This new nationalism concerning education had affirmative substantive and intellectual goals. Its chief concern was to fashion the new citizen appropriate to the new state.

As far as public policy was concerned, this meant decreasing parental influences on children and augmenting state influences, an agenda that was openly – indeed stridently – advocated by many of the era's key progressive reformers. In 1909, one of the era's leading education progressives, Ellwood Cubberly, a professor at Stanford University and an advocate of social evolution through social engineering (he had studied under the famed evolutionary biologist David Starr Jordan), observed in celebration that "each year the child is coming to belong more to the state and less to the parent."[50] For reform Darwinists such as Cubberley and the radical Lawrence Gronlund before him, the processes of social evolution and growing statism were conjoined. Since the state was the thinking head of the evolving social organism, a growing state, heavily involved in education, signaled and made possible the advance of society in a distinctively progressive direction.[51] Arrayed against

[49] Theda Skocpol has demonstrated how state-level efforts can lay the groundwork for later federal control in key policy areas. Skocpol, *Protecting Soldiers and Mothers.*

[50] Ellwood Cubberley, *Changing Conceptions of Education* (Boston: Houghton Mifflin, 1909), 63, cited in David Tyack and Elizabeth Hansot, *Managers of Virtue: Public School Leadership in America, 1820–1980* (New York: Basic Books, 1982), 103. See also Tyack and Hansot, *Managers of Virtue*, 121–8. Cubberley's writings placed a heavy emphasis on the mission of schools to assimilate immigrants into the nation's culture and its workforce. "Illiterate, docile, lacking in self-reliance and initiative, and not possessing the Anglo-Teutonic conceptions of law, order, and government, their coming has served to dilute tremendously our national stock, and to corrupt our civil life." Cubberley, *Changing Conceptions of Education*, 44. Cubberley was one of the leading proponents of educating immigrants for their fit station in life, that is, of vocational education as against what he pejoratively termed "the knowledge curriculum." See Cubberley, *Public School Administration: A Statement of the Fundamental Principles Underlying the Organization and Administration of Public Education* (Boston: Houghton Mifflin, 1916). Cubberley's *Public School Administration*, Diane Ravitch reports, "was the basic text for school administrators for many years." Ravitch, *Left Back*, 98. On Cubberley, generally, see Ravitch, *Left Back*, 95–9, 102–4, 120, 331.

[51] See Hofstadter, *Social Darwinism*, 80, 83, 84. A religious variant of this same dynamic was evident in the reform efforts of many reformers associated with the "social gospel" movement. See Hamburger, *Separation of Church and State*, 379.

this advance, however, were civil society's traditional institutions such as churches and families.

For much of the nineteenth century, it was more likely than not that the claims of religion, family, and intellectual freedom would all be arrayed on the same side. But beginning in the 1840s, critics of the Catholic religion, and Catholic families in particular, had pioneered the view that some religions and some families were actually fetters on the intellectual development of children, a development that gradually came to be identified with the construction of a new American nation itself.[52] By the statebuilding era of the late nineteenth and early twentieth centuries, the sort of pluralism that sustained the alliance of religion and families with the cause of intellectual freedom – a pluralism that was solicitous of the communal pedagogical claims of groups and localities – was under sustained intellectual siege and was well on its way toward being supplanted in status by a novel scientific pluralism that imported different imperatives into American politics and, from there, into American constitutionalism. Scientific pluralism, which was constructed as the indispensable core of American democratic freedom itself, placed less value on the solidarity and autonomy of the group and more value on disagreement among speakers who were ideally situated *within* a contentious and cosmopolitan community of reasoning scholars. The liberation of these scholars was largely defined by the degree to which they were intellectually detached from the old encumbrances of place, of family, and of religion. In this new intellectual environment, the ties of family and religion were less wellsprings of intellectual freedom than fetters. The dynamics of this transformation ultimately toppled religious liberty from its former place as the emblematic civil libertarian freedom and replaced it with freedom of speech, a commitment more consistent with the new scientific pluralism. In importing these new social visions into constitutional law, policy elites came more and more to view religion and the religious liberty of parents and communities of believers as potential menaces to the counterfreedoms of free speech, free inquiry, and free debate, counterfreedoms that considered together, were now placed at the heart of democratic political life.[53]

Indeed, contemporary understandings of "academic freedom" were forged at this very time in direct opposition to the influence of religion upon intellectual life, as that influence had been exercised in American colleges and

---

[52] See, generally, Hamburger, *Separation of Church and State*. See Clement Fatovic, "Liberty and Anti-Popery: The Anti-Catholic Roots of Liberal and Republican Ideas of Freedom," paper presented at the annual meeting of the Northeast Political Science Association, Philadelphia, November 2001.

[53] See, generally, Purcell, *The Crisis of Democratic Theory.* See also John T. McGreevy, "Thinking on One's Own: Catholicism in the American Intellectual Imagination, 1928–1960," *Journal of American History* 84 (June 1997): 97–131, esp. 100–3; Hollinger, *Science, Jews, and Secular Culture* 1, 14–15, 23; White, "Free Speech and the Bifurcated Review Project: The 'Preferred Position' Cases," in *Constitutionalism and American Culture*, eds. VanBurkleo, et al., 99–122.

universities. The concept of academic freedom was invented only in the late nineteenth and early twentieth centuries as a rallying cry of scientific progressives who believed their inquiries and intellectual experiments were impeded by requirements that they tailor their teachings to the religious missions outlined in college charters and enforced by clerical or religious academic administrators and trustees. Drawing in part on German academic traditions of *lehrfreiheit* (freedom for university professors) and *wissenschaft* (the ideal of the scientific search for truth) that many had imbibed during graduate study abroad, these progressives rechristened academic life as a public trust. In fulfilling that trust, intellectuals had a duty to commit themselves to the cosmopolitan project of the advancement of (scientific) truth and, in turn, to the project of using that truth instrumentally to contribute to the imperative of social progress. Religious control of academic life was imagined as propagandistic and attacked as the primary obstacle to the ascertainment of truth and, hence, the achievement of social progress.[54]

The new concept of academic freedom, which pitted social progress and intellectual liberty against tradition-bound religious allegiances, gained an institutional champion with the founding of the American Association of University Professors (AAUP) in 1915, and with the installation of the nation's leading scientific pragmatist, the antireligious John Dewey, as its first president. (The major impetus for the AAUP's founding was the removal of a popular Jamesian pragmatist professor at Lafayette College by the institution's conservative Presbyterian president.) One of the organization's first acts was to issue a report proclaiming academic freedom to be central to the mission of a university community and reconceptualizing the professorial role from employee to public servant. As public servants, the AAUP contended, professors must not be dismissed for teachings at cross-purposes with the more parochial missions of particular colleges. The cause of their intellectual freedom, moreover, would be best served by the creation of a system of tenure, which permitted removal only with just cause, a requirement guaranteed by an elaborate system of due process. In 1940, the AAUP, this time in conjunction with the American Association of Colleges, issued a new statement enshrining its principles of academic freedom and delineating the norms of intellectual inquiry and liberty that today we understand as a fundamental pillar of the civil libertarian constitutional program.[55]

---

[54] George M. Marsden, *The Soul of the American University: From Protestant Establishment to Established Non-Belief* (New York: Oxford University Press, 1994), 296–7, 301–9. See also David Rabban, *Free Speech in Its Forgotten Years* (Cambridge: Cambridge University Press, 1997), 214.

[55] Marsden, *Soul of the American University*, 311; Walter P. Metzger, "The 1940 Statement of Principals of Academic Freedom and Tenure," *Law and Contemporary Problems* 53 (Summer 1990): 3–77. But see Thomas Bender, *Intellect and Public Life: Essays on the Social History of Academic Intellectuals in the United States* (Baltimore: Johns Hopkins University Press, 1994), 61–2 (contrasting the limited, expertise-oriented professional nature of academic freedom

Walter Lippmann's progressive landmark *Drift and Mastery* (1914) illustrated in paradigmatic form the new progressive oppositions that were ultimately reflected in constitutional thought concerning education, the separation of church and state, and intellectual and academic freedom. While the book is well known for its advocacy of a scientific, pragmatic, and optimistic theory of democratic government, what is less commonly discussed is the foil Lippmann made of religion as a counterpoint to the spirit of scientific progressivism.[56] In Lippmann's estimation, the opposition between religious thinking and democratic scientific thinking is between "the old, the inadequate, the foolish, as against what is sane and clean, but unfamiliar."[57] He added that "[t]here is nothing accidental . . . in the fact that democracy in politics is the twin brother of scientific thinking. They had to come together. As absolutism falls, science arises. It is self-government. For when the impulse which overthrows kings and priests and unquestioned creeds becomes self-conscious we call it science."[58]

In *Drift and Mastery*, Lippmann outlined a conception of pluralism that was to shape progressive and (later) liberal thinking for most of the century, both on and off the Court. In its valorization of individual inquiry, this pluralism was individualistic. But in its focus on the individual's neorepublican participation in a search for the social advancement of the public good, it was simultaneously collectivist. What was potentially troublesome for progressives such as Lippmann were intermediate groups and associations in civil society that depending upon their commitments, could short-circuit either intellectual inquiry or the direction of that inquiry toward collective public life. In the progressive imagining, religious allegiances in schools and elsewhere clearly posed a threat to pluralism on both of these fronts.[59]

In chapters tellingly titled "The Rock of Ages," "Poverty, Chastity, and Obedience," and "Modern Communion," Lippmann specifically scored the religious "who flatly refuse to regard Pluralism as a way of life,"[60] and continued (quoting Nietzsche) to characterize religion as a poison to the human

---

as imagined by the AAUP with the much broader civil libertarian defense of it advanced by the ACLU). For the development of the broader view, see Walker, *In Defense of American Liberties*, 124–6, 189–91, 208–9; Ellen W. Schrecker, *No Ivory Tower: McCarthyism and the Universities* (New York: Oxford University Press, 1986).

[56] In his introduction to a contemporary printing of the book, for example, William Leuchtenburg, a prominent liberal historian of the New Deal and of contemporary "civil liberties," all but ignores the plainly antireligious and anti-Catholic tenor and structure of the book. Walter Lippmann, *Drift and Mastery*, ed. William Leuchtenburg (Madison: University of Wisconsin Press, 1985).

[57] Lippmann, *Drift and Mastery*, 155.

[58] Lippmann, *Drift and Mastery*, 151.

[59] On Lippmann's and Herbert Croly's understandings of the nature and proper purpose of education as an outgrowth of the philosophy of education of John Dewey, see Kloppenberg, *Uncertain Victory*, 375–6.

[60] Lippmann, *Drift and Mastery*, 115.

will.[61] Particularly pernicious was the Catholic Church, "[which is] hostile to democracy and to every force that tend[s] to make people self-sufficient."[62] Given the cresting number of Catholic immigrants during the century's early years, including the Irish Catholics ("brutal, greedy, vulgar"), the menace the Roman Catholic Church posed to progress was particularly strong, for, Lippmann notes, "America is a place where their creeds do not work."[63] What is needed is a movement toward what he calls a new "modern communion" in which science is a sacrament and "modern forms of devotion" in which laboratories inspire stronger loyalties than religions.[64] Facts and science – not faith and obedience – are the only foundations upon which a modern pluralism can be built, a pluralism that will "enable men to share their hopes with strangers, to travel about and talk to people of widely different professions and origin, yet to find the assurance that they are part of a great undertaking."[65]

In this vision of scientific pluralism, religion posed a particular menace to education, the *sine qua non* of intellectual and political progress. The chief task of education in the progressive vision was to equip people to accept and master change. In Lippmann's imagining, however, religion was hopelessly wedded to stagnation. Entrusting education to religious leadership and influence was thus a major hindrance to the advancement of the modern, scientific mind.[66]

War, the Educational Imperative, and the State

It is hard to believe that now this war is over we shall be content with a national school system which is a loose aggregation of atoms.[67]

In the 1920s, the Supreme Court handed down its first important decisions involving schools and education – *Meyer v. Nebraska*, involving a restriction on instruction in foreign languages, and *Pierce v. Society of Sisters*, involving a ban on private and parochial education – decisions that have been constructed in traditional narratives of constitutional development as foundations of later civil libertarian commitments to limiting government

---

[61] Lippmann, *Drift and Mastery*, 116.
[62] Lippmann, *Drift and Mastery*, 115.
[63] Lippmann, *Drift and Mastery*, 116–18.
[64] Lippmann, *Drift and Mastery*, 154–5.
[65] Lippmann, *Drift and Mastery*, 155–7.
[66] Lippmann, *Drift and Mastery*, 93–4. Interestingly enough, however, in arguing on behalf of the precedence of education over political reform in the fight for progress, Lippmann criticized the folly of "turn[ing] from education to politics," of "seeking to win votes rather to make converts." Clearly, Lippmann, in spite of himself, could not help but imagine his own program in specifically religious terms. Steel, *Lippmann*, 42.
[67] C. H. Judd, "A National Education System," *Yale Review* 8 (April 1919): 551–63.

authority and, ultimately, to guaranteeing a "right to privacy."[68] *Meyer* and *Pierce* have, moreover, additionally been constructed as the progenitors of the Court's later decisions involving the persecution of ethnic and religious minorities. As such, these early civil liberties decisions have been positioned as forerunners of the Supreme Court's later decisions involving the civil rights of blacks, the civil liberties of religious minorities like Jehovah's Witnesses, and the separation of church and state. Today, scholarly efforts to place *Meyer* and *Pierce* in historical context typically tie the decisions to outbreaks of ethnic and religious bigotry and persecution in the wake of the First World War.[69] The facts more than justify this contextualization. German immigrants were a prime target of Nebraska's Siman law challenged in the *Meyer* case. Oregon's Catholic schools were the chief target of the compulsory public schools law challenged in *Pierce*, a law that was staunchly advocated by the state chapter of the Ku Klux Klan. It does no injustice to these facts, however, to remind ourselves that a focus on the ethnic and religious bigotry behind these cases also serves a contemporary purpose in the construction of Whiggish narratives of American constitutional development.

A genealogy that emphasizes the Court's landmark education decisions of the 1920s as early manifestations of a burgeoning appreciation for civil liberties and civil rights downplays the scope of their antistatism. In a way that serves as ideological ballast for the new regime, when discussing the antistatist thread of these opinions as "judicial Januses" and calling attention to their author, James Clark McReynolds, one of the Court's staunchest opponents of the New Deal, these accounts focus on their nature as old "economic rights" decisions of a sort the modern Court would jettison come the constitutional revolution of the 1930s. What they underemphasize, however, is the

---

[68] Both decisions are cited by the Supreme Court as controlling precedent in *Griswold v. Connecticut*, the birth control case, and *Roe v. Wade*, the abortion case. And in contemporary constitutional history, much of their meaning seems to derive from the support they provided for those two prototypically liberal decisions. *Griswold v. Connecticut*, 381 U.S. 479 (1965); *Roe v. Wade*, 410 U.S. 113 (1973). See Ross, *Forging New Freedoms*, 196–200; Laurence Tribe, *American Constitutional Law*, 2nd ed. (Mineola, NY: Foundation Press, 1988), 1318–19 (*Meyer* and *Pierce* "have remained durable and fertile sources of constitutional doctrine concerning the nature of liberty, the respective rights of social institutions, and the limits of governmental power to homogenize the beliefs and attitudes of the populace"), cited in Ross, *Forging New Freedoms*, 197–8. That the Fourteenth Amendment guarantees of liberty for parents, teachers, and students set out in *Meyer* and *Pierce* against state action were equally applicable under the Fifth Amendment to actions of the federal government was confirmed in *Farrington v. Tokushige*, 273 U.S. 284 (1927) (overturning Hawaiian territorial law severely restricting instruction in schools primarily conducted in a foreign language; Justice McReynolds for the Court).

[69] See, e.g., David Tyack, "The Perils of Pluralism: The Background of the *Pierce* Case," *American Historical Review* 74 (1968): 74–98; William Ross, "A Judicial Janus: *Meyer v. Nebraska* in Historical Perspective," *Cincinnati Law Review* 57 (1988): 125–204; Ross, *Forging New Freedoms*; Lynn Dumenil, *Modern Temper: American Culture and Society in the 1920s* (New York: Hill and Wang, 1995), 212–14.

degree to which these decisions represented acts of resistance to progressive statebuilding and nationbuilding initiatives aimed at gaining increased national bureaucratic control over the lives of children, families, and schools, in the service of constructing a new "American liberty," a stand that – along with protection for "economic rights" – the Supreme Court would abandon in reaching an accommodation with the New American State and the New Constitutional Nation.[70]

Meyer and *Pierce* must be understood in significant part within the stream of early-twentieth-century progressive statebuilding and nationbuilding initiatives concerning education. These initiatives were strengthened by America's preparations to enter the First World War. The drive to One-Hundred-Percent Americanism that the Court had been praised for fighting in the 1920s was not simply an outbreak of irrational and mass hysterical bigotry and race prejudice. Nor was it, as many suppose today, a project identified primarily with the political right. In its public policy incarnations, One-Hundred-Percent Americanism was an important part of a larger progressive nationbuilding and statebuilding project that involved the fashioning of loyal and patriotic citizens fully invested in a newly emergent progressive state.[71]

The American mobilization for World War I brought out anxieties not just about "enemies" or "foreigners" as racial inferiors, but about enemies and foreigners as threats to state solidity.[72] The mobilization and the retrospective reflection upon the nation's readiness led the country's leaders to question whether the powers of the central state as currently constituted were up to modern responsibilities. Although, as we have seen, many were calling for greater federal involvement in education long before the war, it was only after the armistice that a critical mass of policy intellectuals were shocked into action. The military draft, as they saw it, had unexpectedly trained a spotlight on major social problems that called into question the solidity of the New American State: Federal authorities discovered that a full quarter of the soldiers called up for military service were illiterate; more than one-third

---

70 Ross, "A Judicial Janus" (He applies the term to *Meyer*, probably because that case most clearly highlights ethnicity – but it serves just as well for the others); Ross, *Forging New Freedoms*, 197. See also Kenneth B. O'Brien Jr., "Education, Americanization, and the Supreme Court: The 1920s," *American Quarterly* 13 (1961): 161–71 (noting "a conservative court in a conservative decade seem[ing] to exhibit liberal, perhaps even radical, ideas").

71 See John W. Meyer, Francisco O. Ramirez, and Yasemin Soysal, "World Expansion of Mass Education, 1870–1980," *Sociology of Education* 65 (April 1992): 128–50. Dumenil, "Insatiable Maw of Bureaucracy"; Dumenil, *Modern Temper*, 26–31, 46–7 (emphasizing federal education bills as key – and staunchly resisted – parts of the statebuilding program of the 1920s); Ross, *Forging New Freedoms*, 203.

72 The disjunction was apparent in the politics of the Oregon Klan, which, given its ostensible adherence to racist theories of natural inferiority, seemed remarkably optimistic about the promise of public schooling to wipe out these differences.

were found to be physically unfit for military service.[73] Many draftees could not speak English, which, besides raising doubts about their loyalty and patriotism (as this fact did when combined with a dollop of anti-immigrant bigotry), had the concrete effect of slowing down their military training and hobbling their preparedness for battle. The government, moreover, found the technical skills the soldiers needed to operate modern weaponry were also wanting. Government and educational professionals reacted strongly to these inadequacies. And one of their chief targets was the inadequacy of, and the crisis in, American education. "Education in this country is sick," one commentator wrote in a common complaint voiced in the wake of the war. "It is not merely indisposed, it is sick. It has measles, whooping cough, diphtheria, scarlet fever, small-pox, scrofula, erysipelas – like the man in Jerome's story, everything but housemaid's knee. Perhaps it has that." This postwar sense of crisis, spurred on by a perception that the populace had been ill-trained to meet the imperatives of state, gave a renewed impetus to the fight for greater federal initiatives in education.[74]

The pages of the nation's professional education journals (and other magazines) swelled with calls for national action. Writing in the *Yale Review* in 1919, C. H. Judd contended that the cure for the sickness would come in part from the creation of a national system of education. "[N]ational stress," he declared, "has driven all public institutions to recognize their dependence on the central forces which control the nation." "There is no possibility," he added, "of dissociating education from agriculture or commerce or labor and today we all know it."[75] In *School and Society*, Massachusetts Education Commissioner Payson Smith decried the "parochial or neighborhood conception of responsibility" in education. "To think in terms of larger units, and to widen the boundaries of our responsibility, these are definitely the needs of the hour." He then confessed that he was "unable to think of the children of a community in other terms than as potential assets or liabilities of the state or the nation." In support of a national education policy, Smith drew an analogy to the emergence – and efforts to administer – a national

---

[73] H. S. Magill (field secretary, National Education Association), "Education and the Federal Government," *School and Society* 14 (October 8, 1921): 262; George Drayton Strayer (professor, Teachers College, Columbia University; past-president, National Education Association), "Why the Smith-Towner Bill Should Become a Law," *Educational Review* 60 (November 1920): 273.

[74] Winthrop D. Lane, "The National Crisis in Education," *Survey* 44 (May 29, 1920): 299; Strayer, "Smith-Towner Bill," 275. These concerns, as I discussed previously, proved crucial in winning support for Prohibition. On war as an impetus to statebuilding, see *Shaped by War and Trade*, eds. Katznelson and Shefter.

[75] C. H. Judd, "A National Education System," *Yale Review* 8 (April 1919): 551–63, esp. 558–9. Judd, who became head of the education school at the University of Chicago, by the 1930s became a prominent critic of proposals to use schools as instruments of radical social reform. Ravitch, *Left Back*, 233.

market: "Build a wall," he said, "about your boundaries, check the flow of industry and commerce, and speedily you will discover that you are parts of states, and parts of a nation from whose fortunes – good or bad – you are inseparable."[76] "The child left ignorant in Alabama," declared Horace Eaton, a professor at Syracuse University, "is a drag upon the entire country; his vote at a later day tends to lower the standards of democratic action; and it may be that his neglected mind and body may condition for ill his descendants, who, in turn, may settle in any state in the Union."[77] To give all the power to states where education was concerned and none to the national government was, another observed, less constitutional imperative than "blind imitation."[78] "Is it not time," Eaton asked, "to have done with this half-hearted, bungling method of educating our people?" What was needed, he insisted, was "some sort of national control of education, some sort of national department which, far more important than the present Bureau of Education, shall universalize, standardize, and subsidize our school system."[79]

To the many who were similarly inclined, the war mobilization shed light not only on inadequacies, but also on possibilites. As examples to keep in mind when planning national education initiatives, Payson Smith hopefully cited both the huge sums of money drafted into the service of national goals during the war as well as the federal government's wartime stewardship of transportation and industry.[80] Charles Holley of the U.S. Army Psychological Service similarly noted that "we did so well with our food and fuel control during the war" that nothing seemed to stand in the way of a national system of education.[81] S. P. Capen of the U.S. Bureau of Education reminded his readers of the wartime cooperation of America's private colleges in setting up the Student Army Training Corps. "Five hundred and seventeen colleges," he recalled, "voluntarily surrendered their property and their independent educational purposes, abdicated the control of their

---

[76] P. Smith, "Limitations of State Control in Education," *School and Society* 7 (April 6, 1918): 391, 392.

[77] Horace Eaton, "Education a National Problem," *Educational Review* 58 (June 1919): 22. On the political construction of a national market in part through constitutional conceptions, see Bensel, *Political Economy of American Industrialization*, 289–354. On bureaucratic efforts to administer that market, including the administrative innovations undertaken during World War I, see Skowronek, *Building a New American State*; Ellis Hawley, *The Great War and the Search for a Modern Order: A History of the American People and Their Institutions, 1917–1933* (New York: St. Martin's Press, 1979), 20–7.

[78] J. L. McConaughy, "Have We an Educational Debt to Germany?" *Educational Review* 55 (May 1918): 370.

[79] Eaton, "National Problem," 22–3.

[80] Smith, "Limitations," 392.

[81] Charles Elmer Holley, "A National System of Elementary Education," *Educational Review* 60 (November 1920): 324.

affairs, and strove cheerfully, albeit with certain mental reservations, to carry out the will of the government as represented by the War Department. . . . For seventeen months literally the whole country was at school."[82]

It was not long before talk of crisis and possibility in education led to tangible congressional proposals. As the first postwar decade opened, the *Educational Review* pointed optimistically to a veritable legislative "stampede toward an extension of federal participation in educational affairs," the journal's characterization of the more than seventy bills on the subject before the sixty-sixth Congress.[83] The most significant of these was the Smith-Towner bill, centered around a proposal for a cabinet-level federal Department of Education, which in its various incarnations had become the focus of a major political and constitutional battle.

The passage of the Smith-Lever and Smith-Hughes Acts in 1914 and 1917, respectively, had put many education activists advocating a new statism in American education in an optimistic frame of mind. After the war, these acts, which had appropriated large federal grants for agricultural and vocational education, spurred hopes that the old U.S. Bureau of Education might finally be replaced with a federal agency possessed of modern governmental vim and power. To Forest Ensign, the innovative Smith-Hughes Act signaled the start of a movement toward the national control of schooling. In its wake, he predicted it was "probable that Congress will presently be vested with such power as will enable it to establish minimum educational standards throughout the Union."[84]

---

[82] S. P. Capen, "Colleges in a Nationalized Educational Scheme," *School and Society* 9 (May 24, 1919): 613, 615.

[83] "Educational Bills Before Congress," *Educational Review* 59 (May 1920): 438–40.

[84] 38 Stat. 372 (1914); 39 Stat. 929 (23 February 1917); Ensign, *Compulsory School Attendance*, 249. Supporters of the Smith-Hughes Act expressly traced its lineage to the education initiatives of the Civil War Party State such as the Morrill Act. Sanders, *Roots of Reform*, 315–16. Sanders attributes the Smith-Hughes Act's passage to longstanding agitation by farmers working in alliance with the labor movement, with business and labor professionals being latecomers to the fight. Diane Ravitch, however, emphasizes the Act as a classic triumph for progressive educators to separate the forms of education available to the working classes from those available to the elite. Ravitch, *Left Back*, 121–3, 162, 175, 328. Broadly speaking, the stories are compatible, as each of the allied groups that supported the Act had its own agendas and used the Act's passage, practically and rhetorically, for its own purposes. The clear difference between Sanders and Ravitch is that Sanders sees the Act as a triumph for farmers' interests in education, and Ravitch sees it as a step toward consigning them and their children to second-class status as citizens. Ravitch is right to emphasize that, at least as it played out, the movement for vocational education was a broad movement that affected most of the nation's schools – and was specially applied in urban settings – and was not simply a farmer's issue. Sanders relieves farmers from some of this responsibility by chronology, noting that "after 1910 . . . the vocational education movement began to break up into distinct rural and urban components" and that "the final drafting [of the Smith-Hughes Act] was largely the work of middle-class educators." Sanders, *Roots of Reform*, 320, 325–6, 337–8, 339.

For William Bagley, writing in *The New Republic,* the creation of a cabinet-level Department of Education was a step essential to the construction of a modern administrative state; it would be an "instrument for transforming the public schools into a great educational system worthy of the democracy which has recently saved the world and which now bears upon it a large share of the responsibility for insuring that the world's salvation shall be permanent and abiding."[85] In *The Nation,* John MacCracken played to similar sentiments: "[A] nation which deliberately sought international isolation had little need for a national representative of education," he wrote. "A nation which assumes the role of arbiter of the world's destinies and judge of the world's disputes must give the American school a national representative so that the United States may contribute to the world's education whatever it has of value, and learn from the school experience of other nations all that is to be learned."[86] James Abel of the U.S. Office of Education's Foreign School System's Division added a cross-national analysis to the argument: "The establishment of ministries of education represents" he wrote, "changes in an intolerable state of affairs and attempts to better, through education, the condition of the great mass of the people and to train them in ability to manage their matters of common concern. Very frequently ministries of education came into being immediately after great national or international disasters."[87] "England, Germany, France, have national departments of education," another noted. "Why should education in the greatest democracy of them all be left stranded in one sub-bureau of the Department of the Interior?"[88]

England and France may have elicited some interest from reformers, but the clear comparison and competition was with Germany. Germany, birthplace of the Reformation and of Gutenberg, had been an early leader not only in mass education but also in creating a system of compulsory schooling, which it had instituted as far back as the early seventeenth century. In periods of war-driven statebuilding, Germany also moved early on to make the schooling of children the exclusive province of the state (first under Frederick the Great in the eighteenth century and then under Bismarck in the wake of

---

[85] William C. Bagley, "Education: The National Problem," *New Republic* (December 17, 1919): 92. On Bagley's persistently nationalist outlook, see Ravitch, *Left Back*, 192. Bagley, a prominent professor of education at the University of Illinois and later at Teacher's College, Columbia University, became known as a controversial defender of the value of an academic (as opposed to a vocational) curriculum for the nation's schools. For this alone, Ravitch notes, he acquired "an unenviable and unwarranted reputation as an educational conservative." Ravitch, *Left Back*, 121–3, 234–5, 411. This "conservatism" was shared by W. E. B. DuBois and Kenneth Clark. Ravitch, *Left Back*, 223, 406, 380–2.

[86] John H. MacCracken, "A National Department of Education," *Nation* (March 7, 1918): 256.

[87] James F. Abel, "National Ministries of Education," *School Life* 16 (November 1930): 45–6. Abel was writing in the wake of the defeat of the Towner-Sterling bill.

[88] "A Federal Department of Education," *School Review* 26 (April 1918): 296.

Prussia's decisive victory in the Franco-Prussian War, a triumph that many American reformers of this era personally remembered).[89] Jonathan Bourne Jr., a Republican Party functionary, insisted that as far as education was concerned, it was time to have the United States – and not Germany – set the world standard.[90] At the university level, the impressiveness of the German accomplishment was a nagging reproach to America's best minds and to her finest institutions. It was Germany and her state that had invented the Ph.D. program and the research university, which American scholars and educators increasingly admired and which they contrasted with exasperation to the plethora of pious church schools that defined the landscape of higher education at home. Aspiring upward to a German education, many leading American academics came to believe that the only way to learn well was to train abroad. And Ph.D.s from Heidelberg, Freiberg, and Berlin became common on American college faculties of the era. Many Americans hoped for a large dose of Prussian progress in education at home, though some were careful to express reservations about the dark side of German education, with its statist authoritarian and militaristic tendencies.[91]

A characteristic soup of progressive professional and political groups took up the banner of the new nationalism in education. These included government bureaucrats in state and federal education agencies, potential client groups such as the National Education Association and the American Federation of Teachers, women's associations such as the National Congress of Mothers and Parent Teacher Associations, the National League of Women Voters, the National Society of the Daughters of the American Revolution, the Democratic and Republican National Committees of Women, and the American Federation of Labor.[92] The arguments used by these groups to support their cause tracked three characteristic facets of progressive thought: its emphasis on efficiency and expertise; its substantive commitment to broadly ambitious social projects such as the elimination of poverty, disease, and economic inequality; and its moralizing and assimilationist ambitions rooted in an evangelizing Protestantism, whether in its religious or its secular form.

---

[89] See Gabriele Weigand, "The Growth of Compulsory Education in Germany: Some Lessons of History," in J. A. Mangon, *A Significant Social Revolution: Cross-Cultural Aspects of the Evolution of Compulsory Education* (Portland, OR: Woburn Press, 1994), 89–107.

[90] "National Department of Education," *School and Society* 7 (April 6, 1918): 405–6.

[91] See, e.g., J. L. McConaughy, "Have We an Educational Debt to Germany?" *Educational Review* 55 (May 1918): 361–76; Charles Riborg Mann, "The National Organization of Education," *Educational Review* 60 (November 1920): 308–14. See also Ravitch, *Left Back*, 46, 93, 95.

[92] Magill, "Education and the Federal Government," *School and Society* 14 (October 8, 1921): 259; Strayer, "Why the Smith-Towner Bill Should Become Law," *Educational Review* 60 (November 1920): 283.

One promise of a federal department of education that appealed to the progressive attachment to efficiency is that such a department would gather under a single roof in Washington a smattering of education-related programs that at the time were then spread out not only within the Interior Department but also across the government in the Departments of Justice, Treasury, Agriculture, and War, to name only a few. This scattershot organization, reformers argued, bred insalubrious competition between departments, confusion, and a profligate duplication of governing effort.[93] A due regard for efficiency also counseled that research projects currently being undertaken individually by state departments of education, teachers colleges, and university-affiliated schools of education should be coordinated at the national level.[94] Some envisaged a federal department of education as a "cosmic" fact gatherer, which could both set common educational goals and standards and disseminate useful information and the results of a research program targeting those goals to educational professionals, communities, and schools across the country. And, it was presumed, the bigger the fact-gathering apparatus, the more bountiful would be the results.[95] As befit a progressive project, this fact-gathering and research effort would, of course, be run by a team of apolitical policy experts.[96] The money and coordination that came with this project would constitute the backbone of a major national initiative concerning education. And newly massed expertise would constitute its brains. Together, backbone and brains would unite to form a living, thinking body of state that, at long last, had a fighting chance of survival. Progressives expected that through bringing to life a new instrument of state they could now work to advance an array of affirmative and substantive progressive goals such as the mitigation of inequalities in education expenditures between urban and rural areas and between different regions of the country (the South being pegged as especially backward) and the reduction of poverty, squalor, and disease through effective schooling.[97]

[93] See, e.g., S. P. Capen [U.S. Bureau of Education], "Colleges in a Nationalized Educational Scheme," *School and Society* 9 (May 24, 1919): 615.

[94] See, e.g., M. Fairchild, "Federal Education Building," *School and Society* 19 (April 12, 1924): 440–2.

[95] P. Smith, "Limitations of State Control in Education," *School and Society* 7 (April 6, 1918): 391; S. P. Capen, "Do We Need a National System of Public Schools?" *Educational Review* 66 (June 1923): 2–3; Strayer, "Why the Smith-Towner Bill Should Become a Law," 272; Leonard P. Ayres [director, department of education, Russell Sage Foundation], "Education and States Rights," *Survey* 25 (February 4, 1911): 725–7.

[96] H. A. Hollister, "Why and How Should We Federalize Education?" *School and Society* 10 (November 22, 1919): 591–4; Ravitch, *Left Back*, 88–129.

[97] Holley, "National System," 321; "The Federal Interest in Education," *School and Society* 7 (April 20, 1918): 472–3 ; Eaton, "National Problem," 21–30; Strayer, "Smith-Towner"; P. P. Claxton [U.S. Commissioner of Education], "Further Reasons for Federal Aid to Elementary Education," *Child Labor Bulletin* 6 (May 1917): 66–71.

Progressives pushing for a national department of education also touted its promise as a nationbuilding institution that would cement national loyalty and help forge a firm American identity, as Germany's statist school system had famously succeeded in doing under Frederick the Great. In a speech advocating a strong federal department of education in 1910, the president of the University of Illinois told the Minnesota Teachers Association that such a department was needed in part because national unity was being "undermined by foreign currents of thought and feeling." Only a cabinet-level education agency, he concluded, would be strong enough to effectively struggle against these swelling undertows.[98] Similarly, in 1920, the Army's Charles Holley pegged the direction of federal dollars toward education as a crucial means of "prevent[ing] the propagation of foreign culture at the expense of American ideals." In this regard, and with a vaguely ominous nod to issues raised later in the *Meyer* and *Pierce* cases, Holley attempted to reassure those who might be concerned by these centralizing tendencies that a national system of education "should do nothing to handicap local initiative so long as that initiative is directed along progressive lines. It would be only when a community is unwilling to guide its school along the right channels, or does not foster public education, that the hand of the federal government should make itself felt." Individual states might be hard-pressed in the monumental task of Americanizing their charges, but, Holley added hopefully, "it can be cared for easily by federal action without any passion or hard feeling being engendered among those who must become active Americans instead of aliens."[99] After all, said another advocate of a federal education department, "the presence of an electorate speaking a foreign tongue only and more or less ignorant of American institutions [is] a menace to all."[100] In teaching English and inculcating a core of American values (including an appreciation of an "American" understanding of liberty), "[a] centrally subsidized system of schools would be ever ready to meet the emergency by spreading desirable national propaganda.... The central national authority could convert the teachers and the teachers would then reach the people."[101]

For some, clearing the channels for the spread of useful propaganda involved the removal of the barriers to progressive thinking interposed by private and parochial schools. To the Pennsylvania Superintendent of Schools T. E. Finegan, the Sterling-Towner bill proposing a federal department of education was the latest chapter in the grand trajectory of American educational history. "In the early days of our national life," he wrote, "church

---

[98] Edmund J. James, "Education a National Function," *Science* 32 (December 2, 1910): 804.
[99] Holley, "National System," 316–18.
[100] A. J. McKelway [National Child Labor Committee], "The Next Federal Campaign," *Child Labor Bulletin* 6 (Fall 1918): 214.
[101] Holley, "National System," 320.

schools and charity schools prevailed to a large extent. It required a heroic struggle extending over a period of more than half a century to eliminate these influences and establish schools upon a constitutional mandate based upon the inherent right of the child."[102] Along the same lines, progressive social scientist Edward A. Ross explained that only after religion had been removed as an obstacle and society properly modernized through secularization could a secular, centralized, statist, national system of education be built, a system that was prepared to lead the country to a brighter, more progressive future.[103]

Given this reading of history and the progressive construction of the path of progress, it is hardly surprising that Catholics (with their extensive system of parochial education) and leaders in American private education were among the most vocal opponents of Sterling-Towner and of the push for greater control of education by the American central state. And indeed, when it came to education policy at this time, statist progressives, nativist anti-Catholics, and the Ku Klux Klan were political allies. Father James H. Ryan, a professor at Catholic University and one of the era's most prominent public intellectuals, expressed the plausible view that "[a]n unbiased examination of the trend toward federalized education cannot but convince the student that in tendency, at least, the movement is socialistic, if pursued along certain lines, and autocratic and tyrannical if it should develop along other lines."[104] And case-in-point number one for Ryan was the passage of the Oregon compulsory schools law. "Fortunately," wrote Ryan prior to the Supreme Court's decision in *Pierce*, "the judges of our [lower] Federal courts declared the compulsory public school attendance measure unconstitutional – a decision that settles for all time the question to whom the child belongs. He is not a 'national child,' neither has the Federal government nor any individual state the right, under the Constitution, to nationalize the school to such an extent that all private initiative in education must be done away with."[105] Nicholas Murray Butler, the high-profile president of Columbia University and antistatist conservative, seconded Ryan's assessment of the Oregon schools case, wondering "what the future historian will say of the people of the state of Oregon who, 130 years after the adoption of the Constitution, with its Bill of Rights, enact by popular vote a statute which makes education a government monopoly."[106]

---

[102] T. E. Finegan, "State Program in Education and Its Bearing upon the National Program," *School and Society* 14 (August 6, 1921): 62.

[103] Edward A. Ross, *Social Control: A Survey of the Foundations of Order* (New York: Macmillan, 1916), 174–9; Ravitch, *Left Back*, 80.

[104] James H. Ryan, "Dangers of Federalized Education," *Current History* 20 (September 1924): 927 (reprinted from the *New York Times Magazine*).

[105] Ryan, "Dangers of Federalized Education," 930.

[106] Ryan, "Dangers of Federalized Education."

In the same spirit, Butler and other leading private educators warned against the creation of a new education bureaucracy in Washington, calling it a threat both to community control of education and, in turn, to free thought itself. Butler warned that "once more to tap the federal treasury under the guise of aiding the state, and once more to establish an army of bureaucrats in Washington and another army of inspectors roaming at large through the land, will not only fail to accomplish any permanent improvement in the education of our people but will assist in effecting so great a revolution in our form of government as to endanger one day its perpetuity."[107] Political scientist Frank Goodnow, the president of Johns Hopkins University, called the Sterling-Towner bill "a most dangerous usurpation of power in Washington that will undermine the rights of the people."[108] And while visiting Berlin, but with eyes trained toward home, Yale University President Arthur Hadley noted that with a centralized, state-run education system in Germany, "the politicians had become able to throttle free-thought." Hadley characterized the Towner-Sterling bill as "a long step in the Prussianizing of American education."[109]

In opposition to what they saw as a visionary scheme, many appealed to a longstanding and, to them, effective constitutional order that plainly made education a state and local matter. Under the traditional order, "[t]here has been much local experimentation to meet every type of aspiration and need, but somehow . . . there has developed essential national unity, and even uniformity. Yet the child has been the product of its hometown, and the school has been the work and pride of the community itself rather than of any remote bureaucratic central ministry."[110]

Those opposed to the central state control of education took seriously the frank claim of its supporters that such a system would be an effective conduit for propaganda, and they opposed it on those very grounds. The opponents made the Madisonian argument that a decentralized system of education was a constitutional insurance policy against "propagandists of a social, economic, or political cult."[111] To buttress his argument, one opponent of the proposed education department cited the National Advisory Committee on Education, which had concluded that under the traditional

---

[107] Ryan, "Dangers of Federalized Education."

[108] Arthur Hadley, "A Bill to Europeanize Our Public Schools," *Boston Evening Transcript*, July 7, 1922, reprinted in "Documents on the Towner-Sterling Bill," *School and Society* 16 (July 29, 1922): 138.

[109] Hadley, "Bill to Europeanize." As was likely well known by these educators, John Stuart Mill had made a similar argument that state monopolies on education were threats to the liberty of thought. John Stuart Mill, "On Liberty," in Mill, *Three Essays* (New York: Oxford University Press, 1975), 130.

[110] A. W. Atwood, "How Far Should Government Go?" *Saturday Evening Post* (April 18, 1931): 25.

[111] Atwood, "How Far?" 88.

constitutional order:

[o]ne or two states may for a time be the victims of propaganda on a single subject of instruction, but not all states on all subjects. A few misguided local communities may distort their schools with propaganda on a number of subjects. But the state law often, and the examples of other states and communities always, checks this tendency. A class or party may capture a central government by revolution or by some exigency of politics; it cannot as readily capture forty-eight states, or the 120,000 local school communities which really determine American educational policy and procedure.[112]

The danger, as assessed by many, was not so much that the Sterling-Towner proposal, with its generous subsidies, started out this way, but instead that a national system of propaganda and control would be its inevitable result. With federal largesse, it was argued, came a natural federal disposition to control.[113] Added to these concerns was the suspicion that disinterested expertise was less likely to guide the disposition of federal funds than political allegiances. And some of these allegiances were particularly troubling to Southerners, who feared that federal involvement in education would introduce a destabilizing element into race relations.[114]

Advocates of a federal department of education countered this tide of alarm by citing the specifics of the legislative proposals themselves. They did not set up a national system of education, dictated by Washington bureaucrats, but merely conducted research and gathered facts. Boosting aid to education only boosted the power of states and local communities to do as they saw fit. It did not in any way alter the current constitutional order. Prescribing minimal standards – if it came to that – some argued, was not at all objectionable constitutionally and did not interfere with local autonomy, properly understood, which involved a liberty to do what was right in the public interest and not what was wrong and contrary to it.[115]

---

[112] Atwood, "How Far?" 88. See also "Federal Control of Education," *National Republic* 19 (January 1932): 12. This argument echoed the argument made by Madison in Federalist No. 10. Alexander Hamilton, James Madison, and John Jay, *The Federalist Papers*, ed. Clinton Rossiter (New York: Mentor, 1961), 52.

[113] Atwood, "How Far?," 40; Ryan, "Dangers," 926; "Federal Control of Education," *National Republic*, 12.

[114] Atwood, "How Far?" 40; Holley, "National System," 315, 322 (arguing the South would benefit most from the system and reassuring Southerners that under it blacks and whites need not be treated alike); John Dewey, "Federal Aid to Elementary Education," *Child Labor Bulletin* 6 (May 1917): 64–5 (touting aid as of particular benefit to the Northern urban immigrant and the Southern Negro). See also Sanders, *Roots of Reform*, 334–5.

[115] P. P. Claxton, "Further Reasons," 69; Strayer, "Smith-Towner Bill," 282–3; S. P. Capen, "National System," 1; M. G. Clark, "A Nationalized System of Education," *Elementary School Journal* 24 (September 1923): 28–37. An important related development taking place at about the same time outside education, but that linked state and home to an unprecedented degree, was the passage of the Sheppard-Towner Act, 42 Stat. 224 (1921). This Act, which was pushed by – and later implemented by – the Children's Bureau, provided federal

The Child as Creature of the State

By the early twentieth century, the governments in America were assuming unprecedented new authority over schools and the lives of children. At the behest of labor unions and humanitarian reformers, child labor and compulsory schooling laws were being widely championed and passed, and children were being moved off the streetcorners and out of the factories and fields and into public school classrooms at dramatic rates. The rise in mass public schooling put American children to an unprecedented extent under the moral and intellectual sway of public functionaries who, in the process, served as rivals of, and even substitutes for, the authority of clergy and of parents.

These radical alterations in state-society relations sent shock waves through the American psyche, especially through the psyche of American families. Progressives looked favorably upon these developments because they had long regarded the traditional family as a retarding influence on the political maturation of the American people. In the progressive vision, families were prototypically private institutions, with all the debilities they had associated with such institutions, which they took to run against the grain of the new age: They were hierarchical, self-absorbed, and shut-in upon themselves. As such, they encouraged individualism and showed preciously little public-spiritedness. The political development of men and women "who can take an interest in collective property, who can feel personally and vividly about it" would come in large part from getting children out of the parent trap and into the public sphere, the sandlot, and the public school.[116] Along these lines, Walter Lippmann had argued, there were "too few toys that are owned in common, too few group nurseries." "The boy who can talk about 'us fellers,'" he asserted, "has a better start on the modern world than the little girl of the same age who is imitating her mother's housekeeping. From the gang to the athletic team, class spirit, school spirit...they do mean loyalty to something larger than the petty details of the moment."[117]

The passage of compulsory education laws was considered an important step in separating school from home with the aim of modernizing the country by stimulating the intellectual, social, and political development of the

---

grants to the states to promote the health and welfare of mothers and children. The program was terminated in 1929. See Skocpol, *Protecting Soldiers and Mothers*, 494–522.

[116] Lippmann, *Drift and Mastery*, 130.

[117] Lippmann, *Drift and Mastery*, 131. Similarly, Lippmann argued that progress involved weaning women from their traditional position within the bosom of the American family. It was essential that women move beyond the home so they could link up with larger social networks within the public sphere, both by taking up careers and having formerly household tasks such as baking and washing done cooperatively (that is, in the consumer marketplace). And "[i]f they are not satisfied with the kind of work that is done for the home but outside of it," the progressive intellectual argued, "they will have to learn that difficult business of democracy which consists in expressing and enforcing their desire upon industry."

American child. By the 1920s, the changes wrought by the new educational order were pronounced enough to strike sociologists Robert and Helen Merrell Lynd, who charted them in colorful fashion in their study of life in "Middletown" (Muncie, Indiana). In their description of Middletown's "School Life," they cite as a period piece a school board directive from fifty years earlier, declaring:

> Pupils shall not be permitted to remain on the school grounds after dismissal. The teachers shall often remind the pupils that the first duty when dismissed is to proceed quietly and directly home to render all needed assistance to their parents.[118]

In new and different times, such a directive could only seem quaint. By the 1920s, home in Middletown had become akin to a filling station in children's lives. It was no longer the center of their existence but rather a base where they slept and ate, fueling up each night for crowded days in which traditional academic courses were supplemented by new ones in civics and life skills and by a delectable array of extracurricular options, including sports, clubs, and dances.

The new school life in Middletown left many parents feeling that their children were beginning to inhabit a separate world, a world alien to their own experience. In the minds of many, what was worse was that the children seemed to have been tutored at school in a sort of smugness. Their lively experiences there had prompted many to believe that the world of school life was not just different but actually superior to the world they returned to each night. Middletown mothers, for example, complained to the Lynds that after taking home economics classes, their children increasingly mocked their rule-of-thumb homemaking practices as "old-fashioned."[119] After the passage of a compulsory kindergarten law in 1924, one exasperated father complained to the Lynds that "even my youngster in kindergarten is telling us where to get off.... He won't eat white bread because he says they tell him at kindergarten that brown is more healthful."[120]

The compulsory schooling and truancy laws that provided the institutional underpinning for these social trends may have been state laws, but the push to pass them was plainly national. So, too, were the organizations that cheered on school life. New associations of teachers and administrators – such as the National Education Association – now knitted together a network of far-flung and formerly isolated actors who ran schools all across the country.

---

[118] Robert and Helen Merrell Lynd, *Middletown: A Study in Contemporary American Culture* (New York: Harcourt Brace, 1929), 211.

[119] Lynd and Lynd, *Middletown*, 133.

[120] Lynd and Lynd, *Middletown*, 133. For a discussion of how part of the function of new, progressive theories of education was to "reach back into the homes," see Kilpatrick, *Educational Frontier*, 181–2, 193, 250–1.

The Great Schools Cases of the 1920s: Meyer, Pierce, and Scopes

In the 1920s, the Supreme Court and other prominent courts made their first high-profile forays into the most culturally contentious issues of education policy, an involvement that would only increase in intensity in the mid-twentieth century. The Supreme Court's 1920s education decisions are often understood as "judicial Januses." But that characterization itself perhaps places too much emphasis on their forward-looking character as concerned with a "right to privacy" and a solicitude for ethnic minority groups. There is little doubt that, speaking abstractly, these were genuine concerns. But given the context of a cresting call by progressives for a new statism in education, they were virulently antistatist. As such, the later Supreme Court decisions invoking their authority are operating in a world in which the new Court had decidedly repudiated their premises.

The first of the troika great school cases of the 1920s was *Meyer v. Nebraska* (1923), a case involving a constitutional challenge to the state's 1919 Siman law, one of the wave of language laws passed by twenty-one states in the century's early years, most in the wake of the armistice that ended the First World War.[121] The Siman law specifically provided that "[n]o person...shall, in any public, private, denominational, parochial or public school, teach any subject to any person [who has not passed the eighth grade] in any language other than the English language." However severe this law may seem, it was actually passed as a compromise, second-best measure only after the Nebraska legislature came one vote shy of passing a bill that would have totally outlawed all private education in the state.

That draconian prospect was plainly in the Court's mind when it made its decision in *Meyer*. The legislative history of the Siman law was part of the legal record in that case, as was breaking news from the state of Oregon, imported into the dispute in *Meyer* both in oral argument and in an *amicus curiae* brief (not to mention by widespread press accounts). There, in November of 1922, eight months prior to the issuance of the *Meyer* decision, the voters, with the combined support of nativists, the Masons, the Klan, progressives, and newly enfranchised women (squaring off against opposition from the business community and Catholics) had passed a referendum mandating that all children between the ages of eight and sixteen attend public schools.[122]

---

[121] Ross, "Judicial Janus," 133. An earlier wave of such laws was passed in the 1890s in response to pleas by reformist educators eager to homogenize and assimilate an earlier cohort of the children of immigrants. Paul Kleppner, *The Third Electoral System, 1853–1892: Parties, Voters, and Political Cultures* (Chapel Hill: University of North Carolina Press, 1979), 352–3.

[122] Trial Record, *Meyer v. Nebraska*: *Amicus* Brief of William D. Guthrie, 3; Oral Argument of Arthur Mullen. A contemporaneous commentator on the *Meyer* case speculated that the Supreme Court most likely had its eye on the schools dispute in Oregon in reaching its decision. Carl Zollman, "The Fourteenth Amendment and the Part Time Religious Day Schools," *Marquette Law Review* 10 (December 1926): 94–5; See also William G. Hale,

This Oregon law effectively outlawed all private and parochial elementary schools in the state.[123]

It was not long before the Supreme Court, after its warning shot in *Meyer*, was able to pass judgment on the constitutionality of the Oregon law itself. In his opinion for the Court in *Pierce v. Society of Sisters* (1925), Justice McReynolds, referencing the precedent of two years prior, declared:

> Under the doctrine of *Meyer v. Nebraska*, we think it entirely plain that the Act of 1922 unreasonably interferes with the liberty of parents and guardians to direct the upbringing and education of children under their control.... [R]ights guaranteed by the Constitution may not be abridged by legislation which has no reasonable relation to some purpose within the competency of the state. The fundamental theory of liberty upon which all governments in this Union repose excludes any general power of the state to standardize its children by forcing them to accept instruction from public teachers only. The child is not the mere creature of the state.[124]

Justice McReynolds reiterated the same point two years later in the Fifth Amendment case, *Farrington v. Tokushige* (1927), invalidating the Hawaii territorial government's efforts to extensively regulate education in private foreign language schools.[125]

While *Meyer*, *Pierce*, and *Farrington* are significant, the *Pierce* case is clearly the constitutional linchpin of the great Supreme Court education decisions

---

"Educational Regulations and the Constitution: *Meyer v. Nebraska*," *Oregon Law Review* 3 (December 1923): 71–4 (noting applicability of the *Meyer* decision to the recently passed Oregon law).

[123] Hamburger, *Separation of Church and State*, 412–18; Ross, *Forging New Freedoms*, 148–73.

[124] *Pierce*, 268 U.S. at 534–5.

[125] These schools offered language instruction to children (mostly in Japanese but also, in some cases, in Chinese and Korean) as supplements to the children's regular course of study in the territory's public and private schools. An act of the territorial legislature set up not only an elaborate permit and certification scheme for the foreign language schools, but also reached deeply into the day-to-day conduct of their classrooms, prescribing legal limitations on the number of hours of foreign language instruction that were permitted and stipulating acceptable hours during which that instruction could be offered. The legislature also set up a bureaucratic mechanism for monitoring these schools and policing the content of the teaching provided. Hawaii assumed monopoly control over the selection and supply of textbooks. Its territorial government instituted an ascending scale of minimum ages before which instruction in a foreign language was deemed to be criminal. Teachers in Hawaii's foreign language schools were forced to sign a pledge to the government that they would to the best of their ability "direct the minds and studies of pupils in such schools as will tend to make them good and loyal American citizens, and will not permit such students to receive instructions in any way inconsistent therewith." *Farrington*, 273 U.S. 284, 293–4 (1927).

In holding this regulatory scheme unconstitutional, Justice McReynolds cited the *Pierce* case and defended the right of children to receive "instruction deemed valuable by their parents and which is not obviously in conflict with any public interest." He condemned the "deliberate plan to bring foreign language schools under a strict governmental control for which the record," he concluded, "discloses no adequate reason." *Farrington*, 273 U.S. at 298.

of the 1920s. The Court in *Meyer*, aware as it was of both the passage of the Oregon law and the near passage of such a law in Nebraska – anticipating *Pierce*'s arrival on its docket and the ruling in *Farrington*, which used *Pierce* and not the seemingly more relevant language law decision in *Meyer* as its anchoring precedent – was sustained by its memory. That all roads in these decisions lead to *Pierce* suggests the extent to which the Court at this time was concerned with the civil libertarian implications of encroaching statism itself, a focus of the Court's "conservative" jurisprudence that would soon come into conflict with the expansionist statist claims of the New Deal. The antistatist core of these school opinions is only underscored by the strong indignation against these laws expressed by Justice McReynolds, a man known not to have any particular empathy for the ethnic or religious minorities who were these laws' targets.

Within our constitutional order, the conservative court recognized that the government, whether state or federal, was simply not granted the power to standardize its children, prying them away from the influences of churches and parents and seizing possession of their minds. It was not, of course, that such an approach was unheard of. Justice McReynolds explicitly recognized that such standardization had in the past "been deliberately approved by men of great genius." Instead, the problem was that it ran counter to the bedrock commitments of American constitutionalism, that its "ideas touching the relation between individual and state were wholly different from those upon which our institutions rest." Views of education of the sort found in Plato's *Republic* and in Sparta, which the Court saw in embryonic form in the legislation challenged in the *Meyer* and *Pierce* cases, "did violence to both the letter and the spirit of the Constitution."[126]

Under the traditional Constitution, the Court's way of protecting liberties in education and of guarding against the standardization of the minds of students was to aggressively defend the rights of individuals and religious groups to freely associate and to use their property as they wished, subject to only minimal police power regulation. It was to allow individuals and groups to set up their own schools, within which they could teach what they wanted. The old Court, in short, sought to ensure fundamental guarantees of liberty by granting a wide latitude to existing nonstate institutions within civil society, a latitude that included showing a healthy deference for the often hierarchical and exclusionary authority structures within these institutions, even when their beliefs and assumptions ran counter to the prevailing public philosophy.[127]

---

[126] *Pierce*, 268 U.S. at 628.

[127] Recently, as the agenda of the post-1954 Rights Revolution has exhausted itself and communitarianism and multiculturalism became more influential, a civil libertarian vision more consistent with the traditional Constitution, though still a minority position, garnered renewed support, by some and in some areas. See, e.g., Nancy L. Rosenblum, *Membership*

This vision of constitutional freedom concerning schools, which relied heavily on the protection of associational and property rights, represented a rather fragile constitutional *modus vivendi*, which depended for its plausibility on a number of doctrinal commitments in other tenuously related areas of constitutional law. First, it was dependent on a hands-off, accommodationist approach to church-state relations, of the sort illustrated by the Court's early-twentieth-century establishment clause decisions.[128] And, second, it was tied to a limiting interpretation of the Fourteenth Amendment's "state action doctrine," under which the local officials who ran locally controlled schools were not understood to be stand-ins for "the state" when they were making relatively minor, often spur-of-the-moment local decisions. Once every word and whim of teachers, aides, and custodians were understood by lawyers and judges to amount to declarations of "state" policy with all the weight of statutory pronouncements, the conduct of the staff of local schools would become newly porous to governance by the federal judiciary. In sum, when the notion that any involvement of "the state" with matters of religion was combined with an expansive conception of just what constituted "the state," federal judges were handed charter authority to begin to govern American schools. In the guise of limiting the state, the federal judiciary, a powerful instrument of state policy in its own right, thus assumed unprecedented regulatory power over the nation's public schools. Through a

---

and Morals: The Personal Uses of Pluralism in America (Princeton: Princeton University Press, 1998); John T. McGreevy, *Parish Boundaries: The Catholic Encounter with Race in the Twentieth Century Urban North* (Chicago: University of Chicago Press, 1996); Will Kymlicka, *Multicultural Citizenship: A Liberal Theory of Minority Rights* (Oxford: Clarendon Press, 1995); William A. Galston, *Liberal Pluralism: The Implications of Value Pluralism for Political Theory and Practice* (New York: Cambridge University Press, 2002). See also Alan Ehrenhalt, *The Lost City: Discovering the Forgotten Virtues of Community in the Chicago of the 1950s* (New York: Basic Books, 1995). The statist approach, however, continues to prevail in the Rawlsian circles that, until recently, at least, has held the greatest sway within the interpretative community of judges and law professors. See, e.g., Macedo, *Diversity and Distrust.*

[128] See *Quick Bear v. Leupp*, 210 U.S. 50 (1908); *Cochran v. Louisiana State Board of Education*, 281 U.S. 370 (1930). In *Quick Bear*, the Court upheld payments to Indians made by the U.S. Secretary of the Interior out of an Indian trust fund that was used to support Indian parochial (mostly Catholic) schools. Quoting the Court of Appeals, the Supreme Court justified its decision by noting that "it seems inconceivable that Congress should have intended to prohibit [the Indians] from receiving religious education at their own cost if they so desired it; such an intent would be one 'to prohibit the free exercise of religion' amongst the Indians, and such would be the effect of the construction for which the complainants contend." In his short opinion for the Court in *Cochran*, Justice Hughes had no reservations about upholding as constitutional a state's use of taxes to supply children with textbooks, regardless of whether the books were destined for use in public, private, or parochial schools. The schools were not the beneficiaries of the funds, Hughes concluded; the children were. Because the books were not religious books, the case was easy and the decision was unanimous. Philip Hamburger's landmark study of church-state separation, oddly enough, fails to mention either case. Hamburger, *Separation of Church and State.*

legal/doctrinal intercurrence, a new "state of courts" with governing authority over local schools was created.

Meyer and *Pierce* were landmark antistatist Supreme Court decisions that garnered considerable attention in the 1920s. But even their political prominence must be considered small when measured by that of the education decision at issue in *Scopes v. Tennessee* (1926), the Great Dayton "Monkey Trial" case of the 1920s involving the prosecution of a public school teacher for teaching evolution in violation of state law. Along with the Oregon schools law, Scopes became a symbolic touchstone in the struggle between the relative claims of state and civil society over education in the 1920s. Unlike *Meyer* and *Pierce*, of course, the Scopes trial came to symbolize the perils not of statism but rather of unchecked civil society run amok. And as historian Edward Larson has shown, the trial became an allegory of the menace that family and religion posed to modern conceptions of intellectual freedom.[129]

The Scopes trial, for instance, only reinforced for the emblematic progressive Walter Lippmann the threat that "semiliterate, priest-ridden and parson-ridden" people posed to education.[130] Lippmann compared Scopes's trial to Galileo's and raged that the people of Tennessee had snuffed out not only any possibility that their children would learn the truth about the origins of man but also "the spirit and method by which learning [itself] is possible."[131]

Lippmann, in fact, placed teachers such as John Scopes at the center of what he saw as a crisis of modernity. Formerly, he acknowledged, "it was an accepted fact that in Catholic communities the child should learn Catholic dogma, that in Lutheran communities he should learn Lutheranism, that in Calvinistic communities he should learn Calvinism. The growth of science [however] has radically altered all this."[132] Now, Lippmann argued, "wherever science is the accepted mode of thought, the ideal of education must be, not that the child shall acquire the wisdom of his elders, but that he shall revise and surpass it."[133] Lippmann had no illusions that the scientific spirit could be reconciled with what he called "fundamentalism." "The child," he wrote, "is not taught to believe. He is taught to doubt and to inquire, to guess, to experiment, and to verify."[134] In the opposition between

---

[129] Philip Hamburger's account of the separation of church and state does not discuss the Scopes trial, which, although not strictly speaking a lawsuit concerning the Constitution's establishment clause, nonetheless, as a trial that helped set public perceptions of the potential menace of religion in the schools (now Protestantism), must be considered an indispensable part of that history. Hamburger, *Separation of Church and State*.

[130] Quoted from a letter from Lippmann to Learned Hand, in Steel, *Lippmann*, 217.

[131] Quoted in Steel, *Lippmann*, 216, 218.

[132] Walter Lippmann, *American Inquisitors: A Commentary on Dayton and Chicago* (New York: Macmillan, 1928), 83.

[133] Lippmann, *American Inquisitors*, 83–4.

[134] Lippmann, *American Inquisitors*, 83–4.

fundamentalism and modernity, the teacher could not be neutral: "[I]n so far as he is intellectually responsible, [the teacher] must consider himself bound by the code of science. In the scientific method he must find the only true and final allegiance of his mind."[135] And Lippmann recognized that science itself is not neutral and tolerant of all opinions – as many later liberal inheritors on the Court of the earlier progressive mantle would vociferously insist. Forthrightly and forcibly, Lippmann announced that science is partisan, intolerant, or indifferent toward any opinion whose claim does not rest on reason.[136] "To ask the fundamentalist, therefore, to submit his belief to scientific inquiry is to ask him at the outset to surrender the most important attribute of his faith."[137] History had reached a point where the teacher thus faced a clear choice: "[H]e must lead the child either toward the modern spirit or away from it."[138]

The Scopes trial and other aligned events of the 1920s, including popular efforts to rewrite school history texts for political purposes, had led Lippmann away from the easy links he had made in 1914 between science and democracy. The two might coincide in some hard-won future, but for now democracy was arrayed in his thinking as an enemy of the new scientific pluralism. The scientific spirit may "dominate the intellectual classes of the western world," but sovereignty, he recognized, resided in the state and not in the community of scholars.[139] If, as it seemed, freedom of thought and popular rule were in opposition, the early-twentieth-century Lippmann aligned himself clearly with the former. As for those Mencken dubbed the "booboisie," whom Lippmann blamed for trials such as Scopes's, "to dispute their moral authority, to deflect their impact, to dissolve their force, is now the most important task of those who care for liberty."[140] The best one could hope for, in his view, is that once society left a transitional stage and crossed the bridge to modernity, democracy and science would no longer diverge. As best he could, and with prudence, the role of the teacher was to build that bridge.[141]

Precociously for a progressive, Lippmann suggested to federal judge Learned Hand that perhaps one way to advance the scientific pluralism of the "intellectual classes" would be through the activist wielding of the judicial

---

[135] Lippmann, *American Inquisitors*, 84.
[136] Lippmann, *American Inquisitors*, 85.
[137] Lippmann, *American Inquistors*, 86.
[138] Lippmann, *American Inquistors*, 86.
[139] Lippmann, *American Inquisitors*, 84–5. Some contemporary liberals are as admirably frank about this as was Lippmann. See, e.g., Stephen Macedo, "Transformative Constitutionalism and the Case of Religion: Defending the Modern Hegemony of Liberalism," in *Constitutional Politics: Essays on Constitution Making, Maintenance, and Change*, eds. Robert P. George and Sotirios A. Barber (Princeton: Princeton University Press, 2001), 167–92.
[140] Lippmann, *American Inquisitors*, 111.
[141] Lippmann, *American Inquisitors*, 90–6.

review powers by the nation's courts. Lippmann was well aware that one of the pillars of early-twentieth-century progressivism was a deep suspicion of this very power. "Now I know this is progressive dogma as we all accepted it in the days when the courts were knocking out the laws we wanted," he told Hand, "[b]ut I wonder whether we didn't have to develop some new doctrine to protect education from majorities."[142] Hand didn't think so. But it would not be long before the Supreme Court would follow the path advocated by the political pundit.

In the world that Lippmann hoped the courts would midwife into being, the *primus inter pares* of civil libertarian rights was the freedom of speech, which began to far outdistance freedom of religion in the varieties of its intellectual uses.[143] Speech rights, for example, could form ready synergies with a scientific pluralism that invited antagonism, conflict, and intellectual clashes into public spaces such as schools in the service of scientific advance, both individual and collective.[144]

The American Civil Liberties Union played a major role in helping to make speech rights first among equals in the constellation of constitutional rights.[145] An important part of this process involved a prominent initiative on the part of the ACLU to advance the claims of intellectual and speech freedoms when they were arrayed against counterclaims that arose out of religious conviction. More than any other public clash, it was *Scopes* that set these at times opposed claims in starkest relief. *Scopes* was constructed by the ACLU – and many others – as an epic battle between an intellectually fearless teacher who wanted to introduce the provocative scientific theory of evolution into the classroom and the backward and ignorant local school

---

[142] June 1925 letter, Lippmann to Hand, quoted in Steel, *Lippmann*, 216–17.

[143] Oliver Wendell Holmes Jr. announced as much early on when he contended in his famed *Lochner v. New York*, 198 U.S. 45 (1905) and *Abrams v. United States*, 250 U.S. 616 (1919) dissents that restrictions on economic liberty were constitutional if they had a rational basis, but those on free speech were justified only if the ideas "so imminently threaten[ed] immediate interference with the lawful and pressing purposes of the law [and required] an immediate check to save the country." Holmes explicitly advanced his "clear and present danger" test in *Schenck v. United States*, 249 U.S. 47 (1919). See White, "Free Speech and the Bifurcated Review Project," in *New Constitutional History*, eds. Van Burkleo, et al., 99–123; G. Edward White, "The First Amendment Comes of Age," *Michigan Law Review* 95 (1996): 299–392.

[144] Some argued that scientific pluralism promised benefits beyond those of scientific advance. John Dewey, for instance, argued that a scientific pluralism anchored in a liberal approach to free speech served a stabilizing function. Permitting a large degree of contention, he wrote, serves as a social safety valve, according outsiders both respect and a place within the political system, and thus steering them away from the sort of alienation that might lead them to advocate its destruction. John Dewey and James H. Tufts, *Ethics* (New York: Holt, 1932), 446.

[145] The group's origins were in the American Union Against Militarism, which had defended the speech rights of opponents of the First World War. Walker, *In Defense of American Liberties*, 11–45; Rabban, *Free Speech in Its Forgotten Years*, 299–316.

officials (in this case, Protestants) imprisoned in the hardened ways of long-held religious dogmas who opposed him.[146]

As historian Edward Larson has shown, however, the differences between the actual Scopes case of the 1920s and the Scopes case that was later remembered in the Cold War era – when the Warren Court began to actively assume broadranging regulatory authority over schools – were significant. In the 1920s, *Scopes* was – and was known to be – a contrived and even playful test case pitting, in something of a carnival fashion, the claims of science against the claims of religion. During the Cold War era, however, the civil libertarian heirs of scientific progressivism reimagined the case as a dead serious and paradigmatic example of the terrible menace of proto-McCarthyite religious zealotry.

In the actual case, John Scopes, a math teacher and coach who was willing to testify that he taught the doctrine of evolution while serving as a substitute biology teacher (privately, he conceded that he could not remember whether he had done so or not), was recruited as a defendant by the town – which hoped to use the case as a spectacle to put itself back on the map – and by its school board which, in fact, bore him not the slightest ill will. Other than as a test case and media spectacle, the state and town had no real desire to enforce their antievolution law (known as the Butler Act), which was intended more as a symbolic statement of principle than as a serviceable criminal statute. William Jennings Bryan, who was brought in to head the prosecution, had generously agreed to pay John Scopes's fine if he happened to be found guilty. That Scopes would serve time in jail was never a serious possibility.[147] Later, as we shall see, in a wartime atmosphere, the *Scopes* case moved from promoting scoffing and provoking debate, to striking panic in the hearts of progressive-spirited liberal intellectual and legal elites.

Reviving the Progressive Vision after the Lean Years: The Opportunities of the Crash

At the time the threat of a monolithic, bureaucratic state was looming, a state that many feared would move to "standardize its children" and fashion them into its "mere creature[s]," the meaning of a commitment to toleration

---

[146] The leading historian of the group, Samuel Walker, reports, for instance, that the "Scopes 'monkey trial' thrust the ACLU into the spotlight as the defender of the freedom to learn" and "the freedom from state-imposed religious dogma." Walker, *In Defense of American Liberties*, 72. In focusing on the menace of Protestant fundamentalism, rather than Catholicism, Scopes played an important role in reconstituting the sense of menace in a liberal/secularist (as opposed to Protestant, anti-Catholic) direction. Hamburger's account demonstrates that both strains had long histories in American church-state debates and often worked together as intellectual and political allies. Hamburger, *Separation of Church and State*, passim.

[147] Edward Larson, *Summer for the Gods: The Scopes Trial and America's Continuing Debate Over Science and Religion* (New York: Basic Books, 1997), 244.

and pluralism in the context of schools assumed a distinctive cast.[148] On the old Court, hewing to traditional conceptions of constitutional freedom, these virtues were understood to be bulwarks of liberty against new inclinations among influential elements of the polity to strive toward the creation of an "Ideal Commonwealth" along the lines of ancient ones, imaginary and real, where "the wives of [the] guardians are to be common, and their children are to be common, and no parent is to know his own child, nor any child his parent," or where "to submerge the individual and develop ideal citizens . . . the males at seven [are assembled] into barracks and . . . their subsequent education and training [are entrusted] to official guardians."[149] This menace was plainly in the mind of the Court when it issued its famous school decisions of the 1920s.

Statist progressives, of course, rejected the notion that the increasing involvement of the state in education was a trajectory to be feared and decried. They were forward-looking and optimistic on this score and firm believers in their role as midwives to progress. Other moderns, after all, more advanced than the Americans, had done it themselves. Earlier, as we have seen, progressives charted the path of developmental progress for American education by looking to Prussia as a model. But in the wake of the war with the hated Hun, progressives were forced to choose new statist models to emulate. Beginning in the late 1920s and 1930s, the most influential progressive educators thus turned their attention to the Soviet Union. When it came to the development of the life of the mind, the Prussian model was suddenly passé: It was now the Soviets who were repeatedly trumpeted by mainstream progressive educators as putting Americans to shame. After all, it was in the USSR, they lamented, and not in the United States, where the influence of the religious and the "booboisie" on education had been eliminated, and where ideas and intellectuals were taken seriously and put at the center of a vigorously experimental public life. Although he later became a committed anticommunist, at this time the philosopher and educational theorist John Dewey was transfixed by the Soviet embrace of initiatives concerning the relationship between state and family, initiatives that seemed to track so closely those that he and many of his fellow education progressives had for some time been urging upon Americans. Unlike what progressives considered the arid and aloof schoolrooms of America, which focused on the three Rs and moral instruction, the Bolsheviks placed collective social goals at the heart of their pedagogy. Dewey admired the way in which the Soviets had had the courage to take on "the bourgeois family," that "breeder of nonsocial interests."[150] To dismantle that family and give teachers and ideas

---

[148] *Pierce*, 268 U.S. at 573.

[149] *Meyer*, 262 U.S. at 627–8.

[150] John Dewey, *The Later Works, 1925–1953, Vol. 3: 1927–1928*, ed. Jo Ann Boydston (Carbondale: Southern Illinois University Press, 1984), 229–31, cited in Ravitch, *Left Back*, 206.

their proper roles in the creation of a new collective state, it was essential to eliminate not only the bourgeois family, Dewey suggested, but also the private ownership of the means of production. In such a system, the educator concerned with questions of social justice will finally assume his proper role. Dewey wrote:

An educator from a bourgeois country may well envy the dignity that comes to the function of the teacher when he is taken into partnership in plans for the social development of his country. Such an one can hardly avoid asking himself whether this partnership is possible only in a country where industry is a public function rather than a private undertaking.[151]

For Dewey and other cutting-edge progressives who shared his hopes for American education, the prosperous and complacent 1920s were lean years. The Great Crash, by contrast, ushered in a decade of remarkable optimism and hope. In a book Lawrence Cremin has called "[t]he characteristic progressive statement of the decade," *The Educational Frontier*, William H. Kilpatrick of Columbia University's Teacher's College (along with his coauthors, who included John Dewey) noted that "in the days of our prosperity ... we were too flatly prosperous to have any yearnings for reform." Before "the present crisis," there was "a complete inability to conceive of an industrial system except as based on competition and motivated by the desire for personal profit.... This obtuseness," he added, "is too complete to be dismissed offhand as the product of human stupidity."[152] Although himself somewhat more concerned than Dewey over the threats the adoption of a Soviet model of education might pose to individual freedom and development, Kilpatrick similarly gushed about the Soviet success in bridging the gap between school and society. "If we could establish a social program, in the manner of Russia," he declared, "our educational problems would largely disappear."[153]

Joining Kilpatrick and Dewey in announcing a new path of progress purportedly illuminated by the crisis of the Great Depression, George Counts of Teacher's College at Columbia, also a major figure in progressive education, declared in a series of prominent books – *The Soviet Challenge to America* (1931), *Bolshevism, Fascism, and Capitalism* (1932), and *Dare the Schools Build a New Social Order?* (1932) – that effective education could only take place in a system committed to the elimination of property rights, capitalism, and competition, and the public control of industry, natural resources, and the distribution of wealth. Far from being a fringe figure, Counts (also a

[151] John Dewey, *Later Works*, 246, 238, cited in Ravitch, *Left Back*, 208. See also Ravitch, *Left Back*, 204–8.

[152] William H. Kilpatrick, et al., *The Educational Frontier* (New York: D. Appleton-Century, Co., Inc., 1933), 6–7, 84.

[153] Kilpatrick, *Educational Frontier*, 22–3.

collaborator on *The Educational Frontier*) was appointed the head of the American Historical Association's Commission on the Social Studies in the Schools. The Commission's final report, drafted largely by Counts, declared defiantly that "in the United States, as in other countries, the age of individualism and laissez faire in economy and government is closing and...a new age of collectivism is emerging."[154] That same year, education progressives launched the journal *The Social Frontier*, "the most significant forum for politically-minded educators in the 1930s." Its "consistent theme...was the need for a planned, collectivist social order."[155]

As it was, America's education system, the institutional spawn of its atavistic Constitution and outmoded ideologies, stood as a barrier to this grand endeavor. One unmistakable sign of the failure of American schools was that "[e]ven the laboring classes do not regard it as the purpose of their organizations to achieve control of the conditions and plans of industry but merely to get increased pecuniary reward and reduced hours of labor, and if possible to bring it about that their offspring become members of the possessing and employing class."[156] The problem was one of the "Crusoe individual" who did not recognize that "competitive private individualism" is "outworn and irrelevant," as was, incidentally, "competitive nationalism."[157] To move beyond these barriers, traditional conceptions of American creedal commitments had to be abandoned. The new political economy, according to Kilpatrick, "has nullified our democratic ideals in the form in which they were originally stated and held." Even the "conceptions of liberty and equality, of democracy and individualism [held by forward-looking liberals], are derived from past conditions which have been destroyed by the industrialization of the country."[158]

The first step in formulating new definitions of these conceptions was to move from an ethos of "compartmentalization" to one recognizing interconnectivity. This was no easy task, as an ethos of compartmentalization

[154] American Historical Association, *Commission on the Social Studies in the Schools: Conclusions and Recommendations of the Commission* (New York: Scribners, 1934), 16–17, 34, 35, cited in Ravitch, *Left Back*, 228. See also Ravitch, *Left Back*, 214–17; George S. Counts, *The Soviet Challenge to America* (New York: John Day Co., 1931); George S. Counts, Luigi Villari, Malcolm C. Rorty, and Newton D. Baker, *Bolshevism, Fascism, and Capitalism: An Account of the Three Economic Systems* (London: Oxford University Press, 1932); George S. Counts, *Dare the Schools Build a New Social Order?* (New York: John Day Co., 1978 [1932]). Counts came very close to Lenin's views on omelettes and eggs, declaring boldly that revolution cannot "be conducted according to the very latest rules of parlor etiquette." Counts, *Bolshevism, Fascism, and Capitalism*, quoted in Ravitch, *Left Back*, 214.

[155] Ravitch, *Left Back*, 230–1.

[156] Kilpatrick, *Educational Frontier*, 55.

[157] Kilpatrick, *Educational Frontier*, 82–3, 69, 71. On the persistence of the theme of the atavism of nationalism within progressive thought, see this book's concluding chapter.

[158] Kilpatrick, *Educational Frontier*, 47, 50. In these sentiments, Kilpatrick's constitutional ethos distinctly echoes Herbert Croly's.

was reinforced by an array of interests within civil society. As things stood:

Patriotism, for example, in the sense of loyalty to our existing institutions, must be kept separate from sentiments of pacifism or internationalism. Moral and religious standards must be protected against the apparent implications of the natural sciences or psychology. Our economic order must be kept inviolate from criticisms emanating from political or economic history. In a word, this pressure from outside vested interests, being all in the direction of keeping the aims or values represented in the curriculum segregated or compartmentalized, became a sort of intellectual confusion and insincerity. Conflicts could be avoided most easily by maintaining this compartmentalization, in much the same way that a clergyman can avoid trouble by confining himself to "preaching the gospel" and staying away from business and politics. Plain sincerity, as expressed in clear thinking, was sacrificed to expediency.[159]

The problem of religion, as Kilpatrick's metaphor (and express statement) suggests, was a major one for educational progressives in the 1930s. After all, "a person brought up with traditional religious beliefs may also adopt the scientific belief that even the most trifling details of this universe of ours are determined by natural law; yet he may remain completely untouched by what is commonly called the conflict between science and religion." Compartmentalizing "gives us a wide range of freedom and protects our self-respect." But, ultimately, it is delusional. "The beauty of this arrangement," Kilpatrick wrote, "is exemplified by a colored man at a prayer meeting, which was to the effect that, while he had robbed hen roosts and got drunk and slashed folks with razors, he never, thank God, had lost his religion."[160] The authority of religious institutions and other institutions of civil society was waning: "[T]he home, the church, and the community no longer exercise the influence over men's minds that they did in times past. . . . The immediate result of this change is . . . a greater tendency to look to education for guidance." "Our faith in education," Kilpatrick concluded, "has become a faith akin to the faith in religion."[161]

This faith, Kilpatrick makes clear, was evangelical. Educators were itinerant preachers propounding a new gospel. "[Z]eal for action and life devotion in sensitive students of society would," he noted, "in former times have led them into the missionary field, at home or abroad. Now it seems rather to lead into social work and education. And these usually bring with them a zeal for a program, a social program."[162] As reformers in the thick of an intellectual battle, educational progressives such as Kilpatrick had a commendable lucidity not only about who their enemies were, but about the affirmative substantive content of their reformist program.

[159] Kilpatrick, *Educational Frontier*, 5.
[160] Kilpatrick, *Educational Frontier*, 7, 8.
[161] Kilpatrick, *Educational Frontier*, 3, 10.
[162] Kilpatrick, *Educational Frontier*, 76.

Of the 1920s, Kilpatrick asks,

Why did [liberal philosophy] not set up more resistance to the reaction against the social emphasis in thought which prevailed for the decade after the war? It would be bold and probably wrong to proclaim that this failure was due to any one influence alone, but it may be ventured with reason that a chief condition of the effects noted was the absence of defined positive programs in the views of liberalism. The liberal has assumed, and with some justification, that his method is in itself a positive program.... but it has not been enough to conceive in the abstract of better things in society: our subject matter must be this particular society in this particular time and place.... [T]his program must be some position drawn up as of our own times and condition and *for* these times and conditions. Our method must be at work here and now advancing working programs which we are eager to have carried out eventually into experimental practice.[163]

The affirmative and aggressive choice of ends is an essential part of this process, and "[t]he obligation to be impartial is the obligation to state as clearly as possible what is chosen and why it is chosen." "Our position implies that a philosophy of education is a branch of social philosophy and, like every social philosophy, since it requires a choice of one type of character, experience, and social institutions, involves a *moral* outlook."[164] This project, Kilpatrick states plainly, is a statebuilding and nationbuilding project, akin to other statebuilding and nationbuilding projects that have taken place at various interludes since the nation's founding.[165]

In the 1930s, many of the country's leading progressives were pushing hard for a collectivized, planned economy, with some (such as Counts) going as far as toying with revolution, and others for the aggressive indoctrination of children with a new, modern, social and political vision. These progressives were clear about the barriers that they believed need to be vanquished (such as tradition, religion, the bourgeois family, local communities, and patriotic love of country) and about the affirmative moral content of their programs, which they themselves frequently and openly claimed to be a modern substitute for religion. It was in resistance to this aggressive, avowedly substantive and avowedly revolutionary political program undertaken by educational elites in a moment of national crisis and vulnerability – and not during the later McCarthy era – that loyalty oaths were first introduced on a broad scale into American education. They were instituted by states and communities to counter an open commitment to revolution and indoctrination as a professional creed of progressive educators.[166] Such oaths may have been, as Harry Kalven later rather blithely put it, "a gratuitous, unnecessary legal device, the use of which is always suspect," but they were not formulated by the orthodox as against the free thinkers. A real war of substantive political

---

[163] Kilpatrick, *Educational Frontier*, 87.
[164] Kilpatrick, *Educational Frontier*, 287–8, 290 [emphasis in original].
[165] Kilpatrick, *Educational Frontier*, 108–9.
[166] Ravitch, *Left Back*, 230–2.

visions was at stake and, at least in the 1930s, both sides fighting to control the nation's schools very much knew it.[167]

Court and Classroom in the Mid-Twentieth Century: The New State and the New Pluralism

In the wake of Stalin's purges and the Moscow trials of 1936–8 and the 1939 Hitler–Stalin Pact, the latest round of progressive enthusiasms for a statist education policy that would serve as an essential component of a centrally planned, postreligious, postcapitalist order, collapsed. Many education progressives became anticommunists and joined the liberal ranks of supporters of Franklin Roosevelt's New Deal. As patriotism surged after the attack on Pearl Harbor and American entry into the war, and as the economy, through the engine of wartime stimulus, gradually recovered, proposals for direct, centralized, bureaucratic control of education became fewer and fewer. Certainly, statism in general was on the rise in this era. Why, then, did education fall off the progressive agenda? Answers are speculative, but a number of factors were likely at work. First, the choice of a revolutionary, Soviet model by progressives throughout the 1930s left these progressives discredited in the wake of world events. Given this choice, statist education progressives lost much of their authority in public policy debates – at least to the degree that they continued to advocate the same public policies. Moreover, it seems likely that the rise to power of a New Deal Democratic coalition with white Southerners at its core played an important role. Since at least the Civil War, race and sectionalism had always played an important mediating role in setting the shape and parameters of central state involvement in education. With Southern segregationists a key part of the governing coalition, any proposal for nationalizing education would be a nonstarter.[168]

Nonetheless, although statist and transformative visions were no longer available to education progressives, the core commitment of these progressives to science and secularism remained. Indeed, this commitment, in the

---

[167] Harry Kalven Jr., *A Worthy Tradition: Freedom of Speech in America* (New York: Harper and Row, 1988), 341. Part of the reason these clashes have been obscured in constitutional history (apart from the tendency of most contemporary neo-Kantian liberal theorists to theorize away conflicts – or, put otherwise, to remove politics from their theories of politics – is that Dewey, Counts, and others abandoned their appeals to the Soviet model of education and their more revolutionary views following Stalin's purges and the Hitler-Stalin pact in the late 1930s. Counts backed away from his earlier calls for a statist national control of education and became a staunch anticommunist. Similarly, the movement's flagship journal, *The Social Frontier*, came to support the New Deal. Many of the substantive commitments of the movement persisted, however, albeit with a softer, less millennial cast. Ravitch, *Left Back*, 235–7.

[168] Ira Katznelson, Kim Geiger, and Daniel Kryder, "Limiting Liberalism: The Southern Veto in Congress, 1933–1950," *Political Science Quarterly* 108 (Summer 1993): 283–306; Richard Franklin Bensel, *Sectionalism and American Political Development: 1880–1980* (Madison: University of Wisconsin Press, 1984), 222–51.

postwar years was as strong as, if not stronger than, ever. As hopes of implementing this substantive vision through a centrally administered national system of education had fallen away, however, those holding these convictions now needed to consider alternative paths of state construction. National education policy from the war onward became a classic case of failed statebuilding (with success defined by European models) and the subsequent construction of a functioning patchwork. Much of central state policy concerning education in these years came to be formulated as constitutional law in rulings of the federal courts, a path that Walter Lippmann had tentatively advocated to Learned Hand in a hostile institutional and ideological context as early as the late 1920s.

The justices sitting on the Court in the mid-twentieth century would have been well prepared for this key nationbuilding project. The generation of justices who were to formulate and implement the new regulatory order concerning religion and education in the mid-twentieth century were born in the 1880s and 1890s and came of age in the heyday of scientific progressivism. This unique generational baptism distinguished those justices from the shapers of associational and intellectual freedom on the Court in the 1920s, when *Meyer* and *Pierce* were decided. At that time, and as now seemed quaint in the wake of *Scopes* and years of ascendant progressivism, religious schools were imagined by the U.S. Supreme Court to be the fundamental protectors of intellectual freedom. This generational difference would come to have significant effects upon the meaning of the First Amendment in the schoolroom setting.

For the generation of justices who populated the Court at mid-century, science and education were taken to be synonymous. In the early years of the twentieth century, a time of mass immigration and the proliferation of religious and ethnic diversity, the cause of science – with its universalism, secularism, and rationality – seemed especially well suited to serve as the basis for a new Americanism that could at last unite a diverse nation.[169] A new pluralism anchored in science placed less value on the solidarity and autonomy of the group and more value on disagreement among speakers who were ideally situated *within* a contentious and cosmopolitan community of reasoning scholars, scholars whose liberation was largely defined by the degree of their intellectual detachment from the old encumbrances of place, of family, and of religion.[170] In this new mid-century imagining, the ties of family and of religion were taken once again – although now with new

---

[169] See John H. Scharr, *Legitimacy and the Modern State* (New Brunswick, NJ: Transaction Books, 1981), 33–7; James Nolan, *The Therapeutic State: Justifying Government at Century's End*, 19. I follow Philip Hamburger in referring to this as an "American" vision. Hamburger, *Separation of Church and State*.

[170] Michael Sandel has usefully referred to this as "the unencumbered self." Sandel, *Liberalism and the Limits of Justice* (Cambridge: Cambridge University Press, 1982).

judicial and jurisprudential authority – less as wellsprings of intellectual freedom than as fetters. In such a context, free speech was favored and religious freedom, in many contexts at least, was as much a problem as a goal. In this new institutional and intellectual context, religion and religious freedom were imagined by judges, law professors, and other legal elites as potential menaces to the counterfreedoms of free speech, free inquiry, and free debate. Those counterfreedoms were, in turn, placed by academic liberal intellectuals and judges at the very heart of democratic political life.

The displacement of religion by speech as the foundational and iconographic judge-protected civil liberty came about gradually. An important crucible for this transition was, predictably enough, the 1939–46 constitutional crusade of the Jehovah's Witnesses, a religion, of course, but one that was decidedly minority, nonmainstream, and persecuted. Many of the Court's Jehovah's Witness cases involved confrontations over street corner preaching, tract distribution, and door-to-door solicitation, which blended speech issues with those of religious liberty. In these cases, the Court alternated between free speech and free exercise as grounds for its decisions. In *Murdock v. Pennsylvania* (1943), a Witness case in which the Court voided a local license tax on the distribution of religious literature, Justice Douglas, writing for the Court, put religion and speech on a par, asserting that "[f]reedom of the press, freedom of speech, [and] freedom of religion are in a preferred position."[171]

When the setting was switched from the streets to the schoolroom in a case from the same year, the Court, reversing a high-profile decision of only three years earlier, recurred to the rhetoric of free speech and not that of religious liberty to anchor its ruling.[172] In the Jehovah's Witness flag salute case of *West Virginia v. Barnette* (1943), the Court invalidated a state law requiring all children, including Jehovah's Witness children, to salute the flag – even if they believed such conduct to be sinful idolatry. Although the *Barnette* case explicitly involved matters of religious conscience and practice, Justice Robert Jackson's opinion for the Court rested not upon free exercise considerations but rather upon Holmesian free speech principles – principles that appeal to a scientific pluralism associated with the free exchange of ideas in the secular intellectual marketplace. Thus, Jackson considered it dispositive that the exemption of students from an otherwise compulsory flag salute did not create "a clear and present danger that would justify an effort . . . to muffle expression." "To sustain the compulsory flag salute," he added, "[the Court

---

[171] *Murdock v. Pennsylvania*, 319 U.S. 105, 115 (1943). See *Lovell v. City of Griffin*, 303 U.S. 444 (1938) (decided on free speech grounds); *Cantwell v. Connecticut*, 310 U.S. 296 (1940) (decided on free exercise grounds). On the Jehovah's Witnesses cases, see Shawn Francis Peters, *Judging Jehovah's Witnesses: Religious Persecution and the Dawn of the Rights Revolution* (Lawrence: University Press of Kansas, 2000); David Manwaring, *Render Unto Caesar: The Flag Salute Controversy* (Chicago: University of Chicago Press, 1962).

[172] *Minersville v. Gobitis*, 310 U.S. 586 (1940).

would be] required to say that a Bill of Rights which guards the individual's right to speak his own mind, left it open to public authorities to compel him to utter what is not in his mind."[173] Writing against the grain of the view that religion had any sort of preferred constitutional status, Jackson had made it explicit in his *Barnette* opinion that he drew no distinction between religious belief and any other sort of belief, emphasizing that "while religion supplies [the children's] motive for enduring the discomforts of making the issue in this case, many citizens who do not share these religious views hold such a compulsory rite to infringe the constitutional liberty of the individual."[174] All sorts of divisions must be welcomed into the schoolroom, because any other approach to pluralism is inflammable: "Probably no deeper division of our people could proceed from any provocation than from finding it necessary to choose what doctrine and whose program public educational officials shall compel youth to unite in embracing," he declared. "Those who begin in coercive elimination of dissent soon find themselves exterminating dissenters. Compulsory unification of opinion achieves only the unanimity of the graveyard."[175]

As such, in the problems it was directed at and in the weapons it wielded against them, Justice Jackson's opinion in *Barnette* proved to be less a doctrinal building block for later religious freedom opinions than for the Court's pathbreaking latitudinarian free speech cases of the late 1960s, such as *Tinker v. Des Moines* (1969). In *Tinker*, the Court held that schoolchildren had a right to wear black armbands to school in protest against the Vietnam War, a behavior that Des Moines school principals had deemed disruptive and had thus prohibited.[176] In his opinion for the Court in *Tinker*, Justice Abe Fortas, echoing the reasoning of Justice Jackson's *Barnette* opinion, imagined the school as a contentious scientific pluralist polity in microcosm, as a neutral forum denuded of any substantive value commitments of its own but where the allegiances and commitments of its constituent members were respected and invited. This imagining of the school is evident, for instance, in Fortas's refusal to distinguish it from the wider arena of public affairs (neither "students or teachers," he wrote, "shed their constitutional rights to freedom of speech or expression at the schoolhouse gate") and in a defoliated definition of an educational community that would have been utterly alien to the *Meyer* and *Pierce* Court. ("[T]he principal use to which the schools are dedicated is to accommodate students during prescribed hours for the purpose of certain types of activities.")[177] In Fortas's view, to impose

---

[173] *West Virginia State Board of Education v. Barnette*, 319 U.S. 624, 634 (1943).
[174] *Barnette*, 319 U.S. at 635.
[175] *Barnette*, 319 U.S. at 641.
[176] *Tinker v. Des Moines Independent Community School District*, 393 U.S. 503 (1969). See also *Dennis v. United States* 341 U.S. 494, 580 (1951) (Justice Black, dissenting) (referring to the freedom of speech as "the keystone of our Government").
[177] *Tinker*, 393 U.S. at 506, 512.

purposeful limits on the freedom of expression of students is to flirt with tyranny. "In our system," he writes, "state-operated schools may not be enclaves of totalitarianism. School officials do not possess absolute authority over their students. . . . Students may not be regarded as close-circuit recipients of only that which the state chooses to communicate. They may not be confined to the expression of those sentiments that are officially approved."[178]

The Promise of Speech and the Menace of Religion: Academic Freedom and Strict Separation

Try teaching communism in the schools of a community that denounced Tennessee intolerance. . . . Fundamentalism is to the Tennesseean what the profit system is to a Northern middle-class business man – the thing he believes in with all his heart.[179]
– Howard K. Beale

In the wake of the Court's transitional Jehovah's Witness decisions in which the claims of free speech and free exercise were commonly commingled, the Court increasingly began to differentiate between the promise and perils of unfettered secular and religious expression in schools. Whatever its disruptive effects in the classroom, free expression of secular opinions by students and teachers was highly prized in the emergent civil libertarian vision because it brought with it all the advantages promised by the scientific pluralist outlook: contention, conflict, and the prospect of intellectual progress. And in the Court's view, this desirable prospect beckoned whether the contentious secular expression came from the students, whose views presumably did not have the imprimatur of school authorities, or from the teachers, whose views did.

In fashioning its new separationist doctrines concerning church and state, however, the Court began to marry religion to an altogether different model of pluralism, which had distinctive implications for judicial policymaking in the service of the construction of the new child at home in the New Constitutional Nation. Religion brought to the Court's mind not a scientific pluralism in which all views were welcome and contention and diversity were deemed to be good, but instead an exclusionary pluralism, which was fearful of antagonism, contention, and difference and the effects they might have on the peaceable enjoyment of collective life. Both freedoms may have technically been "preferred," but they were preferred in radically different ways, ones that proved to have divergent policy implications.[180]

[178] *Tinker*, 393 U.S. at 511.
[179] Howard K. Beale, *Are American Teachers Free? An Analysis of Restraints upon the Freedom of Teaching in American Schools* (New York: Charles Scribner's Sons, 1936), 258–9.
[180] See Purcell, *Crisis of Democratic Theory*, 61.

Although it took place in the 1920s, the *Scopes* trial played an important part in this process of constitutional reconstruction. For, as historian Edward Larson has shown, the meaning of that trial was reconstructed during the Cold War to lend support to key progressive-spirited nationbuilding imperatives concerning education. In *Summer for the Gods*, Larson deftly charts the construction across time of the memory of the *Scopes* trial. In looking backward, Richard Hofstadter's 1957 collegiate text for students of American history, Larson observes, closely associates "fundamentalism" (an issue Hofstadter discussed solely in terms of the *Scopes* trial) with the Klan, the Red Scare, Nativism, and Prohibition as exemplary illustrations of the intolerance of the 1920s.[181] After the rise of Joseph McCarthy in 1950, influential historians such as Hofstadter, Ray Ginger, and William Leuchtenburg all wrote books linking the religiously motivated antievolutionism of Bryan with McCarthyite anticommunism and associating Clarence Darrow's atheistic attack on the Butler Act with scientific and civil libertarian enlightenment.[182] Perhaps most influential of all, the release of Stanley Kramer's 1960 movie about the trial, *Inherit the Wind* (based on the play by Jerome Lawrence and Robert E. Lee), pits the Constitution-saving Drummond (Darrow) against an ignorant and buffoonish Brady (Bryan), backed solidly by a town ruled by ruthless and authoritarian religious zealots.[183] Out

---

[181] Larson, *Summer for the Gods*, 235–6; Richard Hofstadter, William Miller, and Daniel Aaron, *The United States: The History of a Republic* (Englewood Cliffs, NJ: Prentice-Hall, 1957), 636. This construction built upon the contemporaneous one of religious (white) Southerners as "morons" and "bigots." Walker, *In Defense of American Liberties*, 74–5; H.L. Mencken, *A Mencken Chrestomathy: His Own Selections From His Choicest Writings* (New York: Vintage Books, 1982), 187–8.

[182] Larson, *Summer for the Gods*, 236; William E. Leuchtenburg, *The Perils of Prosperity: 1914–1932* (Chicago: University of Chicago Press, 1958), 217–23; Ray Ginger, *Six Days or Forever? Tennessee v. John Thomas Scopes* (London: Oxford University Press, 1958), 190–217, 238; Richard Hofstadter, *The Age of Reform: From Bryan to FDR* (New York: Knopf, 1955), 286; Richard Hofstadter, *Anti-Intellectualism in American Life* (New York: Knopf, 1963). Ginger characterizes the Butler law as "evil." Ginger, *Six Days or Forever*, 2. Robert Wuthnow has observed in his study of the postwar period that "[e]vidence suggests that rationality, natural science, and the social sciences have all exercised a negative effect on traditional religious beliefs and practices. Not only do scientists – and especially social scientists – demonstrate radically low levels of religious commitment, but scientific and social scientific meaning systems also appear to operate as functional alternatives to traditional theistic ideas for a number of people." Robert Wuthnow, *The Restructuring of American Religion: Society and Faith Since World War II* (Princeton: Princeton University Press, 1988), 301–2.

[183] Jerome Lawrence and Robert E. Lee, *Inherit the Wind* (New York: Bantam, 1960); Larson, *Summer for the Gods*, 240–6. Kramer, who both directed and produced the film version of *Inherit the Wind*, was known for his "message films" that pushed the culture toward confronting as social problems not only (ostensibly) religious fundamentalism, but also anticommunism and McCarthyism (*High Noon* (1952)[as producer]), juvenile delinquency (*The Wild One* (1954)[as producer]), and racism (*The Defiant Ones* (1958)[director and producer]); (*Guess Who's Coming to Dinner* (1967)[director and producer]). Kramer's

of this political and cultural stew arose a civil libertarianism that was solicitous for the protection of secular political opinions in schools, particularly radical – including, most prominently, communist – opinions, and yet
highly sensitive to the slippery slope caused by religious utterances in those
same settings. The commitment to welcoming communist ideas into schools
and removing religious ones became a staple of twentieth-century civil
libertarianism.

As far as Court doctrine was concerned, the elevation of speech over religion in the hierarchy of civil libertarian solicitude (or, put otherwise, the displacement of religion by secular democratic theory within the nationbuilding
project) began with the Court's fashioning of the Preferred Freedoms Doctrine, under which the Court rationalized its aggressive assertion of judicial
review in some areas and its relative hesitance in others. Although the Court's
efforts to determine which rights would have preferred status got off to a
cautious start (in 1937, Justice Cardozo could state only that preference was
due to those "fundamental principles of liberty and justice which lie at the
base of all our civil and political institutions"), new problems eventually
pushed the Court to work to refine state policy concerning the substantive
content of these freedoms.[184]

Judgment at Nuremberg (1961)[director and producer] was both an antiracist film and an
anti–anticommunist film, in its evident conviction that a preoccupation with anticommunism was dangerous. Walker agrees that Mencken's "stereotypes" of religious Southerners
were "exaggerated" in *Inherit the Wind* – and to much effect. Walker, *In Defense of American
Liberties*, 75. Interestingly enough, despite the fact that Bryan was a Protestant and the
Tennessee case swirled around Protestantism, Mencken could not resist characterizing Bryan
in Dayton as "a tin-pot pope in the coca-cola belt." Mencken, quoted in John T. Scopes
and James Presley, *Center of the Storm: Memoirs of John T. Scopes* (New York: Holt, Rinehart
and Winston, 1967), 216.

[184] *Palko v. Connecticut*, 302 U.S. 319 (1937). See, generally, Howard Gillman, "Preferred
Freedoms: The Progressive Expansion of State Power and the Rise of Modern Civil Liberties
Jurisprudence," *Political Research Quarterly* 47 (1994): 623–51. Gillman initially conceptualized the rise of the preferred freedoms doctrine as involving more the removal of barriers
than as an affirmative substantive political program. In doing so, his discussion of preferred
freedoms fit well with traditional narratives of constitutional development. In recent work,
he has placed more emphasis on the substantive political nature of the Court's preferred
freedoms initiative. See Gillman, "Political Development and the Rise of the 'Preferred
Freedoms' Rubric," paper presented at the University of Maryland Discussion Group on
Constitutionalism (College Park, April 2002). See also *Carolene Products*, 303 U.S. 144,
152–3 n. 4 (1938). My own views, however, as set out here, more closely parallel those of
G. Edward White, who has emphasized the special role that free speech came to play in
"modernist" democratic theory between the wars and argued that that role was foundational to the emergence of the doctrine of preferred freedoms. See White, "Free Speech and
the Bifurcated Review Project," 99–122; White, "The First Amendment Comes of Age."
The position of free speech as *primus inter pares* of civil libertarian freedoms was only en-
hanced by the moral glow of the civil rights movement free speech cases. See, generally,
Powe, *Warren Court and American Politics*, chs. 11, 12.

The universalizing scientific pluralist model as applied to schools, which drew directly upon a tradition of scientific progressivism and a conception of academic freedom invented during the Progressive Era, was fashioned by the Court primarily in cases in which public school teachers at both the secondary and university levels were alleged (both accurately and inaccurately) to be Communists.[185]

The importance of secular, scientific inquiry to the functioning of a healthy, forward-looking liberal democracy had once again became an animating theme of intellectual life in the late 1930s and early 1940s, just as it had been in the late nineteenth and early twentieth centuries. As such, it has a pervasive influence on the worldview of elites. This time, the immediate impetus for a broad-ranging defense of secular scientific values was not, at least in the first instance, the perceived menace of religious backwardness, but rather the threat posed by Nazi fascism. Writers including the broadly influential sociologist Robert K. Merton, while continuing to assert that science's unique value came from its unwillingness to "preserve the cleavage between the sacred and the profane," placed most of their emphasis on counterposing the unique service science provides in a liberal democracy to its perverse relationship with the state under a totalitarian political system. Both science and democracy, Merton and others prominently argued, evinced a respect for human dignity and a commitment to human inquiry. Indeed, each made a powerful contribution to the thriving of the other.[186]

In the postwar years, however, the antagonism between the scientific and religious outlooks resumed its wonted place in modern American intellectual and political life. The era's "cosmopolitan intellectuals" seized the initiative to launch "a program for secular culture organized around what its adherents represented as the core values of science."[187] Many of these intellectuals considered Christianity, in both its Protestant and Roman Catholic varieties, to be enemies of that affirmative program. The Catholic Church, however, with its strict system of deferential hierarchies and retrograde politics (not to mention its links to fascist regimes, particularly in Spain), was once again taken to be a special menace. Indeed, "agnostic intellectuals who rallied

---

[185] See Hollinger, *Science, Jews, and Secular Culture*, 164 (noting a fervent commitment to scientific ideals among cosmopolitan intellectuals as a significant part of their response to McCarthyism). See, e.g., Richard Hofstadter and Walter Metzger, *The Development of Academic Freedom in the United States*.

[186] Robert K. Merton, "Science and the Social Order," *Philosophy of Science* 5 (1938): 321–34; Robert K. Merton, "A Note on Science and Democracy," *Journal of Legal and Political Sociology* 1 (1942): 116. See Hollinger, *Science, Jews, and Secular Culture*, 80–92, esp. 82 (arguing at length that "Merton's formulation of the 'ethos' of science – its prevailing ideals for cognitive behavior – constituted a distinctive contribution to the ideology of liberal democracy as that ideological cause was being developed by Anglo-phone intellectuals in the West during the late 1930s and early 1940s").

[187] Hollinger, *Science, Jews, and Secular Culture*, 155.

to the banner of science and democracy... [believed] that Roman Catholic priests and their fellow-traveling intellectuals were a genuine and formidable enemy in a struggle over the future of American culture."[188] The perceived antagonism between Catholicism and secular liberal democratic science at this time assumed a particular prominence within the nation's law schools and law journals, where the legal theory adjuncts of this broader intellectual movement vigorously opposed "a variety of unfortunate provincialisms that some conservative intellectuals had the outrageous audacity to support," including foundationalist theories of natural law.[189]

Part of the secularizing nationbuilding project of the postwar period, as we have seen, involved the intellectual reconstruction of the meaning of the *Scopes* trial. Another part of it, in which the legal academy (and especially Jews within it) played a major role, was the reconstruction of the meaning of the life and work of Justice Oliver Wendell Holmes Jr. That project involved the radical reimagining of a Holmes that Grant Gilmore has described as a "savage, harsh, and cruel, a bitter and lifelong pessimist who saw in the course of human life nothing but a continuing struggle in which the rich and powerful impose their will on the poor and weak" into a progressive pragmatist and proto-civil libertarian.[190] As an agnostic and an unflinching devotee of following science wherever it may lead, who was, through his famous father, hoary New England provenance, and Civil War service, nevertheless closely identified with the nation and its one-hundred-percent American Protestant establishment, Holmes was a constitutional symbol ripe for ideological use.

"The making of the agnostic Holmes into an emblem for American life" was largely the work of Jewish legal and political intellectuals who had a particular interest in both the secularization of American life and, simultaneously, in the construction of both the New American State and an allied New Constitutional Nation, including Max Lerner, Jerome Frank, Morris Cohen, Harold Laski, and, most importantly, Felix Frankfurter.[191] Jews in mid-century America became staunch partisans of the public schools, and, taking the successful litigation campaign of the Jehovah's Witnesses as their

---

[188] Hollinger, *Science, Jews, and Secular Culture*, 159.

[189] Hollinger, *Science, Jews, and Secular Culture*, 160; Purcell, *Crisis of Democratic Theory*, 164–70; Allitt, *Catholic Intellectuals and Conservative Politics in America, 1950–1985* (Ithaca, NY: Cornell University Press, 1993), 8–9, 186; Primus, *American Language of Rights*, 184–5.

[190] Grant Gilmore, *The Ages of American Law* (New Haven: Yale University Press, 1977), 49; Hollinger, *Science, Jews, and Secular Culture*, 42–9; Albert W. Alschuler, *Law Without Values: The Life, Work, and Legacy of Justice Holmes* (Chicago: University of Chicago Press, 2000), 14–40, 181–6.

[191] Hollinger, *Science, Jews, and Secular Culture*, 26–7, 51 ("Jewish intellectuals... helped to reconstitute American intellectual life, and helped construct, in the process, the particular, liberal version of American culture that became a common possession of the American intelligentsia during the middle decades of the twentieth century."); Alschuler, *Law Without Values*, 181–6.

strategic model, they launched a major political initiative to ensure that the secular scientific model of education – as a citizen-building and nation-building initiative – would be institutionalized within federal constitutional doctrine and, as such, set nationwide policies concerning the place of religion in the public schools.[192] In this endeavor, they united with Protestants and secularists. As it soon became clear, their chief antagonists would prove to be – as often was the case when it came to the schools – the Catholic Church and American Catholics. In the crucible of the battle between science and Catholicism at mid-century, mainstream views concerning church-state separation became institutionalized as central state policy through the constitutional rulings of the U.S. Supreme Court. Appeals to Cold War fears, as we shall see, helped make this longstanding assault on religion, at long last, a part of modern constitutional doctrine.

Fears: The Cold War and the Social Construction of a Waxing Roman Catholic Menace

In the late 1930s, the jeremiads of Father Coughlin, the Radio Priest, had sullied Catholicism for many with the anti-Semitism of the emergent German enemy. To make matters worse, at the same time many American Catholics actively supported Franco's Fascists in the Spanish Civil War, in part by staunchly opposing lifting the arms embargo on the Spanish Republic. As journalist George Seldes (who characterized the Spanish Civil War as "the 'dress rehearsal' of the Fascist attempt to conquer the world" and "the ultimate conflict between reaction and progress") noted, this helped once again cast Catholics, particularly in the imagination of the nation's elites, as enemies of the intellect. Looking at Gallup polls and other data, Seldes found it important that "the writers of America voted some 98 percent against Franco." At the same time, the "cardinals and bishops were about 98 percent for Franco."[193] Unlike Vociferous critics of the Catholic Church like *The Nation* magazine writer Paul Blanshard, who – in the aftermath of both the Hitler-Stalin pact and the onset of the Cold War – saw Communism as an enemy of democracy and progress, Seldes, one of the most prominent liberal journalists of his time, declared confidently in the 1930s, in the spirit of many forward-looking thinkers of the era, that "it is Fascism which is the menacing power in the whole world, not Communism."[194] The significance

---

[192] Gregg Ivers, *To Build a Wall: American Jews and the Separation of Church and State* (Charlottesville: University of Virginia Press, 1995), 2–5, 16, 27–8, 55, 74. It should be said that, as Ivers details, there were divisions amongst Jews over these mid-century initiatives. The American Jewish Congress led the way, while the American Jewish Committee and the Anti-Defamation League were concerned about the initiative's anti-Christian thrust and worried about an eventual political backlash.

[193] Seldes, *Catholic Crisis*, 1, 4, 5. See also Hollinger, *Science, Jews, and Secular Culture*, 159 (also citing Catholic support for Mussolini).

[194] Seldes, *Catholic Crisis*, 9.

of the fact that part of Franco's claim to power was his strident defense of Spain's parochial schools was not lost on anyone. The concerns of progressives and liberals with Catholics lasted right through the war and, as new problems and contexts arose, became an important influence on postwar thinking (and, in turn, constitutional law) as well.[195]

In 1950, the Harvard Law School hosted an evening forum on a topic the Law School Forum's president, Anthony Nugent, characterized as "what you [in the audience] know is a 'red hot' subject." The issue was "The Catholic Church and Its Politics." Moderator Henry Aiken of Harvard's philosophy department declared the discussion to be long overdue given "the growing impression . . . that the political power of the Catholic Church is growing, but more important, that the purposes of the Church in the United States . . . are in many ways inimical to the American way of life." The guest of honor was Paul Blanshard, who had just published his highly praised (and bestselling) book, *American Freedom and Catholic Power* (1949) and was then hard at work on his next book, *Communism, Democracy, and Catholic Power* (1951). Joining Blanshard on the panel was a Catholic priest, Father George H. Dunne, a man for whom the moderator expressed some sympathy and gratitude, given that, as Aiken described it, the audience at Harvard was "overwhelmingly Protestant" and the law school's audience, in particular, "probably overwhelmingly secular."[196]

Blanshard was a familiar and popular figure to Harvard law students in the early 1950s. Aiken assumed that most of the audience had read Blanshard's book. And the transcript of the evening records that the rising members of the legal elite burst into applause after Blanshard announced that he had overtaken Fulton J. Sheen on the bestseller lists of both the *New York Times* and the *Chicago Tribune.* Blanshard also called attention to the fact that *American Freedom and Catholic Power* had held the number two position in college bookstores throughout the country for many months. He declared himself "delighted that the new movement against Catholic aggression in the field of politics is rising not on the fringes, the lunatic fringes of religion and fanaticism, but right in the hearts of American university leaders." So was the audience: The expression of delight drew a warm round of applause.

That the Harvard law students would have favored the anti-Catholic crusader rather than the priest was not simply a matter of the religious background of the students and the broad-ranging disposition of the era's secular liberal elite. It was also likely a matter of intellectual training. Since the late

195 Alan Brinkley, *Voices of Protest: Huey Long, Father Coughlin and the Great Depression* (New York: Vintage Books, 1982); Philip Gleason, "Pluralism, Democracy, and Catholicism in the Era of World War II," *Review of Politics* 49 (Spring 1987): 208, citing Blanshard's *American Freedom and Catholic Power* and Seldes's *The Catholic Crisis.*
196 "The Catholic Church and Politics," *The Harvard Law School Forum* (1950), *www.law. harvard.edu/studorgs/forum/church.html.*

1930s, reacting to a rise of totalitarian dictatorships and what for many seemed the imperative of a critique of these systems, a neoscholastic school of legal thought had come to life in the nation's Catholic law schools and in the pages of its Catholic law reviews. This Catholic legal thought, anchored in Thomistic commitments to natural law, represented a challenge to the reformist understandings of the nature of law, the positivism and relativism of the sociological jurisprudence, and the pragmatism and legal realism that by 1950 had become hegemonic within the legal academy, including (despite the presence of Lon Fuller) at the Harvard Law School.[197]

Blanshard, who had worked under John Dewey as a graduate student at Columbia and fit seamlessly into the intellectual architecture of the Harvard Law School, came to Harvard as an avowed partisan of political progress across the board. "All my life I have belonged to those liberal and radical movements that have fought against every kind of discrimination, racial and personal and religious." He cited his work as an anticorruption crusader in New York City and as a labor organizer in Southern cotton mills. He asserted he was neither a bigot nor anti-Catholic, declaring Catholic individuals to be more victims of their church structure than accomplices in the antidemocratically oppressive system that it had set up.

In this, Blanshard was very much in the mainstream of the nation's cosmopolitan liberal intellectual elite. As John McGreevy has chronicled, Blanshard's work was praised in its day by a vertible who's who of the mid-twentieth-century party of progress: Albert Einstein, Bertrand Russell, McGeorge Bundy, John Dewey, Lewis Mumford, Reinhold Niebuhr, and Arthur Schlesinger Jr., among others.[198] Blanshard's mid-century imagination of Roman Catholicism as the enemy "other" was far from idiosyncratic among liberals, intellectuals, and civil libertarians. It was one of the anchors of the thought of the party of progress in the Cold War era. The party of progress, assuming a new identity as "liberals" in their post–New Deal incarnation, defined liberty and progress in significant part in opposition to Catholic tyranny and slavery.[199]

---

[197] See, generally, Purcell, *Crisis of Democratic Theory*, 164–78; Allitt, *Catholic Intellectuals*, 8–9, 186.

[198] McGreevy, "Thinking on One's Own: Catholicism in the American Intellectual Imagination."

[199] David Green, *The Language of Politics in America: Shaping Political Consciousness from McKinley to Reagan* (Ithaca, NY: Cornell University Press, 1987), 119–63. See also Hollinger, *Science, Jews, and Secular Culture*, 159 ("agnostic intellectuals who rallied to the banner of science and democracy had strong reasons for believing that Roman Catholic priests and their fellow traveling intellectuals were a genuine and formidable enemy in a struggle over the future of American culture"); Hamburger, *Separation of Church and State*, 449–54; Ivers, *To Build a Wall*, 26 n. 47 (alluding to "the considerable anti-Catholic literature that emerged in the period immediately following World War II" and discussing the anti-Catholic affinities of Protestants and Other Americans United for the Separation of Church and State [POAU], the main separationist activist group, with which Blanshard was associated. While once

Blanshard's popular progressive liberal critique of Catholicism began with a critique of the public face of Roman Catholicism itself. The notion that one was not removing religion from the schools by simply removing religious rituals and symbols from the schools (an argument made in support of church-state separationism) owes much to the Protestant notion that true religiosity is spare, subdued, and unostentatious. In this conviction, mid-century elite Protestantism defined itself against what it took to be gaudy, symbol-laden Catholic ritual. "The Catholic Church," Blanshard wrote, "is usually a big church, and often an oversized church."[200] "The Roman Catholic Church in America," he added, in a theme that he recurs to repeatedly in his columns and books, "has a great gift for showmanship, and its ceremonials and costumes lend themselves naturally to pageantry in the grand manner." The Catholics, he notes, are devotees of "gigantic religious spectacles," which play on the delight Americans have in such circuses, and "the hierarchy in recent years has learned to give them the kind of displays they want."[201] In his 1966 book on the Second Vatican Council, Blanshard praised the church's decision to de-emphasize the place of the Virgin Mary in Catholic worship, asserting that "Catholic Mariology is, next to papal infallibility, the greatest purely theological stumbling block to Christian cooperation and Christian reunion."[202]

This dazzling pagentry was used to charm the ignorant into signing on to a politics of reaction. Much of the mid-century intelligentsia – an influential number of whom, in the years immediately preceding the Cold War at least, were fellow travelers – read reaction into what it took to be the Church's overzealous and uncompromising anticommunism. "[T]his sharp lining up of the Catholic Church against communism," declared the Protestant theologian Harry Elmer Barnes, "puts it by implication as an ally of Fascism."[203] The Methodist Federation for Social Service declared "The Pope put his

---

justifying its public arguments for a strict separationist constitutional jurisprudence on [anti-Catholic] religious grounds, in subsequent years, the group, in a Rawlsian turn, has since promoted the same constitutional positions through recourse to a discourse of secular, public reason.

[200] Paul Blanshard, *American Freedom and Catholic Power* (Boston: Beacon Press, 1949), 12.

[201] Blanshard, *American Freedom and Catholic Power*, 12. See also Paul Blanshard, *Paul Blanshard on Vatican II* (Boston: Beacon Press, 1966), 3–5.

[202] Blanshard, *Vatican II*, 173. In his 1950 debate with Blanshard at Harvard Law School, Father Dunne sought to demonstrate to the law students the "anti-Catholic tone" of Blanshard's criticism of Catholic display and pageantry by taking passages from Blanshard's writings and substituting the words "Jewish," "synagogue," and "rabbi" for "Catholic," "church," and "priest."

[203] Quoted in George Seldes, *The Catholic Crisis*, 19. See Allitt, *Catholic Intellectuals*, 20–31. None of this is to deny the existence of a strong group of "liberal anticommunists," which included Schlesinger and, most prominently, the group of "New York Intellectuals" associated with the *Partisan Review*. See, generally, Neil Jumonville, *Critical Crossings: The New York Intellectuals in Post-War America* (Berkeley: University of California Press, 1991), *passim*.

attack on Communism in between those of Hitler and Mussolini. He became their ally."[204]

Writing after the onset of the Cold War, Paul Blanshard was less sanguine
about communism in his attacks on the Church than were commentators of
just a few years earlier. Still, Blanshard noted with disapproval the fact that
"Catholic journals could be counted upon to take the most aggressive conceivable line against any attempt to 'appease' communism." And he scorned
"the holy-war-against-Communism eloquence of Cardinal Spellman's recurring speeches at conventions of the American Legion."[205] The pre–Vatican
II Church, Blanshard complained, saw communism as "the Atheist Devil
Incarnate."[206] "In American Catholic propaganda, Russian communism is
literally and figuratively a devil. For the priests it is a happy eventuality that
their fears coincide with American national fears," he wrote. "In the national anticommunist symphony, the double brass of the Catholic section
blares loudly," he declared, in a return to the critique of gaudiness, "and the
Catholic priests obviously enjoy their pro-American role in the noisy performance."[207] "[M]any Catholic organizations," he concluded, "have shown
an unbalanced emotionalism in their anticommunist campaign."[208] This un-
hinged outlook on the part of the Catholic Church toward communism led
to McCarthyism and to Cardinal Spellman's "obnoxious" and "mistaken"
support for "the Catholic dictator of South Vietnam, Ngo Dinh Diem." That
is, it helped set the stage for the Vietnam War.[209]

Despite his repeated attacks on the Church's staunch anticommunism, one
of Blanshard's chief arguments in the highly nationalistic Cold War era, apparent inconsistencies notwithstanding, involved drawing a strong analogy
between Roman Catholicism and communist totalitarianism. Blanshard, in
fact, devoted an entire book to this argument, *Communism, Democracy, and
Catholic Power* (1951), which opens with the declaration that "[p]robably no
aspect of world affairs is more carefully avoided by American writers today
than the fundamental resemblance between the Vatican and the Kremlin."
This book was put forward as a primer in helping to shape Cold War policy
in dealing with these ostensibly twin threats.[210]

Many on the liberal/left had other reasons for treating Catholicism as the enemy "other,"
even if this reason would not serve amongst liberal anticommunists.

[204] Quoted in George Seldes, *The Catholic Crisis*, 18.
[205] Seldes, *Catholic Crisis*, 320.
[206] Seldes, *Catholic Crisis*, 323.
[207] Blanshard, *American Freedom and Catholic Power*, 259.
[208] Blanshard, *American Freedom and Catholic Power*, 262.
[209] Blanshard, *American Freedom and Catholic Power*, 291.
[210] Paul Blanshard, *Communism, Democracy, and Catholic Power* (Boston: Beacon Press, 1951),
    1. Hollinger has observed that "[w]hat was most suspect [to mid-twentieth century liberal
    cosmopolitan intellectuals] about the ostensibly secular Communist movement... was its
    'religious' character, which brought it neatly into place alongside the Catholic Church and
    the old hegemonic Protestantism as rivals to the values of these cosmopolitan intellectuals."
    Hollinger, *Science, Jews, and Secular Culture*, 160.

It was Blanshard's contention that the struggle of the middle years of the twentieth century was oversimplified if conceptualized as a war against Communism alone. Rather, what was taking place was "a war of ideas [that] embrace[d] the whole field of democratic versus totalitarian thought." "The struggle of democracy against the Kremlin is one phase of the war of ideas," he wrote, "and the struggle of democracy against the Vatican is another. The underlying issue in both phases of the struggle is the same – the rule of the world by free minds."[211]

Of essence was what Blanshard considered the plain fact that both the Vatican and the Kremlin are dictatorships, a fact that "no cloudy ecclesiastical effusions can quite conceal."[212] Both were authoritarian hierarchies. Both sought to indoctrinate the young through partisan systems of education (in this, it seemed to Blanshard that the Russians actually had the better claim to educating for freedom, as "[p]robably the Russian communists have done more in a single generation to overcome illiteracy among their... subjects than the Vatican has done for *its* people since the Middle Ages").[213] One taught Marxism-Leninism, the other Saint Thomas Aquinas.[214] But in schools behind the Iron Curtain, the coercion forcing the students to dogmatically venerate Stalin, Blanshard noted, reluctantly throwing a bone to the Catholics, is "even more severe than [the coercion] in the Catholic schools" to venerate the Pope.[215]

He observed, moreover, that Catholic groups frequently moved in communistic ways: They bored and corrupted from within. So, for example, "Catholic Action creates in many non-Catholic as well as Catholic organizations cells of devotees which function in a manner strikingly similar to communist cells."[216] In *Communism, Democracy, and Catholic Power*, Blanshard presented the reader with paired chapters, the first titled, "The Strategy of Penetration: The Kremlin," and the second titled, "The Strategy of Penetration: The Vatican." The latter opens by declaring, "The missionaries of the Kremlin penetrate the jungles of capitalism with the gospel of a classless society according to Lenin, and the missionaries of the Vatican penetrate all non-Catholic countries with a gospel of faith, service, and loyalty which emphasizes almost all Kremlin values in reverse."[217] Blanshard focuses

---

[211] Blanshard, *Communism, Democracy, and Catholic Power*, 5. See also *The God That Failed*, ed. Richard Crossman (New York: Bantam Books, 1959) [originally published 1950], 6 ("The Communist novice, subjecting his soul to the canon law of the Kremlin, felt something of the release which Catholicism also brings to the intellectual, wearied and worried by the privilege of freedom").

[212] Blanshard, *Communism, Democracy, and Catholic Power*, 43.

[213] Blanshard, *Communism, Democracy, and Catholic Power*, 134 [emphasis in original].

[214] Blanshard, *Communism, Democracy, and Catholic Power*, 137.

[215] Blanshard, *Communism, Democracy, and Catholic Power*, 139.

[216] Blanshard, *American Freedom and Catholic Power*, 31.

[217] Blanshard, *Communism, Democracy, and Catholic Power*, 263, chs. 11, 12. Blanshard does qualify the parallel somewhat. After first drawing it, he writes: "It is obvious that the

on Catholic penetration of labor unions, political parties, the diplomatic establishment, and, of course, the provision of education to the young. So far
as parties are concerned, "The question which many observers are asking,"
Blanshard declares, is, "Will such . . . parties be amalgamated and fused into
a Catholic international to parallel the Cominform and dominate western
European politics?"[218]

What's more, in a section of *American Freedom and Catholic Power* that
does not analogize the Church directly to communism, Blanshard seems to
have plainly imagined Catholicism in a similar light by describing it as an
ideology bent on world domination. He even posits the Catholic equivalent of the Domino Theory. "There is no Catholic plan for America distinct from the Catholic plan for the world," he warned. In fact, he claimed,
"[t]here are many worthwhile exhibits of the Catholic plan for America
in our own hemisphere." Though mightily resisted by intellectuals ("John
Dewey's books were burned in Brazil"), Latin America had largely fallen
(Blanshard lists Argentina, Bolivia, Colombia, Costa Rica, the Dominican
Republic, Panama, Paraguay, Peru, and Venezuela). To our immediate south,
only the Mexican Revolution staved off total disaster. And on our northern
border, Quebec is already Catholic through and through. Given these developments, the future of freedom in the United States itself was anything
but certain.[219] The ultimate formation of a united anti-American front was
possible, despite the ostensible anticommunism of the Church. "There is
so much basic kinship between the doctrinal absolutism of the Vatican and
that of the Kremlin that the possibility of ultimate collaboration on a basis
of mutual self-interest cannot be dismissed as unthinkable."[220]

When Vatican II came around in the early 1960s and seemed to signal a
thaw in the Church's traditional doctrines in many areas, Blanshard warned

---

Vatican's techniques of penetration are in sharp contrast to those of the Kremlin. The
Kremlin relies on violence wherever it is deemed to be necessary; the Vatican does not –
or, at least, has not done so in recent times. The Kremlin aims to destroy the governments
which it cannot conquer by persuasion; the Vatican is, on the whole, law-abiding and nonrevolutionary. But the Vatican has one special advantage not shared by any other church or
government. Since it is a church and a state, it can enter into any nation which permits the
free exercise of religion and use its machinery of power to further political as well as religious
ends. Simultaneously, it can use the reservoirs of religious devotion and prejudice among
its people on behalf of strictly political objectives." Blanshard, *Communism, Democracy, and
Catholic Power*, 263.

[218] Blanshard, *Communism, Democracy, and Catholic Power*, 273.

[219] Blanshard, *American Freedom and Catholic Power*, 269, 273–81, 284–8. One of the methods
of Catholic conquest to which "the Kremlin is a very poor second to the Vatican" is what
Blanshard called "conquest by fecundity," a form of "biological penetration and conquest."
He warned that "Canada is rapidly becoming a Catholic nation because of this policy,
and northern New England is being transformed by the Catholic overflow from Canada."
Blanshard, *Communism, Democracy, and Catholic Power*, 286.

[220] Blanshard, *American Freedom and Catholic Power*, 258.

his fellow Protestants not to be duped by calls for Christian unity: "Some potential Protestant negotiators might think of the sad analogy of the Popular Front Movement in American politics in the 1930s when relatively innocent liberals sat down to bargain with the representatives of Stalin and found themselves completely outmaneuvered by a Machiavellian strategy designed for the benefit of Big Brother in Moscow."[221]

The critique by the party of progress of the Church's "reactionary" views concerning Communism, the welfare state, abortion, marriage and divorce, and participatory church government, in characteristic progressive fashion, imagined church-state separationists as critics who see through false doctrines, social delusions, and veils of ignorance, hypocrisy, and superstition. This imagining – which has heavily informed Court-created constitutional doctrine concerning church-state separation since the mid-twentieth century – serves to obfuscate the affirmative substantive (indeed, in many cases, moralistic; and in some cases, antimoral) commitments of the progressive positions advocated by the party of progress. That affirmative, substantive commitment, which was joined to the critique of the affirmative commitments of American Catholics, is apparent throughout Blanshard's influential mid-century writings on church-state separation.

One of Blanshard's attacks on the Roman Catholic Church, for instance, centered around its congenial relation to the game of Bingo and its apparent responsibility for popularizing that game throughout the country. "[T]he game is openly encouraged on church premises in many parts of the United States," he complained. "Even Mayor LaGuardia was not powerful enough to eliminate it from New York City Catholic institutions."[222] Here, Blanshard's concern is not that the Church is imposing its moral views to restrict freedom in private life, but rather that, where penny ante gambling is concerned, the Church is not being morally interventionist enough.

While the progressive attachment to eugenics is often portrayed as a pre–World War II affair, it in fact remained popular among many anti-Catholic church-state separationists right through mid-century. In 1949, Blanshard complained, for example, that "[u]nder [the Catholic] theory of reproduction... eugenics is on the defensive."[223] Indeed, he approvingly cited the Supreme Court's notorious sterilization case of *Buck v. Bell* (1923) in *American Freedom and Catholic Power* ("an historic opinion"), noting that the Court's only dissenting vote was "that of Catholic Pierce Butler." And he warned mid-century political progressives that "the opposition of the hierarchy continues to hamper enforcement of the sterilization laws in the twenty-seven states that now have such laws, and to prevent the passage of adequate sterilization laws in other states." He added further that "Birthright, Inc., the

---

[221] Blanshard, *Vatican II*, 344.
[222] Blanshard, *American Freedom and Catholic Power*, 36.
[223] Blanshard, *American Freedom and Catholic Power*, 148.

national organization which is working for sterilization laws in all states, reports the same kind of threats against legislatures in this field that the Planned Parenthood Federation reports in the field of birth control."[224]

One further bit of evidence Blanshard adduces for the "inelasticity" and "immovable conservatism" of the Catholic Church is its rigid insistence on the "baptism of monstrosities" (what some today would call "the disabled"). "Since monstrosities have souls equal to the souls of mothers," Blanshard writes with disapproval, "every Catholic nurse must baptize every monstrosity if possible." This Catholic practice is cited to demonstrate "how Catholic hospitals are used as partisan and sectarian agencies in spite of the public claims by the clergy that they are common enterprises," and "how priests attempt to impose as much of their moral code as possible on non-Catholic hospitals."[225]

Hopes: Catholics and the Imagined Trajectory of Social and Political Progress

The fear of the power of Catholic schools on the part of the mid-century party of progress was especially acute because the Catholic Church took what it understood to be an antiprogressive stance on a broad array of important social and political issues. At the time, Blanshard was able to quote no less mainstream a source than the *Encyclopaedia Britannica* for the proposition that the Roman Catholic Church was at "war against the modern political and social order."[226] The Church was the prime embodiment to liberals of this era of a belated feudalism. It was totally antidemocratic and, hence, utterly un-American. Blanshard attacked the "absolute rule of the clergy" in the Church, which he declared to be "without parallel in the Protestant Churches."[227]

The genuflections of the faithful before the so-called princes of the Church, and even before simple bishops, annoy and disturb non-Catholic Americans, who are likely to ask: "Is not such servility utterly contrary to the American tradition?" "What good American ever kneels to any man?" "How did this medieval posturing ever get to the United States?"[228]

Blanshard declared the Pope to be "one of the few remaining absolute monarchs in the world."[229]

---

[224] Blanshard, *American Freedom and Catholic Power*, 152. Amongst the parade of horribles Blanshard lists in his "Catholic Plan for America" is that the Catholics will push through a Constitutional Amendment that states that "[s]terilization of any human being is forbidden except as an infliction of grave punishment under the authority of the government for a crime committed." Blanshard, *American Freedom and Catholic Power*, 269.

[225] Blanshard, *American Freedom and Catholic Power*, 121–3.

[226] Blanshard, *American Freedom and Catholic Power*, 23.

[227] Blanshard, *American Freedom and Catholic Power*, 15.

[228] Blanshard, *American Freedom and Catholic Power*, 15.

[229] Blanshard, *American Freedom and Catholic Power*, 19.

The Catholic Church also preached antediluvian notions about sex. Its commitment to priestly celibacy, in fact, was the fount of the Church's entire "antisexual code." ("Many Catholic laymen believe that the whole priestly system of sexual dogma is a direct result of celibacy, a compensation for thwarted instincts and suppressed desires.")[230] The problem apparently was that "Freud's wisdom was not available to the Popes and theologians who first imposed celibacy upon a reluctant clergy and [thus] they could scarcely be held responsible for failing to appreciate the gravity of the effects upon human nature of suppressing the basic human instincts."[231] "Obligatory chastity," Blanshard noted, "is losing some of its appeal as knowledge of psychology and psychoanalysis spreads among those who would normally be considered prospective recruits."[232] Nuns, he declared, "belong to an age when women allegedly enjoyed subjection and reveled in self-abasement. Their unhygienic costumes and their medieval rules of conduct... reflect a medieval attitude of piety and feminine subordination that seems utterly alien to the typically robust and independent spirit of American womanhood."[233]

Priests warped by celibacy inevitably gave bad advice, and a hierarchy so spiritually mangled refused to see the sensibleness of abortion not only to protect the mother's health and in cases of rape or incest but, "most important[ly]," "to prevent the wreaking of a home by the acquisition of a brood too large to support."[234] He added, emphasizing the Church's failure to consider modern conditions, that "[t]he relatively simple and quick dilation and curettage performed by a skilled physician is not more dangerous than a tonsillectomy, and the patient can usually return to work in a few days."[235]

A celibate hierarchy also impeded social progress by its opposition to birth control, and such opposition had consequences not only at home but also abroad: "It would be difficult to imagine a worse *faux pas* than the Pope's figure of speech [in a recent talk] about 'the banquet of life.' One could almost hear the hungry millions of the world jeering in derision: whose banquet?"[236] The Church set itself against religiously mixed marriages by Catholics, and against efforts to reform divorce laws in New York State and elsewhere.[237]

---

[230] Blanshard, *American Freedom and Catholic Power*, 154.
[231] Blanshard, *American Freedom and Catholic Power*, 132.
[232] Blanshard, *American Freedom and Catholic Power*, 18.
[233] Blanshard, *American Freedom and Catholic Power*, 67.
[234] Blanshard, *Vatican II*, 256.
[235] Blanshard, *Vatican II*, 256.
[236] Blanshard, *Vatican II*, 239. Seldes characterizes the Church as the "chief antagonist" of Margaret Sanger. Seldes, *Catholic Crisis*, 56.
[237] Blanshard similarly criticized the Church for its opposition to birth control ("the right to plan a family is one of the basic human rights") and to the reform of state divorce laws ("those of us who have fought in various places for more liberal divorce laws find every

Roman Catholicism was, of course, antiscience; and, what was progressivism but a science for improving society, shorn of superstition and delusions? For example, Blanshard complained, the Church opposed the "hygienic," "economical," and "common sense method of the disposal of the body": cremation. The case for cremation (which was in vogue among white, middle-class, Protestant professionals in the mid-twentieth century) was rooted in the nineteenth-century social reformist project, when it was informed by reformist notions of "purity" and practiced only by the most "advanced thinkers." Jane Addams, Francis Willard, and Eugene Debs were pioneering contributors to the cause. As usual, the Catholic Church, which opposed cremations because of Church doctrine concerning the resurrection of the body, was viewed by burial reformers as obstructing the course of progress as set by the country's most advanced scientific thinkers.[238]

The Church had certainly proved itself hostile to civil liberties through its efforts to ban books, to pressure public schools on the content of reading assignments, and to influence film ratings. In so doing, the Catholic hierarchy has "use[d] American freedom as a cloak for the systematic cultivation of separatism and intolerance among the American Catholic people."[239] The final point in Blanshard's imagined six-point "Catholic Plan for America" reads "The First Amendment to the Constitution of the United States is hearby repealed."[240]

---

time . . . we are blocked in the Legislature in Albany or any where else by the Catholic hierarchy") in his talk at Harvard Law School.

[238] Blanshard, *American Freedom and Catholic Power*, 127, ch. 10 ("Science, Scholarship and Superstition"). See Stephen Prothero, *Purified by Fire: A History of Cremation in America* (Berkeley: University of California Press, 2001). As Prothero notes, the opposition between the vanguard and the Church goes back as far as the French Revolution, when the revolutionaries pushed cremation as part of their efforts to undermine the Church's authority. Beginning in the 1880s and 1890s in the United States, the Church issued three separate decrees against cremation and in favor of burial. By the time Blanshard was writing, the cremation versus burial debate was still alive, albeit in altered, less heated form. In the 1950 Tennessee Williams play, *The Rose Tattoo*, a Catholic priest, Father DeLeo, is depicted calling cremation "an abomination in the sight of God." Blanshard's sanitary justification for cremation had been discredited by modern science twenty or thirty years before he wrote. Despite the falling away of its sanitary justification, many mid-century, white, middle-class Protestants were newly drawn to it on aesthetic grounds. See also Jessica Mitford, *The American Way of Death* (New York: Simon and Schuster, 1963), 161–72, 246. As part of the Vatican II reforms in 1963, Pope Paul VI formally relaxed the Church's ban on cremation that had been in effect since the 1880s. Even with the Vatican II reforms, however, the Church continued to endorse burial as the preferred means of bodily disposal. Prothero, *Purified by Fire*, 109, 129, 134–5, 136, 154, 157–9, 165.

[239] Blanshard, *American Freedom and Catholic Power*, ch. 9.

[240] Blanshard, *American Freedom and Catholic Power*, 267. See also George Seldes, *The Catholic Crisis*, 49–50, 98. See Powe, *Warren Court and American Politics*, 190–3, discussing *Burstyn v. Wilson*, 343 U.S. 495 (1952)(invalidating state ban on sacrilegious films, spearheaded by the Catholic League of Decency); *Kingsley Pictures v. Board of Regents*, 360 U.S. 684 (1959)(invalidating similar ban on grounds of "immorality" of a film version of *Lady Chatterley's*

When a taxpayer suit was launched in 1940 against the City College of New York challenging the appointment to CCNY's faculty of Bertrand Russell, a Catholic judge invalidated the appointment on the grounds of Russell's unfitness, as a sex radical and atheist, to instruct the city's young. Russell's court case was famous – indeed, notorious. It played a significant part in forming the cultural image of American Catholics in mid-twentieth-century America.[241]

To make matters worse, Catholicism had no respect for due process: "A priest can be suspended by his bishop without even a hearing if the reasons seem sufficient to his bishop, and the bishop is not even required to inform the priest of his reasons."[242] It opposed the new trend toward ecumenicism in religion – what Catholics called "indifferentism" – that Blanshard described as "the form of broad-mindedness which permits men to view other religions with calm detachment and to search for a common denominator of agreement."[243]

And finally, the Church had long set itself in opposition both to socialism and to the expansion of the welfare state.[244] Politically, it was joined most prominently in the reformist intellectual imagination with corrupt urban political machines. Seldes, in fact, devoted a chapter of *The Catholic Crisis* to "Catholics and Political Machines," showcasing Jersey City's Mayor Frank Hague, whom Catholic organizations backed "in his fight against free speech and the democratic system of government." "The political machine of Jersey City . . . is corrupt," Seldes wrote. "It is not only financially corrupt but also morally corrupt. The law is broken there, and undue pressure is brought by an arrogant majority against a Liberal and Progressive minority which seeks to uphold the first ten amendments to the Constitution of the United States and the Bill of Rights."[245]

Blanshard saw hope in Pope John XXIII's 1961 encyclical, *Mater et Magistra*, which "placed the Catholic Church on the side of social reform and foreign aid to underdeveloped countries. Equally important, it rambled over the whole field of poverty and social discontent without indulging in the usual tirade against communism."[246] Blanshard was delighted that "the leader of the largest Christian Church had stopped repeating stale anticommunist clichés and recognized the whole world's moral responsibility for destroying poverty."[247]

Lover). See, generally, Gregory D. Black, *Hollywood Censored: Morality Codes, Catholics, and the Movies* (Cambridge: Cambridge University Press, 1994).

[241] Marsden, *Soul of the American University*, 383; Hollinger, *Science, Jews, and Secular Culture*, 159.

[242] Blanshard, *American Freedom and Catholic Power*, 16.

[243] Blanshard, *American Freedom and Catholic Power*, 32. See Allitt, *Catholic Intellectuals*, 12.

[244] Blanshard, *American Freedom and Catholic Power*, 46–8, 240, 242, 248, 265.

[245] Seldes, *Catholic Crisis*, 155. See *Hague v. CIO*, 307 U.S. 496 (1939).

[246] Blanshard, *Vatican II*, 25.

[247] Blanshard, *Vatican II*, 26.

Given all these heresies, it is not surprising that mid-twentieth-century progressives demonized the Roman Catholic "other" by imagining Catholic religious belief not simply as a pillar of reaction but as a form of maladjustment, even of psychological deviance. So, for instance, Blanshard declared it to be "mentally abnormal" for the Pope to claim infallibility. As for the Irish, he opined, "using the Roman system of authoritative power ... compensate[s] for an inner sense of insecurity which still seems to survive from the days when the Irish Catholics were a despised immigrant minority." And deploying the era's Freudianism, he concluded that during the ritual of Catholic confession, "[t]he joy of release for pent-up emotion and the comfort of communion are mingled with personal submission and the yearning of the grown-up child for a substitute father."[248]

Fears and Hopes and the Battle for the Future: Separationism and the Schools

It is essential that this basic issue be seen for what it is – namely, as the encouragement of a powerful reactionary world organization in the most vital realm of democratic life with the resulting promulgation of principles inimical to democracy. We cannot deny that public education needs federal aid in order to equalize opportunity between state and state, and between individual and individual. But it would be a poor bargain indeed to gain material aid at the expense of losing our greatest intellectual and moral heritage.

                                        – John Dewey, *The Catholic Hierarchy vs. the Public School*[249]

Writing at about the time of the *Everson* decision (1947), Paul Blanshard declared that "a tremendous revival of anti-Catholic feeling is taking place in the United States and ... its focal point is the educational policy of the Church." That feeling "is strongest among the liberals who have always stood most courageously for personal tolerance."[250]

The causes of this renewed surge in anti-Catholic feeling, as Blanshard identified it, were the extension of bus transportation at public expense to students traveling to parochial schools and efforts to spread new federal aid for education to parochial and public schools alike. Both initiatives were in large part a product of the mid-century political economy, which was characterized, first, by a radical New Deal and post–New Deal expansion of the distribution of state aid for social services and, second, in the immediate postwar years, by a spiral in prices and, hence, the cost of living. Under these conditions, the question of public money going to parochial schools assumed

---

[248] Blanshard, *American Freedom and Catholic Power*, 23, 27, 39.
[249] John Dewey, "The Catholic Hierarchy vs. the Public School," quoted in Blanshard, *American Freedom and Catholic Power*, 106. Dewey, a key figure, of course, in shaping the intellectual architecture of the Progressive Era, remained a participant in the fight against Catholicism and for "science" and "democracy" through the middle years of the twentieth century. Hollinger, *Science, Jews, and Secular Culture*, 158–60.
[250] Blanshard, *American Freedom and Catholic Power*, 59.

a new political prominence. The proposed Aiken bill would have provided federal funds for parochial school incidentals such as bus transportation, instructional equipment, and supplies. The vigorous opposition of the National Education Association helped to defeat the proposal. In an echo of the earlier proposals of nativist President Grant and Congressman James G. Blaine in the nineteenth century, talk about a constitutional amendment to ban all public aid to churches and church schools was once again in the air.[251]

Given the nature of instruction in the Catholic schools as understood by the mid-century liberals and progressives – the familiar charge long since made by the Ku Klux Klan and others that parochial schools indoctrinated children and that proper schools "taught [children] *how to think, not* what to think" – the provision of public monies to parochial schools posed a problem for the very promise of a free future for the nation. "Often the parochial schools and public schools are on opposite sides of the same street, dividing the children into competing and even hostile groups, conscious of their own differences and suspicious of each other's way of life." "[This] separatism," Blanshard declared, "is particularly harmful when, as so often happens, the Catholic group is largely an immigrant group that needs assimilation and Americanization more than any other part of the community."[252] In these Catholic schools, *The Nation* columnist complained, the teachers are able to evade state laws requiring that instruction take place in English only.[253] What's more, Catholic schools proved a burden to the poor – to whose interests liberals and progressives understood themselves as staunchly committed. After all, allowing Catholics to send their children to parochial schools placed a terrible financial strain on poor Roman Catholic families.[254]

Isolated in parochial schools from their American peers, Catholic students were subjected to "authoritarian" habits of mind because their teachers "never learned to use the intellectual freedom of the unshackled, inquiring mind."[255] One sure sign of the failure of these schools was that Catholicism

---

[251] Blanshard, *American Freedom and Catholic Power*, 93–5.

[252] Blanshard, *American Freedom and Catholic Power*, 60. The quote that proper schools "teach children how to think, not what to think" is from *The Ku Klux Klan Presents Its View of the Free Public Schools*, 2 (n.p., circa early 1920s), quoted in Hamburger, *Separation of Church and State*, 414.

[253] Blanshard, *American Freedom and Catholic Power*, 73.

[254] Blanshard, *American Freedom and Catholic Power*, 62.

[255] Blanshard, *American Freedom and Catholic Power*, 69. In his Harvard Law School debate, Blanshard argued that freedom in America was threatened not simply by some public money going to America's Catholic schools, but, in fact, by the very existence of those schools. At base, the schools were fundamentally undemocratic and, hence, un-American. "We Americans believe in the public school as the foundation of our democracy," he declared, echoing John Dewey. "It isn't merely that we believe in public schools as a place to cram knowledge into children's heads. We believe in the public schools as a democratic community where the children of every creed can gather together and learn how to associate with each other without religious prejudice. We built that system and are proud of it." "Now, I

is the "denomination that has the highest proportion of white criminals in our American prisons of any denomination."[256]

The Constructions of a State of Courts Concerning Education: Nationbuilding in the Supreme Court's Religion Cases

The waxing of anti-Catholicism in mid-twentieth-century America was intertwined in complex ways with the era's much-noted preoccupation with patriotism and national unity. As was the case during the late nineteenth and early twentieth centuries, those who understood themselves as "progressive" were hardly, in any uniform sense, the opponents of One-Hundred-Percent Americanism. What had changed at mid-century was merely that the scientific imperative (in the work of Robert K. Merton and others) had been recast in new forms, and that the Americanization and nationbuilding effort had shifted from a project of bureaucratic statebuilding to a nationbuilding project imposed on the country through court-fashioned constitutional doctrine concerning the separation of church and state.

Even a quarter century after the Supreme Court's *Pierce* decision, it is worth noting, the call for mandatory public schooling was far from dead. Paul Blanshard, for example, lamented in 1949 that "the people have accepted the Catholic schools as substitutes for public education under the state compulsory education laws."[257] Indeed, he worried loudly, blithely disregarding the 1925 Oregon schools decision as a sport, or an Old Court irrelevancy, that we might soon see a "Catholic Amendment to the Constitution of the United States" providing that "[c]ompulsory education in public schools exclusively shall be unlawful in any state in the Union."[258] In 1952, the president of Harvard University, James Bryant Conant, in an overt appeal to nationbuilding, vociferously attacked private elementary and secondary education in the United States as a "threat to our democratic unity." When he was criticized for this by Catholic leaders, the Harvard faculty rose overwhelmingly to his defense.[259]

---

know," he continued, "that these Catholic Parochial Schools have thousands of devoted nuns and priests and many of them render a splendid service. But they are not fundamentally democratic schools. They are controlled entirely by the priests. They are an organic part of the Church system. Their school boards aren't elected as public school boards are. Their nuns are not allowed to read newspapers or magazines or books of their own choice. How can they teach freedom if they don't know freedom of thought themselves?" The issue of public money going to such schools, the progressive declared, "is going to be the great battleground of democracy in the next ten years." "Catholic Church and Politics," *Harvard Law School Forum* (1950).

[256] Blanshard, *American Freedom and Catholic Power*, 81.

[257] Blanshard, *American Freedom and Catholic Power*, 60.

[258] Blanshard, *American Freedom and Catholic Power*, 268.

[259] John T. McGreevy, *Catholicism and American Freedom* (New York: W. W. Norton, 2003), 187–8. See also George H. Nash, *The Conservative Intellectual Movement in America Since 1945* (Wilmington, DE: ISI Books, 1998), 71.

The Court's mid-century nationbuilding inititiative was related in complex ways to the era's peculiar constellation of hopes and fears. As Blanshard's work indicated, that constellation evinced a disposition toward communism that was ambivalent, even contradictory. Intellectuals and opinion leaders of the era, for example, scorned the Catholic Church both for evoking in their minds the horror of Soviet totalitarianism as well as for what they took to be the Church's exaggerated hostility toward it. Along the same lines, Catholics were criticized and even mocked both for their uncritical allegiance to a foreign potentate (the Pope) and the loud and gaudy nature of their patriotism. Given this brew of contradictions, ambivalences, bogies, and fears at mid-century concerning the relationship between religion and state, many historians have recently come to appreciate the implausibility of traditional Whiggish accounts of the Court's twentieth-century establishment clause jurisprudence, an account that posits the Court's realization in these years of the founder's original understanding of the separation of church and state. The dicta and decisions concerning religion in the schools issued by the Court at mid-century were the products of a distinctive approach to American nationbuilding that had deep roots in the unique vision of democracy forged in the crucible of mid-twentieth-century progressive political thought.

That vision represented a marked departure from earlier understandings. In the late nineteenth and early twentieth centuries, the Court had fashioned a civil libertarianism for the school that was especially protective of the association rights of ethnic and religious groups, rights that were menaced by the increasingly insistent claims of an increasingly ambitious interventionist state. The Court fashioned this old pluralism through the use of theories not of group rights, but rather of individual rights, for example by backing the rights of parents, teachers, and property owners in its *Meyer* and *Pierce* decisions. Those individuals could then, in turn, use those individual rights to unite with others sharing like commitments to build the strong communal institutions that would nourish and sustain the little platoons of civil society they valued most.

By the early twentieth century, however, these platoons began to be seen by progressive statebuilders not as the nourishing sustenance of a strong political order but rather as a maddening array of draining and sapping atavisms and obstacles that thwarted the achievement of unified – and highly individualized – statist modern polity.[260] Family and religion, as we have seen, were special bugaboos of progressives. The first choice of many of

---

[260] See William J. Novak, *The People's Welfare: Law and Regulation in Nineteenth Century America.* (Chapel Hill: University of North Carolina Press, 1996), 240. Catholics epitomized for many (Protestant) progressives the danger of a certain "group oriented" approach to social and political life. See Hamburger, *Separation of Church and State*, 194. Of course, as I demonstrated in my previous chapter, they were often great champions of group analysis when it was applied to labor, and, later, categories anchored in race and sex. These

these progressives would have been to vault over these obstacles by creating a centralized and nationalized system of education, as had been done in the presumably more highly developed and advanced European welfare states. That developmental path, however, was foreclosed for an array of reasons that have been canvassed previously. In the wake of this developmental failure, the matter increasingly became a project of constitutional law. Beginning in the 1930s, the Court began to hear an unprecedented number of school cases. In these decisions, the Court clearly involved itself in the affirmative, nationbuilding task of setting policy concerning what it – informed, supported, and (in its failures and hesitations) criticized by progressive law professors – took to be the construction of modern American citizens.

In this project, religion as a whole did not fare well. But some religions ran up harder against the new imperative than others. Catholicism had long been suspect in American education for "teaching children not how to think, but what to think." By the 1930s, the Church had the additional misfortune of being perceived as an ally of a wide variety of forces of reaction and an opponent of a series of progressive reform imperatives. When the staunch anticommunism of America's Catholics was played out in an era of heavy fellow-traveling among intellectual elites, Catholics came to stand for many as arrayed against academic and intellectual freedom and progress itself – along almost every possible political dimension. Moreover, when the civil rights movement moved north in the mid-1960s, and civil rights had fully displaced the "labor problem" as the defining progressive imperative, Catholic efforts to preserve the religious uniformity of their urban parishes came to be interpreted by many as simply the ugly Northern counterpart to a racist system of Southern apartheid.[261] It is only in this context that we can begin to appreciate why parochial schools assumed the menacing aspect they did in the mind's eye of a self-consciously progressive postwar Supreme Court. The Court's commitment to free speech and an antiracist constitutionalism were joined with the simultaneous commitment to church-state separationism that reflected a wariness about religious influence that was unprecedented, if not in the history of the country, then at least in the history of the Court. In this context, parochial schools appeared to raise very serious constitutional problems.

The themes of citizenship, loyalty, and intellectual liberty in the Supreme Court's school cases played themselves out simultaneously in two lines of cases that must be considered together. Those cases involve the constitutional legitimacy of the influence of two types of religions in the schools: the secular religion of communism and the traditional theistic religions.[262]

---

inconsistencies are constitutive of a modern political order characterized by patterns of intercurrence.

[261] McGreevy, *Parish Boundaries*.

[262] In characterizing communism as a "secular religion," I follow, among others, Raymond Aron. Raymond Aron, *The Dawn of Universal History: Selected Essays from a Witness of the Twentieth Century* (New York: Basic Books, 2002), 177–201.

The Court's most explicit considerations of issues of academic and intellectual freedom took place in its cases involving communism. As we have seen, the issue of academic and intellectual freedom was intellectually and politically prominent long before it became a matter of court-enunciated constitutional law. These issues were at the center of the nineteenth- and early-twentieth-century antagonisms between pragmatists, Darwinists, and nativists and both church-run schools and public schools under the control of traditionally minded local communities. Questions involving communism, per se, became ascendant, only following the Bolshevik Revolution (1917) and only after the Court began its sustained involvement in education issues beginning in the 1920s. The Supreme Court's mid-twentieth-century school decisions involving communism are not uniform in their results, although we can say, generally speaking, that what many would now consider the conservative, "anti–intellectual freedom" position predominated during Fred Vinson's tenure as chief justice (1946–53) and the civil libertarian position (typically accompanied by praise of the scientific pluralist outlook) predominated in the Warren years (1953–69). This directionality, culminating in the institutionalization of modern civil libertarianism, of course, informs the traditional Whiggish model of constitutional development concerning civil rights and civil liberties.

Of particular interest for our purposes are the political visions or constitutional constructions underlying these communist-related school cases. In a 1952 opinion striking down a requirement that college professors take a loyalty oath, for example, Justice Black, who was a devoted reader of Paul Blanshard, had a Klan background, and was the chief architect of the Court's mid-twentieth-century establishment clause jurisprudence, penned a full-throated defense of intellectual freedom, declaring that "[t]yrannical totalitarian governments cannot safely allow their people to speak with complete freedom. I believe with the Framers that our free government can."[263] In the same case, Justice Frankfurter, a former professor himself, added:

[I]n view of the nature of the teacher's relation to the effective exercise of the rights which are safeguarded by the Bill of Rights and by the Fourteenth Amendment, inhibition of freedom of thought and of action upon thought, in the case of teachers brings the safeguards of those amendments vividly into operation. Such unwarranted inhibition upon the free spirit of teachers affects not only those who, like the appellants, are immediately before the Court. It has an unmistakable tendency to chill that free play of the spirit which all teachers ought especially to cultivate and practice.[264]

---

[263] *Wieman v. Updegraff*, 344 U.S. 183 (1952). On the depth of Black's Klan background and anti-Catholicism, which have been downplayed as part of the ideological project involving the construction of the legitimacy of modern civil libertarianism, see Hamburger, *Separation of Church and State*, 422–34, 461–78. This construction of Black's Klan allegiances as insignificant should be considered alongside Felix Frankfurter's mythologization of Holmes as essential parts of the ideological construction of twentieth-century American constitutionalism. See Alshuler, *Law Without Values*, 181–6.

[264] *Wieman*, 344 U.S. at 195.

In *Sweezy v. New Hampshire* (1957), the Court, in upholding the rights of a university professor to "academic freedom and political expression" against the demand by state authorities investigating subversive activities that he hand over his lecture notes and give testimony regarding his knowledge of subversives within the state. Justice Warren, writing for the Court, proclaimed:

No one should underestimate the vital role in a democracy that is played by those who guide and train our youth. To impose any strait jacket upon the intellectual leaders in our colleges and universities would imperil the future of our Nation.... Scholarship cannot flourish in an atmosphere of suspicion and distrust. Teachers and students must always remain free to inquire, to study and to evaluate, to gain new maturity and understanding; otherwise our civilization will stagnate and die.[265]

The Court in *Sweezy* was especially solicitous of the political beliefs of teachers, noting,

History has amply proved the virtue of political activity by minority, dissident groups, who innumerable times have been in the vanguard of democratic thought and whose programs were ultimately accepted. Mere unorthodoxy or dissent from the prevailing mores is not to be condemned. The absence of such voices would be a symptom of grave illness within our society.[266]

Justice Brennan, who, along with Justice Black, is one of the chief architects of the modern civil libertarian understanding of free speech, declared in a later case involving university professors that the First Amendment "does not tolerate laws that cast a pall of orthodoxy over the classroom.... The classroom is peculiarly the 'marketplace of ideas.' The Nation's future depends upon leaders trained through wide exposure to that robust exchange of ideas which discovers truth 'out of a multitude of tongues, [rather] than through any kind of authoritative selection.'"[267] These same principles and the reference to the "public interest in having free and unhindered debate on matters of public importance" were applied not just in cases at the college level but also in those involving teachers in the public secondary schools.[268] Interestingly enough, while the Court's

---

[265] *Sweezy v. New Hampshire*, 354 U.S. 234, 250 (1957).

[266] *Sweezy*, 354 U.S. at 251.

[267] *Keyishian v. Board of Regents*, 385 U.S. 589 (1967) (holding loyalty oath requirement for university professors unconstitutional on vagueness and First Amendment "academic freedom" grounds), citing *United States v. Associated Press*, 52 F.Supp. 362, 372 (S.D.N.Y., 1943). See also *Baggett v. Bullitt*, 377 U.S. 360 (1964) (striking down loyalty oath requirement for University of Washington faculty and employees on vagueness and due process grounds and noting that the constitutional violation is particularly pernicious when First Amendment freedoms may be deterred).

[268] *Pickering v. Board of Education*, 391 U.S. 563, 573 (1968) (citing *Time v. Hill*, 385 U.S. 374 (1967))(invalidating on First Amendment grounds the dismissal of a teacher for criticizing his district's school board in a letter to the editor of the local newspaper). See also *Epperson*

secondary schools decisions involving teachers reached the same result as those involving post-secondary education, the Court shied away from anchoring the secondary school decisions in doctrines concerning free speech and notions of academic freedom. In these cases, the Court instead evinced a marked preference for anchoring its reasoning either in constitutional doctrine proscribing overbreadth or vagueness or (in cases involving the teaching of evolution) in the establishment clause.[269] The scientific pluralist outlook seemed to be driving decisions in both sorts of school cases. But given that the countervailing communal and parental claims of the right to transmit local traditions and values to the young were so much stronger when lower-level schools were involved, the Court may have been inhibited from openly deploying soaring legitimating rhetoric of intellectual freedom in these cases.

When one does find eloquent paeans to free speech, inquiry, and expression in cases involving secondary school teachers, they are typically in the dissents, most likely because, there, the individual justices by definition had already given up on forging a consensus and needed to speak only for themselves and not for the Court or for other justices. Thus, in a 1952 case involving the application of an antisubversive civil service law to secondary school teachers, Justice Black's dissent lamented the passage of "another of those rapidly multiplying legislative enactments which make it dangerous – this time for schoolteachers – to think or say anything except what a transient majority happen to approve at the moment." "Basically," he observed, "these laws rest on the belief that government should supervise and limit the flow of ideas into the minds of men." The Constitution, Black emphasized, should "encourage varied intellectual outlooks in the belief that the best views will prevail."[270] In a decision a few years later upholding the dismissal of a Philadelphia schoolteacher following his refusal to answer questions his superintendent had posed on his possible Communist affiliations and activities, Justice Douglas's dissent (joined by Justice Black) quotes Robert Jackson's encomium to "intellectual individualism" from the Jehovah's

---

v. Arkansas, 393 U.S. 97, 106, 104 (1968) (striking down on establishment clause grounds a state statute making it unlawful for public school teachers to teach evolution: "There is and can be no doubt that the First Amendment does not permit the state to require that teaching and learning must be tailored to the principles or prohibitions of any religious sect or dogma." "Our courts... have not failed to apply the First Amendment's mandate in our educational system where essential to safeguard the fundamental values of freedom of speech and inquiry and of belief").

[269] *Shelton v. Tucker*, 364 U.S. 479 (1960) (holding Arkansas statute requiring that all teachers provide state with a list of the organizations to which they belong to be a violation of the teachers' Fourteenth Amendment due process associational rights); *Cramp v. Board of Public Instruction*, 368 U.S. 278 (1961) (striking down on vagueness grounds loyalty oath required of Florida public school teachers); *Elfbrand v. Russell*, 384 U.S. 11 (1966) (striking down on overbreadth grounds loyalty oath required of Arizona public school teachers); *Epperson v. Arkansas*, 393 U.S. 97 (1968).

[270] *Adler v. Board of Education*, 342 U.S. 485, 496–7 (1952).

Witness flag salute case and emphasizes that intellectual inquiry and belief is an area "where government may not probe." "The fitness of a subway conductor for his job depends on his health, his promptness, his record for reliability, not on his politics or philosophy of life." Likewise, Douglas added, "[t]he fitness of a teacher for her job turns on her devotion to that priesthood, her education, and her performance in the library, in the laboratory, and the classroom, not on her political beliefs."[271] It is not the proper place of government to police the beliefs of teachers, even if the failure to police may lead to some danger or harm: "Total security is possible only in a totalitarian regime," Douglas concluded, "the kind of system we profess to combat."[272]

The majority opinions in the secondary school cases that we now classify as hostile to civil libertarian concerns reject the scientific pluralist approach as applied to the beliefs of teachers and, in a vision that is statist in its prejudices, although localist in its forbearance, emphasizes instead the risks the convictions of the teachers pose to their young and impressionable charges. Justice Sherman Minton's opinion for the Court in *Adler v. Board of Education* (1952) is illustrative. "A teacher works in a sensitive area in a schoolroom," Minton explains. "There he shapes the attitude of young minds towards the society in which they live. In this, the state has a vital concern. It must preserve the integrity of the schools . . . to protect [them] from pollution and thereby . . . defend its own existence."[273] The problem is that "propaganda can be disseminated among the children by those who teach them and to whom they look for guidance, authority, and leadership." Subversive organizations, the legislature found, are comprised of members who "use their positions to advocate and teach their doctrines, and are frequently bound by oath, agreement, pledge, or understanding to follow, advocate, and teach a prescribed line or group dogma or doctrine without regard to truth or free inquiry."[274] As for the associational and speech rights of the teachers, Minton says that "[i]t is clear that such persons have the right under our law to assemble, speak, think and believe as they will. It is equally clear that they have no right to work for the state in the school system on their own terms."[275]

Minton's approach to these issues clearly runs counter to the thrust of contemporary civil libertarianism. Although the analogy is not precise, what is striking is that when transferred from the cases involving the secular religion of communism in schools to the cases involving theistic religion that were proliferating before the Court at precisely the same time, Minton's

---

[271] *Beilan v. Board of Public Education*, 357 U.S. 399, 415 (1958).
[272] *Beilan*, 357 U.S. at 416.
[273] *Adler*, 342 U.S. at 493.
[274] *Adler*, 342 U.S. at 489–90.
[275] *Adler*, 342 U.S. at 492.

concerns suddenly transmogrify into the core of church-state separationism. The analogy is not precise, of course, because no laws forbade Catholics from teaching in public schools. This distinction itself, however, can be overstated because, as Philip Hamburger and John T. McGreevy have demonstrated at length, American history is rife with political movements (often progressive movements) calling for bans on Catholic schools, the Catholic Church itself, boycotts of Catholic businesses, and the firing of Catholic employees. There were also efforts to force nuns employed as teachers in Indian schools to remove their "distinctive garb" and even to remove all Catholics from their positions as teachers in public schools – a history that before Hamburger and McGreevy barely served as a footnote in Whiggish, civil libertarian narratives that preferred to focus on the perils of anticommunism.[276] Minton's animating focus on the perils of indoctrination – an anti–civil libertarian concern in schools cases involving communism – was a major concern of the era's civil libertarian establishment clause decisions.

One side of the dynamic at work in cases involving the place of secular and theistic religions in the nation's schools involved the ambivalent attitude toward communism that pervaded the thinking of the liberal/left intellectual elite for much of the century. The other side of it, however, involved a vision of either religion generally or, commonly enough, the Catholic religion in particular, as powerful, dogmatic, and unyielding and hence dangerously combustible. This vision, which has a pedigree in American political thought that long predates the work of John Rawls and his progeny, is profoundly troubled by the possibility of religion entering into a common public space, though it does permit it to do so under carefully specified conditions. For those hewing to this vision, religiosity raises the specter of divisiveness, and often divisiveness unto war, on the model of the often explicitly cited religious wars of sixteenth- and seventeenth-century Europe. Because of these threats, which are augmented by having children indoctrinated in these ill-starred dogmas, modern pluralism – scientific pluralism, that is – needed to take a highly vigilant attitude toward the entry of religion into public spaces, and especially into the public schools.[277]

---

[276] Hamburger, *Separation of Church and State*, 366, 373, and *passim*; McGreevy, *American Freedom and Catholic Power*. For a rare exception, see Donohue, *Politics of the American Civil Liberties Union*; William A. Donohue, *Twilight of Liberty: The Legacy of the A.C.L.U.* (New Brunswick, NJ: Transaction Publishers, 1994).

[277] Rawls has referred to these types of claims, often (and oftentimes improperly) associated universally with religions, as "comprehensive doctrines" or "comprehensive beliefs." John Rawls, *Political Liberalism* (New York: Columbia University Press, 1996), 242–3. For a contemporaneous presentation of this vision as postwar conventional academic wisdom, see Mary McCarthy's fictional account of the discussions in a liberal arts college faculty meeting over what to do in light of charges that a professor is about to be dismissed on the basis of his communist past. Mary McCarthy, *The Groves of Academe* (New York: Harvest Books, 1980) [originally published 1951], 92, 118 ("For everyone but the plaintiff

The Court's modern doctrine concerning religion, which revived Jefferson's "wall of separation" metaphor, was invented during a surge of anti-Catholicism in the 1940s. This surge united intellectuals, liberal Protestants, and Reform Jews, all of whom, drawing upon broad-ranging rhetoric concerning the perils of religious dogmatism and of not thinking for oneself, worked to construct Roman Catholicism as especially divisive and dangerous – in a Cold War context that put a premium on ecumenicism in the service of Americanism.[278]

Led by Justice Black, the Court announced in 1947 for the first time that the First and Fourteenth Amendments, properly interpreted, mandated the separation of church and state. The *Everson* decision, which involved the use of taxpayer funds to bus children to schools, secular and religious alike, was

Van Tour ... Mulcahy's confessed Communist past and the President's right to fire him for it became immediately subordinated to some collateral issue; thus Bentkoop ... was impelled to state, categorically, speaking as a neo-Protestant, that his support for Mulcahy rested, very simply, on his belief that it was important to have at least one theist in the Literature department. On any other occasion, this avowal would have provoked a clamor, since it laid bare a view of education-as-indoctrination that was as shocking to the liberals and pluralists present as would have been the sight of an imported serpent rearing up on Aristede's Coptic rug. But this morning such a response was held in abeyance ... the notion, in fact of a working alliance with God produced an agreeable sensation of jesuitry in everyone, as though it were a pact with the dark Plutonic powers. They felt heartened and stimulated by the very novelty of it ... ; 'Well now, Alma,' [Aristede] allowed, 'I am not sure you have the correct formulation. Intellectual freedom – that is the usual point, isn't it? Can a Communist under discipline have intellectual freedom? We hear that they cannot, that they are under strict orders to promote their infamous doctrine; their minds are not free as ours are.' Van Tour interrupted, excitedly. 'Catholics are not free either,' he protested with heat. Like many teachers of English, he was not able to think very clearly and responded, like a conditioned watch-dog, to certain sets of words which he found vaguely inimical. ... 'Catholics believe in a single truth, too,' he cried, warming. 'They only tolerate opposition in countries where they haven't taken over the government. Look at Spain! Why should we let *them* teach when we won't allow it to Communists?' " See also Kent Greenawalt, who refers to varieties of religious beliefs characterized by "views that are narrow and dogmatic, that leave nothing for dialogue with others" as not belong[ing] in the politics of a liberal democracy." Greenawalt, *Religious Liberty, Non-Establishment, and Political Discourse* (Cincinnati: Judaic Studies Program, University of Cincinnati, 1995), 6. Greenawalt, however, importantly warns against a too easy identification of religion with dogmatism: "When one turns to the quality of political life, one may worry that large injections of religion will cause conflict and dissension, and feelings of exclusion. Certainly the wars at the time of the Reformation show that religion can be a terribly divisive force, and the modern world is far from free of violence related to religion. On the other hand, society is a lot different from Europe in the sixteenth and seventeenth centuries. An open airing of religious positions may enhance understanding of political possibilities and of the relevance of religion for society." Greenawalt, *Religious Liberty*, 7. I would also warn against a too easy identification of dogmatism with religion, as dogmatisms also come in an innumerable array of secular forms.

[278] See McGreevey, "Thinking on One's Own;" Ivers, *Building a Wall*, 43–65; Hamburger, *Separation of Church and State*, 449–54.

brought by the head of a patriotic group with a storied history of nativism and anti-Catholicism and authored by the staunchly anti-Catholic Hugo Black. In that decision, the Court strategically upheld the funding scheme at issue as a Trojan horse for a ringing declaration of the importance of an aggressive commitment to church-state separation. This decision, with both its ambiguities and the interpretations it invited, encouraged a variety of litigation-centered separationist interest groups, including Protestants and Other Americans United for the Separation of Church and State (founded in 1948), to enter the interpretive fray and work to influence the development of the law; the manifesto of the group's founder, Joseph Martin Dawson's *Separate Church and State Now* (1948), in fact, opens with a quotation from Justice Black's *Everson* opinion.[279]

As the litigation campaign involving church-state separation took off, the Court put aside the issue of the provision of public monies to parochial schools for several decades. Instead, it turned its attention to questions involving religion in the schools themselves, questions that touched directly on the same issues of indoctrination and intellectual liberty that were engaging the Court simultaneously in its free speech and free association jurisprudence involving communism. One prominent area in which the Court set out its vision involved "release time" programs, where for one period a week during school hours students were able to receive the religious instruction of their choice from visiting clergy. Release time programs, which were then common in the United States, were voluntary, and students only received religious instruction if they wished to do so.

The Court's key release time opinions of the era, *McCollum v. Board of Education* (1948) and *Zorach v. Clauson* (1952), are manifestly preoccupied with the menace of religion.[280] *McCollum* involved an establishment clause challenge brought by an openly antireligious atheist to the release time program in the schools of Champaign, Illinois. Under that program, students were released for voluntary religious instruction on school grounds. The Court held that the school board's program violated the First Amendment (as applied to the states via the Fourteenth).

The *McCollum* case was brought by an atheist and involved a program that applied to all religions alike, a pattern that would be common enough in the swelling cascade of mid-twentieth-century Supreme Court school cases involving religious issues, many of which would not involve Catholics

---

[279] Hamburger, *Separation of Church and State*, 454–72; Ivers, *To Build a Wall*, 67. See also Charles Epp, *The Rights Revolution*, 50, 68. The ACLU also became heavily involved in the litigation campaign for strict separationism.

[280] *McCollum v. Board of Education*, 333 U.S. 203 (1948); *Zorach v. Clauson*, 343 U.S. 306 (1952). In the immediate aftermath of the Scopes trial, the ACLU raised no objections to release time arrangements. Walker, *In Defense of American Liberties*, 77. On the politics behind the release time litigation, see Ivers, *To Build a Wall*, 66–99.

directly. But even in *McCollum*, as Gregg Ivers notes, Catholicism provided the starting point for thinking about the problems posed by religion in the schools. (In this regard, in many cases, it seems that activist litigators selected plaintiffs of differing religions for strategic reasons, in the process severing the link between the religious affiliation of a particular plaintiff and the broader problem the Court understood itself to be engaging.) In the brief he submitted in the *McCollum* case, for example, Leo Pfeffer of the American Jewish Congress and the ACLU – and the intellectual architect of the mid-twentieth-century church-state separation that was appropriated by law professors and the Court – noted portentiously that "where there is a substantial Catholic population, the Catholics participate in the program to a very large extent, Protestants less, Jews rarely."[281]

In his opinion for the Court in *McCollum*, Justice Black, reviving Jefferson's long obscure metaphor, declared that "the First Amendment has erected a wall between Church and State which must be kept high and impregnable," in the process constructing that metaphor as a core principle of the Court's contemporary establishment clause jurisprudence.[282] Black, however, leaves most of the historical and theoretical heavy lifting to Justice Frankfurter – also no friend of Roman Catholicism – whose concurrence in the case is a plea for peace conceived in light of a particular understanding of the forces that endanger it. Moved by the distinctly modern definition of a locally adopted release time rule as a "state" policy, Frankfurter, a great defender of the social utility of contention involving secular religions, proclaimed in his opinion dealing with theistic religions that "[i]n no activity of the state is it more vital to keep out divisive forces than in its schools."[283] He then goes on to review the history of America's common schools, praising Horace Mann for barring sectarian teaching from those schools, which he says saved them "from being rent by denominational conflict" that was "long and fierce."[284] Frankfurter continued:

The sharp confinement of the public schools to secular education was a recognition of the need of a democratic society to educate its children, insofar as the state undertook to do so, in an atmosphere free from pressures in a realm in which pressures are most resisted and where conflicts are most easily and bitterly engendered.... The

---

[281] Quoted in Ivers, *To Build a Wall*, 72.

[282] *McCollum*, 333 U.S. at 212. On Black's misuse of Jefferson as a surrogate for the Founder's vision – or the textual constitutional vision – of the relationship between Church and State, see Daniel L. Dreisbach, "Sowing Useful Truths and Principles: The Danbury Baptists, Thomas Jefferson, and the 'Wall of Separation,'" *Journal of Church and State* 39 (Summer 1997): 455–501; Daniel L. Dreisbach, *Thomas Jefferson and the Wall of Separation Between Church and State* (New York: New York University Press, 2002); Hamburger, *Separation of Church and State*, 1–17, 486–9.

[283] *McCollum*, 333 U.S. at 231. On Frankfurter and Catholicism, see Hamburger, *Separation of Church and State*, 1–17, 486–9.

[284] *McCollum*, 333 U.S. at 215.

preservation of the community from divisive conflicts requires strict confinement of the state to instruction other than religious, leaving to the individual's church and home, indoctrination in the faith of his choice.[285]

In the preceding passage, Frankfurter (perhaps thinking less of the children than their taxpaying parents) characterizes the pluralist problem in schools as potentially one of strong individuals wedded to firm convictions, fighting, if necessary, to the bitter end. Black emphasized the same point in his dissent in *Zorach*, an unsuccessful establishment clause challenge to New York City's release time program in which, unlike in *McCollum*, the religious instruction took place off school grounds. There, recurring to a longstanding theme, Black declared

It was precisely because eighteenth century Americans were a religious people divided into many fighting sects that we were given the constitutional mandate to keep Church and State completely separate. Colonial history has already shown that, here as elsewhere zealous sectarians entrusted with governmental power to further their causes would sometimes torture, maim and kill those they branded "heretics," "atheists" or "agnostics."[286]

Frankfurter expressed similar views, referring again to "the deeply divisive controversy" occasioned by allowing any links between sectarian instruction and the public schools.[287]

Moving on from these decisions of the 1940s and the early 1950s, it would be too simple to say that the issue of religion in the schools, which in its initial phases was heavily influenced by fears and imaginings of the effects of Roman Catholicism on young minds, remained one of Catholics versus secularists, Jews, and Protestants alone – though these alignments in many ways did continue. The *Everson* decision was equivocal enough, early enough, and focused enough on the single question of taxpayer-financed bus services to leave these divisions more or less intact. Once release time became the issue, many Protestants began to join Catholics in condemning the Court's new initiatives in this area.[288] Various Jewish groups split sharply over the new doctrine of church-state separation, with some, along with activists in the secular civil libertarian movement, supporting separationism, and others condemning it. Jewish groups played an important role in the next move in this area – getting the Court to ban Bible reading in the public schools, a practice that, through their long campaign against aid to parochial schools over the course of much of American history, Protestants had staunchly and vehemently supported.

---

[285] *McCollum*, 333 U.S. at 216–17.
[286] *Zorach*, 343 U.S. at 319.
[287] *Zorach*, 343 U.S. at 323.
[288] Ivers, *Building a Wall*, 82–3, 102–4, 120–1.

The understandings of religion as a divisive force, much to the surprise and chagrin of many who had enthusiastically pushed an anti-Catholic agenda earlier on, came to inform the immensely controversial decisions of the Warren Court banning Bible reading and prayer in the public schools. In *Engel v. Vitale* (1962), a case involving the students' voluntary recitation of a Regent's prayer in New York public schools, the ever-active Justice Black rang alarms about "the anguish, hardship and bitter strife that could come when zealous religious groups struggled with one another," cited battles over the use of the Book of Common prayer in sixteenth- and seventeenth-century England, and noted that the controversy "repeatedly threatened to disrupt the peace of that country."[289] In his concurrence in *Engel*, Justice Douglas warned that "once government finances a religious exercise it inserts a divisive force into our communities."[290] William Brennan, himself a Catholic, made the same point with specific reference to education in the 1963 case that declared voluntary Bible readings in public schools to be not only unconstitutional but, moreover, a threat to the nationbuilding task assigned to the public schools: "It is implicit in the history and character of American public education," he wrote in his concurrence in *Abington v. Schempp* – the case that set the bedrock constitutional test for establishment clause violations – "that the public schools serve a uniquely public function: the training of American citizens in an atmosphere free of parochial, divisive, or separatist influences of any sort. . . ." "This," he added, is "an atmosphere in which, children may assimilate a heritage common to all American groups or religions."[291]

---

[289] *Engel v. Vitale*, 370 U.S. 421, 429, 425 (1962). David Hollinger, looking not at constitutional law but at the nation's general intellectual life, considers the years 1962–1965 to be the breakthrough years in the triumph of contemporary scientific outlooks in postwar America. These years are coincident, of course, with the Supreme Court's landmark church-state "triumphs." Hollinger, *Science, Jews, and Secular Culture*, 99–100, 168–9.

[290] *Engel*, 370 U.S. at 442.

[291] *Abington v. Schempp*, 374 U.S. 203, 222, 241–2 (1963) (to be constitutional, the law must have "a secular legislative purpose and a primary effect that neither advances nor inhibits religion"). See also *Lemon v. Kurtzman*, 403 U.S. 602, 622 (1971) (discussing at length the "divisive political potential" of the state aid at issue); *Board of Education v. Allen*, 392 U.S. 236, 254 (1968) (upholding New York State textbook lending law against Establishment and Free Exercise Clause challenge) ("The First Amendment's prohibition against governmental establishment of religion was written on the assumption that state aid to religious schools generates discord, disharmony, hatred, and strife among our people, and that any government that supplies such aids is to that extent a tyranny") (Justice Black, dissenting). Interestingly enough, in the immediate aftermath of the Scopes trial, many members of the ACLU's National Committee considered compulsory Bible reading in the public schools to be an "unimportant" issue. Other members of the National Committee, such as Progressive sociologist Edward A. Ross, actually defended the teaching of religion in the nation's public schools. To *not* teach religion in the schools, Ross argued, would lead Catholics to withdraw their children from those schools and construct a separate, parallel system of parochial education. In so doing, too strict a construction of the concept of the separation of church

When it came to the possibility that public money might be channeled to private or parochial primary and secondary schools – that is, that "state action" would be involved – the Court took the threat of divisiveness especially seriously. The perceived evil in this case was quite specific: In an abstract sense, of course, the problem was that monies might go to groups with religious convictions with which the citizens who contributed that money via their tax bills might disagree. This abstract problem was experienced as a real menace, however, because of the actual likelihood that money would go not just to any religious schools, but to Catholic schools in particular. Those schools, conceived from the standpoint outlined earlier in the century by Progressives, risked not only disagreement but (in that Court's latent progressive imagining) perhaps the ultimate threat of intellectual despotism.

This turn by the Court in its religion cases involving schools, which, in common with the liberal legal and political theory that reinforced it, placed special emphasis on the social dangers of religious conviction in the public sphere, proved to be among the most politically provocative turns of the Supreme Court's Warren years. During that era, establishment clause decisions spurred a cavalcade of countervailing political initiatives outside the courts in acts of resistance to channel additional public monies to support struggling religious schools. In response, advocates of the Court's new church-state separationism initiatives – advocates who, of course, had helped the Court to invent that separationism in the first place – sued to halt these newly enacted funding initiatives.[292]

To do so, it was imperative that parochial school aid questions (which, narrowly considered, the Court had not dealt with since *Everson* in the late 1940s) be removed from the hands of legislatures, which supported them, and put into the hands of courts, which did not. To do so, however, these groups first had to get the courts to alter a major procedural barrier, the entrenched precedent concerning standing, which barred "taxpayer standing," or lawsuits by taxpayers claiming legal injury from alleged constitutional transgressions by government on the basis of their status as offended taxpayers alone. (Under traditional conceptions of the separation of powers, such injury was shared by all alike and thus was properly addressed in the nation's political branches, not in its courts.) In a startling decision breaking sharply from legal precedent – a 1968 case involving a constitutional challenge to the funding of textbook and instructional material purchases

and state would thwart the project of civic assimilation, fragment the culture, and frustrate initiatives of progressive social reform. By 1930, however, those members of the National Committee opposed to compulsory Bible reading had gained the upper hand. It was still many years before the group, despite its best efforts, was able to drum up a willing plaintiff. Walker, *In Defense of American Liberties*, 76–7.

[292] Ivers, *To Build a Wall*, 113, 149.

provided in the Elementary and Secondary Education Act of 1965 – the Court cast aside its traditional standing requirements and invited taxpayer standing suits in religion and other cases. Such cases then flowed freely into the Court in succession during its Burger years.[293]

In the cases that immediately followed, not all such funding was struck down. In one case that held back, *Board of Education v. Allen* (1968), though, Justice Black not only raised the specter of violence that had long underlaid his fears in this area, but now suggested that violence was the likely consequences of *any* "linkage" between government monies and religious education. This suggestion, in turn, spurred Leo Pfeffer to crystalize it into a new third prong of a test for establishment clause violations, which Pfeffer dubbed "excessive entanglement."[294] Pfeffer hoped that this new addition to the "purpose and effects" test that had been set out in *Schempp* would have broad implications – to the point of invalidating the tax exempt status of religious institutions – a position that he persuaded the ACLU (but not his longstanding sponsor, the American Jewish Congress) to accept.

This, of course, was simply too much for a broad array of religious groups, including the most separationist among them. And the Court rejected it in *Walz v. Tax Commission* (1970) by an 8–1 vote. Nonetheless, in his opinion for the Court in *Walz*, Chief Justice Burger assumed that the establishment clause forbade an "excessive government entanglement with religion." Pfeffer's proposal was now part of American law.[295]

The new entanglement prong served as an invitation to further taxpayer litigation, and, in the succeeding years, civil liberties groups mounted constitutional challenges to federal laws providing aid to religious schools at the elementary, secondary, and university level, with Pfeffer, in the briefs he wrote for those cases, describing such schools as "havens" of prejudice.[296] This new constitutional law, aimed at these old fears, was finally anchored in the Supreme Court's landmark decision of *Lemon v. Kurtzman* (1971), in which Chief Justice Burger warned direly of "the danger that a teacher under religious control and discipline poses to the separation of the religious from the purely secular aspects of pre-college education."[297] In *Lemon*, the Court, with a few minor exceptions, banned all federal aid to parochial elementary and secondary schools. And, in a novel formulation (borrowed from Pfeffer) aimed at casting the decision as a civil libertarian advance, Justice Douglas's concurrence in the case (which was joined by Justice Black) linked its holding

[293] *Flast v. Cohen*, 392 U.S. 83 (1968). See *Frothingham v. Mellon*, 262 U.S. 447 (1923); Ivers, *To Build a Wall*, 150–62.

[294] Ivers, *To Build a Wall*, 163–6; *Board of Education v. Allen*, 392 U.S. 236 (1968).

[295] *Walz v. Tax Commission*, 397 U.S. 664 (1970). Justice William O. Douglas was the lone dissenter. Ivers, *To Build a Wall*, 165–8.

[296] Ivers, *To Build a Wall*, 169–70.

[297] *Lemon v. Kurtzman*, 403 U.S. at 617.

to the quintessentially twentieth-century civil libertarian commitment: free speech. The stakes, these justices determined, were very high. To allow such aid to go forward – and to avoid "excessive entanglement" – it would be necessary to place "a public investigator in every classroom" and to institute "a pervasive monitoring of... church agencies by the secular authorities" lest "the zeal of religious proselytizers... carry the day and make a shambles of the Establishment Clause." This sort of government censorship, Justice Douglas declared, was constitutionally intolerable; and for that reason, the law providing assistance to parochial schools was an affront to intellectual freedom.[298]

On this point, Justice Douglas expressly warned of the perils of Roman Catholic education. In his opinion in *Lemon*, Douglas leaned unabashedly upon a book-length attack on Roman Catholicism by Presbyterian theologian Lorain Boettner. Indeed, Douglas quoted Boettner as an authority for his interpretation that in Catholic schools

indoctrination is included in every subject.... The whole education of the child is filled with propaganda.... Their purpose is not so much to educate, but to indoctrinate and train, not to teach scripture truths and Americanism, but to make loyal Roman Catholics. The children are regimented, and are told what to wear, what to do, and what to think.[299]

---

[298] *Lemon*, 403 U.S. at 627–8. Powe identifies Black and Douglas as the Court's most openly anti-Catholic justices. Powe, *Warren Court and American Politics*, 367–9; Ivers, *To Build a Wall*, 180, 183.

[299] *Lemon*, 403 U.S., at n. 20, quoting Lorain Boettner, *Roman Catholicism* (Philadelphia: The Presbyterian and Reformed Publishing Co., 1962), 360. *Lemon*, 403 U.S. at 627–8. In this, Douglas was only quoting the milder portions of the authority upon which he was relying. Boettner's 450-page tome, published by the Presbyterian and Reformed Publishing Company (a fact not noted by the Court, and a fact highly relevant to a consideration of whether the Court, which is itself a "state actor," is fostering religious division) warns that wherever the Catholic Church gains power in any small way, it moves to establish a "clerical dictatorship" that takes as its enemy all of the values that Americans, who benefit from a priceless Protestant heritage, have come to cherish. Elsewhere in his book, Boettner calls Roman Catholicism "a religious monstrosity" (Boettner, *Roman Catholicism*, 11), a pathway to "ignorance, poverty, superstition, illiteracy, suppression of religious freedom, and legalized prostitution" (Boettner, *Roman Catholicism*, 13), a "totalitarian system" whose "one consuming purpose... is to convert the entire world" (Boettner, *Roman Catholicism*, 3), which it does through an "aggressive policy [of] infiltrating governments, schools, press, radio, etc." (Boettner, *Roman Catholicism*, 16), and calls for the removal of all members of the Catholic faith from teaching positions in the public schools. Parochial schools, the menace of which Boettner treats in a separate chapter, are "the 'secret weapon' by which the Roman Church hopes to control the nation's future citizens so to win the victory over Protestantism" (Boettner, *Roman Catholicism*, 363). For this reason, Justice Douglas's authority adds, "Let it be clearly understood that we do not object to church related schools as such, as they are conducted, for instance, in the Lutheran and some other churches, but only to that form of parochialism that is found in the Roman Catholic Church" (Boettner, *Roman Catholicism*, 359).

Leo Pfeffer had hopes of extending the Court's decision in *Lemon* beyond elementary and secondary education to postsecondary education as well. But the following year the Court demurred on this point, declaring that the "potential for divisiveness inherent in the essentially local problems of primary and secondary schools is significantly less with respect to a college or university whose student constituency is not local but diverse and widely dispersed."[300] Claims involving the perils of educational indoctrination in parochial schools, as were prominent in *Lemon*, it is worth noting, would also be less persuasive in the context of education involving not children but young adults. The establishment clause distinction between aid to education in these two types of institutions persists (albeit in complicated ways) to the present.

Science, Civil Rights, and the Waning of Anti-Catholicism: The Ecumenical Turn

A number of events and intellectual turns taking place in the early 1960s marked the beginning of a decline of the most intense antagonisms between the elite, scientifically oriented partisans of progress and Roman Catholicism – an antagonism that had influenced much of the constitutional jurisprudence involving schools from the 1940s to the 1980s.[301] One such event was the 1960 election of John F. Kennedy to the presidency. Despite the fact that Kennedy was Boston Irish, as one of the bona fide heroes of the Second World War he had certifiably proved himself to be One-Hundred-Percent American. Kennedy also self-consciously styled himself as an intellectual and prototypically cosmopolitan Harvard man who was at home with writers, artists, and scientists to an extent rarely seen until that time among holders of high political office, especially among old-time Catholic politicians such as his grandfather.[302] In positioning himself as an American, Kennedy was replicating in the political sphere a turn in Catholic intellectual life more generally. At the time that Kennedy was serving in the U.S. Senate, Catholic legal scholars, playing off the progressive defense of legal positivism (which had been largely discredited by the rise of the Third Reich), had instigated a revival of natural law theory and had cast that revival as evincing a commitment to fundamental American values, as reflected in

---

[300] *Tilton v. Richardson*, 403 U.S. 672, (1971) 688–9, quoted in Ivers, *To Build a Wall*, 180–1.

[301] Robert Wuthnow, *The Restructuring of American Religion: Society and Faith Since World War II* (Princeton: Princeton University Press, 1988); Allitt, *Catholic Intellectuals*, 12.

[302] Hollinger, *Science, Jews, and Secular Culture*, 5, 167. Nonetheless, Protestants and Other Americans United for the Separation of Church and State (the leading church-state separationist group and frequent participant in Supreme Court litigation) opposed Kennedy's run on the grounds of his Catholicism. Allitt, *Catholic Intellectuals*, 19, 85–6.

the founding document of American national sovereignty: the Declaration of Independence.[303]

The Second Vatican Council also worked, in the mind of scientific secular or Protestant progressives, to defang the long-feared monster of the Roman Catholic Church. At the outset of his later 1966 book reporting on the Second Vatican Council, Paul Blanshard wrote:

> I am often asked: Have you changed your opinion about the Catholic Church? The answer is "yes," but only to the extent that the Catholic Church has changed. . . . I am delighted that during the Council years the Church has begun to break out from its medieval cocoon and that it is showing signs of a willingness ultimately to fly with the wings of true intellectual freedom. It is still feudal but no longer frozen.[304]

In this regard, at the Second Vatican Council one could not help but feel "the healing ecumenical air" served as a balm to the "[o]ld festering sores of prejudice." Sizing up these new developments, Blanshard declared: "In spite of Curial narrowmindedness, Catholics, Protestants, and Jews throughout the world began to engage in a new grass-roots, practical cooperation without benefit of theology."[305]

The position the Catholic Church took during the Second Vatican Council, of course, was welcomed because the Church was moving, there and elsewhere, to adopt an array of public policy positions that aligned more salubriously, if still far from completely, with the public policy program that constituted the core of mid- to late-twentieth-century political liberalism. In Pope John XXIII's encyclical *Mater et Magistra* (1961), for instance, the Pope had praised the welfare state, in the process demonstrating to traditional nemeses such as Blanshard "a new cooperation with European liberals and moderate socialists." At the Second Vatican Council, "When the Fathers came to discuss poverty and economic organization, they sounded like a Social Democratic convention representing a party out of power" in their solicitude for labor movements and concern about world poverty.[306] As evidence that Catholicism had finally arrived, Blanshard noted: "The *New York Times* recognized the importance of the occasion by publishing the entire 25,000-word encyclical in four closely packed pages, and Hubert Humphrey inserted the text in the *Congressional Record*."[307]

---

[303] See Purcell, *Crisis of Democratic Theory*, 203–5; Allitt, *Catholic Intellectuals*, 35; Hollinger, *Science, Jews, and Secular Culture*, 53. See also John Courtney Murray, *We Hold These Truths: Catholic Reflections on the American Proposition* (New York: Sheed and Ward, 1960).

[304] Blanshard, *Vatican II*, ii, iii.

[305] Blanshard, *Vatican II*, 347; Hollinger, *Science, Jews, and Secular Culture*, 5; Macedo, *Diversity and Distrust*, 131–8.

[306] Blanshard, *Vatican II*, 326; Hollinger, *Science, Jews, and Secular Culture*, 5.

[307] Blanshard, *Vatican II*, 25, 26. On the contemporaneous debate on this political turn amongst Catholics, see Allitt, *Catholic Intellectuals*, 89–101.

Moreover, at the same time, the Church had toned down its intransigent anticommunism, coming out against nuclear weapons and staking its claim to being "an ally of internationalism." According to Blanshard, this occasioned "considerable rejoicing among peace advocates throughout the world – and considerable consternation among traditional Catholics." "If the Church had been a pro-war Church in the 1940s," he added, "it now suddenly emerged from the Council as one of the most important and influential pro-peace forces in the world."[308] Blanshard praised the Pope's 1963 encyclical _Pacem in Terris_ for its new openness to "world government" and its willingness to "compromise with communism."[309] Also important was the Church's antiracism, which was not so much an altered stance as a recurring allegiance, now restated in unusually contentious times.[310]

That said, of course, in some very important areas, the Catholic Church continued to hew to its reactionary ways. Perhaps the most important was schools. After asserting "[t]he obvious truth that schools that are segregated by creed tend automatically to promote religious bigotry," Blanshard declared that "America is facing a hundred years war over tax appropriations to Catholic schools."[311] In a way, as he saw it, "the new and uncritical ecumenical spirit produced by Vatican II had actually done some damage on this front. For when federal funds flowed to Catholic schools under the aegis of religiously neutral funding for welfare and poverty programs under the Economic Opportunity Act (1964) and the Elementary and Secondary Education Act (1965), only the ACLU, Protestants and Other Americans United for the Separation of Church and State, and the (Reform) American Jewish Congress could muster any resistance. The aid nonetheless went through unchecked. An impure and dangerous accommodation, in Blanshard's view, had been reached. Despite progress in many areas, one important project of reform remained.[312]

While the issue remained controversial and occupied a great deal of the Supreme Court's time, the great "war" that Blanshard predicted did not take place; although, as we have seen, a series of relatively quick victories invented and institutionalized constitutional doctrine concerning church-state separation. Contention among religions was partially vitiated by interfaith agreement on the era's central reformist (and moral) imperative, the race problem, which went a long way toward cementing a new religious ecumenicism. In the struggle for civil rights, Catholics, Protestants, and Jews united in service of the common purpose that they had long lacked.[313] The new

---

[308] Blanshard, _Vatican II_, 321.

[309] Blanshard, _Vatican II_, 28.

[310] Blanshard, _Vatican II_, 29, 318–19; Allitt, _Catholic Intellectuals_, 110–16.

[311] Blanshard, _Vatican II_, 313, 312.

[312] Blanshard, _Vatican II_, 307–8; Economic Opportunity Act, 78 Stat. 508 (1964); Elementary and Secondary Education Act, 79 Stat. 27 (1965).

[313] McGreevy, _Parish Boundaries_, 60, 90, 147. See also Billy Graham, _Just As I Am: The Autobiography of Billy Graham_ (San Francisco: Harper San Francisco, 1997); Will Herberg,

ecumenicism itself worked to transform cultural understandings of the nature of religious commitment. That ecumenicism devalued those traditional understandings of religion that were tied too closely to doctrines, strictures, and judgments, and emphasized instead a theology of antiracist tolerance and the American creed of democracy, justice, and fairness for all. The Second Vatican Council and the growth of Catholic liberalism generally brought Catholics, the most doctrinal of these mainstream religions, closer to Reform Jews and ecumenical Protestants. Indeed, in his book on Vatican II, Blanshard made much of the Church's condemnations of racial bigotry. And in the 1950 debate at the Harvard Law School between Blanshard and Father Dunne, in introducing Father Dunne to what the transcript makes clear was plainly a pro-Blanshard audience, the Harvard philosophy professor moderating the debate went out of his way to mention *three times* the priest's demonstrable "opposition to racial intolerance." These repeated reminders of the priest's antiracism were taken to what a contemporary reader might consider an almost comical level, as when the moderator, while breaking into the middle of the debate to get the priest's response to Blanshard, feels compelled to state to the audience that "Father Dunne, I remind you again, is well known for his powerful defense of Jews and Negroes."

This new ecumenical turn was conducive to the Court's new separationist jurisprudence concerning schools because only under the sway of such an ecumenical vision could the Court so readily imagine that religious flourishing would in no way be damaged by the removal of its divisive forms – outward signs and symbols – from the public schools. Indeed, in the context of the new ecumenicism, religion was perceived to be stronger for its willingness to forgo the parochial symbols that set one religion off from another. In this context, parochial schools – that is, the highly developed system of Catholic schools – were now understood as the primary obstacles to the achievement of antiracist, American creed ecumenicism; they were seen as divisive and contentious, as barriers to the broader nationbuilding project. Only with a new ecumenical spirit in the air could the Court systematically remove these symbols from public life and at the same time imagine itself not to be stigmatizing but instead serving the convictions of a religious people.

The Limits of Peace: Progress Through Contention

The Supreme Court's mid-twentieth-century establishment clause decisions, which initiated the most successful sustained national policy separating church and state in the country's history, derived much of their plausibility

Protestant-Catholic-Jew: An Essay in American Religious Sociology (Garden City, NY: Doubleday, 1955); Cynthia Ozick, "Who Owns Anne Frank?" *The New Yorker* (October 6, 1997), 85–6 (on the 1955 Broadway production of *The Diary of Anne Frank*, which, Ozick argues, presented a nonjudgmental, ecumenical antiracist message that all but erased Frank's Jewishness).

from the ritual invocation of the special dangers theistic religions posed to the public peace. Fears of this sort, however, proved to have little purchase in the Court's school decisions of the same era involving secular religions. In school cases involving race – also being decided in innovative ways at this same historical moment – the Court treated the possibility of outbreaks of violence altogether differently. Far from being considered a horror to be avoided at all costs, it was treated rather as an eventuality that had to be faced in the interest of hewing, whatever the consequences, to fundamental constitutional standards.

Although racial segregation in the South has typically been discussed as a matter of control and repression, pure and simple, it was not instituted with only the basest of motives. Many reformers supported segregation with the aim of improving black life and nourishing black institutions. Their hope was that creating separate institutions for blacks and whites would lower the level of interracial violence. Jim Crow segregation was, to an extent more than is commonly appreciated, about the preservation of public peace.[314] As early as 1917, however, the Supreme Court had raised doubts about the desirability of peace as an ultimate standard in race cases. At that time, in a case involving the constitutionality of legally mandated racial segregation in housing, the Court noted:

It is urged that this proposed segregation will promote the public peace by preventing race conflicts. Desirable as this is, and important as is the preservation of the public peace, this aim cannot be accomplished by laws or ordinances which deny rights created or protected by the Federal Constitution.[315]

In the school cases that followed – and they constituted the core of the Court's mid-century civil rights cases – far from insisting upon the primacy of the mitigation of violence, the Court frankly acknowledged that its rulings were spurring social contention, and it stuck proudly to its convictions, acknowledging that violence was perhaps unavoidable. The Court's decision in *Brown* (1954) prompted not only Congress's Southern Manifesto but also such massive resistance from Southern civil society that Eisenhower was forced to send federal troops to Little Rock, Arkansas (events that ultimately inspired Norman Rockwell's 1964 *Look* magazine cover – "The Problem We All Live With" – probably the twentieth century's most indelible pictorial representation of American constitutionalism).

In the civil rights school case of *Cooper v. Aaron* (1958), which arose out of the stand-off at Little Rock's Central High, the Court said that in setting up a timetable for desegregation the Court must consider the relevant factors

---

[314] Hugh Davis Graham, *Collision Course: The Strange Convergence of Affirmative Action and Immigration Policy in America* (New York: Oxford University Press, 2002), 14–17. To acknowledge this motivation, of course, is not to justify the segregation.

[315] *Buchanan v. Warley*, 245 U.S. 60, 81 (1917) (invalidating on Fourteenth Amendment property rights grounds a Kentucky law mandating residential racial segregation).

"which, of course, excludes hostility to racial desegregation."[316] That hostility included a school year characterized by "chaos, bedlam, and turmoil," "repeated incidents of more or less serious violence directed against the Negro students and their property," and "tension and unrest among the school administrators, the classroom teachers, the pupils, and the latters' parents, which inevitably had an adverse effect upon the educational program."[317] Despite all of this disruptive contention, the Court concluded, "law and order are not here to be preserved by depriving the Negro children of their constitutional rights."[318] Or as Felix Frankfurter asserted in his concurring opinion in *Cooper* – a direct contradiction of Justice Brown in the landmark *Plessy* (1896) decision that had ratified the constitutionality of Jim Crow by an appeal to considerations of public peace – "the responsibility of those who exercise power in a democratic government is not to reflect inflamed public feeling, but to help form its understanding."[319] In its movement from a policy forbidding racial discrimination to one requiring racial integration of the schools to correct for past *de jure* discrimination (when other practical remedies were unavailable), the Court, in the service of an insistent constitutional fidelity, continued to discount the social unrest, which it acknowledged had been caused by its decisions.[320]

Clearly, the issue of "divisiveness," a problem the Court recurred to consistently in its nationbuilding mid-century establishment clause decisions, was not imagined to be a problem when looked at across the wider spectrum of the Court's civil liberties and civil rights decisions. In the Court's modern free speech jurisprudence, including that involving schools and secular speech, contention was imagined in most cases, in a scientific pluralist vein, as a positive good – as a spur to intellectual (and, hence, social) progress. This was true despite any divisiveness it might cause. In the establishment clause cases, however, as we have seen, the Court imagined divisiveness as the paramount evil, to be avoided at all costs, and not to be tamed through exhortations to tolerance and mutual respect. The context surrounding the Court's civil rights cases made it all but impossible to deny the violence its antidiscriminatory rulings would entail; in them, the horrors prognosticated

---

[316] *Cooper v. Aaron*, 358 U.S. 1, 7 (1958).

[317] *Cooper v. Aaron*, 358 U.S. at 13, citing the findings of the District Court.

[318] *Cooper v. Aaron*, 358 U.S. at 16.

[319] *Cooper v. Aaron*, 358 U.S. at 26 (J. Frankfurter, concurring).

[320] See *Green v. County School Board*, 391 U.S. 430 (1968). See also *Keyes v. School District No. 1*, 413 U.S. 189, 253 (1973) ("The single most disruptive element in education today is the widespread use of compulsory transportation, especially at elementary grade levels. This has risked distracting and diverting attention from basic educational needs, dividing and embittering communities, and exacerbating rather than ameliorating, interracial friction and misunderstanding"). See also Lino Graglia, *Disaster by Decree: The Supreme Court Decisions on Race and the Schools* (Ithaca, NY: Cornell University Press, 1976); J. Anthony Lukas, *Common Ground: A Turbulent Decade in the Lives of Three American Families* (New York: Knopf, 1985).

by Justice Black in his establishment clause decisions plainly became real. The problem for the Court, then, became one of justifying its rulings in light of the very real divisiveness that its civil rights school decisions created. To do so, it needed to formulate a theory of pluralism that was tailored to the cause of civil rights and fit into its broader constitutional project in other areas, including speech and religion.

Prior to 1954, the Court's civil rights opinions scrupulously avoided the express advocacy of novel theories of racial pluralism, thus striving to palliate a polity in which the meaning of pluralism itself, so far as race was concerned, was a transparently contentious issue, with no clear common ground. Decisions like *Missouri ex rel. Gaines* (1938), *McLaurin v. Oklahoma* (1950), and *Sweatt v. Painter* (1950) were devoid of the freewheeling disquisitions on history and the nature of civil society that came to suffuse the Court's establishment clause jurisprudence. Rather, the early civil rights decisions were cast in the abstract legalistic language of classical liberalism, which characterized the segregation laws at issue as negative barriers to the freedom of motion and opportunity. In the early civil rights case of *Missouri ex rel. Gaines*, for example, Chief Justice Charles Evans Hughes, writing for the Court, refused to consider whether a black man might have received an equal or better legal education outside the state (at the state's expense) once he was denied admission to the law school at the University of Missouri. "The basic consideration," he wrote, "is not as to what sort of opportunities other states provide, or whether they are as good as those in Missouri, but as to what opportunities Missouri itself furnishes to white students and denies to negroes solely upon the ground of color." "Sending them out of state for their legal education," he added, "may mitigate the inconvenience of the discrimination but cannot serve to validate it."[321] In a similar tenor, the opinions in both *Sweatt* and *McLaurin* focused on equality of opportunity, with the latter stating modestly but firmly that "[t]he removal of the state restrictions will not necessarily abate individual and group predilections, prejudices, and choices. But at the very least, the state will not be depriving [the black plaintiff] of the opportunity to secure acceptance by his fellow students on his own merits."[322]

In the aftermath of the breakthrough of *Brown*, these early, formalistic civil rights decisions had a progeny: a succession of antisegregation opinions

[321] *Missouri ex rel. Gaines v. Canada*, 305 U.S. 337, 349, 350 (1938).

[322] *McLaurin v. Oklahoma*, 339 U.S. 637, 641–2 (1950) (striking down Oklahoma law that admitted black students to the state university's graduate program but segregated them from other students within it); *Missouri ex rel. Gaines v. Canada*, 305 U.S. 337 (1938) (striking down Missouri law denying blacks admission to the state university's law school but providing for the legal education of black students out of state); *Sweatt v. Painter*, 339 U.S. 629 (1950) (striking down Texas law denying blacks admission to the University of Texas law school but providing them the opportunity to attend a new law school specifically set up to accommodate them).

that opened various social spaces so that blacks could legally enter them. In this progeny, the Court deployed an abstract liberal legal analysis (when there was any analysis at all) that deliberately kept at arm's length any discussion of the model of pluralism most applicable to racial issues.[323] In this regard, however, the *Brown* decision was Janus-faced. On the one hand, as has often been noted, the opinion was written in distant legalistic prose, devoid of a sweeping social vision or a didactic model concerning how and why diverse groups – perhaps contentiously – should be brought together.[324] At the same time, however, the Court tentatively began to fashion a pluralist social vision that would effectively undergird its civil rights constitutionalism concerning schools. This justification would tilt away from an emphasis on external barriers to motion and tilt toward a notion of internal barriers to educational achievement, barriers that had been at issue in the Court's religion and speech cases (and in education generally) since at least the time of John Dewey.

While the Court's confidence in its mid-century initiative on race seemed to deepen with each passing year, the public philosophy it advanced to justify that initiative, a formalistic jurisprudence at odds with its initiatives in other areas, seemed increasingly untenable. To claim, first, that public peace and order were irrelevant to constitutional decision making and to then, through the adoption of the highly abstract language of traditional liberalism, avoid a theoretical confrontation with the plain consequences of its decisions, no longer provided a politically suitable foundation for the Court's provocative new initiatives on civil rights. The task was to shore up this foundation with a richer and more robust social theory.

The first place the Court looked in its search for a supplementary social vision for schools in race cases was to the forms of arguments it was using in speech cases arising in similar settings. In the latter cases, the civil libertarian wing of the Court had advanced a scientific pluralism under which conflict and contention were not only accepted but praised as positive goods. The problem was that in the speech cases conflict was deemed to be good because it served instrumentally to advance scientific understanding and the search for truth, an instrumentalism that seemed inapplicable to outbreaks of racial tension.[325]

---

[323] See *Mayor and City Council of Baltimore v. Dawson*, 350 U.S. 877 (1955) (beaches); *Holmes v. Atlanta*, 350 U.S. 879 (1955) (golf courses); *Gayle v. Browder*, 352 U.S. 903 (1956) (buses); *New Orleans v. Detiege*, 358 U.S. 54 (1958) (parks); *Burton v. Wilmington Parking Authority*, 365 U.S. 715 (1961) (restaurants in public buildings); *Johnson v. Virginia*, 373 U.S. 61 (1963) (seating in courtrooms); *Watson v. City of Memphis*, 373 U.S. 526 (1963) (public parks and playgrounds).

[324] See Cass R. Sunstein, *One Case at a Time: Judicial Minimalism on the Supreme Court* (Cambridge, MA: Harvard University Press, 1999), 37–9.

[325] The truth, though, was that as a functioning instrumentalism, it did not necessarily work in the speech context either. Or, rather, it worked in the speech context only until it didn't. Conflict, that is, was a wonderfully useful thing until it was perceived as destroying the

The scientific pluralism of many of the Court's speech cases assumed a bedrock of political and social stability for which, in light of a totalitarian menace, opponents of a latitudinarian approach to speech desperately feared.[326] Racial conflict, which had no ties to the search for truth, commonly crossed the dividing line between talk and violence. And in this way, at least in the civil libertarian imagining, it had to be seen as different from speech and as possibly even analogous to the Court's reading of religious conflict in seventeenth-century Europe in its establishment clause decisions. Since no bedrock of political and social stability could plausibly be assumed in the Court's race cases, it would seem that the Court would have to revert to the arguments of *Plessy*, which emphasized social contentiousness concerning race as a justification for the constitutional reasonableness of segregation. This, however, it had decided, was not an acceptable option.

These tensions in the race cases drove the Court to shoehorn race issues into the scientific pluralism model by constructing novel theories of the social meaning of racial integration. The Court started down the road to this new construction of race by acknowledging the obvious conflict and contention that race provoked. But then, in a novel twist, it moved to define that contention as a prelude to, and, perhaps, even a necessary concomitant of, peace. This new construction of the meaning of social disorder arising from race implicitly appropriated John Dewey's "safety valve" justification for free speech, which Dewey had advanced in the early twentieth century to supplement his other arguments in defense of contentious speech. In its Dewey-esque turn, the safety valve approach claimed in essence that whatever the perils occasioned by the Court's aggressive policymaking concerning integration might be, they paled in comparison to what James Baldwin (borrowing the apocalyptic biblical imagery of a Negro spiritual) later called "the fire next time," to the eruptions of violence, including quite possibly

---

stability of the ordered public space that served indispensably as its stage. These necessary limits to toleration were recognized early on by even by its early advocates like John Locke, who was advocating not free speech but religious toleration. For Locke, though, toleration of Catholics and atheists was beyond the pale; in his view, this overly broad toleration unacceptably threatened the very cohesiveness of the political order. See John Locke, "Letter Concerning Toleration," in Locke, *Treatise of Civil Government and a Letter Concerning Toleration* (New York: Irvington Publishers, 1979), 165–224. See David J. Lorenzo, "Tradition and Prudence in Locke's Exceptions to Toleration," *American Journal of Political Science* 47 (April 2003): 248–58.

[326] See, e.g., *Wieman v. Updegraff*, 344 U.S. 183, 194 (1952) ("Tyrannical totalitarian governments cannot safely allow their people to speak with complete freedom. I believe with the Framers that our free Government can") (Justice Black, concurring); *Adler v. Board of Education*, 342 U.S. 485, 493 (1952) (Justice Minton for the Court, defending the right of a school "to defend its own existence"). See also Willmoore Kendall, "The 'Open Society' and Its Fallacies," *American Political Science Review* 54 (December 1960): 972–9.

a race war, that would occur should the nation cling conservatively to an unintegrated status quo.[327] This outlook is clearly reflected in the early work of Louis Lusky, a young Columbia University law professor, who, as a law clerk to Justice Stone, had penned the *Carolene Products* footnote, and who became one of the century's seminal legal/constitutional theorists of civil rights and civil liberties.[328] In a 1942 article in the *Yale Law Journal*, Lusky cited a best-selling book by black writer Richard Wright for the sociological proposition that racial exclusion can lead to pathological murder. Wright's 1940 novel, *Native Son* – in which a poor young black man from the ghetto, deformed by a racist society, ends up killing a liberal white woman – in Lusky's view "present[ed] a powerful description of the problems created by a failure to inculcate a sense of political obligation."[329] Lusky's article advanced an extended argument, made in time of war, for the "public stake in the cessation of discrimination against minorities." Only by confronting race head-on, whatever the tensions it created, Lusky argued, could the greater harm, "the possibility of national suicide," be avoided.[330]

In fact, it was becoming increasingly apparent from works such as Wright's, Lusky argued, that a consensus on the value of adhering to the rule of law itself ("the creation and preservation of a general sense of political obligation") could only be maintained by solving the problems posed by racial minorities.[331] "[T]he lawmaking agency is organized to serve the whole community, and if it is honestly striving to do so, the people find it more practical to obey than to resist or disregard its laws."[332] The preservation of the authority of law and, indeed, of political authority itself could only be achieved, Lusky contended – in a frank, nationbuilding formulation that liberals and progressives would later jettison – by the "elimination of minorities." Alluding to events in Europe, Lusky continued:

In some countries serious efforts are being made to eliminate them by extermination. The future will show whether the horror and resentment aroused by these tactics will in the end cause the rulers more trouble than even the continued existence of intransigent minority groups. In this country, we are adopting a different means to

---

[327] James Baldwin, *The Fire Next Time* (New York: Laurel Books, 1962).

[328] Footnote Four in the *Carolene Products* case proposed a distinction between the level of constitutional scrutiny the Court would apply to economic legislation and legislation that ran contrary to a specific provision of the Bill of Rights, restricted the free operation of the democratic process, or involved prejudice against "discrete and insular minorities." *United States v. Carolene Products*, 304 U.S. 144, 152–3 n. 4 (1938).

[329] Louis Lusky, "Minority Rights and the Public Interest," *Yale Law Journal* 52 (December 1942): 1–41, 5 n. 7.

[330] Lusky, "Minority Rights," 1.

[331] Lusky, "Minority Rights," 6.

[332] Lusky, "Minority Rights," 4.

the same end. Our policy is to eliminate minorities, not by exterminating them but by doing away with the irrational prejudices and fears to which they owe their existence. The Supreme Court has assumed jurisdiction over the problem because a national interest is at stake. The Court has taken the lead both in explaining the methods which the political branches must adopt in dealing with minority groups, and in exploring the policies on which that choice of methods is founded.[333]

Lusky was arguing that obedience to law – the ultimate guarantor of peace – could only be achieved by fully assimilating racial minorities into the mainstream of American public life. Only then would racial conflict and contention abate. At that point, the very existence of minorities *qua* minorities, the very persistence, that is, of rivalrous domestic "cultures," would end, and quietude would prevail over conflict.

Over the next two turbulent decades, however, what Lusky called the "final solution" to the minority problem proved naggingly elusive. This was plain both on the Court and in the broader field of American politics. Given the civil disobedience campaigns of the Southern Christian Leadership Conference (SCLC) and the Student Non-Violent Coordinating Committee (SNCC) – and Southern resistance to them – the Little Rock school crisis, the Watts Riot of 1965, and the "long, hot summers" of urban rioting of the next few years, integration and civil rights were not proving conducive to social peace. And by the mid-1960s, the rise of the black power movement exacerbated the sense that it was chimerical to hope that minorities would be culturally "eliminated" or that racial contention and conflict would soon abate.

This context complicated the Court's ongoing search for a serviceable public philosophy of racial pluralism. Mindful now that in contravention of Lusky's hopes minorities seemed here to stay and that contention would continue for the foreseeable future, the Court recurred to scientific models of the social utility of contention that had been tested in the doctrinal battle for free speech. While the Deweyan "safety valve" theory seemed implausible in light of ambient political events, however, there remained another justification for contentiousness in free speech cases: That was the understanding that contention was socially useful in a scientific sense in conducing to the discovery of truth. The new construction of the social meaning of racial integration, contentious or peaceful, was explored most prominently in the Supreme Court's school decisions involving race.

The argument for a new scientifically inclined racial pluralism in schools went as follows: The Court not only concluded but emphasized that racial

---

[333] Lusky, "Minority Rights," 40. For a discussion of the progressive notion that the existence of minorities is a problem (a notion rooted in the imagining of a "minority" on the role of European nationalist minorities), see Philip Gleason, "Minorities (Almost) All: The Minority Concept in American Social Thought," *American Quarterly* 43 (September 1991): 392–424. See also Mazower, *Dark Continent*, 41–75.

prejudice was first and foremost irrational. In arriving at this conclusion and committing itself to this emphasis (a new departure, incidentally, in the understanding of race, even among progressives), the Court chose to echo the findings of new and much discussed social scientific studies motivated by efforts to make sense of the roots of German anti-Semitism in the wake of the nation's military triumph over the Third Reich. This scholarship aimed at understanding Nazism (undertaken, in many cases, by German Jewish scholars in exile in the United States) spurred other scholars to strive for a scientific understanding of racial prejudice within the United States itself.[334]

This new scholarship, like the work on "mass society" prompted by National Socialism in Europe, assumed: first, that race prejudice was as widespread in America as it had been in the Europe that had exterminated most of its Jews and provoked a world war; and, second, that the distinguishing characteristic of that prejudice was its irrationality. In its focus on irrationalism, this social scientific literature thus transmogrified prejudice into a problem of truth. Racial prejudice, that is, was not only judged or constructed as unfair, immoral, or (as translated into law) unconstitutional; its foremost failing was that it was false. The next step in this construction of the political imperative of integration was to recognize that belief in this falsehood caused social damage, and it emphasized the damage done by the failure to integrate the victim group, American blacks. The Court, most notably in the era's most celebrated school case, *Brown v. Board of Education* (1954), found evidence for the damage caused by this animating irrational falsehood in the contemporaneous social science literature on prejudice. In *Brown*, the Court famously cited as authority for its opinion Kenneth Clark's doll studies, which, in the words of Chief Justice Warren for the Court, represented a significant advance upon "[w]hatever may have been the extent of psychological knowledge at the time of *Plessy v. Ferguson.*"[335] These studies, he wrote, demonstrated that "[t]o separate [black children] from others of similar age and qualifications solely because of their race generates a feeling of inferiority as to their status in the community that may affect their hearts and minds in a way unlikely ever to be undone."[336] Racial segregation in

---

[334] See T. W. Adorno, *et al.*, *The Authoritarian Personality* (New York: Harper, 1950); T. F. Pettigrew, "Regional Differences in Anti-Negro Prejudice," *Journal of Abnormal and Social Psychology* 59 (1959): 28. See also Gordon Allport, *The Nature of Prejudice* (Cambridge, MA: Addison-Wesley, 1954).

[335] *Brown v. Board of Education*, 347 U.S. 483 (1954).

[336] Albert Murray referred to this approach as "degradation by other means." Albert Murray, *The Omni-Americans: New Perspectives on Black Experience and American Culture* (New York: Outerbridge and Dienstfrey, 1970), 23. The Court's adoption in *Brown* of a vision of blacks as damaged and degraded is emphasized in Daryl Michael Scott, *Contempt and Pity: Social Policy and the Image of the Damaged Black Psyche, 1880–1996* (Chapel Hill: University of North Carolina Press, 1997), ch. 7. For a roughly contemporaneous example of the focus on black damage in the schools offered outside of the Court, see Report of the U.S. Commission

schools, in short, amounted to a tort that left a maimed human being in its wake.

This social vision, which had been absent from the more formalistic racial integration opinions involving schools prior to *Brown*, began to loom much larger in its aftermath, despite pleas for formalism in some quarters, accompanied by sustained critiques of the Court's use of the doll studies cited in Footnote Eleven.

By the late 1960s, an affirmative policy aimed at remedying this injury – as opposed to ending racial discrimination – came to predominate on the Court. This was apparent in Justice Brennan's opinion for the Court in *Green v. County School Board* (1968) in which the Court struck down on equal protection grounds a Virginia freedom of choice plan that did not significantly alter the racial attendance patterns in the county that had, in the past, been shaped by *de jure* segregation. Brennan wrote:

It is of course true that for the time immediately after *Brown II* the concern was with making an initial break in a long-established pattern of excluding Negro children courageous enough to break with tradition a place in the "white" schools. See, e.g., *Cooper v. Aaron*. Under *Brown II* that immediate goal was only a first step, however. The transition to a unitary, non-racial system of public education was and is the ultimate end to be brought about.[337]

In short, Brennan called for "a unitary school system in which racial discrimination would be eliminated root and branch" through an affirmative duty to integrate.[338]

As far as blacks alone were concerned then, in the mid-twentieth-century constitutional imagining, legally mandated segregation had been premised on a social scientific falsehood that damaged the psyche of American blacks. From here, however, progressive elements on the Court went on to argue in its school decisions not only that *de jure* discrimination injured blacks by lowering their sense of self-worth but that both legal segregation and a *de facto* failure to integrate injured both blacks and whites by suppressing the truth of the equal worth of the races in a biracial polity. By not actively importing blacks into white schools, this social truth was suppressed in the

on Civil Rights, *Racial Isolation in the Public Schools* (Washington, D.C.: U.S. Government Printing Office, 1967), 103–11, 114, 193, 196. Recent work by Rogers Smith has criticized this emphasis on black damage and argued that a broader theory premised on more broad-ranging social damages to whites and blacks alike would have been more appropriate. Even had this approach predominated at the time, as I argue it did (in a sense) subsequently, it would not have altered the basic scientific search-for-truth construction of the desirability of integration that I discuss here. See Rogers M. Smith, "Black and White after Brown: Constructions of Race in Modern Supreme Court Decisions, *University of Pennsylvania Journal of Constitutional Law* 5 (May 2003): 709–33.

[337] *Green v. County School Board*, 391 U.S. 430, 435–6 (1968).
[338] *Green*, 391 U.S. at 438. See also *Keyes*, 413 U.S. 189, 225–6 (1973) (Justice Powell, concurring).

education of both races. Moreover, as Walter Lippmann had precociously suggested to Learned Hand in the old days of scientific progressivism, an important means of advancing the discovery of truth would be court activism undertaken by judges who belonged to the "intellectual classes . . . to protect education from [retrograde] majorities."[339]

By the end of the Warren era, this campaign for racial integration as an imperative in the search for truth was well under way. In *Swann v. Charlotte-Mecklenberg* (1971), for instance, Justice Burger suggested that placing racially diverse students in the confines of a single school, even via the use of explicit racial quotas, might work well "to prepare students to live in a pluralistic society."[340] In *Keyes v. School District # 1* (1973), Justice Powell emphasized that the law might serve to "promot[e] the values of an integrated school experience," adding that "[i]n a pluralistic society such as ours, it is essential that no racial minority feel demeaned or discriminated against and that students of all races learn to play, work, and cooperate with one another in their common pursuits and endeavors."[341] He emphasized clearly that it was the consciousness of both whites and blacks that the Court hoped to transform, suggesting that the earlier in a child's life integration began, the better, "as young children may be less likely than older children and adults to develop an inhibiting racial consciousness."[342]

The culmination of the peculiar imperatives of this new constitutional imagining of the race problem is that eventually the Court came to imagine black people as abstract symbols and vessels of truth. Each black person, by the mere fact of his existence, came to be imagined by late-twentieth-century liberal-progressive thought as the living embodiment of a truthful but unpopular idea.[343] As such, racial integration itself was accorded the status of a progressive-spririted intellectual, scientific project. The end (and the beginning) of all this would become evident in the Court's 1978 decision in *Regents of the University of California v. Bakke*.[344] There, returning full circle to the issues at the core of the debates over education in the late nineteenth and early twentieth centuries, Justice Powell defended race-based preferences in medical school admissions as an issue of "academic freedom" in which those preferences were closely linked with the process of "select[ing] those students who will contribute the most to the "robust exchange of ideas," an

---

[339] Lippmann, *American Inquisitors*, 84–5. See also Steel, *Lippmann*, 216–18.

[340] *Swann v. Charlotte-Mecklenberg*, 402 U.S. 1, 16 (1971).

[341] *Keyes*, 413 U.S. at 242.

[342] *Keyes*, 413 U.S at 251 n. 31. See also *Milliken v. Bradley*, 418 U.S. 717, 783–814 (1974) (J. Marshall, dissenting).

[343] In this regard, Albert Murray's contention that "an ever increasing number of U.S. intellectuals . . . seem absolutely convinced that all knowledge and certainly all guidelines for the perplexed are found only in blacks. . . . " applied as well to the ersatz intellectuals of the Supreme Court, who by and large parroted the commonplaces of the prevailing elites. Murray, *Omni-Americans*, 114.

[344] *Regents of the University of California v. Bakke*, 438 U.S. 265 (1978).

exchange, of course, typically considered to be a First Amendment issue. The alternatives – first, that race was (as far as the Constitution was concerned) not a truth, an idea, a belief, or an opinion, but instead an irrelevant physical trait; or, second, that, even if it were imagined in some sense as a belief, race was more akin to a religious conviction that because of its social explosiveness, should be outwardly removed by physical segregation as a point of contention from the public schools – were rejected as models for constitutional civil rights. Speech and civil rights (itself imagined on the model of free speech) were to constitute the core of the new imperative in constitutional civil rights and civil liberties.[345]

Conclusion

In part because of their orientation around the labor problem and the related question of "why no socialism?" and in part because of the notable failures of efforts to fashion national education policy and create a national school system, scholars of American political development have devoted little attention to paths of development (both sustained and aborted) concerning education. Nonetheless, those paths exist and – in the Supreme Court's twentieth-century jurisprudence involving the separation of church and state, free speech, and racial segregation in schools – have played an important part in American politics. To the extent that the subject is treated at all, it is assimilated within studies of American constitutional development into a linear, Whiggish narrative of progress, which has the Supreme Court, after ending its solicitude for the protection of economic liberties at the time of the New Deal, gradually moving, pursuant to the agenda set out in Footnote Four of the *Carolene Products* case (1938), to vindicate the core meaning of the freedom of speech, establishment, and equal protection clauses.

---

[345] *Bakke*, 438 U.S. at 312–13. Although Powell represented a single voice on the Court, his approach, far from being idiosyncratic, actually served to recognize "diversity" arguments that were by this time becoming broadly influential in institutions and amongst elites outside the courts. Influential law professors had already been making the argument. See, e.g., Ronald Dworkin, *Taking Rights Seriously* (Cambridge, MA: Harvard University Press, 1978), ch. 9. See also Ronald Dworkin, *A Matter of Principle*, part 5 (Cambridge, MA: Harvard University Press, 1985). And, as his opinion in *Bakke* makes clear, Powell essentially accepted the decision by the Harvard University admissions office to adopt the procedure as authority for the legitimacy of the practice. *Bakke*, 438 U.S. at 316–23. See also Frederick R. Lynch, *The Diversity Industry: The Drive to Change the 'White Male Workplace'* (New York: Free Press, 1997); Elizabeth Lasch Quinn, *Race Experts: How Racial Etiquette, Sensitivity Training, and New Age Therapy Hijacked the Civil Rights Revolution* (New York: W. W. Norton, 2001), 161–93. The Court as a whole (once again citing free speech and academic freedom decisions) ultimately held the "educational benefits that flow from a diverse student body" to be a "compelling state interest" in *Grutter v. Bollinger*, 539 U.S. 306 (2003). See also Schuck, *Diversity in America*, 15–16, 160–9.

The path of state development concerning education presented here, however, is considerably different. It demonstrates that from the founding onward, important political figures had grand ambitions for the construction of national education systems on a continental European model. These ambitions, however, were soundly thwarted by a wide array of institutional debilities, including issues of revenue, sectionalism, and race. In periods of war, however, instruments of national education policy were created and aimed at a variety of tasks, including the integration of the freedmen and, more coercively, of Roman Catholics (and immigrants) into the mainstream of political life. In the statebuilding era, and especially in the wake of World War I, there were extensive efforts by statist progressives to create a national, centrally administered system of education with the aim of constructing citizens suitable for life in the New Constitutional Nation, particularly citizens who were freed of the fetters forged by church and family, and fit to participate in a science-centered republic. When this bureaucratic initiative was thwarted, Progressives such as Walter Lippmann, with frankly antidemocratic aims, suggested that the statebuilding task in this area now be turned over to the courts, who could shape it via constitutional rulings that would have nationwide implications. Plainly influenced by old (scientific) progressive imperatives, shifting intellectual hopes and fears concerning the path of progress, and an altering institutional environment, the Court negotiated new constitutional doctrine deeply suspicious of the place of theistic religions in the schools and generally welcoming of secular religions. To advance civil rights, the Court reimagined black people as contributors to the search for truth. The Court's initiatives concerning the establishment clause, free speech, and segregation in the schools ultimately gelled as part of a single political ideology and, as such, stood for an important period of time as binding precedent. These initiatives, indeed, succeeded in becoming broadly identified with a commitment to "civil liberties and civil rights." Contrary to the Whiggish developmental model, which posits these idiosyncratic settlements as the essence of the meaning of the First and Fourteenth Amendments as applied to the schools, the genealogy presented here demonstrates that these settlements are shot through with political (and typically reformist) constructions and the product of a cascade of intercurrences of institutions and ideas. Constitutional development concerning education, if failing in its ultimate tasks of full nationalization and secularization, nonetheless achieved these goals to a notable extent.

5

Conclusion

In the late nineteenth and early twentieth centuries, in response to profound changes in the nature of the nation's political economy and an array of social and political forces influencing and arising out of them, a New American State was built. Although it never achieved the unity and solidity of the benchmark continental European states, its centralized, bureaucratic, and administrative features nonetheless marked a radical departure from the constitutional system of governance – the state of courts and parties – that preceded it. This preexisting state of courts and parties was structured by the provisions of the original Constitutional text (as amended) as understood in light of traditional and relatively stable (if not always purely original) constitutional principles as set out in the nation's founding texts and in writings about those texts, such as *The Federalist Papers*, key Supreme Court opinions, and the learned and authoritative glosses of the great nineteenth-century treatise writers, such as Kent, Story, and Cooley. The building of the New American State – with its radically centralizing tendencies, its transformative, radically statist commitment to a government of general, rather than enumerated, powers, and its affinity for the promise of administration – severed the relationship between the prevailing institutions of state and the sources of its legitimacy in traditional American constitutionalism.

The severing of state from Constitution at this time provided the impetus for the creation of modern constitutional theory. The traditional Constitution had served as the central discourse around which the authority of the old state was constructed. Now, a new constitutional vision was needed to legitimate the institutional arrangements and the proliferating policy initiatives of the New American State. Since the break of the statebuilding era, constitutional theorists have offered a profusion of such visions: radical, conservative, and moderate; simple and elaborate; clause-bound and comprehensive; monist and pluralist; principled and pragmatic; and so forth. These visions, which have typically been tied to a succession of reformist political programs and seek to legitimate them in light of other such programs and altering institutional, political, and intellectual contexts, have been influential, ignored, held, fallen apart, adopted in whole or in part, and advanced consciously and unconsciously.

Many of these visions were negative and were advanced largely as critiques of the traditional constitutionalism, which they characterized as formalistic and out of touch with contemporary social and political reality. Such visions, with their focus on the inadequacies, barriers, and obstacles of what went before, to this day comprise the spine of Whiggish narratives of the trajectory of constitutional development. Others, however, were affirmative substantive visions fashioned on the run to construct as constitutionally legitimate a trajectory of development that was now largely unmoored. These affirmative visions were commonly informed by theories of progress. The first prominent vision of this sort was advanced by Herbert Croly. Croly succeeded in crafting a more or less cogent and politically plausible argument explaining why the radical departure marked by the building of the New American State – which had been defended on nonconstitutional grounds by him, as by others – was *constitutionally* legitimate under the conditions of an altered political economy and an altered modern world. Croly's successors today are primarily law professors and other allied political philosophers (such as John Rawls) whose task in the New Constitutional Nation is, after accepting statism as a given, to provide a succession of ingeniously serviceable legitimating rhetorics for whatever progressive-spirited reform imperative is imagined to be of moment.

From the statebuilding era onward, as a spur to political reform and further flights of central state construction, progressive elites have argued repeatedly that the United States, as measured by the benchmark standards of European ideas and European states, was underdeveloped. Indeed, in these circles the desire to match such standards in a particular institutional or policy area, whether it involved building a modern social welfare or regulatory state or a Prussian- or Soviet-style education system, was commonly the measure of an individual's cultural or public policy sophistication, if not of "reasonableness" itself. For the constitutional adjuncts of these reformist campaigns, the task in perpetuity was to construct these successive developmental imperatives as constitutionally legitimate.

Progressive efforts to push the United States to measure up to the standards of continental European statism commonly ran up hard against highly institutionalized commitments to traditional constitutional structures and, often, to traditional constitutional rights. The antagonism progressive intellectual elites have evinced toward basic rights as part of their reformist campaigns has heretofore been minimized in Whiggish developmental narratives, which characterizes the reformers as interested chiefly in jettisoning outmoded "economic" rights, while evincing a tireless – and admirable – solicitude for the cause of "personal" rights. As this book has shown, however, the reformers themselves, when in the heat of battle, were much more frank. They boldly and repeatedly animadverted against both economic and personal rights that seemed to them to stand in the way of the trajectory of progress. Once the political battle had been won and the necessary institutional reforms accomplished, however, the theorists of the New Constitutional Nation then stepped forward to perform the institution-sustaining task of reconstituting reforms sold as restrictions of rights as, first – and upon further reflection – an apotheosis of rights, and, second – for those with the proper interpretive theory – as triumphs of constitutional principle, expanded, deepened, and updated. The path of reform was, in this way, continually both constitutionalized and Americanized.

It has not been my purpose here to claim that these dynamics were always operating in all areas of the law or that they always succeeded. As illustrated by the historical narrative presented here, I subscribe to Orren and Skowronek's assertion that intercurrence and multiple orders are defining features of American political and constitutional development. Some reformist campaigns took hold and succeeded as lines of development, and some were either partial or spectacular failures. Some progressive-spirited people were rather consistently prorights, rather than antirights. Some modern constitutional theorists, of course, are traditionalists and opponents of progressive-spirited campaigns. My claim is simply that the dynamics I describe here are important and much neglected. As such, a focus on them, where they are operating, will prove illuminating.

Along the same lines, I would not claim that American legal and intellectual elites are always in the grip of an *idée fixe* concerning the path of reform that broadly sets the institutional and constitutional agenda – though such elites have long evinced a demonstrable affinity for leaping onto such campaigns. As we have entered the twenty-first century, it does seem like a new reformist project along the lines of many of the important reformist imperatives chronicled in this book is indeed beginning to transfix American intellectuals. The idea taking root in a number of disciplines is that the United States, in the nature of its federalism, in its adherence to notions of national sovereignty, in its refusal to grant and protect social and economic rights, and in its stunted interpretation of the scope of rights in other important areas (such as same-sex marriage, abortion, and the death penalty), is an atavism and a global laggard that has fallen behind the curve in the trajectory of world historical (and moral) development. This idea originated outside of the law schools. But it has already begun to work its way down to them, where it is beginning to exert a concrete political influence on the path of American law. For the many law professors in the grip of this idea, a set of new imperatives is at hand. The intellectual and practical task, as they conceive it, is first, to document U.S. deficiencies in this regard, and, second, to formulate political and constitutional theories that demonstrate that the United States is bound both morally and legally to alter its laws and its constitutional rules to meet these more advanced world standards.

As legal adjuncts of this broader intellectual project, the special task of constitutional scholars within this broader reformist intellectual movement is to argue that there is nothing novel about this endeavor and that integrating the nation into the emergent "global constitution" is a project as old as the nation itself, that enhances rather than constricts the rights of Americans.

Following, as a coda to my broader study and prior to presenting a more general conclusion to the book as a whole, I present a brief précis of this newly crystalizing reformist imperative.[1]

The Rise of Global or World Constitutionalism

In recent years, one of the most striking turns in elite intellectual life in the United States, particularly within political science and constitutional law, has been a rapidly burgeoning interest in the concept of "global" or "world" constitutionalism. These terms have been used in various ways in the literature evincing this turn, but approaches to the concept fall roughly into two categories. The first chronicles and considers the spread of the commitment to constitutional government in sovereign nations across the globe in the post–World War II (and, subsequently, post-1989) era. The second, in contradistinction, both chronicles empirically and, in many cases, normatively advocates, the construction of a unifying "global" constitution that has broken the atavistic shackles of sovereignty (much as the New Deal ostensibly shattered the old constitutional order) and strains toward the apotheosis of a post-national constitutional order embracing the entire world. Although these two approaches are distinguishable, they are often blended together in the literature. Prominent strands of the turn toward global constitutionalism, for example, blur the distinction between domestic constitutional commitments and some notion of a world constitution by criticizing American lawyers and judges for not "learning" from the constitutionalism of other nations and for disregarding the ostensible requirements of international law or international "norms." Indeed, the normative pull of a world constitution is typically so palpable in this literature that the two understandings are perhaps best taken not as separate or complementary, but rather as ultimately antagonistic.[2]

The increasing attractiveness to people around the world of the idea of organizing and anchoring their political lives by a commitment to constitutional government and the rule of law has drawn the attention of many scholars interested in democratic transitions, both in the developing world

---

[1] See also Ken I. Kersch, "Multilateralism Comes to the Courts," *The Public Interest* 154 (Winter 2004): 3–18.

[2] See, e.g., Bruce Ackerman, "The Rise of World Constitutionalism," *Virginia Law Review* 83 (1997): 771–97.

and in Eastern Europe.³ But scholars most likely to influence the trajectory of *American* constitutional development have evinced a special attraction to work, often undertaken by Europeans, that posits either the empirical emergence or the normative imperative of a unified transnational legal and constitutional order. At the moment, this work seems to be exciting to progressively inclined American scholars because it promises a route for importing into American law public policy commitments concerning social and economic rights and the death penalty (among others) that are pervasive among foreign NGO activists and European and transnational bureaucratic and intellectual elites, but have by and large been rejected within the domestic politics of the United States.⁴

---

³ See, e.g., Jennifer Widner, *Building the Rule of Law: Francis Nyala and the Road to Judicial Independence in Africa* (New York: W. W. Norton, 2001); Herman Schwartz, *The Struggle for Constitutional Justice in Post-Communist Europe* (Chicago: University of Chicago Press, 2000); A. E. Dick Howard, "Judicial Independence in Post-Communist Central and Eastern Europe," in *Judicial Independence in the Age of Democracy*, eds. Peter H. Russell and David M. O'Brien (Charlottesville: University of Virginia Press, 2001), 89–110.

⁴ See Andrew Moravcsik, "Why Is U.S. Human Rights Policy So Unilateralist?" in *The Cost of Acting Alone: Multilateralism and U.S. Foreign Policy*, eds. Shepard Forman and Patrick Stewart (Boulder, CO: Lynne Riener Publishers, 2001), 352–9. See, e.g., Ackerman, "World Constitutionalism," 773 ("Over the past decade, we have been grappling with the original understanding of the Constitution of 1787, the Bill of Rights, and the Reconstruction Amendments with a new intensity. Whatever the utility of this debate for Americans, it does not engage the texts that have paramount constitutional significance for the rest of the world...the Universal Declaration of Human Rights, or the European Convention, or the German Constitution.... [T]hese beacons of a new era do not appear on American radar screens. The standard judge or lawyer would hardly raise an eyebrow when told, for example, that existing American law on capital punishment or welfare rights offends basic constitutional principles as the rest of the civilized world has come to understand them. What has *that* got to do with the Bill of Rights or the Equal Protection Clause?"); Stanley N. Katz, "Constitutionalism and Human Rights: The Dilemma of the United States," Second Annual Walter F. Murphy Lecture in American Constitutionalism, James Madison Program in American Ideals and Institutions, Princeton University (28 February 2002). ("But the rights revolution, seen in retrospect, was basically a movement toward civil rights, with scant impact on social and, especially, economic rights. Progress was made in those areas through legislation, but there is a big constitutional difference between statutory entitlement programs and rights-based programs. And... for the past thirty years the Court has been moving in directions that are hardly suggestive of the creation of even modest social or economic rights of the sort that are the staple of [the International Covenant on Economic, Social and Cultural Rights] – unless the reinvigoration of property rights can be counted.... [The] historic Federalist sense of the tight fit between popular sovereignty and constitutional validity [in the United States] makes it hard for us to accept the constitutional legitimacy of even the most admirable exogenous constitutional institutions and norms. We simply cannot accept that the United Nations or any other international body embodies the will of the American people sufficiently for it to establish rules enforceable in American courts.") See also Robert A. Dahl, *How Democratic Is the Constitution?* (New Haven: Yale University Press, 2002), 116–18, 168–9. Dahl has long been critical of the promise of judicial leadership in matters of public policy, but after finding the United States inferior to other democratic nations in such areas as social expenditures, state welfare measures, energy efficiency, foreign aid, "family policy," and "the representation

This inclination among progressive-spirited American social scientists and legalists is shared by influential political theorists around the world, many of whom, animated by a commitment to a common reformist public policy agenda for the United States, have united across longstanding intellectual divides. In recent years, neo-Hegelians, utilitarians, Rawlsian liberals, cosmopolitans, and multiculturalists have all become transfixed by the promise of a transnational and postnational world. Neo-Hegelian Marc Weller, for instance, has recently posited a three-part trajectory of progress in world history, with a worldwide constitutional order as its end point and apotheosis. In the initial stage, which Weller calls "the classical period of international law," the world order was dominated by governments – of which he expressly counts the United States to be a contemporary atavistic example – which "believe[d] themselves to be the exclusive representatives of a fully sovereign entity, endowed with a full panoply of natural rights and only bound by the very rules they have positively accepted." In the next stage, the world order is comprised primarily of "governments which have rediscovered modernity." In this stage, the sovereign state remains the principle ordering unit, although "legal rules and institutions can now fulfill functions that go beyond the narrowly defined self-interests of the individual members of the system and instead serve common values where it has been possible to achieve universal agreement on them." Finally, the world will enter – indeed, is now entering – the "third paradigm; that of the emerging universal constitution," involving "the empowerment and self-regulation of literally all mankind through the creation of a global social process which is conducted by all under the rule of law." "This emerging system," Weller writes, "features an infinite number of constitutionally authorized actors which are empowered to fulfill certain public functions within the universal [constitutional] system." This transition now under way represents a major step forward for mankind, since popular sovereignty (such as that which anchors the American constitutional tradition) is a "legitimating myth." In helping the world to move beyond this myth, the European Union is leading the way, though Weller notes "that some of the very actors who were disenfranchised by the traditional concept of sovereignty are rushing to its defense." "It is as if," he adds, "the slaves were rallying to save the practice of forced labor."[5]

---

of women in the national legislature," he concludes that the U.S. Constitution may need to be radically revised. "Perhaps not since Progressive scholars such as Justice Allen Smith wrote at the beginning of the twentieth century," Gordon Wood wrote of Dahl's book, "has anyone condemned the Constitution so harshly." Gordon S. Wood, "Rambunctious American Democracy," *New York Review of Books* (9 May 2002). As always, there are exceptions. See Michael Walzer, *Spheres of Justice: A Defense of Pluralism and Equality* (New York: Basic Books, 1983), 61–2, 281–311.

[5] Marc Weller, "The Reality of the Emerging Universal Constitutional Order: Putting the Pieces of the Puzzle Together," *Cambridge Review of International Affairs* (Winter/Spring

What will this new world constitutional order look like? At the moment, it "must be acknowledged" that "governments [remain] the principal representatives of their respective constituents in the universal law-creating process." The state is "the principal layer of delegated competence." In time, however, it will be governed from above by a complex "ordering of competences," which will work in service of norms set by "customary international law" administered by "universal mechanisms of public administration." In this new global system, at least as it concerns "areas of regulation essential to mankind, such as the maintenance of international peace and security, of essential humanitarian values and the global environment... it is no longer necessary to achieve the active consent of all participants in the law creating process." "Such rules," Weller concludes, "permit no derogations and demand compliance under all circumstances."[6]

Proceeding from utilitarian as opposed to Hegelian premises, philosopher Peter Singer has recently published a book, *One World* (2002), whose title is offered not only as an empirical description of the increasing interconnectedness of the world, but also "as a prescription of what the basic unit of our ethical thinking should be." "Is the division of the world's people into sovereign nations a dominant and unalterable fact of life?" Singer asks, before calling for, among other things, "a global system of criminal justice, so justice does not become the victim of national differences of opinion" and a new worldwide deference to global public opinion. Indeed, Singer announces that now is the time "we should be developing the ethical foundations of the coming era of a single world community," culminating in the construction of a "world government" that takes "all humans, or even all sentient beings, as the basic unit of concern."[7]

For Singer, as for Weller, a powerful obstacle stands like Cerberus at the gate, thwarting the passage of the world's people to a more advanced future on a global scale: the United States of America. "When the world's most powerful state," Singer writes in conclusion, "wraps itself in what – until September 11, 2001 – it took to be the security of its military might, and arrogantly refuses to give up any of its own rights and privileges for the sake

1997): 40–63, 41–2, 45. See also David Held, "Law of States, Law of Peoples: Three Models of Sovereignty," *Legal Theory* 8 (2002): 1–44. Hegel made the nation-state the culmination of his developmental trajectory. Weller, by contrast, envisages a densely interactive system comprised of an "infinite" number of actors. Weller would likely not consider this a dense network to be a "world government" or a "world state." In being staffed by an emergent, relatively autonomous world-governing class with similar worldviews, nomenclatures, and policy preferences, however, it would likely assume many of the characteristics (including legitimacy) that we associate with states and amount, in some significant respects, to a system of governance. See also Alexander Wendt, "Why a World State is Inevitable," *European Journal of International Relations* 9 (December 2003): 491–542.

[6] Weller, "Emerging Universal Constitutional Order," 46, 50, 53.

[7] Peter Singer, *One World: The Ethics of Globalization* (New Haven: Yale University Press, 2002), ix, x, 4, 7, 198, 199.

of the common good – even when other nations are giving up their rights and privileges – the prospects of finding solutions to global problems are dimmed."

One can only hope that when the rest of the world nevertheless proceeds down the right path, as it did in resolving to go ahead with the Kyoto Protocol, and as it is now doing with the International Criminal Court, the United States will eventually be shamed into joining in. If it does not, it risks falling into a situation in which it is universally seen by everyone except its own self-satisfied citizens as the world's "rogue superpower."[8]

Can a world government and a world ethical system be created without slipping into tyranny? If so, the answer lies with the Europeans, who have pioneered the principle of "subsidiarity." Singer acknowledges that that principle "is still being tested" in Europe. "But if it works for Europe," he concludes, "it is not impossible that it might work for the world."[9]

Rawlsian liberalism, whose abstractions begin by defining identity and conflict out of the model as a starting point for a theory of justice, has also proved amenable to a globalist turn. This has been the case despite the fact that in *The Law of Peoples* (1999) John Rawls himself flinched, insisting upon the continuing relevance of the political communities within nation-states as part of a "political liberalism" and refusing to take his ethical system beyond the boundaries of the nation to the global, world-universalist level. For his insistence on maintaining this distinction, Rawls has been roundly criticized by non-Rawlsians.[10] Rawlsians, on the other hand, have set themselves to an increasingly influential scholarly agenda that builds upon Rawls's work,

---

[8] Singer, *One World*, 198–9.

[9] Singer, *One World*, 199, 200. The principle of subsidiarity was pioneered by the Roman Catholic Church. See Encyclical Letter, Pope Pius XI, *Quadragesimo Anno* (15 May 1931). Singer's views are often taken to be extreme. *One World*, however, is well within the mainstream of current progressive opinion. See, e.g., Andres Martinez, "Home Planet Security" [book review], *New York Times*, Sec. 7, p. 27, col. 1 (1 December 2002) (calling *One World* a "timely and thoughtful book" and "a stimulating tour of the moral and practical challenges posed by the world's accelerating contraction," but lamenting Singer's "failure to dwell on the experience of the European Union...the one cutting-edge research lab for many of Singer's core issues, especially the need to subjugate national interests to the welfare of the broader community"); G. John Ikenberry, [book review], *Foreign Affairs* (March/April 2003); Gregg Easterbrook, "Greatest Good for the Greatest Number," [book review], *Washington Monthly* (November 2002); Morag Fraser, "The Question of Singer," [book review], *The Age* [Australia] (1 February 2003) (asserting that *One World* outlines "the direction [the] world might take – if we were brave and just"). See also Andrew Moravcsik, "In Defense of the 'Democratic Deficit': Reassessing Legitimacy in the European Union," *Journal of Common Market Studies* 40 (2002): 603–24; Andrew Moravcsik, "The EU Ain't Broke," *Prospect* (2003): 38–45 (arguing that, by standards of advanced industrial democracies, the EU has been largely successful in avoiding a "democratic deficit"). For a contrary view, see Larry Siedentop, *Democracy in Europe* (New York: Columbia University Press, 2001).

[10] See, e.g., Singer, *One World*, 8–9, 176–80 (Singer laments, for example, that Rawls chose to pursue a book titled "*The Law of Peoples*, not... *A Theory of Global Justice*"). John Rawls,

"pay[ing] homage," as one recently put it, "by being more royalist than the King," by extending the reach of Rawlsian justice to a global level, in the process articulating "a moral vision of a cosmopolitan world order."[11] Reflecting the characteristic abstraction of the Rawlsian project, this literature, unlike that of the neo-Hegelians, utilitarians, and others, has refrained from frankly proclaiming European civilization to be the embodiment of the world of tomorrow. The most enterprising Rawlsian scholars have instead turned much of their attention to the task of setting up new global deliberative forums that are free of the sorts of people who have caused them so much trouble at home (such as those who persist in disagreeing over the concrete policy requirements stemming from a commitment to "equal concern and respect" and "justice"), and are well stocked with more congenial, like-minded foreign judges, bureaucrats, and NGO activists. In these forums, the Rawlsians have correctly concluded, consensus among "reasonable people" concerning the requirements of "global," "cosmopolitan," or "universal" justice is now possible.[12]

Rawlsian ethics is centered upon a stated commitment to rational deliberation discovering the overlapping consensus about matters of justice. The

---

The Law of Peoples: The Idea of Public Reason Revisited (Cambridge, MA: Harvard University Press, 1999).

[11] See, e.g., Andrew Kuper, "Rawlsian Global Justice: Beyond _The Law of Peoples_ to a Cosmopolitan Law of Persons," _Political Theory_ 28 (October 2000): 640–74; Charles Beitz, _Political Theory and International Relations_ (Princeton: Princeton University Press, 1979); Charles Beitz, "Social and Cosmopolitan Liberalism," _International Affairs_ 75 (1999): 515–29. The cosmopolitan turn in Rawlsian political theory seems to be a special imperative for the Rawlsian political project, as by now sustained disagreement outside the academic conference circuit about such issues as the welfare, abortion, affirmative action, and other salient political issues has rendered it all but moribund in domestic political debates.

[12] Much of the initial work in this area has focused on finding a consensus concerning "serious crimes under international law," such as "piracy, slavery, war crimes, crimes against peace, crimes against humanity, genocide, and torture." See, e.g., _Princeton Principles of Universal Jurisdiction_ (Princeton: Program in Law and Public Affairs, Princeton University, 2001) (available at www.princeton.edu/~lapa/) (project chaired by Rawlsian political theorist Stephen Macedo) announcing that judges should have "universal jurisdiction" worldwide to prosecute serious crimes under international law, free of a statute of limitations, regardless of state boundaries, with no exception for heads of state and government officials, "even if their national legislation does not specifically provide for it." Nations, however, may refuse extradition to countries where the defendant is likely to face the death penalty. The meeting that crafted these principles and "debated" them included no critics of the new universalism or skeptics of international institutions. The vote on the principles was 29–1 (with an English judge voting no primarily because of prudential concerns involving immunity for heads of state). If anything, the single "no" vote following these deliberations served usefully to lend the project the veneer of legitimacy, without causing it the least bit of trouble. Of course, where, as here, the group is self-selected and nonrepresentative of any democratic political constituency, the vote tally is meaningless. See also _Universal Jurisdiction: National Courts and the Prosecution of Serious Crimes under International Law_, ed. Stephen Macedo (Philadelphia: University of Pennsylvania Press, 2003).

political problem, though, becomes one of positing a functional deliberative polity. It is here that the burgeoning interest in "cosmopolitanism" comes in. Whereas the task of drawing political boundaries reasonably calculated to conduce to effective democratic deliberation was once a major concern of political scientists, the new cosmopolitans, with a manifestly religious sensibility, argue that the next step for political theory is to imagine a polity that comprises all of humanity.[13] Martha Nussbaum, for example, posits as the "ideal that is...[most] adequate to our situation in the contemporary world...the person whose allegiance is to the worldwide community of human beings." Citing the Stoics and Kant, Nussbaum calls for the construction of a global "community of dialogue and concern" that will transcend barriers to "rational deliberation" (such as patriotism and primary allegiances to family, friends, and fellow citizens).[14] As with others transfixed by the promise of a global polity and a universal constitution, the cosmopolitans, like the Europeans, do not call for the end of the nation-state – at least not yet. They understand that that state might prove serviceable, pursuant to the subsidiarity principle, for administering delimited geographic districts. But, in this new world, the loyalities of persons and their ultimate ethical and political commitments would not run to either the bureaucratic authorities of, or their geographic neighbors within, these adminstrative units. Rather, their primary allegiance would be to the entire, complex, worldwide network of authorities, arranged at the global level, to serve as a constitution for all humanity.[15]

Some scholars, while sympathetic to much of the new cosmopolitanism, also seem to harbor a continuing commitment to multiculturalism, a commitment that attributes special importance to the role of group identity in lending meaning to human life. While cosmopolitans in their purer forms emphasize commitments to a unitary polity administered by a complex network of global institutions, multiculturalist globalists such as Rogers M. Smith emphasize a world of multiple allegiances and multiple potential memberships, which would recognize primary commitments to religions, political movements, cultures, races – or nations. Smith argues that the "constitutive stories" concerning the meaning of the group that bind members of identity groups together are both a permanent feature of human political life and normatively valuable to human flourishing. Smith's multiculturalism remains part of the globalist intellectual project in two ways. First, it

---

[13] See Held, "Law of States, Law of Peoples," 23–32. In acknowledging the distinction between *regnum* and *sacerdotium*, Christian thought, from its inception, has been much less ambitious. On the importance of delimitations of space in effective political science concerning successful liberal democracies (especially in the writings of Montesquieu and Madison), see Siedentop, *Democracy in Europe*, 1–46.

[14] Martha C. Nussbaum, *For Love of Country?* (Boston: Beacon Press, 2002), 4, 9, 13.

[15] See Held, "Law of States, Law of Peoples," 33, 39.

finds its ultimate justification in a political commitment to all humanity.[16] And, second, it accords no special political value (and no special debility) to nation-states against any other associational grouping that is supported by a compelling constitutive story.[17]

Although his approach is distinctive, Smith's destination is familiar. "In the years ahead," he writes:

> [I]t might foster acceptance of various sorts of transnational political arrangements to deal with problems like exploitative and wildly fluctuating international financial and labor markets, destructive environmental and agricultural practices, population control, and the momentous issue of human genetic modifications.... Greater acceptance of such arrangements would necessarily entail increased willingness to view existing governments at all levels as at best only "semi-sovereign," authoritative over some issues and not others, in the manner that acceptance of multiple particularistic constitutive stories would also reinforce. In the resulting political climate, it might become easier to construct the sorts of systems of interwoven democratic international, regional, state and local governments that theorists of "cosmopolitan democracy" ... all envision.[18]

Integrating the United States into the Global Constitution: How Lawyers and Judges Can Help

One of the familiar and persistent themes in modern American progressive political thought is the notion that the United States, as measured by the standards set in continental Europe, is a laggard nation that has yet to develop a social welfare state worthy of the name and to fully respect (as modern Europeans do) social, economic, civil, and political rights. As the Europeans have moved in recent years to build a world beyond the nation-state, in the process providing a blueprint for a world constitution that respects basic rights, the United States has stubbornly hewn to what many openly describe

---

[16] Rogers M. Smith, "Cosmopolitan Patriotism, Constitutive Stories, and Norms of Allegiance," paper presented at the Center for Human Values, Princeton University (25 April 2002), 3. ("[W]e should insist that all constitutive stories justifying more particular political memberships must be connected to larger constitutive stories defining the identity and interests of the human species.")

[17] Smith, "Cosmopolitan Patriotism." See also Rogers M. Smith, *Stories of Peoplehood: The Politics and Morals of Memberships* (New York: Cambridge University Press, 2003). It should be said that Smith's multiculturalism is more ecumenical and more tolerant than many forms, particularly in its welcoming of the constitutive stories of patriots and even religious groups. At his presentation at Princeton, he was roundly attacked for this ecumenicism.

[18] Smith, "Constitutional Patriotism," 37. See, generally, Keith E. Whittington, "Dismantling the Modern State? The Changing Structural Foundations of Federalism," *Hastings Constitutional Law Quarterly* 25 (Summer 1998): 483–527, esp. 511–13 (arguing that the increasingly apparent limits of the nation state in the context of globalization creates space for the construction of new constitutional understandings better adapted to emergent conditions).

as atavistic notions of sovereignty, antistatism, and a truncated understanding of basic human rights, particularly as they pertain to matters of positive liberty. The frustration within progressive political and intellectual circles, born of the persistence of American exceptionalism and the marginality of the liberal-left in contemporary domestic politics, has come to pervade elite intellectual life in the United States to the point where the "problem of the United States" has become a robust successor to "the labor problem" and "the race problem" as a major, world-defining axis of orientation for influential American intellectuals.

Law professors have recently caught the wave of these trends in the social sciences and the humanities and set themselves to the task of finding ways to do their part in integrating the United States into the global constitutional system. While, of course, this project of legal elites involves many areas of law, including commercial law, which I do not address here (but which will prove quite helpful to their project), interest has, unsurprisingly enough, been particularly strong in areas of constitutional law that seemed to hold promise during the Warren and early Burger years (such as welfare rights and the elimination of the death penalty), but have since fallen upon hard times in the Reagan and Rehnquist years. It is during these hard times that legal scholars have developed a strong interest in the penetration of American law by foreign sources of law and, indeed, of foreign public opinion and foreign institutions, all of which are understood in the nature of things to be a potential force for evolution and progress in American law.[19] One part of this campaign involves a scholarly push to have international law – and especially the highly malleable and rapidly evolving (evolving, that is, through elite intellectual influence) modern version of "customary international law" – held binding on American courts. A second and related part involves a broader effort to integrate American judges into a global "conversation" among judges, so they can "learn" from other judges, becoming more cosmopolitan and, in due course, evince that cosmopolitanism by applying what they have learned as sitting judges of the U.S. Constitution's Article III courts. Unlike the global conversations imagined by Nussbaum, which are wholly fantastical, these more delimited conversations among elites (such as those among the new global Rawlsians), as part of an emergent academic and professional conference circuit, are eminently practical.

---

[19] This burgeoning preoccupation, in many respects, is simply a move in a classic strategic political game, involving efforts by the losing side in a political fight to alter the scope of the conflict by welcoming into the ring (previously nonparticipating) like-minded players from abroad. See E. E. Schattsneider, *The Semi-Sovereign People: A Realist's View of Democracy in America* (New York: Holt, Rinehart, and Winston, 1960). For elaboration of this argument, see Jeremy Rabkin, *Why Sovereignty Matters* (Washington, DC: AEI Press, 1998); Ken I. Kersch, "The Semi-Sovereign People," paper presented at the Conference on the Declaration of Independence, James Madison Program in American Ideals and Institutions, Princeton University (April 2002).

Some of the efforts to effectuate domestic political and constitutional change through international law involve appeals to U.S. ratified treaties. This route to reform, of course, is relatively unproblematic from the standpoint of traditional approaches to constitutional construction and American (popular) sovereignty, though it is often wielded with a patent disdain for American constitutional arrangements (Peter Singer, for instance, has denounced Article II creating the electoral college as a plain violation of the "equal suffrage" provision of Article 25(b) of the Universal Declaration of Human Rights).[20] The treaty approach is of some use as a pathway to domestic political reform, as some human rights treaties, such as the International Covenant on Civil and Political Rights, the Genocide Convention, the Convention on Torture, and the International Covenant on all Forms of Racial Discrimination, have been both signed and ratified by the United States. This route, however, has its limits as a means of reform. One problem is that the United States (for various reasons that these elites persistently denounce) has refused to ratify enough of these agreements (including the Convention on the Elimination of All Forms of Discrimination Against Women and the Convention on the Rights of the Child).[21] Another is that, after what progressive legalists typically regard as an unconscionable delay, the United States frequently attaches a series of legally binding reservations to the articles of ratification, such as statements that "nothing in the Constitution requires or authorizes legislation or other action by the United States of America prohibited by the Constitution of the United States as interpreted by the United States." Reservations like this are commonly criticized by these scholars (and NGO activists) as effectively vitiating the potential of the treaties.[22]

Given the frustrations inherent in the most legitimate routes to domestic policy change via international law, law professors – beginning about the time that Ronald Reagan was elected president of the United States – have developed an intense interest in the once arcane subject of customary

---

[20] Singer, *One World*, 100–1.

[21] This is the grounds for the now rather commonplace charge that the United States is a "laggard state" when it comes to human rights. See, e.g., Katz, "Constitutionalism and Human Rights," 4–5. In guaranteeing the rights of women, the United States lags behind Angola, China, Libya, Yemen, and Zaire [Congo], which, unlike the United States, have ratified the Convention on the Elimination of All Forms of Discrimination Against Women. In recognizing the rights of children, the United States lags behind Convention signatories Cuba, Ethiopia, Cambodia, Rwanda, the Sudan, Vietnam, Zaire [Congo], and Zimbabwe. Barry E. Carter and Phillip R. Trimble, *International Law: Selected Documents and New Developments* (Boston: Little Brown and Co., 1994), 379, 400. Unlike Rwanda, which leaped at the chance to participate in setting new global norms, the United States was a late and reluctant signatory to the Genocide Convention.

[22] See Moravcsik, "Why Is U.S. Human Rights Policy So Unilateralist?" 345–6. See, e.g., Katz, "Constitutionalism and Human Rights," which treats this reservation appended by the U.S. Senate to the ratification of the Genocide Convention this way.

international law. That law (or one of its related variants) has the advantage of being available for ready use by judges in the absence of any affirmative acts of Congress or the president (indeed, some scholars are now beginning to argue that customary international law is binding on American judges even in direct opposition to the wishes of the nation's political branches).[23] In the past quarter century, a consensus has emerged in the legal academy (minus the "curious broadsides" of a handful of "utterly mistaken... revisionists" whose views have "superficial appeal for those not well steeped in the field of international and foreign affairs law") that customary international law is binding on the United States as a form of federal common law.[24] As such, this customary international law potentially "preempts inconsistent state law pursuant to the Supremacy Clause... provides a basis for Article III's 'arising under' jurisdiction... [and may even] bind the President under Article II's Take Care Clause... [and] supercede prior inconsistent federal legislation."[25]

As Harold Koh, a prominent proponent of the view that international law, including customary international law (traditionally considered a subset of the "law of nations") is binding upon American judges, properly notes that law has long been considered part of American law. His "revisionist"

---

[23] See Curtis A. Bradley, "The Status of Customary International Law in U.S. Courts – Before and After *Erie*," *Denver Journal of International Law and Policy* 26 (Winter 1998): 807–26, esp. 809–10 (citing examples). As such, this is perhaps more accurately seen as an appeal to *jus cogens* or natural law than as an appeal to custom. See Mark Janis, *Introduction to International Law*, 41–82. For an explanation of customary international law and its variants, see Anthea Elizabeth Roberts, "Traditional and Modern Approaches to Customary International Law: A Reconcilation," *American Journal of International Law* 95 (October 2001): 757–91; The literature in this area, at least as developed so far, seems to shift amongst appeals to "customary international law," "*jus cogens*," "international norms," "the law of nations," and other variants, each of which has distinctive claims to authority and derogability. In this introductory discussion, I forbear from tracing out the implications of these shifting appeals. On the way in which political actors have used judges to institutionalize policy gains they see as under siege, see Howard Gillman, "How Political Parties Can Use the Courts to Advance Their Agendas: Federal Courts in the United States, 1875–1891," *American Political Science Review* 96 (2002): 511–24.

[24] Harold Hongju Koh, "Is International Law Really State Law?" *Harvard Law Review* 111 (1997–8): 1824–61, esp. 1824, 1827. See also Jordan J. Paust, "Customary International Law and Human Rights Treaties Are Law of the United States," *Michigan Journal of International Law* 20 (Winter 1999): 301–36, esp. 306 (characterizing these "revisionist" arguments as "astonishing" and "bizarre and unreal").

[25] Bradley, "The Status of Customary International Law in U.S. Courts"; Curtis A. Bradley and Jack L. Goldsmith, "Customary International Law as Federal Common Law: A Critique of the Modern Position," *Harvard Law Review* 110: 4 (February 1997): 815–76. Bradley and Goldsmith are critics of these claims and the chief "revisionists" criticized by Harold Koh, whom Bradley and Goldsmith, conversely, describe as one of the inventors of the "modern" position. For an anatomy of the Koh–Bradley/Goldsmith debate, see Daniel H. Joyner, "Note: A Normative Model for the Integration of Customary International Law into United States Law," *Duke Journal of Comparative and International Law* (Fall/Winter 2001): 133–56, esp. 135–41.

antagonists, Jack Goldsmith and Curtis Bradley, however, properly counter that the current turn to international law is altogether different in its spirit, objectives, and context than the domestic uses of international law in the past. For most of American history, they correctly assert, the law of nations was not used by American judges as a vehicle for seeking to effectuate broad, transformative, and purportedly progressive policy objectives that had been rejected by the American people through their domestically constituted democratic political institutions. The law of nations, in these earlier years, was deployed by American courts as gap fillers – much needed prior to the creation of the modern, positive, statutory state – in commercial law, admiralty, maritime, and prize cases.[26] Customary international law was not considered applicable as public law, that is, as law ordering the relationship between the United States and its citizens.[27]

World War II and its aftermath transformed the potential for leveraging old doctrine concerning customary international law to effectuate progressive-spirited, judicially initiated political change. The Nuremberg trials (1945), the Universal Declaration of Human Rights (1948), and the development of an international human rights movement, along with an attendant series of international covenants and agreements, broadly challenged the legitimacy of a prevailing legal positivism that both held sway within progressively oriented legal thought and, at the same time, held that international law had nothing to say about the way a sovereign nation treated its own citizens. As we have seen in our earlier discussion of the path of development concerning criminal process rights, these postwar initiatives immediately triggered efforts by American legal academics and lawyers to leverage them and import them into American law to advance the cause of civil rights. That effort, however, ultimately foundered in the face of domestic

---

[26] See Edwin D. Dickinson, "The Law of Nations as Part of the National Law of the United States," *University of Pennsylvania Law Review* 101 (1953): 26–56; Harold H. Sprout, "Theories as to the Applicability of International Law in the Federal Courts of the United States," *American Journal of International Law* 26 (1932): 280–95.

[27] On this gap-filling function in private law adjudication, see *The Paquette Habana*, 175 U.S. 677 (1900). ("[W]here there is no treaty, and no controlling executive or legislative act or decision, resort must be had to the customs and usage of civilized nations; and, as evidence of these to the works of jurists and commentators.... Such works are resorted to by judicial tribunals, not for the speculations of their authors concerning what the law ought to be, but for trust in or evidence of what the law actually is.") What's more, prior the Supreme Court's New Deal–era decision in *Erie v. Tompkins*, 304 U.S. 64 (1938), customary international law was considered part of the general common law, not federal law, per se. As such, it was not considered "the Supreme Law of the land." Nor was it considered part of the "laws of the United States," which would give rise to Article III jurisdiction. The federal government and, indeed, the states both had the authority to override this law. Bradley and Goldsmith, "Customary International Law." See also Edward A. Purcell Jr., *Brandeis and the Progressive Constitution: Erie, Judicial Power, and the Politics of Federal Courts in Twentieth Century America* (New Haven: Yale University Press, 2000).

political resistance (the push for the Bricker Amendment) and the Supreme Court's decision to pursue the sought-after reforms by means of a more aggressive interpretation of the Fourteenth Amendment. The current reformist movement to effectuate legal change through appeals to international authority, however, began in earnest only with the election of Ronald Reagan. In the Carter administration's waning days, its Justice and State Departments submitted an *amicus* brief in *Filártiga v. Peña-Irala* (1980), a case involving the torture by a Paraguayan against another Paraguayan in Paraguay, that was audaciously brought to an American court pursuant to the eighteenth-century Alien Tort Claims Act. In an opinion written by liberal Brooklyn federal judge Irving Kaufman, the U.S. Court of Appeals for the Second Circuit adopted the Carter brief's view that customary international law is binding on federal judges. The Second Circuit's *Filártiga* opinion has since been singled out by progressive legal academics and political activists for lavish praise (Harold Koh, for instance, called *Filártiga* "the *Brown v. Board of Education*" of the transnational human rights movement).[28] The passion for *Filártiga* is understandable, since it opens up vast new vistas for domestic judicial policymaking. The customary international law route to judge-led political change has two signal advantages that make it especially promising. First, since customary international law in certain senses has long been considered part of domestic law, the courts, in following it, can make rhetorically persuasive claims to humility and legitimacy. And, second, since the content of customary international law in recent years is increasingly set on a transnational conference circuit attended by bureaucratic, academic, and political elites, that content can be massaged out of public view, under the guise of scholarly authority, without the retarding interference of domestic political actors and institutions.

The *Filártiga* case involved a dispute between two foreign nationals over events that took place in a foreign country. The domestic political agenda of

---

[28] *Filártiga v. Peña-Irala*, 630 F.2d 876 (2nd Cir. 1980). The Alien Tort Claims Act (1789) gives federal courts jurisdiction "where an alien sues for a tort only in violation of the law of nations or a treaty of the United States." The Act was used to support federal jurisdiction in only two cases prior to *Filartiga*. The only case in which it was invoked prior to the 1960s was an admiralty case. The *Filartiga* court held that the proscription was part of a broader body of customary international law that protected individuals in their fundamental human rights, and that that body of law was part of the law of nations, hence triggering federal jurisdiction under the Act. Andrew M. Scobie, "Enforcing the Customary International Law of Human Rights in Federal Court," *California Law Review* 74 (January 1986): 127–87, esp. 127. Kaufman, who, as a young man, had sentenced the Rosenbergs to death, was execrated for that act by the liberal-left and was perpetually striving to redeem himself. Yale's Geoffrey Hazard noted Kaufman's "strong inclination to be in the public eye." He added, "I think his inclination in that regard diminished the professional appreciation of his judicial abilities." Marilyn Berger, "Judge Irving Kaufman, of Rosenberg Spy Trial and Free-Press Rulings, Dies at 81," *New York Times* (3 February 1992), Sec. D, p. 10.

those who are committed to "bringing international law home," however, is, clear. In the wake of *Filártiga*, Harold Koh asks frankly, for instance,

To what extent... should we acknowledge that police brutality by local American police or prison conditions in state penitentiaries should meet not only the standards of the Constitution and 42 U.S.C. Sec. 1983 jurisprudence, but also the international standards of torture or arbitrary detention acknowledged by international bodies? To what extent should our practice of executing juveniles or people with mental retardation under the Eighth Amendment meet evolving standards of international decency? To what extent should our understanding of the legality of same-sex marriage be informed by European or Australian standards construing treaties and protocols using phrases that are also in international instruments to which we are a party? And to what extent should our Supreme Court's recent decision in *Bush v. Gore* be subjected to the international standards of electoral fairness that we apply in Croatia or Peru or Ukraine, or the universality of the counting procedures applied in South Africa?[29]

The path to bringing these policies "home" is a two-step process. First, like-minded scholars and activists, acting transnationally, convene and formulate commitments that they declare to be global "customs." And second, these scholars and activists then work to bring about a "dialogue" between themselves and judges, and between judges in different countries who "share" insights and understandings as part of a goal-directed "transnational legal process" that reconstitutes legal meanings and understandings of the judicial role within the nation-state itself – as of U.S. judges sitting on Article III federal courts. "[A] nation's repeated participation in transnational legal process," Koh makes clear, alluding specifically to Robert Cover's notion of "law creating" jurisgenerativity, "is internalizing, normative, and constitutive of identity." "By domesticating international rules," he announces hopefully, "transnational legal process can spur internal acceptance even of previously taboo political principles."[30]

Law professors, both American and foreign, play a major role in the process of inventing the contemporary "customs" and "norms," while insisting, against their frank declarations elsewhere, that they are not inventing law, but simply describing it. The late Richard Lillich of the University of Virginia, who described himself "[a]s one who has prepared affidavits, been an expert witness, and helped to draft numerous amicus curiae briefs in many of the U.S. cases that have *developed* the customary international law of human rights over the past fifteen years," in a typical jurisgenerative instance,

---

[29] Harold Hongju Koh, "The Globalization of Freedom," *Yale Journal of International Law* 26 (2001): 305–12, esp. 307; Harold Hongju Koh, "The 1998 Frankel Lecture: Bringing International Law Home," *Houston Law Review* 35 (1998–9): 623–81. See Moravcsik, "Why Is U.S. Human Rights Policy So Unilateralist?" 354, 370 (providing empirical evidence of the alignment of the policy preferences of multilateralists with the policy preferences of the contemporary Democratic Party).

[30] Koh, "Bringing International Law Home," 641, 643.

convened an influential symposium on "the growing importance of customary international human rights law" and then cited "the near-unanimous support of the contributors to the Symposium" as authority for the proposition that there was an agreement among scholars that customary international law was binding upon states. He then went on, citing "the consensus that emerges from this Symposium," to declare that contrary views "would appear to be well outside the 'mainstream' of contemporary international law scholarship."[31]

In recent years, the making of customary international law has become something of a cottage industry. Indeed, the term "custom" is a misnomer, because within this industry "custom" (like "norm," another term that is frequently used) is no longer used to refer to the actual, longstanding practices of nations, businesses, and individuals. For Lillich, and for reform-minded elites fixated on a clear path of political progress, customary international law has little to do with custom as traditionally understood (just as the current enthusiasm for "international norms" among reformist political scientists has little to do with actual norms). If it did, after all, it would hardly have been taken up with such zeal, since merely reading widespread practice into law, while useful for resolving disputes in cases involving admiralty and the law merchant, lacks any sort of transformative potential.

The content of contemporary customary international law, rather, is adduced from an array of sources. Traditionally, custom was defined as a widespread, general practice that was understood to be binding as law. Whether a certain behavior was a general practice was determined inductively, through observation. The content of traditional customary international law may have changed over time, but that change was evolutionary: It tended to take place slowly and imperceptibly. After the Second World War, however, in the wake of United Nations efforts to codify international law and the proliferation of international agreements and conventions, the boundary between written international law and unwritten customary international law began to blur. This blurring was accentuated by the terms of the UN Charter itself, which announced that the United Nations would give precedence in its activities to efforts to codify not only well-settled practices but what was adjudged to be the "progressive development of international law." In this new world, practice was still relevant in determining the content of customary international law. But in line with the new commitment to "progressive development," it was emphasized that that practice need not have been longstanding. Greater emphasis was placed on the question of whether that practice had come to be accepted as law. And that was to be

---

[31] Richard B. Lillich, "The Growing Importance of Customary International Human Rights Law," *Georgia Journal of International and Comparative Law* 25 (1995–6): 1–30 [italics added]. See also *Princeton Principles of Universal Jurisdiction*. The primary, initial focus in this case is on serious international crimes of the sort outlined in the Princeton Principles.

determined on a case-by-case basis by weighing the evidence from a proliferating array of sources, including international agreements and covenants (including UN opinions, actions, and resolutions), the opinions of judges of international and national courts, the pronouncements of states, and the opinions of scholars. Today, many of these sources of law are highly dynamic and aggressively reformist. The content of modern customary international law, accordingly, now changes relatively rapidly.

Among the most prominent sources of evidence of customary international law are international pronouncements such as the Universal Declaration of Human Rights. Such pronouncements, as Richard Lillich puts it, "constitute important indications that an international consensus... that [those conventions] reflected customary international law was *evolving*" (emphasis added).[32] The Declaration's provisions range beyond issues involving "serious international crimes" to cover freedom of opinion, expression, and religion, and freedom from arbitrary arrest, and they assert a right to an adequate standard of living, equal pay for equal work, and other such rights. That these rights may be honored more in the breach than in practice has little bearing on the Declaration's status as a reflection of global custom, since the content of modern customary international law is defined in terms of "progressive development." The Declaration's status as, in part, declarative of evolving customs, in turn, is held to be the source of its authority as a source of law. If assent to a pronouncement evincing a commitment to a right or principle is evidence (and sometimes, as some argue, the most important or even sole evidence) of its status as custom; and, if as is often the case, that assent has no relation to actual social practice, there is little that prevents the creation of "instant customary international law." In addition, the ultimate source of the law in the postwar environment in which modern customary international law is created is unclear. These two characteristics, needless to say, make contemporary customary international law an immensely serviceable concept in the modern world.[33]

Another wellspring of authority for the content of customary international law is opinions of legal commentators. (The status accorded to these "international law" commentators, it is worth noting, tracks that accorded to legal scholars in continental civil law systems – which is not the system

---

[32] Lillich, "Growing Importance of Customary International Human Rights Law," 2.

[33] See Gary L. Scott and Craig L. Carr, "Multilateral Treaties and the Formation of Customary International Law," *Denver Journal of International Law and Policy* 25 (Fall 1996): 71–94; Anthony D'Amato, *The Concept of Custom in International Law* (Ithaca, NY: Cornell University Press, 1971). For a critique, see Jonathan I. Charney, "International Agreements and the Development of Customary International Law," *Washington Law Review* 61 (July 1986): 971–96. See, e.g., *Grutter v. Bollinger*, 539 U.S. 306 (2003) (Justices Ginsburg and Breyer, concurring) (although not referring specifically to "customary international law," citing U.N. General Assembly Resolutions and the Convention on the Elimination of All Forms of Discrimination Against Women – which was signed but not ratified by the United States – as evidence of "the international understanding of the office of affirmative action").

out of which the American legal order arises). These professors often have close ties to transnational advocacy groups and work in tandem with them and other like-minded academics. Both play significant roles in limning in authoritative books and articles the "evolving" understanding of the covenants and noncovenanted customs and norms. These evolving understandings and progressive developments, now given the imprimatur of "international law," are then ripe to be applied as law by the judges of the world's international and domestic courts.[34]

The imperative of joining a worldwide "constitutive" process of "bringing international law home" has become very popular among foreign judges.[35] American academics have worked hard to persuade American judges to follow a similar path by praising efforts of American judges to overcome their "provincialism" and develop productive "transjudicial relations" to "help the world's legal systems work together, in harmony, rather than at cross purposes."[36] Steps in this direction have been warmly praised in law review articles.[37] They have also been placed at the core of cutting-edge programs, such as Yale Law School's Global Constitutionalism Seminar and NYU Law School's Hauser Global Law School Program (whose founding director was former ACLU head Norman Dorsen), which bring together academics and foreign and American judges – including Supreme Court justices – to share

[34] On this, Koh once again speaks frankly, describing the importance of networks of "transnational norm entrepreneurs" and "interpretive communities" (among other factors) for "bringing international law home." Koh, "Bringing International Law Home," 647–9.

[35] See, e.g., speech by Murray Gleeson [Chief Justice of Australia], to the Australian Bar Association Conference, "Global Influences on the Australian Judiciary" (Paris, France, 8 July 2002) (www.hcourt.gov.au/speeches/cj/cj_global.htm). ("I believe there is a growing awareness within the Australian profession, of the importance of looking beyond our own statutes and precedents and our traditional sources of law, in formulating answers to legal problems.... The forces of globalization tend to standardize the questions to which a legal system must respond. It is only to be expected that there will be an increasing standardization of the answers.")

[36] Ackerman, "World Constitutionalism," 773; Anne-Marie Slaughter, "Court to Court," *American Journal of International Law* 92 (October 1998); 708–12, citing *Howe v. Goldcorp Inves., Ltd.*, 946 F.2d 944, 950 (1st Cir. 1991) (opinion of Judge Stephen Breyer); Anne-Marie Slaughter, "40th Anniversary Perspective: Judicial Globalization," *Virginia Journal of International Law* 40 (Summer 2002): 1103–24; Anne-Marie Slaughter, *A New World Order* (Princeton: Princeton University Press, 2004), ch. 2; Heinz Klug, "Model and Anti-Model: The United States Constitution and the Rise of World Constitutionalism," *Wisconsin Law Review* (2000): 597–616. See also Mary Ann Glendon, *Rights Talk: The Impoverishment of Political Discourse* (New York: The Free Press, 1991), 145–70.

[37] See Slaughter, "Court to Court," at 710, praising Judge Calabresi's decision in *U.S. v. Then*, 56 F.3d 464 (1995), advocating that American judges "join a global trend and pay more attention to foreign decisions" and noting that the belief they should do so "is shared in high places"; Anne-Marie Slaughter, "A Global Community of Courts," *Harvard International Law Journal* 44 (Winter 2003): 191–219; Harold Hongju Koh, "Forward: On American Exceptionalism," *Stanford Law Review* 55 (2003): 1479–527, esp. 1513–15; Harold Hongju Koh, "Rights to Remember," *The Economist*, 1 November 2003, 24–6.

information and forge personal and institutional bonds.[38] Briefs submitted to the Supreme Court now not only increasingly urge the Court to follow international law, but also to look to foreign experience and even foreign public opinion. These briefs, and the scholarly praise that comes from following their lead, as the Court's recent gay rights and affirmative action decisions indicate, are already leading the Court to new sources of authority, sources that seem well on their way to altering the nature and path of American constitutional development.[39]

[38] See *Democracy and the Rule of Law*, eds., Norman Dorsen and Prosser Gifford (Washington, DC: CQ Press, 2001) (NYU conference proceedings); Slaughter, "A Global Community of Courts"; Slaughter, *A New World Order*, ch. 2. See also American Civil Liberties Union, National Training Conference, "Human Rights at Home: International Law in U.S. Courts" (Carter Presidential Center, Atlanta, Georgia, 9–11 October 2003) ("All practicing lawyers and advocates engaged in social justice work in the U.S. will find training workshops relevant to their work. In depth training will be offered on using a human rights framework to advance racial equality, women's rights, workers' rights, and economic justice; environmental justice; gay, lesbian, bisexual and transgender rights; and disability rights.... The emphasis throughout the conference will be on using international law and human rights norms to advance justice in United States courts or on behalf of United States clients. Today, 'human rights' means much more than the struggle to free political prisoners in undemocratic nations. Human rights laws and strategies can be usefully applied on behalf of clients in the United States in conjunction with constitutional protections.") (ACLU Conference announcement, on file with author). See, generally, Ken I. Kersch, "The Synthetic Progressivism of Justice Breyer," in *The Structure of the Rehnquist Court Jurisprudence*, ed. Earl Maltz (Lawrence, KS: University Press of Kansas, 2003); Ken I. Kersch, "Justice Breyer's Progress," paper presented to the Program on Constitutional Government, Harvard University (15 November 2002); Kersch, "Multilateralism Comes to the Courts."

[39] *Lawrence v. Texas*, 123 s.ct. 2472 (2003), citing European Court of Human Rights precedent and amicus brief surveying foreign precedent submitted by Mary Robinson, former United Nations High Commissioner for Human Rights (Harold Hongju Koh, Counsel of Record), in holding unconstitutional Texas statute criminalizing consensual same-sex sodomy; *Grutter v. Bollinger*, 539 U.S. 306 (2003), citing the International Convention on the Elimination of All Forms of Racial Discrimination and the Convention on the Elimination of All Forms of Discrimination Against Women (which the U.S. has not ratified) as evidence of "the international understanding of the office of affirmative action," in upholding the constitutionality of the admissions policies at the University of Michigan Law School (Justices Ginsburg and Breyer, concurring); Ruth Bader Ginsburg, "Affirmative Action as an International Human Rights Dialogue," *Brookings Review* (Winter 2000); Stephen Breyer, "The Supreme Court and the New International Law," speech to The American Society of International Law (Washington, D.C., 4 April 2003); Sandra Day O'Conner, speech to the Southern Center for International Studies (Atlanta, GA, 28 October 2003) ("I suspect that over time, we will rely increasingly – or take notice at least increasingly – on international and foreign law in resolving domestic issues."). See also *Atkins v. Virginia*, 536 U.S. 304 (2002), fn. 21, citing Harold Koh, and noting "within the world community, the imposition of the death penalty for crimes committed by mentally retarded offenders is overwhelmingly disapproved."); *U.S. v. Lopez*, 514 U.S. 549 (1995) *Printz v. United States*, 521 U.S. 898, 977 (1977) (Justice Breyer, dissenting); *Knight v. Florida*, 528 U.S. 990, 997 (1999) (Justice Breyer dissenting from denial of *certiorari*); *Washington v. Glucksberg*, 521 U.S. 702 (1997), 710, 718 n. 16, 785–7 (Chief Justice Rehnquist) *Thompson v. Oklahoma*, 487 U.S. 815 (1988), 830, 851 (Justice Stevens). See also

Conclusion: Constructing Civil Liberties in the New Constitutional Nation

In the late nineteenth and early twentieth centuries, the United States underwent a profound transformation from a rural and agricultural to an urban and industrial society. This transformation was accompanied by a transformation in the character of the American state itself from a state of courts and parties to an unwonted and patchwork centralized and bureaucratized New American State. These tectonic political-economic and governmental shifts shook the American constitutional order to its foundations. During the statebuilding era, a relatively stable and continuous traditional constitutional order constitutively structured by political and institutional tensions was gradually drained of authority as a source of order and governmental legitimacy. When this happened, constitutional arguments appealing to the traditional order's ethos lost their cachet. By contrast, constitutional arguments that aspired audaciously to reconcile conflicting commitments in service of progressive-spirited national goals and national movements were newly appealing. Under these conditions, reconciliation in the service of progress became the new constitutional coin of the realm within the precincts of American constitutional thought. Such reconciliations, of course, were dependent upon robust understandings of the nature and trajectory of progress. These understandings were the product of highly protean political and intellectual trends and enthusiasms that typically originated outside the courts. In the New Constitutional Nation, constitutional thought and progressive political fashion were thus tied to each other and mutually constitutive to an unprecedented extent.

Constitutional theorists, both within the legal academy and outside of it, were players in this process and came to play a distinctive role within

Justice Sandra Day O'Connor, *The Majesty of the Law: Reflections of a Supreme Court Justice* (New York: Random House, 2003), 231–5; O'Connor, "Keynote Address Before the Ninety-Sixth Annual Meeting of the American Society of International Law," *American Society of International Law Proceedings* 96 (2002): 348–50; William Rehnquist, "Constitutional Courts – Comparative Remarks (1989), in *Germany and Its Basic Law: Past, Present, and Future – A German-American Symposium*, eds. Paul Kirchof and Donald P. Kommers (1993), 411, 412; John Cushman Jr., "O'Connor Indicates She Will Remain on the Court," *New York Times* (6 July 2003) Sec. A, p. 9, col. 1 (quoting Justice Breyer, in an unprecedented joint network television interview held with Justice O'Connor on ABC's *This Week*, asserting that "whether...and how [our Constitution] fits into the governing documents of other nations...will be the challenge for the next generations"). See also Koh, "Paying 'Decent Respect' to World Opinion on the Death Penalty," *U.C. Davis Law Review* 35 (June 2002): 1085–130. Key media outlets such as the *New York Times* have also begun to publish articles noting this trend and framing it in a positive light. See Linda Greenhouse, "The Supreme Court: Overview; In a Momentous Term, Justices Remake the Law and the Court," *New York Times* (30 June 2003) Sec. A, p. 1, col. 1; Linda Greenhouse, "Ideas and Trends: Evolving Opinions; Heartfelt Words from the Rehnquist Court," *New York Times* (6 July 2003), Sec. 4, p. 3, col. 1.

the constitutional politics of the New Constitutional Nation. The central task of these theorists – once outsiders, but now insiders – was to realign the mainstream of American constitutional thought with the ideological requirements and governing facts of the New American State. Herbert Croly laid the cornerstone for the edifice of contemporary constitutional theory by fashioning an emotionally and politically plausible ideological defense of a level of statism in American politics that previously would have been taken, emotionally and politically, to be fundamentally incompatible with a creedal antistatist conception of freedom. Croly's successors, in turn, laid the reconciling ideological groundwork for the imperatives thrown up by one reformist campaign after another, in a succession that persisted throughout the twentieth century and (as the new push for global constitutionalism suggests) continues onward right through the present day. In the twentieth century, in short, constitutionalism became identified with often protean (and contradictory) understandings of the march of social and political progress itself.

Constitutional development in the New Constitutional Nation proceeded simultaneously on two tracks, both of which may be readily assimilated into broader studies of American political development. One involved the building of the physical institutions and coercive apparatus of the modern New American State. And the second involved the ongoing ideological work of constructing that state – not only as it was initially created, but also as it subsequently developed – as a legitimate source of national governing authority. Constitutional theorists and Whig historians fashioning regime-sustaining constitutional narratives of the trajectory of twentieth-century constitutional development have been endogenous and invested participants in this process.

In the twentieth century, the constitutionalism of a particular set of rulings that came to be reified as a theoretically coherent whole known as "civil rights and civil liberties" stood at the core of this process. Linear and unidimensional Whiggish narratives of twentieth-century constitutional development have imagined that development as consisting in significant part in the Supreme Court's cresting solicitude for this coherent and normatively desirably category. The actual paths of development I have presented here, however, demonstrate that this ostensibly coherent endpoint – often understood as a "matter of principle" – is considerably more idiosyncratic than regime-sustaining scholars have judged it politic to admit. Those paths, I have shown in my genealogies of contemporary constitutional morals, are the issue of complicated patterns of intercurrences, unintended consequences, path dependencies, and (antiprogressive) pockets of resistance. They were, moreover, the issue not of a simple effort of right-thinking people to stand up for rights and liberties (or even "personal" rights and liberties) in the face of rear-guard actions to restrict those rights. Rather, they involved a cascade of often stark choices made by reformers in distinctive political, social, and intellectual contexts with particular and highly protean imperatives in mind. These choices were political choices, and as such, they involved not issues of fidelity to a single monistic principle. They involved choices between incommensurables (as important political choices are wont to do), choices between rights and rights, liberties and liberties, and rights and liberties. The nature of these choices made in the name of progress was often frankly acknowledged by reformers themselves acting during the heat of reformist campaigns. In the reconciling and institutionalizing mopping-up that followed, however, their conflictual nature was commonly erased from constitutional memory in the service of a regime-sustaining linear, unidimensional narrative of progress.

As my illustrative genealogies of contemporary constitutional morals show, the path of institutional development identified by scholars in other areas of politics and law are not magically absent from patterns of development involving civil rights and civil liberties. Normative convictions have their place. But, as many scholars are now beginning to realize, they should not work to constrict the agendas of those aspiring to chart significant developmental patterns concerning vitally important areas of American constitutional law. As our Whiggish narratives have collapsed, the field has opened. Much work remains to be done.

Cases

Note to readers: This table of cases includes all cases mentioned in either substance or name in the body of the text. In addition, for the convenience of readers whose point of entry may be case law, it contains references to U.S. Supreme Court decisions noted in the book's footnotes. Omitted from this table are state court decisions (as well as some foreign court decisions) referenced only in the footnotes.

Abington v. Schempp, 374 U.S. 203 (1963), 318, 320

Abrams v. United States, 250 U.S. 616 (1919), 230, 276

Adair v. United States, 208 U.S. 161 (1908), 145, 182

Adams v. Tanner, 244 U.S. 590 (1917), 152

Adler v. Board of Education, 342 U.S. 485 (1952), 311–12, 330

Allen-Bradley Local v. Board, 315 U.S. 742 (1942), 216

American Communications Association v. Douds, 339 U.S. 382 (1950), 227

American Federation of Labor v. Swing, 312 U.S. 32 (1941), 216

American Steel Foundaries v. Tri-City Central Trades Council, 257 U.S. 184 (1921), 167

American Tobacco Co. v. United States, 221 U.S. 106 (1911), 157

Ashcraft v. Tennessee, 322 U.S. 143 (1944), 125

Atkins v. Virginia, 536 U.S. 304 (2002), 358

Badders v. United States, 240 U.S. 391 (1916), 67

Baggett v. Bullitt, 377 U.S. 360 (1964), 310

Bailey v. Alabama, 219 U.S. 219 (1911), 71, 247

Bakery Drivers' Local v. Wohl, 315 U.S. 769 (1942), 216

Barkus v. Illinois, 359 U.S. 121 (1958), 131

Barron v. Baltimore, 32 U.S. 243 (1833), 35, 66

Bartemeyer v. Iowa, 85 U.S. 129 (1873), 142

A. S. Beck Shoe Corp. v. Johnson, 274 N.Y. Supp. 946 (Sup. Ct., 1934), 212, 213, 214

Bedford Cut Stone v. Journeymen Stone Cutters'Association of North America, 274 U.S. 37 (1927), 167

Beecher v. Alabama, 389 U.S. 35 (1967), 124

Benton v. Maryland, 395 U.S. 784 (1969), 87

Berea College v. Kentucky, 211 U.S. 45 (1908), 86, 143

Index